Reviving Businesses With New Organizational Change Management Strategies

Nuno Geada
College of Business Administration, Polytechnic Institute of Setúbal, Portugal

Pedro Anunciação
College of Business Administration, Polytechnic Institute of Setúbal, Portugal

IGI Global
PUBLISHER of TIMELY KNOWLEDGE

A volume in the Advances in Logistics, Operations, and Management Science (ALOMS) Book Series

Published in the United States of America by
IGI Global
Business Science Reference (an imprint of IGI Global)
701 E. Chocolate Avenue
Hershey PA, USA 17033
Tel: 717-533-8845
Fax: 717-533-8661
E-mail: cust@igi-global.com
Web site: http://www.igi-global.com

Library of Congress Cataloging-in-Publication Data

Names: Geada, Nuno, 1983- editor. | Anunciação, Pedro Fernandes, 1967- editor.
Title: Reviving businesses with new organizational change management strategies / Nuno Geada, and Pedro Anunciacao, editors.
Description: Hershey, PA : Business Science Reference, [2021] | Includes bibliographical references and index. | Summary: "This book analyzes the sensitivity of organizations to change management based on methodologies and tools to control impacts and investigates how employees are impacted by their environment discussing issues such as technology communication and business continuity and the importance of collaborative and interactive relationship pertaining to change management"-- Provided by publisher.
Identifiers: LCCN 2020055695 (print) | LCCN 2020055696 (ebook) | ISBN 9781799874522 (hardcover) | ISBN 9781799874539 (paperback) | ISBN 9781799874546 (ebook)
Subjects: LCSH: Organizational change--Management.
Classification: LCC HD58.8 .R4954 2021 (print) | LCC HD58.8 (ebook) | DDC 658.4/063--dc23
LC record available at https://lccn.loc.gov/2020055695
LC ebook record available at https://lccn.loc.gov/2020055696

This book is published in the IGI Global book series Advances in Logistics, Operations, and Management Science (ALOMS) (ISSN: 2327-350X; eISSN: 2327-3518)

British Cataloguing in Publication Data
A Cataloguing in Publication record for this book is available from the British Library.

All work contributed to this book is new, previously-unpublished material. The views expressed in this book are those of the authors, but not necessarily of the publisher.

For electronic access to this publication, please contact: eresources@igi-global.com.

Advances in Logistics, Operations, and Management Science (ALOMS) Book Series

John Wang
Montclair State University, USA

ISSN:2327-350X
EISSN:2327-3518

Mission

Operations research and management science continue to influence business processes, administration, and management information systems, particularly in covering the application methods for decision-making processes. New case studies and applications on management science, operations management, social sciences, and other behavioral sciences have been incorporated into business and organizations real-world objectives.

The **Advances in Logistics, Operations, and Management Science** (ALOMS) Book Series provides a collection of reference publications on the current trends, applications, theories, and practices in the management science field. Providing relevant and current research, this series and its individual publications would be useful for academics, researchers, scholars, and practitioners interested in improving decision making models and business functions.

Coverage

- Networks
- Organizational Behavior
- Production Management
- Information Management
- Finance
- Computing and information technologies
- Risk Management
- Operations Management
- Political Science
- Marketing engineering

IGI Global is currently accepting manuscripts for publication within this series. To submit a proposal for a volume in this series, please contact our Acquisition Editors at Acquisitions@igi-global.com or visit: http://www.igi-global.com/publish/.

The Advances in Logistics, Operations, and Management Science (ALOMS) Book Series (ISSN 2327-350X) is published by IGI Global, 701 E. Chocolate Avenue, Hershey, PA 17033-1240, USA, www.igi-global.com. This series is composed of titles available for purchase individually; each title is edited to be contextually exclusive from any other title within the series. For pricing and ordering information please visit http://www.igi-global.com/book-series/advances-logistics-operations-management-science/37170. Postmaster: Send all address changes to above address.

Titles in this Series

For a list of additional titles in this series, please visit:
http://www.igi-global.com/book-series/advances-logistics-operations-management-science/37170

The Role of Islamic Spirituality in the Management and Leadership Process
Mahazan Abdul Mutalib (Islamic Science University of Malaysia, Malaysia) and Ahmad Rafiki (Universitas Medan Area, Indonesia)
Business Science Reference • © 2021 • 335pp • H/C (ISBN: 9781799868927) • US $195.00

Global Perspectives on Change Management and Leadership in the Post-COVID-19 Era
Ebtihaj Al-Aali (University of Bahrain, Bahrain) and Meryem Masmoudi (University of Bahrain, Bahrain)
Business Science Reference • © 2021 • 374pp • H/C (ISBN: 9781799869481) • US $215.00

Handbook of Research on Innate Leadership Characteristics and Examinations of Successful First-Time Leaders
Matthew Waritay Guah (South Carolina State University, USA)
Business Science Reference • © 2021 • 500pp • H/C (ISBN: 9781799875925) • US $285.00

Handbook of Research on Recent Perspectives on Management, International Trade, and Logistics
Güner Koç Aytekin (Ufuk University, Turkey) and Çağlar Doğru (Ufuk University, Turkey)
Business Science Reference • © 2021 • 490pp • H/C (ISBN: 9781799858867) • US $345.00

Handbook of Research on Multidisciplinary Perspectives on Managerial and Leadership Psychology
Rick D. Johnson (Johnson Professionals, Inc., USA)
Business Science Reference • © 2021 • 742pp • H/C (ISBN: 9781799838111) • US $285.00

Transforming Corporate Governance and Developing Models for Board Effectiveness
Qaiser Rafique Yasser (Centre for Rural Economy, Pakistan) and Abdullah Al-Mamun (University of Wollongong, Australia)
Business Science Reference • © 2021 • 345pp • H/C (ISBN: 9781799866695) • US $195.00

Encyclopedia of Organizational Knowledge, Administration, and Technology
Mehdi Khosrow-Pour D.B.A. (Information Resources Management Association, USA)
Business Science Reference • © 2021 • 2734pp • H/C (ISBN: 9781799834731) • US $3,950.00

Corporate Leadership and Its Role in Shaping Organizational Culture and Performance
Azza Bejaoui (High Institute of Management of Tunis, Tunisia)
Business Science Reference • © 2021 • 350pp • H/C (ISBN: 9781522582663) • US $195.00

IGI Global
PUBLISHER of TIMELY KNOWLEDGE

701 East Chocolate Avenue, Hershey, PA 17033, USA
Tel: 717-533-8845 x100 • Fax: 717-533-8661
E-Mail: cust@igi-global.com • www.igi-global.com

I want to dedicate this work to my wife and my son, because without them none of this would make sense, as they are my path of light and my driving force.

I dedicate this work to all my students, hoping to have contributed to their personal and professional development, for the benefit of the economy and society.

Table of Contents

Detailed Table of Contents

Technologies and digital transformation are the forces that have transformed societies. In a world where everything seems to be under "control," the unexpected occurs and forces rapid changes without proper time for planning. The future becomes uncertain, and the present becomes an excellent opportunity to upgrade and maximize profit by changing the way organizations work and especially how organizations communicate. The new world highlights the relevance of information systems flexibility and the powerful role that communication plays in the success of organizations.

This chapter seeks to explore the key strategic change lessons organizations can learn ahead of implementing digital transformation initiatives. The chapter will review the digital transformation literature and associated challenges organizations are confronted with in implementing large-scale information systems-enabled change. Key enterprise system lessons are taken from implementation, where the McKinsey 7-S framework is introduced as a lens to support organizations adopting digital transformation. Critical success factors are identified that seek to provide leaders with a more holistic arsenal when leading digital transformation initiatives. The chapter concludes with reflections for the strategic change field.

The objective of this work is, on the one hand, to study the new competitive forms that correspond to the development of the different markets linked to electronic platforms and social networks on the internet and, on the other hand, to develop a proposal for social welfare for the positive and negative impacts produced by the development of these markets. In the first part, the main social and economic changes inherent to political and social evolution are addressed. The main logical trends of the market are presented about production and modalities of information appropriation, in particular the new forms of information asymmetries in the electronic market.

This chapter analyzes the characteristics of the strategic greening and social responsibility of organizational development. The main assumption of the analysis is based on the consideration that the strategic organizational development should take into consideration the greening of organizations and the corporate social responsibility. Using a holistic and humanistic approaches on individual and organizational development, the analysis focuses on individual freedom, lifetime education and training, consciousness on human values, and ethical concerns related to the implementation of the organizational greening and corporate social responsibility. Finally, it proposes a strategic organizational development model.

Digitalization is changing the way we live, work, our relationships, and it couldn't be otherwise if we talk about competitiveness in the maritime transport sector. The world faces considerable technological challenges; so does the maritime sector, turning information technologies into opportunities by using countless data inputs, thus allowing more control, better planning, and a reduction in operational costs while enhancing environmental sustainability. According to Carbone and Martino, ports have been naturally used for transhipment, consisting of the transference of cargo from one mean of transport to another, which has led to a series of new demands and challenges in port management concerns, since goods temporarily remain within the area under the influence of the port. Before its expedition, port activity faces diverse challenges in the management of storage, availableness, and handling, among other issues.

Information is the driving force of organizations because it is in information systems that the decisions are made. The need to have adequate infrastructure for collection, storage, processing, and distribution in an organization means that an appreciable part of the organization's effort in terms of human and financial resources is channeled in this direction. This chapter aims at the development and consequent application of change management, for optimization of information and process management based on the Lean methodology in information systems. The analysis and implementation of infrastructure for information management is based on eliminating waste and activities without added value, thus imparting continuous improvement, in order to achieve the goals/objectives proposed towards excellence and success and optimization processes and services. In order to achieve the objective of this project, a survey and analysis of the requirements of the IT processes to be able to construct and implement change management are done.

With increased competition, speculation, changes in customer expectations, and world events that significantly disturb the markets, managers have more technical difficulties in coordinating/monitoring organizational processes and practices. The lean philosophy made it possible, through the identification of the most recurring problems within the company under study, to understand the restructuring needs of the organizational culture, the revision of fundamental key processes, the significant improvement in response times, and the assumption of a commitment by stakeholders from the various areas of activity in the company. In this context, this work, carried out in the scope of internship, aims to analyze and evaluate the importance of adopting the lean concept in a multinational company, inferring about the benefits achieved and the improvements felt with regard to competitiveness and service level. In this sense, it was clear that the adoption of lean allows the optimization of key processes.

Sustainable development is one of the greatest challenges facing our generation and the next, and achieving this goal will force society to continuously challenge and overcome itself. In order to attain the required sustainable objectives, many companies are investing in new methodologies, such as the Kaizen-Lean methodology. This chapter focuses on a case study in the food retail industry, a strategic and one of the largest and oldest industries in the world able to thrive even in the face of substantial adversity. The authors systematized the case study in three different stages via an action-research intervention. In a first stage, they identified the most sensitive areas, which enabled them to detect and target the intervention. In a second stage, they implemented and monitored several actions supported by the Kaizen/Lean methodologies. In a third stage, a survey was applied to workers whose work areas had changed in order to analyze and assess the impact of the implemented measures.

This study aims to analyze the concerns of the largest companies operating in the Portuguese market regarding technological developments and artificial intelligence in the context of replacing human work with machines. More specifically, this study targets the reference to these concerns in these companies' codes of ethics and/or codes of conduct. The codes of ethics of 20 large companies operating in Portugal were thus analysed and classified according to their turnover, adopting an analytical method based on three dimensions identified as relevant for the respective evaluation: social responsibility, technological innovation, and commitments to employees. The conclusions from this study are that the companies analysed do not show in their codes of ethics any concern in mentioning the safeguarding of jobs if these are ever to be replaced by machines.

The information society requires governance. The complexity of the markets is bringing complexity to the functioning of economic organizations. The pressure of technological innovation challenges the need for governance on organizational systems, in particular on information systems. But the role of technological innovation is pressing for the re-qualification and re-balance of jobs and professions themselves. This process has come to assert itself as a result of the affirmation of Industry 4.0, where, evidently, technologies accelerate the replacement of human presence in the production system.

The teaching management of higher education institutions (HEIs) has traditionally focused on processing compliance with regulated curricular conditions rather than normalizing the learning and knowledge developed to be transferred to society. The motivation of knowledge management in HEIs should be oriented to the strengthening of knowledge preservation strategies. In recent decades, this model has been a growing interest on the part of academics and academic institutions at the international level. The main objective of this study is to analyze the research trends on knowledge management in HEIs worldwide during the period 2000-2019. Bibliometric techniques were applied to a sample of 1,836 articles from scientific journals selected from the Scopus database. The study documented a rapidly growing knowledge base, mostly written by academics located in developed societies. This chapter provides a point of reference for future research on this topic, as well as revealing the intellectual structure of this interdisciplinary field.

Preface

With the gradual resumption of economic activity noticed by the World Governments, most businesses are facing a range of challenges associated with implementing measures to protect the health and safety of their employees. So, some employers had to put certain business activities on hold and even start new ones to keep their organization flowing. The global COVID-19 pandemic has challenged companies to manage their organizations in newfound ways. In the short term, they are facing enormous scope changes to their business plans, in the long term, they must adapt and continue to make progress on their original goals. To this end, it is important to understand how changes can be associated with methodologies traditionally adopted with the support Information Systems and Technologies. This book aimed to analyze the sensitivity of organizations to the change management based on methodologies and tools to control impacts; Understand how employees will be impacted in their environment, and how technology will help; Which types of frameworks were built for communication and business continuity; The Importance of Collaborative and Interactive Relationship for Change Management; Paradigm Shift in Business Strategic Programs to Change Management; Emotional Factors and People Issues for Change Management. These macro key objectives are focused on the following variables:

- Focus on the big picture. The strategic business goals and objectives that mattered yesterday matter more now. Tactics may need to be updated but staying focused on the big picture is critical for business performance.
- Adapt to new ways of productivity. This may include building new virtual dashboards on project or team progress, remote status meetings and team brainstorming sessions, or utilizing different collaboration tools to support remote communications. Whatever the case remains flexible and provide support to project teams and impacted team members.
- Clearly and consistently communicate. Creating a structured communications format and setting expectations for remote work will help keep people focused and productive during times of uncertainty.
- Increase ways for employees to provide feedback and escalate issues or concerns. This will help to gauge communications effectiveness, adoption, and areas of resistance.
- Enable continuous improvement. Training and development, such as virtual team management coaching and collaboration management, helps employees pivot to adopt new ways of working and operate productively.
- Build in elasticity. Adjusting business continuity plans, ensure program is sustainable for the long term with the ability to evolve as developments, continue to change.

The book structure is composed by 16 chapters, that encompass studies which approach theoretically focused chapters that attempt to discuss fundamentals, conceptual definitions and relationships and set new levels correlated to nowadays issues. It permits understanding how contents could be addressed by researchers and practitioners to develop further comprehension over changes in organizations management field. Finally, opens a reflection where practical results from field implementations can be detailed, exposed, and evaluated by authors, defining an actual point of technological application in real cases, completing a context where theory reaches practices, enabling a deeper understanding of concepts, methodologies, and holistic approaches to *Reviving Businesses With New Organizational Change Management Strategies.*

Chapter 1, authored by Albérico Travassos Rosário, describes the Increased global concerns about climate change and environmental degradation have attracted attention to sustainable development strategies. Sustainability involves maintaining ecological balance, requiring organizations to integrate social, political, economic, and environmental concepts in their business models. This research aims to explore the new business models associated with increased awareness of sustainability. Despite the differences in definition and implementation of these modern frameworks, innovation and sustainability remain the central concepts of enhancing value creation and capturing. While these business models aim to enhance organizations' capability to optimize new opportunities and overcome challenges, they also aim to improve society and protect the environment.

Chapter 2, authored by Neeta Baporikar, Knowledge Management is crucial in this knowledge-based society. Further knowledge is a critical resource when it comes to business competitiveness and sustainability. Hence, to reach the sustainability aims, knowledge management (KM) may be regarded as central for any business organization. Therefore, adopting an in-depth literature review method with a grounded theory approach the aim of this chapter is to discuss the role and significance of knowledge management to ensure business growth and sustainability. The chapter also provides a holistic framework of knowledge management for business sustainability.

Chapter 3, authored by Ana Catarina Lopes da Silva, Technologies and digital transformation are the forces that have transform societies. In a world where everything seems to be under "control", the unexpected occurs and forces rapid changes without a proper time for planning. The future becomes uncertain, and the present becomes an excellent opportunity to upgrade and maximize profit by changing the way organizations work and especially how organizations communicate. The New world highlights the relevance of information systems flexibility and the powerful role that communication plays in the success of organizations.

Chapter 4, authored by John Loonam, this chapter seeks to explore the key strategic change lessons organizations can learn ahead of implementing digital transformation initiatives. The chapter will review the digital transformation literature and associated challenges organizations are confronted with in implementing large-scale information systems-enabled change. Key Enterprise System lessons are taken from implementation, where the McKinsey 7-S framework is introduced as a lens to support organizations adopting digital transformation. Critical success factors are identified that seek to provide leaders with a more holistic arsenal when leading digital transformation initiatives. The chapter concludes with reflections for the strategic change field.

Chapter 5, authored by José Poças Rascão has the objective of this work is, on the one hand, to study the new competitive forms that correspond to the development of the different markets linked to electronic platforms and social networks on the Internet. On the other hand, to develop a proposal for social welfare for the positive and negative impacts produced by the development of these markets. In the first part, the main social and economic changes inherent to political and social evolution are addressed. The main logical trends of the market are presented about production and modalities of information appropriation, in particular the new forms of information asymmetries in the electronic market.

Chapter 6, authored by José G. Vargas-Hernández, this study has the aim to analyze the characteristics of the strategic greening and social responsibility of organizational development. The main assumption of the analysis is based on the consideration that the strategic organizational development should take into consideration the greening of organizations and the corporate social responsibility. Using a holistic and humanistic approaches on individual and organizational development, the analysis focus on individual freedom, lifetime education and training, consciousness on human values and ethical concerns related to the implementation of the organizational greening and corporate social responsibility. Finally, it is proposed a strategic organizational development model. Keywords: Corporate social responsibility, organizational development, organizational greening, strategy.

Chapter 7, authored by Cátia Sofia Salgado, Digitalization is changing the way we live, we work, our relationships, and it could not be otherwise if we talk about competitiveness in the maritime transport sector. The world faces considerable technological challenges; so does the maritime sector, turning information technologies into opportunities by using countless data inputs, thus allowing to have more control, a better planning and a reduction in operational costs while enhancing environmental sustainability. According to Carbone & Martino (2003), ports have been naturally used for transshipment, consisting on the transference of cargo from one mean of transport to another, which led to a series of new demands and challenges in what port management concerns, since goods temporarily remain within the area under the influence of the port, before its expedition, port activity faces diverse challenges in what regards the management of storage, availableness, and handling, among other issues.

Chapter 8, authored by Nuno Geada, Information is the driving force of organizations because it is based in Information Systems that the decisions are made. The need to have adequate infrastructure for collection, storage, processing, and distribution in an organization means that an appreciable part of the organization's effort in terms of human and financial resources is channeled in this direction. This chapter aims at the development and consequent application of change management, for optimization of information and process management based on the Lean methodology in information systems. The analysis and implementation of infrastructure for information management is based on eliminating waste and activities without added value, thus imparting continuous improvement, to achieve the goals/objectives proposed towards excellence and success and optimization processes and services. To achieve the objective of this project, a survey and analysis of the requirements of the IT processes to be able to construct and implement the change management on digital.

Chapter 9, authored by Denise Lopes Pereira, with an increased competition, speculation, changes in customer expectations and world events that significantly disturb the markets, managers have more technical difficulties in coordinating/monitoring organizational processes and practices. The lean philosophy made it possible, through the identification of the most recurring problems within the company under study, to understand the restructuring needs of the organizational culture, the revision of fundamental key processes, the significant improvement in response times and the assumption of a commitment by stakeholders from the various areas of activity in the company. In this context, this work carried out in the scope of internship, aims to analyze, and evaluate the importance of adopting the lean concept in a multinational company, inferring about the benefits achieved and the improvements felt regarding competitiveness and service level. In this sense, it was clear that the adoption of lean allows the optimization of key processes. Keywords: Organizational culture, Lean, reviewed processes, Lean implementation models.

Chapter 10, authored by Pedro Silva, Alexandra Braga, Sara Mota, Miguel Soares and Marisa Ferreira, Sustainable development is one of the greatest challenges facing our generation and the next, and achieving this goal will force society to continuously challenge and overcome itself. In order to attain the required sustainable objectives, many companies are investing in new methodologies, such as the Kaizen-Lean methodology. Our chapter focuses on a case study in the food retail industry, a strategic and one of the largest and oldest industries in the world, able to thrive even in the face of substantial adversity. We systematized the case study in three different stages via an action-research intervention. In a first stage, we identified the most sensitive areas, which enabled us to detect and target our intervention. In a second stage, we implemented and monitored several actions supported by the Kaizen/Lean methodologies. In a third stage, a survey was applied to workers whose work areas had changed, in order to analyse and assess the impact of the implemented measures.

Chapter 11, authored by Nuno Cruz, Ana Carvalho and Sandra Duarte This study aims to analyze the concerns of the largest companies operating in the Portuguese market regarding technological developments and artificial intelligence in the context of replacing human work by machines. More specifically, this study targets the reference to these concerns in these companies 'codes of ethics and/or codes of conduct. The codes of ethics of twenty large companies operating in Portugal were thus analyzed and classified according to their turnover, adopting an analytical method based on three dimensions identified as relevant for the respective evaluation: social responsibility, technological innovation, and commitments to employees. The conclusions from this study are that the companies analyzed do not show, in their codes of ethics, any concern in mentioning the safeguarding of jobs if these are ever to be replaced by machines.

Chapter 12, authored by Pedro Fernandes Anunciação, Fernando Gonçalves and João Pimenta, the Information Society requires Governance. The complexity of the markets is bringing complexity to the functioning of economic organizations. The pressure of technological innovation challenges the need for governance on organizational systems, on information systems. But the role of technological innovation is pressing for the re-qualification and re-balance of jobs and professions themselves. The dismissal of employees in general economic sectors and in industry. This process has come to assert itself because of the affirmation of Industry 4.0, where, evidently, technologies accelerate the replacement of human presence in the production system.

Chapter 13, authored by Pedro Fernandes Anunciação, Vitor Manuel Lemos Dinis and Francisco Madeira Esteves, Industry 4.0 marks the beginning of the so-called 4th industrial revolution. The new emerging information technologies, such as Internet of Things, Cloud computing, Machine Learning, Artificial intelligence, among others, have challenged the management and organization of industrial companies. They have now shorter market response times, higher quality requirements and customization needs, which challenges many industrial areas, from production to maintenance, from design to asset management. The maintenance and asset management condition, and the reliability of production lines are closely linked and constitute key areas of good industrial operation. This work seeks to present a roadmap proposal for the management of industrial assets from maintenance management. In addition, seeks also identify the key elements for a roadmap design, and proposes a set management questions to assessing the maintenance maturity.

Chapter 14, authored by Nuno Geada, after the World Health Organization declared the coronavirus disease in 2019 (COVID-19) outbreak as a pandemic, digital transformation is a process in which entities make use of technology to improve their performance, reach and guarantee better results. It is a structural change in organizations, giving an essential role to the technology, digital transformation engages processes where organizational actors engage in digital innovation and transform their organizations to respond to change in their business and technology environments. So, just like in all changes must have models and frameworks that support it in transition, it is a path in this case, under constantly pressure, to achieve goals and have an efficient management of the processes that it contains.

Chapter 15, authored by Ricardo Jorge Travassos, Nuno Sérgio Martins, João Pedro Sousa and Ricardo Barata Mota, the present markets affect organizations by triggering the need for change. However, in addition to flexibility, it is considered the implementation of procedures to alleviate the 'weather'. So, change management is fundamental in organizations that move in innovative and disruptive environments. The present work seeks to provide a tool that will allow the collection and structuring of the constituent data necessary for the management of new projects / products, creating relevant information to strategic decision makers, stating that the exploratory cycle of the process, intends to create organizational knowledge that will 'situate' all team members within the various projects. It will consist of a literary review, followed by the presentation of a case study, which can be applied in an SME due to its technical simplicity. The objective is to support the proposal as a promoter of information and knowledge management. The work ends with a critical analysis of the contents, exposure of limitations, and suggestions for possible future work associated with the current theme.

Chapter 16, authored by Mariana Gonzalez-Zamar and Emilio Abad-Segura the teaching management of higher education institutions (HEIs) has traditionally focused on processing compliance with regulated curricular conditions, rather than normalizing the learning and knowledge developed, to be transferred to society. The motivation of knowledge management in HEIs should be oriented to the strengthening of knowledge preservation strategies. In recent decades, this model has been a growing interest on the part of academics and academic institutions at the international level. The main objective of this study is to analyze the research trends on knowledge management in HEIs worldwide during the period 2000-2019. Bibliometric techniques were applied to a sample of 1836 articles from scientific journals selected from the Scopus database. The study documented a rapidly growing knowledge base, mostly written by academics located in developed societies. This chapter provides a point of reference for future research on this topic, as well as revealing the intellectual structure of this interdisciplinary field.

As a final consideration this book project, a though one itself, aimed to contribute with this important discussion, publishing studies of academic, researching, consulting practitioners around change management actual challenges and holistic models. This book will permit to develop a consistent theoretical and practical background that can be considered as a basis for further studies, organizations, support future studies related to the change management area, support organization managers to create tools through methodologies that apply good practices to control the change, allow sharing of experiences to support other investigations. At the end, the main vision behind developing this project is not to have just simple transfer of knowledge but to engage those who used these books to engage actively in improving the quality this book.

Nuno Geada
College of Business Administration, Polytechnic Institute of Setúbal, Portugal

Acknowledgment

I want to thank IGI Global for the opportunity to be able to publish this book. I also want to pay my thanks to Prof. Pedro Anunciação, for the availability and team spirit.

Finally, to all who may have somehow contributed to the accomplishment of this work, my respectful thanks.

Chapter 1
New Business Models Sustainability

Albérico Travassos Rosário
https://orcid.org/0000-0003-4793-4110
GOVCOPP, ESGT, Instituto Politécnico de Santarém, Portugal

ABSTRACT

Increased global concerns about climate change and environmental degradation have attracted attention to sustainable development strategies. Sustainability involves maintaining ecological balance, requiring organizations to integrate social, political, economic, and environmental concepts in their business models. This research chapter aims to explore the new business models associated with increased awareness of sustainability. Literature review methodology was used as the primary data collection method. Four main new business models were identified, including sustainable business model innovation (SBMI), triadic business model (T-Model), circular business model, and Web 2.0-based business model. Despite the differences in definition and implementation of these modern frameworks, innovation and sustainability remain the central concepts of enhancing value creation and capturing. While these business models aim to enhance organizations' capabilities to optimize new opportunities and overcome challenges, they also aim to improve society and protect the environment.

INTRODUCTION

Sustainable development refers to development where social, political, and economic activities are combined with environmental stability and balance to ensure the satisfaction of basic needs for both current and future generations. The high rise in climate change, global warming, and environmental degradation concerns have led to the establishment of sustainable business models that aim to reduce the impact of business activities on the natural environment (Pajula et al., 2017). Nosratabadi et al. (2019) define a business model as an abstract representation of the value flow and interconnection of value elements of creation, proposition, value capturing, and delivering within a company's unit. These elements make business sustainability a continuous process because they need to understand how they interplay amidst changing environments and conditions. The primary goal of sustainable business models is to highlight

DOI: 10.4018/978-1-7998-7452-2.ch001

and enforce transformational and long-term changes instead of short-term plans and strategies (Høgevold et al., 2014). Organizations are thus required to understand the correlation between political, environmental, social, and economic elements, their evolution, and their impact on organizational change processes.

Technological advancements and internationalization have played a major role in promoting the global implementation of sustainable business models by raising competition in worldwide markets that drive firms to find appropriate solutions. Consumers' increased use of the internet and improved access to information has increased their awareness of current environmental, economic, political, and social activities, and further pressuring companies to identify and implement appropriate alternative measures (Attias & Mira-Bonnardel, 2016). Therefore, sustainable business models ensure maximum productivity and profitability and achieve sustainable development goals by creating value for the triple bottom line, that is, the environment, society, and economic (Nosratabadi et al., 2019). They contribute to reducing harmful effects by employing a proactive multi-stakeholder leadership, long-term strategies and innovation, and incorporating sustainability principles and goals into value creation and proposition.

The objective of this research is to promote the improvement of knowledge in new sustainable business models.

METHODOLOGICAL APPROACH

Conducting a literature review enables researchers to understand the depth and breadth of existing literature regarding the topic of study and aids the identification of explorable knowledge gaps (Rosário, 2021, Rosário et al., 2021; Rosário & Cuz, 2019; Sacavém, et al., 2019). The methodology involves analyzing, synthesizing, and summarizing multiple related works of literature to develop new information, theories, or test hypothesis. It can also assess the quality and validity of available information related to the topic, thus, identifying inconsistencies, weaknesses, and contradictions. In this study, the literature review process involved the eight steps recommended by Rosário, (2021), Rosário et al., (2021); Rosário and Cuz, (2019); Sacavém, et al., (2019); Xiao and Watson (2019), summarized in Table 1.

Table 1. Process of systematic literature review.

Phase	Step	Description
Phase One	Step 1	Formulate the problem
	Step 2	Develop and validate the review process
Phase Two	Step 3	Search for relevant literature
	Step 4	Search for inclusion
	Step 5	Quality evaluation
	Step 6	Data extraction
	Step 7	Data analysis and synthesize
Phase Three	Step 8	Report Findings

Source: own elaboration

A meta-search engine (MetaLib) was used to identify relevant scientific articles for analysis. The study used the SCOPUS database in January 2021 due to the robustness and the peer-reviewed nature of the electronic database.

However, we consider that the study has as a limitation only to consider the SCOPUS database, thus excluding other academic databases. The key terms used include "Sustainability," "Business models," "new business models," and "sustainable business models." The search was limited to the subject area "Business, Management and Accounting", while the publication year 2010- was used to limit the publication period. After a screening process, 96 relevant sources were identified, Article (53); Conference Paper (18); Book Chapter (13); Review (7); Book (4); and Note (1). Since the goal of this paper is to promote knowledge advancement in new, sustainable business models, careful evaluation of the existing resources was ensured to increase the accuracy and quality of data synthesized.

PUBLICATION DISTRIBUTION

Peer-reviewed articles on the subject can be traced 2010-2021. 2019 was the year with the largest number of peer-reviewed articles on the subject, reaching 18.

Figure 1 summarizes the peer-reviewed literature published for the period 2010–2021.

The publications were sorted out as follows: Journal Of Cleaner Production (13); Proceedings Of The International Conference On Industrial Engineering And Operations Management (3); Proceedings Of The Summer School Francesco Turco (3); publications 2 (2018 IEEE International Conference On Engineering Technology And Innovation ICE Itmc 2018 Proceedings; British Food Journal; Business Strategy And The Environment; Emerald Emerging Markets Case Studies; Journal Of Business Strategy; Journal Of Fashion Marketing And Management; Production Planning And Control; Technology Analysis And Strategic Management) the remaining publications 1 (2010 IEEE International Technology Management Conference ICE 2010; Accounting Auditing And Accountability Journal; Advances In Enterprise Inmation Systems II; Advances In Science Technology And Engineering Systems; Automobile Revolution Towards A New Electro Mobility Paradigm; Benchmarking; Business Horizons; Competitiveness Review; Corporate Sustainability Inclusive Business Approaches Contributing To A Sustainable World; Driving Agribusiness With Technology Innovations; Dynamic Supply Chain Alignment A New Business Model Peak Permance In Enterprise Supply Chains Across All Geographies; Dynamics Of Long Life Assets From Technology Adaptation To Upgrading The Business Model; Emerging Market Multinationals And Europe Challenges And Strategies; Entrepreneurship Concepts Methodologies Tools And Applications; Euromed Journal Of Business; Global Bioethanol Evolution Risks And Uncertainties; Handbook Of Research On Strategic Fit And Design In Business Ecosystems; Handbook Of Research On Strategic Innovation Management Improved Competitive Advantage; Handbook Of Sustainable Luxury Textiles And Fashion; Hybrid Organizations New Business Models Environmental Leadership; Icitm 2020 2020 9th International Conference On Industrial Technology And Management; International Journal Of Arts Management; International Journal Of E Business Research; International Journal Of Economic Research; International Journal Of Electronic Business; International Journal Of Innovation And Sustainable Development; International Journal Of Integrated Supply Management; International Journal Of Logistics Management; International Journal Of Production Research; International Journal Of Productivity And Quality Management; International Journal Of Public Sector Permance Management; International Journal Of Service Science Management Engineering And Technology; International Journal Of Technology Management; Intrinsic Capability Implementing Intrinsic Sustainable Development An Ecological Civilisation; Italian Utilities Industry Success Stories And Future Perspectives; Journal Of Business And Retail Management Research; Journal Of Business Research; Journal Of Evolutionary Economics; Journal Of Islamic Marketing; Journal Of Management Development; Journal Of Product And Brand Management; Journal Of Service Management; Journal Of Sustainable Tourism; Logistics And Supply Chain Innovation Bridging The Gap Between Theory And Practice; Management Decision; Manufacturing And Service Operations Management; Networked Business Models In The Circular Economy; Organization And Environment; Picmet 2018 Portland International Conference On Management Of Engineering And Technology Managing Technological Entrepreneurship The Engine Economic Growth Proceedings; Proceedings 2020 IEEE 22nd Conference On Business Inmatics CBI 2020; Proceedings Of The 2013 2nd International Conference On Inmation Management In The Knowledge Economy Imke 2013; Proceedings Of The 28th International Business Inmation Management Association Conference Vision 2020 Innovation Management Development Sustainability And Competitive Economic Growth; Proceedings Of The 33rd International Business Inmation Management Association Conference Ibima 2019 Education Excellence And Innovation Management Through Vision 2020; Proceedings Of The European Conference On Innovation And Entrepreneurship Ecie; Quality Access To Success; Revista De Administracao Mackenzie; Rivista Di Studi Sulla Sostenibilita; Strategic Change; Strategic Direction; Technological Forecasting And Social Change; Tourism Analysis).

We can see that there was a growing interest until 2019 by New Business Models Sustainability publications.

Figure 1. Documents by year
Source: own elaboration

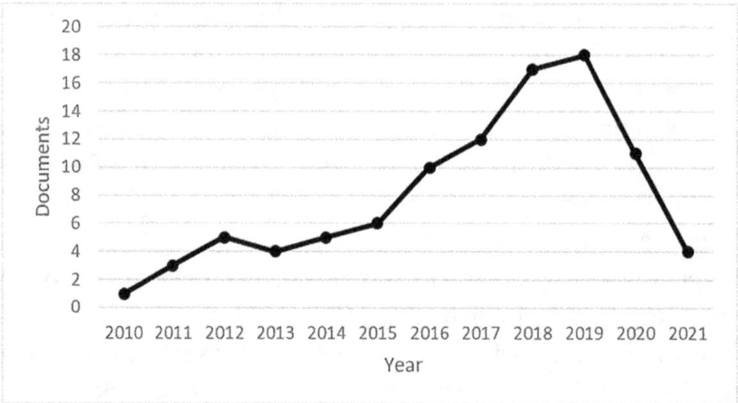

In Table 1 we analyze for the Scimago Journal & Country Rank (SJR), the best quartile and the H index by publication. The Sustainable manufacturing: Trends and research challenges is the most quoted publication with 1,390 (SJR), Q1 and H index 70. There is a total of 23 journals on Q1, 8 journals on Q2, 9 journals, Q3, 4 journal on Q4 and 23 no data . Journals from best quartile Q1 represent 32% of the 72 journals titles; best quartile Q2 represents 11%, best quartile Q3 represents 13%, and finally, best Q4 represents 6% each of the titles of 72 journals.

As evident from Table 2, the significant majority of articles o rank on the Q1 best quartile index

Table 2. Scimago journal & country rank impact factor.

Title	SJR	Best Quartile	H Index
Manufacturing And Service Operations Management	5,730	Q1	77
Organization And Environment	2,080	Q1	55
Journal Of Cleaner Production	1,890	Q1	173
Journal Of Business Research	1,870	Q1	179
Business Strategy And The Environment	1,830	Q1	94
Technological Forecasting And Social Change	1,820	Q1	103
International Journal Of Production Research 1,790	1,780	Q1	125
Journal Of Service Management	1,710	Q1	53
Accounting Auditing And Accountability Journal	1,460	Q1	92
Business Horizons	1,400	Q1	76
Production Planning And Control	1,390	Q1	70
Journal Of Sustainable Tourism	1,330	Q1	93
International Journal Of Logistics Management	1,060	Q1	72
Advances In Science Technology And Engineering Systems	0,140	Q3	7
Management Decision	0,860	Q1	91
Journal Of Product And Brand Management	0,840	Q1	75
Competitiveness Review	0,710	Q1	23
Journal Of Fashion Marketing And Management	0,710	Q1	47
Euromed Journal Of Business	0,630	Q1	19
Technology Analysis And Strategic Management	0,630	Q2	64
Journal Of Evolutionary Economics	0,610	Q1	69
British Food Journal	0,580	Q1	74
Benchmarking	0,550	Q2	57
Journal Of Management Development	0,520	Q1	55
Journal Of Business Strategy	0,490	Q2	36
Strategic Change	0,480	Q2	12
Tourism Analysis	0,470	Q2	33
International Journal Of Arts Management	0,460	Q1	11
International Journal Of Productivity And Quality Management	0,450	Q2	25
International Journal Of Technology Management	0,410	Q1	54
International Journal Of Integrated Supply Management	0,390	Q2	20
Journal Of Islamic Marketing	0,370	Q3	34
International Journal Of Innovation And Sustainable Development	0,280	Q3	19
Quality Access To Success	0,280	Q3	20
International Journal Of Service Science Management Engineering And Technology	0,250	Q2	5
International Journal Of E Business Research	0,220	Q3	20
International Journal Of Public Sector Permance Management	0,200	Q3	6
Proceedings Of The Summer School Francesco Turco	0,190	-*	7
Journal Of Business And Retail Management Research	0,180	Q3	7
Emerald Emerging Markets Case Studies	0,170	Q3	4
Rivista Di Studi Sulla Sostenibilita	0,170	Q3	10
International Journal Of Electronic Business	0,160	Q3	7
2018 IEEE International Conference On Engineering Technology And Innovation ICE Itmc 2018 Proceedings	0,150	-*	5
Proceedings Of The European Conference On Innovation And Entrepreneurship Ecie	0,130	-*	4
International Journal Of Economic Research	0,120	Q4	19
Proceedings Of The International Conference On Industrial Engineering And Operations Management	0,120	-*	6
Strategic Direction	0,120	Q4	10
2010 IEEE International Technology Management Conference ICE 2010	0,100	-*	2
Revista De Administracao Mackenzie	0,100	Q4	1
Advances In Enterprise Inmation Systems II	-*	-*	4
Automobile Revolution Towards A New Electro Mobility Paradigm	-*	-*	-*
Corporate Sustainability Inclusive Business Approaches Contributing To A Sustainable World	-*	-*	-*
Driving Agribusiness With Technology Innovations	-*	-*	-*
Dynamic Supply Chain Alignment A New Business Model Peak Permance In Enterprise Supply Chains Across All Geographies	-*	-*	-*
Dynamics Of Long Life Assets From Technology Adaptation To Upgrading The Business Model	-*	-*	-*
Emerging Market Multinationals And Europe Challenges And Strategies	-*	-*	-*
Entrepreneurship Concepts Methodologies Tools And Applications	-*	-*	-*
Global Bioethanol Evolution Risks And Uncertainties	-*	-*	-*
Handbook Of Research On Strategic Fit And Design In Business Ecosystems	-*	-*	-*
Handbook Of Research On Strategic Innovation Management Improved Competitive Advantage	-*	-*	-*

continued on following page

Table 2. Continued

Title	SJR	Best Quartile	H Index
Handbook Of Sustainable Luxury Textiles And Fashion	-*	-*	-*
Hybrid Organizations New Business Models Environmental Leadership	-*	-*	-*
Icitm 2020 2020 9th International Conference On Industrial Technology And Management	-*	-*	-*
Intrinsic Capability Implementing Intrinsic Sustainable Development An Ecological Civilisation	-*	-*	-*
Italian Utilities Industry Success Stories And Future Perspectives	-*	-*	-*
Logistics And Supply Chain Innovation Bridging The Gap Between Theory And Practice	-*	-*	-*
Networked Business Models In The Circular Economy	-*	-*	-*
Picmet 2018 Portland International Conference On Management Of Engineering And Technology Managing Technological Entrepreneurship The Engine Economic Growth Proceedings	-*	-*	-*
Proceedings 2020 IEEE 22nd Conference On Business Inmatics CBI 2020	-*	-*	-*
Proceedings Of The 2013 2nd International Conference On Inmation Management In The Knowledge Economy Imke 2013	-*	-*	3
Proceedings Of The 28th International Business Inmation Management Association Conference Vision 2020 Innovation Management Development Sustainability And Competitive Economic Growth	-*	-*	-*
Proceedings Of The 33rd International Business Inmation Management Association Conference Ibima 2019 Education Excellence And Innovation Management Through Vision 2020	-*	-*	-*

Note: *data not available.
Source: own elaboration

The subject areas covered by the 19 scientific articles were: Business, Management and Accounting (96); Engineering (33); Economics, Econometrics and Finance (24); Environmental Science (23); Decision Sciences (19); Energy (15); Social Sciences (14); Computer Science (12); Agricultural and Biological Sciences (3); Mathematics (2); Arts and Humanities (1); Materials Science (1); Multidisciplinary (1); Physics and Astronomy (1); Psychology (1).

The most quoted article was "Sustainable manufacturing: Trends and research challenges" from Garetti et al. (2012) with 404 quotes published in the Production Planning and Control 1,390 (SJR), the best quartile (Q1) and with H index (70). The article addresses the challenges expected in the sustainable manufacturing of the international IMS 'IMS2020' project: Global Research Support for IMS2020 Vision", promoted by the European Commission to prepare a roadmap for future manufacturing.

In Figure 2 we can analyze the evolution of citations of articles published between 2005 and 2020.

The number of quotes shows a positive net growth with an R2 of 51% for the period 2010-2021, with 2020 reaching 741 citations.

Figure 2. Evolution of citations between 2010 and 2021.
Source: own elaboration

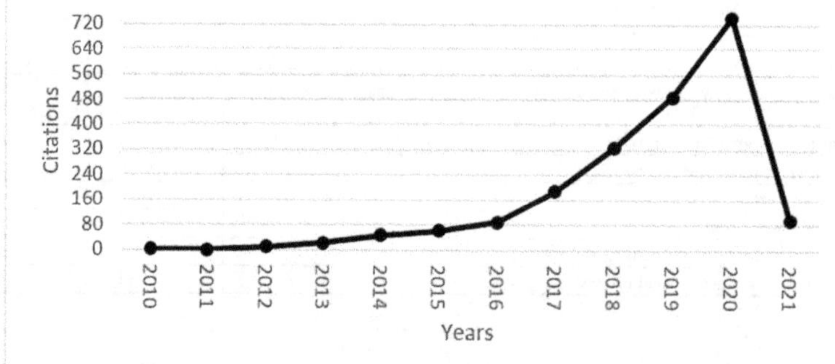

Figure 3. Network of all keywords

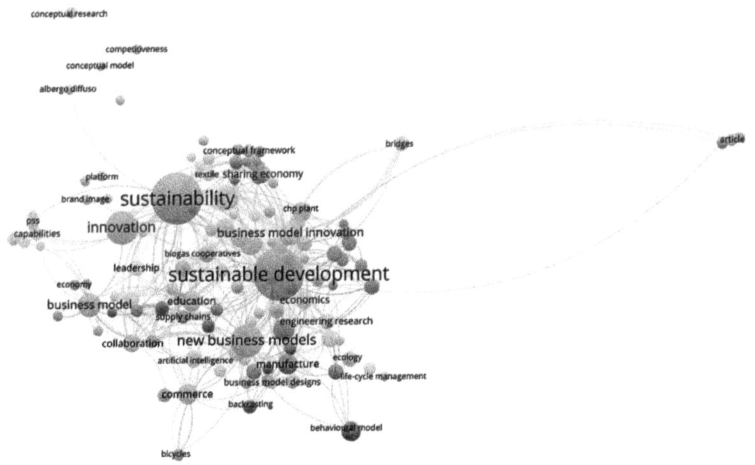

The h-index was used to ascertain the productivity and impact of the published work, based on the largest number of articles included that had at least the same number of citations. Of the documents considered for the h-index, 21 have been cited at least 21 times. 1

In Appendix 1, the citations of all scientific articles from the 2010 to January 2021 period are analyzed; 33 documents were not cited until January 2021, until ≤2010, 1; 2011, 0; 2012, 10; 2013, 23; 2014, 46 2015, 62; 2016, 90; 2017, 188; 2018, 327; 2019, 488; 2020, 741; and 2021, 96, with a total of 2072 citations.

Figure 4. Network of Linked Keywords

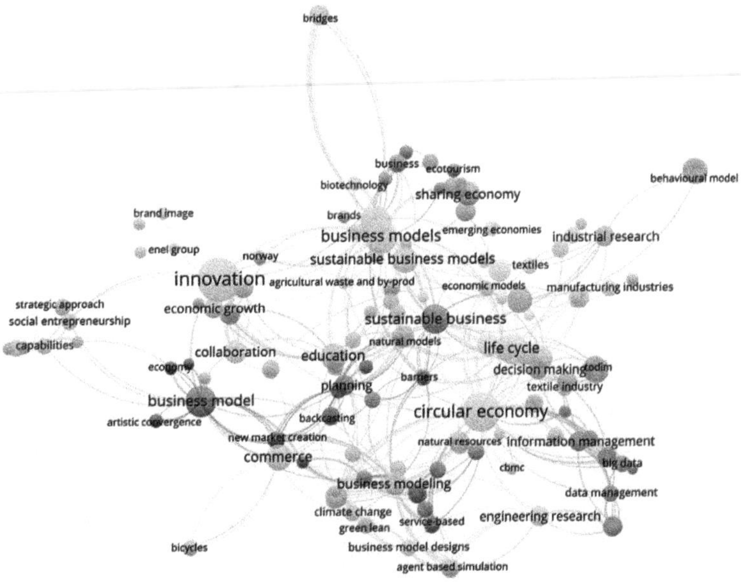

Appendix 2 examines the self-citation of the document during the period ≤2010 to January 2021, 96 documents were self-cited 122 times, the article Sustainable manufacturing: Trends and research challenges by Garetti and Taisch (2012) published in Production Planning and Control was cited 37 times each.

In Figure 3, a bibliometric study was carried out to investigate and identify indicators on the dynamics and evolution of scientific information using the main keywords. The study of bibliometric results using the scientific software VOSviewe, aims at identifying the main research keywords in studies of Sports marketing and Sponsorship.

The research was based upon the studied articles on Sports marketing and Sponsorship. The linked keywords can be examined in Figure 4 making it possible to make clear the network of keywords that appear together / linked in each scientific article, allowing to know the topics studied by the researches and to identify future research trends. In Figure 5, it is presented a profusion of bibliographic coupling with a unit of analysis of cited references.

Figure 5. Network of bibliographic coupling

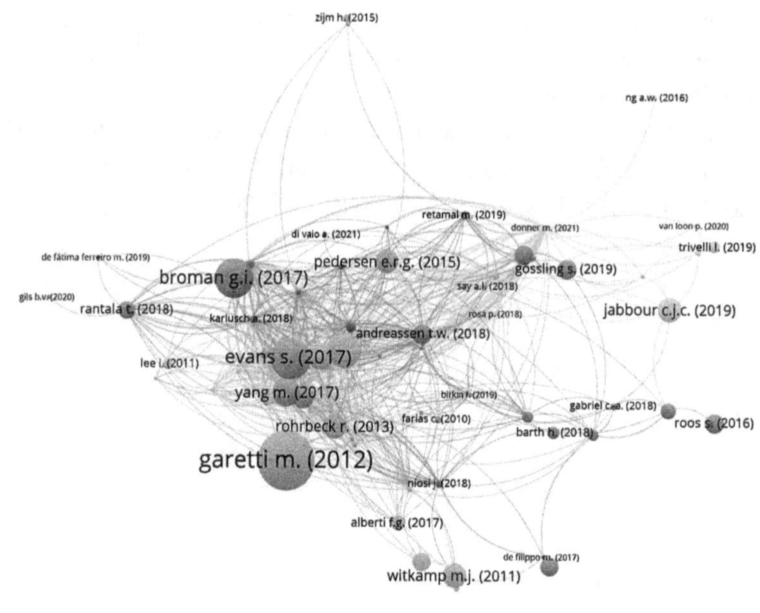

THEORETICAL PERSPECTIVES

The growth of e-commerce and internationalization has led to the popularity of the concept of a sustainable business model. Andreassen et al. (2018) define a business model as an architecture employed by organizations to create, deliver and capture value. It involves specified activities or systems used to satisfy the need of a particular market segment alongside those of key stakeholders, such as the firm and its partners (Kankaanpää et al., 2016). Management use business models to identify crucial business activities and illustrate how they relate to each other (Gjøsæter et al., 2021). In modern-day business environments, firms must implement sustainable business models that integrate environmental and social concerns into their operations and objectives (Breinbauer et al., 2019). Comin et al. (2019) explain that the growth in the global population accelerated economic development, while Lacy et al. (2012) notes its contribution to higher demand for resources to sustain industrial and economic activities and eventually causing environmental problems. Government agencies, NGOs, activists, and consumers require firms to maintain responsibility and accountability towards promoting the welfare of the society by reducing harmful activities (Bouma & Wolters, 2018). Organizations are seeking alternative strategies of improving their productivity and profitability while maintaining a balance between environmental, social, and economic elements. As a result, new business models have emerged to enable organizations to highlight and integrate fundamental changes required to maintain a competitive advantage.

The primary goal of the new business models is to improve the alignment and information inefficiencies, which affect the sustainability performance of existing business models. Girotra and Netessine (2013) recommend using 4Ws, i.e., what, when who and why to understand the decisions needed to implement the necessary changes. Yang et al. (2017) indicate that these four attributes of organizational choices are critical design parameters of establishing a profitable business model. This argument aligns with Comin et al. (2019) recommendation that sustainable business practices should be operationalized throughout management-related activities. Notably, organizational failure or success relies on implementing decisions and strategies, including business models that differentiate its products or services from those of incumbent competitors (Lopes de Sousa Jabbour, 2019). Boyd et al. (2017) indicate that new business models are built from the old ones since identifying new models involves analyzing weaknesses, strengths, and differences. They are used to develop, deliver, and communicate value in modernized ways, including innovations such as new technologies (Marín-García et al., 2020). The new business models, therefore, involve the invention or adoption of innovative technologies that support sharing the ideas and resources throughout the production chain, enhancing delivery channels, and consumer involvement in value-creation processes.

THE IMPACT OF FANS PERCEPTIONS AND ATTITUDES TOWARDS SPORTS SPONSORS

Sports teams and players have loyal fan bases, which attract marketers and appeal to sports sponsors. The relationship between sports entities and fans is characterized by emotional attachment. For instance, fans have positive feelings towards players, teams, and management when they win and are promoted, while they present negative emotions, such as hatred, frustration, and anger, when they lose and are relegated. As a result, fans define their identity based on their attachment with a sports team, making it an integral component of personal identity (Dalakas & Melancon, 2012).

The negative behaviors such as mocking the referee or yelling obscenities can lead to a negative brand image and creating reputational damage. Davies et al. (2006) explain that effective sponsorship that successfully associates a particular team or club with the sponsor can alienate competitors' fans, turning them against the sponsor's products, services, or ideas. The emotional connection between fans and their favorite athletes and teams can cause them to hate their rivals. These feelings can influence how the opposition fans feel about the sponsoring brands, affecting their connection with a potential target audience. The inability to control fan activities, behaviors, and attitudes can, therefore, pose a threat to the rapidly growing sports marketing field.

Sustainable Business Model Innovation (SBMI)

SBMI refers to organizational strategies used to address environmental and social issues resulting from business activities. Baldassarre et al. (2020) define SBMI as an approach that uses a strategic viewpoint to integrate social and environmental concerns into organizational operations and objectives. Different organizations operating in varying sectors adopt SBMI as a strategy to promote cleaner production. For instance, a company can turn waste into a resource, thus changing negative social and environmental impacts into business opportunities. SBMI combines concepts from business model innovations and sustainable business models (Geissdoerfer et al., 2018). The integration increases efficiency, leading to higher returns than process or product innovations and risk mitigation and resilience (Kerem & Sternad, 2011), increased value co-creation, and diversification opportunities (Rantala et al., 2018). These additional benefits enable organizations using SBMI to achieve and maintain a competitive advantage over competing firms by achieving a balance between environmental demands, access to resources, productivity, and profitability.

Additionally, SBMI enables firms to meet societal demands that require them to choose between profitability and societal impacts, making sustainability goals a useful trade-off. The model allows firms to exploit the rapidly growing opportunities of sustainable and socially responsible investments by encouraging corporate strategists and managers to align profitability and sustainability (Banda et al., 2019). Pressures for sustainability requires organizations to show their rational positioning on sustainability and incremental responsibility towards improving society and reducing the negative impacts resulting from business activities (Roome & Louche, 2016). In the United States, socially responsible investments have grown into a $3 trillion industry while sustainable products and services are worth $290 billion (Alberti & Varon, 2017). These statistics indicate the massive exploitable opportunities available for firms that align their organizational practices and objectives with societal demands of environmental and social stability and sustainability. However, De Fátima Ferreiro and Salavisa (2019) note that the transitioning process from traditional models to new models is challenging due to the latest innovative strategies required to implement sustainable solutions. In this case, organizations should optimize their networks and entrepreneurial values to drive sustainable business activities and processes that satisfy the new demand and offerings.

Organizations implement SBMI as a long-term strategy of achieving sustainable development by relating their operations or entity with the surrounding or supporting environment. It involves the triple-bottom-line (people-planet-profit) thinking, which considers sustainability as the central component of development ("Sustainability for future growth...," 2012). While satisfying consumers' current needs is critical, organizations using SBMI also understand the significance and impact of their process of other environmental and societal aspects. Evans et al. (2017) identifies sustainability innovations as innovation in technologies, processes, systems, business models, operating practices and procedures, and thinking. From this perspective, SBMI is not only a framework that tells how firms do businesses and conduct their activities but also how they use innovations to reconfigure their business capabilities. The various sustainable innovation approaches integrated into SBMI frameworks include green product development, social enterprises, and the blue economy (Baldassarre et al., 2020). These innovations require firms to consider activities that can potentially create environmental, economic, and social value and how they may influence the surrounding environment and communities.

Triadic Business Model (T-Model)

The T-model creates value through transactions and interactions between actors through a platform. The model links buyers and sellers of products, services, and other essential resources such as data. Examples of organizations using this model include Uber, Alibaba, Craigslist, and TaskRabbit (Andreassen et al., 2018). The emergence of this business model has shifted focus from the traditional mono-organizational logic to creating two-sided markets. For instance, in T-model, the sellers provide assets or labor to buyers in exchange for a fee or another resource, while the platform organization creates a value proposition to the purchasers based on the availability of the demanded asset. The multi-sided platforms (MSPs) bring together partners with heterogeneous roles and interests, creating a network that facilitates interactions in different markets and access to knowledge and competencies that enhance organizational success (Barni et al., 2018). Value creation occurs by establishing the infrastructure that connects producers and consumers, thus, reducing transaction costs and enabling interactions that would have otherwise not occurred.

The platform company in T-model assumes the role of intermediaries, increasing connectivity and access to resources. Andreassen et al. (2018) explain that this new middleman role facilitates the identification, selection, centralization, and standardization of services flow and equips and pairs actors to reduce search, information, and bargaining costs. As a multi-sided business model, T-model enhances an organization's competency by increasing access to improved distribution channels and access to the market. Johannsdottir (2014) indicates that moving away from the linear way of doing business enhances an organization's capability of understanding how its activities and processes contribute to sustainability. Global demand for products and services, internationalization, and the booming high-tech business have been major contributors to the model's development (Gattorna, 2016). "Innovate your business model or die" is a famous phrase used by practitioners and academics to advise investors to implement new business strategies that accommodate modern changes (Hoveskog et al., 2018). The T model can be perceived as an effective response to this mantra, where organizations understand the significance of outsourcing services to increase global consumer demand. In this framework, the producers share the value creation and delivery responsibilities with the platform company, enhancing consumer experiences.

T model promotes collaborative consumption since it operates in a triangle of actors, which can be used to enhance sustainability. T-Model can disrupt the traditional business models by encouraging higher levels of market capitalization and potentially reducing wastage of products and resources (Andreassen et al., 2018). Firms can use the platforms for marketing their excess productions and encouraging sharing of products, such as cars (Toma & Tohanean, 2019). These activities involve optimizing modern innovations and technologies and can influence consumer behaviors, leading to sustainable and responsible actions (Popescu et al., 2016). The use of the T model to promote sustainable business requires organizations to holistically evaluate their operations and how they influence all stakeholders and the environment (Johannsdottir, 2014). Barni et al. (2018) argue that multi-sided platforms implement business models that enable management of different relationships and tools that provide details of each stakeholder and value components. These aspects of the new business model facilitate communication and interactions that promote socially acceptable behaviors and the provision of sustainable products and services (Gruchmann & Seuring, 2018). Compared to traditional business models, the T model's engagement of multiple players in an industrial facilitates effective communication that builds trust and enhances mutual understanding. As middlemen, the platform companies gather consumers' feedback, complaints, and demands and communicate the same to the producers (De Filippo et al., 2017). Data collected through these platforms can include consumers' opinions of the provided products or services and potential improvement areas. Producers can also use the platform companies to communicate changes in product design, usage, and other critical elements. This two-sided communication can be used by either party to encourage sustainability, where consumers encourage sustainable production and producers encourage responsible consumption.

Circular Business Models

Companies, civil society, and policy-makers recognize circular business as a popular concept of sustainable development. The new model aims to change the traditional 'take-make-dispose' production model, which leads to enormous wastage of products and resources (Donner & de Vries, 2021). The model promotes sustainability by encouraging recycling and reusing products, materials, and components, thus, developing sustainable economic systems. Jabbour et al. (2019) recognize circular economy to integrate economic activities and environmental wellbeing by eliminating waste and reducing leakages. It helps organizations reduce the environmental burden and its potential implications on economic growth. Nasution, Aula, and Ardiantono (2020) further explain that the circular economy business model is designed to be generative and restorative, thus maintaining the value of resources, products, and materials for the longest period to reduce waste. As a result, it increases efficiency and enhances the exploration of new potential business opportunities (Gopal & Thakkar, 2016). Although some companies have implemented this strategy as a competitive strategy, environmental protection and management policies have been the primary driver of changes (Jabbour et al., 2019). Local and international environmental agencies have established policies that regulate the amount of waste disposed of by manufacturing companies and to reduce environmental concerns.

Reduction of waste in the manufacturing processes and plants and supply chain can occur in varying ways depending on the framework implemented by an organization. For instance, firms can partner to implement industrial symbiosis where an organization reuses another firm's by-product as input material (Rosa et al., 2018). In another case, firms can focus on remanufacturing or refurbishing products thrown away, thus, adding value by resetting the product's lifetime or enhancing its functionalities (Garetti & Taisch, 2012). This procedure is mostly applicable for products with short commercial life, such as electronics, which Canetta et al. (2018) argue that people often throw them away when still in operating form. Reusing and refurbishing materials under circular business models provides a practical alternative for reducing waste and exploiting natural resources. This framework enhances an organization's capacity to maintain a balance between economic, social, and environmental demands while maintaining steady profits and productivity (Broman & Robèrt, 2017). For instance, a firm using waste as secondary raw material creates quality products that meet the needs of the target market while reducing environmental degradation resulting from pollution and maintaining steady sales that ensure the firm's financial wellbeing. The practice enables the organizations to achieve the triple-bottom-line, i.e., the people-planet-profit concept of sustainability.

Although circular economy new business models (CENBM) are still in their infancy stage, the availability of large-scale data provides a support mechanism for enhanced implementation. Unlocking the potential of the circular economy model relies on innovative, complex, and large dynamic data gathering and analysis to develop knowledge and skills and identify valuable opportunities and challenges (Pedersen et al., 2019). The emergence of the internet of things and the integration of the smart industry has made the management of large amounts of data a critical component of organizational leadership (Belui Essimengane et al., 2016). Recycling of products to recover secondary raw materials involves different market actors to engage in three activities of collecting, sorting, and secondary production (Rosa et al., 2018). Big data can facilitate a smooth flow of these activities by increasing the actors' knowledge and skills regarding their particular area of operation and ensuring interconnectivity throughout the production chain and systems (Polesie & Birkin, 2019). In addition, Brendzel-Skowera (2019) indicates that the circular economy involves deep transformations of manufacturing and consumption chains and redesigning industrial systems. These activities require a thorough evaluation of data to minimize challenges associated with transitioning from the traditional "produce - consume - throw away" model to the new loop model that involves recycling, refurbishing, and remanufacturing to enhance functionality and product life cycle.

However, companies utilizing the circular economy business model struggle to maintain profitability during the transitioning process. Van Loon and Van Wassenhove (2020) indicate the firms rely on external conditions such as consumer behavior, legislation, and competition to shift to sustainable production. These external conditions undermine organizations' capability to identify and implement a feasible transitioning plan that does not affect their profitability (Gils & Weigand, 2020). For instance, local and international environmental bodies have established environmental and natural resources protection and management policies that define, and shape business models implemented across different sectors (Wójcik & Olejko, 2019). Besides, consumer awareness and empowerment has significantly improved due to enhanced access to information, increasing their involvement and engagement in business processes and decisions (Ng, Wong, & Wut, 2016). As a result, transitioning from traditional business models to new models has become a critical component of achieving success and competitiveness (Pedersen & Netter, 2015). However, despite the pressure from these external factors, their contribution is an important driving force in implementing circular business models. For instance, consumers' attitudes towards sustainable products produced from recycled materials can influence the success of the circular economy. Rosa et al. (2018) note that recycling can lead to either downcycling (low quality) or upcycling (high quality) depending on the quality of the material recycled. These aspects can influence the target market's response to the business model and, consequently, its profitability. However, firms can collaborate with policy-makers to create awareness campaigns to enhance people's understanding of the circular economy and its significance to the environment, economy, and society.

Web 2.0-Based Business Models

The increased growth of technology and the internet has shifted business models from being business-oriented to consumer-oriented. Lee (2011) defines Web 2.0 as a website that has evolved beyond the functionalities of Web 1.0 and promotes dynamic user interactions through features that support online communities and user-created content. The evolution of Web 2.0 has enhanced organizational capability to adopt new business models, manage partner and customer relationships, and support business processes and knowledge management. Gössling and Michael Hall (2019) explain that the use of web-based business models began in the 2000s with the emergence of a 'sharing economy.' Sharing economy focuses on transforming production and consumption cultures and interactions between consumers and producers (Petrini et al., 2017). During this period, organizations began optimizing infrastructures such as Information and Communication Technologies (ICT) that connected actors within a network economy. Karlusch et al., (2018) identify technology as an essential element of effective implementation of a business idea, especially in specifying how an organization creates and captures value to achieve and maintain sustainability. Web 2.0 model promotes the implementation of business ideas by providing new multiple methods of using the internet to develop and host software applications and develop and exchange digital contents between consumers and businesses (Lee, 2011). This new business model has enhanced companies' capability to survive and improve competencies throughout the digital period (Moore & Hawarden, 2020). For instance, internet-based communication platforms such as a website's comment section facilitate interactions between a company and its consumers, increasing empowerment and involvement (Ramanathan et al., 2019). The strategy helps build a strong relationship between an organization's key stakeholders, consequently enhancing stability and financial performance.

Web-based business models enable organizations to shift focus from the cost-based competition, which is incompatible with maintaining sustainability and social values, to added value product-services competition. Global competition in business environments has increased the need for consumer-focused solutions (Starace, 2020). It has also led to a paradigm shift where companies integrate products and services rather than considering them independently (Say et al., 2018). Marques and Cunha (2014) identifies this model as 'Product-Service Systems' (PSS). Companies use integrated product-service systems to enhance the life cycle (Gabriel et al., 2018). Under this business model, customers have access to customized products and services (Wirawan et al., 2018). Besides, it is characterized by newer functionalities and higher quality (Wirawan et al., 2020). Personalization is a major development of Web 2.0 due to increased access to data through user-generated content (UGC). While UGC is considered to increase consumer empowerment and promote freedom of expression and democracy, it also benefits companies through enhanced access to consumer data (Farias & Farias, 2010). Internet-based networking platforms such as Facebook gather users' data such as name, age, location, and interests, shared with third-party organizations such as advertisers (Sen & Ongsakul, 2017). Despite the criticism associated with this practice based on violation of privacy, the data enables firms to customize marketing messages and products based on the interests of the target market.

Web-based business models promote sustainability through the industrial and scientific application of technological knowledge to optimize new opportunities. It is an innovative model that can influence various organizational aspects, such as revenue generation practices, value chain structure, and value proposition. Innovation is an undeniable component of all sustainable new business models. It promotes analysis of positive feedback relationship between various actors, firms and attributes, and highlights the complexity and dynamics of a system (Niosi & McKelvey, 2018). Innovation spurs industrial growth and the establishment of different forms of businesses. However, Rohrbeck et al., (2013) argue that most sustainability innovations do not create a positive impact on organizations' competitiveness unless they create a new market and solve societal problems. Zehir et al., (2019) indicate that positive response can only occur with a change of mindset and the creation of new systems. This notion suggests the potential implication of the Web 2.0-based business model as a way of enhancing awareness among consumers and organizations. Economic agents such as firms, governmental, and non-governmental can utilize interactive websites to spur discussions associated with sustainability and innovation to influence consumer attitudes and behaviors (Bogers et al., 2020). For instance, ICT has brought a fundamental shift in the economic and social lives of producers and consumers through multi-faceted and interactive communication that influences behavior (Basl et al., 2012). This paradigm shift changes consumers' status from passive recipients of services and products to active participants throughout the production and delivery processes. Consequently, organizations have more capacity to explore sustainable opportunities that resonate with their target populations.

Additionally, Web 2.0-based business models have escalated competition and influenced drastic structural changes in various industries. The interactivity promoted by this model has led to consumer empowerment, enabling them to affect the nature and quality of products and services offered and the processes used. This condition has increased organizational accountability and responsibility (Rohrbeck et al., 2013). For instance, Kwon and Hong (2015) note that competition in the smartphone industry has increased efficiency levels regarding the utilization of resources and the corresponding output. Competition prompts manufacturers and their networks to align their production and delivery strategies with the needs of the public to gain a competitive advantage (Elia et al., 2019). Achieving this goal requires maximum utilization of digital goods, which Tan and Morales-Arroyo (2014) define as online knowledge-based and knowledge-enhanced products, such as software, databases, computerized art, information, and literature. This paradigm's features facilitate a digital computerized environment where companies and users share interactive media that combine text, graphics, sound, and moving images (Filice & Young, 2012). These components enhance understanding of the communicated message and influence responses. Therefore, Web 2.0-based business model can enhance an organization's transitioning process from traditional to new business models through increased access to data on potential markets and trends and increased consumer awareness and empowerment that support responsible consumption.

FACTORS INFLUENCING THE DEVELOPMENT OF THE NEW BUSINESS MODELS

Sustainable Innovation

The availability of innovative technologies that facilitate the development of products and services that contribute to the wellbeing of society and the environment has been a significant driver of new business models. Tadeu and Silva (2018) indicate that organizations are prompted to develop business processes and frameworks that incorporate these innovations to achieve competitive advantage and enhance quality and productivity. Wilburn and Wilburn (2014) explain that the primary goal of the new business model is to create an enterprise that integrates business engine and social mission without compromising on either front. The new frameworks aim to balance productivity, profitability, and environmental and social stability and sustainability. Witkamp et al. (2011) categorizes these technologies as 'social innovations' used to aid 'social entrepreneurship,' which Carvalho (2017) describes as processes of creating social value while maintaining a financial profit. Social entrepreneurial is characterized by the capacity to recognize and exploit new opportunities that serve a social mission, participation in innovation processes, thinking beyond the limitations of current resources, and enduring risks.

Innovation challenges the values, strengths, and weaknesses of the existing business models within specific industries. For instance, strategic niche management as innovation was established to understand and influence the early acquisition of technologies with the capacity to enhance sustainable development (Witkamp et al., 2011). The innovative strategy facilitated easy transitioning from the traditional way of doing business to modern tech-focused processes (Trivelli et al., 2019). Zijm and Klumpp (2015) indicate that transitioning to sustainable strategies is a challenging process since it requires a real paradigm shift characterized by new business models, cultural change, technological integration, and diverse skills and knowledge. Given the rapid changes experienced in the global business environment, sustainable innovation has become a critical managerial aspect (Choi et al., 2015). It is a continuous process used to enhance the life cycle of products and services and ensure that the firm maintains its competitive edge (Fidan et al., 2021). Roos et al. (2016) suggest that firms should install control systems that provide feedback on performance in relation to their goals. Measuring performance is a critical stage of achieving sustainable development as it enables the firms to maintain productivity while ensuring social and environmental objectives are achieved (Verenikin et al., 2020). Besides, the measurement can highlight underperformance areas that require interventions, thus, promoting a consistent process of sustainable innovation.

Consumers' Awareness and Demands

In the modern digital period, consumers are aware of the various environmental, social, and economic issues caused by business activities. As a result, they have increasingly partnered with activists, NGOs, and other policy-makers to encourage organizational responsibility and accountability. Vallone and Veglio (2019) prove this notion by explaining that the hospitality sector is implementing new models that focus on understanding the customers' voice as a strategic asset of evaluating organizational success. Understanding the consumers' opinions and perceptions of the quality of products and services offered can influence performance and service provision (Di Vaio et al., 2021). There has been a rapid growth of the middle-class population globally, especially in emerging economies, influencing consumption behaviors and access to consumer goods (Retamal, 2019). With current technologies and widespread adoption of the internet as a major source of information, purchasing decisions among this population are well-informed. This condition has significantly influenced new business models since the frameworks adopted must accommodate buyers' demands and expectations. For instance, Tieman (2015) notes that the halal industry's success is influenced by consumers' ability to separate halal from non-halal during purchase and their willingness to pay for the halal goods. Models such as the circular economy business model are heavily reliant on consumers' perceptions of products manufactured from recycled or refurbished materials. Plewnia and Guenther (2018) explain that people participate in sustainable economic activities either as a community to receive, give or jointly own resources while others participate to ensure maximum use of resources or convey experiences, feelings, knowledge, and ideas. The success of a new business model, therefore, depends on the organization's understanding and involvement of its target audience. The management should adopt a new model that is consumer-focused since it will reflect on the organization's commitment to achieving a balance between economic, social, and environmental sustainability.

Laws and Regulations

The escalating of environmental and ecological issues have attracted the attention of policy-makers from across the world. Both governmental and non-governmental agencies continue to push for reforms in regulations to enhance environmental protection and increase organizational responsibility. For instance, the Brazilian government created the PROÁLCOOL in November 1975 to decrease oil dependency and increase domestic production of liquid oil (Cortez & Baldassin, 2016). Although this regulation served other purposes such as creating jobs, reducing socio-economic inequalities, and saving hard currency, its environmental consequence is reflected in Brazil's current use of renewable energy. Compared to fossil fuels, renewable energy has minimal adverse environmental impacts, making it a practical alternative. Therefore, policies aimed at encouraging alternative energy sources play a significant role in strengthening environmental protections. Although these policies are often regarded as external factors that drive change, Barth and Melin (2018) recommend using industry-based and organization-based policies that regulate practices within a particular scope. For example, the agricultural sector's industrialization has led to environmental degradation (Antonaras & Kostopoulos, 2017). While national and international agencies should enforce protection laws, actors in this particular industry should be proactive in enforcing regulations that protect the environment and surrounding communities (Ardley & May 2020). This sustainability initiative requires firms to shift their focus from traditional profit-maximizing business models and integrate corporate social and environmental components (Powell & Tilt, 2017). The regulations prompt organizational management to establish new routines, beliefs, traditions, and values that align with the requirements.

Additionally, the policies serve as barriers to control business activities that would further the already troubling negative impacts. For example, governments use legal channels to protect specific areas such as forests from exploitation, thus, barring companies in the wood or furniture sectors (Papadopoulos et al., 2014). The barriers encourage managers and other staff to understand environmental issues associated with their areas of operations. Consequently, the business models adopted are environmentally and eco-friendly. Governments and international bodies such as United Nations Commission for Sustainable Development have increasingly considered manufacturing firms responsible for the sustainability of their products and services through legal statutes that explicitly indicate their responsibilities and limitations (Negri et al., 2013). Policies and regulations push organizations to establish a long-term business framework that not only focuses on current consumer needs but also their future stability (Ivan et al., 2015). As a result, value-added from sustainable strategies has become a competitive edge (Dupada et al. 2013). Therefore, these laws' availability turns the responsibility of ensuring a better future for coming generations into a shared and collaborative initiative.

CONCLUSION

The modern business environment requires an organization to implement strategies that integrate economic, political, social, and environmental concepts into their business models. This condition ensures that the firms understand their responsibilities in enhancing the wellbeing of the communities served and the environment. Business models are used to identify and specify the various activities or systems required to meet the needs of the target population. Changes in the world resulting from developments, such as the emergence of the internet and globalization, have increased the public's awareness of sustainability and organizations' contribution to the existing problems. These conditions have made creating new models a necessity in the current competitive environment. Sustainable business model innovation (SBMI), Triadic business model (T-Model), Circular business model, and Web 2.0-based business model are the new business frameworks identified in this research paper. SBMI addresses social and environmental issues by making them central components of organizational operations and objectives. For instance, the firm can integrate a strategy of turning waste into raw materials as part of its operations. T-Model focuses on creating two-sided markets through platforms that add and deliver value via improved interactions and transactions. The platforms link buyers and sellers, thus, bringing together heterogeneous market actors. The circular business model promotes sustainable development by encouraging recycling and reusing of waste products. It is a framework that focuses on establishing sustainable economic systems by integrating environmental wellbeing and economic activities. Modern technological innovations are used to improve the functionality of waste products and resources by either remanufacturing or using them as secondary raw materials. Web 2.0-based business models involve the use of websites that increase interactions between organizations and their target markets. It promotes user-generated content and online communities characterized by dynamic interactions. The development of these new business models has been driven by several factors such as continued development of sustainable innovation, consumer awareness and empowerment, and the enforcement of laws and regulations. The public, government, and non-government agencies, activists, and firms are collaborating to achieve sustainable development and ensure the wellbeing of current and future societies.

ACKNOWLEDGMENT

We would like to express our gratitude to the Editor and the Referees. They offered extremely valuable suggestions or improvements. The author were supported by the GOVCOPP Research Center of Universidade de Aveiro.

REFERENCES

Alberti, F. G., & Varon Garrido, M. A. (2017). Can profit and sustainability goals co-exist? New business models for hybrid firms. *The Journal of Business Strategy*, *38*(1), 3–13. doi:10.1108/JBS-12-2015-0124

Andreassen, T. W., Lervik-Olsen, L., Snyder, H., Van Riel, A. C. R., Sweeney, J. C., & Van Vaerenbergh, Y. (2018). Business model innovation and value-creation: The triadic way. *Journal of Service Management*, *29*(5), 883–906. doi:10.1108/JOSM-05-2018-0125

Antonaras, A., & Kostopoulos, A. (2017). Stakeholder agriculture: Innovation from farm to store. In Driving agribusiness with technology innovations (pp. 125-147). doi:10.4018/978-1-5225-2107-5.ch008

Ardley, B., & May, C. (2020). Ethical marketer and sustainability: Facing the challenges of overconsumption and the market. *Strategic Change*, *29*(6), 617–624. doi:10.1002/jsc.2372

Attias, D., & Mira-Bonnardel, S. (2016). Extending the scope of partnerships in the automotive industry between competition and cooperation. In The Automobile Revolution: Towards A New Electro-Mobility Paradigm (pp. 69-85). doi:10.1007/978-3-319-45838-0_5

Baldassarre, B., Konietzko, J., Brown, P., Calabretta, G., Bocken, N., Karpen, I. O., & Hultink, E. J. (2020). Addressing the design-implementation gap of sustainable business models by prototyping: A tool for planning and executing small-scale pilots. *Journal of Cleaner Production*, *255*, 120295. Advance online publication. doi:10.1016/j.jclepro.2020.120295

Banda, G., Mittra, J., Tait, J., Watkins, A., & Omidvar, O. (2019). Understanding the emergence and evolution of new business models in the UK regenerative medicine sector. *Technology Analysis and Strategic Management*. Advance online publication. doi:10.1080/09537325.2019.1685087

Barni, A., Montini, E., Menato, S., Sorlini, M., Anaya, V., & Poler, R. (2018, June). Integrating agent-based simulation in the design of multi-sided platform business model: a methodological approach. In *2018 IEEE International Conference on Engineering, Technology, and Innovation (ICE/ITMC)* (pp. 1-9). IEEE. 10.1109/ICE.2018.8436360

Barth, H., & Melin, M. (2018). A green lean approach to global competition and climate change in the agricultural sector – A Swedish case study. *Journal of Cleaner Production, 204*, 183–192. doi:10.1016/j.jclepro.2018.09.021

Basl, J., Buchalcevova, A., & Gala, L. (2012). Conceptual model of the impact of enterprise information systems innovation on sustainability. *Advances in Enterprise Information Systems, II*, 27–34. doi:10.1201/b12295-5

Belui Essimengane, J., Mushiri, T., & Mbohwa, C. (2016). Improving the management of operations at the "office des ports et RAdes du Gabon" (OPRAG). The road to achieve and sustain quality service delivery. *Proceedings of the International Conference on Industrial Engineering and Operations Management*, 1004-1007.

Bocken, N. M., & Geradts, T. H. (2020). Barriers and drivers to sustainable business model innovation: Organization design and dynamic capabilities. *Long Range Planning, 53*(4), 101950. doi:10.1016/j.lrp.2019.101950

Bogers, M., Chesbrough, H., & Strand, R. (2020). Sustainable open innovation to address a grand challenge: Lessons from Carlsberg and the green fiber bottle. *British Food Journal, 122*(5), 1505–1517. doi:10.1108/BFJ-07-2019-0534

Bouma, J. J., & Wolters, T. (2018). *Corporate sustainability: Inclusive business approaches contributing to a sustainable world*. Routledge., doi:10.4324/9781315639185

Boyd, B., Henning, N., Reyna, E., Wang, D. E., Welch, M. D., & Hoffman, A. J. (2017). Hybrid organizations: New business models for environmental leadership. doi:10.4324/9781351279246

Breinbauer, A., Leitner, J., & Becker, K. (2019). Sustainable location development: How do investment promotion agencies go about attracting sustainable foreign direct investment? In Emerging market multinationals and Europe: Challenges and strategies (pp. 143-158). doi:10.1007/978-3-030-31291-6_9

Brendzel-Skowera, K. (2019). Circular economy in the development of sustainable entrepreneurship. *33rd International Business Information Management Association Conference, IBIMA 2019: Education Excellence and Innovation Management Through Vision*, 8390–8399.

Broman, G. I., & Robèrt, K. (2017). A framework for strategic sustainable development. *Journal of Cleaner Production, 140*, 17–31. doi:10.1016/j.jclepro.2015.10.121

Canetta, L., Fontana, A., Foletti, M., & Tschanen, M. (2018). Sustainability assessment of various circular economy scenarios in the consumer electronics sector. *2018 IEEE International Conference on Engineering, Technology, and Innovation, ICE/ITMC 2018 – Proceedings*. 10.1109/ICE.2018.8436270

Carvalho, J. M. S. (2017). Social innovation and entrepreneurship: The case of Porto region. In Entrepreneurship: Concepts, methodologies, tools, and applications (pp. 850-887). doi:10.4018/978-1-5225-1923-2.ch036

Choi, H. R., Le, T. M. H., Alfaro, L. A., Cho, M. J., & Kim, C. S. (2015). Challenges and opportunities for port logistics in using BPAAS based on the TCO model. *International Journal of Economic Research, 12*(3), 559–581.

Comin, L. C., Aguiar, C. C., Sehnem, S., Yusliza, M., Cazella, C. F., & Julkovski, D. J. (2019). Sustainable business models: A literature review. *Benchmarking*, *27*(7), 2028–2047. doi:10.1108/BIJ-12-2018-0384

Cortez, L. A. B., & Baldassin, R. (2016). Policies towards bioethanol and their implications: Case brazil. Global bioethanol: Evolution, risks, and uncertainties (pp. 142-162) doi:10.1016/B978-0-12-803141-4.00006-X

De Fátima Ferreiro, M., & Salavisa, I. (2019). *Innovation and business models towards a sustainable food system.* Paper presented at the Proceedings of the European Conference on Innovation and Entrepreneurship. doi:10.34190/ECIE.19.119

De Filippo, M., Colangelo, D., & Farnia, L. (2017). Innovation and new business models in tourism. *Rivista di Studi sulla Sostenibilità*, (1), 149–168. doi:10.3280/RISS2017-001010

Di Vaio, A., Palladino, R., Pezzi, A., & Kalisz, D. E. (2021). The role of digital innovation in knowledge management systems: A systematic literature review. *Journal of Business Research*, *123*, 220–231. doi:10.1016/j.jbusres.2020.09.042

Donner, M., & de Vries, H. (2021). How to innovate business models for a circular bio-economy? *Business Strategy and the Environment*, *30*(4), 1932–1947. Advance online publication. doi:10.1002/bse.2725

Dupada, S., Gedela, R. K., Aryasri, R. C., & Acharya, R. (2013). Building value chain through actionable benchmarking for sustainability and excellence. *Proceedings of the 2013 2nd International Conference on Information Management in the Knowledge Economy,* 24-30.

Elia, V., Gnoni, M. G., & Tornese, F. (2019). Exploring the benefits of productization in public services utilities. *Proceedings of the Summer School Francesco Turco*, *1*, 41–45.

Evans, S., Vladimirova, D., Holgado, M., Van Fossen, K., Yang, M., Silva, E. A., & Barlow, C. Y. (2017). Business model innovation for sustainability: Towards a unified perspective for creation of sustainable business models. *Business Strategy and the Environment*, *26*(5), 597–608. doi:10.1002/bse.1939

Farias, C., & Farias, G. (2010). Cycles of poverty and consumption: The sustainability dilemma. *Competitiveness Review*, *20*(3), 248–257. doi:10.1108/10595421011047433

Fidan, F. Ş., Aydoğan, E. K., & Uzal, N. (2021). An integrated life cycle assessment approach for denim fabric production using recycled cotton fibers and combined heat and power plant. *Journal of Cleaner Production*, *287*, 125439. Advance online publication. doi:10.1016/j.jclepro.2020.125439

Filice, M., & Young, S. (2012). From mainstage to movies to media: Sustaining the live and performing arts through artistic convergence and the Balaban and Katz philosophy of continuous performance. *International Journal of Arts Management*, *14*(2), 48–56.

Gabriel, C., Bortsie-Aryee, N. A., Apparicio-Farrell, N., & Farrell, E. (2018). How supply chain choices affect the life cycle impacts of medical products. *Journal of Cleaner Production*, *182*, 1095–1106. doi:10.1016/j.jclepro.2018.02.107

Garetti, M., & Taisch, M. (2012). Sustainable manufacturing: Trends and research challenges. *Production Planning and Control*, *23*(2-3), 83–104. doi:10.1080/09537287.2011.591619

Gattorna, J. (2016). *Dynamic supply chain alignment: A new business model for peak performance in enterprise supply chains across all geographies*. Routledge. doi:10.4324/9781315578316

Geissdoerfer, M., Vladimirova, D., & Evans, S. (2018). Sustainable business model innovation: A review. *Journal of Cleaner Production, 198*, 401–416. doi:10.1016/j.jclepro.2018.06.240

Gils, B. V., & Weigand, H. (2020). Towards sustainable digital transformation. *Proceedings - 2020 IEEE 22nd Conference on Business Informatics, CBI 2020,* 104-113. 10.1109/CBI49978.2020.00019

Girotra, K., & Netessine, S. (2013). Business model innovation for sustainability. *Manufacturing & Service Operations Management, 15*(4), 537–544. doi:10.1287/msom.2013.0451

Gjøsæter, Å. S., Kyvik, Ø., Nesse, J. G., & Årethun, T. (2021). Business models as a framework for sustainable value-creation: Strategic and operative leadership challenges. *International Journal of Innovation and Sustainable Development, 15*(1), 50–74. doi:10.1504/IJISD.2021.111549

Gopal, P. R. C., & Thakkar, J. (2016). Analyzing critical success factors to implement sustainable supply chain practices in the Indian automobile industry: A case study. *Production Planning and Control, 27*(12), 1005–1018. doi:10.1080/09537287.2016.1173247

Gössling, S., & Michael Hall, C. (2019). Sharing versus collaborative economy: How to align ICT developments and the SDGs in tourism? *Journal of Sustainable Tourism, 27*(1), 74–96. doi:10.1080/09669582.2018.1560455

Gruchmann, T., & Seuring, S. (2018). Explaining logistics social responsibility from a dynamic capabilities perspective. *International Journal of Logistics Management, 29*(4), 1255–1278. doi:10.1108/IJLM-08-2017-0200

Hedstrom, G. S. (2018). *Sustainability: What it is and how to Measure it.* Walter de Gruyter GmbH & Co KG. doi:10.1515/9781547400423

Høgevold, N. M., Svensson, G., Wagner, B., Petzer, D. J., Klopper, H. B., Varela, J. C. S., ... Ferro, C. (2014). Sustainable business models: Corporate reasons, economic effects, social boundaries, environmental actions, and organizational challenges in sustainable business practices. *Baltic Journal of Management, 9*(3), 357–380. doi:10.1108/BJM-09-2013-0147

Hoveskog, M., Halila, F., Mattsson, M., Upward, A., & Karlsson, N. (2018). Education for sustainable development: Business modeling for flourishing. *Journal of Cleaner Production, 172*, 4383–4396. doi:10.1016/j.jclepro.2017.04.112

Ivan, C., Mukta, R., Sudeep, C., & Burak, C. (2015). Long-term sustainable sustainability in luxury. Where else? In Handbook of Sustainable Luxury Textiles And Fashion (pp. 17-34). doi:10.1007/978-981-287-742-0_2

Jabbour, C. J. C., Jabbour, A. B. L. D. S., Sarkis, J., & Filho, M. G. (2019). Unlocking the circular economy through new business models based on large-scale data: An integrative framework and research agenda. *Technological Forecasting and Social Change, 144*, 546–552. doi:10.1016/j.techfore.2017.09.010

Johannsdottir, L. (2014). Transforming the linear insurance business model to a closed-loop insurance model: A case study of Nordic non-life insurers. *Journal of Cleaner Production, 83*, 341–355. doi:10.1016/j.jclepro.2014.07.010

Kankaanpää, T., Shamsuzzoha, A., Carneiro, L., Almeida, R., Helo, P., Fornasiero, R., ... Chiodi, A. (2016). Methodology for non-hierarchical collaboration networks for complex products manufacturing. *2010 IEEE International Technology Management Conference, ICE 2010*. 10.1109/ICE.2010.7477018

Karlusch, A., Sachsenhofer, W., & Reinsberger, K. (2018). Educating for the development of sustainable business models: Designing and delivering a course to foster creativity. *Journal of Cleaner Production, 179*, 169–179. doi:10.1016/j.jclepro.2017.12.199

Kerem, K., & Sternad, D. (2011). Deal of the day at cherry. *Emerald Emerging Markets Case Studies, 1*(3), 1–13. doi:10.1108/20450621111170630

Kwon, H., & Hong, P. (2015). Comparative efficiency assessment and strategic benchmarking of smartphone providers with data envelopment analysis. *International Journal of Productivity and Quality Management, 15*(2), 185–202. doi:10.1504/IJPQM.2015.067762

Lacy, P., Haines, A., & Hayward, R. (2012). Developing strategies and leaders to succeed in a new era of sustainability: Findings and insights from the United Nations global compact-accenture CEO study. *Journal of Management Development, 31*(4), 346–357. doi:10.1108/02621711211218997

Lee, I. (2011). Overview of emerging web 2.0-based business models and web 2.0 applications in businesses: An ecological perspective. *International. Journal of Business Research, 7*(4), 1–16. doi:10.4018/jebr.2011100101

Lopes de Sousa Jabbour, A. B. (2019). Going in circles: New business models for efficiency and value. *The Journal of Business Strategy, 40*(4), 36–43. doi:10.1108/JBS-05-2018-0092

Marín-García, A., Gil-Saura, I., & Ruíz-Molina, M. E. (2020). How do innovation and sustainability contribute to generate retail equity? Evidence from Spanish retailing. *Journal of Product and Brand Management, 29*(5), 601–615. doi:10.1108/JPBM-12-2018-2173

Marques, P. C., & Cunha, P. F. (2014). Integrating product-service systems with new business models definition for manufacturing industries. *International Journal of Service Science, Management, Engineering, and Technology, 5*(2), 66–86. doi:10.4018/ijssmet.2014040105

Moore, A. F., & Hawarden, V. (2020). Discovery digital health strategy: COVID-19 accelerates online health care in South Africa. *Emerald Emerging Markets Case Studies, 10*(3), 1–18. doi:10.1108/EEMCS-06-2020-0197

Nasution, A. H., Aula, M., & Ardiantono, D. S. (2020). Circular economy business model design. *International Journal of Integrated Supply Management, 13*(2-3), 159–177. doi:10.1504/IJISM.2020.107848

Negri, E., Holgado, M., Wagner, D., Grefrath, C., & Macchi, M. (2013). Life cycle-based and triple bottom line assessment of sustainability impacts in product-service systems. *Proceedings of the Summer School Francesco Turco,* 139-144.

Ng, A. W., Wong, A. K. L., & Wut, T. M. (2016). Second-movers' advantage of utilizing big data to enhance sustainability performance: The case of the elevator industry. *Proceedings of the International Conference on Industrial Engineering and Operations Management*, 2569-2579.

Niosi, J., & McKelvey, M. (2018). Relating business model innovations and innovation cascades: The case of biotechnology. *Journal of Evolutionary Economics*, *28*(5), 1081–1109. doi:10.100700191-018-0561-9 PMID:30613125

Nosratabadi, S., Mosavi, A., Shamshirband, S., Kazimieras Zavadskas, E., Rakotonirainy, A., & Chau, K. W. (2019). Sustainable business models: A review. *Sustainability*, *11*(6), 1663. doi:10.3390u11061663

Pajula, T., Behm, K., Vatanen, S., & Saarivuori, E. (2017). Managing the life cycle to reduce environmental impacts. In Dynamics of long-life assets: From technology adaptation to upgrading the business model (pp. 93-113). doi:10.1007/978-3-319-45438-2_6

Papadopoulos, I., Karagouni, G., Trigkas, M., & Beltsiou, Z. (2014). Mainstreaming green product strategies why and how furniture companies integrate environmental sustainability? *EuroMed Journal of Business*, *9*(3), 293–317. doi:10.1108/EMJB-12-2013-0058

Pedersen, E. R. G., Earley, R., & Andersen, K. R. (2019). From singular to plural: Exploring organizational complexities and circular business model design. *Journal of Fashion Marketing and Management*, *23*(3), 308–326. doi:10.1108/JFMM-04-2018-0062

Pedersen, E. R. G., & Netter, S. (2015). Collaborative consumption: Business model opportunities and barriers for fashion libraries. *Journal of Fashion Marketing and Management*, *19*(3), 258–273. doi:10.1108/JFMM-05-2013-0073

Petrini, M., De Freitas, C. S., & Da Silveira, L. M. (2017). A proposal for a typology of sharing economy. *Revista De Administracao Mackenzie*, *18*(5), 39–62. doi:10.1590/1678-69712017/administracao.v18n5p39-62

Plewnia, F., & Guenther, E. (2018). Mapping the sharing economy for sustainability research. *Management Decision*, *56*(3), 570–583. doi:10.1108/MD-11-2016-0766

Polesie, T., & Birkin, F. (Eds.). (2019). *Intrinsic Capability: Implementing Intrinsic Sustainable Development for an Ecological Civilisation*. World Scientific. doi:10.1142/9789813225589

Popescu, D. I., Popa, I., Ştefan, S. C., & Vlăsceanu, C. (2016). Innovative Business Models and Responsible Consumption–Case Study. *28th IBIMA Conference, Vision 2020: Innovation Management, Development Sustainability, and Competitive Economic Growth*, 4275-4290.

Powell, L., & Tilt, C. (2017). The examination of power and politics in a conservation organization. *Accounting, Auditing & Accountability Journal*, *30*(3), 482–509. doi:10.1108/AAAJ-01-2015-1933

Ramanathan, R., Duan, Y., Ajmal, T., Dong, F., Ransbeeck, S. V., Valverde, J. M. M., & Valverde, S. B. (2019). IoT sensors in aquaculture-barriers and facilitators for sustainability in the brazilian context. *Proceedings of the International Conference on Industrial Engineering and Operations Management*, 465-467.

Rantala, T., Ukko, J., Saunila, M., & Havukainen, J. (2018). The effect of sustainability in the adoption of technological, service, and business model innovations. *Journal of Cleaner Production, 172*, 46–55. doi:10.1016/j.jclepro.2017.10.009

Retamal, M. (2019). Collaborative consumption practices in Southeast Asian cities: Prospects for growth and sustainability. *Journal of Cleaner Production, 222*, 143–152. doi:10.1016/j.jclepro.2019.02.267

Rohrbeck, R., Konnertz, L., & Knab, S. (2013). Collaborative business modeling for systemic and sustainability innovations. *International Journal of Technology Management, 63*(1-2), 4–23. doi:10.1504/IJTM.2013.055577

Roome, N., & Louche, C. (2016). Journeying toward business models for sustainability: A conceptual model found inside the black box of organizational transformation. *Organization & Environment, 29*(1), 11–35. doi:10.1177/1086026615595084

Roos, S., Zamani, B., Sandin, G., Peters, G. M., & Svanström, M. (2016). A life cycle assessment (LCA)-based approach to guiding an industry sector towards sustainability: The case of the Swedish apparel sector. *Journal of Cleaner Production, 133*, 691–700. doi:10.1016/j.jclepro.2016.05.146

Rosa, P., Sassanelli, C., & Terzi, S. (2018). Circular economy in action: uncovering the relation between Circular Business Models and their expected benefits. In 23rd Summer School" Francesco Turco"-Industrial Systems Engineering 2018 (pp. 228-235). Academic Press.

Rosário, A. (2021). Research-Based Guidelines for Marketing Information Systems. *International Journal of Business Strategy and Automation, 2*(1), 1–16. doi:10.4018/IJBSA.20210101.oa1

Rosário, A., & Cruz, R. (2019). Determinants of Innovation in Digital Marketing, Innovation Policy and Trends in the Digital Age. *Journal of Reviews on Global Economics, 8*, 1722–1731. doi:10.6000/1929-7092.2019.08.154

Rosário, A., Fernandes, F., Raimundo, R., & Cruz, R. (2021). Determinants of Nascent Entrepreneurship Development. In A. Carrizo Moreira & J. G. Dantas (Eds.), *Handbook of Research on Nascent Entrepreneurship and Creating New Ventures* (pp. 172–193). IGI Global. doi:10.4018/978-1-7998-4826-4.ch008

Sacavém, A., Cruz, R., Sousa, M., & Rosário, A. (2019). An integrative literature review on leadership models for innovative organizations, innovation policy and trends in the digital age. *Journal of Reviews on Global Economics, 8*, 1741–1751. doi:10.6000/1929-7092.2019.08.156

Say, A. L., Guo, R., & Chen, C. (2018). Disruption or new order? The emergence of the unicorn bike-sharing entrepreneurship in china. *PICMET 2018 - Portland International Conference on Management of Engineering and Technology: Managing Technological Entrepreneurship: The Engine for Economic Growth, Proceedings*. 10.23919/PICMET.2018.8481864

Sen, S. K., & Ongsakul, V. (2017). Emerging frontiers in entrepreneurship through retail-E-business: 'centripetal momentum' engaged product life cycle model. *The Journal of Business and Retail Management Research, 12*(1), 13–25. doi:10.24052/JBRMR/V12IS01/EFIETREBCMEPLCM

Starace, F. (2020). From national champion to global player. In The Italian Utilities Industry: Success Stories and Future Perspectives (pp. 71-83). doi:10.1007/978-3-030-37677-2_4

Sustainability for future growth: A key element of successful business strategies. (2012). *Strategic Direction, 28*(8), 6-8. doi:10.1108/02580541211249538

Tadeu, H. F. B., & Silva, J. T. M. (2018). Improving productivity by adopting existing technologies and sustainability. In Handbook of Research on Strategic Innovation Management for Improved Competitive Advantage (pp. 331-341). doi:10.4018/978-1-5225-3012-1.ch018

Tan, M., & Morales-Arroyo, M. (2014). Understanding distributional disruptions in the interactive digital media eco-system. *International Journal of Electronic Business, 11*(1), 42–62. doi:10.1504/IJEB.2014.057900

Tieman, M. (2015). Halal clusters. *Journal of Islamic Marketing, 6*(1), 2–21. doi:10.1108/JIMA-05-2014-0034

Toma, S., & Tohanean, D. (2019). Green business models: The case of a German automaker. *Quality - Access to Success, 20*(S2), 635–640.

Trivelli, L., Apicella, A., Chiarello, F., Rana, R., Fantoni, G., & Tarabella, A. (2019). From precision agriculture to industry 4.0: Unveiling technological connections in the agrifood sector. *British Food Journal, 121*(8), 1730–1743. doi:10.1108/BFJ-11-2018-0747

Vallone, C., & Veglio, V. (2019). Customer perceptions of the albergo diffuso concept: What makes the difference in terms of service excellence? *Tourism Analysis, 24*(3), 367–375. doi:10.3727/108354219X15511864843902

Van Loon, P., & Van Wassenhove, L. N. (2020). Transition to the circular economy: The story of four case companies. *International Journal of Production Research, 58*(11), 3415–3422. doi:10.1080/00207543.2020.1748907

Verenikin, A. O., Makhankova, N. A., Finley, J. T., & Verenikina, A. Y. (2020). Evaluation of sustainable development of Russian largest companies. *ICITM 2020 - 2020 9th International Conference on Industrial Technology and Management*, 37-41. 10.1109/ICITM48982.2020.9080388

Wilburn, K., & Wilburn, R. (2014). The double bottom line: Profit and social benefit. *Business Horizons, 57*(1), 11–20. doi:10.1016/j.bushor.2013.10.001

Wirawan, C., Yudoko, G., & Lestari, Y. D. (2018). Developing a conceptual framework of product-service system management toward firms' sustainability for Indonesian industrial estate firms. *Advances in Science, Technology and Engineering Systems, 3*(5), 128–139. doi:10.25046/aj030517

Wirawan, C., Yudoko, G., & Lestari, Y. D. (2020). Determining an appropriate product-service system management to encourage firms' sustainability: A conceptual framework (case for Indonesian industrial estate firms). *International Journal of Public Sector Performance Management, 6*(4), 488–507. doi:10.1504/IJPSPM.2020.109300

Witkamp, M. J., Raven, R. P. J. M., & Royakkers, L. M. M. (2011). Strategic niche management of social innovations: The case of social entrepreneurship. *Technology Analysis and Strategic Management, 23*(6), 667–681. doi:10.1080/09537325.2011.585035

Wójcik, E. B., & Olejko, K. (2019). Legal and ethical aspects of CSR: Potential in new business models development. In Networked Business Models in the Circular Economy (pp. 200-223). Academic Press.

Xiao, Y., & Watson, M. (2019). Guidance on conducting a systematic literature review. *Journal of Planning Education and Research, 39*(1), 93–112. doi:10.1177/0739456X17723971

Yang, M., Evans, S., Vladimirova, D., & Rana, P. (2017). Value uncaptured perspective for sustainable business model innovation. *Journal of Cleaner Production, 140*, 1794–1804. doi:10.1016/j.jclepro.2016.07.102

Zehir, C., Zehir, M., & Zehir, S. (2019). New strategies for evolution of business eco-systems: Platform strategies. In Handbook of Research on Strategic Fit and Design In Business Eco-Systems (pp. 98-122). doi:10.4018/978-1-7998-1125-1.ch005

Zijm, H., & Klumpp, M. (2015). Logistics and supply chain management: Developments and trends. *Logistics and Supply Chain Innovation: Bridging the Gap between theory into practice*, 1–20. doi:10.1007/978-3-319-22288-2_1

APPENDIX 1

Table 3. Overview of document citations period ≤ 2010 to 2021

Documents		≤2010	2011	2012	2013	2014	2015	2016	2017	2018	2019	2020	2021	Total
The role of digital innovation in knowledge management syste ...	2021	-	-	-	-	-	-	-	-	-	-	1	-	**1**
Addressing the design-implementation gap of sustainable busi ...	2020	-	-	-	-	-	-	-	-	-	-	7	3	**10**
Sustainable open innovation to address a grand challenge: L ...	2020	-	-	-	-	-	-	-	-	-	-	3	2	**5**
How do innovation and sustainability contribute to generate ...	2020	-	-	-	-	-	-	-	-	-	-	3	-	**3**
From precision agriculture to Industry 4.0: Unveiling techno ...	2019	-	-	-	-	-	-	-	-	-	4	11	1	**16**
Going in circles: new business models for efficiency and vai. ..	2019	-	-	-	-	-	-	-	-	-	1	3	-	**4**
From singular to plural: exploring organisational complexiti ...	2019	-	-	-	-	-	-	-	-	-	1	7	-	**8**
Unlocking the circular economy through new business models b ...	2019	-	-	-	-	-	-	-	-	2	21	38	8	**69**
Collaborative consumption practices in Southeast Asian citie ...	2019	-	-	-	-	-	-	-	-	-	1	9	-	10
Sustainable business models: a literature review	2019	-	-	-	-	-	-	-	-	-	-	4	1	5
Sharing versus collaborative economy: how to align ICT devei. ..	2019	-	-	-	-	-	-	-	-	-	6	34	4	**44**
A Green Lean approach to global competition and climate chan ...	2018	-	-	-	-	-	-	-	-	-	5	13	1	**19**
Relating business model innovations and innovation cascades: ...	2018	-	-	-	-	-	-	-	-	1	5		2	**8**
Explaining logistics social responsibility from a dynamic ca ...	2018	-	-	-	-	-	-	-	-		6	10		**16**
Business model innovation and value-creation: the triadie wa ...	2018	-	-	-	-	-	-	-	-	5	11	25	4	**45**
Sustainable business model innovation: A review	2018	-	-	-	-	-	-	-	-	6	31	81	15	**133**
Disruption or new arder?: The emergence ofthe unicorn bike- ...	2018	-	-	-	-	-	-	-	-	-	-	2	-	**2**
Integrating Agent Based Simulation in the Design of Multi-Si ...	2018	-	-	-	-	-	-	-	-	-	1	2	-	**3**
How supply chain choices affect the life cycle impacts of me ...	2018	-	-	-	-	-	-	-	-	-	4	3	-	**7**
Educating for the development of sustainable business models ...	2018	-	-	-	-	-	-	-	-	2	1	3	-	**6**
The effect ofsustainability in the adoption oftechnologica ...	2018	-	-	-	-	-	-	-	-	7	15	15	-	**37**
Education for Sustainable Development: Business modelling fo ...	2018	-	-	-	-	-	-	-	-	4	2	7	-	**13**
Developing a conceptual framework of product-service system ...	2018	-	-	-	-	-	-	-	-		1			**1**
Mapping the sharing economy for sustainability research	2018	-	-	-	-	-	-	-	-	2	13	26	3	**44**
Emerging frontiers in entrepreneurship through Retail-E-Busi. ..	2017	-	-	-	-	-	-	-	-	-	2	-	-	**2**
Business Model Innovation for Sustainability: Towards a Unif...	2017	-	-	-	-	-	-	-	1	33	58	101	15	**208**
Managing the life cycle to reduce environmental impacts	2017	-	-	-	-	-	-	-	-	-	2	5	-	**7**
Stakeholder agriculture: Innovation from farm to store	2017	-	-	-	-	-	-	-	-	1	-	3	-	**4**
Social innovation and entrepreneurship: The case ofporto re ...	2017	-	-	-	-	-	-	-	1	-	1	-	-	**21**
Hybrid organizations: New business models for environmental ...	2017	-	-	-	-	-	-	-	-	1	-	4	-	**5**
A pro posai for a typology of sharing economy	2017	-	-	-	-	-	-	-	-	1	1	3	1	**6**
The examination of power and politics in a conservation erga ...	2017	-	-	-	-	-	-	-	-	1	3	-	-	**4**
Can profit and sustainability geais co-exist? New business m ...	2017	-	-	-	-	-	-	-	2	5	7	14	-	**28**
Value uncaptured perspective for sustainable business model ...	2017	-	-	-	-	-	-	-	9	21	31	30	6	**97**

continued on following page

Table 3. Continued

Documents		≤2010	2011	2012	2013	2014	2015	2016	2017	2018	2019	2020	2021	Total
A framework for strategic sustainable development	2017	-	-	-	-	-	-	1	24	44	53	55	6	**183**
A life cycle assessment (LCA)-based approach to guiding an i ...	2016	-	-	-	-	-	-	-	5	10	13	13	3	**44**
Analysing criticai success factors to implement sustainable ...	2016	-	-	-	-	-	-	-	3	8	7	9	2	**29**
Policies Towards Bioethanol and Their lmplications: Case Bra ...	2016	-	-	-	-	-	-	-	-	1	2	-	-	**3**
Methodology for non-hierarchical collaboration networks for ...	2016	1	-	-	-	-	-	-	-	-	-	-	-	**1**
Dynamic supply chain alignment: A new business model for pea ...	2016	-	-	-	-	-	-	-	-	-	1	2	-	**3**
Journeying Toward Business Models for Sustainability: A Cone ...	2016	-	-	-	-	-	-	3	5	20	27	25	2	**82**
Second-movers' advantage of utilizing Big Data to enhance su ...	2016	-	-	-	-	-	-	-	-	-	1	-	-	**1**
lnnovative business models and responsible consumption - Cas ...	2016	-	-	-	-	-	-	-	-	2	-	-	-	**2**
Extending the scope of partnerships in the automotive indust...	2016	-	-	-	-	-	-	-	1	-	1	-	-	**2**
Long-term sustainable sustainability in luxury. Where else	2015	-	-	-	-	-	-	-	-	-	1			**1**
Logistics and supply chain management: Developments and tren ...	2015	-	-	-	-	-	-	-	-	4	2	2	-	**8**
Comparative efficiency assessment and strategic benchmarking ...	2015	-	-	-	-	-	-	-	-	1	1	1	-	**3**
Challenges and opportunities for port logistics in using BPA ...	2015	-	-	-	-	-	-	-	-	-	-	1	-	**1**
Collaborative consumption: Business model opportunities and ...	2015	-	-	-	-	-	-	4	6	15	20	17	3	**65**
Halal clusters	2015	-	-	-	-	-	2	3	9	7	9	10	-	**40**
Transforming the linear insurance business model to a closed ...	2014	-	-	-	-	-	-	-	1	3	3	4	-	**11**
lntegrating product-service systems with new business models ...	2014	-	-	-	-	-	-	-	-	2	-	1	-	**3**
Understanding distributional disruptions in the interactive ...	2014	-	-	-	-	-	-	-	-	1	1	2	-	**4**
Mainstreaming green product strategies why and how furniture ...	2014	-	-	-	-	-	-	-	2	4	6	3	-	**15**
The double bottom line: Profit and social benefit	2014	-	-	-	-	-	3	4	3	12	7	11	**1**	**41**
Building value chain through actionbale benchmarking for sus ...	2013	-	-	-	-	-	-	-	-	-	-	1	**-**	**1**
Business model innovation for sustainability	2013	-	-	-	1	1	4	5	12	13	13	17	**2**	**68**
Collaborative business modelling for systemic and sustainabi ...	2013	-	-	-		1	3	8	10	16	10	19	**3**	**70**
Developing strategies and leaders to succeed in a new era of...	2012	-	-	1	2	4	3	1	3	4	5	3	**-**	**26**
From mainstage to movies to media: Sustaining the live and p ...	2012	-	-	-	-	-	-	1	-	-	-	-	-	**1**
Sustainable manufacturing: Trends and research challenges	2012	-	-	1	14	32	42	50	75	54	63	67	**6**	**404**
Overview of emerging web 2.0-based business models and web 2 ...	2011	-	-	1	1	3	-	3	4	1	-	-	-	**13**
Strategic niche management of social innovations: The case o ...	2011	-	-	7	4	4	4	7	12	11	8	10	**2**	**69**
Cycles of poverty and consumption: The sustainability dilemm ...	2010	-	-	-	1	1	1	-	-	2	-	1	**-**	**6**
	Total	**1**	**0**	**10**	**23**	**46**	**62**	**90**	**188**	**327**	**488**	**741**	**96**	**2072**

Source: own elaboration

APPENDIX 2

Table 4. Overview of document self-citation period ≤ 2010 to 2021

Documents		≤2010	2011	2012	2013	2014	2015	2016	2017	2018	2019	2020	2021	Total
Addressing the design-implementation gap of sustainable busi ...	2020	-	-	-	-	-	-	-	-	-	-	3	-	**3**
From precision agriculture to Industry 4.0: Unveiling techno ...	2019	-	-	-	-	-	-	-	-	-	1		-	**1**
From singular to plural: exploring organisational complexiti ...	2019	-	-	-	-	-	-	-	-	-	-	1	-	**1**
Unlocking the circular economy through new business models b ...	2019	-	-	-	-	-	-	-	-	-	2	5	-	**7**
Sustainable business models: a literature review	2019	-	-	-	-	-	-	-	-	-	-	1	-	**1**
Green business models: The case of a german automaker	2019	-	-	-	-	-	-	-	-	-	-		-	
Sharing versus collaborative economy: how to align ICT devei. ..	2019	-	-	-	-	-	-	-	-	-	-	2	-	**2**
A Green Lean approach to global competition and climate chan ...	2018	-	-	-	-	-	-	-	-	-	-	1	-	**1**
Explaining logistics social responsibility from a dynamic ca ...	2018	-	-	-	-	-	-	-	-	-	-	2	-	**2**
Business model innovation and value-creation: the triadie wa ...	2018	-	-	-	-	-	-	-	-	-	-	2	-	**2**
Sustainable business model innovation: A review	2018	-	-	-	-	-	-	-	-	-	-	1	-	**1**
The effect ofsustainability in the adoption oftechnologica ...	2018	-	-	-	-	-	-	-	-	-	1	1	-	**2**
Education for Sustainable Development: Business modelling fo ...	2018	-	-	-	-	-	-	-	-	-	-	1	-	**1**
Emerging frontiers in entrepreneurship through Retail-E-Busi. ..	2017	-	-	-	-	-	-	-	-	3	-	2	-	**7**
Business Model Innovation for Sustainability: Towards a Unif...	2017	-	-	-	-	-	-	-	-	1	-		-	**1**
Can profit and sustainability geais co-exist? New business m ...	2017	-	-	-	-	-	-	-	-	-	1	1	-	**2**
Value uncaptured perspective for sustainable business model ...	2017	-	-	-	-	-	-	-	6	23	1		-	**30**
A framework for strategic sustainable development	2017	-	-	-	-	-	-	-	9	-	1	2	-	**12**
A life cycle assessment (LCA)-based approach to guiding an i ...	2016	-	-	-	-	-	-	-	-	1	1	1	-	**3**
Analysing criticai success factors to implement sustainable ...	2016	-	-	-	-	-	-	-	-	1	1	-	-	**2**
Logistics and supply chain management: Developments and tren ...	2015	-	-	-	-	-	-	-	-	3	1	-	-	**4**
Collaborative consumption: Business model opportunities and ...	2015	-	-	-	-	-	-	-		1	2	1	-	**3**
Halal clusters	2015	-	-	-	-		1		1	-		-	-	**2**
Transforming the linear insurance business model to a closed ...	2014	-	-	-	-	-	-	-	-	-	1	-	-	**1**
Mainstreaming green product strategies why and how furniture ...	2014	-	-	-	-	-	-	-	-	1		-	-	**1**
Business model innovation for sustainability	2013	-	-	-	-	1	-	-	-	-	1	-	-	**2**
Collaborative business modelling for systemic and sustainabi ...	2013	-	-	-	-	2	-	2	1	-	-	-	-	**3**
Sustainable manufacturing: Trends and research challenges	2012	-	-	-	10	1	17	4	3	1	-	1	-	**37**
Strategic niche management of social innovations: The case o ...	2011	-	-	1	-	-	-	-	-	-	--	-	-	**1**
	Total	**-**	**-**	**1**	**10**	**4**	**18**	**6**	**20**	**35**	**14**	**28**	**-**	**122**

Source: own elaboration

Chapter 2
Knowledge Management for Business Sustainability

Neeta Baporikar
https://orcid.org/0000-0003-0676-9913
Namibia University of Science and Technology, Namibia & University of Pune, India

ABSTRACT

Knowledge management is crucial in this knowledge-based society. Further, knowledge is a critical resource when it comes to business competitiveness and sustainability. Hence, to reach the sustainability aims, knowledge management (KM) may be regarded as central for any business organizations. Therefore, adopting an in-depth literature review method with a grounded theory approach, the aim of this chapter is to discuss the role and significance of knowledge management to ensure business growth and sustainability. The chapter also provides a holistic framework of knowledge management for business sustainability.

INTRODUCTION

An increasing number of companies have started to transform into more sustainable ones (Tideman *et al.*, 2013). Investments in sustainable practices are expected to increase both firm competitiveness and operational performance (Schoenherr, 2012; Iasevoli & Massi, 2012). Regarding the latter, performance is not only considered in terms of economic performance (e.g. savings or profitability) but also in non-economic terms such as eco-efficiency (Iasevoli & Massi, 2012). Given the interconnectedness of economic, business and social issues that form the pillars of sustainability, organizations have to attune to an even stronger involvement of the different stakeholders (Van Kleef & Roome, 2007).

To reach the sustainability aims, knowledge management (KM) may be regarded as central (Gloet, 2006; Seow, Hillary, Robinson, Anumba, Carrillo & Al-Ghassani, 2006). There are many different perspectives as how to define KM. One of the practical definitions is to see KM as a systematic way of creating, sharing and leveraging knowledge within and around organizations (Bounfour, 2003). This clarifies that KM has a long-term orientation and therefore fits nicely with one of the underlying assumptions of sustainability and sustainable management, namely, durability (Chow & Chen, 2012). KM practices,

DOI: 10.4018/978-1-7998-7452-2.ch002

such as knowledge creation, knowledge dissemination, knowledge storage and knowledge application, are expected to support a continued development of knowledge that is up-to-date and relevant. Hence, KM can be regarded as a strategic lever to ensure business sustainability; where the primary role of KM is to treat current and future knowledge resources sustainably by considering social, economic and business aspects (Ch, Holland, & Fathi, 2010). This brief discussion also leads us to the importance of formulating suitable KM strategies to achieve the aims set. It would also underline the critical need of having incorporated these KM strategies in the overall company strategy (Hansen *et al.*, 1999).

In today's dynamic competitive environment, KM research and implementation have grown rapidly in recent years. Even though several disciplines have studied KM from their own perspectives, there are only limited systematic efforts to study the interfaces of KM from an interdisciplinary perspective. Against this background, it might be interesting to study how the KM can enhance business sustainability.

More precisely, we are interested in the adoption of KM approaches supporting and improving business sustainable practices. Having this in mind, the aim of this chapter is to review existing research on KM activities in the context of business sustainable practices to establish the current body of knowledge. The main research question is: *RQ1*. What is the role of KM for enhancing business sustainability?

The above research question has been addressed through a structured review of the extant literature on the above topic. The review allows the establishment of the current body of knowledge and, on this basis, to identify gaps in our understanding. Based on this, the present chapter will list a number of promising future research avenues.

The remainder of the chapter is organized as follows. The next section briefly summarizes extant literature on KM. Then, in Section 3, the main focus is on the link between KM strategies and business sustainability. Section 4 provides a critical discussion and presents the main findings. Section 5 discusses the solutions and recommendations and provides future areas for research. The final section terminates with the conclusion of the chapter.

BACKGROUND

Knowledge is the key to effective competition. The challenge for companies requiring participation in knowledge-intensive sectors of the global company is to organize them so that they can recognize that, for example, commercial knowledge is different in kind from philosophical and scientific knowledge. The aim is effective performance, not eternal truths since commerce is about the transitory (Baporikar, 2019). All commercial knowledge is social and is traded. In fact all companies have knowledge economies working within the organization. There are four stages -discerning knowledge, choosing a container, dissemination and the use made of the knowledge. Understanding how the stages operate in the company is essential to the successful knowledge management process. In addition, to be successful the process has to be explicitly supported, managed and measured. Knowledge actually comprises multiple networks or nodes of knowledge linked together (Baporikar, 2020a). The four categories of knowledge are imperative or cultural, predictive, or having a pattern, bound by rules and prescriptions for performance. All are tacit or shared, embodied in "raw" materials, mechanisms, business practices and processes and environment and culture, and will move from softer to harder forms of embodiment. To be useful, knowledge must be distributed; only that way can it increase company performance in the market place (Baporikar, 2018b). Knowledge management is the systematic underpinning, observatism, measurement and optimization of the company's knowledge economies.

Knowledge can be seen as a key source of advantage. Its importance has been recognized for a long time. Some scholars have realized that information can create wealth. What is happening today is that there has been a qualitative change in the way in which vast amounts of data can be collected and communicated. The risk is of information overload. To help avoid this, a discipline is needed which can distinguish between data and knowledge, can find ways to reduce the overload and can organize itself. At present, little consideration is given to whether and how individuals and organizations can manage knowledge. Knowledge management is a process of continually managing knowledge of all kinds and requires a company-wide strategy which comprises policy, implementation, monitoring and evaluation. Such a policy should ensure that knowledge is available when and where needed and can be acquired from external as well an internal source. Activities such as these have management implications at all organizational levels and functions; thus culture, people, process, and technology have all to be considered (Baporikar, 2018a). In this, the fact that much information that is used is not in computers but in heads needs to be recognized. Indeed, companies are now aware that traditional database structures can hold only a fraction of what is available. This in turn leads to increased emphasis on information and communication technologies (ICTs) and the need to realize that to be accessible information has to be organised in the same way as the human brain. This is very important in the case of collecting tacit knowledge. In addition, organizations have to solve the "boundary paradox", in other words, they must be open to receive information on both an informal and formal basis from the outside. It is difficult, of course, to find solutions and processes which are completely outside individual experience. To be successful, it is necessary to recognize that knowledge is a process or set of relationships. Knowledge can be seen as a product of power relations. Knowledge management comprises information, communication, human resources, intellectual capital, brands etc. It involves facing a number of challenges such as its usefulness, its transfer to others and its quantity. It is necessary to develop an organizational capability which may be costly. It does not mean managing all that is known. It does mean formulating and implementing strategies, improving business processes, and monitoring and evaluating what knowledge exists, and its effective management. It is important yet difficult to scope, define and understand the processes, but to do so is necessary if organizations are going to be able to cope.

Innovation begins, as shown by 3m's post-it notes, with the construction of a new kind of knowledge within the firm. But the need is for repeated innovation with increasingly high levels of re-use. Business process re-engineering is a necessary precursor to innovation. This means that time-to-market and time-to-decide is the two most critical time metrics today. Too often the end of the process has been managed alone; it is now necessary to manage the front-end, market identification; product and service design. Knowledge management has a crucial role in this.

Leaders of successful organizations are consistently searching for better ways to improve performance and results. Frequent disappointments with past management initiatives have motivated managers to gain new understandings into the underlying, but complex mechanisms - such as knowledge - that govern an enterprise's effectiveness. Knowledge Management, far from being a management "fad", is broad, multi-dimensional and covers most aspects of the enterprise's activities. To be competitive and successful, experience shows that enterprises must create and sustain a balanced intellectual capital portfolio (Wig, 1997; Baporikar 2020b).

Knowledge may be viewed from several perspectives like state of mind, an object, a process, condition of having access to information, or a capability. It has also been described as "a state or fact of knowing" with knowing being a condition of "understanding gained through experience or study; the sum or range of what has been perceived, discovered, or learned". The perspective on knowledge as a state of mind focuses on enabling individuals to expand their personal knowledge and apply it to the organization's needs (Alavi & Leidner, 2001).

Research Methods

Given the situation that the topic under investigation is in its infancy, we need to apply research methods that can support theory development. Qualitative research methods are particularly suitable for meeting this aim. Qualitative methods would also give the opportunity to understand better the motives behind any actions or non-actions regarding the linkages between KM and business practices.

KM STRATEGIES

There is a general consensus in extant literature that KM is the basis on which companies can transform knowledge into useful actions. KM supports in delivering knowledge to the right people at the right time to enhance productivity and decrease supply chain cost and thus can improve the competitive advantage of companies. Consequently, KM forms the necessary fundament for developing and executing KM strategies. As a result, by having a proper KM strategy in place, companies can manage their knowledge more effectively. KM strategies are used to help companies in determining "what to do" with their knowledge to reach certain objectives. KM strategies address the "how to do it" question as well. When dealing with KM strategies, it is important to distinguish between different types of strategies. However, it is important that KM strategies should be aligned with the company's business strategies as exploiting internal knowledge is the most economic knowledge strategy companies can apply.

These companies (so-called internal exploiters) have sufficient knowledge resources to keep themselves competitive in their industries. On the other hand, companies that focus both on exploring external knowledge resources to develop new knowledge bases and exploiting internal knowledge bases to seek business opportunities can be thought of as using the most aggressive knowledge strategies. These companies ("unbounded innovators") focus on both acquiring knowledge capitals from their external environment and creating benefits by utilizing it. Hansen *et al.* (1999) identified two kinds of KM strategies: "codification" and "personalization" strategies. A codification strategy is IT-oriented, it emphasizes the codification of knowledge and its storage into databases, so people working in the company can easily retrieve it. Personalization strategy is human-oriented, it is focused on knowledge sharing between people, and IT systems are used for helping people communicate knowledge, thus their application goes beyond pure knowledge storage.

The utilization of a personalization strategy is a kind of strategic thinking that starts from and around people. The business activities of companies adopting this strategy mainly depend on their employees' tacit knowledge rather than on their existing explicit knowledge.

The work of Choi & Lee (2002) investigated the influences of knowledge strategy to knowledge creation processes in a sample of 58 Korean companies. The authors identified "system" and "human" KM-oriented strategies. The system strategy emphasizes knowledge codification, storing, information system, etc., and tries to share knowledge formally with IT network, software, documents, etc. The human strategy focuses on dialogues between people in social networks, and tries to recruit knowledgeable and experienced employees and emphasizes informally shared knowledge in knowledge communities, discussion teams/confrontation meetings, etc.

Many studies have also highlighted the steps required to develop "system"- or "human"-oriented strategies. These studies can be divided into three categories: balanced, dynamic and focused. These studies recommend companies to choose a type of strategy that is predominant or one which best serves the knowledge creation, sharing and utilization requirements and use the other one as a form of support.

The balanced view suggests that firms need to strike a balance between the two strategies.

The dynamic perspective suggests that firms adjust their strategies according to the characteristics of the knowledge present. For example, managers should align KM strategies with tasks characteristics. The focused perspective suggests companies to focus on a single strategy. By contrast, the balanced and dynamic visions insist that companies should apply both types of strategies. The concentrated and balanced perspectives, however, do not take into account the dynamic nature of knowledge. The dynamic perspective suggests that the choice of the strategy type will vary depending on the characteristics of knowledge Choi & Lee (2002). When a firm attempts to implement both strategies, with equal emphasis given to both, the consequences can result in risking a complete strategy failure. Both strategies can in fact be implemented, but this argument is apparently valid only for multinational corporations that have relatively complex and information and communication technology (ICT)-intensive functions to link the two strategies, but it is not valid for small and medium-sized enterprises. In sum, one can conclude that any KM strategy should be implemented in accordance with the structure and characteristics of the company concerned.

Many authors argue that companies can improve organizational performance by strategically aligning their business strategies with their KM strategies. Using different KM strategies at different stages of the business life cycle is also essential, as companies have different knowledge needs in different stages (Baporikar, 2018b). As such, the adoption of KM strategies can lead to better performance. In this context, another important element to generate, achieve and maintain a sustainable company is the creation of organizational architectures and KM systems that are capable of capturing, processing and making sense of business data and information. Given the fact that KM has a long-term orientation, it fits nicely with sustainability and sustainable management (Chow & Chen, 2012).

Considering the link between KM and innovation, when it comes to implementing, the lines between traditional functional areas have blurred, while at the same time, an even greater need for extensive collaborative interactions between organization members is required. In addition, a mere employee specialization may not be a suitable approach to knowledge and its management; instead, a broad knowledge base is needed that is supported by all organization members and their different types of knowledge (Baporikar, 2019). Therefore, firms can derive performance improvements through appropriate KM systems to support organizational learning as an important parameter in contributing towards innovation and sustainability. Thereby, an appropriate KM system is defined as a system that comprises a set of procedures, infrastructures, technical and managerial tools, which are designed towards the creation, sharing and leverage of information and knowledge within and around organizations (Bounfour, 2003). From a research point of view, most studies on sustainability issues have focused on manufacturing sectors and little attention has been paid to other sectors. The overall view is that KM must aim at all kinds of business sustainability be it manufacturing or service.

In conclusion, businesses are becoming are increasingly complex and knowledge-intensive in today's dynamic competitive environment. Knowledge assets have become critical to attain performance goals. Thus, it is crucial to implement KM approach for developing sustainable business strategy. It seems that a strategic approach to KM has the potential to help businesses in addressing the complexity connected with sustainability challenges. In particular, the management and understanding of knowledge processes may support the integration, rapid development and exploitation of sustainable and business knowledge by organization members (internally) and other stakeholders and participants (externally) to meet the challenges ahead.

SUSTAINABILITY

Literally, sustainability means a capacity to maintain some entity, outcome or process over time. However, in development literature, most academics, researchers and practitioners (Gray, 2010; Tjarve, & Zemīte, 2016; Mensah & Enu-Kwesi, 2018; Thomas, 2015) apply the concept to connote improving and sustaining a healthy economic, ecological and social system for human development. Stoddart (2011) defines sustainability as the efficient and equitable distribution of resources intra-generationally and inter-generationally with the operation of socio-economic activities within the confines of a finite ecosystem. Ben-Eli (2015), on the other hand, sees sustainability as a dynamic equilibrium in the process of interaction between the population and the carrying capacity of its environment such that the population develops to express its full potential without producing irreversible adverse effects on the carrying capacity of the environment upon which it depends. From this standpoint (Thomas, 2015) continues that sustainability brings into focus human activities and their ability to satisfy human needs and wants without depleting or exhausting the productive resources at their disposal. This, therefore, provokes thoughts on the manner in which people should lead their economic and social lives drawing on the available ecological resources for human development.

Hák, Janoušková, and Moldan (2016) have argued that transforming global society, environment and economy to a sustainable one is one of the uphill tasks confronting man today since it is to be done within the context of the planet's carrying capacity. The World Bank (2017) continues that this calls for innovative approaches to managing realities. In furtherance of this argument, DESA-UN (2018) posits that the ultimate objective of the concept of sustainability, in essence, is to ensure appropriate alignment and equilibrium among society, economy and the environment in terms of the regenerative capacity of the planet's life-supporting ecosystems. In the view of Gossling-Goidsmiths (2018), this dynamic alignment and equilibrium must be the focus of a meaningful definition of sustainability.

However, as argued by Mensah and Enu-Kwesi (2018), the definition must also emphasize the notion of cross-generational equity, which is clearly an important idea but poses difficulties, since future generations' needs are neither easy to define nor determine. Based on the foregoing, contemporary theories of sustainability seek to prioritize and integrate social, business and economic models in addressing human challenges in a manner that will continually be beneficial to human (Tosun & Leininger, 2017). In this regard, economic models seek to accumulate and use natural and financial capital sustainably; business models basically dwell on biodiversity and ecological integrity while social models seek to improve political, cultural, religious, health and educational systems, among others, to continually ensure human dignity and wellbeing (Evers 2018), and for that matter, sustainable development.

Economic Sustainability

Economic sustainability implies a system of production that satisfies present consumption levels without compromising future needs (Lobo, Pietriga, & Appert, 2015). Traditionally, economists assuming that the supply of natural resources was unlimited placed undue emphasis on the capacity of the market to allocate resources efficiently (Du & Kang, 2016). They also believed that economic growth would be accompanied by the technological advancement to replenish natural resources destroyed in the production process, which is not true. Moreover, it has now been realized that natural resources are not infinite; besides not all of them can be replenished or are renewable. The growing scale of the economic system has overstretched the natural resource base, prompting a rethink of the traditional economic postulations (Du & Kang, 2016). This has prompted many academicians to question the feasibility of uncontrolled growth and consumption.

Economies consist of markets where transactions occur. There are guiding frameworks by which transactions are evaluated and decisions about economic activities are made. Three main activities that are carried out in an economy are production, distribution and consumption but the accounting framework used to guide and evaluate the economy with regard to these activities grossly distorts values and this does not augur well for society and the environment. Allen and Clouth (2012) echo that human life on earth is supported and maintained by utilizing the limited natural resources found on the earth. However, due to population growth, human needs like food, clothing, housing increase, but the means and resources available in the world cannot be increased to meet the requirements forever. Furthermore, Retchless and Brewer (2016) argue that, as the main concern seems to be on economic growth, important cost components like the impact of depletion and pollution, for example, are ignored while increasing demand for goods and services continues to drive markets and infringe destructive effects of the environment. Economic sustainability, therefore, requires that decisions are made in the most equitable and fiscally sound way possible, while considering the other aspects of sustainability (Zhai & Chang, 2019)

On the other hand, KM initiatives also seem to help SMEs while facing challenges such as qualified human resource. For instance, KM main processes seem to allow active preparedness while streamlining operations (Wiig 1997). KM enables human resources to get involved in discussions of strategy development and not as administrators only. KM organic growth of knowledge helps to define better scenarios and vision for the firm, while promoting the analysis of long-term opportunities. Therefore, KM permits to expand firms' perceptions – knowledge, by continually measuring performance, and thus to improve its sustainability operations (Hansen, Nohria, and Tierney 2000). Basically KM through its main continuous processes, such as, capture relevant knowledge, storing information, disseminates information and generation of ideas; allow linking massive updated knowledge to improve, to avoid errors (Davenport and Glaser 2002) and to foster eco-innovation for more sustainable operations.

For this to happen, a knowledge-based approach that permits creativity for innovative changes is required, managing an effective change of mindset both in society and in the industry. For this reason, from the academic literature, it is implied that a new awareness or knowledge is required for a revolution of current practices to occur. In order for firms to create improvement and care of our planet's prosperity, they have to know and be aware of the negative impacts of their operations and committed to minimizing them. This leads to the urgency of including the role of workers so they acknowledge their roles' impacts onto a whole sustainable development approach.

In fact, this challenge of integrating sustainability in firms' operations represents a source of new knowledge, innovation and inspiration, to adapt general operations strategies, concepts, methods and/or tools (Baporikar, 2018b). Similarly, companies have reported value creation practices while implementing sustainable practices. However, information is particularly deficient regarding quantification of benefit, implementation difficulties and knowledge management about sustainability in companies (Baporikar, 2020b).

Environment-Economy-Society Relationship

The concept of sustainability appears poised to continue to influence future discourse regarding development science. This, implies that the best choices are likely to remain those that meet the needs of society and are business and economically viable, economically and socially equitable as well as socially and business bearable. This leads to three interconnected spheres or domains of sustainability that describe the relationships among the business, economic, and social aspects of SD as captured in Figure 1.

Figure 1. Environment-economy-society relationship
Source: Wanamaker (2018)

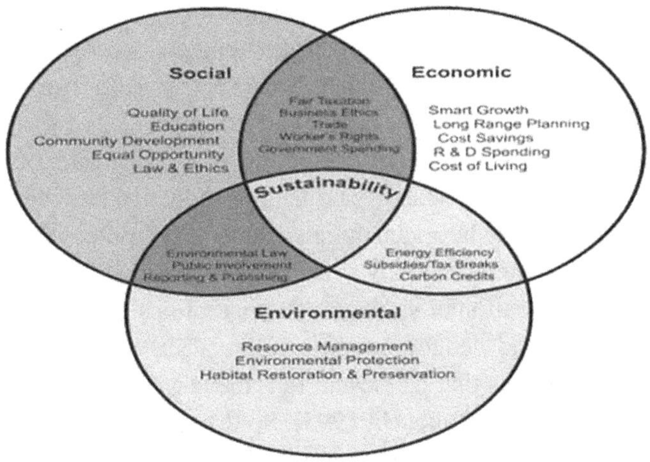

Basically, it can be concluded from the figure that, nearly everything man does or plans to do on earth has implications for the environment, economy or society and for that matter the continued existence and wellbeing of the human race. Akin to this, as argued by Wanamaker (2018), the spheres constitute a set of interrelated concepts which should form the basis of human decisions and actions in the quest for SD. Yang (2019) supports the argument by opining that basically, the figure depicts that proper decisions on sustainable resource management will bring about sustainable growth for sustainable society. Examples of these include decisions on land use, surface water management, agricultural practices, building design and construction, energy management, education, equal opportunities as well as law-making and enforcement (Montaldo, 2013).

The argument is that, when the concepts contained in the three spheres of sustainability are applied well to real world situations, everybody wins because natural resources are preserved, the environment is protected, the economy booms and is resilient, social life is good because there is peace and respect for human rights (DESA-UN, 2018). When this link is in synch then there is good life for all within the boundaries and the planet will be well protected (O'Neill, Fanning, Lamb & Steinberger, 2018).

KNOWLEDGE MANAGEMENT FOR BUSINESS SUSTAINABILITY

To improve their sustainability performance, companies need to ensure they incorporate sustainability into their vision. Accordingly, they require to be 'aware' of why and how to incorporate it, then to translate its overall objective into specific sustainability practices for each area of performance; finally, to control and measure indicators to assess actual achievement for each area. In fact, knowledge is defined as 'awareness of something' and it has been classified into tacit and explicit; the tacit knowledge is mental models, beliefs and perspectives, whereas, the explicit knowledge is the articulated knowledge. The transition from tacit to explicit is essential by firms in order to produce innovations (Nonaka and Takeuchi 1995). In this regard, knowledge is considered the firms' survival power, and the foundation of firms' capabilities.

KM appears as a potential framework to pursue sustainability due to its action learning orientation (Gloet 2006), which can define how a company fits, implements and operationalizes strategies with sustainability initiatives. Hence, KM represents an effective way to help firms to be educated about the incorporation of sustainability in operations, which means to improve its awareness and understanding of the issues involved in the required transformation. Thus, KM is any intentional and systematic process or practice of acquiring, capturing, sharing and using productive knowledge, wherever it resides, to enhance learning and performance in organizations. Hence, KM processes: discovering, capturing, sharing and applying knowledge are more likely to impact sustainability by enabling the creativity and innovation required for a transformation of strategies and operations.

In the creation or discovery of knowledge, workers are crucial since they are not only users of a system but captors and creators of know-how that is relevant to achieve a company's objectives and it depends on personal commitment (Nonaka and Takeuchi 1995). So they have the freedom to actually select the relevant knowledge for later dissemination for sustainable practices.With the proper knowledge, (e.g. training) workers can innovate, for example, designing new techniques that will potentially become the new specifications (product, method). Among the reported techniques to foster personal commitment, on which knowledge creation depends, are the use of figurative language from metaphors, analogies, models, umbrella concepts and qualitative criteria to product specifications (Nonaka and Takeuchi 1995).

The capture of knowledge is another relevant process in KM, since firms need to extend their knowledge base in order to create innovation. This should help in not only summarizing information in reports but to make sure tacit and explicit knowledge interact, while from this innovation can emerge. This is, firms should help workers to articulate part of their tacit knowledge and know-how through policies and tools.

Knowledge sharing is another KM process that seems to be the key for supporting improvements in sustainable development, through making personal (tacit) knowledge available or explicit, which is reported to be the central activity in a knowledge-creating company (Nonaka and Takeuchi 1995). This comes from the basic fact that knowledge that is not frequently discussed becomes obsolete (Baporikar, 2020a).

Further literature provides evidence that he enhancement of knowledge sharing can be promoted, according to the literature, mainly by observation, imitation practice, and socialization (tacit and explicit knowledge interacting). The application of knowledge is important and representative for sustainable operations to ensure people actions in the company are actually based on adequate top-down management of information. Besides the limited evidence regarding the general understanding and utilization of KM to support the transition towards more sustainable operations, exposed in the introduction section, the literature review showed that limited research has also been conducted to specifically study the link between knowledge management and business sustainability. From the literature, KM seems to help increase awareness of workers' practices, particularly for business sustainability and firms' operations. In this line, KM could also serve and facilitate the achievement of more business sustainability. Therefore, the present research focused on understanding the influence of KM on business sustainability, because to date, there has been little agreement on the effect and contribution of KM to achieve more sustainable business. The investigation of this phenomenon is considered the main theoretical contribution derived from this work.

SOLUTIONS AND RECOMMENDATIONS

Considering the above discussion, for businesses to be sustainable the three basic areas that may be considered include customer relationship management, quality of human resources and the adoption of ICT tools and systems through which an appropriate KM strategy is essential to enhance business sustainability. For each of the areas, KM solutions are identified and given below.

Customer relationship management: It is widely recognized that customer plays a critical role in driving sustainability programs and actions by companies. To reach this objective, KM is essential to manage and maintain effective relationship with customer. Firstly, it is necessary for companies to have an appropriate level of knowledge on sustainability and green issues to understand better the customer sustainability and green requirements. Secondly, collaborative programs among customers and companies a shared stock of knowledge on business sustainability issues that may be build-up through mixed teams comprising managers and employees of both customer and companies. These teams may work through periodic meetings aimed at exchanging knowledge and experiences on actions undertaken in collaboration to understand which kind of improvements are needed to overcome program weaknesses. Finally, customers are even more interested in performance measurement of collaborative initiatives undertaken. Communication skills and expertise hereby serve as a means for facilitating the exchange and share information about green performance.

Quality of human resource: The adoption of successful business sustainability programmes in any company as well as in businesses is dependent on leveraging employees' knowledge. From this perspective, education and training of employees play a critical role in the creation and development of business knowledge within and outside the company. It is then important to provide employees with training and education programs to anchor business sustainability thinking into the staff's minds. This may also facilitate the integration of sustainability issues in the service design and development process. Such programs should be focused on different aspects (economic, ecological and social) and functions (e.g. sales and marketing). Another solution may be the implementation of job rotation approach allowing employees to switch jobs with colleagues to understand the main characteristics of different kind of works and establish the conditions for creating new solutions through the exchange and transfer of knowledge. This may also facilitate the service innovation process and transfer of useful knowledge from one division to another. To support efforts to sustain and enhance the quality of human resource, a number of tools may be used such as e-learning tools with digital media for presenting and distributing learning materials between employees. The use of knowledge-database platforms can be also used to guarantee the easy access to relevant business knowledge and information to employees at all levels in the company.

Adoption of ICT tools and systems: Technologies are important too for supporting the business sustainability orientation of any businesses and service companies. The transfer of information is crucial for sharing knowledge within and outside the company. The use of appropriate ICT tools is essential for spreading knowledge. For example, the use of fleet management systems may not only provide accurate information on truck fleet but also stimulate truck drivers to save fuels and lorry wear out. The use of KM ICT systems and tools supports the exchange of information and sharing of knowledge and experiences facilitates a common understanding of the most appropriate actions to be implemented and the setting-up of collaborative initiatives and decision-making as well. Moreover, the adoption of ICT tools and systems may allow for the monitoring and improvement of business performance at both company and supply chain level.

The expected benefits that KM can bring in the area of business sustainability open up a huge potential for researchers from different disciplines. Some of these promising research opportunities are presented next.

FUTURE RESEARCH DIRECTIONS

This chapter has reviewed existing papers on KM in business sustainability practices. Against the expected benefits, KM approaches can bring more specific provision for research is called for. The review conducted reveals that the body of knowledge regarding the topic chosen is rather poor. Indeed, one can argue that the topic that resembles a white spot on the map which can be assessed be considered unacceptable. Given the fact that extant research provides only fragmented insights into KM in business sustainability practices, the topic offers scholars a variety of promising research avenues. Some of them include the research methods, analysis of factors hampering/supporting the implementation of KM in practices related to business sustainability, development of measures to demonstrate the impact of KM on sustainability practices and role of different stakeholders in the implementation of KM in business sustainability practice. As KM should not have an internal focus, business and companies should also think of how to best integrate different stakeholders in the KM approach to improve the effective use of existing and future knowledge. An example would be the creation of communities of practice that are attended by different stakeholders that are active to advance KM. Thus, research could focus on suitable governance models to meet this issue. This will also raise the questions of suitable KM strategies that can help in improving the management of this issue.

CONCLUSION

The authors are aware of the fact that the present study is not without limitations. By restricting the review to the databases Web of Science, ABI Inform, Business Premier Source and Scopus, this study may not have allowed complete coverage of all articles in the topic under investigation. Yet, it seems reasonable to assume that the review process covered a large proportion of the studies available. In addition, reviewing the literature was sometimes disconcerting, as many papers do not specify whether they are discussing SMEs or large firms.

To conclude, many organizations have lost business opportunities due to poor 'Knowledge Management' (KM) practice. Poor documentation on workflows, procedures and processes together with an inability to retain critical Human Capital are cited as the most common problems for such organizations. The purpose of this study was to explore the importance of the KM for business sustainability and recommend a new KM framework that will allow both the explicit and tacit knowledge to be identified, retained and levered off to ensue business sustainability. At its core, the new KM framework emphasized retention and optimal utilization of all resources especially the human capital and ICT, as these resources provide the key strength to any organization and for inculcating a knowledge-sharing and performance-driven workforce for the betterment, prosperity, and sustainability of an organization. The success of the Knowledge Management process always depends on how well the organizational culture allows for knowledge and experience sharing. The organizational leaders need to be the champions of KM so that the employees will be committed to sharing knowledge. The IT infrastructure must provide a workable common platform that captures, distributes and allows for the application. To ensure success and to bridge the gap between the people and the infrastructure, the organization needs to identify KM framework along with KM working groups at all levels in the organization.

REFERENCES

Alavi, M., & Leidner, D. E. (2001). Knowledge management and knowledge management systems: Conceptual foundations and research issues. *Management Information Systems Quarterly*, *25*(1), 107–136. doi:10.2307/3250961

Allen, C., & Clouth, S. (2012). Green economy, green growth, and low-carbon development – history, definitions and a guide to recent publications. *UNDESA: A Guidebook to the Green Economy*. Retrieved from https://sustainabledevelopment.un.org/content/documents/GE%20Guidebook.pdf

Baporikar, N. (2018a). Innovation and Sustainability in SMEs. In R. Perez-Uribe, C. Salcedo-Perez, & D. Ocampo-Guzman (Eds.), *Handbook of Research on Intrapreneurship and Organizational Sustainability in SMEs* (pp. 163–181). IGI Global. doi:10.4018/978-1-5225-3543-0.ch008

Baporikar, N. (2018b). *Global Practices in Knowledge Management for Societal and Organizational Development*. IGI Global. doi:10.4018/978-1-5225-3009-1

Baporikar, N. (2019). Knowledge Management Dynamics and Public Sector Organization Development. In Y. Albastaki, A. Al-Alawi, & S. Abdulrahman Al-Bassam (Eds.), *Handbook of Research on Implementing Knowledge Management Strategy in the Public Sector* (pp. 55–71). IGI Global. doi:10.4018/978-1-5225-9639-4.ch003

Baporikar, N. (2020a). Learning Link in Organizational Tacit Knowledge Creation and Dissemination. *International Journal of Sociotechnology and Knowledge Development*, *12*(4), 70–88. doi:10.4018/IJSKD.2020100105

Baporikar, N. (2020b). Sustainability of Social Enterprises. In J. Saiz-Álvarez & J. Gámez-Gutiérrez (Eds.), *Senior Entrepreneurship and Aging in Modern Business* (pp. 148–169). IGI Global., doi:10.4018/978-1-7998-2019-2.ch009

Ben-Eli, M. (2015). Sustainability: Definition and five core principles a new framework the sustainability laboratory. Academic Press.

Bounfour, A. (2003). *The management of intangibles: The organisation's most valuable assets* (Vol. 16). Psychology Press.

Ch, F. A., Holland, A., & Fathi, M. (2010, September). Advanced knowledge management concept for sustainable environmental integration. In *2010 IEEE 9th International Conference on Cybernetic Intelligent Systems* (pp. 1-7). IEEE.

Chow, W. S., & Chen, Y. (2012). Corporate sustainable development: Testing a new scale based on the mainland Chinese context. *Journal of Business Ethics, 105*(4), 519–533. doi:10.100710551-011-0983-x

Davenport, T. H., & Glaser, J. (2002). Just-in-time delivery comes to knowledge management. *Harvard Business Review, 80*(7), 107–111. PMID:12140850

DESA-UN. (2018, April 4). *The Sustainable Development Goals Report 2017.* https://undesa.maps.arcgis.com/apps/MapSeries/index.html

Du, Q., & Kang, J. T. (2016). Tentative ideas on the reform of exercising state ownership of natural resources: Preliminary thoughts on establishing a state-owned natural resources supervision and administration commission. *Jiangxi Social Science, 6*, 160.

Evers, B. A. (2018). *Why adopt the Sustainable Development Goals? The case of multinationals in the Colombian coffee and extractive sector* (Master Thesis). Erasmus University Rotterdam.

Gloet, M. (2006). Knowledge management and the links to HRM. *Management Research News, 29*(7), 402–413. doi:10.1108/01409170610690862

Gossling-Goidsmiths, J. (2018). *Sustainable development goals and uncertainty visualization* (Master's thesis). University of Twente.

Gray, R. (2010). Is accounting for sustainability actually accounting for sustainability … and how would we know? An exploration of narratives of organizations and the planet. *Accounting, Organizations and Society, 35*(1), 47–62. doi:10.1016/j.aos.2009.04.006

Hák, T., Janoušková, S., & Moldan, B. (2016). Sustainable development goals: A need for relevant indicators. *Ecological Indicators, 60*(1), 565–573. doi:10.1016/j.ecolind.2015.08.003

Hansen, M. T., Nohria, N., & Tierney, T. (2005). What's your strategy for managing knowledge. *Knowledge Management: Critical Perspectives on Business and Management, 77*(2), 322.

Iasevoli, G., & Massi, M. (2012). The relationship between sustainable business management and competitiveness: Research trends and challenge. *International Journal of Technology Management, 58*(1/2), 32–48. doi:10.1504/IJTM.2012.045787

Lobo, M.-J., Pietriga, E., & Appert, C. (2015). An evaluation of interactive map comparison techniques. In *Proceedings of the 33rd Annual ACM Conference on Human Factors in Computing Systems - CHI '15* (pp.3573–3582). ACM Press. 10.1145/2702123.2702130

Mensah, J., & Enu-Kwesi, F. (2018). Implication of environmental sanitation management in the catchment area of Benya Lagoon, Ghana. *Journal of Integrative Environmental Sciences.*

Montaldo, C. R. B. (2013). *Sustainable Development Approaches for Rural Development and Poverty Alleviation & Community Capacity Building for Rural Development and Poverty Alleviation.* Academic Press.

Nonaka, I., & Takeuchi, H. (1995). *The knowledge-creating company: How Japanese companies create the dynamics of innovation*. Oxford university press.

O'Neill, D. W., Fanning, A. L., Lamb, W. F., & Steinberger, J. K. (2018). A good life for all within planetary boundaries. *Nature Sustainability, 1*(2), 88–95. doi:10.103841893-018-0021-4

Retchless, D. P., & Brewer, C. A. (2016). Guidance for representing uncertainty on global temperature change maps. *International Journal of Climatology, 36*(3), 1143–1159. doi:10.1002/joc.4408

Schoenherr, T. (2012). The role of environmental management in sustainable business development: A multi-country investigation. *International Journal of Production Economics, 140*(1), 116–128. doi:10.1016/j.ijpe.2011.04.009

Seow, C., Hillary, R., Robinson, H. S., Anumba, C. J., Carrillo, P. M., & Al-Ghassani, A. M. (2006). STEPS: A knowledge management maturity roadmap for corporate sustainability. *Business Process Management Journal*.

Stoddart, H., Schneeberger, K., Dodds, F., Shaw, A., Bottero, M., Cornforth, J., & White, R. (2011). *A pocket guide to sustainable development governance*. Stakeholder Forum 2011.

Thomas, C. F. (2015). *Naturalizing Sustainability Discourse: Paradigm, Practices and Pedagogy of Thoreau, Leopold, Carson and Wilson* (PhD Thesis). Arizona State University.

Tideman, S. G., Arts, M. C., & Zandee, D. P. (2013). Sustainable leadership: Towards a workable definition. *Journal of Corporate Citizenship, 2013*(49), 17–33. doi:10.9774/GLEAF.4700.2013.ma.00004

Tjarve, B., & Zemīte, I. (2016). The Role of Cultural Activities in Community Development. *Acta Universitatis Agriculturae et Silviculturae Mendelianae Brunensis, 64*(6), 2151–2160.

Tosun, J., & Leininger, J. (2017). *Governing the inter-linkages between the sustainable development goals: Approaches to attain policy integration*. Global Challenges.

Van Kleef, J. A., & Roome, N. J. (2007). Developing capabilities and competence for sustainable business management as innovation: A research agenda. *Journal of Cleaner Production, 15*(1), 38–51. doi:10.1016/j.jclepro.2005.06.002

Wanamaker, C. (2018). *The Environmental, Economic, and Social Components of Sustainability: The Three Spheres of Sustainability*. U.S. Army Corps of Engineers. https://soapboxie.com/social-issues/The-Environmental-Economic-and-Social-Components-of-Sustainability

Wiig, K. M. (1997). Knowledge management: An introduction and perspective. *Journal of Knowledge Management, 1*(1), 6–14. doi:10.1108/13673279710800682

World Bank. (2017). *Atlas of sustainable development goals 2017*. World Development Indicators.

Yang, L. X. (2019). From general principles of civil law to general provisions of civil law: A historical leap in contemporary Chinese civil law. *Social Sciences in China, 2*, 85–91.

Zhai, T. T., & Chang, Y. C. (2019). Standing of environmental public-interest litigants in China: Evolution, obstacles and solutions. *Journal of Environmental Law, 30*(3), 369–397. doi:10.1093/jel/eqy011

KEY TERMS AND DEFINITIONS

Decision-Making: A rational and logical process of choosing the best alternative or course of action among the available options.

Impact: To have effect on, effect of coming into contact with a thing or person; the force exerted by a new idea, concept, technology, or ideology, the impression made by an idea, cultural movement, social group, it is to drive or press (an object) firmly into (another object, thing, etc.) so as to have an impact or strong effect (on).

Imperative: Absolutely necessary; urgent; compelling; a rule; principle; or instinct that compels a certain behavior.

Information Technology (IT): The umbrella term that encompasses the entire field of computer-based information processing: computer equipment, applications, and services, telecommunication links and networks, digital databases, and the integrated technical specifications that enable these systems to function interactively. IT is study or use of systems (especially computers and telecommunications) for storing, retrieving, and sending information.

Knowledge: The fact or condition of knowing something with familiarity gained through experience or association, acquaintance with or understanding of a science, art, or technique, the range of one's information or understanding, the circumstance or condition of apprehending truth or fact through reasoning or the fact or condition of having information or of being learned. Knowledge is acquaintance with facts, truths, or principles, as from study or investigation; general erudition, familiarity or conversance, as with a particular subject or branch of learning including acquaintance or familiarity gained by sight, experience, research or report.

Knowledge Development: The development of knowledge includes not only processes of external knowledge procurement (i.e., through cooperative efforts, consultants, new contacts, etc.) or the creation of specific knowledge resources like research and development departments. The formation of personal and technical knowledge networks is also part of the development of knowledge.

Knowledge Exchange: The act, process, or an instance of exchanging acquaintance with facts, truths, or principles, as from study or investigation for and including general erudition creating, involving, using, or disseminating special knowledge or information.

Knowledge Management: The systematic process of finding, selecting, organizing, distilling, and presenting information that improves the comprehension in a specific area of interest. It is used also as a synonym for content management or information management, but incorporates communities of practice, learning from experience, and knowledge retention and transfer.

Sustainability: Sustainability is the ability or capacity of something to be maintained or to sustain itself.

Tacit: Expressed or understood without being directly stated or put into words, to involve or indicate by inference, association, or necessary consequence, to contain potential sense.

Chapter 3
The Digital Bridge:
The Way We Work and Communicate in the Digital Age

Ana Catarina Lopes da Silva
Deloitte, Portugal

ABSTRACT

Technologies and digital transformation are the forces that have transformed societies. In a world where everything seems to be under "control," the unexpected occurs and forces rapid changes without proper time for planning. The future becomes uncertain, and the present becomes an excellent opportunity to upgrade and maximize profit by changing the way organizations work and especially how organizations communicate. The new world highlights the relevance of information systems flexibility and the powerful role that communication plays in the success of organizations.

"The outpouring of global solidarity and support sparked by this shared challenge has been phenomenal." (World Health Organization, n.d.)

INTRODUCTION

The market positioning and the success of the organizations are clary linked to the capability to answer to market changes and the ability to deal with the uncertainty generated. The faster and better is the answer to signals of change, the better will be your positioning. Think about it. Most of the strategies implemented by the organizations are focused on two things only: deliver the best service/product of the market and build strong relationships with their customers by establishing clever market positioning.

The organizations already face and adapt their structure due to a range of factors like legal, political or demographic changes and now mainly directed to the speed of the technology where in one click

DOI: 10.4018/978-1-7998-7452-2.ch003

everything is available and the communication is done instantly. New trends in digitalization emerge and a new world of computing, what we also call the cloud environment, brings the possibility to run a business more easily and efficiently in order to respond to the Big Data paradigm. In this scope, it is now possible the introduction to new markets like e-Commerce and run a total digital business and this is just one slice of the big picture.

Nowadays and according to the World Health Organization, the world is facing an unprecedented challenge with the most recent global COVID-19 pandemic. This new reality brings along the classic need to change and adapt the current structures of the information systems and spotlights not only the relevance of technology and Big Data trends to give special attention to where everything begins: the people.

Deloitte, a multinational professional services network, addresses and highlights the relevance of resilience with growth mindsets as a way to adapt and face the new reality. The uncertain future becomes an opportunity *that enables to respond to changes in customer demands, economic and market landscapes, and evolving talent and capability areas* (Deloitte, 2020) by changing the way we communicate, sharing and collaborating in a way we never did before.

Google also shared the need to adapt the structure and the importance of "thinking outside of the box" by reinvent the way they connect with audiences using innovative and compassionate approaches that brings closer their customers and communities (Google, 2020). Gartner also reinforces the need to partner with digital giants and increase automation by given as an example the successful Chinese companies that adopted these key characteristics to face the COVID-19 pandemic (Gartner, 2020).

Unexpectedly, the world becomes online, and new routines and ways of work are adopted in a scenario never considered before. Companies are forced to think and implement new ways to communicate that change the current information systems structure with the special focus on the people and the way they field. We run our daily lives uncertain of the future and we don´t know the future outcomes of the new realities but we do know that remaining flexible and adapting with agility is our key to stay connected and create a global network of solidarity never seen before.

THE REMOTE CULTURE

The global COVID-19 pandemic as challenged not only the way we work but also the way we run our daily lives. If we thought that before the pandemic, we lived in online world full of possibilities, we did not have a clear picture of how this could be possible. According to (Google, 2020) in the US, staying home has led to a 60% increase in the amount of content watched and consumers across the globe are spending 20% more time in apps than they did a year ago.

50% of US consumers said they used video to communicate with family and friends in March 2020 and YouTube platform raised new contents related to "with me" videos, where people film themselves going about ordinary tasks like cleaning or cooking, and "study with me" videos to stay connected and not feel alone (Google, 2020).

Every routine is now full online including shopping through digital supermarkets, the workout and education with full online classes and online gyms, the communication with family and friends through our tablets, self-phones and/or computers and the work online most known by the Work From Home (WFH). These new structures take full advantage of technology tools to run our daily and business lives with the transition of operations to virtual and the adoption of flexible ways of work.

The new way of work (WFH) is implemented and successfully adopted with the correct structure and adequate software however, it creates a bigger impact to the sectors that cannot have their activities done remotely without a loss of productivity. According to research done by (McKinsey Global Institute, 2020) the finance, management, professional services and information sectors in US have the highest potential for remote work where most of their activities do not require physical presence and can be done remotely without losing effectiveness (figure 1).

The potential and the possibility to transact the operations to a virtual environment not only is related to the sector and also to the advanced economies, where the technology reigns in its role, but most importantly are the productivity challenges that employers have to focus on.

Figure 1. Sectors with potential share of time working remotely by sector in US (McKinsey Global Institute, 2020)

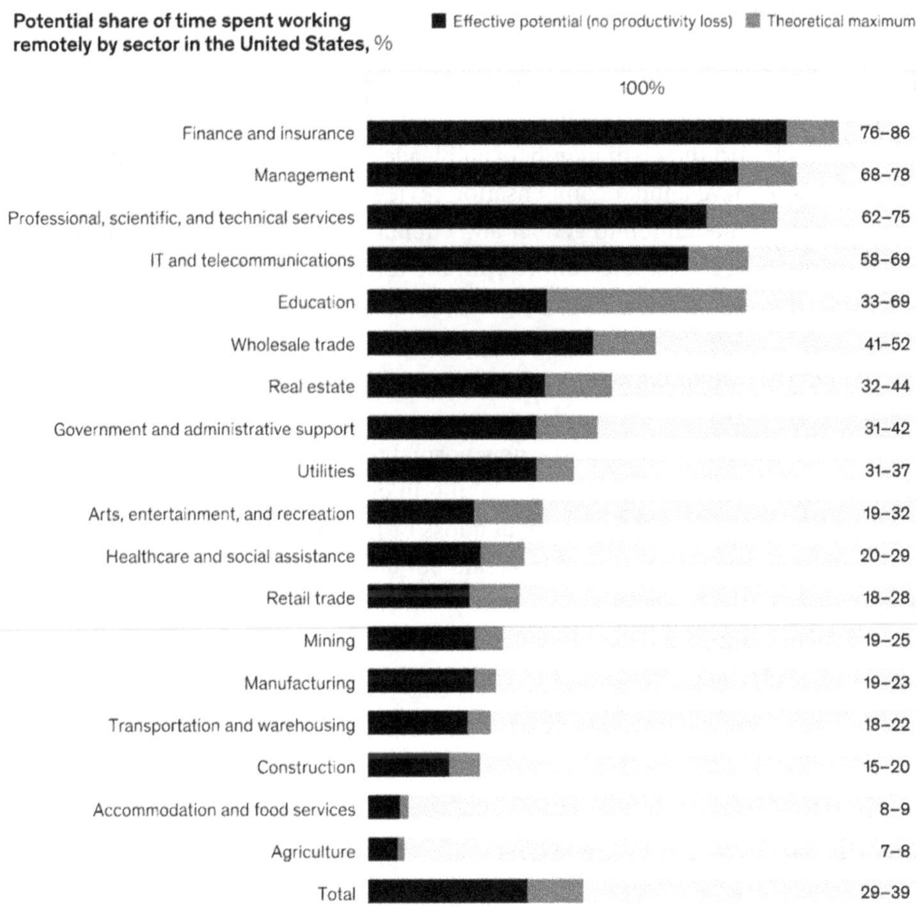

Even with the best technology implemented to stay connected, like Skype, Microsoft Teams or Zoom, and considering the work from home opportunities, these new structures of work needs to be adapt to the people, being imperative recognize their needs, prioritize communication to know their concerns and adjust the model in order to keep their motivation and boost their productivity.

Mark Read, Chief Executive Office of WPP - the world's biggest advertising agency, announced that the returning to the office is voluntary, taking into account individual situations, and decisions are being made in consultation with local leadership (Read, 2020). They adopted a number of measures design to respond to the new challenge of the world, focus not only on the company but also on their employees.

"While I am concerned about the wellbeing of our people, I am confident in the future of WPP" (Read, 2020)

The WPP Board and Executive Committee took a voluntary 20% cut in their fees or salary for an initial period of three months and further actions where consider in order to mitigate the impact on cash flow. The new structure of work that the pandemic forced WPP not only made the Company more resilient and more future-facing but also created as Mark Read affirms, a "much simpler structure that is easier for clients to navigate and easier for us to manage" (Read, 2020).

InVision a digital product company, with people in more than 25 countries around the world, is centered on remote culture with a set of collaboration tools to build strong lines of communication that never was experience before in in-house. Jennifer Aldrich, employee of InVision announced in 2019 that the company have a "cultural centered on happiness" with an official Director of Employee Happiness, certified life coach to support the team members and leaders in the company (Aldrich, 2019).

Additionally, InVision have annual compensation reviews to balance and ensure equal pay between team members, with special attention to gender and ethnicity. This strategy proved to be a very valued factor for their employees in the remote culture with the reference that these measures created stronger connections between the team members that what was experienced in the traditional offices.

"For a remote company, maintaining positive company culture is especially imperative." (Aldrich, 2019)

The WFH is now a flexible strategy of the new normal that should be adjustable to the organization and planned accordingly to the business needs, taking in consideration how much of the work can be done remotely and how to operate safety without a loss of productivity. This also requires a clear view of employees needs and generates the need to create policies to support not only the business but also their workers.

The trend of remote work intends to grow with new challenges for the organizations and especially to their leaders. The need to adopt new ways of communication and production is imperative in order to minimize losses, addressing the remote work as an opportunity for the business and a way to adapt and improve the motivation of their employees.

COMMUNICATION AND LEADERSHIP

"Interactions between leaders and teams provide an essential locus for creating the social cohesion and the unified hybrid virtual culture that organizations need in the next normal." (McKinsey Global Institute, 2020)

In a world where everyone is isolated and the only contact that we have is through digital platforms, the management and the leadership are now a critical factor to boost their employees and ensure efficiency and motivation on a daily basis. Now, is not only about having better control of what is happening and how their employees are responding to their customers. The remote work highlights the need for trust and challenges the management to enforce and create communication priorities where questions like "How are you?" and "How are you feeling?" becomes crucial for their employees.

Think about how the information flow in the traditional office: the way we talk to each other and the way we move and express gives us a greatest amount of information in a short period of time. Now make a switch to the virtual environment, where in some cases, only the voice is used to express and communicate and the interaction is planned using meetings and scheduled calls to stay "in touch".

According to a study made by (Bohns, 2017), an associate professor of Organizational Behavior at the ILR School at Cornell University, the communication face-to-face is "34 times more effective than emailed ones". Nowadays, the video meetings become the new face-to-face that the leadership can use and encourage their workers to do the same for a better understand of their needs and promote honest and consistent communication.

With this in mind, managers have now to communicate differently and embrace new behaviors with their teams to facilitate team cohesion and minimize the impacts of physical distance and dispersion. As mentioned by Michael Jenkins in (EngageRocket, 2020), CEO of Expert Humans, HR Thought Leader, "Some middle managers may well have struggled to provide their people with the support they might have needed – as the middle managers themselves are 'learning by doing'."

In a world where companies tend to have a better control of their outcomes, the unexpected becomes more unsafe to their plans and it will always be something inevitable that companies have to deal with. In this context, the flexibility becomes a key to adapt and try new methods of work, respond to market changes with success and learn to maximize which opportunity to their benefit.

EngageRocket, an Asian leader in employee engagement analytics that helps leaders and organizations make better people decisions, collected 880.000 survey responses from organizations of a large range of industries in order to study the impacts of the WFH paradigm and better understand employee's challenges. This study revealed that "manager support has a "high" to "very high" impact on employee loyalty, particularly through clear and regular feedback" (figure 2).

Figure 2. Communication and care to strengthen engagement
(EngageRocket, 2020)

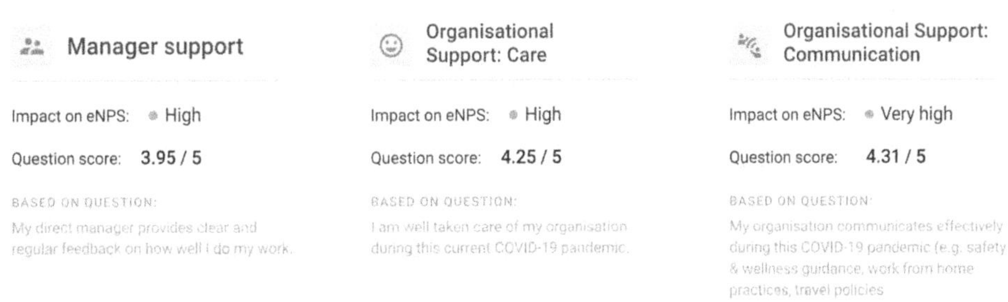

The new normal not only changes the way the information flows and accelerates the use of technologies but also brings the relevance of mental wellbeing to build resilience and set up the necessary digital bridge of the physical workspaces forced by the new challenge of the world. According to Peck Kem

Low, Chief HR Officer and Advisor, leaders are the bridge that can "make this path easier for their teams by embracing change and better preparing for the future" (EngageRocket, 2020).

Organizations are creating new strategies and implementing programs like career counselling, coaching, regular check-ins or mental wellness to better understand employee's needs, reduce negativity, keep teams together and boost productivity. In parallel, new solutions are arising in the market to monitor work, support the management and increase profitability.

The Bank of Ireland, along with a "Career Development Program" designed to promote professional wellbeing, provided to their employees a "Colleague Wellbeing App" and created new initiatives as "You as a Manager" program and a pilot Female Leadership Program, "Rise" (Bank of Ireland, 2021) to improve engagement and employee health.

Wipro, an Indian multinational corporation of information technologies, makes use of the technology such as automation (RPA), artificial intelligence (AI) and augmented reality (AR) to transform the new normal not only in caring for their employees but also for investment in the health and wellness industry, following areas that according to (Damani & Khaira, 2020) intend to emerge, namely:

- **Analysis of Behavioral Patterns**, used to suggest measures to managers related to employee's well-being profile and performance;
- **Sentiment Analysis**, used to analyze the context of replies given by the employees and alert Counselors, HR stakeholders, and line managers;
- **Interest Profiling,** used to study the different types of personas in the organization and their social behavior, tracking possible changes and alert the right stakeholders;
- **Facial Expressions & Speech Analysis**, used to analyze individual feelings like anxious or stress.

It is important to highlight that the wellbeing of employees and organizations is not a recent intervention to take into consideration but quite the opposite. A definition of mental wellbeing used by National Institute for Health and Clinical Excellence (NICE, 2009) is "Mental wellbeing is a dynamic state in which the individual is able to develop their potential, work productively and creatively, build strong and positive relationships with others and contribute to their community. It is enhanced when an individual is able to fulfil their personal and social goals and achieve a sense of purpose in society"

COVID-19 pandemic enforced the evidence of the effectiveness and the impact of leadership and communication in the wellbeing of employees and organizations, bringing an excellent opportunity to upgrade ourselves and use a critical resource directly related to success and within reach of all.

FOUR WAYS TO STAY CONNECTED

In an organization context, the technology never was so crucial to break the physical distance, manage and monitor work and empower productivity. When we talk about "connectivity", the first think we can think of is the use of digital platforms to interact and talk with each other like Skype for Business, Microsoft Teams or even Zoom to share and discuss our work.

However, connectivity can be more than one call or regular meetings to clear goals and assign tasks. The globalization and the COVID-19 pandemic raised new ways to collaborate and build strong bonds of trust with the customers and the employees, emerging in the market new solutions to help organizations synchronize team works and increase profitability in what we call the new normal. Today, effective connectivity can be the key to a more flexible and agile business and the secret ingredient to benefit with the best work of the employees and a more productive and happy working environment.

Even before we had the concepts of machine learning or advance analytics in a world flooded by a wave by information, the famous designer Charles Eames mentioned that "Eventually everything connects - people, ideas, objects. The quality of the connections is the key to quality per se".

- **Project Management Tools**

Tools to mitigate the challenges of Working from Home trend and improve remote team collaboration are a new strategy implemented by the organizations to stay nearly of their employees work and quickly updated.

Weekdone, a tool dedicated to periodic planning and track the activities for the week, update progress and provide/receive feedback and recognition. It is possible to integrate the progress with external tools like JIRA software or Google Task and provide leaders a better understanding of what problems their teams are facing, while users can see and track all the activities of each team member.

Time Doctor, a tool design not only to help the business but also to help their employees to be more efficient and avoid distractions with alerts that detects when the user is inactive or when it detects non-work related activities for a long period during working hours. With a range of functionalities, it enables to track the time spent on each project, client or task including easy-to-read summary reports and also with the possibility to integrate external tools to interact with Time Doctor.

- **Monitor Wellbeing**

As mentioned, wellbeing programs are also the new approach for the organizations to mitigate the impacts of the WFH paradigm and improve employee health. This strategy helps the management build strong relationships with their employees, support team members and create strong bonds of trust and loyalty.

Some approaches are for example sharing and promoting guidelines/suggestions of good practices in the WFH context, adjusted to the business time gaps and responsibilities within the organization. Considering some examples that highlights the importance to keep a routine and set a clear definition of the goals of each meeting to improve effectiveness and promote efficiency, incorporate breaks to recover and/or schedule meeting only during the work hours.

Create forms/communities to share common activities related for example to physical exercise or cooking that brings employees together in a non-work related context and helps to build relationships and meet new people that they could meeting in the traditional office in a simple coffee or lunch time.

These are simple and "small" interactions of the management to share awareness and recognition of the wellbeing of their employees, creating an indirect connection with emotional support.

- **Create Informal and Social Interactions**

The core of the organization culture are associated to the relationships between team members that are not only work related but also establish by the casual conversions about work or personal topics. The casual conversions also helps to build integration, promoting collaborative work and team spirit.

When switch to the work from home context, the casual conversions are typically lost when our coffee machine zone is our home and our "office hauls" are now empty. In this context, the organizations need to recreate these shared areas in the virtual environment and support casual interactions.

We can think about the creation of informal meetings to join team members or groups where the idea is to promote the casual interactions lost by the remote work. Set up a 10 minutes break for a coffee in the morning or a 30 minutes call by the end of the week to relax with a bear after a full week of work.

Additionally, organizations can implement initiatives to create shared knowledge meetings in order to improve outcomes, reduce costs by empowering the employees and promote closer collaborations between the teams. This enables also the creation of network in the organization and helps the team members to get the right information to the right people when facing challenges out of their field of knowledge.

- **Dedicate Time for Feedback**

Feedback proof to be one powerful strategy to maintain the effectiveness of leadership and mitigate the impact of the pandemic. It helps not only the management to understand the positive and negative reviews of their employees but also helps workers to improve and get a clear view about their performance on a daily basis.

The new normal upgrades the feedback strategy, adding a new approach that requires not only a formal feedback directed to the business goals but also an informal structure with a support policy to share our feelings, needs and concerns around the new ways to work and operate.

With this in mind, individual needs have to be addressed by the management and take in consideration when adopting a remote work operation. Regular feedback can also provide the ability to adapt and respond quickly to the business and individual needs, promote the integration and build strong relationships between the team members and their leader.

HYBRID MODEL

Organizations have already experienced the combination with the work from the office with the work from home, what is called the Hybrid model, and are now open to adopt and implement the benefits of this structure, starting to think about the longer term and decide the best way to structure work communication as well as physical presence required.

Kissflow, a global Software as a Service product company, start to elaborate a feedback exercise with their teams to express the advantages and disadvantages of the WFH that they experience during the lockdown. Based on that feedback, Kissflow created the REMOTE+ for their employees, an "industry-first work model for the After-COVID era" that combines the work from anywhere with work in-office, given the freedom to their teams to decide and explore the benefits of the hybrid model (Kissflow, 2020).

According to a research made by Hibob (Hi bob Inc., n.d.), a people management platform that helps companies to understand the work structures and take the best of their employees, four types of hybrid models can be adopt, namely:

- **Week-by-Week**: this model switches the WFH and the work from the office (WFO) on a weekly basis, which means that employees can opt to work side-by-side during a week and work from home in the next one, according to their needs.

- **Split-Week**: this model splits the week to give the possibility to WFH and WFO. It especially directed to companies that need to meet on a weekly basis and enables managers to stay in touch with their teams with face-to-face group meetings.
- **Shift Work**: using this model, employees work in shift, which means that they can WFH and WFO on the same day. For example, working in home during the morning and working in the office in the afternoon to meet the team face-to-face.
- **At-Will**: this model gives 100% freedom to their employees to adopt the best work structure on any given day. It brings a range of benefits for those who do not need meet people frequently on a daily basis and needs a quiet place to work.

Figure 3. Hybrid, WFH and WFO arrangements
(Hi bob Inc., n.d.)

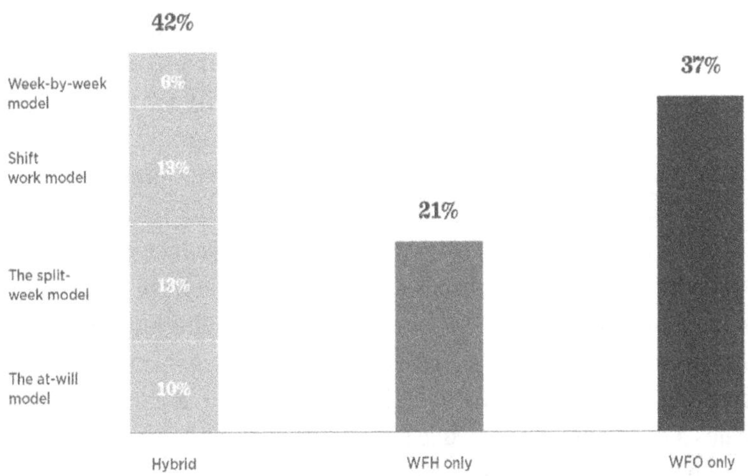

In order to understand the relevance of the Hybrid models to the business and their employees, Hibob surveyed 1,000 UK-based companies across all industries that had full-time employees and were challenged by the lockdown to adopt the remote work. According to this study, 42% of the UK employees were working according to a hybrid framework where the shift work and split-week were the models more adopted after the lockdown. Additionally, they also concluded that at-will model was more appreciated by the employees, given the trust and the flexibility to do their jobs with more support from the leadership when compared to in-office structures.

Hybrid models challenges the organizations with the use of technology to innovate and restructure their own network according to the business and workers needs. This new wave accelerated by the pandemic claim to persist as a new way of working which brings benefits not only to organizations but also to their employees with the freedom and autonomy provided by this model and the gain of confidence that improves their productivity.

CONCLUSION

In a world where the COVID-19 does not choose sectors or the profit level of a company, redefining the information system becomes imperative by just being part of this new world and the technology is used as the best ally to adapt and become continually more prosperous.

The remote work increases in order to survive to the unexpected and the effective communication between the management and leadership becomes imperative to boost productivity and morale in the process. The success is not only about the planning and the budged but specially related to authentic communication and by embracing flexibility.

In the business perspective, new industries in the field of natural language processing and artificial intelligence intend to emerge for example analyze behavior patterns, study different types of profiling or sentiment analysis tasks to extract and monitor subjective information for a better management and performance.

In the organization context, different ways to stay connect and collaborate were adopted to better meet individual and business needs. Build productive relationships by adopting intensive models of feedback and/or monitor wellbeing enables to build trust and security for the business and to retain their employees. New ways to manage the teams work and promote integration through informal and social interactions are used to increased productivity, creativity and keep employee engagement.

To summarize, we are now able to talk and implement the hybrid models where virtual workspaces are a commonplace and the companies can adapt their structure to reduce cost, create a balance between remote and office work and increase probability. Organizations can have a plan about which days they attend to work from home, managing by week or month and including business and individual needs.

What we thought was not a possible scenario to adapt in the organizations' structure is currently a new model that is considered to drive business and obtain productive gains. The new reality generated by the pandemic creates a different way to awake and clarify that what determinates the best structure of information systems is not only the technology involved but especially the management and the people who are part of the system.

REFERENCES

AldrichJ. (2019, February 1). Retrieved from https://www.invisionapp.com/inside-design/remote-life-whats-it-all-about/

Bank of Ireland. (2021). Retrieved from https://www.bankofirelanduk.com/about/responsible-business/colleagues/

Bohns, V. K. (2017, April 17). *Harvard Business Review.* Retrieved from https://hbr.org/: https://hbr.org/2017/04/a-face-to-face-request-is-34-times-more-successful-than-an-email

DamaniM. D.KhairaS. (2020, December). Retrieved from https://www.wipro.com/business-process/proliferating-new-age-digital-technologies-to-boost-mental-health-and-wellbeing/

Deloitte. (2020). Retrieved from https://www2.deloitte.com/content/dam/Deloitte/global/Documents/About-Deloitte/RECOVER-TAL-STRAT-Reimagine-talent-strategy-op-modelPDF1.pdf

EngageRocket. (2020). Retrieved from https://www.engagerocket.co/hubfs/Resilience%20of%20SG%20workforce%20Whitepaper_Aug%2020_EngageRocket.pdf

Foresight Mental Capital and Wellbeing Project. (2008, October). Retrieved from https://assets.publishing.service.gov.uk/government/uploads/system/uploads/attachment_data/file/292453/mental-capital-wellbeing-summary.pdf

Gartner. (2020, October 21). *Smarter With Gartner.* Retrieved from www.gartner.com: https://www.gartner.com/smarterwithgartner/how-successful-chinese-companies-adapted-to-covid-19/

Google. (2020). Retrieved from https://services.google.com/fh/files/misc/2020_covidadsplaybook_en-us.pdf

Hi bob Inc. (n.d.). Retrieved from https://www.hibob.com/guides/hybrid-working-model-advantages/

Kissflow. (2020, June 8). Retrieved from https://kissflow.com/news/kissflow-launches-remoteplus/

McKinsey Global Institute. (2020, July 7). Retrieved from https://www.mckinsey.com/business-functions/organization/our-insights/reimagining-the-postpandemic-workforce

McKinsey Global Institute. (2020, November 23). Retrieved from https://www.mckinsey.com/featured-insights/future-of-work/whats-next-for-remote-work-an-analysis-of-2000-tasks-800-jobs-and-nine-countries

Meulen, R. v., & Pettey, C. (2018, January 25). *Gartner.* Retrieved from www.gartner.com/en: https://www.gartner.com/en/newsroom/press-releases/2018-01-25-gartner-says-self-service-analytics-and-bi-users-will-produce-more-analysis-than-data-scientists-will-by-2019

NICE. (2009, November 5). Retrieved from https://www.nice.org.uk/guidance/ph22/chapter/1-Recommendations

ReadM. (2020, April 29). Retrieved from https://www.wpp.com/-/media/project/wpp/images/investors/2020/annual-report/download-files/wpp_annual_report_2019_strategic_report-2.pdf?la=en

World Health Organization. (n.d.). *World Heath Organization.* Retrieved from https://www.who.int/emergencies/diseases/novel-coronavirus-2019/donate

Chapter 4
Towards Digital Transformation:
Implications for Strategic Change

John Loonam
Dublin City University, Ireland

ABSTRACT

This chapter seeks to explore the key strategic change lessons organizations can learn ahead of implementing digital transformation initiatives. The chapter will review the digital transformation literature and associated challenges organizations are confronted with in implementing large-scale information systems-enabled change. Key enterprise system lessons are taken from implementation, where the McKinsey 7-S framework is introduced as a lens to support organizations adopting digital transformation. Critical success factors are identified that seek to provide leaders with a more holistic arsenal when leading digital transformation initiatives. The chapter concludes with reflections for the strategic change field.

INTRODUCTION

This chapter seeks to explore the key strategic change lessons organizations can learn ahead of implementing digital transformation initiatives. The chapter begins by reviewing the literature and the key technologies associated with digital transformation. The chapter then introduces the challenges organizations are confronted with in implementing large-scale information systems-enabled change. With a view to overcoming these challenges, the chapter will introduce the key lessons learned from the implementation of enterprise-wide systems, where the McKinsey 7-S framework is introduced as a lens to support organizations adopting digital transformation. Critical success factors are identified that seek to provide leaders with a more holistic arsenal when leading digital transformation initiatives. The chapter concludes with reflections for the strategic change field.

DOI: 10.4018/978-1-7998-7452-2.ch004

TOWARDS DIGITAL TRANSFORMATION

To explore the rise of digital transformation within work organizations, it is firstly important to review the evolution of information systems (IS). According to Porter & Millar (1985) and Porter & Hepplemann (2014), there have been three waves of evolution associated with IS-driven competition. The first wave occurred between the 1960s and late 1980s, where organisations sought to improve operational effectiveness by automating information-based processes, or as Somogyi and Galliers noted 'early commercial computers were used mainly to automate the routine clerical work of large administrative departments' (1987: 30). Early computer systems were based on centralised stand-alone machines, which were used principally for data processing. The advent of such databases and more sophisticated and powerful mainframe computers during this era gave rise to the idea of developing corporate databases in order to supply management with information about the business (Somogyi and Galliers, 1987). Initially, centralised information systems from the 1960s and 1970s were deployed by organisations to assist in single application functionality, such as manufacturing or accounting systems. However, from the 1980s onwards, added pressures to deliver greater strategic and competitive advantages meant that typical business applications had grown exponentially[1] (Slee and Slovin, 1997). What started out as 'islands of automation' (McKenney and McFarlan, 1982), i.e., applications running separately from each other, by the 1980s these were often put into a single system in order to manage and centralise data better. Accordingly, such centralised databases afforded organisations an opportunity to think more strategically about information system implementation and the respective ability of leveraging greater organisational competitive advantage (McFarlan, 1984).

With the development of end user computing, which would assist in disseminating information throughout the entire enterprise, the 1980s witnessed the emergence of the second wave of IS-driven competition. Enterprise-wide information systems emerged, from vendors such as SAP, Oracle, Baan, and JD Edwards, which promised to unite disparate information systems into a single database. As noted by Loonam et al, 'enterprise systems are the internal technological hub of the enterprise allowing data from different business functions, mainly from finance, human resources, logistics, manufacturing, and sales and marketing to be manipulated and processed by a single software package such as SAP (2018: 186-187). According to Shang & Seddon (2000), Enterprise systems (ES) provide organizations with a number of benefits, most notably (i) operational, (ii) managerial, (iii) strategic, (iv) IS infrastructure, and (v) organizational. From an operational perspective, ES facilitate a casual connection between a visual model of business processes and the software implementation of those processes, and therefore they ensure a level of integration, data integrity and security, which is not easily achievable with multiple software platforms (Parr and Shanks, 2000). From a managerial perspective, ES would enable senior leadership teams to view organizational information more holistically, where data from across all functions and divisions can be revealed in real-time to enable more effective decision-making (Loonam et al, 2014). From a strategic perspective, ES packages assist in building strategic partnerships and supporting alliances, and according to Kraemmergaard et al, they have the potential to integrate beyond the organisations own value chain, delivering inter-enterprise integration (2003). This form of integration allows a single organisation to integrate with customers and suppliers along its value chain and to other organisations with similar areas of interest thus creating opportunities for competitive advantage. From an IS infrastructure perspective, ES packages allow organisations to implement an integrated IS plan. In other words, the ES package rids the firm of old legacy systems, unstable IS architectures, and expenditure related to maintenance of these systems. Finally, from an organizational perspective, ES implementations allow organizations to adapt more enterprise-oriented change visions, supporting a more transparent and data-centric culture.

The third wave of IS-driven competition began in the mid 2000s as organizations increasingly looked to digital technologies to transform their offerings. This has given rise to the era of Digital Transformation (DT). Westerman et al, describe digital transformation 'as the use of technology to radically improve performance or reach of enterprises' (2014). Research by the authors, which "surveyed 391 large companies with revenues of $500 million or more across 30 countries, found that organizations with successful digital strategies were 26% more profitable than their industry peers and generated 9% higher revenue from their physical assets (2014, 17–18). Hess et al, advance our understanding of DT, viewing it 'as being concerned with the changes digital technologies can bring about in a company's business model, which result in changed products or organizational structures or in the automation of processes' (2016). Central to our understanding of DT is the significant structural, process, system, and cultural organization-wide changes associated with implementation. Such profound changes are felt both inside and outside the organization, where DT not only transforms business activities with reassess the very essence of value capture and creation and as such afford the formation of new business models and strategic opportunities. In essence, this is the key difference between second wave and third wave IS-driven competition. Second wave change centres primarily on internal transformation whereas third wave IS-driven competition adopts both an inside-out and an outside-in perspective of strategic thinking. This point is furthered by Vial, who from a review of 282 works on digital transformation within the IS literature, developed a conceptual definition of DT as "a process that aims to improve an entity by triggering significant changes to its properties through combinations of information, computing, communication, and connectivity technologies" (2019: 118).

In order to fully appreciate the transformational potential associated with DT initiatives, it is important to explore the range of information systems that are engaged during implementation. Sebastian et al, refer to these digital technologies with the acronym SMACIT (which stands for social, mobile, analytics, cloud and the Internet of Things [IoT]) (2017: 197). Figure 1 below seeks to illustrate the range of technologies involved in the delivery of digital transformation. The figure depicts an enterprise system in the centre with the surrounding SMACIT technologies. The enterprise system acts as an operational backbone, where all internal organizational data is integrated into a single database. The SMACIT technologies are able to leverage off the enterprise system, where each technology can align and integrate its data to the operational core of the organization. For example, the combination of social media tools, for example, Facebook, mobile computer applications, for example, smartphones and tablets, and virtual data analytics and cloud computing, referred to as Enterprise Social Systems (Kumar et al, 2016), can provide organizations with a new stream of data and insights into how their customers perceive respective products and service offerings and how the organization can improve to build more enduring relationships with customers and prospective customers and help to leverage greater organizational value. As Westerman et al note, 'the successful introduction of ESS technologies allows organizations to create new forms of value by transforming their entire customer experience, exploiting greater value from organizational operations, and creating new business models that reconfigure value chains and offer new competitive advantages' (2014).

Perhaps the most significant technological development to enable digital transformation has been the growth and performance of both analytic and cloud computing capabilities. For decades, organizations struggled with two key computing challenges, namely how to continue to store large volumes of data and process it in real time. In recent years significant improvement to big data and cloud computing systems has resolved these challenges and given rise to an era of smart connected products (also referred to as The Internet of Things) (Porter & Hepplemann, 2014). As the authors note, "Information Technology (IT) is becoming an integral part of the product itself. Embedded sensors, processors, software, and connectivity in products (in effect, computers are being put inside products), coupled with a product cloud in which product data is stored and analyzed and some applications are run, are driving dramatic improvements in product functionality and performance" (Porter & Hepplemann, 2014: 67). By deploying a suite of digital technologies conventional product manufacturers are able to digitize their offerings and accordingly devise new value creating opportunities. Digitized products keep the manufacturer closer to customers, allow design to feed modifications into product development faster, which in turn fosters new layers of innovation and potential new product offerings. Central to reshaping how organizations deliver their respective product and service offerings is the emerging role data will play in shaping strategy. As Porter & Hepplemann note, "to create products and get them to customers, manufacturers perform a wide range of activities, which generally take place in a standard set of functional units: research and development (or engineering), IT, manufacturing, logistics, marketing, sales, after- sale service, human resources, procurement, and finance. The new capabilities of smart, connected products alter every activity in this value chain. At the core of what is reshaping the value chain is data" (2015: 99). As a consequence, the most significant opportunity for organizations in implementing digital transformation initiatives, resides in how product-centric organizations can start to focus on service offerings as a result of new data insights. Such insights have significant strategic implications for conventional organizations, offering new growth opportunities, business models, and product innovations.

Figure 1. Technologies used for digital transformation
(Author, 2021)

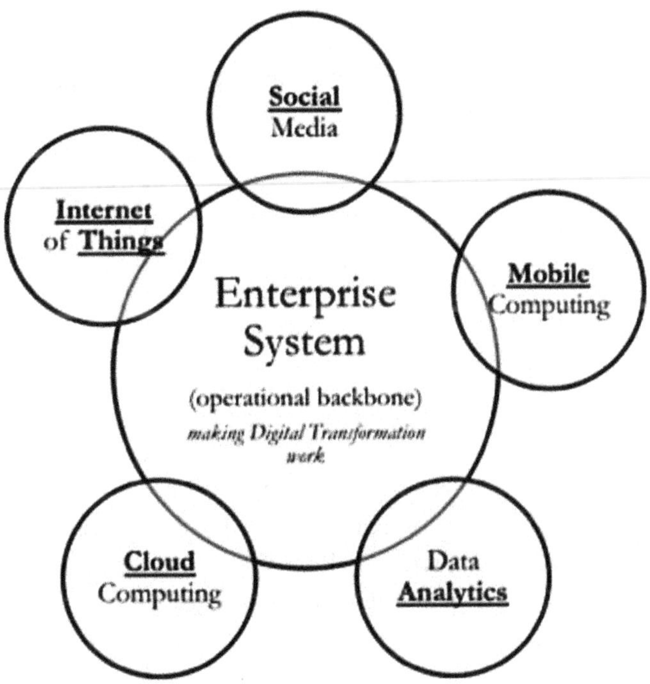

AN ORGANIZATIONAL DILEMMA-DIFFERING PERSPECTIVES OF INFORMATION SYSTEMS

According to a McKinsey survey, the author estimates "that by 2025 IoT will have a potential total economic impact of as much as $11.1 trillion per year. In fact, IoT will be the biggest source of value of all disruptive technologies, ahead of mobile Internet, knowledge-work automation, cloud computing, and advanced robotics" (Menard, 2017: 32). Yet, as pointed out by Loonam et al, "many organizations have struggled with the emergence of digital technologies and the respective transformation initiatives required by organizations" (2018: 102). A historical tour of the IS literature reveals the enduring dilemma for organizations involved in the introduction of new technologies. According to Markus and Benjamin, in their seminal article on IT-enabled change, the authors note that "it is widely known that many large-scale change management projects involving new information technology (IT) fail" (1997:55). More specifically, Iveroth notes that "as much as 70 percent of IT-enabled change projects fail" (2010: 136). Central to this challenge is the differing perspectives held by organizations in implementing information systems.

This chapter identifies three different perspectives as to how IS-enables change within organizations, these include; (i) the technological determinism, (ii) the organisational imperative and (iii) socio-technical interactionism. Technological determinism is used by Campbell (1996), but it is also referred to as the 'technology imperative' (Markus and Robey, 1988) and the 'determinist' perspective (Symons, 1991). This perspective of information systems is imbued with the sense that technology is intrinsically good and in turn will affect the organisation positively. Implementation is used to mean the actual installation of IS applications into the organisation, focusing entirely on the technical aspects of IS (Gintzberg, 1981). This perspective views organisations as 'machines', where human behaviour is highly predictable and determined by clearly defined rules (Morgan, 1997). Consequently, the introduction of new technology does not pose any problems as long as these rules are adhered to. The technological deterministic perspective is dominated by an engineering worldview (Keen and Scott Morton, 1978). Implementation is regarded as a straight forward task where the human and the organisational components are given little priority in relation to the machines and the methods for making the transition from manual tasks to automated tasks (Orlikowski and Baroudi, 1991). As human behaviour is predictable and organisations can be structured to accommodate new technology, implementation is just the final stage in the technical process of getting the technology to work. However, technological determinism has been criticised due to its strong bias towards technology and lack of attention to the human and organisational issues demanded from IS implementations. Consequently, other perspectives have emerged, most notably the organisational imperative and socio-technical interactionism perspectives, which seek to address the deficits of a technological deterministic bias.

The second perspective, referred to as the organisational imperative, adopts a top-down approach to implementation, which began with the rise of the strategic management school from Harvard (Chandler, 1962). The label 'organisational imperative' was created by Markus and Robey (1988), but this perspective has also been labelled the 'systems perspective' (Symons, 1991), or 'managerial rationalism' (Campbell, 1996). It is referred to as a top-down approach because implementation begins at the strategic level and works its way down the organisation. The basic assumption about this perspective is that through strategic planning all organisations will be effective and efficient. Invariably, this perspective relies on organisational engineering through strategy, structure, and systems. IS implementation is, therefore, planned at a strategic level and then filtered down through the organisation using specific structures and systems. Such an approach to implementation is envisaged to lead to greater organisational competitive advantage.

The final perspective, referred to as socio-technical interactionism, adopts a bottom-up approach to IS implementation. The socio-technical perspective, which was first proposed by Emery and Trist in 1965, places an emphasis on the necessity of attending to the social structuring of work groups to maximise the fit between technology and human systems (2005). In other words, 'what occurs within the group is somewhat determined by the technology, but the persons within the group have some agency of choice with the constraints that are imposed by the technology' (Clegg et al, 1996: 365). Laudon and Laudon note that 'in a socio-technical perspective, the performance of a system is optimised when both the technology and the organisation mutually adjust to one another until a satisfactory fit is obtained' (2002: 15). This means that technology must be changed and designed in such a way as to fit organisational and individual needs. Similarly, organisations and individuals must also be changed through training, learning, and planned organisational change in order to facilitate the operation and prosperity of the technology (Laudon & Laudon, 2015).

The socio-technical perspective provided the first real evidence that IS implementation involved more than just a technological deterministic approach (Mumford, 1996). Instead, implementations would need to pay attention to the organisational and human aspects involved in applying information systems to the workplace. While the 'technology determinism' perspective focused on machines and the 'organisational imperative' perspective recognised the importance of developing a strategic approach to implementation, the socio-technical perspective focused more on the people within the organisation and their interaction to the machines. As Iveroth noted, "managers often think that IT will take care of itself once it is implemented. What they tend to forget, however, is that IT is intimately interlinked with the organization and the way people go about their daily work. As a result, successful IT-enabled change implies managing both the IT itself *and* its social and organizational implications" (2010: 136). Similarly, digital transformations typically require large-scale change, owing to the scale and scope of implementations. Accordingly, organizations conducting such implementations will need to be cognisant of the socio-technical demands from digital technologies.

LEARNING LESSONS FROM ES TRANSFORMATIONS

As noted in figure one above, in order for organizations to implement digital technologies successfully, an enterprise system typically resides at the operational core that supports data integration between and across all systems. Therefore, this chapter seeks to take lessons learned from previous large-scale Enterprise System (ES) transformations, which were notable for their implementation scale and scope, and apply to the introduction of digital technologies into organizations. Specifically, the chapter will focus the discussion on the pre-implementation phase where the organization is preparing for digital transformation configuration. Such configuration involves assessing an organizations' ability to change, "a well-known means of considering this is the McKinsey 7-S framework, which highlights the importance of fit between strategy, structure, systems, staff, style, skills and superordinate goals" (also referred to as shared values) (Waterman et al, 1980: 14-cited in Johnson et al, 2018). Lessons from ES transformations are taken from the critical success factors (CSF) required to successfully implement such change initiatives. Loonam et al (2018), from a review of the literature, identified 34 CSFs for ES implementation, which are adapted to each element of the McKinsey 7-S framework to support assessing an organizations readiness for change (see Figure 2 below). A review of the literature further extends CSFs for digital transformation initiatives to the framework.

Figure 2. McKinsey 7-S Framework and digital transformation critical success factors
Adapted from Waterman et al, 1980 and Loonam et al, 2018

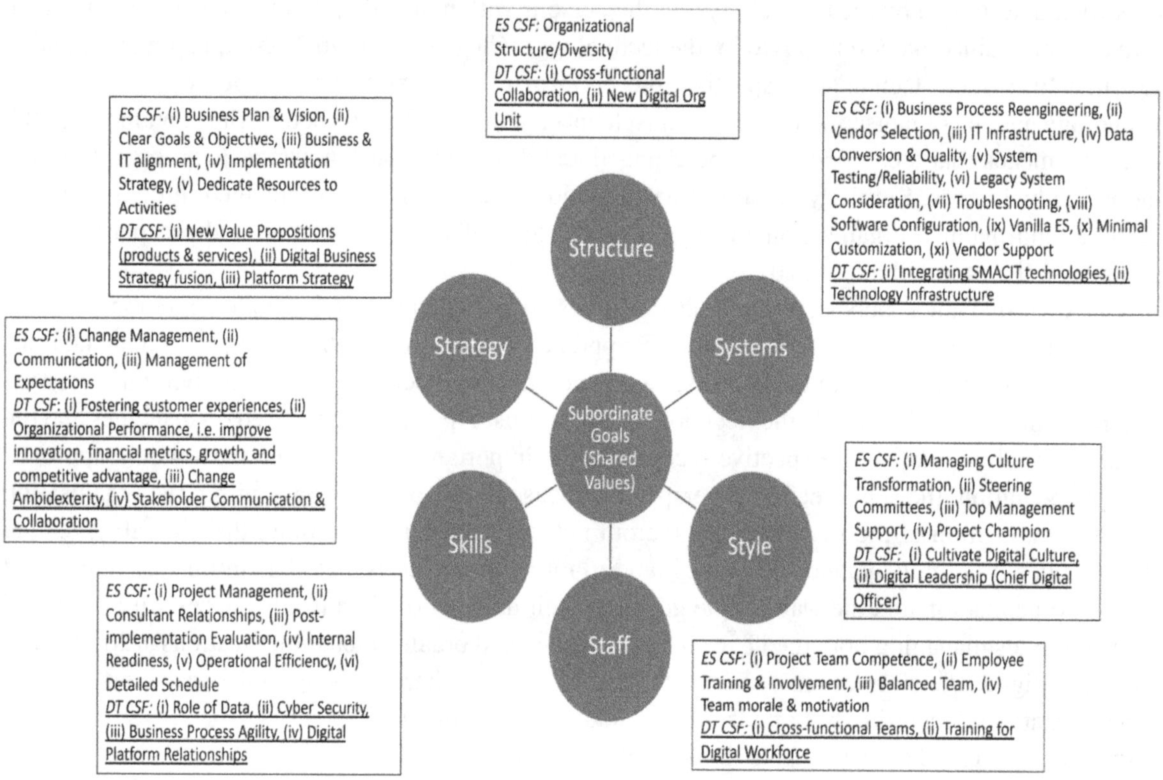

A central tenet of the McKinsey 7-S framework is how all elements carry equal weighting in terms of organizational attention and consequently management support in ensuring effective fit and alignment between each element. Each element of the framework will be discussed in order to advance discussion on the key CSFs for digital transformation initiatives.

1. *Strategy*: ES implementations focus on attaining a clear organizational vision, measurable goals and objectives, strategic alignment between the system and the business, and an implementation strategy that is supported with dedicated resources to change activities. These CSFs reflect the scale and scope of such transformation projects, where ES tends to influence every aspect of the organization and its respective processes, systems, structures, and indeed culture. Central to effective strategic thinking for such transformations is the importance of aligning the 'organization' to the 'system'. This concept of IS and business strategy alignment has remained an enduring topic within the literature, with Reich and Benbasat noting that 'the establishment of strong alignment between information systems and organisational objectives has consistently been reported as one

of the key concerns of IS managers' (2000: 81). Yet, the DT literature suggests a different approach for ensuring successful transformation. As many digital transformations create new value propositions, in particular for product-centric organizations moving to service-centric opportunities, there is significant scope to involve platforms to increase value network. Platform strategies promise to move the organization away from traditional 'make one, sell one' business models and support the introduction of networking ecosystems, where co-opetition becomes a key strategic approach. Parker et al, refer to this traditional approach to business as a 'pipeline', where organizations 'employ a step-by-step arrangement for creating and transferring value, with producers at one end and consumers at the other' (2017: 6-7). Therefore, for strategists, capturing value becomes less about linear value chain thinking, with greater emphasis placed on creating new value opportunities across the platform. To support such value creating opportunities, Bharadwaj et al, call for a move beyond strategic alignment of organizational strategy and IS strategy and towards greater fusion for a 'digital business strategy' (2013). The authors believe that the pervasiveness and ubiquity of digital across, and beyond, the organization needs to move past a separate view of IS and business strategy and create a synergy between both perspectives.

2. *Structure*: The ES literature notes the importance of organizational structure in aligning to process and system changes. Understanding organizational structure allows ES initiatives to judge the scale and scope of change required, the levels of management and the respective roles and responsibilities throughout. The literature tells us that cross-functional collaboration is important for the introduction of digital technologies in order to support transformation. Lorsch and Lawrence note that "every organizational structure must combine two basic elements: differentiation and integration. Dissimilar tasks, such as sales and engineering, need to be 'differentiated', or organized into distinct units. At the same time, the activities of those separate units need to be 'integrated' to coordinate and align them" (cited in Porter & Hepplemann, 2015: 108). Therefore, cross-functional collaboration has been key to effective organizational structuring. Yet, Porter and Hepplemann remind us that with the emergence of 'smart, connected products', the classic approach to organizational structure breaks down. "The need to coordinate across product design, cloud operation, service improvement, and customer engagement is continuous and never ends" Therefore, the authors recommend 'a new functional unit focused on data management' (2015: 108-109). The inclusion of a new unit to the organizational structure portfolio illustrates the enormity of task for leaders of digital transformation. However, the classic approach to cross-functional collaboration and organizational restructuring will not be sufficient in embracing digital and embedding data at the centre of the organization.
3. *Systems*: From an ES perspective, 'systems' refers to the technical nature of initiatives. The literature focuses on three broad issues when focusing on technical prerequisites for ES implementation, namely (i) data and its quality, reliability and troubleshooting capacity, (ii) legacy systems and the necessary IT infrastructures and software configurations required, and (iii) business process reengineering and the level of organizational customization and vendor support required. From a DT perspective, the primary areas for attention include (i) extracting effective data from SMACIT technologies and (ii) building a new IT Infrastructure that can align legacy IT systems and the emerging nature of SMACIT technologies. Similar to ES initiatives, digital transformations will need to ensure systems are in place that can harvest and interpret emerging data. While ES implementations tended to focus internally capturing organization-wide data, SMACIT technologies are externally oriented. The development of technology platforms can support multi-system and multi-data interaction and allow for more effective storage, processing, and analysis. The second key critical success

factor for DT initiatives, is to focus on building a new approach to IT infrastructure that integrated the organizations operational core and digital technologies. Porter and Hepplemann refer to this as a "technology stack, made up of multiple layers, including new product hardware, embedded software, connectivity, a product cloud consisting of software running on remote servers, a suite of security tools, a gateway for external information sources, and integration with enterprise business systems" (2015: 101). It is critical for digital transformation that the technology infrastructure is integrated to the operational core, otherwise value creating opportunities are unlikely to be yielded by the organization. From a McKinsey 7-S 'systems' perspective, a successful IT infrastructure will integrate internal organizational data into a single database and harness, process, and analyse externally created data to support future planning and innovation, improve product performance and growth.

4. *Style*: Within the McKinsey 7-S framework, 'style' "refers to the leadership style of top managers in an organization" (Johnson et al,2018: 218). From an ES transformation perspective, top management support and effective steering committees were viewed as critical factors, where the large-scale nature of these projects would require organization-wide cultural change for ensuring successful implementation. Equally, the large-scale and disruptive nature of digital transformation requires leaders that can cultivate a digital mindset to permeate the organizational culture. As Vial notes, "organizational leaders must work to ensure that their organizations develop a digital mindset while being capable of responding to the disruptions associated with the use of digital technologies" (2019: 129). Due to the enormity of the leadership task, organizations can develop a shared digital space (steering committee) across the strategic leadership team, as conducted for ES transformations. While such a process would support the digital champion it also supports respective functional-level leaders to share emerging challenges and unite as a team in overcoming obstacles. Porter and Hepplemann call such engagement a 'cross business-unit steering committee', where "thought leaders across the various business units, who champion opportunities, share expertise, and facilitate collaboration" (2015: 112). Another approach for escalating the importance of digital transformation is with the creation of a new leadership role. Vial emphasises that "the creation of a chief digital officer (CDO) position signals the strategic nature of DT for the entire organization. CDOs are tasked to ensure that digital technologies are properly leveraged and aligned with the objectives of the organization" (2019: 129). Similarly, Rickards et al, note that the CDO is now a 'transformer in chief', whose responsibilities include (i) making digital integral to the strategy, (ii) deepening customer relationships, (iii) building a digital mindset into operational processes, (iv) extend networks both inside and outside the organization, and (v) ability to execute on plans and 'get stuff done' (2015). Clearly, effective leadership that appreciates the transformational capacity of digital technologies will be a critical success factor for implementing organizations.
5. *Skills*: Within the framework 'skills' refers as much to organizational level capabilities as it does to individual skills. As Johnson et al, note "the concept of capabilities here raises not only staff skills but also issues to do with how these skills are embedded in and captured by the organization as a whole" (2018: 218). ES transformations offer organizations an opportunity to reflect on key skills and capabilities that are required to successfully implement change, for example, (i) project management skills, (ii) fostering effective relationships with external consultants, vendors and stakeholders, and (iii) the skills of assessing and evaluating operational efficiency and implementation effectiveness. These skills and capabilities are organization-centric, they focus on project, system, and process change. A review of the DT literature reveals a different suite of required skills

and capabilities for implementing organizations. Specifically, the importance of data is revealed, where organizations can leverage data-driven algorithmic decision-making to leverage competitive advantage (Günther et al., 2017) and foster new value propositions. As noted by Loonam et al, "as organizations increasingly view information as one of their most valuable assets, which supports the creation and distribution of their products and services, information security will be an integral part of the design and operation of organizational business processes (2020: 1). The authors go on to reveal that as organizations rely increasingly on data for attaining competitive advantage, 'cyber resiliency' will become a key strategic capability of DT transformations. Organizations need to protect their data reservoirs from cyber threats and attacks, and ensure their most valuable strategic asset is not compromised or suffers from loss of trust among organizational stakeholders and customers. Another key capability will be in creating agile business processes that can work across different platforms. ES transformations tend to focus on internal business process reconfiguration and adjustment to suit requisite organization-specific changes. However, DT transformations will require a more agile business process landscape that can move across organization functions but equally onto external platforms to allow new value propositions to be fulfilled. Therefore, in re-configuring business processes to meet the needs of digital transformation, organizations need to foster agility within process activities and across the value chain.

6. *Staff:* This element refers to the people in the organization and their ability to cope with digital transformation. The ES literature notes a number of critical factors for ensuring staff can support project implementation and organization-wide change, these include (i) employee training and involvement, (ii) ensuring effective project team competence, (iii) measuring team morale and motivation throughout project implementation, and (iv) ensuring balanced teams are in place with high levels of ES knowledge and competency. From a digital transformation perspective, the literature notes that digital literacy is critical amongst employees to foster buy-in and prepare individuals and teams for new roles and responsibilities. Specifically, with the arrival of new organizational structures to meet data management needs, teams will need to engage cross-functionally in order to collaborate and conduct work. Cross-functional collaboration is supported with training and development to meet the needs of a digital workforce. As Vial notes, "as digital technologies enable new forms of automation and decision-making processes, questions on the need to develop the skills of existing workers as well as the skills required for future workers who will form the digital workforce are also becoming increasingly relevant" (2019: 129).
7. *Shared Values*: The final element of the McKinsey 7-S framework is the organizations' subordinate goals or shared values. As Johnson et al note, this final element, which is placed in the centre of the framework, "refers to the overarching goals or purpose of the organisation as a whole, in other words the mission, vision and objectives that form the organisational purpose" (2018: 219). From an ES transformation perspective, the organizations shared values must be communicated to align to the proposed change management programme and support the management of project expectations. Similarly, the organizations' DT goals and objectives can play a significant role, where the benefits of improved financial performance and growth, opportunities for new value propositions, and the potential for fostering sustained competitive advantage need to be incorporated into shared values. The transformative nature of digital technologies offers customers an 'experience', particularly for product-centric organizations, therefore organizations will need to ensure this shapes their 'purpose' in applying digital lessons. Finally, but perhaps most significantly when setting DT goals and objectives, is for the organization to be prepared to embrace change ambidexterity.

For example, Sebastian et al, found that ambidexterity is founded upon a firm's ability to maintain both an operational backbone as well as a digital services platform (2017-in Vial). As noted in figure one above, effective digital transformation requires the unison of both operational and digital technologies, where the programme of change will adopt a 'dual operating system' (Kotter, 2012) that combines the ability to exploit existing resources and explore opportunities for digital innovation (Vial, 2019).

IMPLICATIONS FOR STRATEGIC CHANGE

As illustrated above, the IS literature over the past decades has revealed three different perspectives on implementation and as a result the corresponding outcomes for organizational change. The 'technology deterministic' perspective, views technology as inherently good, where organizations are viewed as 'machines' and where human behaviour is highly predictable and determined by clearly defined rules. Consequently, senior leadership teams often delegate responsibility for the implementation process to the IS executive, who typically leads a 'technology-centric' approach to implementation. Yet, denied management attention and skirting organization-wide change issues, it is unlikely for IS initiatives to be ever significantly transformative. The 'organizational imperative' perspective seeks to overcome the weaknesses of the technology-centric view by adopting a top-down approach to implementation. It is referred to as a top-down approach because implementation begins at the strategic level and filters its way down the organisation. The basic assumption about this perspective is that through strategic planning all organisations will be effective and efficient. Consequently, senior leadership teams support IS implementations by aligning the IS strategy to the business strategy, where it is expected that successful implementation will flow down through the organisation. However, one of the core challenges to such an implementation perspective is that some of the best laid plans are often simply left 'sitting on shelves'. The IS executive believes that top management are taking the initiative serious, while top managers feel they are supporting the initiative by incorporating the IS strategy into the business strategy. However, plans alone cannot secure successful implementation, action is also required. Mintzberg, for example, believes that a top-down approach to strategy formulation and implementation simply separates strategy from implementation and keeps the top management team isolated from the rest of the organisation (1990). Similarly, such an approach only separates the 'organization' from 'information systems', thus resulting in an over-dependence on strategy that is isolated from the organisation. Consequently, calls have been made for a more collaborative approach to implementation, where both the organisation and technology aspects of implementation are united. As a result, the 'socio-technical interactionism' perspective emerged to fill this gap in practice. This perspective focuses on aligning the organisation and the technology to suit the people who will be using the new system, i.e. end-users. In other words, 'the performance of a system is optimised when both the technology and the organisation mutually adjust to one another until a satisfactory fit is obtained' (Laudon & Laudon, 2002: 15). However, a core challenge with this implementation perspective is that it is a bottom-up approach to implementation. In other words, this perspective is often accused of lacking the top-down direction required to lead transformational level initiatives.

Therefore, the differing perspectives on implementation are often applied in an ad hoc hybrid manner, where leaders and organizations engage in piecemeal and incremental change rather than going for all out technological transformational. This is understandable given the enormity of many digital transformation programmes, but it can result in poor returns on investment due to project drift or scope creep that leads to eventual digital 'fatigue'. Instead, a more balanced and holistic approach to implementation is called for. Applying the McKinsey 7-S framework to the case of digital transformation will support leaders in preparing and readying the organization for change, where each element of the framework is supported with factors deemed critical for successful implementation. The framework also helps to provide a more balanced view for digital transformation critical success factors, uniting the disparate IS perspectives of 'technological determinism', the 'organizational imperative', and the 'socio-technical' approaches. The hard 'S' elements (structure, strategy, systems) are reflective of the technological deterministic perspective, where strategic plans are centrally focused on the technology and maximizing its functionality to garner efficient and effective organizational advantages. Equally, the soft 'S' elements (skills, staff, style) are similar to the socio-technical perspective, viewing bottom-up engagement from employees across the organization as a key pillar for embracing a digital culture. The third perspective of the organizational imperative is similar to the final 'S' element (shared values), where a top-down approach is adopted to inform the organization as to the purpose and vision for digital transformation.

Balogun et al, identify four generic types of strategic change, namely (i) adaptation, (ii) turnaround, (iii) evolutionary, and (iv) revolutionary (2015). All four approaches to strategic change can fit into two perspectives when considering the extent of change required by implementing organizations. Typically, the authors note that change that occurs in line with the organizations current business model and culture is considered a realignment of strategy, which fits with the 'adaptation' and 'turnaround' perspectives. Implementation is carried out to realign the organizations' strategy, culture, and processes in order to cope with change. Whereas, change that goes beyond the current business model or culture is transformational in nature, requiring more 'evolutionary' and/or 'revolutionary' approaches to implementation. The scale, magnitude, and complexity of digital initiatives requires transformational change. The McKinsey 7-S framework reminds organizations to adopt a balanced approach in preparing for change while the critical success factors provide a holistic arsenal of tools for leading digital transformation.

CONCLUSION

Digital transformation continues to grow in importance for traditional organizations. It offers many traditional businesses an opportunity to break free from the confines of their respective industry structure limitations and move towards more value innovative approaches to strategic thinking. By adopting digital technologies, traditional product-centric organizations can reimagine their offerings, where data insights foster new service-centric opportunities. Yet, there is a lack of understanding as to the key critical factors required to successfully implement such digital transformation initiatives. This chapter seeks to bridge this gap by adapting the McKinsey 7-S framework to support leaders in identifying these success factors. Due to the high levels of project failure associated with large-scale IS-enabled change, the chapter also emphasizes the importance of adopting a more holistic approach to strategic change in order to support leaders in successfully adopting digital transformation.

REFERENCES

Balogun, J., Hailey, V. H., & Gustafsson, S. (2015). *Exploring strategic change* (4th ed.). Pearson Education.

Bharadwaj, A., El Sawy, O. A., Pavlou, P. A., & Venkatraman, N. (2013). Digital business strategy: Toward a next generation of insights. *Management Information Systems Quarterly, 37*(2), 471–482. doi:10.25300/MISQ/2013/37:2.3

Campbell, H. (1996). A Social Interactionist Perspective on Computer Implementation. *Journal of the American Planning Association, 62*(1), 99–107. doi:10.1080/01944369608975673

Chandler, A. D. (1962). *Strategy and structure: Chapters in the history of the industrial empire*. MIT Press.

Clegg, S., & Hardy, C. (1996). *Handbook of Organisational Studies*. Sage Publications Ltd.

Ginzberg, M. J. (1981). Early diagnosis of MIS implementation failure: Promising results and unanswered questions. *Management Science, 27*(4), 459–478. doi:10.1287/mnsc.27.4.459

Günther, W. A., Mehrizi, M. H. R., Huysman, M., & Feldberg, F. (2017). Debating big data: A literature review on realizing value from big data. *The Journal of Strategic Information Systems, 26*(3), 191–209. doi:10.1016/j.jsis.2017.07.003

Hess, T., Matt, C., Benlian, A., & Wiesböck, F. (2016). Options for formulating a digital transformation strategy. *MIS Quarterly Executive, 15*(2).

Iveroth, E. (2010). Inside Ericsson: A framework for the practice of leading global IT-enabled change. *California Management Review, 53*(1), 136–153. doi:10.1525/cmr.2010.53.1.136

Johnson, G., Scholes, K., Whittington, R., Angwin, D., & Regner, P. (2018). *Fundamentals of Strategy* (4th ed.). Pearson Education.

Keen & Scott-Morton. (1978). *Decision Support Systems*. Addison-Wesley.

Kotter, J. P. (2012). Accelerate! *Harvard Business Review, 90*(11), 44–52. PMID:23155997

Kraemmerand, P., Møller, C., & Boer, H. (2003). ERP implementation: An integrated process of radical change and continuous learning. *Production Planning and Control, 14*(4), 338–348. doi:10.1080/0953728031000117959

Kumar, V., Loonam, J., Allen, J. P., & Sawyer, S. (2016). Exploring enterprise social systems & organisational change: Implementation in a digital age. *Journal of Information Technology, 31*(2), 97–100. doi:10.1057/jit.2016.13

Laudon, K. C., & Laudon, J. P. (2002). *Management information systems*. Pearson Publications.

Laudon, K. C., & Laudon, J. P. (2015). *Management information systems*. Pearson.

Loonam, J., Eaves, S., Kumar, V., & Parry, G. (2018). Towards digital transformation: Lessons learned from traditional organizations. *Strategic Change, 27*(2), 101–109. doi:10.1002/jsc.2185

Loonam, J., Kumar, V., Mitra, A., & Abd Razak, A. (2018). Critical success factors for the implementation of enterprise systems: A literature review. *Strategic Change, 27*(3), 185–194. doi:10.1002/jsc.2194

Loonam, J., McDonagh, J., Kumar, V., & O'Regan, N. (2014). Top managers & information systems: 'Crossing the Rubicon'! *Strategic Change*, *23*(3-4), 205–224. doi:10.1002/jsc.1971

Loonam, J., Zwiegelaar, J., Kumar, V., & Booth, C. (2020). Cyber-Resiliency for Digital Enterprises: A Strategic Leadership Perspective. *IEEE Transactions on Engineering Management*, 1–14. doi:10.1109/TEM.2020.2996175

Markus, M. L., & Benjamin, R. I. (1997). The magic bullet theory in IT-enabled transformation. *Sloan Management Review*, *38*(2), 55–68.

Markus, M. L., & Robey, D. (1988). Information Technology and Organisational Change: Causal Structure in Theory and Research. *Management Science*, *34*(5), 583–598. doi:10.1287/mnsc.34.5.583

McFarlan, F. W. (Ed.). (1984). *The information systems research challenge: Proceedings*. Harvard Business School Press.

McKenney, J. L., & McFarlan, F. W. (1982). The information archipelago-maps and bridges. *Harvard Business Review*, *60*(5), 109–119.

Menard, A. (2017). *How can we recognize the real power of the Internet of Things?* McKinsey Consulting.

Mintzberg, H. (1990). The design school: Reconsidering the basic premises of strategic management. *Strategic Management Journal*, *11*(3), 171–195. doi:10.1002mj.4250110302

Morgan, G. (1997). *Images of Organisation*. SAGE.

Mumford, E. (1996). *Systems Design: Ethical Tools for Ethical Change*. Macmillan. doi:10.1007/978-1-349-14199-9

Orlikowski, W. J., & Baroudi, J. J. (1991). Studying information technology in organizations: Research approaches and assumptions. *Information Systems Research*, *2*(1), 1–28. doi:10.1287/isre.2.1.1

Parker, G. G., Van Alstyne, M. W., & Choudary, S. P. (2016). *Platform revolution: How networked markets are transforming the economy and how to make them work for you*. WW Norton & Company.

Parr, A. N., & Shanks, G. 2000, January. A taxonomy of ERP implementation approaches. In *Proceedings of the 33rd Annual Hawaii International Conference on System Sciences*. IEEE. 10.1109/HICSS.2000.926908

Porter, M. E., & Heppelmann, J. E. (2014). How smart, connected products are transforming competition. *Harvard Business Review*, *92*(11), 64–88.

Porter, M. E., & Heppelmann, J. E. (2015). How smart, connected products are transforming companies. *Harvard Business Review*, *93*(10), 96–114.

Porter, M.E., & Millar, V.E. (1985). *How information gives you competitive advantage*. Academic Press.

Reich, B. H., & Benbasat, I. (2000). Factors that influence the social dimension of alignment between business and information technology objectives. *Management Information Systems Quarterly*, *24*(1), 81–113. doi:10.2307/3250980

Rickards, T., Smaje, K., & Sohoni, V. (2015). *'Transformer in chief': The new chief digital officer*. McKinsey Consulting.

Sebastian, I., Ross, J., Beath, C., Mocker, M., Moloney, K., & Fonstad, N. (2017). How big old companies navigate digital transformation. *MIS Quarterly Executive, 16*(3).

Shang, S., & Seddon, P. B. (2000). A comprehensive framework for classifying the benefits of ERP systems. AMCIS 2000 Proceedings, 39.

Slee, C., & Slovin, M. (1997). Legacy asset management. *Information Systems Management, 14*(1), 12–21. doi:10.1080/10580539708907024

Somogyi, E. K., & Galliers, R. D. (1987). Applied information technology: From data processing to strategic information systems. *Journal of Information Technology, 2*(1), 30–41. doi:10.1177/026839628700200107

Symons, V. (1991). Impacts of Information Systems: Four Perspectives. *Information and Software Technology, 33*(3), 181–190. doi:10.1016/0950-5849(91)90132-U

Trist, E., & Emery, F. (2005). Socio-technical systems theory. *Organizational Behavior 2: Essential Theories of Process and Structure, 169.*

Vial, G. (2019). Understanding digital transformation: A review and a research agenda. *The Journal of Strategic Information Systems, 28*(2), 118–144. doi:10.1016/j.jsis.2019.01.003

Waterman, R. H. Jr, Peters, T. J., & Phillips, J. R. (1980). Structure is not organization. *Business Horizons, 23*(3), 14–26. doi:10.1016/0007-6813(80)90027-0

Westerman, G., Bonnet, D., & McAfee, A. (2014). *Leading digital: Turning technology into business transformation*. Harvard Business Press.

ENDNOTE

1 According to the authors typical business applications grew by 5,400%.

Chapter 5
Social Networks and Well-Being in Democracy in the Age of Digital Capitalism

José Poças Rascão
https://orcid.org/0000-0003-2448-2713
Polytechnic Institute of Setúbal, Portugal

ABSTRACT

The objective of this work is, on the one hand, to study the new competitive forms that correspond to the development of the different markets linked to electronic platforms and social networks on the internet and, on the other hand, to develop a proposal for social welfare for the positive and negative impacts produced by the development of these markets. In the first part, the main social and economic changes inherent to political and social evolution are addressed. The main logical trends of the market are presented about production and modalities of information appropriation, in particular the new forms of information asymmetries in the electronic market.

THEME AND SEARCH PROBLEM

Studying the relationships between technologies, social networks, stored data, surveillance, and fundamental rights (especially about security and privacy), is something of great relevance to the Social Sciences. The exploitation of digital capitalism is a reality, based on the knowledge of the behavior of internet users and digital platforms, their decisions and their privacy (it is not the individual who chooses whether to share such data or not, which relate to facets of their way of being, which go beyond the conscious, penetrating even in the area of desires and attitudes personally unnoticed). Legally, such a study is relevant because it is focused on forms of social communication and economic generation that challenge the constitutionally established norms in democracy: respect for private life and contractual adhering.

Every social network, application and/or website that captures data exposes its intentions in electronic contracts of association so long and complex that it becomes impossible, in normal daily life, to have sufficient time and knowledge to understand such obligations. This threat to rights is aggravated, the

DOI: 10.4018/978-1-7998-7452-2.ch005

fact that technological tools are less and less dispensable for the realization of life in society, economic / labor activities, entertainment, etc.

Questions for Debate

1. What will be the impact of social networks on the digital society?
2. What will be the purpose of the data collected by digital platforms?
3. What will be the purpose of the data collected by digital surveillance?

OBJECTIVES AND APPROACH METHODOLOGY

To achieve its objectives, the article was divided into three parts. The first is the description of technological forms based on personal and behavioral data generated in individuals' online communications. The second studies the relationship between the digital economy and the business world, users' rights, and their privacy. Finally, the third party seeks to understand how states and private organizations use electronic data surveillance. As for the nature of the work, it is qualitative, since it does not claim to quantify anything, nor does it favor statistical study. The theoretical framework of this work was constructed through the research technique of the literature review. Its nature is exploratory and its method of hypothetical-deductive procedure.

FUNDAMENTAL CONCEPTS

Data, Information and Knowledge

Information is not the same as data, although the two words are often confused, so it is understood that the subtle distinction between these concepts is essential. The data do not convey sense or meaning of the facts, images, or sounds, since they lack relational elements essential to the establishment of a complete meaning, lacking an internal relational structure for a cognitive purpose. This structure is one of the attributes of the information. Data is transformed into information when its creator adds meaning to it Davenport and Prusak (1998). Wiliam G. Zikmund (2000, p.19) defines knowledge as "the mixture of information, experience and understanding that provide a structure that can be applied in the evaluation of new information or new situations". Information "feeds" knowledge. Knowledge can thus be defined as a person's ability to relate complex information structures to a new context. New contexts imply change, action, and dynamism. Knowledge cannot be shared, although the technique and components of information can be shared. When a person internalizes information to the point that he can use it, we call it knowledge Zikmund, (2000). This is a fluid mix of experiences, values, contextual information, and expert judgment, structured that provide a framework for evaluating and incorporating new experiences and information. Organizations are found not only in documents and reports, but also in organization routines, processes, practices, and standards. Knowledge has its origin and is applied in the minds of connoisseurs (Davenport and Prusak, 1998), (William Zikmund, 2000). Knowledge is information as valid and accepted, integrating data, acts, information and sometimes hypotheses. Knowledge needs someone to filter, combine and interpret information. Information can be considered as a "substance" that can be acquired, stored, and owned by a person or group and transmitted from person to person or from group to group.

Information has a certain stability, and it may be better viewed as existing at the level of society (Davenport and Prusak, 1998). Although we can store it using various physical supports, the information itself is not physical, but rather abstract and neither purely mental. Knowledge is stored in people's memory, but information is out there in the world. Whatever it is, there is somewhere between the physical world around people and the mental of human thought.

Knowledge = Internalized information + ability to use it in new situations.

Knowledge is found fundamentally and intrinsically within people. These are more complex and unpredictable at the individual level than an entire society, so it is not surprising that knowledge is much more difficult to obtain than information. Knowledge exists mainly within people; it is an integral part of human complexity and unpredictability. Knowledge has a fundamental duality: it is something storable (at least sometimes we intend to do it) and something that flows (something that communicates from person to person). It is possibly the duality of knowledge (something that flows and storage process) that makes its treatment and management difficult. According to (Dahlberg, 2006), knowledge is organized into units of knowledge (concepts) according to its characteristics (objects / subjects / subjects). The organization of knowledge is related to a process of conceptual analysis of a domain of knowledge and from there, it is structured / architected generating a representation of knowledge about that domain that will be used for the organization of information about that domain of knowledge.

Figure 1. Data, Knowledge, and Information.
Source: Davenport, 1998.

Given	Information	Knowledge
Simple observations on the state of the world: • easily structured. • easily obtained by machines. • often quantified. • easily transferable	Data with relevance and purpose: • requires unit of analysis. • requires consensus on meaning. • necessarily requires human mediation.	Valuable information from the human mind. Includes reflection, synthesis, context. • difficult to structure. • difficult to capture on machines. • often tacit. • difficult to transfer.

Data, information and knowledge should be seen and analyzed from the continuing perspective of values and fundamentally marked by the growing human contribution – processing, management, action, result, learning and feedback, that is, human empowerment for actions that generate the desired results at the organizational level

Information Imperfections

Humans are not only rational, but they also assume some opportunistic behaviors. Williamson (1975) describes opportunism as "the search for one's own interest, with cunning" involving "disbelief of threats and opportunities", so as, to realize individual, advantages. These advantages are also suitable for "selecting and distorting discovered information or discrediting the opportunities leading to the fu-

Figure 2. Data, Information, Knowledge, Actions - Results
Source: Adapted from Choo, (2002, p.258).

	Data Processing	Information Management	Knowledge Management	Stocks/Results
Activities	• Data capture • Data definition • Data Storage • Data Modeling.	• Information Needs • Acquisition of information • Information Organization • Distribution of Information	• Knowledge Creation • Sharing of Knowledge • Use of Knowledge	• Strategies, alliances and initiatives • Products and Services • Processes • Systems • Structures • Values
Values	• Precision • Efficiency "Once we have the data, we can analyze it"	• Access • Relevance "Bringing the right information to the right person"	• Enables action • Value generation "If only we knew what we know"	• Innovation • Learning The ability to learn is the only sustainable advantage"

ture" (Williamson 1975, p.26). The claim is that, even if not all humans, behave opportunistically, it is difficult to predict in advance, whether they will be have or not, as such.

These types of behaviors reflect the relationship between the economic interest of the search engine operator, but also the public interesting accessing information in a search on a person's name. The combination of opportunist and rational behavior, is the, main cause, for the three types of imperfections of information:

- **Asymmetric** information – an asymmetric distribution of information from the parties involved in a relationship, causes an opportunity. The critical impact of the information, on the optimal allocation of risk, is not merely its presence or absence, but its inadequacy between the actors, together two conditions under which, the asymmetry of the information, provides an opportunity, for example, the relationship, between the economic interest of the search engine operator, but also the public interest, in accessing the information, in a research on the name of a person:
    - High costs to obtain equal information.
    - Propensity of the part's opportunistic behavior. In other words, asymmetric information occurs when one party has information that is unknown to the other and difficult to obtain by the other party and provides an opportunity to exploit this advantage of information through possible alternatives.

Asymmetric information can result from a favorable situation for suppliers or customers depending on who has that information. The opportunity is caused by the hidden information, for the current relationship. One party in a relationship is better informed about one relevant variable than the other. It is the invisibility of this private information that constitutes the essence of information imperfections and introduces the risk to the other party.

Considering the possibility of opportunistic behavior, the party that possesses the hidden information has no incentive to re-image the information, if it is harmful to it. Therefore, for example, if the economic interest of the search engine operator, but also the public interest, in accessing information in a search on a person's name. is particularly appropriate for a determined organization, will end up with the main benefits of the actors who benefit from this hidden information. The imperfections of information are known as enemies of the selection.

- **Ambiguous Information –** The ambiguity of information in a relationship can cause an opportunity. Although in the case of complete information, different interpretations, about the same information, may occur. As a result of opportunism, these representations can be opportunistic in the sense that they can lead to an individual advantage for either party (e.g. the economic interest of the search engine operator, but also the public interest in accessing information in a search on a person's name.

The opportunity for one of them is discovered, when such opportunistic interpretation, is not recognized by the other and results in:

1. Will of one of them to pay a high price, for information.
2. One of them will offer a "product" at a low price.

As a result of this opportunistic behavior, the part with opportunistic interpretation has no incentive to share that information if it becomes a disadvantage to it.

- **Incomplete Information** – The opportunity of incomplete information is hermetically related, with the assumption of rationality. The limits of rationality are certainly interested in the extent that the limits of rationality are reached – i.e. under conditions of uncertainty and/or complexity. In the absence of any of these conditions of ownership of contingent actions may be completely specific to this principle.

In a universe characterized by a high degree of complexity and uncertainty, the possibility of certain events quickly become numerous. Under these circumstances, it is impossible for humans to acquire and analyze the relevant complete information. As explained before, this impossibility leads to "satisfactory" behavior. The opportunity for incomplete information occurs, when someone is incomplete informed, about the range of possibilities. Therefore, one of the actors who allows an incomplete comparison of the parties and their reciprocal differences can move towards a situation of abyss.

Information Economy

For the economy, the need is "the feeling of a certain lack united with the desire to be eliminated". The need is thus "the desire to have a means capable of preventing or stopping an unpleasant sensation or provoking, preserving or increasing a pleasant sensation" (Sabaté, F. Tarragó, 1989).

The means used by people to meet their needs are designated by economists as goods. A *good* is therefore all that is recognized, as apt to satisfy a need, regardless of any other judgment (e.g. moral judgment). Goods can be classified in several ways. The first one that interests us is the one that distinguishes the so-called free goods (e.g. the air we breathe, the water) from economic goods. An economic good is one that is characterized by its scarcity, that is, it is one that exists in quantities lower than those required, given the need felt" (Sabaté, F. Tarragó, 1989).

"The usefulness of *a good* refers to the quality and capacity of that good to meet the needs that is proper to that good. The usefulness of a good is the aptitude of this good to meet the needs and the needs are subjective sensations, it follows that a same *good* may have different utility for different people, depending on the intensity with which they can experience or feel the needs that can satisfy with this *good"*, (Sabaté, F. Tarragó, 1989).

Associated with the concept of utility is the concept of *"economic value"* from which it can be said that it is the quality of everything that is granted importance, because it is considered to deserve esteem. Therefore, the value of a particular good also depends on each person, since each one can feel a distinct appreciation for the same good, (Sabaté, F. Tarragó, 1989).

Organizations seek to achieve economic return by selling their products or services on the market. In a competitive environment, an organization can achieve a better performance than its competitors, because it has better resources or because the organization makes better use of its distinctive competencies, (Penrose 1959, p.54). A distinctive competence is defined as a differentiated qualification, complementary asset and organization routines that together allow the company to coordinate a specific set of activities that provide the basis of competitive advantages, (Dosi and Teece, in: Williamson 1999, p.1094).

Competitive advantage is referred to as economic profitability (Porter 1980). Profitability is then defined, as the excess return of a resource that owns an opportunity cost, (Mahoney and Pandian 1992). In other words, profitability can be measured, like a normal financial return. To differentiate the possible sources of profitability, some types are distinguished. For example, profitability can be realized by, (Mahoney and Pandian 1992):

- Superior management capacity to coordinate resources (Penrose 1959).
- Possession of a valuable resource that is rare.
- Government protection when barriers to entry of new competitors are high.
- Taking risks and business acumen in uncertain and complex surroundings.
- Make better use of the organization's resources, any of the physical assets and human capital.

In short, the base resource is an attempt to explain why organizations differ in terms of resources and capabilities and how these differences can lead to sustained profitability positions, producing superior financial return. The base resources therefore serve the purpose of explicitly focusing on the role of the resources and capabilities of organizations, such as the origin of strategy and organizational performance. This exploration of the relationship between resources, competition and profit includes, among other issues, the role of imperfect information in creating profitability differences between competitors, (Grant 1991, p.3, Barney 1986, Itami 1987). Information imperfections are some of the competitive imperfections that shock the economic ideal of the perfect market, (Yao, 1988). The perfect market is characterized by numerous customers and suppliers of homogeneous products and or services and whose price mechanism determines the most efficient organization of the market. Looking at the information, all customers and suppliers are completely and perfectly informed about all relevant aspects of business transactions.

While the market ideal serves as the most important appropriation of neoclassical economic theory, contemporary economic theories tend to consent to this as opposed to the appropriation of unrealistic theories. Therefore, we assume that the perfect market and that perfectly informed customers and suppliers are a myth. For this reason, it is proposed that markets are characterized by imperfect competition and that information imperfections are an important trend. (Yao, 1988).

Network Economics and Social Welfare

The economy of social networks is the emerging economic order of the digital society. The name derives from a key attribute – products and services are created and value is added through social networks that operate on large scales or globally. This contrasts sharply with the economy of the industrial era, in which existed the right of ownership over physical property right Business models for capturing value added rights to products and services created on social media are being widely explored.

The economy of social networks can be seen from a number of perspectives: transition from the industrial economy to the digital economy on a global scale, value networks and intellectual property rights. From the point of view of transition, (Malone and Laubscher, 1998) claim that the information revolution changed the nature of business activity. As information can be shared instantly and economically on a global scale, the value of centralized decision-making and expensive bureaucracies is greatly reduced. Second, (Brand, 1999), trade is being accelerated by the digital and social media revolution. The role of trade is to exploit and absorb these shocks. Some efforts focus on developing new infrastructure, while other activities emphasize governance and evolving culture. (Rifkin, 2000), notes that real estate has become a commercial burden in network-based markets. From an infrastructure point of view, (Tapscott, 1996) compared the information networks of the new economy with the highways and the electricity grid of the industrial economy, so no country can succeed without a state-of-the-art electronic infrastructure. According to, (Schwartz, 1999), in the future, large companies make their purchases, invoice, document exchange and logistics, will be made through global networks that connect n computing devices. Companies will be able to provide 24-hour service because customer requests are transferred from one time zone to another, without customers being aware that the work is being done on the other side of the world. (Boyett and Boyett, 2001) state that the larger the network, the bigger the market and its value. According to, (Kelly, 1998), in a network economy, value is created and shared by all members of the network, not by individual companies. Economies of scale derive from the size of the network and not from the enterprise. Similarly, the value flows from connectivity. According to (Shapiro and Varian, 1999), the network economy raises important questions about intellectual property, since the first copy of the information was produced, the production of additional copies costs virtually nothing. (Rifkin, 2000) proposes that as markets pave the way for networks, ownership is being replaced by access rights because ownership becomes increasingly marginal to business success and economic progress.

Social well-being is the set of factors a person needs to enjoy a good quality of life. These factors lead the subject to enjoy a quiet existence and in a state of satisfaction. Social well-being therefore encompasses the things that focus positively on quality of life: decent employment, economic resources to meet needs, a home to live, access to education and health, **tempo** time **ser** for **leisure,** etc. Although the notion of well-being is subjective (what is **good** for one person may not be it for another), social well-being is associated with objective economic factors.

The role of any State is to promote social welfare among all its citizens in that country. To this end, measures and policies are needed to correct the injustices of the capitalist market. The distribution of income and the development of free and free social services for all people are necessary conditions to achieve social well-being. The possibility of expanding social well-being to all social strata of each country implies the existence of wealth (to respond to state spending). With each government ensuring the equitable distribution of the wealth created.

Democracy

According to Plato, (in:Werner Jäeger, 1979, 1936), the essence of democracy, as he saw it in his hometown, is that "all citizens attain equal rights and public office were filled by lot. He appreciated the knowledge of the experts, but democracy as a symbol of a regime gave the judgment of each one an equal participation in the resolution of the supreme problems of the State."

Plato viewed the ideal society as a society stratified by merit, incompatible with the proposals of equality, and the resentment of what affected it in the face of the circumstance that led to Socrates death could not be lessened. In this context Plato's criticism, the essence of the Greek concept of democracy is extracted: *"the idea of absolute equality, the apex* of which was manifested in the provision of public office by lot".

According to Plato, *"The city exudes freedom and within it everyone can do what it gives them in Ghana*". The freedom it is about is to feel free from all the class of duties, to organize life as it best comes. It is the triumph of the individual. The Greek democratic man criticized in Plato would correspond to the contemporary *individualistic type*, ambitious, able to become miserly and tortuous; thus, a risk for democracy to degenerate in its impure form. Equal rights for the filling of public offices, so that everyone is guaranteed to participate in the government. This is the essence that was bequeathed to us by Greek antiquity to guide the evolution of the concept of democracy. Since that date, the dilemma of how to achieve equality has been discussed without stifling the difference; how to include the individual as a social unit, without denying the person, as a universe of aspirations. The concept of democracy as conceived by the Greeks, in their transition to modern democracy, maintains in its entire the titration of the power of the people, but alters the way or the procedure of how that right is exercised. From direct democracy to representative democracy. (Madison, 1791-1795), defends representative democracy in texts such as: "The scheme of representation as a substitute for a meeting of citizens in person being at most but very *imperfectly known to ancient polity, it is in more modern times only that we are to expect instructive examples*"

This shows the imperfections of direct democracy for the exercise of government (elitist view), poorly disguised under logical arguments, such as the territorial dimension and professional specialization. The territorial dimension constitutes a physical obstacle to the exercise of direct democracy. Likewise, participation in government business is not harmonizable with the individual concern of the citizen to resolve their private affairs that take him most of the time.

Digital Capitalism

Technological changes are always accompanied by narratives in which optimistic interpretations predominate, whose function is essentially legitimizing, hiding the power relations that drive or that are underlying the processes of technological change, relationships with social consequences, based on the generalized digitization of processes, products, and services.

The decade of the years and seventy was lavish in diagnoses that pointed to the relevance of a series of technological developments and economic trends – then manifested mainly in the United States – on the basis that it was argued that advanced industrial societies were undergoing a fundamental social transformation, equivalent in scale and importance to the transition to industrial society during the eighteenth and nineteenth centuries. The most diverse denominations then began to refer to this new society: an active society, a service society, a knowledge society, a technocratic society, an interconnected society, a telematic society, a leisure society, a post-capitalist society, an interactive society, a multimedia society, a post-industrial society. The most successful name was the information and knowledge society. Most of the research was based on the consideration that new information and communication technologies as "technologies open par excellence, regardless of economic, social and cultural weights", so that the evolution of everyday life was also open to a plurality of futures. Open future full of optimism, until one could conceive a whole saga of post-industrial utopias according to which, together with the hand of new information and communication technologies, the expected human liberation in the form of productivity and material abundance, communicative fluidity and personal self-realization, would arise. Some went further in considering the revolutionary nature of the transformations that were being experienced by the more developed countries. The communicator of the new society, Alvin Toffler, expressed it in this way: It has become a cliché to say that we are living "a second industrial revolution". With this sentence, we intend to describe the speed and depth of change around us. But besides being vulgar, you can cheat. Because what is happening now is most likely bigger, deeper, and more important than the industrial revolution. In fact, a growing and trustworthy opinion group argues that the present moment represents nothing less than the second crucial milestone of the digital society.

THEORETICAL–METHODOLOGICAL FRAMEWORK FOR RESEARCH

The Information Economy

The notion of information is polysemic. It is, according to the case, simple sign or already knowledge. She answers codes and signs up for a social relationship. It not only makes sense in relation to this social relationship, but also the exchange of information is itself a major component of this relationship. Of course, the perspectives that the social sciences can take to analyze the notion of information are multiple. The economy, in addition to the diversity of approximations, can never reduce this plurality. The information marks at various levels the individual and collective components of the agents. Each school of thought makes a different point about this or that aspect, but it cannot therefore pretend to take care of the set of situations where, in production, consumption or exchange activities, the notion of information is involved.

This finding is based on the start of the contemporary debate on the information economy, with information highways, virtual enterprises and their teleworkers exploring the various facets of the way different theoretical approaches deal with information. Somewhat paradoxically the bet is to make the diversity of the approximations of the information economy allow to clarify an important but dedicated debate on the digital information society, better than could do it a specific theoretical construction, too spontaneously ad *hoc*. In order to understand the nature and breadth of the transformations of our society that are aware of our ways of treating, storing and circulating information, it is useful to resort to relevant theoretical research tools, although the field to which they are addressed is partial.

This need for theoretical tools is all the clearer as the phenomena in question are, at first glance, perceived as brutal and contradictory. And so it is with telework, for example, often presented as a threat of massive job destruction as a result of the shift in of strictly codified tasks thanks to new information and communication technologies, but also as anew opportunity to better aped and adjust working times by developing other socio-professional, family and civic benefits. Another reason for debate is the accelerated and broad functioning of markets on a global scale and, first, financial markets where transactions are of increased effectiveness, are mixed with fears that the brutal adjustments under development will generate financial crises. It is by no means the resumption of the eternal debate on the advantages and disadvantages of technological progress. The evolution of information and communication technologies has been spectacular in the continuous increase in the capacity to store, treat and transmit information, so the number of issues that arise are inherent in the development of markets, the growth of the division of labor and the accumulation of knowledge. The multiple aspects of contemporary economic transformations concern the production, transmission, treatment and use of information, as well as the theoretical problems that these changes cause. With the complexity of modern economies, information is being a determining factor. In order to understand the economic transformations, some relevant questions raised by some economic theories and the contribution of some experts with complementary approximations in the field of information or knowledge to better contribute to the debate on the impact of information on the economy are presented. The aim is to introduce some issues related to economic analysis, but also to the implications of economic policy, into an economy where information and knowledge represent an added value, even strategic. These issues start from several stylized facts, about the use of new information and communication technologies or in the mobilization of knowledge both in production processes and in the functioning of the market and labor. But this pragmatic approach can only be read in view of the great structural transformations that mark the contemporary period.

What Is Information Economics?

It is useful to analyze the contributions to recall the essential question: how to characterize what we can qualify as a knowledge-based and information-based economy? A whole set of discourses on the information economy seems relatively sick of a tautological approach where the information economy is explicitly defined by the reference to the importance of the use of information and communication technologies. Different theoretical approaches to the notion of information allow us to understand the way economic agents use, treat, or spread information and knowledge. Talking about the information economy has at first sight several possible meanings. From the perspective described here, the notion of information economics is used to emphasize that one of the best characteristics of contemporary developed economies has expanded and diversified their use of information in all forms and at all levels. In a more complete way, the information economy considers the set of knowledge and the added value of knowledge that goes alongside technological developments. The notion of information economics then qualifies a certain historical phase of the development of our economy. All the characteristics of such economies undergo an analysis of the growth scenarios that correspond to it. These scenarios are connected to several levels, according to what the analysis involves on productive activities, the functioning of the market or the evolution of wages. If this perspective is with given, the notion of information economics is still poorly defined. Certainly, the economy has no affinity for information and knowledge so specific, to significantly influence how it works. On the contrary, changes that consider affinities, have strong impacts on how they operate. If the issue deserves to be put the threads of the causes to the effects that result, are at least poorly established and deserve further investigation. This research can progress by questioning the rule that the different theoretical approaches in the economy confer on information and knowledge and by confronting these analyses with the observable changes in the functioning of markets or the organization of production and consumption. There is also another perspective to address the notion of information economics. It considers the central object of the economy of the entire system that produces, disseminates, and interprets information. From this point of view, information is a natural or produced resource, from which one can follow the dissemination and the conditions that preside over it. We then talk about information economics without reference to a precise historical period, a little, as is done for education, health, or safety, to claim to cover all its aspects. Thus, there is a whole set of approaches dealing centrally with information. We will use these various approaches to illustrate some characteristics of the advantages of information in the confidence of the functioning of markets and in the placement of productive organizations, as well as ways of life and consumption. The notion of information economics has come out of the heart of contemporary debate that largely addresses the circle of economists. Indeed, the echo of global debates underlines Mondial the greater importance of the new structural distribution that these technologies are. These questions start from the observation of rapid dissemination and in all areas of economic activity through information and communication technologies. But this is not just structural change that has led to giving information a more important role in the economy. The evolution of territorial activities (services), the extension of markets and productive combinations on a planetary scale (globalization), such as the accumulation of information and knowledge (education) thus play a decisive role in the characterization of a new structural distribution.

Tertiarization

There are several ways to address this structural change, according to the observation of the growing importance of third-rate activities at the heart of productive activities or in the way markets work with their logistics, processing activities and dissemination of information. This gives the impression that information in various forms plays an increasing role in economic development, not only in services, but also in a whole set of tertiary activities that have been regulating productive activities and changes. This phenomenon is contemporary with the spread of a new technical system centered around ICT's. This phenomenon has long been a trend in developed economies, the growth of service activities within organizations and intermediation services (such as banking, insurance, transport, and communications). Between 1970 and 1993 service activities between organizations, including financial services, nearly doubled, and accounted for about 18% of total employment in large OECD countries, (Castells et Aoyama,1994). Economic operators are aware that only economic activities increasingly deal with information and knowledge, mobilizing multiple knowledge, but also that the functioning of markets participates in this complexity, calling for a whole range of qualities that can benefit those who possess the information or can acquire it. The globalization of banking and financial activities supported by ICT's provides new information on a global scale, 24 hours a day and 365 days a year, completes this image of a virtual sphere where information flows propel the world economy.

Information as an Economic Category

Making the theory of what you might call the information economy is not an easy thing. The analysis of what is meant by information economics cannot in any way progress on the basis of empirical finding on the growing place it occupies in all the activities of our economy, linked more or less directly to the collection, treatment and transmission of information, knowledge and knowledge of all nature. It is necessary to know more the specificities that such an economy will have: the economic status it confers on information in the different activities; the determinants of value and the modalities of the production of the different forms of information are integrated into the economic sphere. It is not safe that one can achieve the goal and produce a theory of the information economy, but one can undoubtedly pursue more thoroughly than is customary, the specificities of the gains of contemporary developed economies of information.

To advance in this direction it is proposed to confront a whole set of issues, such as the greater and plural function of information in the economy and the treatments of the notion of information in the various contemporary economic theories. In fact, the economic literature has for three decades seen work on the role of information multiply. These works are increasingly diverse and elaborate and deserve in some way the attention on whether they only want to broaden our perception of this so-called information economy in a structured way.

The Evolution of Technologies

Information and Communication Technologies (ICT's) were an important instrument for the transformation of industrial society in the information and knowledge society. It is a networked society, emerging a new social morphology, and gains economic, social, political, and cultural primacy. According to Orth, (2002, p. 22), one lives in a culture and a society that is constantly changing, either because the economic, social, political, and cultural contexts are increasingly massified, internationalized and globalized, or because the relations of life, study, work and capital are changing rapidly and constantly.

According to (Santos, 2013), it is possible to prescribe that from the technical uniqueness (unique technical model), based on the capitalist system and the form, as the process of globalization is configured, there is a significant transformation of consumption into ideology of life, making citizens consumers, massifying and standardizing culture, and form that often contributes to the concentration of wealth, in the hands of a few. According to (Ney Jr, 2002), "the current information revolution is based on the rapid technological advances of the computer, communications and software, which in turn led to extraordinary reductions in the cost of processing and transmitting information", as well as, "in ideal terms, the Information Revolution will repeat the successes of the Industrial Revolution. Only this time, part of the brain's work, not the muscles, will be transferred to the machines." For (Cardoso, 2007, p. 102), information seems to have replaced energy as a central element of economic life, first of the most developed countries and then for all areas of the planet and subject to market rules. It is observed in this panorama that the Internet was the apex of the Information and Knowledge Society since it allowed the free movement of information throughout the world. Furthermore, "the first stages of ***Internet*** use int he 1980s were announced, such as the arrival of a new era of free communication and personal fulfillment in virtual communities, formed around communication, mediated by the computer", (Castells, 2003, p. 100). According to, (Lojkine, 1995), "the transfer to machines of a new type of abstract brain functions is at the heart of the informational Revolution", emerging the need for restructuring capitalism that drives the adoption, diversification of media and the development of information and communication technologies and their networking.

ICT's provides the great legitimacy of the expansive political power, which assumes all spheres of culture. In this Universe, ICT's also provides great rationalization of man's lack of freedom and demonstrate the "technical" impossibility of being autonomous, of determining people's lives. This lack of freedom does not arise, either irrationally, or as politics, but rather as work. Technological rationality protects, the legality of domination, rather than eliminating it, and the instrumentalist horizon of reason opens to a ***rational totalitarian society.*** According to (Gonçalves, 2003, p. 138), *cyberspace* is the main vector of the Internet, and its striking characteristics are invisibility, intangibility and intercommunicability. The processing of information by computer gave rise to legislative and judicial movements to protect rights over information and the regulation of access and use. The Internet is characterized by being a communication space without mediator, structured according to an "all-all relationship". Thus, relationships between peoples are given and interaction with the worldwide network of ***computers, which*** stores the most diverse types of content, whether they are made available by the users themselves about their *preferences and their private life or by the servers themselves.* ***It turns out that by the interaction generated on the network, its storage, and the distribution of content, it becomes virtually impossible to remove information once posted online.***

According to (Nissenbaum, 2010, p. 21), the great difficulty faced in this context is to separate the public and private spheres from each individual from what should or should not be available, and available to all, in a virtual environment. Therefore, "information technology considers itself a major threat to privacy, because it allows for ubiquitous surveillance, gigantic databases and a rapid distribution of information around the world". For (Habermas, 1997, p. 92), the public sphere can be "described as an appropriate network for content communication, decision-making and opinion; in it the communication flows are filtered and synthesized, to the point of condensing into public opinions encased at specific times." It is in this sense that the aspirations of the next design of the text are given, aiming to provide a debate between the right to privacy and intimate life, of what may or may not be, linked to the existence of each person, characterizing what is of private interest or what can generate, a right ***to forgetfulness.***

The Digital Society

It will not be an exaggeration or a blatant mis understanding, to affirm that the current society is increasingly qualified by the digital adjective, where new information and communication technologies (ICT's) have constant daily influence, configuring themselves as, mediators of social relations, the economy and even the way to produce / disseminate knowledge. There are forms of knowledge absorption about users in a ubiquitous way, in which ICT's be new forms of surveillance (Lupton, 2015, p. 02; p. 189). Digital ICT's play a crucial role in the process of globalization, as a phenomenon characterized by the wide circulation of people, ideas, and habits, which although it has not started historically with technologies, develops at high speed through them (De Mul, 2015, p. 106).

The increasing insertion of Information, and Communication Technologies (ICT's) in people's daily lives has promoted a deep dependency relationship between them. In this context, daily, actions have become essentially informational, given the need for mediation for their performance.

The society original is a complex society of technological innovation and communication, in which there is the creation of new environments and changes in, the organizational dynamics of people, in the way people understand reality, changing the way they relate to the environment, with other people and how, they conceive in the face of reality itself. Both senses can be understood, as arising from the informational revolution, promoted mainly from the attempts to understand human intelligence, via computational bases.

The works developed by (Turing,1950), had great influence in the studies of the second half of the twentieth century, including in Philosophy, mainly by its algorithmic approach to the nature of thought, in which he proposes the thesis, according to which, "thinking is calculating" (Turing, 1950, p. 436). This is that, given that digital computers operate from calculations and manipulate rules for the organization of symbols, if we consider that thinking consists, in the activity of manipulating symbols, according to a set of logical rules, constituting algorithms, then digital computers could, in principle, think. Once intelligent thinking is understood mechanically, it would be possible to construct mechanical models of the structure and dynamics of this type of thought. This understanding allowed the development of mechanical models of the mind, which initially generated two aspects in Cognitive Science, (Teixeira, 1998):

- Strong Artificial Intelligence - is one in which mechanical models of the mind, when successful, not only simulate/ emulate mental activities, but explain and instantiate such activities.
- Weak Artificial Intelligence – is one in which the model is only an explanatory tool, limited to intelligent mental activity.

The common point of such nodes is that both accept the thesis that to simulate is to explain, in order to attribute to mechanical models, the value of theories, in which the computer is used, as a fundamental tool. As for the social sphere, the development of studies of information theory promoted the social changes that are currently experiencing and that have generated new types of problems, especially those that relate to action / technology / environment. Given its impact on the academic and social spheres, the approximation between Philosophy and Information Science, and the role of computers in the development of theories, theoretical production occurred concomitantly with technological improvement.

(Floridi, 2008, p. 3-4), states that during the second half of the 20th century events such as: the massification of the computer, which promoted the generation of the "personal computer"; the advancement of scientific discoveries in function of the use of ICT's; and the emergence of new ways of expert meant the world, from such technologies. These events illustrate the influence of ICT's in various areas of society (sociological, economic, scientific, and cultural), providing elements for the characterization of it, such as the information and knowledge society. According to (Floridi, 2002, p. 127): "Post-industrial societies are nourished, by information".

ICT's acquire a central role in the characterization of the digital society, to the extent that they are present and related to the person and their well-being, and in their continuous use in everyday situations (e.g., leisure, work, etc.), constituted relationship of dependence, between the person and the TIC's. This relationship is strengthened, according to Floridi, from the following factors:

- Increasing the power of ICT's, while reducing their cost of production and marketing.
- Improvement of ICT's in their interaction potential (machine-machine and mem-machine).
- The rise of the zettabyte's era (dated 2010).

The factors indicated are responsible for the approximation between people and ICT's, generating deep relationship of dependence for the performance of routine actions in today's world. This dependence is based on the digital presence, as a mediator of common actions, such as financial movement (home banking), the acquisition of products and services (virtual stores, e-commerce), personal and professional interrelationship (via social networks, such as Facebook, Twitter, or dating apps such as Tinder), access to movies (via streaming, YouTube, Netflix, etc.), urban mobility (via app, Uber, Taxi 99), making connections (using the network, via Skype, WhatsApp), the practice of physical activity (Run keeper, for example), professional activities via SOHO (small office / home office), political organization (via websites or social networks), among others. Situations in which there is no mediation of s internet-connected artefacts by the **person**s, but which require technological mediation by the service to be requested, such as: payment by credit card for face-to-face purchases, biometric systems for the removal of books in libraries, among others.

In addition to understanding the influence of ICT's on the constitution and alteration of people's self, the three types, of self-highlighted by (Floridi, 2014, p. 60) are explained:

- **Personal Identity** - it concerns "who we are". We live in an era where people spend a great deal of time transmitting information about themselves, interacting digitally with other people, which is a good example of how ICT's is affecting and shaping people's identity.
- **Self-conception** - consists of "who we think we are".
- **Social elf** - concerns what we are, from the thought of other people.

It is mainly this third notion of self that ICT's have a deeper channel of action in the conception of people's identity, because there is a growing support and overvaluation of social networks, illustrated, for example, by the intensification of a "narcissistic culture".

The Web enhances narcissistic culture, typical of our time, by expanding the forms of self-celebration and self-promotion. Relationship sites, in turn, end up encouraging vanity and competition. [...] young people strive to show in their profiles, photos and texts that value them and promote the increase in the number of people they add as "friends". [...] This type of behavior is justified by a constant search for attention and recognition. The ease of access to information about themselves generated by third parties, promotes self-understanding from others (social self), constitutes a scenario in which people, especially those corresponding to Generation Z, feed the network, with personal information intensely.

The greatest of all changes is the transformation of the information and knowledge society into the digital society. The center of work was 'distance work - telework'. In developed country societies, access to good jobs and a professional career will increasingly depend on a university degree with distance work, anywhere, in a country, in the globalized world. That is, the logical result, since we stopped working in the office and in large urban centers, it was through intellectual work and teleworking was reached at home or elsewhere, outside the large urban centers. This last step represents a break with the past.

- The fact that knowledge and education have been a passport to the achievement of good jobs and a career has meant above all that in society, companies are no longer the only way for someone to progress in life and have become one of several opportunities available.
- Knowledge has become the capital of developed economies and knowledge workers, which determines the values and norms of society.

The big challenge is to maintain the commitment, with the economic performance necessary for organizations and countries to remain competitive. Governance and entrepreneurship contain the entrepreneurial spirit. They are not antagonistic concepts, nor mutually exclusive. Both are always necessary and at the same time. Both must be coordinated, i.e. both must work together. No existing organization can survive without innovation and at the same time without being managed.

Digital Capitalism

According to (Gary T. Marx, 2015, p. 735), surveillance is tied to verbs such as "look", "observe", "supervise", "control", "inspect", "monitor", "guard" or even "follow". Many of the examples for understanding contemporary ways of obtaining, information is based on cognitive skills through technological artifacts, such as software and automated processes. However, such technical means may also involve sophisticated forms of manipulation, with seduction, coercion, deception, unambiguous information, and other special forms of observation, (Marx, 2015, p. 735-737). Surveillance has become more deceptive over time and be something harder to defeat than before, after all many forms are so ubiquitous that Marx's omnipotent are generally presumed. Surveillance can, succinctly, take place on the human routine, the semi-conscious "autopilot" and often even the biological instinct of our sensory receptors that are ready to constantly receive information from whoever is territorially close, (Marx, 2016, p. 16). With the development of language, numerical and written, and of different forms of social organization involving larger political entities, more complex and systematic forms of surveillance emerged, based on counting, registration, interrogation, information, infiltration, confessions, and the expanded use of tests (Marx, 2016, p. 17).

With the emergence of industrial society, new tools of surveillance and communication emerged, individuals, groups, and contexts using technological means to extract, infer or create information, (Marx, 2016, p. 19-20). Examples can be found in computer profiles, which have large data sets, video cameras, data about DNA analysis, GPS, electronic monitoring, drug testing and monitoring made possible by social media and mobile phones.

The BIG data industry establishes a system in contemporary society, where the world and life are transformed or mediated by data, and this is a fundamental paradigm shift for contemporary society, (Beraldo; Milan, 2019, p. 01). The nature of databases is inherent to any software, which basically performs programming of data that can be divided into four operations, (De Mul, 2015, p. 106): a) add; b) search; c) change; and d) destroy (command that can be sorted by the options of insert, select, update, and delete). Together, these commands constitute the dynamics of database ontology.

In the age of BIG data, databases are increasingly connected to each other and with connected data streams such as Google searches, social media interactions (Twitter, Facebook, Instagram, LinkedIn, Reddit, etc.) and online commerce. These connections derived from BIG data are tracked and used for the purpose of configuring user profile and real-time data mining by private and public organizations, (De Mul, 2015, p. 107-108). From this same logic it can be inferred-se that, due to data from production processes, money transfers, GPS devices, surveillance cameras, biometric measurements and the use of smartphones and other localizable devices, an immense global database is being formed and will transform the ways of life, work and thinking (De Mul, 2015, p. 107).

It can be understood that the impact of databases is vast, since it is not limited only to the universe of computing, since they evoke acts in the material world. Examples of this are the biotechnological databases used for genetic engineering purposes, implementations in industrial robots and the airport profile design system, with the aim of identifying potential terrorists, (De Mul, 2015, p. 107). In thesis everything that can be identified through data becomes an object of control of such databases. Celebrities, politicians and other public figures are subject to constant monitoring (whether in public or private) and the great facilitators of this exhibition are not only the paparazzi, after all, but anyone with some mobile device can also make an instant live broadcast. 21st century capitalism has found a massive new raw material to appropriate: stored data, (Srnicek; From Sutter, 2016, p. 106). Through a series of developments, the electronic platform has become an increasingly dominant way to organize business, monopolizing, extracting, analyzing, using, and selling data. The business models of the Fordist era were capable, only in a rudimentary way, of extracting data, from the production process or from the customer's use. The era of lean production changed this slightly, as global supply chains 'just in time' required data on the status of stocks and the location of supplies. The problem is capitalism, not technology.

The Dominant Discourse

Dados outside the company remained almost impossible to obtain; and even within the company, most of the activities were not recorded. The electronic platform, on the other hand, has data extraction incorporated into DNA, as a model that allows other services, goods, and technologies to be built on it, as a model that requires more users to obtain network effects, and as a digital medium that simplifies registration and storage. All these characteristics make platforms, a central model, to extract data as raw material. Data can be used in several ways to generate revenue. For companies like Google and Facebook, data is a feature that can be used to attract advertisers and other stakeholders. For companies like Rolls Royce and Uber, data is at the heart of beating the competition: it allows these companies to offer better products and services, control workers and optimize their algorithms for a more competitive business.

With Google's system in place and Facebook's development in the online landscape — targeted advertising, surveillance capitalism adds new logic of accumulation where its guidelines and financial prowess dominate the virtual sphere of connected networks and this grossly disfigures the previous dream of digital technology as a empowering and emancipatory force, (Zuboff, 2019, p. 01). Today, this surveillance capitalism can no longer be identified punctually, as it was, until some time ago, Google exclusivity, a pioneer in this form of data capitalization), since, this logic has expanded, in a way with which Silicon Valley has expanded to various sectors of the economy and its vast options of products and services (Zuboff, 2019, p. 01). Both capitalism and surveillance can no longer be confused, as belonging to an individual corporation, after all digital technologies today can take many forms and reproduce various reflexes, depending on their social and economic orientation. For (Zuboff, 2019, p. 01) economic guidance is the master, while technology is the puppet. From change in the logic of the global economy and the global technological market, we currently have a work environment characterized by less job security, stagnant wages and where the nature of work has become more intense and idiosyncratic; several employers believe that they must obey a market imperative that constantly pushes for greater productivity, so that their organizations remain competitive (Connolly, 2017, p. 69).

Therefore, attempts to satisfy such demand, foster an unceasing search for efficiency, and the emergence of strict performance quotas. Surveillance capitalism is not the same as algorithms, sensors, machine intelligence or platforms, although it relies on all of this to express its will; soon surveillance capitalism is indeed an economic creation and is therefore subject to democratic contestation, debate, review, restriction, supervision and may even be illegal in many cases (Zuboff, 2019).

The New Forms of Surveilance

Society is interconnected due to the digital technologies that serve to meet the most diverse human needs. While users are often aware of the risks they run with such technologies, they do not understand the complexity of the online permissions they grant or the destination of their personal data.

Surveillance is a terminology that has not emerged with the digitization of technologies but has expanded through such technologies. Not only security cameras and real estate cameras are able to capture images and sounds, after all applications and mobile devices are the most common among technological devices today. The evolution of technological surveillance was linked to the process of individualization and self-responsibility of the capitalist economy, in which it is the user who produces the data of his own surveillance, being subject to the process that his data is necessary for improvement of the systems, producing value for the algorithms. Surveillance configures a constant situation, which increasingly evolves beyond the paradigm of work and public safety to the core of everyday life, analyzing and conditioning behaviors, causally linked to utility applications and social networks. The search for increased utility and satisfaction of desires, consequently, drives an economic logic of the market. Entrepreneurship is focused on the commercialization and production of new technologies that adapt to the needs of consumers. Capitalism that emerges from such logic presents several contrasts, and among them, the threat against people's privacy. Information stored in databases that will serve various purposes, including policy-related purposes, is exploited.

THE DEVELOPMENT OF THE DIGITAL SOCIETY AND DEMOCRACY

Introduction

Considering the assumption that, in the global sphere, the convergence of information and communication technologies (ICT's) does not necessarily lead us to the identification of ethical, cultural, social, and democratic values. A new model of socioeconomic organization is observed, the model of global digital capitalism, through the instrumentalization of information and communication technologies, to develop new forms of increasingly sophisticated exploration (Basso, 2005). Related to the structural changes in the globalized economy, most of the Gross Domestic Product (GDP) of a country to be generated by the information sector, surpassing the other sectors of the economy (Moore, 2014).

This social organization assumes that a large part of the economically active population works in activities related to production, marketing, information-related services. In the United States of America, in 2016, about two-thirds (2/3) of the workforce was directly or indirectly linked to the information sector (École..., 2020). From this angle, telecommunications and information have become a vital resource for the country's social well-being, national security, and competitiveness (Aguadero, 1997).

Digital capitalism is based on an economic model based on the development of new mechanisms for exploiting the value produced by work, through the instrumentalization of disinvolvement, without precedents financial type accumulation, 'ICT's. result in massive indebtedness of governments and families (Santos, 2013; Mef, 2017). For more than 20 years, government spending has exceeded revenues. This situation can be explained by the state's desire to adopt an expansionary fiscal policy with the aim of stimulating economic growth and job creation from the perspective of the new structural changes of the globalized capitalist project (Ministère..., 2017).

The development of the information-based digital economy is conditioned by the ability to produce market value. From this perspective, countries operate structural changes in their economies, and aim to increase their market shares in world trade in goods and services, as well as the global opening of these markets, (Porras, 2015, Ventura, Ventura, Ventura. Broner, 2016). The penetration of digital capitalism is not linear. Capitalist relations of production do not replace non-capitalist production relations. The penetration of digital capitalism partially destroys them and adapts them. The dematerialization of the economy for the economic activities of the service sector (with complex apprehension of market values: financial institutions, transport and communication, domestic and business services) results in a (re) mechanization of capitalism.

THE ECONOMIC DEVELOPMENT OF SOCIAL NETWORKS

In the 1990s, in the initial phase, the Internet could not find a viable business model, which would provide it with a minimum of stability and coherence, that is, an aesthetic techno system that ensured coherence between the modalities of production, consumption and financing, (Leroy, 1980 Herscovici, 1995). These difficulties characterize all activities that work in network: in the initial phase*(startup),* while the number of users is insufficient, the network knows a period of deficit (Herscovici, 2013).

In the consolidation phase, from the 2000s on, the system overcame the deficit phase and managed to reach the critical mass from which the networks became profitable. The system has succeeded in building an economically viable mode of sectoral regulation, based on the development of intermarket, i.e. On the sale of audience to the different advertisers, and data relating to those audiences. The various electronic platforms have developed a double-sided markets strategy to reach specific audiences and ensure better quality when it comes to receiving the advertising message.

The development of algorithms and the sale of the collected data have allowed the diversification and expand in of the sources of financing of electronic platforms and thus creating markets in which access modalities and audience data are sold. The increasing use of increasingly complex and sophisticated algorithms had the following implications:

- reach specific audiences, which has enabled the diversification of funding sources and, therefore, to intensify the market for social spaces built by those users.
- Collect a series of data and determine the social and cultural trajectories of different users, which represents the different sources of financing of electronic platforms. These data are sold to different actors and used by these actors for economic and/or political purposes.
- The informative efficiency of these algorithms allows to elaborate more reliable expectations, from a much more representative sample of the public: the larger the sample from which the predictions are drawn, the lower the statistical errors, and the more reliable these predictions are, and that allow a greater appreciation of their products and / or services, in the market.

Digital capitalism is implemented outside of products and or services. In the different markets, information is valued from its specificities, based on the concrete work applied to it (HerscovicI, 2014). Being the object of exchange, information can be associated with products and or services, in the sense defined by classical economists. From a more general point of view, information is heterogeneous, and is valued in different markets based on its heterogeneity.

Evolution translates into profound changes, with regard to the modalities of production, distribution and management, of the social value of information, which corresponds to the abandonment of the classical (and Marxist) theory of work value (Marx, Grundisse, 2011).

From a theoretical point of view, it is not possible to study the economics of social networks according to the concepts of classical economists, whose maximum exponent is Marx, for the following reasons:

- The "production" of information by users is valued socially and economically from specific works, i.e. that "production" cannot be associated with a specific commodity. It is not valued because of, the amount of abstract work contained therein. This type of "production" does not correspond to the concept of physical merchandise: it is a production that is valued from its specificities and that cannot be produced by the application of abstract work.

- Since it is not a physical commodity, it is not possible to speak of exploitation of workers (users), according to Marx's theoretical concepts. Capital gains is one of the components of the value of the commodity, and in the absence of goods, it is not possible to conceive capital gains.

The only productive work (strict sense) is one that is directly linked to the "construction" (constitution) of the infrastructures that correspond to the implementation of networks and the design of the different algorithms that allow storing and valuing, in secondary markets, the data that relate to the different audiences. These works are abstract works, because they are not valued from their specificities, but from their functionalities: they are the ones that allow access, treatment, storage and disseminate the raw information initially produced by users.

The extent of market logic and the economic nature of information, from audience sales to tracking, are the different modalities of expanding market logic. This extension of market logic originated from two dimensions: the first relates to the social and geographical extension, from the New Law and Economics of Chicago, when markets were created linked to the exchange of pollution rights between different countries. Digital capitalism developed during the first industrial revolution, from the exploitation of natural resources, and currently expands its logic to immaterial and symbolic resources, information.

During Fordism, the main media outlets consisted of selling the modalities of access to audiences, and became adios an important source of financing, and the first endless markets that developed with the press, radio and open television emerged. Today, there is an intensive expansion of market logics: in addition to selling access to certain audiences, it consists in developing and expanding other sources of financing linked to the traceability of users' behavior, whose social trajectories are sold to other agents, for commercial and/or political purposes.

There are different types of market, depending on the different types of information. Each type of market corresponds to a certain type of information and a certain type of exchange relationships. The primary market has a direct relationship with the final consumer: the newspaper reader, the traditional media audience, and the social media user, who produces raw information. This information can be produced on the network or off the network, but distributed free of charge or almost, by platforms such as YouTube videos, photos on Instagram, articles published in magazines and accessible on Google, which will be exploited by electronic platforms and different agents in the intermediary markets. On the other hand, users of social networks produce information relating to their social and cultural trajectories, which will be tracked, collected, and organized by digital platforms and the different data collection systems, "Big Data".

The raw information produced by consumers is an abundant and non-economic good, which is why it is free. However, digital platforms take ownership of this raw data, providing users with free or semi-free access to certain services. In primary markets, the information also presents the characteristics of non-exclusion, indivisibility and collective good:

- No deletion - users have free access to the information available on the network.
- Indivisibility - the service is not destroyed at the time of consumption.
- Very collective - the stock available to users depends on the number of users.

Secondary markets are located between the final consumer and other economic agents: they exist from the moment that the raw information produced in the primary markets has already been stored, organized, and codified. Once encoded, this raw information becomes the subject of trade. One of the paradoxes of this economy is, on the one hand, these goods are traded on the markets, but on the other, depending on the character of the public good, it is impossible to attribute individual property rights to them. Agents operating in these nonterm markets benefit from a dominant position, in terms of information and receipt of, to the detriment of users who produce raw information; those markets deviate from the characteristics of pure and perfect competition. From an economic point of view, information can be compared with natural resources since it is available free of charge. It is produced from the tacit knowledge of users and, therefore, from concrete work, as defined by Marx, and is characterized by its heterogeneity. As a raw data, information does not produce value, just as forest trees also produce no economic value; while it does not become a "raw material" in a given commercial production process, it is useless and does not generate economic value until it is the object of transformation, from the application of work. The role of social networks is to collect, process, process and disseminate, from increasingly powerful and sophisticated algorithms, raw information. This process only occurs from the moment the information was encoded. Networks develop economic stratagems at two levels:

- **Primary markets** - offering a free service to users (end consumer);
- **Secondary markets** – sale of services to access highly segmented audiences and information relating to the economic, social, and political trajectories of platform users.

In the digital economy, the consumer/user produces the "raw material" that will be sold in secondary markets, depending on the very operation of the system. Its presence in networks is the necessary condition to generate economic value. For this reason, that consumer benefits from free or almost access to the stock of the encoded and available information. From the implementation of physical networks and the construction of algorithms, the role of networks is to generate economic value, in secondary markets, from the social value created in the primary markets; it is from (abstract) work linked to the distribution, codification and processing of raw information, that information becomes the object of commercial exchange.

SOCIAL NETWORKS AND BUSINESS

Undoubtedly, one of the most changed activities in recent years around the world, there are social relationships, through online social networks, such as Facebook, Twitter, YouTube, etc. Most users who interact in these social networks, do so for different purposes, but mainly, to socialize and maintain relationships with colleagues, family, and friends, (Miralbell, 2014).

However, the opportunities and challenges that online social networks present vary from global economic activity, supported by Information and Communication Technologies (ICT's), which stimulate innovative dynamism (Lladós, Jiménez & Garay, 2008) and become one of the main foundations of the process of change experienced by the economy and social structure in the last decade, because they become a resource of massive use and application,, by all economic and social agents, and as such, are the basis of the new innovative substrate that "transforms the structure of basic in sums and relative production costs" (Torrent and Sellens, 2009).

In the globalized economy and the digital networked society, the dynamics of the structure of social networks is generated from the exchange of digitally processed information and using information and communication technologies (Castells, 2009). Companies take advantage of knowledge transfer, to improve competitiveness, through the innovation of their products and / or services and production processes. The competition stimulates the generation of new knowledge, which allows to preserve the preferred position of owners, on the Internet. This does not mean that there is a long way to go in most companies, in terms of promotion and socialization, through social networks, although existing studies have shown that this favors the sharing of knowledge, improving the performance of the company and its professionals (Miralbell, 2013).

INFORMATION ASYMMETRIES

In the digital information economy, the existence of imperfections in information is systematically translated by information asymmetries, opportunistic behaviors appear, which are incompatible with a socially optimal situation: informed agents benefit from additional revenue to the detriment of uninformed or uninformed agents. On the other hand, depending on the nature of the public good of the goods and services produced on social networks, it is not possible to apply an efficient and individualized system of Property Rights (DP). This situation means that the contracts established between users and digital platforms are, by their very nature, incomplete.

Social media users are unable to control all the uses that are made of data relating to their social and cultural trajectories. Thus, the different laws on the protection of individual data (the latest measures adopted in the European Union) are not efficient because the isolated individual is unable to control these uses.

Social media users are unable to control all the uses that are made of data relating to their social and cultural trajectories. Thus, the different laws on the protection of individual data (the latest measures adopted in the European Union) are not efficient because the isolated individual is not able to control these uses. These contracts are incomplete, in the sense employed by (Williamson, 2002): they are not fully efficient, and this partial control implies high transaction costs (Barzel, 1997). The screening modalities are distributed in an unequal way, which translates into inequalities, about the modalities of appropriation of the economic value created.

In primary markets, consumers / users are harmed because they are unable to negotiate a favorable breakdown of the value generated with digital platforms. The negotiation between users and digital platforms is based on the exchange of free-or semi-free access modalities against the use and exploitation of the data produced. The way to reduce information asymmetries will be the implementation of forms of collective administration.

Information asymmetries are produced by the dynamics of digital markets. When consumers / users use social networks, they leave track that algorithms, increasingly powerful and sophisticated, will use, so it is possible to track, in an exhaustive way, these trajectories.

When they go to social networks, users cannot escape or control the tracking mechanisms. The data collected and organized by the platforms or by specialized agents are, thus, another type of information which will be traded in the intermediate markets. These secondary markets are characterized by the presence of strong and large information asymmetries. Consumers/users cannot trade trading in those markets, so platforms benefit from a dominant position. Their opposition can only express itself, in a form of voluntary exclusion from the public space, in not attending the social network. The consequences of these asymmetries are as follows:

- Increase in transaction costs related to the modalities of contract establishment and management of participants' behavior.
- Users are unable to make rational decisions, since they do not know the context, from which they will make those decisions.
- *Fake news,* etc., are forms of manipulation, distortions, which make it impossible for users to make rational decisions.

For example, political choices are to maximize the utility function on the part of voters, as voters have a distorted knowledge of reality, and are unable to assess in advance the usefulness attached to their political decisions.

DATA CAPITALISM AND PRIVACY

21st century capitalism has found a massive new raw material to appropriate: data (Srnicek; by Sutter, 2016, p. 106). Through a series of developments, electronic platforms have become an increasingly dominant way to organize business, monopolizing, extracting, analyzing, using, and selling data.

Fordist-era business models were able to extract data from the production process or customer use. The era of lean production changed this slightly, as global supply chains "***just in time***" required data on the status of stocks and the location of raw materials.

However, data outside the company remained almost impossible to obtain; and even within the company, most of the activities were not recorded. Electronic platforms, on the other hand, have data extraction embedded in their DNA, as a model that allows other services, goods, and technologies to be built on it, as a model that requires more users to achieve network effects, and as a digital medium that simplifies registration and storage. All these characteristics make platforms a central model for extracting data as raw material to be used in various ways.

Data can be used in several ways to generate revenue. For companies such as Google and Facebook, data is primarily a resource that can be used to attract advertisers and other interested companies / organizations. For companies like Rolls Royce and Uber, data is at the heart of beating the competition, as it allows them to offer better products and services, control workers and optimize their algorithms for a more competitive business. Today, the data shape a scenario where mass production or those, with economic dominance, however, generate alternatives, but increasingly controversial, since it comes within generic parameters of the policy (for example, against mapping and critical cartography), or are under the influence of factors that foster crucial contemporary struggles, such as against racial discrimination by algorithms), (Beraldo; Milan, 2019, p. 03).

Today the systems of Google and Facebook in the online scenario of targeted advertising, surveillance capitalism adds a new logic of accumulation where financial guidelines and prowess dominate the virtual sphere, of connected networks and this grossly disfigures, the previous dream of digital technology, as a empowering and emancipatory force, (Zuboff, 2019, p. 01).

Today, this surveillance capitalism can no longer be identified on time, as a specific company (as it was, until some time ago, Google's exclusivity, a pioneer in this form of data capitalization),since this logic has expanded, so that Silicon Valley has expanded to various sectors of the economy and its vast options of products and services, (Zuboff, 2019, p. 01).

Digital capitalism and electronic surveillance cannot be confused as belonging to an individual corporation. The end digital technologies can take many forms and reproduce various reflections, depending on their social and economic orientation. For (Zuboff, 2019, p. 01) economic guidance is the master, while technology is the puppet.

In the global economy and in the global technological market, the labor market is characterized by less job security, stagnant wages and the nature of work has become more intense and idiosyncratic. Several employers believe that the market imperative requires greater productivity, so that their organizations remain competitive (Connolly, 2017, p. 69).

To meet demand, they foster an unceasing search for efficiency and effectiveness, and strict performance quotas emerge. Electronic surveillance capitalism is not the same as algorithms, sensors, machine intelligence or platforms, although it relies on all of this to express its will, since it is indeed an economic creation and is therefore subject to democratic contestation, debate, review, restriction, supervision and may even be illegal in many cases (Zuboff, 2019).

Second, (Lupton and Michael, 2017, p. 254), digital data is influencing people's concepts about themselves, their bodies and even their social relationships; the use of personal digital data in surveillance activities is a controversial topic, after all electronic data surveillance is carried out both on a personal and interpersonal level, involving self-surveillance or straight surveillance, and this phenomenon is driven, fostered and co-opted by companies, security and policing institutions and agencies, transport organizations, employers, educational institutions, etc. (Lupton; Michael, 2017, p. 255).

Second, (Zuboff, 2019, p. 02), Google has capitalized, and its success derives from the ability to predict the future of human behavior, and the way to translate its interactions outside the market, with users as "raw material" intended for its real customers, advertisers (Zuboff, 2019, p. 03). In other words, the "**Meta data** "that is generated by search engine users (e.g. questions on the platform, peak times for the use, gender, gender, age, race of platform users, geo-positioning.), which until recently were considered as residue of operations or, at most, useful information for Google itself to improve its-product, became a true "behavioral surplus" (behavioral surplus),highly valued by Google, to form user profiles and, increasingly accurately, target ads to potential consumers.

The internet of things has gained great potential for realization, as well as in real-time, data collection. Wearable devices *are* a step towards the realization of the **so-called Internet of Things,** which is characterized by maintaining constant connectivity between the different types of common objects, in people's daily lives, such as glasses, watches, shoes, bracelets, shirts etc. There are several examples of how mobile technology can be inserted into different accessories, whether as a source of information, communication, or entertainment, for its users. *Smartwatches,* for example, are wristwatches that work from hybridism with technology present in smartphones and *tablets. Wearables,* as defined by the concept of the Internet of Things, help to build an environment in which technology is now intrinsically connected to people's day-to-day lives, in an **imperceptible way.**

The Internet of Things is a technological concept in **which all objects of everyday life are connected to the internet,** acting intelligently and sensorially. It consists of the idea of merging the "real world" with the "digital world", making individuals can be in constant communication and interaction, whether with other people or with objects such as appliances, cars, clothing, keys, tables, mirrors, etc. There are countless possibilities to attach computing to the things that belong to one hundred people's daily lives.

This technological revolution is considered by many scholars to be the last step in the computer development process. As Mark Weiser, one of the most important computer science scholars, **described, the Internet of Things** is at the stage in which computer science is ubiquitously consolidated in people's lives. However, it was scientist Kevin Ashton in 1999 who first used the expression "internet of **things**" to refer to the use of technologies that could interconnect various devices and different objects, helping to facilitate and organize people's lives.

However, privacy, internationally recognized as a human and constitutional right by various democracies as a fundamental right, is devalued on issues such as national security and the effective administration of companies, (Rahman et al., 2019, p. 965)

For (Cowls, 2018, p. 145), the Right to Privacy has always been associated with technologies and their skills in capturing data or even valuable information. Simpler forms of technology, such as typing, are indeed far from contemporary forms that can collect and store data, such, as security cameras. In this sense it is very pertinent to question, how surveillance and privacy relate. In common sense, surveillance is often mistakenly seen as just the opposite of privacy (Marx, 2016, p. 23); however, it implies the existence of something that accesses personal data (through discovery tools, rules or logistical configurations); while privacy, on the contrary, involves an agent capable of restricting access to personal data through the most varied complex devices.

It is possible to point out that both surveillance and privacy are factors that involve efforts to control information (such as discovery or protection) and can be connected in several ways. Surveillance is capable of abusively invading privacy, but also can be a useful means to protect privacy (e.g., biometric identification and audit trails, video cameras that film those with access to sensitive data); and privacy, in turn, can also protect surveillance (e.g. undercover police officers who use fake IDs, and forwarding anonymous calls to protect the identity of witnesses), as well as, can override it (e.g., encryption, whispers, and disguises). Thus, depending on the way in which it is used, surveillance can affect the presence of privacy and/or advertising, depending on the context and role played.

Surveillance and Data Analysis

Society is interconnected in its most diverse forms, through digital technologies that serve to meet the various needs. While users are often aware of the risks they take with the use of such technologies, they do not understand the complexity of such online permissions they grant and the destination of their personal data.

The term "surveillance", which designates surveillance, is derived from the French verb "surveillir", which in turn is related to the term "vigilare" from Latin. According to (Gary T. Marx, 2015, p. 735), this terminology is tied to verbs such as "look", "observe", "supervise", "control", "inspect", "monitor", "save" or even "follow". Many of the examples for understanding contemporary ways of obtaining information are guided by cognitive skills, through technological artifacts, such, as software and automated processes. However, such technical means may also involve sophisticated forms of manipulation, such as seduction, coercion, deception, unambiguous information, and other special forms of observation (Marx, 2015, p. 735-737).

Surveillance has become more deceptive over time. Surveillance can, succinctly, take place on the human routine, the semi-conscious "autopilot" and often, even the biological instinct of our sensory receptors that are ready to constantly receive information, from whoever is territorially close (Marx, 2016, p. 16). These purposes make it possible to distinguish two forms of surveillance, at least:

- Traditional surveillance relies on unassisted senses and is characteristic of pre-industrial societies. With the development of language, numerical and written, and of different forms of social organization involving larger political entities, more complex and systematic forms of surveillance emerged, based on counting, registration, interrogation, information, infiltration, confessions, and the expanded use of tests (Marx, 2016, p. 17).

- With the emergence of industrial society, new tools of surveillance and communication have emerged, which have improved the senses and cognition Visual is usually an element of surveillance, even when, is not the initial means of data collection, so the new surveillance can be defined, as the scrutiny of individuals, groups and contexts, through the use of technological means to extract, infer or create information (Marx, 2016, p. 19-20).

Examples of such a phenomenon can be found in computer profiles, which have large data sets, video cameras, data about DNA analysis, GPS, electronic monitoring, drug testing and monitoring made possible by social media and mobile tele. The new surveillance is more intensive and extensive, expanding the senses, thus reducing costs, and reaching more remote locations; it is based primarily on aggregating data in **Big Data;** thus, it has less visibility and directly involves the involuntary conformity of the individual (Marx, 2015, p. 735-736).

The new surveillance established in contemporaneity is the thorough examination of individuals and groups, using highly sophisticated technological means, capable of extracting information. In this sense, the use of technical means to extract and create information implies the ability to go beyond what is naturally offered to the senses and minds or what is voluntarily reported (Marx, 2015, p. 736).

The **big data industry establishes** a system in contemporary society, where the world and life are transformed or mediated by data, and this is a fundamental paradigm shift for contemporary society (Beraldo; Milan, 2019, p. 01). The nature of databases is inherent in any software, which basically uses software programs to store data that can be divided into four operations (De Mul, 2015, p. 106): a) add; b) search; c) change; and d) destroy (command that can be classified by the options of insert, select, update, and delete). Together, these commands constitute the dynamics of database ontology. The dynamics of databases is not necessarily digital, since phone books and indexes are ways of grouping data as well.

Surveillance is a terminology that has not emerged with the digitization of technologies but has expanded through such technologies. Not only security cameras and real estate cameras are able to capture images and sounds, after all applications and mobile devices are the most common among the technological media today. The evolution of technological surveillance was linked to the process of individualization and self-responsibility of the capitalist economy, in which it is the user who produces the data of his own surveillance, being subject to the process that his data is necessary for improvement of the systems, producing value for the algorithms.

Surveillance configures a constant situation, which increasingly evolves beyond the paradigm of work and public safety, to the core of everyday life, analyzing and conditioning behaviors, causally linked to social networks. The search for increased utility and the satisfaction of desires, drives an economic logic of the market. Entrepreneurship is focused on the commercialization and production of new technologies that adapt to the needs of consumers. Capitalism that emerges from such logic presents several contrasts, and among them, the threat against people's privacy. Information stored in databases that will serve various purposes, including policy-related purposes, is exploited.

Data Export

The electronic security of society involves not only the private sector, but also the State and relations between people. Electronic surveillance leads us to ask the question, is it good or bad? The use of data by government, security, commercial and even criminal agencies are examples of how new forms of registration reach the hands of private initiative or even individuals, with only one smartphone in their hands (Lupton, 2016, p. 114). Surveillance, as such, is not ontologically good or bad, it is the context and behavior that will characterize it in one way or another (Marx, 2015, p. 734), and the same can be said for the concept of privacy.

The context refers to the type of institutions and organizations and their objectives, rules, and expectations. Behavior refers to the type of behavior expected (either based on the law or less formal cultural expectations). Differences in surveillance contexts involving coercion (government), assistance (parents and children), contracts (work and consumption) and accessible and free personal data (personal and private in public) need to be considered, as surveillance is a generic process characteristic of living systems with information boundaries, and not something restricted to governments, espionage, or secrecy.

Surveillance and privacy are not opposite concepts, in fact the latter can be a means of ensuring the first, as well as access controls to information. Uncritical acceptance of algorithms can end autonomy, and the potential for free data collection and processing can greatly harm privacy. In this sense, it is noteworthy that algorithms are capable of exacerbating discriminatory actions against minorities and other social groups (although it may not be the programmer's intention).

The challenge of designing algorithms that maximize human flourishing in the context of justice and security without causing harm should not be taken lightly, but the rewards are potentially great. Lives and properties can be protected if the design, implementation, and deployment of algorithms can be executed effectively and ethically. These challenges will not always be possible to be solved with mathematical solutions, as some problems require philosophical deliberation.

Digital networks and the paradigmatic change brought about by so-called ICT's have placed for movements, groups, collectives, and social agents a new territory for alternative radical media action (Downing, 2002). However, the internet, far from neutral, becomes a platform configured by the socio-metabolic reproduction system of capital. It centrifuges the denial and affirmation of the order, leading the economy of attention, to the information provided by internet users, monetized in the trade of Big **Data Capitalism,** (Fuchs; Chandler, 2019).

The activities developed on the Internet are the object of a mechanism of profitability of profitable corporations, which are extended according to the lifetime destined to them. To give you an idea, the five most valuable companies in the world are Apple, Amazon, Microsoft, Alphabet (Google conglomerate) and Facebook, all expressive and dominant players in the ICT's as an industry. The media concentration, which was already identified in broadcasting, is based on the digital environment of social networks, and limits any democratizing role that it could have (Martins, 2020).

Second, (Castells, 2007), there is a confusion about the architecture of networks, seen as neutral, as well as growing a naturalization, via common sense of the activists, the Internet, as free territory (givenness by the possibility of producing content without previous limits, easily identifiable). So, avoiding the notion of class struggle, has led the activism of many social movements to a small-scale posture of action, spurred by a rejection of the problem's stems from the contradiction of capital / labor. The problem lies in the fact that, while the movements surf them in the nets, an **increasingly powerful plutocratic class dominates the world without being challenged.** What is more, it relies on the "old" mechanisms of police power and the repressive state, which receives support from the main digital surveillance tools available.

In the field of politics, what we see is that communicative capitalism, instead of leading to a greater equitable distribution of wealth and influence, has allowed the emergence of a richer variety of ways of life and practices of freedom, leads most people of the world to give in to spectacle and political resignation (Dean, 2005). A utopian techno ideology is based on the illusion of a classless world by the digitization of life, something that seeks to hide the mining of waste, in the form of data that leverages the profitability of large Silicon Valley companies

"As long as the dominant cultural narrative considers technology as the weapon of the weak and the poor, and not as the weapon pointed at the weak and the poor, there is little hope that phenomena such as data extraction are actually taken into account" (Morozov, 2018, 173). The algorithms of social networks, for example, concentrate power in platforms, since they are private agents seeking profits from the commercialization of data and profiles, mapping behaviors, and scaling the model of citizen participation.

The exercise of power of these private organizations that regulate symbolic exchanges and express the models of conduct takes place in the control of information traffic and, under a false appearance of participatory egalitarianism. Generates profitability over free time. These institutions also have as characteristic the execution of interconnected activities of work exploitation, in a complex cooperation format. Platforms set out the rules that determine who can participate and what conditions; decide what types of communication are allowed and which are not [...]" (Thompsom, 2018, p. 37).

Digital platforms act with high selection power, which does not transpose by their sophisticated camouflage, since they do not directly operate communicative content, but allow a circulation of information configured by their economic interests. Whoever controls the algorithms controls the network. The automation of human behavior symbolizes the political technology of cementing strange preferences, of a public probed in their apparent preferences, which intensifies a network architecture facilitating reification devices. As a result of this action occurs the cementation of capitalist logics in the digital environment.

It was the Internet that created globalization and as such the formation of digital capitalism. The global village has never materialized, but we ended up in a feudal domain, clearly shared between technology companies and intelligence services (Morozov, 2018, p. 14-15). These digital fiefdoms create bubbles that crystallize and feed, in a strange way, versions of reality not necessarily sustained by a critical reading of social reality. The intentional fragmentation of networks has led to the intensification of a policy of affections that are easily eased in the social media environment.

The Dilemma of Social Networks

Is It Possible to Escape Them?

People are increasingly online, dependent on likes and ready to consume information, not validated. According to George RR Martin, social networks have terrible effects on our society... and in political discourse. The effects of social networking problems lower the human level, caused by the intensive use of social networks: addiction, deconcentrating, isolation, polarization, misinformation, etc.

The internet knows everything about people, but they have the false notion that the use of social networks is free, but someone is paying for them: advertisers. These are therefore the real customers of these companies. People think they are using a tool, but they are being sold. This is an old market maxim: If you are not paying for the product, it is because you're the product.

Computer scientists and multimedia artists are the creators of virtual reality: the product is the gradual change in human behavior and its perception of reality; what social networks want is to "change what people do, what they think, what they are", gradually and imperceptible. As? Through the algorithm.

To be sure that an ad is effective you have to be able to predict who needs the product that is being advertised, who is already interested in it, who may be interested, who is more likely to be influenced by the ad. For this forecast to be increasingly accurate, a lot of information is needed. The companies of the technologies have this information and so can sell accurately to advertisers. Social networks know everything network users do online. All. You know what people see, when they see it, where and for how long. You know when people see pictures of their ex-boyfriends, if they're looking for a boyfriend in a dating app, if they order food for one or six, if they prefer sushi or burgers, what time they go to work, what they do at night, if they have insomnia. They know all that and more. All this data is archived, crossed, and used to make increasingly, accurate predictions about their behaviors.

Digital has advantages, but it is devouring the human essence. The monsters of technology companies such as Google, Facebook, Instagram, YouTube, Twitter, and others are devouring the human essence since it is virtually impossible to escape social networks unless you have an iron will. In Silicon Valley designers, ages 20 to 35, located in California, have made, and made decisions that impact many billion people. The people behind the screen have a lot more power than people think.

The computer builds models that predict people's actions and begin to interfere with them. The algorithm knows what video can show them that will hold them for a little while longer. What emotions encourage them to continue online. The goal is not, as some optimists say, to give things that please them to make them happy. Yes, the algorithm gives them what they want, but their goal is to increase their use of networks and the interaction they establish to give them more advertising and ultimately make money - make a **lot** of money, it is no accident that technology companies are the most powerful and that their **leaders top the lists of millionaires.**

Using the Internet is not an addiction, but always being online, from morning to night. The business model of social networks is simple: keep people on screen. On social networks nothing happens by chance. The algorithm knows everything people look for on the internet and will therefore give them suggestions that meet their interests. Likes, tags, emojis, are ways to provoke interaction; the ellipsis that appears when someone is writing keeps people on hold (and connected). Everything is designed to keep people online if possible.

The "infinite scroll", for example, acts in people's minds creating a kind of addiction that prevents them from turning off, just as the player in a slot machine always thinks that in the next move will win, by scrolling, the fact that they do not know what to follow, creates suspense. The release of dopamine (also known as pleasure hormone) is common to both situations. People can spend 12, 16, sometimes even 24 hours in a row, without sleep, using a technology. These are obviously pathological cases, but what is observed is that consumption is widening among all people. As the phone is a minicomputer, which people use for everything, whether as an alarm clock, to talk to others or to see the news, what is happening is a normalization of its use. This trend was sharpened in the confinement period.

Children learn how to unlock parental control tools in... that people are online in the order of 70%, which is very worrying. Prevented from leaving home, people were online to work, to study, to shop, to socialize, to watch movies or to play. In late 2019, a study in the United States found that people were on average more than six hours a day online. This year, due to the pandemic, this average will surely have increased. Do you check the phone before you pee in the morning or while you pee in the morning? Because those are the only two hypotheses," asks one of the interviewees in the film.

The Digital " Suck" and the Dangers

The risks of this excessive consumption of internet and social networks are, first and foremost, mental. People who were born from 1996 are the first generation who grew up with internet and who got used to having "a digital suck " to solve all their problems. However, replacing face-to-face contacts with digital contacts will deepen loneliness, depression, and anxiety. The need to always have a reaction from the other, the pressure of the image, all this will generate mental problems, to which, in the case of young people and vulnerable people, can be joined the real dangers of safety. Besides, living on your phone, controlled by the algorithm, each person has their world, their reality. There is no contradiction. There is no way of knowing what is true and what's a lie. Utopia gives way to dystopia. This vulnerability has been exploited by political regimes and ideological campaigns.

There has always been marketing and advertising, but social networks allow you to spread manipulative narratives with incredible speed, on a global scale. Of course, with a little regulation, network managers will be able to control the proliferation of false information and rumors, but misinformation generates interest and interaction in users and makes a profit.

If nothing is done to stop fake news, the dangers are enormous for democracy, for the environment, for the economy and for all people. The only solution will be that everyone disconnects from social networks forever. But of course, that is not going to happen. It is impossible to put the oxygen us back in the bottle. That is the dilemma. How to take advantage of the good that technology gives people without being completely manipulated? First tip: turn off notifications. Second, never follow the recommendations. Always choose and control the use. Search for other sources of information. Confirm the information before sharing something. Stimulate critical sense. Have other sources of pleasure. Enjoy the wonders of the world without using a screen.

The Implications of Social Well-Being

Economic Models and Type of Goods

The goods of social networks are not destroyed in the act of consumption. The externality of demand characterizes the economy of networks. The usefulness of each user's information depends on the total number of users, (Katz; Shapiro, 1985; Herscovici, 2013).

The digital economy is the economy of demand, as opposed to the supply economy, and its dynamics is based on the number of network users. The concept of social utility is one of the key elements of the dynamics of these markets. The value of the exchange, or the market value, is determined from this social utility, that is, from the value of social use. This simply means that the valuation in the different intermarket (the market value) depends on the prior creation of a certain value of social use.

The value is produced socially, but part of this value will be redistributed by the networks, through the modalities of access to the stock of the stored data. On the other hand, it is an extension of the commercial logic for these new public spaces, to the extent that the stratagems of double sided markets consist of valuing, in the intermediate markets, the different components of this social utility.

The Social Welfare Function

What is the social impact linked to the development of the digital economy? Is it globally positive or negative? The Pareto criterion, used in neoclassical economics, is not satisfactory for the following reasons:

- Since it is an approach characterized by methodological individualism, it is impossible to consider utility as the product of inter-individual relationships.
- Analyses carried out on the Pareto criterion consider that the initial. distribution of revenues is determined exogenously.
- In this type of approach, the utility value is limited, since it is conceived from an ordinal design, which does not allow the aggregation of individual values.

Depending on the limitations, social well-being depends on the level of available stock of the information stored and the degree of democratic openness of the user community. From an approach linked to philosophy, the degree of democratic openness implies the recognition of the autonomy of the citizen (defined by the private sphere), of the public space, in the sense defined by Habermas, of the political and legal sphere.

All the limitations of the democratic space, the whole mechanism that threatens this autonomy will have to be interpreted as a negative externality. ***Fake news and*** the use of robots, hurt this autonomy, resemble rough forms of manipulation, and a decrease in the "quality" of information provided. These relationships indicate the negative or positive impact of each of these components about the level of stock available to the collective, or the degree of democratic openness.

Transaction costs represent, in their most general definition, the costs that companies have to bear in order to be able to operate in the market: costs related to the design, implementation and management of contracts (Williamson, 2002), as well as those linked to the implementation of an intellectual property system (Barzel, 1997). As the entire user community must bear these costs, they represent a decrease in well-being, i.e. a negative externality.

Interference is directly linked to the definition and limits of the disclosure of users' personal data by electronic platforms: how far does current legislation allow such data to be stored and disclosed by the companies that control these electronic networks, and what are the limits that these companies must respect? In this regard, in most cases, national laws are not respected, as the recent data disclosure scandals by some companies (e.g. Cambridge Analytica, Facebook, etc.) show.

Interference can go beyond further, from the development of sophisticated algorithms, and become a generalized and exhaustive control system; this control can be both external and linked to a self-censorship mechanism. Interference can also influence political choices, as was the case of the election of Trump in the United States or Bolsonaro in Brazil. In this case, this mechanism translates into a limitation of individual freedom, and constitutes a negative externality. Interference can be a particularly efficient system for Big Data, but it allows:

- Reach specific audiences.
- Know the trajectories of users in advance.
- Certain audiences are the target ***of fake news*** that seems plausible to them. Generally, this type of stratagems is used for political purposes.

With regard ***to fake news,*** we can talk about manipulation: it is not just about trying to impose a certain view of the world and reality from a rational argument, but of radically falsifying this reality, and of trying to impose this view as the only possible: the denialist theses defended by the neo-Nazi parties, which deny the existence of concentration camps, etc.

It is interesting to observe the way the public space has changed (Habermas, 1978). In the eighteenth century, the public space was a democratic space of discussion in which citizens had the same rights, regardless of their economic condition. Its function was to protect the citizen from the arbitrary power of the State. Today, the nature and function of the public space represented by social networks is transforming deeply. There is a loss of autonomy in relation to economic power, there is a strong interdependence between political and symbolic power, and economic power. Due to the very characteristics of the digital economy, symbolic power has become indispensable to ensure economic power, from the creation of social utility; but this symbolic and political power has become increasingly dependent on economic power. This movement translates a loss of autonomy of the public space, in its political and symbolic dimensions, in relation to economic power.

The information disclosed on social networks influences the political decisions of users, social networks are used to guide the vote. The autonomy of the new public space, in relation to the political one, is relative and partial. We must also recall the problems linked to tax evasion. Electronic platforms operate in the global market. The ploy is to use the agencies in tax havens and thus escape the national tax rules, benefiting from those in force in tax havens.

The political dimension is related to the concept of interference and has implications in terms of social well-being. Faced with the expansion of mercantilist logic, with the intensification of the different modalities of interference, the political sphere is progressively losing its autonomy in relation to the economic sphere; this underscores the fragility of democratic processes in today's capitalism, and its growing inability to maintain the conditions conducive to maintaining the democratic game. A restriction of democratic spaces must be regarded as a negative externality. These observations lead us to question the nature of the social bond built in the digital age: in addition to the fact that it presents itself as a social manifestation of individualism and subjectivity, in the context of an increase and decentralization of accessible information, it is the product of opacity that characterizes the whole system of intrinsically asymmetric and fully merchandized relationships.

The Right to Privacy

Privacy is the subjective feeling of human beings about their personal space that is dimensional – territorial, physical, mental or psychological and should be considered a mechanism developed, throughout life in the context of social interaction and coexistence with other human beings In this way, if we consider that all cultures have their particularities and differences, in particular, in the communication processes obtained by education and socialization, also privacy, the way it is understood by each person and collectively varies according to time and cultures.

In the individualistic view of the State, privacy is taken as a reserved area of the individual without any ethical or solidary requirement in its exercise, therefore a privacy with a selfish and antisocial accent; on the other hand, privacy in the European matrix occupies a high place in human rights, coexisting with several others of the same nature, such as, the rights to the inviolability of the domicile, the secrecy of correspondence, to the image, unfolding in various restrictions and prohibitions, being therefore a fundamental defensive right.

Privacy can be understood as the ability or ability that any human being has to manage his physical and mental space of well-being, in a balance between what he wants to expose of himself (his identity) and the invasion of what he does not want. The feeling of privacy is somehow linked to the feelings of comfort and trust, which you have in relation to others, and it is in these two measures that the management of the same is made, on a basis of choosing the permanence or absence of these same people, as Friedrich Nietzsche tells us: The solitude has nothing to do with the presence, or absence, of people. [...] In fact, I'm not going to I hate those who steal my loneliness, without in return offering me truly company." Yalom, (2015).

Certainly, privacy go hand in hand with values, such as, the reservation of the intimacy of private life, in any domain, be it the intimate and personal sphere (family, affective and sexual life, health status, religious and political beliefs). At present, the privacy of individuals/citizens and organizations as a consequence, given that they hold "private" information from these same citizens, is a very present concern of democratic states, particularly public authorities, to be able to manage this information, for specific purposes, namely for the construction of public policies, and at the same time to protect the protection of people's privacy.

Indeed, because in the last sixty years new mechanisms and communication and information technologies (ICT's) have been developed, in particular wireless technologies (computers, mobile phones) with internet access, new forms of interaction without constraints of space and time, various forms of exposure of individuals and information sharing, however, in view of this greater exposure has been provided to men, organizations and States, the territory of privacy has become more vulnerable.

In other words, this amplification of communication, exposed by the Internet promoted new forms of freedom, with emphasis on the freedom of expression of individuals, but likewise, has raised many risks in the exercise of the right to privacy, which in its traditional form is broad and vague, when it is addressed to ICT's and this territory that is nobody's (network), opens up a new range of questions about these two fundamental rights, namely what is privacy on the Internet? what is its nature and limits? How is privacy protected in this exhibition area, how to minimize the damage caused by new forms of crime *(cybercrime),* how to protect information? How is the right to privacy of citizens guaranteed by the full exercise of their freedom of expression? And how should users act in this digital world, in which their private sphere is more diverse?

The right to privacy can be divided into several subgroups, pursuant to Article 17 of the ICCPR, that is, the right to privacy, identity, integrity, intimacy, autonomy, communication, and sexuality.

- **Privacy** - The right to privacy, as defined in Article 12 of the UDHR, protects the field of individual existence with respect to the sphere of privacy of others. It can also be understood as the element that does not fall into any of the following categories.
- **Identity** - Identity includes personal 'characteristics', such as name, appearance, clothing, hair, gender, genetic code, as well as religious confession or belief of each.
- **Integrity** - Personal integrity is protected by Art. 17 of the ICCPR. It means that, for example, medical treatment without consent or even against the patient's will should be considered as an infringement of the right to privacy.
- **Intimacy** - Intimacy is first and foremost ensured by the protection of home and correspondence, as well as through data protection. A person is protected against the publication, without prior consent, of his/her personal data.

- **Autonomy** - Contemplates the area of personal achievement of human beings. It is the right to your own body that also gives you the right to act against your own body, including the right to commit suicide.
- **Communication** - Covers interaction with others and confers, in addition to the special protection of the family, a right to develop relationships with other people.
- **Sexuality** - Sexual autonomy is a special and particularly important part of the right to privacy. Any regulation of sexual behavior constitutes an interference with the right to privacy. Interference, if necessary, is only permitted to protect those affected (e.g. children). (Source: Manfred Nowak. 2005. CCPR Commentary, art. 17 CCPR.)
- **Especially Vulnerable Groups**
    - **People with disabilities – People with disabilities who need special care and help are often likely** to suffer interference with their rights to privacy, for example if they are in closed facilities.
    - **People affected by diseases and the** elderly – People affected by illnesses or the elderly living in hospitals, clinics or homes face a particular risk of affecting their right to privacy.
    - **Children** – About new media, children are likely to suffer violations of their privacy rights if they reveal personal information on social networks or on the internet.

Privacy in Digital Environments

In digital environments, private data is provided to a system that records and stores the data. The data provider will have little or no control over, how, and for how long, the recorded and stored data will be used, leading to the asymmetries of the information flows. In many cases, the data provider is obliged to agree to assign the data, otherwise it will not have access to the services offered. In this context, the violation of privacy derives, in most cases, from the asymmetric flow of information between the company that records and stores the data and the data provider, (Jiang; Hong, Hong, Landay, 2002).

This issue is compounded as there is increased data flows, system speed, and low data maintenance costs over time. Many companies design and employ their own regulatory policies with regard to the use and privacy of their users / customers data and make public those policies to detail how the data is recorded and stored and what their use will be before they are required by law.

However, data is often recorded and stored before users have access to privacy policies or have the means to follow up, if companies comply with what they promise in their control policies, data confidentiality. The dynamics of the Internet itself and the constant updates of computer programs expose the system to risks that compromise privacy (Pollach, 2007, p. 188).

The streams of data recorded and stored on the Internet brings many benefits to consumers and citizens, but also increases the risk of abuse through discrimination, manipulation and/or cybercrime. Digital privacy laws should provide users with control and co-ownership of their data, as well as facilitate their deletion when claimed. Although it has advanced in regulating menthe right to forget over digital networks, in practice, the lack of supervision allows companies to carryout manipulations, with the data of their users, which have not been previously agreed, such as, the sale to third parties.

CONCLUSION AND CLUES TO NEW INVESTIGATIONS

It can be concluded that the digital economy and the development of social networks produce mixed, some positive and some negative externalities. Positive externalities are related to the expansion of the modalities of access to information, with the social and cultural diversification of the audiences reached, the different components of the offer, and the decentralized production of information. In this sense, it is possible to assimilate the digital economy to a logic of social inclusion. Nevertheless, exclusion will take other forms: depending on the asymmetries of information that are inherent in the functioning of these markets, there is a partial exclusion of consumers/users.

From a perspective linked to Political Sociology, it is also possible to speak of exclusion in relation to the modalities of access and understanding of a particular social and political reality. Fake ***news represents*** a brutal distortion of reality, the imposition of a narrow, unique, and exclusive worldview: it is a means of guiding the political choices of users/citizens, regardless of any rationality. The dual character of the Digital Economy is emphasized, and the opacity inherent to its dynamics. This opacity is causally related to interference, in addition to the economic sphere, extends to private life, politics and legal structure.

It translates into lower efficiency and a higher cost of control systems. Common sense assimilates the strengthening of democracy to the expansion of access to information by members of the collective. The Digital Economy allows to refute, in part, this statement: the expansion of the modalities of access to information occurs in parallel with a "weakening" of democratic spaces. Moreover, it is necessary to question the pertinence, the "veracity", that is, the "quality" *of accessible information: fake news* and the use of robots constitute a form of manipulation, in the sense defined by Political Sociology, and directly threaten democratic processes. Does the Big Data **of** the Digital Economy represent a real, not virtual, real-life achievement of The Big **Brother** evoked by George Orwell?

The new digital platforms are new products of mediated routing and control instruments associated with the use of computers, being one of the uses the digital mediation of workplaces on the web. Radical social movements are trying to broaden the goal of their flags on the internet and social networks to advance the anti-capitalist flag. Network communications provide the tools that can be used in the fight for political change. Political change requires a break with the fantasies that bind us to communication capitalism, (Dean, 2005, p.71).

Capital is not built on the Internet, although it is used in the production and reproduction of a huge range of information-related businesses. The expansion of the accumulation of capital is achieved through neoliberal reforms supported by a postmodernist hegemony in culture, aesthetics, and behavioral practices. These two combines contradictorily in digital territory. The decommodification of the logic of the Internet requires the fenestration of alternatives, in favor of new forms of social relations with their own dynamics.

Second, Marx, those responsible for these transformations are the freely associated workers. The coordination of material and intellectual production by them is not only the desirable end of a movement directed to overcome the socio-metabolic system of capital, it becomes the mediation for new social relations, capable of operationalizing technology for emancipatory purposes, guided not by the expansion of capital, but by the development of human capacities.

The challenge will be to build another social and global digital project alternative to the capitalist system, as well as another way of using the digital network, appropriate to the new civilizational parameters collectively built, in addition to the paralyzing dynamics of digital social networks in capturing free time.

REFERENCES

Barney, J. B. (1986). Strategic Factor Markets: Expectations, Luck and Business Strategy. *Management Science, 32*(10), 1231–1241. doi:10.1287/mnsc.32.10.1231

Beraldo, D., & Milan, S. (2019). From data politics to the contentious politics of data. *Big Data & Society, 6*(2), 1–11. doi:10.1177/2053951719885967

Boyett, J.H., (2001). *Lo mejor de los gurús. Las ideas clave de Covey, Drucker, Bennis, Champy, Hammer, Kaplan, Mintzberg, Peters, Porter, Senge y los demás gurús del management*. Academic Press.

Brandt, C. (2019). I Heard You Paint Houses. The Irishman. In The Strategic Management of Intellectual Capital and Organizational Learning. Oxford University Press.

Cardoso, F. (2016). Citizens: the new urban leaders. *Smart Cities*.

Cardoso, L. (2007). *Requiem for the lone navigator*. Don Quixote.

Castells, M. (1996), The rise of the network society. Oxford: Blackwell.

Castells, M. (1999), The network society (2nd ed., vol. 1). São Paulo: Peace and Earth.

Castells, M. (2003). The Internet Galaxy: Reflections on the Internet, Business and Society. Rio de Janeiro: Jorge Zahar Ed.

Castells, M. (2007). *The network society*. Peace and Earth.

Castells, M. (2010). *Networking: the age of information, economy, society and culture*. Peace and Earth.

Castells, M. (2013). *Networks of indignation and hope: social movements in the internet age*. Zahar.

Castells, M. (2015). *The power of communication*. Peace and Earth.

Choo, C. W. (2002b). *Information Management for the Intelligent Organization: The Art of Scanning the Environment* (3rd ed.). Information Today, Inc.

Choo, C. W. (2008). *Social use of information in organizational groups, information management: Setting the scene* (A. Huizing & E. J. De Vries, Eds.). Elsevier.

Dahlberg, I. (1978). Theory of concept. Information Science, 7(2).

Dahlberg, I. (2006). Feature: Interview with Integrant Dahlberg, December 2007. *Knowledge Organization, 35*(2/3).

Davenport, T. H. (1998). Ecology of Information: why technology alone is not enough for success in the information age (6th ed.). São Paulo: Futura.

Davenport, T. H., & Prusak, L. (1998). *Business knowledge: how organizations manage their intellectual capital*. Campus.

De Mul, J. (2015). Database Identity: Personal and Cultural Identity in the age of Global Datafication. In *Crossroads in new media, identity, and law: the shape of diversity to come* (pp. 97–118). Palgrave Macmillan. doi:10.1057/9781137491268_6

Dean, J. (2005). Communicative Capitalism: Circulation and the foreclosure of politics. *Cultural Politics, 1*(1), 51–74. doi:10.2752/174321905778054845

Devlin, K. (1991). *Logic and Information*. Cambridge University Press.

Devlin, K. (1999). *Info Sense: turning information into knowledge*. W. H. Freeman and Company.

Downing, J. D. H. (2002). *Radical media: rebellion in communications and social movements*. Editora Senac.

Floridi, L. (2010). The philosophy of information: ten years later. *Metaphilosophy, 41*(3), 402-419.

Floridi. (2014a). *The fourth revolution: how the infosphere is reshaping human reality*. Oxford University Press.

Floridi. (2014b). *What is the philosophy of information*. Academic Press.

Fuchs, C. (2016). Towards a Marxist problem of internet studies. *Marxist Criticism*, (43), 67–93.

Fuchs, C., & Chandler, D. (2019). *Digital Objects. Digital Subjects. Interdisciplinary perspectives on capitalism, labour and politics in the age of Big Data*. University Westminster Press.

Gonçalves, N. C. (2015). *Strategic knowledge management: case study at the Federal Institute of Brasília. Course Completion Work (Graduation in Business Administration)*. IESB University Center.

Grant, R. (1991). The Resource-based Theory of Competitive Advantage: Implications for Strategy Formulation. *California Management Review, 33*(3), 114–135. doi:10.2307/41166664

Habermas, J. (1978). *Raison et legitimité: problèmes de légitimation dans le capitalisme avancé*. Payot.

Habermas, J. (1987). Technique and science as ideology (70th ed.). Academic Press.

Habermas. (2017). *The post-national constellation: political essays*. doi:10.5433/2178-8189.2017v21n3p323

Hayes, P., & Poel, V. D. (2020, September). Algorithms and values in justice and security. *AI & Society, 35*(3), 533–555. Advance online publication. doi:10.100700146-019-00932-9

Itami, H. (1987), Mobilizing Invisible Assets. Harvard University Press.

Jaeger, W. (1962). *Early Christianity and Greek Paideia. Cambridge (Mass.): Harvard University Press*. Oxford University Press.

Link, K. (2005). *Magic for Beginners*. Small Beer Press.

Lojkine, J. (2002). *The Informational Revolution*. Cortez.

Lupton, D. (2015). *Digital Sociology*. Routledge Taylor & Francis Group.

Lupton, D. (2015). *Digital Sociology*. Routledge Taylor & Francis Group.

Lupton, D. (2016). The Diverse Domains of Quantified Selves: Self-tracking Modes and Dataveillance. *Economy and Society, 45*(1), 101–122. doi:10.1080/03085147.2016.1143726

Lupton, D. (2017). Williamson, Ben., (2017b) The Datafile child: The dataveillance of children and implications for their rights. *New Media & Society, 19*(5), 780–794. doi:10.1177/1461444816686328

Lupton, D. (2019a). "It's made me a lot more aware": A new materialist analysis of self-tracking health. *Media International Australia, 171*(1), 1–14. doi:10.1177/1329878X19844042

Lupton, D. (2019b). Data mattering and self-tracking: What can personal date do? *Continuum (Perth)*. Advance online publication. doi:10.1080/10304312.2019.1691149

Lupton, D., & Michael, M. (2017a). 'Depends on Who's Got the Data': Public Understandings of Personal Digital Dataveillance. *Surveillance & Society, 15*(2), 254–268. doi:10.24908s.v15i2.6332

Madison, J., (2017). *Life Before the Presidency—Miller Center*. millercenter.org

Mahoney, J., & Pandian, J. R. (1992). The Resource-Based View Within The Conservation of Strategic Management. *Strategic Management Journal, 13*, 363–380. doi:10.1002mj.4250130505

Malone, T. W., & Laubacher, R. J. (1999). The Dawn of the E-Lance Economy. *Wirtschaftsinformatik Proceedings,* 2. https://aisel.aisnet.org/wi1999/2

Martins, H. (2020). *Communications in times of crisis*. Popular Expression, Rosa Luxembourg Foundation.

Marx, G. T. (2015). Surveillance Studies. In N. J. Smelser & P. B. Baltes (Eds.), *International Encyclopedia of the Social & Behavioral Sciences* (2nd ed., pp. 733–741). Elsevier. doi:10.1016/B978-0-08-097086-8.64025-4

Marx, G. T. (2016). *Windows into the Soul: Surveillance and Society in at Age of High Technology. Chicago, Chicago, Chicago.* The University of Chicago Press. doi:10.7208/chicago/9780226286075.001.0001

Marx, K. (1976). *Le Capital, Critique de l'économie politique*. Socialeditions. (Original work published 1875)

Marx, K. (2008), Contribution to the critique of political economy (2nd ed.). São Paulo: Popular Expression.

Marx, K. (2011). *Grundrisse*. Boitempo.

Marx, K. (2013). *The capital: critique of political economy. Book I.* Boitempo.

Nissenbaum, H. (2010). *Privacidad amenazada. Tecnología, política y la integridad de la vida social.* Ocean.

Penrose, E. (1959). *The Theory of the Growth of the Firm.* Basil Blackwell.

Rifkin, J. (2000). *The Age of Access*. Puntnam.

Sabaté, F. T. (1989). *Fundamentals of Economics de la Empresa* (2nd ed.). Librería Hispano Americana.

Santos, A. D. G. (2018). Interview given to Paulo Victor Melo. *Eptic: network of political economy of information, communication, and culture.* Available in: http://eptic.com.br/entrevista-com-anderson-santos-presidente-da-ulepicc-brasil/

Santos, A. D. G., & Mota, J. S. (2020). 10 years of ULEPICC-Br: Contributions to EPC from its events and its praxis. *EPTIC Magazine, 16*(1), 57–75. doi:10.18617/liinc.51222

Santos, E. A. (2013). Credit to death: The decomposition of capitalism and its criticisms, by Anselm Jappe. *Plural, 20*(2), 219–222. doi:10.11606/issn.2176-8099.pcso.2013.76370

Santos, F. R. L. (2017), Intellectual vices and social networks: does constant access to information make us intellectually vicious? Veritas, 62(3), 657-682.

Shapiro, C., & Varian, H. R. (1999). *Information Rules - a Strategic Guide to the Network Economy.* Harvard Business School Press.

Srnicek, N., & Sutter, F. L. (2016). Platform Capitalism. Polity Press.

Tapscott, D., & Tapscott, A. (2016). *Blockchain Revolution: How the chnology behind bitcoin is changing Money, business, and the world.* Penguin Random House LLC.

Tapscott. (2014). *The Digital Economy Anniversary Edition: Rethinking Promise and Peril in the Age of Networked Intelligence.* McGraw-Hill.

Teixeira, J. F. (1998). *Minds and machines: an introduction to cognitive science.* Medical Arts.

Teixeira, R. A., & Rotta, T. N. (2012). Valueless knowledge-commodities and financialization: Productive and financial dimensions of capital automatization. *The Review of Radical Political Economics, 44*(4), 448–467. doi:10.1177/0486613411434387

Turing, A. M. (1950). Computing machinery and intelligence. *Mind, 59*(236), 433–460. doi:10.1093/mind/LIX.236.433

Uber x Taxi. (2018). Understand the differences in costs and services between taxi and the app. *G1 News.* Available in: http://especiais.g1.globo.com/saopaulo/2015/uber-x-taxi/

Williams, R. (1979). *Marxism and Literature.* Zahar.

Williamson, O. E. (1975). *Markets and Hierarchies: Analysis and antitrust implications.* The Free Press.

Williamson, O. E. (1999). Strategy Research: Governance and Competence Perspectives. *Strategic Management Journal, 20*(12), 1087–1108. doi:10.1002/(SICI)1097-0266(199912)20:12<1087::AID-SMJ71>3.0.CO;2-Z

Williamson, O. E. (2002). The Theory of the firm as governance structure: from choice to contract. *Journal of Economic Prospective, 16*(3).

Williamson, B. (2017). The Datafile child: The dataveillance of children and implications for their rights. *New Media & Society, 19*(5), 780-794.

Yao, D. A. (1988). Beyond the Reach of the Invisible Hand: Impediments to Economic Activity, Market Failures and Profitability. *Strategic Management Journal, 9*, 59-70.

Zikmund, W. G. (2000). *Business. In Research Methods* (6th ed.). Dryden Press Harcourt College Publishers.

Chapter 6
Strategic Greening and Social Responsibility of Organizational Development

José G. Vargas-Hernández
https://orcid.org/0000-0003-0938-4197
University Center for Economic and Managerial Sciences, University of Guadalajara, Mexico

ABSTRACT

This chapter analyzes the characteristics of the strategic greening and social responsibility of organizational development. The main assumption of the analysis is based on the consideration that the strategic organizational development should take into consideration the greening of organizations and the corporate social responsibility. Using a holistic and humanistic approaches on individual and organizational development, the analysis focuses on individual freedom, lifetime education and training, consciousness on human values, and ethical concerns related to the implementation of the organizational greening and corporate social responsibility. Finally, it proposes a strategic organizational development model.

INTRODUCTION

In global competitive markets, many organizations undertake efforts to survive creating conditions in a destructive dynamic conditions and developing into an organizational unsustainable development. Organizational development change due to decisions that are made unstained, becomes unsustainable development change.

A holistic and humanistic approaches on organizational development is focused on individual development, individual freedom and lifetime education and training, more consciousness on human values about the worth of workers as an active partner in innovation and creativity and committed and collaborative participant to the organization and ethical concerns related to the employment relationship. Changes on organizational values and external variables transform the practices and activities leading to the emergence of organizational collaboration and new ideas not contradicting the organizational logic and setting to support the work processes.

DOI: 10.4018/978-1-7998-7452-2.ch006

Sustainable organizational development is becoming possible through consecutive and evolutionary periods of steady growth with different dominant management styles to solve the problems leading to the emergence of different organizational structure arrangements and forms. The green organizational management philosophy is one tendency becoming one of this dominant organizational management model linked to sustainable organizational development practices. This green organizational management model is within an interdisciplinary theoretical framework supporting a holistic sustainable organizational development integrating the corporate social responsibility with competitive advantage strategy.

The content of this study first analyzes the implications between organizational transformation, change and development to characterize them. After this characterization, the notion of greening organizations is considered to be transformed into one of the core competencies and become the competitive advantage of any organization. It continues to analyze the corporate social responsibility as a strategy to implement the sustainable organizational development. Finally, the study proposes a strategic organizational development framework before presenting the conclusions.

ORGANIZATIONAL TRANSFORMATION, CHANGE AND DEVELOPMENT

The concept of organizational development encompasses the overall organizational health which has effects on the motivation, communication organizational cohesion and organizational behavior of workforce and the structure. A heightened sense of motivation enables organizational development as adaptability. The sustainable organizational development and growth has effects on the overall organizational performance and growth.

Sustainable organizational development should be decided between the top management and the operational working areas, including the staffing personnel, to spot opportunities of individual and organizational growth and development. The top-down sustainable organizational development initiatives supported by bottom-up implementation process builds on current work experiences and the workers become more responsible and committed to carry on more actively on the activities and practices of the development projects and becoming (Argyris, 1998).

Organizational change and organizing is a central characteristic of the contemporary organizational context of a global economy (Ahrne and Brunsson, 2006). A sustainable organizational and individual development in the new economy most generate the changing capacity to adapt to an environment subject to the development elasticity. Management of sustainable organizational development in the context of the new economy and environment requires new organizational management principles and behaviors to develop organizational capacities and capabilities. Organizational development focus on managing flexible planned changes and an adaptive process approach due to the constant flow of information, changes and developments (Cummings & Worley, 2014).

Organizational change theory (Hatch 1997, 350) has dimensions of radical and incremental change based on their outcomes (Buhanist 2000). The organizational transformation and development processes based on the organizational structures development differ in relation to the specificities of the national economic system and the synergetic processes created between the sustainable organizational development and the level of innovation development. Organizational structure has a relevant role in organizational social and cognitive sustainable development (Ahadi, 2011). Individual and organizational approaches lead more meaningful, comprehensive and manageable work system supported by a post-bureaucratic organizational structure embedded in individual and organizational sustainable development.

Hiring and the constant development of individuals with the best job criteria and mindset moving in the same direction, enables the organizational development. Organizational practices based on a humanistic approach makes more emphasis on communication, commitment, collaboration, self-regulation and self-control. Organic and flexible organizational collaboration emerge accidentally not focusing on conflicting organizational philosophy, visions and physical setting or experiencing uncertainty on the goals and other issues.

An organizational innovative model is based on self- organizational management processes, scientific and technological non-linear developments are more efficient and make contributions into the economic system development and growth. An organizational model on actions and institutions (Barley and Tolbert 1997) and model of organizational learning (Crossan et al. 1999) analyze in contradiction each other the nature of work in organizational settings. Sustainable organizational development need to accomplish indicators related to efforts to measure costs, value of production, human development, customer, revenue, profits, competition, etc., aimed to achieve a market position and share.

The nature of organizational development and transformation depicts a problem maze across private, public and third sectors which can be studied from evolutionary, involutionary, revolutionary and holovolutionary transformations (Li, Lin, 2011). Sustainable change and development in organizations is a multidisciplinary approach in which any discipline perspective complements the others resulting in a more balanced and complete framework and models (Burnes 2014, p. xiv). A balanced organizational behavior and structure development increase the benefits of the organizational core competencies.

The action research approach is a practical problem-solving process has the possibility to create generative theories that enable organizations to question conservative beliefs of what is wrong and can be fixed towards transformational organizational change (Cooperrider & Srivastva, 1987). Organizations can self-transform and change themselves into some work systems to solve their problems and provide opportunities and possibilities for the workers and stakeholders to growth and prevent individual and organizational sustainable development.

Organizational harmony is concerned with a friendly and cooperative agreement in terms and conditions on working relationships between employers and employees at the work place for their mutual benefit (Ladan, 2012). Organizational harmony conceived as cordial relationships of trust and cooperation between employers and workers is a critical factor in the organization pursuit of performance.

Organizational cooperation through bilateral and multilateral networks for certification in all activities of sustainable development according to the different areas to meet the challenges of the new economy. Oneness of purpose and mutual trust between employers and workers in an organization allow to participate in planning and management, collective productivity agreements and may accept austerity measures for the overall benefit of all the stakeholders for the sustained organizational development and growth.

For maintaining good organizational relations between management and workers must prevail an organizational environment of mutual respect and trust, understanding and goodwill in such a way that the expectations of both are fulfilled for sustainable personal and organizational growth and development. The elasticity of development considers the environmental opportunities taken into action, thus, the higher the elasticity the better the opportunities.

Development of a sustainable height to get the desired rewards results from being part of a collective relationships. Sustainable personal or individual development is supported by the driving energy he is able to commit in the physical, psychological and emotional life with harmony and stability in the work. Sustainable organizational development may reduce the workload influenced by the new life styles and the quality of working life which also may be in conflict with improvements in the workplace but not in the work and for that, may be required other types of development initiatives.

Organizational steady growth and a comfortable and stable atmosphere with compatible goals among the different stakeholders, encourages personal development without conflicts of structural power and avoiding frustrations. Development of new projects with challenging methods, tasks and processes derives in motivation towards the organizational vision and purpose.

The planning and control model has a rationalistic assumption on a set of stages required to follow up for sustainable organizational change and development, free to issues of organizational power, politics and conflicts (March and Simon, 1958; Lindblom, 1959; March and Olsen, 1976). The rationalistic model is normative and has legitimacy in organizational change and development initiatives (Winter et al., 2006; Brulin and Svensson, 2012).

These two organizational change models have limitations as well as tensions between them. Planning and control models of organizational change underestimate the complexities, emergency, interactive nature and proactive and reactive modifications (Weick and Quinn, 1999). Vulnerability of organizations is in part due to its capacity to deal with crises. Process and learning organizational change models emphasize open and emergent organizational change.

Heterogenic organizational groups may lead to dysfunctional feelings related to their performance which may be managed by creating a more accepting organizational environment and climate through recruiting of diverse individuals, use of codes of conduct, integration strategies and policies, implementing practices of organizational development and transformation, etc. Sustainable organizational development can be initiated as the way to alleviate existent imbalances and dysfunctionalities when the work system is more rationalized with the organizational outcomes, the workload becomes extremely high and high stress levels appear persisting as organizational burnout (Maslach and Leiter 1997).

Dysfunctional behaviors emerge from the incompatibility between the individual and organizational interests. Sustainable organizational development is supported by a reciprocal ongoing commitment between the individuals and the organization. The development form is depending from the type of commitment scholastic, national, egocentric, group and organizational.

Organizational commitment is a personnel and managers' emotional bonds and duties with the organization (Hersi, Blanchard, 1988). Organizational commitment has a direct relationship with the job performance and organizational obedience behavior. The model of organizational commitment of Miyer and Allen includes the emotional commitment implying the emotional bond in the engagement of activities, the constant commitment on assuming value and share organizational life and the norm-based commitment (Al-Hosseini, 2002) including the need to stay with the organization (Moghimi, 1999).

Achieving goals through reinforcement of practices enable better relationships and a higher level of organizational performance (Mahal, 2009) leading to a more cohesive environment. Sustainable organizational performance is an approach to attain the best performance while taking care of the environment. Organizational performance meets the needs and wants of all the involved stakeholders that provide resources (Cummings & Worley, 2014).

The concepts of communication, commitment, structure, motivation and cohesion are tied together such as the coexistence of a cohesive team and communication, and motivation with commitment. The concepts of organizational behavior, motivation, communication, cohesion and organizational structure are factors linked to and organizational development framework, and thus, linked also to sustainable organizational growth which encompasses the concept of sustainability (Han et al. 2010 and Hill & Bowen 1997).

The internal determinants of sustainable organizational growth have an impact on the indicators of infrastructure sustainability which in turn influences sustainable organizational development also (Ugwu & Haupt 2007 and Pitt, Tucker, Riley & Longden 2009). Sustainable organizational growth provides stability between the position and the level of competition of the organization (Bianchi, 2012). However, there are some internalities derived from these organizational developments towards a less bureaucratic expression of collective action, but in contrast, at the cost of becoming more standardized and centralized in organizational operations.

Sustainable organizational development is leading towards supporting organizational changes through the application of experimental methods of standardization and managerial solutions with different implications of specific workplaces and conditions, such as organizational autonomy and leadership, flexible management practices, human resources training and development, etc. Resource based view argues that the most important organizational source of sustainable development is the human resources development.

The organizational development is tied to its human resources and talent development. Human resources management practices and policies shape the organizational structure of working conditions to deliver individual and team innovativeness in new procedures and high sustainable organizational development performance. The ability of organizations to exercise human resource development practices is a relevant factor for shaping the workplace, in such a way that workers utilize their capabilities to deliver innovative practices and processes aimed to achieve the organizational goals and to attain the sustainable organizational development performance. Leadership needs for a sustainable workplace to operationalize sustainable organizational practices aimed to improve competitiveness while receive the benefits of being committed to sustainability.

Sustainability as a process intends to reach long term organizational development effects consuming the same resources. Sustainable organizational growth requires a synergistic balance on resource provision and management capability to use and improve them without reducing availability (Bianchi, 2012). Digitalization has become significant in organizational development leading to top management to provide a continues actualization of the staff to attain common goals and organizational growth. Organizational digitalization supports development of the tools to enable information and communication technologies leading to top management not only for making decisions but to provide continuous actualization of management tools aimed to attain the organizational goals and growth.

The concept of sustainable development is not a synonym and does not encompass the concept of growth (Daly, 1996). Sustainable development is meeting present needs without compromising the ability of future generations to meet their own needs. A sustainable development from the content perspective balances results orientations and working conditions such as gender conditions, health, learning and development, etc. However, sustainable development may balance conflicting needs associated with a change process (Elg, Ellström, Klofsten and Tillmar, 2020)

Organizational sustainability is a framework that can be developed to be used for creating knowledge as a competitive strategy enabling organizations to continuously change and improve value creation through processes (Moore & Manring, 2009). Innovative organizational sustainability initiatives can be implemented on human capital development, organization effectiveness, culture change and corporate strategy (Savitz & Weber, 2006). Sustainable development in organizations need to be focusing on development initiatives and efforts within organizations and in the development process between networks and clusters of organizations.

The core of sustainability is an issue that needs organizational and cultural change (Hitchcock & Willard, 2006) interventions conducted by facilitation processes, management and cultural change, conflict management skills and other processes and system tools. Cultural diversity of workers in the work place is a goal that leads to sustainable organizational development and growth. At operational level, organizational development interventions focus more on improving the ability to solve procedural problems and issues (Cummings & Worley 2014). The ability to overcome difficulties in organizational changes occurring in the procedures and business models are more dependent on resources including human capital and core values (Moore & Manring, 2009).

Organizational change toward sustainable organizing development in the vision of a policy and broad societal interrelated content and process perspectives. Organizational structure has a significant impact on organizational sustainable development (Gumora and Arsenio, 2002) although Jahmurataj (2015) found the opposite. Traditional organizational arrangements have to change organizational structures and practices to organize, guide and control the post-bureaucratic regenerative work systems to enhance the positive effects of individual and organizational sustainable development.

The post-bureaucratic characteristics and elements of work systems may emerge in more traditional and mature organizations such as uncertainty, complexity fluidity, invisibility, etc., leading to a gradual organizational sustainable development. Moreover, the low organizational levels are the receivers of rather than the makers of the decisions on the development change.

A sustainable organizational development line should be set by top management after creating a dialogue and a collaboration process on visions and values with the operational levels to create goals, strategies and policies for the organizational change. Participation in organizational change of all the stakeholders aims to provide a transitional space to work through their organizational working relations concentrating more in the existing possibilities for organizational sustainable development rather than the existing problems (Ludema et al. 2001).

The origins of organizational development can be traced back to the early 19th century during the Industrial Revolution when industrial methods undergone changes (Toosi, 2002) in manufacturing production and organization processes of an industrial economic system. Organizational development deals with findings that emerged during and after the second world war (Majidi, 1998, Toosi, 2002) some of the practices are related to creating and developing mutual support and trust among members, enhancing motivation, communication and leadership, improving personal behaviors, attitudes, values, norms, skills, capabilities, etc., improving satisfaction and enthusiasm, group based making decisions, etc.

Organizational development as a constant change process aims to create greater organizational effectiveness confirming that the organization adapts well to changes. Sustainable organization development must be incorporated by the commitment of top management to fulfill changes in the whole organization aimed to improve the organizational structure and communication (Cummings & Worley, 2014). Any organizational development change intervention aims to design, formulate, modify, implement and evaluate strategies (Pettigrew et al., 2001) and to improve abilities at the top management level to solve structure and strategy problems (Cummings & Worley, 2014) and to improve effectiveness in interactions, motivation, communication, leadership within the group (Brown & Harvey, 2011).

Development initiatives contrasts with change at early organizational development and the rational planned development based on rationalistic assumptions and expecting desired effects. Organizational development is related to changes in the organizational structure, processes and strategy of the whole organizational system. Organizational change at the individual and organizational level is facilitated by cohesion of needs through organizational development (Denison & Spreitzer, 1991).

Organizational development is an intervention based on transfer of behavioral capabilities and competences aimed to change structure, organizational design, technological innovation, management consulting, leadership, group dynamics, (Cummings & Worley, 2014), personal and social traits (Pettigrew et al., 2001). Creativity and innovation provides development of talents and contributes to sustainable development (Rezaeian Fordoie, 2014). Organizational development helps to modify organizations for the better (Pettigrew et al., 2001). Organizational development has methodologies and practices that are different of organizational change (Brown & Harvey, 2011; Cummings & Worley, 2014).

Organizational sustainable change and development initiatives and projects being accepted, adopted and incorporated into procedures and standards, although varies in specific organizations with many scopes and setbacks. However, most of the initiatives and projects do not meet the expectations, are considered risky and abandoned the sustainable practices. Implementing organizational sustainable development plays a critical role in setting up sustainable practices to use and manage natural, human, technological and organizational resources as the drivers in developing sustainability. Resources and processes management is vital for the financial benefit and sustainable growth in any organization (Chinta & Kloppenborg, 2010).

Organizational development is a transfer of behavioral capabilities and competences aimed to promote change at top management level to solve problems of structure and strategy become more effective in interactions based on motivation, communication and leadership (Cummings & Worley, 2014; Brown & Harvey, 2011). Organizational development enables to reach the goals of high technological, financial and productivity outcomes, lower the costs and increase profits by implementing social and behavioral sciences (Cummings & Worley, 2014).

Technological advances enable to improve sustainable organizational development (Vanegas, DuBose & Pearce, 1996). The new development perspective is a total development beyond the economic development based on properties of material goods evolving through scientific and technological advances, but expanding the personal-internal dimensions of using, having and possessing to become more satisfied, healthier and happier.

The economy development and growth depends on the level of institutional quality, the organizational structure synergetic order leading to the economic system organizational development (Lisichkina and Goloktionova 2015). At the stage of implementing the organizational development intervention, creating, designing and supporting and constantly changing processes are required for a change program, which lead to long-term institutionalization of new procedures and activities. The level of development of organizations in any economic system is given by indexes such as the level of order depending on institutions controlling the economic system such as of laws, regulations and obedience of laws, the rule of law, law enforcement by government, the primacy of law (Novikova, 2013) control of corruption.

Sustainable organizational development contributes to plan and implement changes in niche strategies, regulations and increases in competition (Han, Kin, Jang & Choi, 2010). Models to manage and organize change programs in sustainable organizational development have been proposed under different approaches, among others the planning and control model and the process and learning model, making each one relevant contributions to development through the strategic design and implementation employing rational structured methods for overcoming inertia and promote change and development (Czarniawska and Sevón, 1996a, 1996b; Røvik, 2011).

Organizational development planning is related to changes on behaviors, attitudes and functions to modify practices, procedures, processes, etc. The evaluation of the organizational development intervention is related to the success achieved by the strategy of change, the resources involved, the focus and management of issues and the results assessed through audits, meetings, interviews, discussions, etc., on what has been changed and what needs to be done to enhance development and improve performance. Internal evaluation is an independent form of action research that supports change in organizational sustainable development (Sonnichsen 2000).

The rational evaluation of sustainable development projects requires structures that may hinder creativity and innovation for sustainable development changes (Eisenhardt and Bourgeois, 1988). Ongoing evaluations of sustainable organizational development projects have the potential for experimentation on sustainability with the expectations of the unanticipated, deviant and unexpected (Svensson and Brulin 2013).

GREENING THE ORGANIZATION

The green organizational management philosophy studies human behavior in environmental management and sustainable development (Jackson and Seo, 2010; O'Donohue and Torugsa, 2016). Mishra, (2017) explores green human resource management linked to sustainable organizational development practices in manufacturing organizations and proposes an interdisciplinary theoretical framework for a holistic sustainable organization by integrating green management and corporate social responsibility with competitive advantage strategy.

Green organization is an interdisciplinary theoretical framework used to develop human resource environmental-friendly behaviors, green competencies and attitudes, eco-friendly practices, policies, tools aligned with an environmental strategy crucial for pro-environmental performance (Subramanian et al., 2016). A green organization environmental sustainable behaviors require not only perceptions but investments for green initiatives and practices such as training, purchasing, etc., aimed to earn brand reputation and value, control the impacts on the environment, acquisition and motivation of talent (Dechant and Altman 1994, Hewitt and Associates 2010).

Organizational greening and environmental management requires the cooperation and participation of all the stakeholders although the management level involvement is crucial to exercise influence in organizational decision-making promote the environmental behaviors towards green organizations (Zibarras and Coan, 2015; Markey *et al*, 2016). The job description may include pro-environmental and green behaviors included in the duties aimed to promote organizational green and environmental initiatives as an important organizational greening goal.

Green stakeholders' empowerment motivates organizational citizenship behaviors to pursue green activities and enhance the greening of organization's outcomes (Tariq et al., 2016), which have an impact an environmental impact (Paillé et al., 2014). Sustainable organizational development is related to effectiveness of empowered workers making organizational decisions who feel more positive towards the management and use of their own capabilities.

Green organization policies, practices and systems can be represented as green human resource management designed to develop a workforce promoting green behavior in the organization for the benefit of natural environment, employees, individuals, business organizations and society at large (Opatha and Arulrajah 2014; Mathapati,2013). Development of strong ties between the organization and the society contributes to feel the sense of identity and purpose. The new development is conceptualized as the elasticity of development as the variation sensitiveness to the variation of an influence factor.

The development elasticity is dependent on an entrepreneurial behavior involving organizational and individual development factors.

Organizational greening initiatives for sustainable development should be cost-saving to attain a competitive advantage in specific areas such as product design, process and service innovation (Yarahmadi and Higgins, 2012) involving the participation of the stakeholders in flexible initiatives and innovation process of organizational greening. Greening organizational initiatives can be implemented through change principles and human resource practices at all the organizational levels.

Teamwork has the potential to promote sustainable organizational development in the new economy challenging the functional structures of the traditional bureaucratic organizations (Katzenbach & Smith, 1993).

Promoting environmental management and sustainable development is based on green performance management system (Gholami et al. 2016) aligned with green behaviors, attitudes and activities within the organization, attuning the individual with the organizational goals (Berrone and Gomez-Mejia,2009). The Global Reporting Initiative (GRI) on sustainable development are practices geared towards large organizations and business companies to report their sustainable performance and sustainable activities such as social justice, environmental degradation, etc.

The organizational pro-environmental vision and mission statements should emphasize the involvement and participation of top management (Ramus and Steger, 2000) and their integrated initiatives in organizational interrelations on green strategies and sustainable green growth practices (Mercer et al., 2017; Erhabor and Don, 2016; Stern et al., 2014). Formalization and documentation of green recruitment, education and training, appraisal and rewards practices of a green human resource system provided by organizations may aim to promote sustainable environmental behavior.

Green organizational practices accepted as innovative measures by management supporting the greening of the organization and involving green teams help to attain a desirable benefits and green outcomes. Organizational top-management involvement and support is crucial to motivate all the stakeholders involved in facilitating green environmental behaviors in the integration between green practices and activities in the greening of organizations (Robertson and Barling, 2013).

Green purchasing is another organizational green practice focusing on the suppliers (Lee, 2008) and green supply-chain. A green organization collaborates with its suppliers inculcating green initiatives and practices and in terms of environmental funding for joint research and development, learning and training, etc.

Organizational green practices and initiatives in environmental behavior need to be evaluated in terms of the environmental impact (Ones and Dilchert, 2012).

Green organizations are social and environmentally responsible organizations that value environment-friendly strategies, have the reputation of being green employers and attracting responsible environment-friendly talent (Phillips, 2007; Stringer, 2009; Guerci et al., 2016; Brekke and Nyborg 2008, Grolleauetal., 2012). Organizational reputation can be the result of a good organizational motivation and communication systems leading to enable the development of organizational identity (Balmer & Gray, 1999). Developing a sense of individual knowledge, motivation, reputation, communication, education and teamwork aligned with the organizational reputation is key to enable organizational development.

CORE COMPETENCIES AND COMPETITIVE ADVANTAGE

Sustainable organizational development and growth can be enabled through different factors of strategies, capabilities, resources and maturity leading to diverse sustainable core competencies that impact the abilities. Promotion of leadership and team development as a strategy to manage the organizational intrinsic core competencies requires that the organizational intrinsic motivation is tied to productivity levels (Mahal, 2009). Sustainability is an opportunity to implement operational competencies and strategic leadership (Losey, Meisinger & Ulrich, 2005).

Management of organizational capabilities and core competencies such as behavior, motivation, communication, structure and others have an impact on organizational growth and enables sustainable organizational development. The management of sustainable core competencies focusing on the needs and development of the workforce lead to obtain longevity and sustainable organizational development and growth.

Organizational core competencies are intrinsic and inherently embedded with the abilities and functions of regional industries to achieve long term sustainable organizational development and growth. Alaqra and Leveau (2018) reported the impact of the organizational communication, structure and behavior, and motivation and cohesion considered as organizational intrinsic competencies in the internal development leading to sustainable organizational growth. Organizational communication is an emerging theoretical framework within organizations of some industrial sectors that have not been empirically explored and analyzed the benefits. The usage of communication tools develops behavioral ties and enables the organization to structure individual behaviors.

The organizational core competencies allow organizational development enabling organizations to adapt, maintain, manage or lead the organizational sustainability changes to the environment, vital to improve the value creation for sustainable organizational growth and development (Pettigrew, Woodman & Cameron, 2001).

Organizational tangible assets and funding require competencies, high level of cohesion and motivation of individuals at the workforce to develop and create a career. The organization emphasis on the social purpose encompasses the involved individuals with a sense of pride to be part of the organization working to achieve goals that also improves the society as a whole.

Developing and enhancing cohesive and motivated teams with efficient communication patterns based on individuals and organizational needs by creating and improving sustainable organizational core competencies, leads to higher level of productivity and improved sustainable organizational development (Denison & Spreitzer, 1991). The sustainable organizational development and growth framework encompasses the concepts of motivation, communication, organizational behavior, structure, strategy, leading to the development of core competences and sustainable organizational growth.

Organizational development is an application resulted de several behavioral and procedural interventions to transfer capabilities and competences to strengthening organizational structures, process, strategies and to encourage organizational effectiveness (Cummings & Worley, 2014).

Organizational sustainable value creation is attained by the capability to create and maintain the knowledge regarding its competencies on processes (Chinta & Kloppenborg, 2010). Organizational motivation, communication, structure and strategy provide the continuous value creation within an organization (Chinta & Kloppenborg, 2010). The competencies of motivation and cohesion, organizational communication and organizational structure and behavior and strategies which encompasses the organizational core competencies are elements of sustainable organizational development and growth.

Motivation of all the stakeholders and a cohesive environment in the organization enable sustainable organizational development and growth while improving the levels of adaptability and productivity and shifting from environmental to internal sustainability based on core competencies. Organizational core competencies development needs the development of its organizational workforce though organizational structure, motivation, communication, team cohesiveness, and others (Michellon & Zollo, 2000; Osterloh & Frey, 2000).

Compensation methods to motivate employees need to be implemented by organizational management besides other practices to encourage competencies to improve performance and sustainable organizational outcomes. The organizational management must instill the values to develop the sense of community development through a cohesive organizational climate. Organizational climate enables the practices to achieve goals (James et al., 2008) and coincide with behavior affecting motivation (Mahal, 2009).

Resources allocation by the top management of the organization is critical to attain stability in the position and competition towards the development of sustainable core competencies. Allocation of human resources is done in function of competencies, motivation and passion of individual candidates to assess the eagerness to work in specific projects and willingness to continue education regarding technical, culture and diverse nature issues. Sustainable organizational development and growth considers the combination of organizational tangible and intangibles resources contributes to value creation through the development of organizational capabilities and competencies, which is leading to the development of the internal output and processes (Schmiedinger, Valentin & Stephan, 2005).

The organizational capabilities and competencies management system have an impact on sustainable organizational development and growth. The organization should know the individual needs and competencies of all the workforce involved to maintain a high level of motivation and continues to the individual growth consistent with the organizational development. Projects such as sustainable product process and competence development although difficult to implement to meet the goals may result in long term benefits (Brulin and Svensson, 2012).

A theoretical framework of reference that may be used for the development of sustainable competitive advantages though the management of core competencies realized by the organization itself (Barney, 1991). A multi-dimensional approach to organizational Sustainable Development (SD) combined with some initiatives and procedures is an integrated strategy designed to address long-term global challenges and achieve a sustainable competitive advantage (Baumgartner and Korhonen, 2010; Clulow, et al., 2003).

Creation and sustainability of competitive advantage for sustainable organizational development in specific environments need knowledge learning and development for design and implementation of strategies and policies. The organizational resources and capabilities which are inimitable, non-substitutable, rare and valuable are also sources to create competitive advantages and organizational sustainable development. The customer's needs lead to service concepts in organizational opportunities, to design and implement a business model and create competitive advantage to be entirely implemented for sustainable organizational development.

Sustainable organizational development performance is the capacity to create value and achieve sustainable competitive advantages (Wigginsand Ruefli 2002). A sustainable organizational competitive advantage pools together the energies of workers to achieve goals and objectives of a sustainable organizational development. The developed organizational climate is a motivating tool to create organizational commitment as one of the best precursors to the sustainable organizational core competencies and encompassing other events to enhance performance (Patterson et al, 2005).

CORPORATE SOCIAL RESPONSIBILITY

The organization of the work system is changing drastically and rapidly to meet the sustainable organizational development process more in accordance to the organizational vision and values developed by the top management and the stakeholders involved. Any contradiction in vision and values may lead into conflicts if they are not allowed to be expressed at the organizational level and the involved do not take responsibility in their work and their workplace.

Greening of the of the organization though initiatives such as green corporate social responsibility, green competitive advantage, product development and packaging, etc. creates common wealth through synergies leading to sustainable development and growth. Green corporate social responsibility in association with human resource management are responsible for promoting organizational green activities and behaviors in production and to curtail environmental deterioration with a direct impact on preservation and development of the environment.

The organizational development capacity has the ability to offer sustainable and social responsibility within a specific context. Organizational competency development can embed social sustainability as a strategy of corporate social responsibility (Redington 2005).

Some organizations are committed to attain more common value besides their goal of profit –making though voluntary activities of corporate social responsibility (Lieberwitz 2005). Many organizations are more focused on profit-making although they are using green corporate social responsibility initiatives only in the external area of the organization (Mintzberg et al. 2002) and outside the organizational boundary at the level of customer and client pressures, government regulations, etc. These green corporate social responsibility initiatives are very difficult to assess the real impact of a green organization.

In order to make a shift from unsustainable organization to more sustainable one by supporting sustainable organizational development requires to identify the challenges that a specific organization faces regarding sustainable practices and corporate social responsibility by designing and implementing strategies and policies to transform the organization and achieve sustainable results. A top-down sustainable organizational development initiative may be implemented by supporting a bottom-up process to place the responsibility of the initiative on the operational workers that consume more of the natural resources and energy, although they need the guidance so that they do not lose the perspective.

The organizations have the responsibility to avoid over exploitation of natural resources causing environmental deterioration by planning sustainable development, environmental improvement and benefiting from environmental management interventions (Khanna and Anton, 2002; Christmann, 2000; Shrivastava,1995) and integrating economic, social and environmental agendas (Elkington, 2006).

Management and personnel are committed responsible to improvements in organizational development, adopting a visionary planning, acquiring reputation, attracting support, supporting personnel honesty and loyalty, sharing and shoulder responsibilities, augment organizational responsibilities in fulfilling the organizational commitments. Sustainable organizational planning requires acquiring information about trends and tendencies of markets, customers, competitors, etc.

Ownership arrangements have effects on sustainable organizational development initiatives. Active ownership is a mechanism that gives relevance to the owner´s role in financing the sustainable development initiatives although it may be insufficient (Van de Ven et al., 2000; Svensson and Brulin, 2013) and the project leader may perform better as an agent. The agent role is more dependent but risky, which can be corrected by the owner´s active responsibility for the sustainable development of the project.

Sustainable organizations design and implement strategies for sustainable organizational employer branding, strategic management and corporate social responsibility for sustainable development.

STRATEGIC ORGANIZATIONAL DEVELOPMENT

An organizational development aims to design and implement strategy towards improvement of the whole organization (Pettigrew et al., 2001). Organizational sustainable development designs and implement strategies to meet the goals of the organization and its stakeholders while protecting, sustaining and enhancing the bio socio ecological systems and natural resources that the next generations will need in the future. Organizational development is a process of work and environmental evaluation of an organization to enable rebuilding their structures, processes and strategies to achieve organizational competitiveness (Cummings & Worley, 2014).

Organizational change is a developmentative process (Seppänen-Järvelä 1999), that requires a strategy leading to the organizational strategic management. The nature of the organizational strategic management can be designed and implemented following the process consultation (Schein, 1999) and the interaction-oriented proposed in the development model (Murto 1991; 2001). Sustainable organizational human resources development practices have an influence on organizational strategic management (Barney 1991). Some non-governmental organizations, society, stakeholders' groups, investors, regulators, law makers, customers, etc., are driving the need for sustainable organizational and environmental practices.

Organizational change and development is a foundation strategy upon which other strategies are designed and implemented. The organizational sustainable development intervention has to reinforce strategic change thinking in the nature of the administrative and top-management. Some of the principles supporting the perspective of a sustainable organizational development are the implementation of the best strategies, capacities development and personal efficiency.

Resource management includes personal and organizational development management to be implemented through strategies aimed to optimize established the management system of systematically structured, documented and communicated organizational processes. Organizational motivation and cohesion is related to the managerial strategies based on the structure and communication and designed to have an impact on the sustainable organizational core competencies and to achieve sustainable organizational development and growth.

Developing workers to enhance their skills centered on the core of sustainable organizational systems and processes, provides opportunities to unlimited growth and development and secure the achievement of strategic objectives and results through the appropriate governance mechanisms. The results of the educational system governance include the organizational relationships and the cultural instruction that embraces the flow of education (Morrar, 2015). Personal grow must be aligned with the organizational grow to deliver results.

Organizational sustainable development strategies must integrate continuous evaluation during the whole change process. The internal evaluation of an organization must take into account for any management development intervention, the nature of the organizational change, the data quality on human resources, operations, organizational culture and the strategies and tools for enhancing the organizational sustainable development.

The corporate restructuring and technological development challenge the organizational sustainable development which require the design and implementation of strategies to use innovative resources and capabilities to deal with uncertain, complex and turbulent environment (Weldy and Gilles, 2010; *Weldy, 2009*; Kriegesmann et al., 2005; Pfeffer, 1994).

Organizational strategy impacts organizational sustainable development (Gino and Staats, 2015). Organizational sustainable strategy considered as the use of resources, methods and techniques to attain internal and external environmental goals of the organization, plays a vital role on organizational sustainable development (Hotho et al., 2015). The development of the organization is subject to synergic and entropic effects and depending of other conditions such as the external environment. The organizational entropy is created by the operating forces of order and disorder creating destructive tensions and disorganizations and interacting simultaneously in organizations.

According to Vansina (1998) an organizational sustainable strategy allows a transitional space for employees and for management to design, initiate and give support to the whole organizational structures, rules and processes and to involve all the stakeholders.

Organizational development focuses to support top-management to improve the ability to unravel the problems in structure and strategy, the effectiveness in communication interaction, and problem-solving procedures within the groups (Brown & Harvey, 2011; Cummings & Worley, 2014).Raising the organizational capacity for more sustainable organizational development is a task of top management implementing a holistic strategic change though process consultation with the support of external consultants, hired or funded by local government (Schein, 1999). Organizational consultancy has designed new insights and approaches that are practices aimed to implement strategies aimed to use the valuable resources to contribute to the sustainable organizational development.

Top management must have objectives aligned with all the organizational workers and motivated for all involved to develop cohesion through organizational ties, as a managerial strategy to develop sustainable organizational development and growth.

One of this approaches is the total quality management aimed to enhance operations of firms to enable organizations to become excellence. Production and logistics organizational strategies such as green and sustainable supply-chain oriented provides creates a competitive advantage leading to long-term to profitability.

Organizational social responsibility is being implemented as strategy to develop long-term vision, mission and purpose to the organization in the society, which in turn leads to provide a sense of motivation enhancing the level of identity and cohesion to the teams. Organizational communication contributes to form a collective identity among all the involved individuals facilitating a more cohesive team (Postmes, 2003) which needs to be managed and invested to attain the benefits (Balmer & Gray, 1999). Organizational teams have to develop a coinciding identity through strong communication that enable to motivate and develop a higher sense of commitment among talented people (Postmes 2003; Balmer & Gray, 1999).

These strategies have an impact and affect all the long- term organizational practices and processes, the stakeholder-employer-employee relationships considered as corporate partners (Kryger Aggerholm, Esmann Andersen, and Thomsen, 2011).

A sustainable organizational development planning has to be founded in a sustainable strategy, practices, processes and procedures centered on changing and improving behaviors, attitudes and performance of individuals and groups (Mir-fakhrae, 2000).

CONCLUSION

Organizations require innovative, flexible and adaptive management development to identify the different options for implementing decisions in actions to meet the global new economic challenges.

Transformation of workplaces to become more sustainable organizations requires commitment to develop organizational competencies and capabilities supported for collaborative strategies. Individual and organizational growth and development of resources is supported in the creation of collaborative and regenerative work practices depending of specific internal and external factors as the condition for sustainable individual and organizational development. These collaborative and regenerative work practices lead to create better individual working life quality and organizational competitiveness.

To improve the sustainable organizational development, it is necessary to take into account the priorities, needs and understandings existing in a complex system to create and develop a well-functioning shared management and organizational structure. Organizational settings may mismatch work activities leading organizational negative consequences, and therefore is necessary to reconsider the work realities and the new collaborative dialogue approaches to diagnose and redesign structures, practices, processes, etc., at all levels on organizational priorities and goals.

A holistic and humanistic approaches are viable framework of reference to propose a strategic organizational development based on the green organizational management philosophy and the studies of human behavior in human resource management linked to environmental management and sustainable organizational development practices by integrating green management and corporate social responsibility with competitive advantage strategy.

REFERENCES

Ahadi, S. (2011). Relationship between empowerment and organizational learning among academics in Malaysian research universities. *Journal of Business and Management*, *22*(2), 226–241.

Ahrne, G., & Brunsson, N. (2006). Organizing the world. In M.L. Djelic & K. Sahlin-Andersson (Eds.), Transnational Governance: Institutional Dynamics of Regulation. Cambridge, UK: Cambridge University Press.

Al-Hosseini, H. (2002). *Organizational Development*. Bahariye Press.

Alaqra, F., & Leveau, P. (2018). *Management of intrinsic competencies for sustainable organizational growth The study of the Swedish construction industry* (Master's thesis). 15 HE Business Administration Master Programme in Business Administration (MBA).

Argyris, C. (1998). Organizational behavior: Production of knowledge for action in the world of practice. In J. McKelvey & M. Neufeld (Eds.), *Industrial relations at the dawn of the new millennium* (pp. 54–61). New York State School of Industrial and Labor Relations.

Balmer, J. M., & Gray, E. R. (1999). Corporate identity and corporate communications: Creating a competitive advantage. *Corporate Communications*, *4*(4), 171–177.

Barley, S. R., & Tolbert, P. S. (1997). *Institutionalization and structuration: Studying the links between action and institution.* Retrieved from Cornell University, ILR School site: http://digitalcommons.ilr.cornell.edu/articles/130/

Barney, J. (1991). Firm resources and sustained competitive advantage. *Journal of Management, 17*(1), 99–120.

Baumgartner, R.J., & Korhonen, J. (2010). *Strategic thinking for sustainable development.* Academic Press.

Berrone, P., & Gomez-Mejia, L.R. (2009). Environmental performance and executive compensation: an integrated agency-institutional perspective. *Academy of Management Journal, 52*(1), 103-126.

Bianchi, C. (2012). Enhancing performance management and sustainable organizational growth through system-dynamics modelling. In *Systemic management for intelligent organizations* (pp. 143–161). Springer Berlin Heidelberg.

Bianchi, C. (2016). Fostering Sustainable Organizational Development Through Dynamic Performance Management. In *Dynamic Performance Management. System Dynamics for Performance Management* (Vol. 1). Springer.

Brekke, K. A., & Nyborg, K. (2008). Attracting responsible employees: Green production as labor market screening. *Resource and Energy Economics, 30*(4), 509–526.

Brown, D. R., & Harvey, D. F. (2011). *An experiential approach to organization development.* Academic Press.

Brulin, G., & Svensson, L. (2012). *Managing Sustainable Development Programmes: A Learning Approach to Change.* Gower Publishing.

Buhanist, P. (2000). *Organisational Change, Development Efforts and Action Research. HUT Industrial Management and Work and Organizational Psychology. Report 12.* Helsinki University of Technology.

Burnes, B. (2014). *Managing Change* (6th ed.). Harlow, UK: Pearson Education.

Chinta, R., & Kloppenborg, T. J. (2010). Projects and processes for sustainable organizational growth. *S.A.M. Advanced Management Journal, 75*(2), 22.

Christmann, P. (2000). Effects of "bestpractices" of environmental management on cost advantage: The role of complementary assets. *Academy of Management Journal, 43*(4), 663–680.

Cooperrider, D., & Srivastva, S. (1987). Appreciative inquiry in organizational life. In R. Woodman & W. Pasmore (Eds.), Research in organizational change and development (Vol. 1, pp. 129–169). Academic Press.

Crossan, M. M., & Berdrow, I. (2011). Organizational learning and strategic renewal. *Strategic Management Journal, 24*(11), 1087–1105.

Cummings, T. G., & Worley, C. G. (2014). *Organization development and change.* Cengage Learning.

Czarniawska, B., & Sevón, G. (Eds.). (1996). *Translating Organizational Change.* New York, NY: Walter de Gruyter.

Czarniawska, B., & Sevón, G. (1996a). Introduction. In B. Czarniawska & G. Sevón (Eds.), *Translating (organizational change)* (pp. 1–12). DeGruyter.

Czarniawska, B., & Sevón, G. (1996b). *Translating Organizational Change*. De Gruyter.

Daly, H. E. (1996). 14 sustainable growth: an impossibility theorem. *Valuing the earth: Economics, ecology, ethics*, 267.

Dechant, K. and Altman, B. (1994). Environmental leadership: from compliance to competitive advantage. *The Academy of Management Executive*, *8*(3), 7-20.

Denison, D. R., & Spreitzer, G. M. (1991). Organizational culture and organizational development: A competing values approach. *Research in Organizational Change and Development*, *5*(1), 1–21.

Eisenhardt, K. M., & Bourgeois, L. J. (1988). Politics of strategic decision making in high- velocity environments: Toward a midrange theory. *Academy of Management Journal*.

Elg, M., Ellström, P., Klofsten, M., & Tillmar, M. (2020). *Sustainable development in organizations*. Downloaded from Elgar Online.

Elkington, J. (2006). Governance for sustainability, Corporate Governance. *International Review (Steubenville, Ohio)*, *14*(6), 522–529.

Erhabor, N. I., & Don, J. U. (2016). Impact of Environmental Education On the Knowledge and Attitude of Students Towards the Environment. *International Journal of Environmental and Science Education*, *11*(12), 5367–5375.

Gholami, H., Rezaei, G., Saman, M. Z. M., Sharif, S., & Zakuan, N. (2016). State-of-the-art green HRM system: Sustainability in the sports center in Malaysia using a multi-methods approach and opportunitiesforfutureresearch. *Journal of Cleaner Production*, *124*, 142–163. www.sciencedirect.com/science/journal/09596526/124?sdc=1

Gino, F., & Staats, B. (2015). Why organizations don't learn. *Harvard Business Review*, *11*(November). https://hbr.org/2015/11/why-organizations-dont-learn

Guerci, M., & Carollo, L. (2016). A paradox view on green human resource management: Insights from the Italian context. *International Journal of Human Resource Management*, *27*(2), 212–238.

Gumora, G., & Arsenio, W. F. (2002). Emotionality, emotion regulation, and schoolperformance in middle school children. *Journal of School Psychology*, *395*, 413.

Han, S. H., Kim, D. Y., Jang, H. S., & Choi, S. (2010). Strategies for contractors to sustain growth in the global construction market. *Habitat International*, *34*(1), 1–10.

Hatch, M., Ji, B., & Shu, O. (1997, September). Do Standing, Lifting, Climbing, or Long Hours of Work during Pregnancy Have an Effecton Fetal Growth? *Epidemiology (Cambridge, Mass.)*, *8*(5), 530–536.

Hersi, P. & Blanchard, K. (1988). *Management of Organizational Behavior – Utilizing Human Resources* (5th ed.). Prentice-Hall Inc.

Hewitt., & Associates. (2010). Hewitt and Associates establishes strong relationship between employee engagement and CSR. Academic Press.

Hill, R. C., & Bowen, P. A. (1997). Sustainable construction: Principles and a framework for attainment. *Construction Management and Economics*, *15*(3), 223–239.

Hitchcock, D., & Willard, M. (2006). *The Business Guide to Sustainability: Practical Strategies and Tools for Organizations*. Earthscan.

Holbrook, M.B. & Hirschman, E.C. (1982). *The experiential aspects of consumption*. Academic Press.

Hotho, J.J., Lyles, M.A., & Easterby-Smith, M. (2015). The mutual impact of global strategyand organizational learning: current themes and future directions. *Glob. Strat. J.,* 85–112.

Jackson, S.E. & Seo, J. (2010), The greening of strategic HRM scholarship. *Organization Management Journal*, *7*(4), 278-290.

Jahmurataj, V. (2015). Impact of culture on organizational development: Case study Kosovo. *Acad. J. Interdis. Stud*, *4*, 206–210.

James, L. R., Choi, C. C., Ko, C. H. E., McNeil, P. K., Minton, M. K., Wright, M. A., & Kim, K. I. (2008). Organizational and psychological climate: A review of theory and research. *European Journal of Work and Organizational Psychology*, *17*(1), 5–32.

Katzenbach, J. R., & Smith, D. K. (1993). The Discipline of Teams. *Harvard Business Review, 71*(2), 111-20.

Khanna, M., & Anton, W.R.Q. (2002). Corporate environmental management: regulatory and market base dincentives. *Land Economics*, *78*(4), 539-558.

Kriegesmann, B., Kley, T., & Schwering, M. G. (2005). Creative errors and heroic failures: capturing their innovative potential. *Journal of Business Strategy, 26*(3), 57-64. doi:10.1108/02756660510597119

Kryger Aggerholm, H., Esmann Andersen, S., & Thomsen, C. (2011). Conceptualising employer branding in sustainable organisations. *Corporate Communications*, *16*(2), 105–123. https://doi.org/10.1108/13563281111141642

Ladan, M. T. (2012). The imperatives of industrial harmony and academic excellence in a productive educational system. The National Orientation Agency, University of Calabar.

Lee, S. Y. (2008). Drivers for the participation of small and medium-sized suppliers in green supply chain initiatives. *Supply Chain Management*, *13*(3), 185–198.

Li, M., & Lin, K. A. (2011). New Paradigm of Organizational Transformation: Enacting Wholeness Praxis in the Oneness of Problem and Possibility. *Systemic Practice and Action Research*, *24*, 107–132. https://doi.org/10.1007/s11213-010-9179-z

Lieberwitz, R. L. (2005). What social responsibility for the corporation? A report on the united states. *Managerial Law*, *47*(5), 4–19.

Lindblom, C. E. (1959). The science of 'muddling through'. *Public Administration Review*, *19*(2), 79–88.

Lisichkina, N.V., & Goloktionova, Y. G. (2015). Synergetics as a way to solve forecast problems of complex social-economic systems. *Fundamental Research, 7*(2), 413 – 417.

Losey, M., Meisinger, S., & Ulrich, D. (2005). *The Future of Human Resource Management, Hoboken*. John Wiley and Sons, Inc.

Ludema, J., Cooperrider, D., & Barrett, F. (2001). Appreciative inquiry: The power of the unconditional positive question. Reason and Bradbury, 189–208.

Mahal, P. K. (2009). Organizational culture and organizational climate as a determinant of motivation. *IUP Journal of Management Research, 8*(10), 38.

Majidi, M. A. (1998). *Effect of Displacement on Organizational Commitment and Job Satisfaction*. Tarbiyat Modarres Press.

March, J. G., & Olsen, J. P. (1976). *Ambiguity and Choice in Organizations*. University Press of Norway.

March, J. G., & Simon, H. A. (1958). *Organizations*. Wiley.

Markey, R., McIvor, J., & Wright, C. F. (2016). Employee participation and carbon emissions reduction in Australian workplaces. *International Journal of Human Resource Management, 27*(2), 173–191.

Maslach, C., & Leiter, M. P. (1997). *The truth about burnout: How organizations cause personal stress and what to do about it*. Jossey-Bass.

Mathapati, C. M. (2013). Green HRM: A strategic facet. *Tactful Management Research Journal, 2*(2), 1–6.

Mercer, T. G., Kythreotis, A. P., Stolte, T., Robinson, Z. P., George, S. M., & Haywood, S. K. (2017). The use of educational game design and play in higher education to influence sustainable behaviour. *International Journal of Sustainability in Higher Education*.

Michellone, G., & Zollo, G. (2000). Competencies management in knowledge-based firms. *International Journal of Manufacturing Technology and Management, 1*(1), 20–41.

Mintzberg, H., Simons, R., & Basu, K. (2002). Beyond selfishness. *MIT Sloan Management Review, 44*(1), 67-74.

Mir-fakhrae, T. (20009. Song of the silent discourse of advertising. In *Advertising Industry Conference Proceedings Persian*. Tehran: Ministry of Culture and Islamic Guidance, Propaganda Department.

Mishra, P. (2017). Green human resource management: A framework for sustainable organizational development in an emerging economy. *The International Journal of Organizational Analysis, 25*(5), 762–788. https://doi.org/10.1108/IJOA-11-2016-1079

Moghimi, M. (1999). *Organization and Management: a Research Approach*. Termeh Publication.

Moore, S. B., & Manring, S. L. (2009). Strategy development in small and medium sized enterprises for sustainability and increased value creation. *Journal of Cleaner Production, 17*(2), 276–282.

Murto, K. (1991). *Towards the well functiong community. Studies in education, psychology and social research*. University of Jyväskylä.

Novikova, E. N. (2013). *The rule of law as a challenge of time*. Thought.

O'Donohue, W., & Torugsa, N. (2016). The moderating effect of 'green' HRM on the association between proactive environmental management and financial performance in small firms. *International Journal of Human Resource Management, 27*(2), 239–261.

Ones, D. S., & Dilchert, S. (2012). Environmental sustainability at work: A call to action. *Industrial and Organizational Psychology: Perspectives on Science and Practice, 5*(4), 444–466.

Opatha, H. H. D. N. P., & Arulrajah, A. A. (2014). Green human resource management: Simplified general reflections. *International Business Research, 7*(8), 101.

Osterloh, M., & Frey, B. S. (2000). Motivation, knowledge transfer, and organizational forms. *Organization Science, 11*(5), 538–550.

Paillé, P., Chen, Y., Boiral, O., & Jin, J. (2014). The impact of human resource management on environmental performance: an employee-level study. *Journal of Business Ethics, 121*(3), 451-466.

Patterson, M. G., West, M. A., Shackleton, V. J., Dawson, J. F., Lawthom, R., Maitlis, S., Robinson, D. L., & Wallace, A. M. (2005). Validating the organizational climate measure: Links to managerial practices, productivity and innovation. *Journal of Organizational Behavior, 26*(4).

Pettigrew, A. M., Woodman, R. W., & Cameron, K. S. (2001). Studying organizational change and development: Challenges for future research. *Academy of Management Journal, 44*(4), 697–713.

Pfeffer, J. (1994). *Competitive Advantage through People Unleashing the Power of the Workforce*. Harvard Business School Press.

Phillips, L. (2007). Go green to gain the edge over rivals. *People Management*, p. 9. Available at: www2.cipd.co.uk/pm/peoplemanagement/b/weblog/archive/2013/01/29/gogreentogaintheedgeoverrivals-2007-08.aspx

Pitt, M., Tucker, M., Riley, M., & Longden, J. (2009). Towards sustainable construction: Promotion and best practices. *Construction Innovation, 9*(2), 201–224.

Postmes, T. (2003). A social identity approach to communication in organizations. *Social identity at work: Developing theory for organizational practice, 81*, 191-203.

Ramus, C. A. (2002). Encouraging innovative environmental actions: What companies and managers must do. *Journal of World Business, 37*(2), 151–164.

Redington, I. (2005). Making CSR Happen: the contribution of people management. In C. I. O. P. A. Development (Ed.), *The Virtuous Circle*. Chartered Institute of Personnel and Development.

Rezaeian Fordoie, S. (2014). *Innovation, Innovation System and Needs*. Secretary of the High Council of the Cultural Revolution.

Robertson, J. L., & Barling, J. (2013). Greening organizations through leaders' influence on employees' pro environmental behaviors. *Journal of Organizational Behavior, 34*(2), 176–194.

Røvik, K. A. (2011). From fashion to virus: An alternative theory of organizations' handling of management ideas. *Organization Studies*, *32*(5), 631–653.

Savitz, A. W., & Weber, K. (2006). *The triple bottom line*. Jossey-Bass.

Schein, E. H. (1999). *Process consultation revisited: Building the helping relationship*. Addison-Wesley.

Schmiedinger, B., Valentin, K., & Stephan, E. (2005). Competence based business development-organizational competencies as basis for successful companies. *Journal of Universal Knowledge Management*, *1*, 13–20.

Seppänen-Järvelä, R. (1999). Kehittämistyön luonne sosiaali- ja terveysalalla. Tutkimuksia 104, Helsinki: Stakes.

Shrivastava, P. (1995). The role of corporations in achieving ecological sustainability. *Academy of Management Review*, *20*(4), 936–960.

Sonnichsen, R. (2000). *High Impact Internal Evaluation. A Practitioner's Guide to Evaluating and Consulting Inside Organizations*. Sage.

Stern, M.J., Powell, R.B. & Hill, D. (2014), Environmental education program evaluation in the new millennium: what do we measure and what have we learned? *Environmental Education Research*, *20*(5), 581-611.

Stringer, L. (2009). *The Green Workplace: Sustainable Strategies That Benefit Employees, the Environment, and the Bottom Line*. Macmillan.

Subramanian, N., Abdulrahman, M. D., Wu, L., & Nath, P. (2016). Green competence framework: Evidence from China. *International Journal of Human Resource Management*, *27*(2), 151–172.

Svensson, L., & Brulin, G. (2013). Effects of programmes and projects. In L. Svensson, G. Brulin, S. Jansson, & K. Sjöberg (Eds.), *Capturing Effects of Projects and Programmes* (pp. 15–33). Studentlitteratur.

Tariq, S., Jan, F. A., & Ahmad, M. S. (2016). Green employee empowerment: A systematic literature review on state-of-art in green human resource management. *Quality & Quantity*, *50*(1), 237–269.

Toosi, M. A. (2002). Organizational Development. Publication of the Center for Scientific Management Training.

Ugwu, O. O., & Haupt, T. C. (2007). *Key performance indicators and assessment methods for infrastructure sustainability—a South African construction industry perspective*. Academic Press.

Van de Ven, A. H., Angle, H. L., & Poole, M. S. (Eds.). (2000). *Research on the Management of Innovation: The Minnesota Studies*. Oxford University Press.

Vanegas, J. A., DuBose, J. R., & Pearce, A. R. (1996, November). Sustainable technologies for the building construction industry. *Proceedings, Symposium on Design for the Global Environment*.

Vansina, L. (1998). The Individual in Organisations: Rediscovered or Lost Forever? *European Journal of Work and Organizational Psychology*, *7*(3), 265–282.

Weick, K. E., & Quinn, R. E. (1999). Organizational change and development. *Annual Review of Psychology, 50*(1), 361–386.

Weldy, T. G. (2009). Learning organization and transfer: Strategies for improving performance. *The Learning Organization, 16*(1), 58–68.

Weldy, T. G., & Gillis, W. E. (2010). The learning organization: Variations at different levels. *The Learning Organization, 17*, 455–470.

Wiggins, R. R., & Ruefli, T. W. (2002, January–February). Sustained Competitive Advantage: Temporal Dynamics and the Incidence and Persistence of Superior Economic Performance. *Organization Science, 13*(1), 63–105.

Winter, M., Smith, C., Morris, P., & Cicmil, S. (2006). Directions for future research in project management: The main findings of a UK government- funded research network. *International Journal of Project Management, 24*(8), 638–649.

Yarahmadi, M., & Higgins, P. G. (2012). Motivations towards environmental innovation: A conceptual framework for multiparty cooperation. *European Journal of Innovation Management, 15*(4), 400–420.

Zibarras, L. D., & Coan, P. (2015). HRM practices used to promote pro-environmental behavior: A UK survey. *International Journal of Human Resource Management, 26*(16), 2121–2142.

KEY TERMS AND DEFINITIONS

Competitive Advantage: A competitive advantage is any characteristic of a company, country or person that differentiates it from others, placing it in a superior relative position to compete.

Core Competencies: Core competencies are the strengths that define an organization. A company may have more than one core competency. Core competencies, sometimes called core competencies or distinctive competencies, help create a sustained competitive advantage for organizations.

Corporate Social Responsibility: It is a way of directing companies based on managing the impacts that their activity generates on their customers, employees, shareholders, local communities, the environment and on society in general.

Organizational Development: Organizational development is a systematic and planned process in which the principles of the behavioral sciences are used to increase individual and organizational effectiveness.

Organizational Greening: A green organization is one that believes in a double purpose: it generates economic wealth, but it also conserves natural resources. It is the one that worries you a lot and questions the impact that your product causes on the consumer, on natural resources, on your collaborators, etc.

Strategy: It is the direction or orientation that is given to the internal resources of an organization depending on the demands of its environment and surroundings to develop a competitive advantage that allows it to survive, lead, etc.

Sustainable Organizational Development: Sustainable organizational development focuses on value creation, environmental management, environmentally friendly production systems and the formation of human capital, social responsibility is linked to transparency, dialogue with stakeholders and care for the environment and the social inclusion.

Chapter 7
Information Management in a Relational Context Innovation and Digitalization

Cátia Sofia Salgado
Port of Sines and Algarve Authority, Portugal

ABSTRACT

Digitalization is changing the way we live, work, our relationships, and it couldn't be otherwise if we talk about competitiveness in the maritime transport sector. The world faces considerable technological challenges; so does the maritime sector, turning information technologies into opportunities by using countless data inputs, thus allowing more control, better planning, and a reduction in operational costs while enhancing environmental sustainability. According to Carbone and Martino, ports have been naturally used for transhipment, consisting of the transference of cargo from one mean of transport to another, which has led to a series of new demands and challenges in port management concerns, since goods temporarily remain within the area under the influence of the port. Before its expedition, port activity faces diverse challenges in the management of storage, availableness, and handling, among other issues.

INTRODUCTION

Digitalization is changing the way we live, we work, our relationships, and it couldn't be otherwise if we talk about competitiveness in the maritime transport sector. The world faces considerable technological challenges; so, does the maritime sector, turning information technologies into opportunities by using countless data inputs, thus allowing to have more control, a better planning and a reduction in operational costs while enhancing environmental sustainability.

According to Carbone & Martino (2003), ports have been naturally used for transshipment[1], consisting on the transference of cargo from one mean of transport to another, which led to a series of new demands and challenges in what port management concerns, since goods temporarily remain within the

DOI: 10.4018/978-1-7998-7452-2.ch007

area under the influence of the port, before its expedition, port activity faces diverse challenges in what regards the management of storage, availableness, and handling, among other issues.

Historically, ports were endowed to provide a connection between maritime, inland, rail, road, and river transport. Nowadays, ports play an essential role in the management and co-coordination of both the goods and internal information flows, within its area of influence and outwards since transport is part of the whole supply chain. In this manner, it is now needed to promote synergies among the diverse interests of the stakeholders thus associated to the port community, in order to guarantee the continuous improvement of the services while assuring high production levels.

We also mustn't forget that not only the port's internal strengths deriving from cargo handling efficiency and connections to the hinterland determine its competitiveness, since it is equally influenced by the connections to the supply chain. Consequently, ports risk to lose important clients not only due to flaws on the port infrastructure, port operators and land connections, but also due to the reorganization of network services and incoming services' rendering partners, who might always use a different hub. In other words, ports' competitiveness is becoming more and more reliant on the coordination and control of the whole supply chain.

Carbone & Martino (2003) comprehends the port as a member of the supply chain. Ports are considered as a cluster of organizations where different transport and logistic operators are committed in adding value to the final consumer. Porter (1993, cit João, Belmiro, N., M., 2008) considers that the approach of the so-called industrial clusters, supported on the Diamond Model concept, endows a new dynamic for converging to the achievement of the nations' competitive advantage, in a broader way. Porter (1998, cit João, Belmiro, N., M., 2008.) states that the competitiveness of a nation depends on its industry capacity to innovate and develop and recognizes that clusters' comprehension cannot be dissociated from a broad understanding of the competition theory and the influence of location in global economy.

In this scope, Porter (1998, cit Belmiro (2008) considers that a cluster derives from the Diamond Model and influences competition in three levels: firstly, by increasing companies and industries' productivity; secondly by enhancing innovation capacity, thus increasing productivity and thirdly, by stimulating new businesses supporting innovation and expanding the cluster. Competitive advantage is achieved whenever demand provides a clearer view to organizations, thus anticipating both its emerging needs and the buyers'.

Besides, the most demanding clients pressure enterprises to quickly innovate, thus achieving more sophisticated competitive advantages towards external competitors; ports are no exception under this perspective.

Belmiro (2008) comprehends corelated industries as the ones in which organizations may coordinate or share activities within the value chain, while competing, or those comprising complementary products or services. This fact allows for an information flow and an extremely advantageous technological exchange for the innovation and modernization of organizations, and the country.

Maritime logistics is thus a key sector for digital transformation, taking into consideration the high network level and its diverse interfaces, offering a wide range of applications for digital technologies. Digitalization and logistics 4.0 endow maritime transport enterprises with a high potential (Binder, 2016c). Traffic and port logistics and just in time delivery will change due to electronic revolution, shaping up with Big Data and the increasing technology network (Berg & Hauer, 2015).

WORLDWIDE MARKET EVOLUTION

The growth of international maritime trade faces considerable challenges, leading to the acceleration of several measures aiming at enhancing world economy, due to economic and world trade slowdown.

According to the World Bank – Mobility and transport connectivity series (December 2020) report, the volumes of goods handled by the maritime transport increased, in average, 3% between 1970 and 2018. Plus, the total volume of goods handled by the maritime transport reached the 11 billion of metric tons in 2017, enhanced by the increasing volumes of bulk commodities, followed by containerized cargo, other dry bulks, crude oil, gas, and chemical products (UNCTAD 2020). Despite the slightly volumes' decrease in 2018, pre-COVID-19 forecasts appointed a continuous increase of 2,6% for 2019, and a 3,4% growth rate for the period from 2019 to 2024. Notwithstanding, during the UN conference on trade and development (Geneve, 2020), world economy was forecasted to suffer a 4,3% contraction in 2020, leading more than 130 million of people to extreme poverty, which would be felt by the poorer and more vulnerable for a longer period. In this manner, the consequences to maritime transport result on a loss of 4,1% in 2020, due to COVID-19.

UNCTAD secretary-general, Mukhisa Kituyi, stated that the spreading of the COVID-19 virus has benefited from the interconnectivity and vulnerabilities of globalization, thus turning a global health crisis into an economic distress, affecting both the more vulnerable and the strongest. Within this scope, UNCTAD developed a road map towards recovery, stating that the health crisis is also a catalyst for the needed change. According to the secretary-general, it is time to approach the weakest issues of globalization, which led to the quick dissemination of the virus across the world, and its unequal economic impacts. It was also enhanced that the pandemics may act as a catalyst for new and more resilient production networks, based on shorter and more regional value chains, both sustainable and digital. UNCTAD expects growth to return in 2021, reaching the 4,8%. However, uncertainties are enormous and, on his statement, Mukhisa Kituyi mentions that global maritime transport industry will lead the efforts towards a sustainable recovery, while the world should be ready to be a different place after the pandemics; industry, one of the chiefs interested parts, must help adapting efficiency logistics. At the peak of the crisis, the sector has shortened capacity and reduced costs, to maintain profitability, while the rates of the services remained stable, despite the sharp drop on demand. Besides, governments, port authorities and customs have adapted themselves, aiming at maintaining the trade flow, while keeping people safe.

Many of the adopted measures require more investments on digitalization and automation, providing digital copies instead of paper documents, clearances before the vessels' arrival, electronic payments, and customs procedures, aiming at helping to accelerate global trade.

Considering the deep impact of COVID-19 in economy, almost leading to its paralisation, a series of disruptions in people's lives must also be enhanced, as well as considerable economic and social costs. The damages in economy are already visible, representing the greatest economic crash the world has witnessed in decades. The World Bank Economic Prospects Report (WB 2020) report forecasts a 5,2% contraction on the global Gross Domestic Product in 2020, the greatest recession in decades, despite the efforts governments have taken, aiming at restraining and respond through supporting fiscal and financial policies. The forecasts are no better when analyzed in the long term; the deep recession caused by the pandemics shall leave profound scars in what concerns the decrease on investment, the loss of human capital because of increasing unemployment, significant impacts in education and world trade fragmentation and its connections to the supply chain.

Figure 1. Patterns of world trade sea voyages
(source: UNCTAD, 2020)

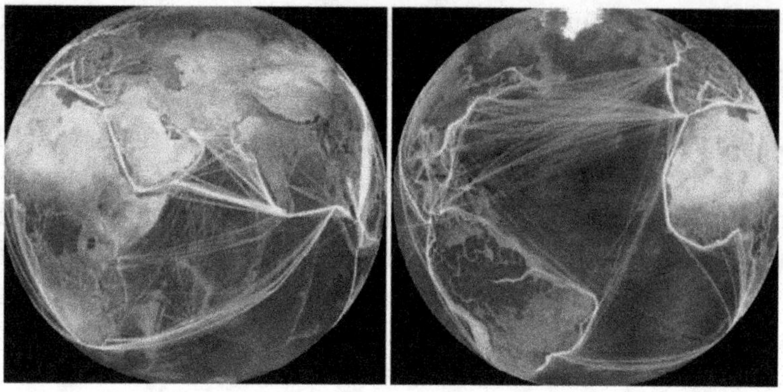

The lesson to be learned from this pandemic, focuses on the critical role maritime ports and related infrastructures play in the supply chain and vessels' capacity to transport big volumes of goods, if adequate and effective measures are taken both in ports and in logistics, along the hinterland. The lack of basic products in highly developed countries, during the first days of the pandemics, was unquestionable, thus clearly attesting the vulnerability of the current logistic system, plus the need to guarantee business continuity, as well as to enhance the resilience of those infrastructures, towards the future.

The "Review of maritime transport 2020" (UNCTAD) report provides data evidencing how much maritime trade has weakened in 2019, and how much it remained under pressure during 2020, due to both economic and global trade slowdown, having reached its lower level since the financial crisis from 2008-2009. Figure 2 shows how maritime trade slowed down along with the downturn of global GDP. The beginning of the pandemics in 2020, and its consequences in worldwide economies, travel, transport, and consuming patterns, as well as industrial activities and supply chains, have caused a global recession in 2020.

Figure 2. Maritime trade
(source: UNCTAD, 2020)

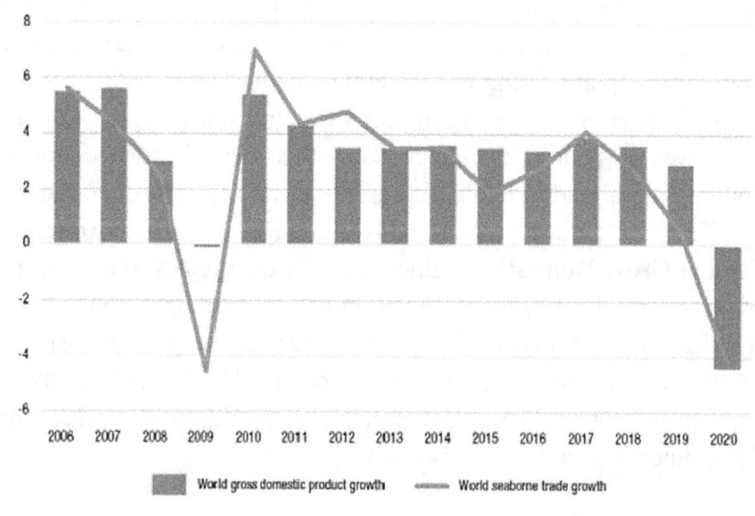

The disruptions in vessels, ports and the supply chain led to a comparison with the 2008-2009 financial crisis; they are similar in certain issues while diverging in other. In both cases, governments have intervened by injecting funds in economies, to stimulate recovery; they were both accompanied by an increasing protectionism and skepticism feeling towards globalization. However, they diverge on the type, scope, dissemination speed and scale; a crisis like no other surpassing the financial crisis of 2008-2009. The International Monetary Fund 2020a) (IMF) called the COVID-19 related crisis the "Great Lockdown", considering that the pandemics has swept the whole world in record time. The 2020 crisis was a double-impact rupture which transformed a disruption from the supply side in China, to become a global crash in what concerns demand. During previous crisis, there were no restrictions in travelling whatsoever, nor to economic activities, and its impact was only notorious 8 months later, while the COVID-19 impact was almost immediate. In what concerns maritime transport and trade, the fundamental difference was the industry's feedback to suppress demand; while during the first crisis shipowners have focused on preserving their market shares, current crisis has changed the focus to supply management and maintaining the rates.

Bearing in mind the uncertain times we are living, the differences on forecasts technics, and while depending on how the pandemics will continue to evolve and on whether the political measures taken are effective or not, UNCTAD forecasted a loss of 4,3% on global GDP in 2020; the International Monetary Fund 2020a) forecasted a loss of 4,4%. On the other hand, both forecasts expect the GDP of all developed and under development countries to decrease, with exception to East Asia, including China, which is expected to grow 1,1%.

The repercussions and impacts of the pandemics, resulting from globalization, have raised some issues in what concerns maritime transport and trade, this being the backbone connecting supply chains. While facing a pandemic such as COVID-19, the sector is now acting as a transmission channel sending shock waves towards supply chains and regions. The restrictions introduced on the reply to the pandemics have raised some obstacles hindering both commercial flows and supply chains operations, a fact that might considerably undermine maritime transport and trade, and the achievements for liberalization and trade facilitation accomplished along the years. In this scope, pandemics and its consequences have accelerated an inexistent debate on the advantages of globalization and the supply chains, a debate which has been triggered by the enormous commercial tension between China and the USA, since 2018. It must also be enhanced that the pandemics has brought up a deep concern towards the production in distant locations, and the need to diversify production and concerning production locations and suppliers.

The redirection of land freight transport services to air transport were re-established (Aylor et al., 2020). The measures taken were traduced in the redirection of vessels, changes in schedules and calls, as well as on the variations of the transported volumes, the world have seen the Suez Canal blockade the canal is becoming more significant for oil flows and supply deliveries than they previously concluded, with seriously impacts at the oil market, said Paola Rodriguez-Masiu, vice president of oil markets at Rystad Energy. The 39.2 million barrels per day of crude imported by seaborne methods in 2020, 1.74 million barrels per day passed through the Suez Canal, according to data from research firm Kpler, this represents under 5% of total flows, but as the build-up stretches on, the impacts rise. The Ever Given was pulled free from the Suez Canal after cutting off traffic in the vital waterway for six days, but experts say the disruptions to global trade will continue to reverberate, including congestion at ports as well as vessels not being in the right place for their next scheduled journey. Most importantly, it further exacerbates supply chains from a container shortage amid the Covid-19 buying boom.

Stephen Flynn, professor of political science at Northeastern University, who is also founding director at the Global Resilience Institute, noted that this is one of the challenges of a just-in-time system, around 12% of global trade flows through the Suez Canal on massive ships like the Ever Given, which can hold 20,000 containers. In addition, it was evidenced that the challenges related to freight transport are sensitive to time, whenever there are disruptions in the supply chains and how the integration level of the supply chains in the different countries can change the results. The changing of the production centers for closer locations is a complex process, which must take in consideration a series of factors besides labor costs.

Before the pandemics, structuring changes such as digitalization and services (Haven e Van Der Marel, 2018) were underway as an imperative of increasing sustainability, while an ever more uncertainty became the major topic for 2021; the impact on maritime trade, the times and the scaling recovery are fully uncertain. On the other hand, the forecasts for 2021 maritime trade also depend on the economic growth projections, and this scenario might change. UNCTAD expects global GDP to recover in 4,1%, while maritime trade is forecasted to grow nearly 4,8%.

Maritime transport needs to adapt itself, making sure to be ready to bear the changes on the supply chains promoting more resilience and robustness. Maritime transport and ports must re-evaluate its business strategies and investment plans, also in what concerns port capacity, transport networks configurations, vessels, and development capacity, thus allowing a better absorption of digital technology. The endeavor towards digitalization will, not only, enhance transport efficiency and productivity, but also ports and smart navigation. Some support must be given to less developed countries, to minimize divisions while guaranteeing that they also can explore and benefit from the advantages of digitalization in building their own resilience. Leverage the crisis will require investments in technology, as well as the adoption of solutions allowing to respond to the needs of the supply chain of the future, supporting development and resilience efforts (Egloff, 2020).

Historically, both innovation and technology have been playing a crucial role in enhancing the sea industry efficiency, while in a social approach, technological development and automation also represent opportunities and challenges. Even though a series of emergent technologies are expected to enhance maritime transport safety and efficiency, labor market is expected to experience some disruptions due to the changes on human resources requirements, which will change routines and work schedules. A possible reduction on human resources shall be compensated by an increase on other aspects of the transport system; this impact will depend on the professional skills of low and medium qualification workers, such as cargo handlers, stevedores, or cranes' operators, all of them facing a higher redundancy risk, due to automation. On the other hand, highly qualified workers will be less affected by increasing automation and harder to substitute. In this manner, countries with lower levels of automation and technological development shall register a considerably lower risk in reducing human resources than those countries highly industrialized, due to an increasing automation and digital technology. The future working scenario of the maritime sector is likely to be quite different in the years to come; there will be less jobs onboard the vessels and more onshore, thus requiring higher adaptation capacity skills. Within this scope, requalification and training shall be determinant for the transformations yet to come, as the results of advanced technology and automation implementation begin to be noticed.

THE CREATION OF STRATEGIC VALUE AND GLOBALIZATION

The current tendency that "all is competition" clearly results from globalization, economic activity, and the use of information technologies, which led to a massification of everything that is digital and a considerable set of economic and social actions and decisions, thus introducing changes on organizational structures. As previously mentioned, maritime transport continues to be the backbone of global trade while the supply chain represents more than four-fifths of global freight trade (per volume) carried by sea.

The available comparing indexes on the impact of international trade inefficiency, analyzed by the World Bank Logistics Performance (LPI) index, the Doing Business index (DBI), and the World Economic Forum`s for competitiveness (GCI) 4.0 on the efficiency of port services and customs clearance, point out to what extent the inefficiencies of a country's maritime borders may impact world trade competitiveness. Technological innovations and digitalization offer opportunities for the development of a holistic approach, in order to integrate the port ecosystem, thus comprising facilitation and cooperation among governments and private stakeholders, aiming to achieve significant results in port transactions.

Acknowledging the benefits of foreign trade for economic development, Elorza (2012) states that a company's export capacity may be blocked by a series of factors, such as the lack of an adequate infrastructure, an inefficient port management, excessive documentation and long customs procedures, thorough inspections, and a series of fiscal investigations from governmental parties. Considering the high competition in export businesses, any obstacle, delays, extra costs along the products trading process may hinder or even prevent business accomplishment (Elorza, 2012). In this manner, countries are demanded to work hard on the improvement of all factors closely related to trade facilitation.

Gallegos (2015) states that globalization plays a determinant role in trade, as world economies advance, integrated, and interconnected among them, in what concerns import and export of both goods and services. Multinational companies represent two thirds of global export flows, and almost 10% of domestic sales all over the world.

Globalization in the logistics of import and export of goods' trade, with maritime activities on one hand, and hinterland related on the other, attest that export companies struggle to comply with the export contracts due dates, not only due to constraints on the good's physical flows, but also in what regards the processing of the documentation accompanying the goods' flows. The congestion of goods is mainly due to the lack of adequate storage areas in maritime ports. In order to overcome this situation, essentially deriving from markets globalization, logistic areas named dry ports were developed, consisting on an extension of maritime ports and comprising logistic centers including storage, transport and other value added services (Woxenius, Roso & Lumsden, 2004).

On the other hand, information management is ever more fundamental, if we consider the area of influence of a port and its hinterland, where smooth operations of the means of transport and cargo handling along the whole logistic chain are key factors for the port competitiveness (Simão, 2013).

With digitalization offering new services complying with nowadays and future legal requirements, it is crucial to assure a prime cooperation among maritime transport, ports and logistics, aiming at enhancing both efficiency and sustainability of the maritime sector, thus facilitating trade and, not less important, promoting global economy recovery.

Digitalization and new technologies are the key to standardization, thus enhancing transport efficiency through electronic messages' harmonization while reducing administrative burden for shipowners and the remaining stakeholders involved in the process. Dias J. Q., (2003) considers that logistics can act as an interface for ports, whose performance results from an inner and complex set of systems and sub-systems influencing the whole chain, both upstream and downstream, thus behaving like a traction rupture in the whole flow. Plus, a port interface constitutes a discontinuity, a breaking point in the logistic chain.

Resultant from the needs evidenced by the crisis, the WB, IAPH and WPSP in Accelerating Digitalization, (December 2020) developed a road map so that any port, country or port community may move forward towards the implementation of digitalization in the maritime logistic chain. The following diagram shows the short-, medium- and long-term measures aiming at protecting public health, assuring businesses continuity and also to enhance and protect the system's resilience.

Figure 3. Digitalization road map
(source: World Bank, IAPH e WPSP,2020)

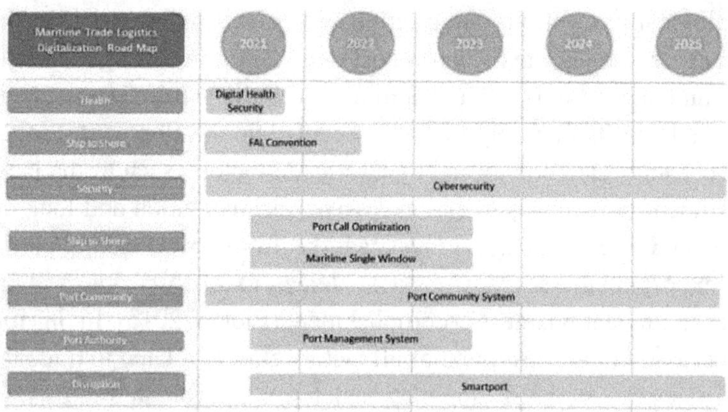

1st Phase

The first phase comprises crucial emergency measures in what concerns digital monitoring, safety in health and in the establishment of crisis centers with intergovernmental agents. The main goal is to protect vessels' crews, port workers, cruise passengers.

2nd Phase

The second phase introduces a short-term model, to acknowledge the requirements defined at the International Maritime Organization`s (FAL) convention IMO (1965), aiming at supporting transmission, reception and response to the information required for the transition to the single window, thus minimizing the number of paper documents and contacts among people; this has been one of the compulsory requirements for all the ports since April 2019, despite being still partially implemented.

For Fine, Vardan, Pethick and El-hout, (2002), cit by Anunciação & Zorrinho, the creation of strategic value demand organizations to control, protect and defend the vulnerable parts of the value chain, through alliances strategically meaningful.

In parallel, and since ports must be acquainted to the FAL convention requirements, discussion must be focused on the nine key data elements related to the so called "port call optimization", allowing the

Figure 4. Maritime single window
(source: World Bank, IAPH e WPSP,2020)

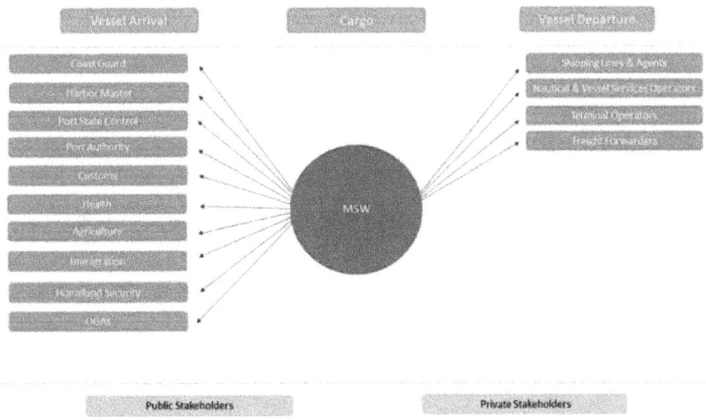

vessels to manage transit times during the trip, so that the arrival occurs as closer as possible to the just-in-time concept, thus consisting of an attractive feature of the port while enhancing its competitiveness.

The risk management, higher safety levels, more incomes and the increasing compliance of the world trade players allow all the involved parts to benefit from an interpretation and adoption of more transparent and predictable standards, plus a more accurate use of both human and financial resources, thus resulting in considerable gains in what concerns competitiveness and productivity.

Sykes (1993) cit by Anunciação & Zorrinho, (2006), states that the relational logic in creating strategic value allows the value creation to extend itself far beyond the limits of the organization. As the products or services pursue their way in collecting value, and while this value is added in each knot of the chain, the different partakes on the net are fully justified until the combination the consumer is looking for is dully achieved, by deeply understanding the importance of the client, the technological innovation, competitive positioning, related strategic competencies, and the development of an adequate architecture.

In this manner, ports must introduce the port community system (PCS), consisting of a platform thus optimizing, managing, and automating both ports and logistic procedures, with a unique data submission for transport and the logistic chain. The benefits resulting from a PCS can be traduced in efficient and quick port processes, specially by reducing the tasks related to paper assembling, thus eliminating unnecessary paper exchange, which potentially causes considerable disruptions in the cargo handling process.

By using a real time exchanging data system, the PCS becomes an efficient, quick, and smooth tool, focused and versatile, primarily aiming at optimizing the processes resulting from the supply chain, by improving efficiency and transparency standards in all the cargo handling process stages, thus including cargoes' loading, and unloading, customs clearances, health formalities and the delivery and collection of goods at the terminals. In this manner, the PCS contributes for a sustainable transport logistics, while playing an important role in carbon reduction process.

Plus, PCS are crucial in programming multimodal transport solutions. In 2015, IPCSA published a guide concerning the development of a PCS, identifying twelve steps towards its accomplishment and implementation. The broad scope of the document allowed it to be applicable to any type of organization, whether it might be a maritime authority, airport, customs, governmental, agents, maritime ports, or dry ports.

Figure 5. The twelve actions for a PCS
(source: World Bank, IAPH e WPSP,2020)

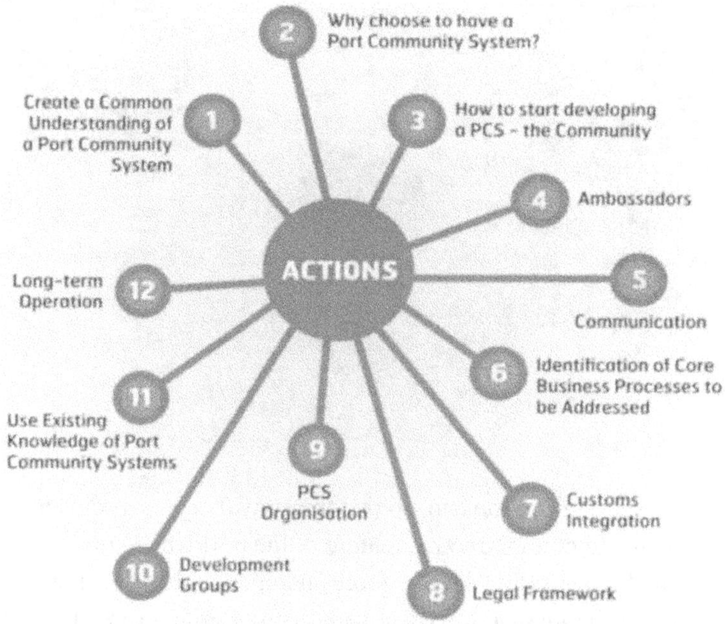

The stages and short-term recommendations for the development of both port community systems and digitalization, towards the achieving of a more resilient sector, comprise the development and introduction of a Port Management System (PMS), as well as the implementation of technologies able to develop smart ports. The urgent requirements related to digital safety are identified as medium-term measures, while a PMS allows a port authority to control traffic, manage the port infrastructure thus comprising calls' management, tariffs, diaries, incidents, wastes, dangerous cargoes, cargo planning, inspections, authorizations, safety, and services, by acceding in an integrated way by a single system. Bearing in mind that the PMS is endowed a port authority regulatory mission, along with the PCS it will facilitate cargo handling from the maritime port to its hinterland, thus comprising a key competitiveness factor to any port.

Figure 6. Port management system
(source: World Bank, IAPH e WPSP,2020)

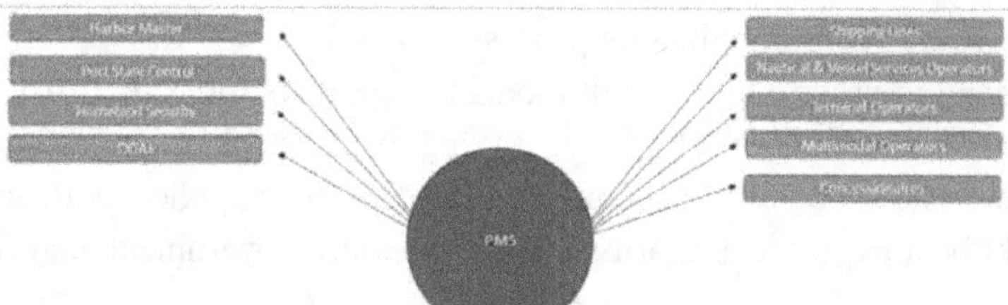

It must also be enhanced that a PMS system improves traffic control, thus helping the planning of vessels' arrivals and departures while reducing delays to the minimum, through real time and precise frames of the port and main approximation routes.

The necessary consistency among port community system, port management system and the single window (SW) must be guaranteed, thus allowing maritime trade and logistic players to benefit from digitalization procedures and processes, while achieving smart ports.

Figure 7. Port community system: optical architecture
(source: World Bank, IAPH e WPSP,2020)

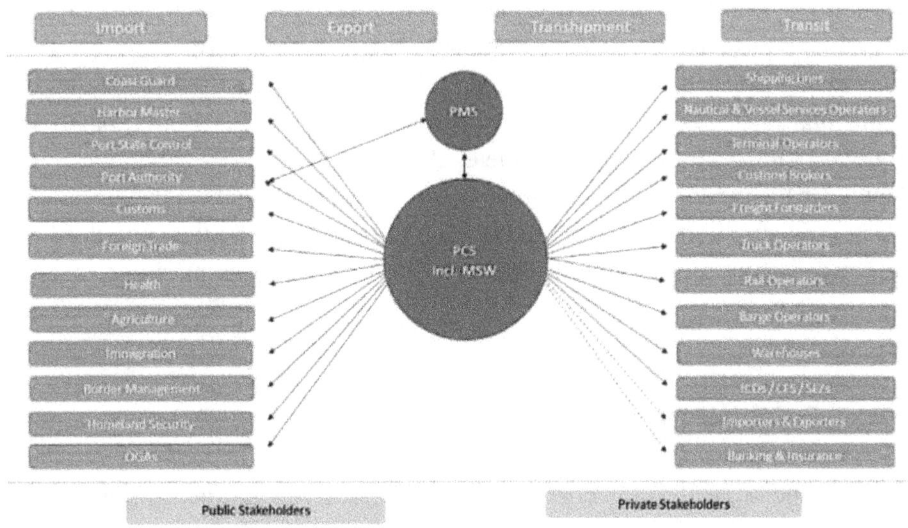

Within this global transport net, "doors" are becoming "nodes". During the last decade, considerable efforts have been done towards a better coordination, synchronization, and optimization of port scale operations, being the Port collaborative Decision Making (portCDM) one of them. The portCDM is an independent international organization whose aim is to enhance the exchange of digital data almost in real time, focusing in promoting guiding lines and patterns which might be adapted both local and regionally, to assure higher efficiency levels. Thanks to digitalization, it is possible to offer interoperable tools and systems to the users, thus allowing the whole world active "doors" to communicate.

Bearing in mind the importance of both organizational urbanism and the architecture of port information and management systems, Laudon & Laudon (2010) state that to enhance real benefits, information systems must be built with a clear comprehension of the organizations, including their environment. In what concerns SW solutions, the framing involves considerable challenges both technological and organizational related, interorganizational, management oriented, political, and legal.

Anunciação and Zorrinho (2006) perceive the concepts of organizational urbanism and architecture to manage this complexity. According to the authors, these solutions must be implemented and performed in a sustained and efficient way, under the management of the available resources aiming at guaranteeing the alignment between information systems development and business strategy (architecture), thus considering national and international context, to assure long term success (urbanism).

Zachman (2016), states that the presentation of the architecture must be considered as a logic structure classifying and organizing the organization's described representations, which are meaningful not only for the management of a company but also for the development of its systems. The author's proposal consists of a benchmark correlating, on a 6x6 matrix, the perspectives of several players involved in the process (Planener, Owner, Designer, Builder, Subcontractor) with a set of basic questions (What, How, Where, Who, When and Why), where each cell comprises a series of relevant artefacts and representations so that the architecture characterization of an organization or system can be thoroughly defined.

We are quite aware of the key role performed by ports within global trade, having become fundamental for critical infrastructures, according to the United Nations Conference on Trade and Development (UNCTAD) "Review of maritime transport 2020" report. The document considers that approximately 90% of the world trade is performed by maritime transport; nearly 8 billion tons of cargo is carried by containerships, oil tankers and bulk carriers (Gopfert & Braun, 2008).

According to the last data available by UNCTAD, in 2020 10.7 billion tons were handled by maritime transport, and the total capacity of the world's container fleet increased to approximately 20.5 billion of twenty-foot equivalent unit (TEU) in 2015 (Grote et al., 2016).

When compared to the world's GDP and global trade, maritime transport registered an increase twice as fast in the last few years. In this manner, and despite representing less than one third, containerized cargo was the type of cargo registering a higher growing rate, as far as maritime transport concerns (N.U., 2011).

THE EXCHANGE OF INFORMATION

Cooperation, communication, and collaboration among the different parties, aiming at preserving and develop this project was formalized by a cooperation agreement signed in March 2020 by IMO, World Customs Organization, the United Nations Economic Commission for Europe, and the International Organization for Standardization (ISO).

UN/CEFACT recommendation nº33 (2005), defines SW as a capacity allowing the parties involved in trade and transport to present, in a standardized way and in a unique point of contact, the needed information to comply with the regulatory requirements concerning import, export and transshipment.

SITPRO (2005) Cit. in Wang, Yingli, & Pettit, Stephen (2016), defines SW as a platform allowing all parties to submit the international import, export and transshipment data requested by governmental departments or agencies, a single time, through a unique electronic interface, thus complying with all the legal requirements related to each transaction.

The relation between the SW concept and the global approach of the supply chain for Wang, Yingli, & Pettit, Stephen (2016), implies that the success of the supply chain requires an efficient exchange of information among the different players involved. From an international perspective, the management of the global supply chain is highly related to this fact; the system emerging like a new Information and communication technologies (ICT), type was the SW.

In what concerns the maritime transport and port activity, the exchange of information among the various players is achieved through EDIFACT[2] messages. Nevertheless, and bearing in mind technological development, we are currently experiencing a gradual evolution towards the use of XML[3] messages. A paperless and standardized communication is, not only, a pre-requirement for the accomplishment of more efficient port operations, but also a way to improve supplying, integration, coordination, and performance of the whole chain. The main ports adopted the exchange of electronic data, based on international standards. The UN/CEFACT[4], one of the organizations responsible for the standardization of electronic messages for the sector, aware that guidelines are, indeed, able to harmonize and simplify the exchange of information between governments, invites countries to consider the possibility to implement a SW concept (recommendation N°33), thus allowing:

- The parties involved in the trade and transport of goods to submit standardized information with a unique access point, implying that, should this information be electronic, individual data shall be issued a single time.
- That the sharing of information thus related with international trade transactions, shall be supported by a legal frame assuring privacy, safety and exchange of information.
- There shall only be a unique access point to disseminate and accede information, thus guaranteeing the access to relevant information, from a governmental point of view, also to authorities, or duly authorized agencies.
- To facilitate and enhance the exchange of information concerning the receiving and payment of rates.

The facilitation of this information exchange, in such a way that companies involved in maritime transport can interact and communicate, through these systems and based on a single window concept, despite the standard established.

In conclusion, SW concept does not correspond to an information system; SW is otherwise a governance philosophy in which traditional structures or governmental and regulatory organizations are challenged to develop a transformation process, aiming at improving the services offered to citizens and economy as a whole, (cite., Pinto, Cláudio. Organizational, informational, and technological impacts while implementing directive 2010/65/EU).

The SW can highly benefit governments and trade. From a governmental point of view, it can enhance risks management while obtaining a higher control towards safety levels, thus increasing incomes thanks to procedures standardization, a more accurate and effective human and financial resources management, thus resulting on considerable gains in productivity and competitiveness (cite Recommendation and Guidelines on establishing a Single Window in United Nations Centre for Trade Facilitation and Electronic Business, Geneva, 2005).

The implementation of the SW concept required viability studies, analysis of both the scopes and potentialities, as well as the nature of the data demand and other information, legal frames, with various options on "how" to implement and the definition of the implementation phases. The pre-requirements for a successful implementation would never succeed without the direct involvement and political willingness of the governments, relevant governmental authorities and without the support and participation of stakeholders from diverse countries.

ADVANTAGES OF THE SINGLE WINDOW

Deepening the scope of the compulsory requirement of the Convection of Facilitation of international Maritime Traffic (FAL Convention), from International Maritime Organization IMO (in force since April 8, 2019), which allows the governments from different countries to introduce the electronic exchange

Table 1. Advantages of the single window

Government/Regulator (public sector)	Enhanced human resources and financial management;
	Improved management risk;
	Higher safety levels;
	More transparency and integrity.
Economic Operators (Private Sector)	More transparency and predictability in standards interpretation and applicability.
	Quicker dispatches/clearances;
	Enhanced human resources and financial management;
	Gains in efficiency and competitiveness.

(source: UN/CEFACT, 2005)

of information between vessels and ports, aiming at facilitating the quick and smooth dispatch of vessels, cargoes, passengers and crews, IAPH has issued a global research aiming at assessing the current FAL requirement conformity level, in order to identify some challenges the ports might face along the process. In June 2020, IAPH plead for the accelerating of the digitalization process in maritime trade and logistics, bearing in mind that the majority of countries had not yet begun the implementation of the data exchange systems among the various authorities involved in the process, each one with its own roles, responsibilities, data needs, culture and established practices, which might impact both EU and IMO guidelines.

According to FAL, the SW concept is encouraged to be adopted by all public authorities connected to the arrival, staying in port and clearing of vessels, passengers, crews and cargoes, sharing and reusing data on a single system (SW) in order to avoid data duplication. Nowadays, this concept is recommended by FAL, but it will quite probably be mandatory in the future; IMO has already issued guidelines towards the development of a maritime single window. As a response to the pandemics, IAPH brought together the prime international ports, transport industries and associations and issues a plea to accelerating digitalization, by the letter IMO Nº 4204/add.20, thus identifying nine priority areas towards the accomplishment of this digitalization process:

1. To assess the state of implementation and find ways to enforce the already mandatory.
2. Requirement defined in the IMO FAL Convention to support transmission, receipt, and response of information required for the arrival, stay, and departure of ships, persons, and cargo, including notifications and declarations for customs, immigration, port and security authorities, via electronic data exchange, making the transition to full-fledged SW;
3. To ensure harmonization of data standards beyond the IMO FAL Convention to facilitate sharing of data for just-in-time operation of ships and optimum resource deployment;
4. To strive for the introduction of Port Community Systems and secure data exchange platforms in the main ports of all IMO Member States;
5. To review existing IMO guidance on Maritime Cyber Risk Management on its ability to address cyber risks in ports, developing additional guidance where needed.

6. To raise awareness and promote best practices on the application of emerging technologies in ports (e.g. artificial intelligence, advanced analytics, internet of things, digital twins, robotics process automation, autonomous systems, blockchain, virtual reality and augmented reality);
7. To facilitate the implementation of such emerging technologies.
8. To facilitate the implementation of digital port platforms for secure data sharing.
9. To establish a coalition of willing stakeholders to address standardization, starting with the long overdue introduction of the electronic bill of lading.
10. To set up a capacity building framework to support smaller, less developed, and understaffed port communities.

The effort and understanding required to all the parties involved in the process, may affect reports and operational activities inside the ports. Should this happen, common interest must prevail over individual interests, thus imposing a change in mentalities and the fear that data exchange might be seen as a loss of power, somehow. Notwithstanding, if all the players contribute, the prime goal of "give and take" shall be accomplished in a quicker and more efficient way, thanks to a harmonized way in communicating data.

The jointly report of the World Bank and IAPH (January 21, 2021 Antwerp) shows that a better digital cooperation among the public and private players, along the whole maritime supply chain shall result on significant efficiency gains, safer and more resilient supply chains, while diminishing CO2 emissions. The digitalization of the sector shall considerably benefit economy and will play a determinant contribution to its sustainable recovery. The acceleration of digitalization aims at strengthening the maritime supply chain, making it more collaborative, which may help streamlining maritime transport process, namely documental and border procedures related to the communication between vessels and land, especially in what ports concern.

The report also enhances that the COVID-19 crisis has evidenced that benefit in digitalizing maritime and land operations, the urgent need of minimizing human interaction while enhancing the resilience of the supply chain towards future crisis. Makhtar Diop (2021) considers that besides the immediate benefits for the maritime sector, digitalization will help countries to actively take part in worldwide economy, thus helping them developing.

The investment in more efficient infrastructures and transport services is a fundamental part of the goal; sustainable transport is an opportunity to unlock economic growth, connect people to jobs and essential services thus facing critical challenges, such as climate change or the COVID-19.

Bearing in mind the global initiatives' context we are currently facing, the decarbonization of maritime transport, with the optimizing of port calls, suggests digitalization as one of the most important short-term measures aiming at significantly reduce CO2 emissions, by reducing the volume of paper used in maritime trade procedures.

INFORMATION SECURITY

Technological development, informatization and digitalization through the nets and internet connections have considerably benefited every industry sector, namely the maritime, despite the risks associated being plenty and complex. Even though current technologies are essential in data monitoring, collection and transmission, information systems are needed to storage, analyze, and disseminate information and knowledge, in order to support the decision processes of the different stakeholders; we are aware that there is information which requires to be classified according to the significance of its content.

It is important to note that, despite being essential, the increasing digitalization of the maritime logistic chain also represents some risks. Between February and May 2020, cyberattacks to the maritime industry have increased 400% (captive international, 2020); fighting this risk is now a priority to port authorities and concerning port communities, thus demanding to enhance port ecosystems' safety.

As maritime sector moves towards a bigger and broader digitalization of the processes along the whole value chain, more vulnerabilities shall arise. What happened to *NotPetya* is a good example; the virus resulted on a loss of 300 million dollars to Maersk. We could also refer the attacks to the ports of Barcelona and San Diego, as well as the one to COSCO, which tore down half the shipowner's network in the USA, plus the malware over MSC, which resulted on the closing of the Geneva Head Office for five days.

In what concerns the economic impact and the "wave" effect of the cyberattacks on port infrastructures, we must consider that unlike IT infrastructures, there is no control panel for Terminal Operator (TO) network allowing operators to assess the vulnerabilities of all the systems connected. Antivirus systems are completely irrelevant when the aggressor is anonymous and discrete, thus enhancing the use of network systems, the bigger the risks will be; this evolution might stress the disconnection among IT and TO in what concerns security, thus realizing that succeeded attacks to IT network result from a penetration on the initial TO system.

According to Accelerating Digitalization from World Bank, IAPH and WPSP (December, 2020), members of port communities ecosystems are able to reduce risks by implementing cybersecurity, with the development of blocks like cybersecurity frameworks, developed in five steps, by the Nacional Institute of Information and Communications Technology (NIST):

- Identify, thus providing the needed basis for any organization to begin with or either professionalize its cybersecurity measures, by identifying systems, assets, data and resources which, when interrupted, may jeopardize port operators' activities.
- Protect, by taking some measures towards the identification and management of access control systems, thus assuring that data and systems shall only be acceded by the ones duly authorized. This issue is equally relevant to comply with national and international legal frames, such as the General Data Protection Regulation (GDPR). Protection issues are closely related to preserve services such as firewalls, endpoints as well as managing vulnerabilities and correction procedures. The investment in professional training for IT and OT human resources must always be preserved, aiming at providing the company with highly qualified personnel, duly aware of the risks and challenges close related to cybersecurity, and of the fact that people are always the weakest link in this issue, whenever there is an attack.

When we think of systems' violations involving phishing, social engineering or other forms of human contact, it is crucial to guarantee that the company's human resources are duly informed, aware and trained to detect these situations and any other suspicious behaviors, emails and IT changes; should this happen, and they will be a solid defense line. Protection and risks control measures must be implemented, as well as contingency planning, in order to protect events while guaranteeing the continuity of port operations.

- Detect, because despite the protection measures implemented by the organization, it always has the risk of being attacked; the only way to minimize the damages caused by an attack is to detect it as soon as possible. A research performed by IBM in 2018 concluded that the losses caused by a cyberattack are only detected 197 days (in average) after having occurred; the same research revealed that, in average, it takes 69 days to control the attack. It is determinant that both the IT and the OT are deeply acquainted with organization's base structure, so they can detect and prevent potential malicious activities.
- Respond and Recover, which, after a cyberattack, will only be possible if the organization has previously identified the need to perform backup and information restore processes, thus decreasing incidents' impact on port operations. Statistics data attest that the needed time to control a breach in security is extremely important, being mandatory to work on incidents' response and recovery, being these the two last steps to comply with the (NIST) framework. To properly plan the response to incidents and training is determinant for minimizing the time a breach in security takes to be controlled, as well as to prevent extreme damages, including the ones endangering the reputation of the organization. The teams endowed to respond to IT incidents must be ready to act according to predefined answer and a recovery strategy, which must always involve the Communication Department of the company, thus assuring an adequate internal and external communication strategy, surely helping to preserve and protect the company's image and reputation.

In conclusion, the goal of cyber-resilience is to reduce risks, while the cybersecurity teams' job is to contribute for decreasing the risk towards the compromise to guarantee confidentiality, integrity and data, processes, and business availableness. The lack of a true awareness and compromise from top management towards cybersecurity might prove to be incompatible with the achieving of cybersecurity maturity, due to a tendency from top management to neglect these issues, thus avoiding increasing costs by performing the needed investments.

According to the World Economic Forum, economic losses closely related to cybercrime are expected to reach $3 trillion US dollars in 2020, thus representing nearly 3,4% of the gross domestic product (GDP), as stated on the World Economic Forum 2020, which took place in Davos.

The scope of the International Safety Management Code (ISM) - Guidelines on Maritime Cyber Risk Management, has been broadened in 2017 with specific guiding lines, fifteen of which recognizing that cybertechnologies have become crucial for operating and managing various critical systems in what concerns the safety and protection of maritime transport, as well as for the protection of maritime environment. These guiding lines have attested that vulnerabilities arising from the access or interconnections, or through the systems network, may provide for the risks to be handled. We must also enhance IMO's decision to broaden the ISM Code, thus comprising cybernetic risks in maritime transport (MSC-FAL.1/Circ.3), plus the NIST Cyber Security Framework approach, thus widening the scope to port authorities. Also, to refer that IMO considers that the next approach shall consist of the definition on how these issues must be managed within the ISPS code context.

JUL – LOGISTIC SINGLE WINDOW

In compliance with the recommendations mentioned on the previous chapter, the JUL – Logistic Single Window was developed in Portugal. The Council of Ministers resolution nº 175/2017 (November 24), approved the strategy aiming at enhancing the Portuguese ports competitiveness.

Aiming at proceeding with the project, the Council of Ministers approved the dispatch n. 2061/2017 (17 February), thus creating a Work Group focused on the implementation of the JUL, and comprised of the following parties:

- The Director General of the General Administration for Natural Resources, Safety and Maritime Services, as the Coordinator
- The Director General of the General Administration for the Sea Policy
- The CEOs of the national Port Authorities
- The CEO of Docapesca – Portos e Lotas, SA

The main goal of the JUL project is to accomplish a digital transformation strategy, duly aligned with the state-of-the-art tendencies in what concerns the development of port business, thus supporting collaboration and interoperability processes in what concerns logistic networks, comprising ports' hinterland and foreland. It also aims at harmonizing procedures, technology, and information exchange mechanisms among national ports. The Logistic SW (JUL) project aims at implementing a unique IT integrated solution in all Portuguese ports, supported by a new version of the JUP – Port SW (JUPIII), whose goal is to update and broaden the JUP system along the whole logistic chain, thus comprising the land means of transport while developing connections to the dry ports and logistic platforms, bearing in mind an intermodal logistics. On the other hand, the JUL also aims at assuring a flow of information while enhancing both the Portuguese ports and the concerning logistic chains efficiency, through procedures simplification and dematerialization in transports, whether nationally or internationally, by reducing administrative costs and freight transit times and, lastly, the increase of efficiency and competitiveness in logistic chains.

The fulfilment of the project comprises the development of a new National Reference Model (MRN2) and the implementing of the JUL in each Port Authority, thus including the settlement of both the basic Hardware and Software, required for the platform's operation.

In order to put the project in practice, the Presidency of the Council of Ministers establishes the JUL on Decree-Law N. 158/2019 (22 October). The document defines the operational conditions and access credentials to the JUL, as well as the concerning governance and operation, while transposing the European Parliament and Council Directive 2010/65/UE, from October 20, 2010, which relates to the declaration formalities required to vessels when arriving or leaving the ports form the Member States, as for what is established on the European Parliament and Council Directive 2017/2109, from November 15, 2017.

Within the scope of this project, and in order to define the Enterprise Architecture (EA) of the Logistic JUL, defined on the National Reference Model (MRN2), a series of phases were planned:

- Phase 1 – Project Organization and Management
- Phase 2 – Definition and creation of the MRN2
- Phase 3 – Implementation of the JUL System
- Phase 4 - Tests, Training, Trainers and Pilots

- Phase 5 – Training of final users and operation of the PRD JUL System
- Phase 6 – JUL System Guarantee

On October 19, 2020, the JUL began operating in the Port of Sines; a significant milestone and the culminating of more than two years of intensive teamwork between the various stakeholders of the national port and maritime sector, thus contributing to the accomplishment of the strategy defined to enhance port competitiveness, approved by the Government.

The collaboration among the different players and authorities in the maritime logistic network allows to register real time events, thus achieving a more accurate processes' alignment while enhancing the synchronism of each player's operations.

Figure 8. JUL logistic single window
(source: APS – Port of Sines and Algarve Authority, 2019)

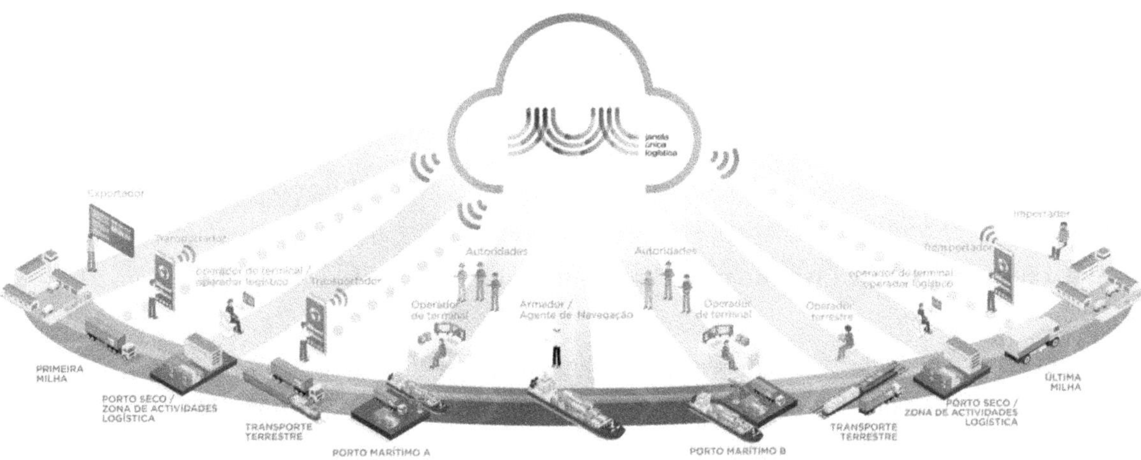

CONCLUSION

This research evidenced that the accomplishment of digital transformation requires the implementation of a series of measures involving considerable financial investments in digitalization and innovation. At a national level, the "Implementation of the Port Single Window III/Logistic SW" project is co-financed by COMPETE 2020, within the scope of the Priority Axis IV, under Notice 03/RAIT/2016. The total estimated investment for this project amounts to 5,1 million Euros, with an eligible investment of 4,3 million Euros.

It is expected that both the maritime-rail and maritime-road integration result on direct benefits to the port related economic players of more than 50 million Euros, in the first three years. In this manner, the JUL will allow the sharing of real time information among the players and authorities in the logistic network, thus aligning procedures to guarantee an improved level of synchronization in what regards operations. In what concerns the hinterland, Portuguese ports shall benefit from harmonized and optimized processes, while enabling the development of synchro modal cross-border corridors, comprising Portugal and Spain. This solution will also allow for the development of new agile and dematerialized layouts in what concerns the relationship with the authorities, while last mile processes shall also be covered by simple and low-cost applications.

Only with the commitment of governments and public entities and concerning legislation is possible to push forward Portuguese ports towards the leadership of digitalization processes, embodying the role of multimodal business' innovation accelerating platforms, by exploring last generation concepts and cargo collaborative ecosystems, Smart Ports, Extended Gateways, synchro modal networks, and Physical Internet. This commitment also provides for the sharing of real time information, as well as the alignment of network processes, in order to guarantee an enhanced synchronizing level between planning and multimodal services execution management, the support to cross-border corridors in the hinterland, and the consolidation of foreland tracking events, with information supporting the global experience of the JUL users, as well as the articulation with PCS from other countries and aggregating platforms (marketplaces, cargo, etc).

REFERENCES

Anunciação, P., & Zorrinho, C. (2006). *Urbanismo Organizacional: Como Gerir o Choque Tecnológico nas Empresas*. Edições Silabo.

Carbone, V., & de Martino, M. (2003). *The Changing role of ports in supply-chain management: an empirical analysis*. Taylor & Francis.

Comissão europeia. (2017). Livro Branco sobre o futuro da europa, reflexões e cenários para a EU – 27 em 2025

Decreto-Lei nº 158/2019 de 22 de outubro. Diário da República nº 203, Serie I – Presidência do Conselho de Ministros – "Cria a Janela Única Logística, transpondo a Diretiva n.º 2010/65/EU"

Decreto-Lei n.º 53/2019 de 17 de abril. Diário da República nº 76, Série I - Presidência do Conselho de Ministros – "Estabelece o conceito de porto seco e define as regras, os procedimentos e a desmaterialização necessários para a sua implementação

Dias, J. C. Q. (2003). *Integração Logística em Tempo de Globalização: Que Estratégias e Políticas para Portugal*. Camarate, Cargo Edições.

Accelerating Digitalization. (2020). *Critical Actions to Strengthen the Resilience of the Maritime Supply Chain*. World Bank Group (WB), International Association of Ports and Harbours (IAPH), World Ports Sustainability Program (WPSP).

Diretiva 2010/65/EU do parlamento Europeu e do conselho – Formalidades de declaração exigidas aos navios à chegada e/ou à partida dos portos dos Estados-Membros e que revoga a Diretiva 2002/6/CE

Framework for Improving Critical Infrastructure Cybersecurity. (2018). *Nacional Institute os Information and Communications Technology*. NIST.

*Guidelines on Maritime Cyber Risk Management – ISM (*MSC-FAL.1/Circ.3)

How to Develop a Port Community System Guide. (2015). International Port Community System Association (IPCSA).

Pinto, C. J. (2016). *Impactos organizacionais, informacionais e tecnológicos da implementação da Diretiva 2010/65/EU (dissertação de mestrado).* Instituto Politécnico de Setúbal. Escola Superior de Ciências Empresariais.

Porter, M. E. (1993). A Vantagem Competitiva das Nações. Rio de Janeiro: Campus.

Porter, M.E. (1998). On competition. Boston: Harvard Business School Publishing.

Recommendation and Guidelines on establishing a Single Window. (2005). United Nations Centre for Trade Facilitation and Electronic Business.

Resolução do conselho de ministros nº 175/2017 Diário da República – Nº 227/2017, Série I de 2017-11-24. Estratégia para o aumento da competitividade da rede de portos comerciais do continente – Horizonte 2026

UN/CEFACT, recomendação nº 33 (2005)

UNCTAD. (2019). *Review of Maritime Transport.* United Nations Publications.

UNCTAD. (2020). *Review of Maritime Transport.* United Nations Publications.

Wang, Y., & Pettit, S. (2016). *E-Logistics – Managing Your Digital Supply Chains For Competitive Advantage.* London: Kogan Page.

ENDNOTES

1 Transhipment: The shipment of goods or containers to an intermediate destination.

2 EDIFACT: Electronic Data Interchange for Administration, Commerce and Transport.

3 XML: Extensible Markup Language.

4 United Nations Centre for Trade Facilitation and Electronic Business.

Chapter 8
Change Management:
Lean Digital Transformation

Nuno Geada
https://orcid.org/0000-0003-3755-0711
Polytechnic Institute of Setúbal, Portugal

ABSTRACT

Information is the driving force of organizations because it is in information systems that the decisions are made. The need to have adequate infrastructure for collection, storage, processing, and distribution in an organization means that an appreciable part of the organization's effort in terms of human and financial resources is channeled in this direction. This chapter aims at the development and consequent application of change management, for optimization of information and process management based on the Lean methodology in information systems. The analysis and implementation of infrastructure for information management is based on eliminating waste and activities without added value, thus imparting continuous improvement, in order to achieve the goals/objectives proposed towards excellence and success and optimization processes and services. In order to achieve the objective of this project, a survey and analysis of the requirements of the IT processes to be able to construct and implement change management are done.

INTRODUCTION

Over the years, automation and evolution of the industry, results from great technological changes, which allow the creation of bounding between human resources and financial resources. It is possible to produce more and better and at lowest costs, leading companies to invest increasingly in their Information Systems. The pressure on the industrial business sector is increasing nowadays, there is a strong competitiveness among sectors. Oftentimes, we have better-informed customers demanding, for short and tight delivery times at lower costs, and a very high level of quality standards of excellence. The implementation of the Lean methodology comes with the scope of reducing operations with no added value, by eliminating waste from processes, through methods, techniques, and tools (Whomack & Jones, 2003; Bell & Orzen, 2012).

DOI: 10.4018/978-1-7998-7452-2.ch008

This paper aims to the objective to apply the principles of the Lean methodology and concept to the processes that leads to manage digital transformation, in order to create the strategies, methods, processes and increase the efficiency and effectiveness of the processes associated to the level business, eliminating or avoiding generated the traditional waste. So, Lean Digital concentrates instead on eliminating digital waste while maximizing data profit.

LEAN METHODOLOGY

The Lean concept emerged after the Second World War with the Toyota brand. So, after the Second World War, with the Japanese economy devastated, Toyota defined 7 types of waste and adopted a strategy to eliminate it (Ohno, 1988); (Teresko, 2006). This concept of waste elimination became the basis of the Toyota Production System. This concept was taken to the west under the name of Lean Manufacturing (Womark et al, 1990); (Dennis, 2002) ;(Liker & Meirer, 2007). Lean Management aims to satisfy customers in terms of product and service quality and to reduce simultaneously process lead times (Fane, 2003).

The predefined objective of reducing non-productive times, disorganization, uncontrolled production that fosters and creates excesses. The lack of quality standards and excess production, creates tools and concepts discussed in all organizations of our era, either by consulting firms organized by internal teams of continuous improvement (Bell S., 2006). So, the main objective is to produce flexibly at the lowest possible costs, so it can be possible to become a competitive company. (Liker, 2004).

For an example, after the end of the Second World War, the Japanese industry had very low production levels, and suffered from an excessive scarcity of resources, after been defeated by the Allied forces, by the other way the United States of America and Europe applied mass production policies (Pinto J. P., 2010) and the economy was growing faster. So, in order to overcome the market instability and the post-war crisis, a Japanese company called Toyota Motor Corporation emerged.

Lean Thinking

Toyota had some emerging problems, (Ohno, 1988) and like today, which is an example in terms of efficiency and quality in the production of motor vehicles. Eiji Toyoda visited the Ford plant in Detroit in the United States of America and considered using the knowledge gained in his organization, but, after several observations and discussions with his best engineer, Taiichi Ohno, realized that mass production would not be the best path solution for Toyota, so the Japanese ended up realizing that it was necessary to face other markets, because they had to produce at low cost and price, and diversify the variety as best as they can.

Based on this innovative production model that the Toyota Production System was created. The term "Lean Thinking" was used to refer to the evolution of Toyota Production System (TPS) and the introduction of new concepts (Dennis, 2002) ; (Fane, 2003). Lean Production was defined as a production system that combined the advantages of the mass production system with the advantages of the handmade production system (Liker, 2004). Lean seeks a constant elimination of all types of waste, it is considered an "antidote to waste" according to (Whomack & Jones, 1996-2003), where waste refers to any human activity that does not add value. As far as known the concept was expanded to include not only human activities, but also all types of activities, resources, and processes that are used improperly, that contribute to increased costs, time, and customer satisfaction. One of the core principles of Lean Thinking is exactly the creation of add-value for individuals, enjoying their products or services.

There are five fundamental principles for the success of the Lean Thinking methodology, (Whomack & Jones, 1996-2003) ; (Dennis, 2002) ; (Bell & Orzen, 2012) ; (Pinto J. P., 2014); (Shingo & Ohno, 2017):

- **Create Value**: it is necessary to understand what the customer needs, since is who defines the value, and not the company itself;
- **Define the Value Chain:** organizations must satisfy all stakeholders (person or group, who manage the actions of an organization and who have a direct or indirect role in the management and results of that same organization, for example, people or companies that are related to a specific action or project (employees, managers, and the State), understanding the value chain of each stakeholder, in order to provide value;
- **Optimize the Flow**: the production flow must be continuous, without interruptions, to avoid creating intermediate stocks, which reduces lead time and increases quality;
- **Pull System**: the customer leads the process, that is, the production corresponds exactly to the quantity and the date the customer wants, which allows for a reduction in stocks and an appreciation of the product;
- **Perfection**: encourage continuous improvement at all levels of the organization until it is possible to provide only what the customer considers value, instantly and with zero waste.

According to picture below Lean focuses on eliminating traditional waste while maximizing customer value.

Figure 1. Lean waste
Source (Jameel, 2018)

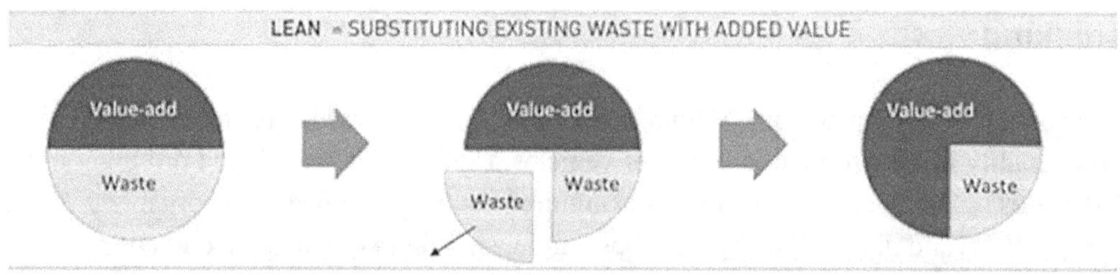

Companies that fail to anchor their continuous improvement efforts with principles rather than tools may experience short-term localized results, but will not achieve the broad acceptance needed for sustained improvement. Without a clear grasp of Lean principles, focus on Lean tools is like sailing a ship without a rudder (Dennis, 2002) ; (Bell S., 2006). Although, none of the fundamental principles will work 100% sure if the essential critical factors are not properly controlled (Shingo & Ohno, 2017).

So, according to authors below, here is the following:

- **Customer Value** - As one of the founders of the TPS, Taiichi Ohno (Liker, 2004, p. 7), formulated to add value to the customer and reduce waste. One of lean's main pillars is to create an operation where the work adds value for the customer and reduce the work that does not;
- **Great People** - Several sources e.g. Liker and Meier (2007), Sun (2008), explain that Toyota believes that their competitive differentiation comes from the great people they develop. Talented people that are taught the TPS from the beginning;
- **Think Long-Term and Substantial** - The philosophy, goals, expectations, openness, and outcomes must be long-term and understood by everyone (Liker, 2004), (Sun, 2008), (Dennis, 2002).
- **Change with Small Improvements** - According to Liker and Meirer (2007), Sun (2008) lean is about making small, but continuous improvements. Change is essential in order to survive in today's developing world;
- **Understand and Commit** - Also must the entire organization understand and be committed to the philosophy of lean in order to improve it. For an example when managers use the principle Genchi genbutsu (Dennis, 2002).
- **Involve Shop Floor Workers** - In order to make change sustainable and successful it is essential to involve workers in the decision-making process. Adapting the principle of involving from the bottom and up (Sun, 2008), Fane et al. (2003) emphasizes the knowledge that the shop-floor workers have and the importance of them sharing it;
- **Standardized Work** - According to Liker and Meirer, (2007) standardized work facilitates the process of improvements. This also facilitates the possibilities of several people to learn the same work.
- **Leaders Must Teach** - Toyota believes that the leader's most important job is to teach others. The organization must develop a learning culture, which should never stop, Liker and Meirer, (2007)
- **Communication** - Once again, communication is brought up in order to succeed in an organization. According to several sources (e.g. Liker and Meirer (2007) and Liker (2004)) communication is important in order to learn, support, listen and much more which is essential in a developing organization.
- **Job Security** - Dennis (2002) states that Toyota is clear with the message to its employees, that no changes will ever risk their job security. The only thing that may happen is other tasks and responsibilities.
- **Lean Everywhere** - In order to implement Lean and gain its benefits, it must exist in the entire organization (Teresko, 2006).
- **Educate and Train** - As mentioned, the people are the most valuable resource which if they are continuously trained and educated, will result in a great long-term investment. (Fane et al. 2003) (Liker and Meirer, 2007).

So, the objective of Lean methodology is to focus on the continuous improvement of processes and services, and the respective use of a set of tools and methods to achieve continuous improvement, so it is necessary to understand customers and what they value, in order to define the value flows and processes within the organization that constitute the services that customers envision, as well as their supply chain (Bell S., 2006) ; (Bell & Orzen, 2012) ; (Jameel, 2018) . To satisfy customers, organizations must eliminate or at least reduce unnecessary activities that customers do not want to pay for. Identifying and eliminating waste is fundamental to being a Lean organization, as the systematic attack on waste is also a systematic attack on the underlying factors such as poor quality and fundamental management problems. In this way, we can say that the Lean thinking is a system that aims to create organizations that are constantly learning, through continuous improvement processes generating value (Meier & Liker, 2005) (Bell S., 2006).

Lean Digital Thinking

Speaking of continuous improvement processes, the Lean methodology itself undergoes mutations and changes, using digital technology generating waste and profit.

Digital waste is defined as all the data that is not accounted for, or combined in redundant, wrong, or misleading information, while data profit is defined as all data combined with relevant information for the user, permitting to make the correct choices. Even structured data may be in some cases perceived as digital waste. Digital waste accumulation may even render a system unaffordable to maintain both technically and economically. So, in order for a digital transformation to succeed it is advisable to follow a lean digital strategy which focuses on eliminating digital waste while maximizing data profit (Angelopoulos, et al 2019).

According to Jameel (2018), digital waste is defined as all the data that is not accounted for, or combined in redundant, wrong, or misleading information: whoever is unable to harness the 'wealth' of data available, wastes precious assets. So, the scope is to extracting\removing waste and create more data profit (called in traditional Lean Add-Value) that is defined as all data combined with relevant information for the users. (Figure 2)

Figure 2. Digital waste
Source (Jameel, 2018)

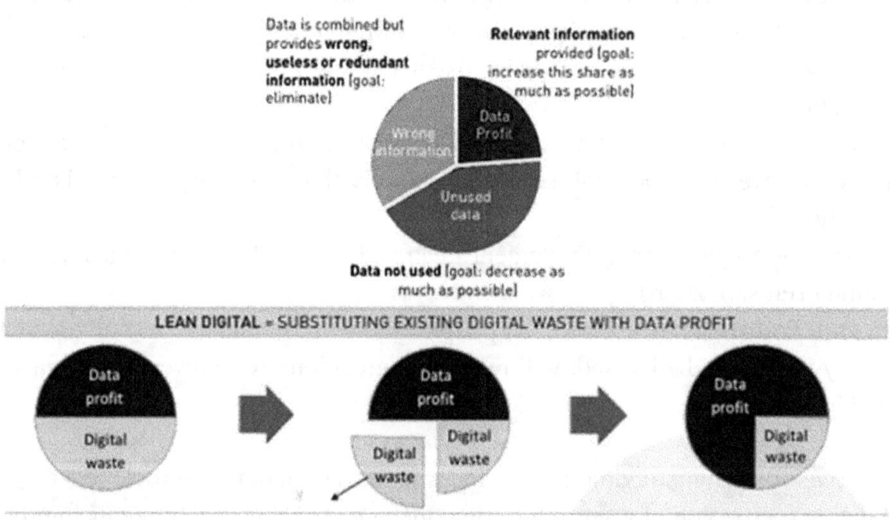

So, from the standard Lean principles emerged the fundamental Lean principles for the success of the Lean Thinking methodology on digital world (Jameel, 2018):

- **Generation of transparency on strategy**, at corporate and business level, which is supported by the definition of the future state Lean Digital vision;
- **Design of different Lean digital value streams**, which will be the basis to analyse and to understand interactions and customers' needs along the value streams;
- **Definition of a Lean Digital agenda**, enabling the organization to achieve the desired results;
- **Implementation** of traditional Lean projects to ensure that processes, structure, products, and services are optimized in parallel to the definition and execution of the Lean digital projects guaranteeing mindset change and sustainability;
- Implementation of Lean Digital projects to **define and establish systems of engagement.**

The figure below illustrates a schema of the lean digital principles.

Figure 3. Lean digital principles
Source (Jameel, 2018)

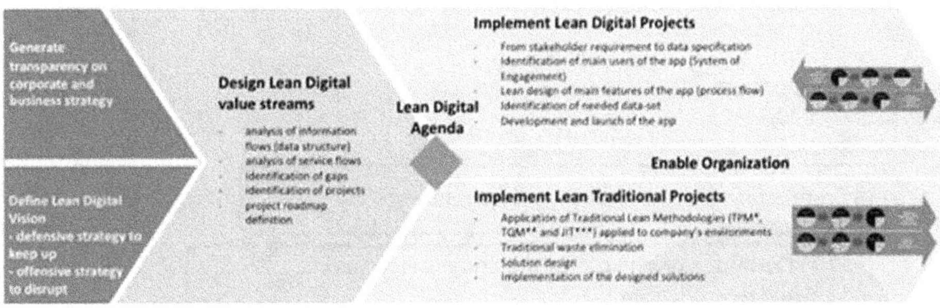

Companies are experiencing the constant pressure to go digital, and know that they need to do so quickly before they are overthrought by innovative and digitally-focused competitors and new entrants as well. So, to achieve equilibrium to the principles this is not an easy process, there are some barriers and challenges to overtake (Jameel, 2018):

- Improving the customer experience;
- Running tighter cost controls;
- Achieving higher performance from the workforce and changing the 'legacy mindset.';
- Generating higher employee engagement;
- Retaining current talents and attracting new ones;
- Acquiring entirely new capabilities in:
  - data analytics;
  - mobile technologies;
  - social media.
- Rethinking business models and strategies;
- Continuously launching new ideas;

The creation of systems of engagement and the increase of data profit is challenging for most companies because traditionally they are more used to evolve their IT systems rather than revolutionizing them.

Most businesses have understood that they need to generating high-level engagement of their ecosystem of users, but most of the time they fail in their attempt due to a lack of attention in designing the right user experience. The experience is a must because it provides advantages to overtake the impacts generated by all processes and events associated to lean digital transformations.

IMPACTS OF LEAN DIGITAL TRANSFORMATION

In order to carry out the analysis on the impact of digital transformation, according to Schumacher, et al (2020) an approach of four steps has been used. As a first step, hypothesis for the specific analysis to be carried out are postulated with regard to the latest academic findings. To address these hypotheses in the literature review, the second step is the definition of feasible criteria to characterize the existing literature. The third step is the execution of the literature review with central positions and relevant contributions. As a last step, the evaluation of the hypotheses is carried out with regard to the literature review. Indicators for digital transformation-induced development are derived (Schumacher, et al, 2020).

Figure 4. Lean digital approach
Source (Schumacher, et al 2020)

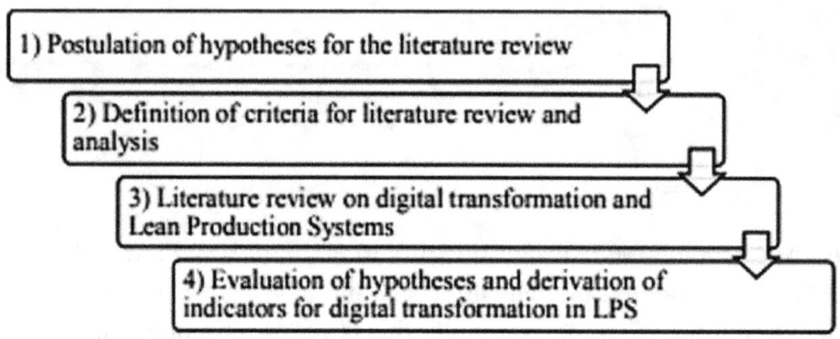

- **Processes** are becoming more agile and will be adapted to 4.0 technologies characteristics;
- **Principles** are of general nature and seem to be compatible to 4.0 technologies. IT can improve performance, especially the efficiency of processes. Difficulties in the integration process and implementing Lean tools;
- **Methods and tools** are subject to significant change induced by digital transformation.
- **Framework** is set and its productivity converges towards saturation; 4.0 seems to enhance it. Digital transformation as a third wave in Lean (isolated analog, holistic analog, digital) Challenge: lean is a static set of rules, 4.0 technologies advance dynamically;
- **Shop floor** elements are digitally integrated and should be represented in Lean frameworks.
- **Strategy** remains enterprise-specific; production strategies are influenced by digital transformation, 4.0 framework for SME with significant innovations on process, method & tool level and Holistic approach with humans-technology organization needed;

Lean digital drives impact by architecting how enterprises run beyond the front-office into middle- and back-offices, by focusing on what generates step-change business outcomes and by avoiding the rest. This is particularly important in large enterprises that, as described in the "digitizing broken processes" box above, have tiered and often organizations, and rely on complex legacy systems for their operations (Genpack Research Insitute, 2017).

Please analyse Figure 5.

Figure 5. Lean digital drives digital impact by harnessing design thinking and lean principles
Source (Genpack Research Insitute, 2017)

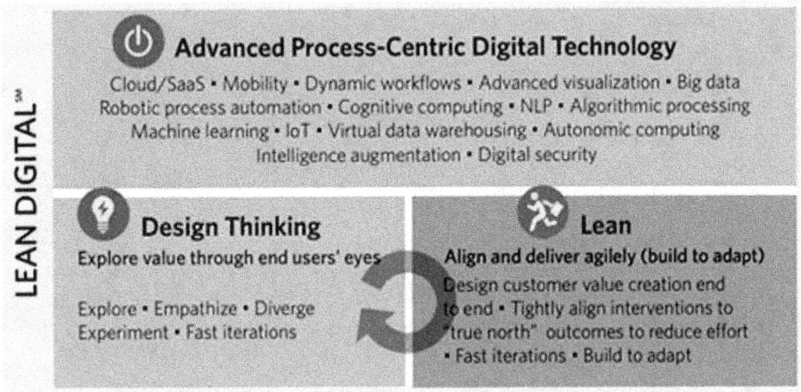

The return of information is very important both within a recursive path from action, to visibility, to adaptation and subsequent action and across them. It is normal to see mature processes that have adopted Six Sigma to at some point require redesigning through design thinking and Lean strategy models.

DIGITAL LEAN STRATEGY MODELS

The organizational environment is evolving toward an integrated and hybridized network that contains elements of old and new technologies working synergistically to provide reliable, affordable, and sustainable businesses, and communities around the world (Angelopoulos, 2019).

According to Angelopoulos, et al (2019) the starting point for digitalization is the designing a digital strategy, based on mythologies that permits to apply good practices. Digitalization drivers are often the IT departments, but specialist departments and management must also support the digital strategy since all areas of the company are affected by digitalization. The digital strategy forms the basis for developing digital business models. Modern methods are used to analyze challenges and problems, create ideas and fine approaches to resolving issues. It is important to have a methodological expertise to the entire organization. Normally, methodologies should be used to enable the application of good practices, such as Information Technology Infrastructure Library, (ITIL). So, based on ITIL it is possible to create models of management that will help to control and implement strategy.

For instance, it can be used a model like "Improvement Idea Implementation Methodology (IIIM)". This model is designed to support information system managers in managing change and predicting possible impacts, as corroborating the data returned by the applied survey all change projects must be managed. Today there are still organizations \ institutions that do not adopt ITIL-associated practices. The origin of the creation of this model is based on the combination of procedural variables that constitute the ITIL cycle versus the Plan-Do-Check-Act (PDCA) and Standardize-Do-Check-Act (SDCA) cycle (Geada, 2019).

Figure 6. "Improvement Idea Implementation Methodology (IIIM)"
Source (Geada, 2019)

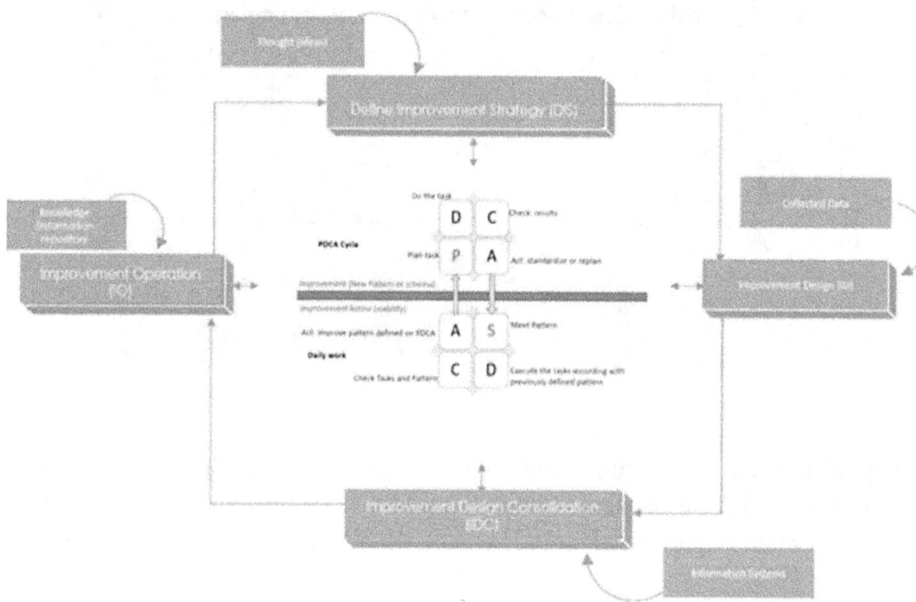

The first phase of the model, "Define Improvement Strategy" (DIS), which consists in defining the objectives and requirements of the thought improvement. Therefore, DIS fits into the first phase of cycle ITIL, *Service Strategy* that all requirements and business needs are surveyed, and where three important variables are used:

The fase ID permits:

- Provide guidance for the design and development of services and service management practices;
- Cover design principles and methods for converting strategic objectives into service portfolios and service goods.

It should be noted that service design is not only limited to new services and processes, but also includes the changes and improvements necessary to enable value to be increased or maintained during the model cycle, giving continuity and achieving service levels, positioning themselves in accordance with the rules and regulations. In this sense, it is possible to create guidance for companies and / or organizations on how to develop and improve design capabilities for change management. At the most transitional level, it is the phase where a service is tested and employed and activated and changed in the real and production environment, providing guidance for developing and enhancing capabilities to introduce new and modified services and processes.

In the Consolidation of Improvement Design (CID) phase that the validation of all variables designed and designed for operationalization is ensured. Therefore, the value identified in the DIS phase, and built in the ID phase, namely in the design, are carried over so that they can be put into service by describing the good practices. The transition provides guidance on managing complexity related to changes in change and meeting management processes, avoiding unintended consequences, and allowing constant innovation. In the Improvement Operation (IO) is when improvement is finally implemented, based on knowledge, and consolidated design.

This applies within a certain methodology "X", minimizes the impact, on the three important variables of change, the people, the environment, and the processes, so the following assumptions should be considered:

- Choose terms used to describe concepts in the context, namely instead of calling change or change, the term "Improvement Idea" (II) as it has a more positive impact when conveying the information that a change will happen;
- Ensure that the continuous improvement process is applied at all stages, not just the last one;
- We must always involve everyone in the improvement process;
- Always adapt improvement to the surrounding environment.

There is another model suggested by the author Angelopoulos, et al (2019), to complement it based on agile methods, see figure 7.

Figure 7. Digital business model
Source (Angelopoulos, et al 2019)

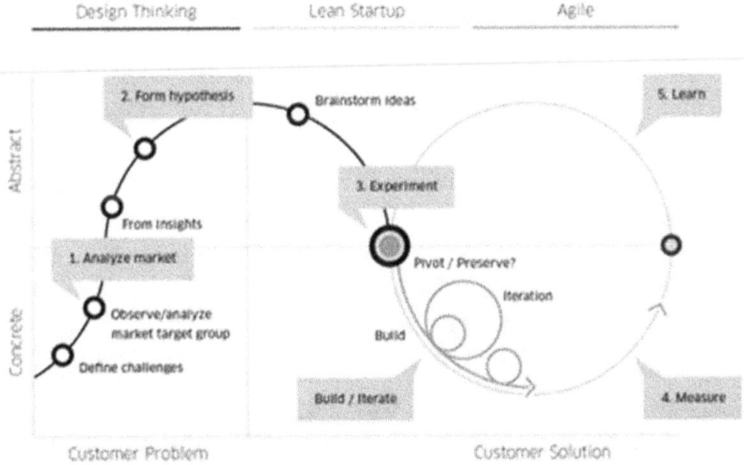

This model consists in scope of business software and some parts of business core items as follows:

- **Design Thinking:** is an approach to problem solving and finding ideas, based on user perception, as well as user needs and motivations. Design Thinking assumes that the collaboration of people of different disciplines in a creative environment can solve problems better.
- **Lean Startup**: is a method for the rapid development of organizational units or products with the leanest possible processes and little capital expenditure. The focus is on a reduced conceptual phase, a short time-to-market, and the fastest possible creation of a prototype on the market. The prototype is continuously developed in short, iterative product release cycles while, it is possible to react quickly to validated learning-by-doing experiences and customer feedback and wishes at no great cost.
- **Establishing Agile Methods:** The appropriate methodological competence is of fundamental importance for the success of a digital organization. It is needed to meet challenges as well as to develop and efficiently implement digital business models.

This applies to structures, methods, and processes as well as the culture within the company. In order to implement digital business models efficiently and effectively, to bring prototypes to the market quickly and to react flexibly to customer feedback and market changes, an iterative approach with agile methods offers a considerable advantage. The establishment of agile methods applies to the methodology of software development and project management, including processes and structures, as well as corporate culture. These two models presented when combined can be very powerful and useful. They allow to control the entire digital business transition environment.

CONCLUSION

This literature review on the digital transformation and its impact on Lean Digital Transformation presents valuable insights on the latest scientific literature and contributes to research, while praising the benefits achieved by lean manufacturing implementation, also made it clear that it is quite challenging to transform to lean. The main reason behind this challenge is the involvement of change in many aspects and stages within the organisation. The authors have designed the evolution of lean manufacturing from its root core in Toyota and its evolution into a more complex and successful concept that is applicable in many industries and countries.

Digital changes the fundamentals of competition in many industries, from manufacturing to financial services. However, today's challenge is not only digital technology; it is also the organizations' ability to reimagine and reinvent how businesses can run scale harnessing digital's power to adapt and compete. It is imperative that organizations do not digitize wrong processes and construct their recursive action-data-insight-action flows. A practical Lean Digital approach can not only produce digital technologies. The business and given that Information Systems are a dynamic and versatile area, so we only need to know what we want, how we want it and the way we want it to be built.

At the business level, the advantage of having the application of these methodology is the fact that it affects business processes making them efficient, guaranteeing the quality of service delivery, process optimization, productivity, customer satisfaction, and in growth, contributing to the stability and survival of the organization, erasing the waste that is created by incomplete processes and tasks.

Lean Digital Transformation can lead more to a customer centricity rather product. This happen because on customer centricity approach, the primary goal to a company is to establish a long-term relationship with the customer, rather than market share. In terms of strategy, therefore, customer-centricity adopts a buyer-driven pull approach as against a sales-driven push approach.

REFERENCES

Alaerds, R., Grove, S., Besteman, S., & Bilderbeek, P. (2017). *The Foundations of our Digital Economy*. Wouter Pegtel & Splend.

Anand, G. a. (2009). Development of a framework for lean manufacturing systems. *International Journal of Services and Operations Management, 5*(5), 687–716.

Anand, G. a. (2010). Analysis of lean manufacturing frameworks. Advanced Manufacturing Systems, 9(1), 1–30.

Angelopoulos, M., Kontakou, C., & Pollalis, Y. (2019, August 12). *Digital Transformation and Lean Management. Challenges in the Energy Industry of Utilities. A Review*. MPRA.

Axelos. (n.d.). Retrieved from https://www.axelos.com/: https://www.axelos.com/

Azharul, K.-U.-Z. (2013). A methodology for effective implementation of lean strategies and its performance evaluation in manufacturing organizations. Business Process Management Journal, 19, 169-196.

Bell, S. (2006). *Lean Enterprise Systems: Using IT for Continuous Improvement*. John Wiley & Sons.

Bell, S. C., & Orzen, M. A. (2012). *Lean IT: Enabling and Sustaining Your Lean Transformation*. BP Trends.

Burnes, B. (2017). *Managing Change* (7th ed.). Pearson Education Limited.

Cartlidge, A., Hanna, A., Rudd, C., Macfarlane, I., Windebank, J., & Rance, S. (2007). *An Introductory overview of ITIL*. The UK Chapter of the itSMF.

de Ven, A. V., & Hargrave, T. (2000). Social, Technical, and Institutional Change. Academic Press.

Dennis, P. (2002). *Lean Production Simplified - A Plain Language Guide to the World's Most Powerful Production System*. Productivity Press.

Fane, G. R., Vaghefi, M. R., Deusen, C., & Woods, L. A. (2003). Competitive advantage the Toyota way'. *Business Strategy Review, 14*(4), 51–60. doi:10.1111/j..2003.00286.x

Galpin, T. J. (1996). *The Human Side of Change: A Practical Guide to Organization Redesign*. Academic Press.

Geada, N. (2019). Change Management in the Digital Economy: Model Proposal. *International Journal of Innovation in the Digital Economy, 11*(3), 4.

Genpack Research Institute. (2017). *Putting Digital to Work - The Lean Digital Way*. Author.

Greenan, N. (2003). Organisational change, technology, employment and skills: an empirical study of French manufacturing. *Cambridge Journal of Economics, 27*(2), 287–316.

Hammer, M., & Champy, J. (1994). *Reengineering the Corporation: A manifesto for business revolution*. Nicholas Brealy.

Imai, M. (1997). *Gemba Kaizen: A Commonsense, Low-Cost Approach to Management*. McGraw Hill Professional.

Imai, M. (2006). *Gemba Kaizen*. MT Biznes.

Jameel, A. L. (2018). *Four Principles Management Consulting FZ-LLC*. Lean Digital Transformation.

Jones, G. (2007). *Organisational Theory, Design, and Change*. Pearson Prentice.

Kling, R., & Lamb, R. (1999, Setembro). IT and Organiacional Change in Digital Economies. *A Socio-Technical Approach*, 17-25.

Laudon, K. C., & Laudon, J. P. (2014). Managment Information Systems - Managing the Digital Firm (13th ed.). Pearson.

Liker, J. F. (2004). *The Toyota Way - 14 Management Principles from the World's Greatest Manufacturer*. McGraw-Hill.

Liker, J. F., & Meirer, D. P. (2007). *Toyota Talent - Developing your People The Toyota Way*. McGraw-Hill.

Meier, D., & Liker, J. (2005). *The Toyota Way Fieldbook*. McGraw Hill Professional.

Motwani, J. (2003). business process change framework for examining lean manufacturing: Case study'. *Industrial Management & Data Systems, 103*(5), 339–346. doi:10.1108/02635570310477398

Narang, R. (2008). Some issues to consider in lean production. *2008 First International Conference on Emerging Trends in Engineering and Technology*, 749–753.

O'Brien, J., & Marakas, G. M. (2011). *Management Information Systems*. Mcgraw-Hill.

Ohno, T. (1988). *Toyota Production System: Beyond Large-Scale Production*. CRC Press.

Pinto, J. P. (2010). Gestão de Operações Na Indústria e nos Serviços (3rd ed.). Lisboa: Lidel -Edições Tecnica Lda.

Pinto, J. P. (2014). *Pensamento Lean-A filosofia das organizações vencedoras*. Lidel.

Plenert, G. (2007). Reinventing Lean: Introducing Lean Management into the Supply Chain. Elsevier.

Requeijo, J. F., & Pereira, Z. L. (2008). *QUALIDADE: Planeamento e Controlo Estatístico de Processos*. Prefácio.

Schumacher, S., Bildstein, A., & Bauernhansl, T. (2020). The Impact of the Digital Transformation on Lean Production Systems. *53rd CIRP Conference on Manufacturing System*. 10.1016/j.procir.2020.03.066

Shingo, S., & Ohno, T. (2017). *Fundamental Principles of Lean Manufacturing*. Productivity Press.

Sun, W. (2008). Lean changes mindsets. *Industrial Engineering (American Institute of Industrial Engineers), 40*.

Teresko, J. (2006). *Learning From Toyota - Again' Rebuilding U.S. Manufacturing* (Vol. 225). www.industryweek.com

Ustundag, A., & Cevikcan, E. (2018). *Industry 4.0: Managing The Digital Transformation*. Springer. doi:10.1007/978-3-319-57870-5

Van Haren - Publishing. (2011). *ITIL Foundations - Best Practice*. Author.

Weick, K., & Quinn, R. (1999). *Organizational Change and Development. Annual Revision Psychology*.

Whomack, J. P., & Jones, D. T. (1996-2003). *Lean Thinking*. Free Press.

Womark, J. P., Jones, D., & Ros, D. (1990). *The Machine that Changed the World*. Macmillan Publishing Company.

Chapter 9
Analysis and Evaluation of Lean Culture Adoption:
The Industrial Multinational Company Case Study in Portugal

Denise Lopes Pereira
Polytechnic Institute of Setúbal, Portugal

ABSTRACT

With increased competition, speculation, changes in customer expectations, and world events that significantly disturb the markets, managers have more technical difficulties in coordinating/monitoring organizational processes and practices. The lean philosophy made it possible, through the identification of the most recurring problems within the company under study, to understand the restructuring needs of the organizational culture, the revision of fundamental key processes, the significant improvement in response times, and the assumption of a commitment by stakeholders from the various areas of activity in the company. In this context, this work, carried out in the scope of internship, aims to analyze and evaluate the importance of adopting the lean concept in a multinational company, inferring about the benefits achieved and the improvements felt with regard to competitiveness and service level. In this sense, it was clear that the adoption of lean allows the optimization of key processes.

INTRODUCTION

The concept and the Lean approach defined uncontroversial themes of the reality of management in economic associations. Although Lean has emerged in the automotive industry, its relevance has been rapidly adopted in other sectors of economic activity, currently being found in most organizational concerns as a guiding axis for efficiency and effectiveness gains. We can thus say that Lean aims to improve economic competitiveness.

Strong competition and pressure from markets to reduce prices permanently challenges management to optimize the respective organizational practices in order to free unnecessary activities to increase

DOI: 10.4018/978-1-7998-7452-2.ch009

efficiency and effectiveness. Lean encourages the use of the necessary resources, that is, nothing more than the identification of what is necessary to carry out a certain activity, process or project. In this way, it is possible to minimize waste, reduce costs and increase competitiveness.

Its adoption should not be developed through specific and targeted approaches to the specificity of existing problems. Lean must have a holistic or systemic perspective at its base that facilitates the increase of benefits to the entire organization, which presupposes the contextualization of problems within a broader scope of organizational functioning or of the value chain. Its correct adoption and application by management, by providing a better use of resources, (human, material, financial), allows direct gains to be obtained associated with the specificity of the problems treated and improved situations, but also the generation of synergistic gains by systemic effects in other organizational areas.

Referring to some examples of benefits that can be obtained with the adoption of Lean, we can consider the identification and elimination of obstacles that restricts the normal execution of processes, the clarification of workflows and the consequent improvement of communication between the respective stakeholders; the adequacy between the inputs and outputs associated with the various activities that integrate the processes, the adequacy of demand to the products or services requested, guarantee of the quality levels associated with the final products and services, among others.

The Lean approach thus assumes three central ideas in the scope of management: delivering value from the customer's perspective; the elimination of waste (everything that does not add value to the final product) and continuous improvement.

In general, nowadays organizations are driven by hundreds of business processes. However focusing on a core and restricted number of business process will create a Lean culture. Lean methodology cannot be implemented in the same way in every situation: it needs to be adjusted to the particular characteristics of each sector of business and be able to respond effectively to what customer demands.

Lean is about a mindset that must be established among all organization's areas - dealing openly with mistakes to improve processes. In fact, learning from the mistake is only identifying ways to progress, thinking about doing things better, quicker, at economical cost, generating minimal waste in terms of materials, time and rework.

Everyone in an organization is called upon to contribute to sustain the "Lean approach" (its practices and tools) for a lasting period, transforming conceptual thinking into concrete actions where leaders and followers are actively participating in the search for solutions. Leadership in this context of cultural change must be consistent and persevering. Lean manager leads by example, takes initiative and demonstrates that there will always be a better way to go between points A and B. He also leads by empowerment, delivering more responsibility to employees and at the same time more autonomy.

Processes aligned with well-defined boundaries and tasks translate into an advantageous support for effective time management, reducing the complexity of the actions and consequently the waste that result from them. In fact, trainings and coordination with department managers contributes for bring a team to the same level of Lean understanding - together they all recognize the benefits of adopting Lean as a model and management tool. Above all, lean reinforces business process management supporting decision making and ensuring process optimization along the value chain.

The main objective of the present work is to highlight the study carried out in relation to the analysis and evaluation of the importance of adopting the lean concept by a multinational company, identifying which improvements have been achieved for the company with regard to competitiveness and service level.

This multinational company operates in the world of process measurement technology, automation solutions and service provision. For the company, it is very important to realize that everything starts and ends with the customer, so aligned processes mean positive experiences for customer and consequently his satisfaction and loyalty for the brand. BPM (Business Process Management) is one of the areas to be implemented in the Group with focus on process alignment. In this context, Lean emerges as an BPM's ally of in the relentless pursuit of general improvement in the structure and quality of the organization itself, with a focus on change management.

This work is composed of a general theoretical framework, identifying the objective and the pertinence of the choice. This is followed by the part of the specific theoretical framework of the theme, using a literary review that supports and contextualizes the concepts and studies already carried out in this area. Then more specifically we talk about the field where the research was inserted - the automation industry. The following chapter presents the objectives and methodology used to carry out this work. The results obtained are described in the next chapter, based on the improvement proposals discussed and presented. Finally, some considerations regarding the topic studied are presented and in the last chapter the bibliographic sources that served as the basis for the research are presented.

THEORETICAL FOUNDATION OF LEAN

Lean thinking comprises a complex set of ideas. It is based on creating a culture of continuous improvement in the work environment, where all members of an organization actively contribute to improving business performance.

In other words, lean is a set of good practices that, together with an adequate management model, bring great benefits, mainly from the perspective of cost reduction (Teixeira &Melim, 2014). Coming from the Toyota company, Lean is seen as a productive philosophy that organizes the company from the customer's point of view, reducing losses that do not add value to the product. Ohno (1997) argues that the main basis of the system is precisely the elimination of waste.

Lean is not about reducing staff and resources, first of all, it is about focusing people's efforts interactively by accelerating operations through the progressive elimination of waste and downtime created by bureaucratic processes.

If managed effectively, Lean can be the main philosophy that unites the organization in a relentless search for improvements (Atkinson, 2010). For Damrath (2012) the difference of a lean operating system has to do with the fact that the company learns through changes, in the search for solutions to problems, coordination and standardization.

According to Hines et al. (2004), the development of the Lean concept in general can be represented by dividing it into four stages. The following figure illustrates these four stages and provides an insight into how the Lean concept has gradually expanded over the past three decades (see Figure 1).

Over almost three decades, lean, initially implemented in the automobile sector, has expanded to other production areas (Damrath, 2012), giving rise today to a concept that has been expanded to include the perspective of organizational learning on two principles main: "continuous improvement" and "respect for people".

Teixeira and Melim (2014) quote Justa and Barreiros (2009) to demonstrate that Lean culture is the construction of an organizational culture aimed at the elimination of what does not add value, reducing stocks, transforming the behavior of leaders and followers for active participation in problem solving, standardization, cost reduction and innovation, therefore and as previously mentioned, continuous im-

Figure 1. Stages of lean evolution
(Belfrage & Hedberg, 2006)

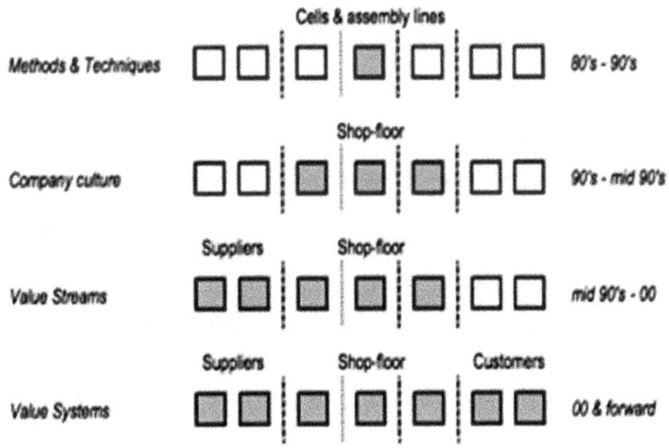

provement. In fact, Liker and Meier (2005) clarify that culture only changes after some successful change is made in people's actions and that they will come to realize that the new behavior brings advantages.

To build a Lean culture, it is necessary to organize practices and tools so that they give rise to a system (see Figure 2). Isolated applications usually give a very quick response, while not being kept for a long time, because if people do not understand the concept of the application of the tool, they will leave it in disuse in the short term. Only from the system that seeks the interaction of all tool applications can culture change be found (Teixeira & Melim, 2014).

Figure 2. Building dimensions of lean culture
(Justa & Barreiros, 2009)

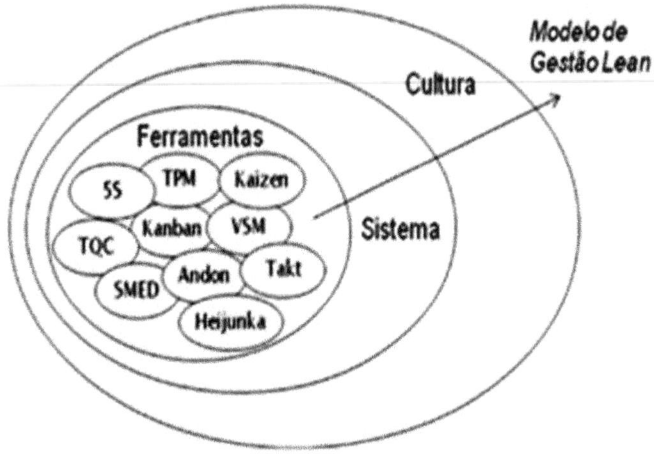

The true implementation of Lean culture is what gives sustainability to the system and ensures that it will continue. Although the application of Lean techniques is an important part of its success, a lean transformation is more about developing leadership behaviors, styles and strategies as the basis for creating a "Lean culture" (Testani & Ramakrishnan, 2012). Mann (2005) states that 80% of Lean success is changing the mindset or thinking of the organization's leaders, with senior leaders paving the way for the new Lean culture. In this sense, it is necessary to permanently monitor the change in culture as a way of directing implementation activities, based on methodologies and tools that support the control of critical factors for the business.

The transition to a Lean organization requires a significant investment of time (Womack & Jones, 1996). Locher (2011) adds that in fact the implementation of Lean only gains sustainability after normally 5 to 10 years. Considering then the fact that a Lean culture implementation process is long and presupposes a series of aligned activities, it is necessary that there is an evaluation reference. Therefore, the implementation as already mentioned will be continuous - a journey with a beginning, but never an end. It is a long-term journey that requires a perfect alignment between organizational strategy and business objectives (Locher, 2011).

However, many critical determinants need to be considered before an organization can embark on a Lean transformation (Dunn, 2009). Many of these aspects have been structured and are displayed in an iceberg model for implementing Lean (see Figure 3).

Figure 3. Iceberg model for lean implementation
(Grove et. al., 2010)

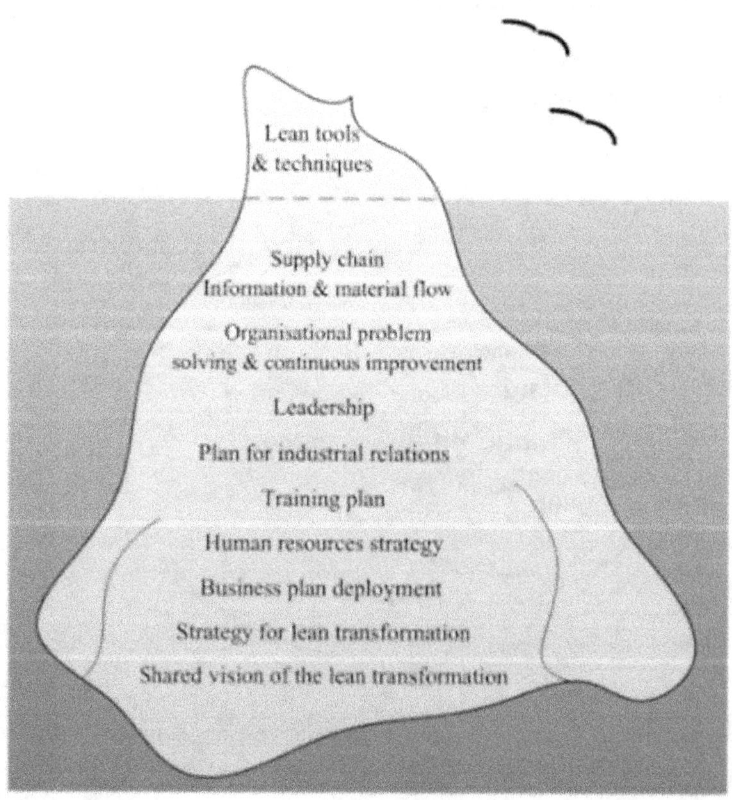

The iceberg model presented in the previous figure alludes to the essential elements/factors to be considered for a successful implementation of Lean. A deep Lean implementation requires that all tasks be implemented in an upward direction - from the bottom of the iceberg to the top (Grove et al., 2010). All essential components and tasks located below the waterline need to be considered before applying the "tools and techniques" (Damrath, 2012).

A solid foundation for Lean implementation needs to be established initially at a strategic level. From top management to operational management, the vision must be shared in terms of managing the changes that will occur.

Lean Principles and Implementation Phases

It is necessary to apply Lean in all aspects of the business, realizing exactly what the customers' needs are, from the first contact to the delivery of the good or service - only then will it be possible to sustain Lean practices over the years and the changes that all of this will imply management (Locher, 2011). Gustafsson et al. (2018) cite authors such as Womack and Jones (1996), Kessler (1999) and Sassanelli et al. (2015) to mention that being able to think Lean according to the literature, consists of five principles, as illustrated in Figure 4:

1. Determine value - identification of customers and specification of values is the most important step to know what the customer really values;
2. Value Stream Identification - identify the value stream. It is the understanding of the processes of delivering value to the customer;
3. Create Flow - eliminate waste in the value stream, which is usually found in the way the work is done;
4. Respond to pull - allow the customer to "pull" the value on demand;
5. Pursue perfection - the focus of perfection must be on continuous and incremental improvement, and through interaction and adaptation to changes in customer value.

According to Locher (2011), in addition to the 5 principles mentioned above, the implementation of Lean, requires the revision of 4 stages considered, equally essential:

- Stabilize,
- Standardize;
- View;
- Continuous improvement.

Stabilize

Initially, it is important to carefully identify a starting point, where it is necessary to create stability. It is necessary to ensure that the outputs are predictable and repetitive. Delivering to the customer what they want and when they want - to do it at the right time with appropriate resources and with quality - clearly implies clarifying and identifying their real needs, documenting key processes in a simple way (checklist), providing adequate training for all in the office and in the services - definition of a specific and transversal process that all employees understand and follow (Locher, 2011).

Figure 4. The five principles of lean thinking
(Damrath, 2012)

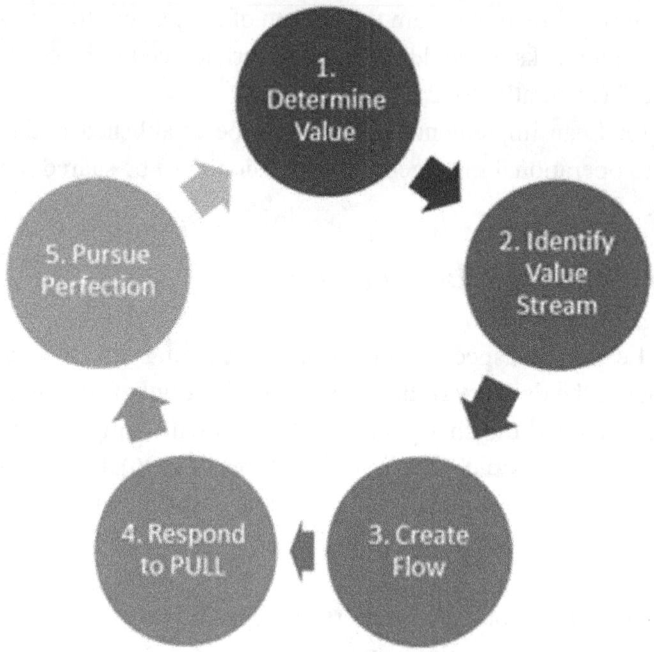

Standardize

The next step is to standardize processes, developing consistent practices that are categorically followed by everyone. At this stage, all stakeholders are able to accurately recognize and compare the "non-standard conditions" that may be interfering with activities. For this, it is extremely necessary to identify the waste that is generated as each specific process is taking place.

Lean, in this context, is seen as a problem solving system, capable of identifying and eliminating inefficiency or waste. If not verified, waste in processes can divert time to perform value-added work and, even worse, lead to a decrease in the value - product or service - that customers receive or perceive.

When it comes to eliminating waste, it is essential to know the concept of the 7 Muda (Locher, 2011). Japanese "waste" or "changes" are all activities that consume resources without creating value for the customer (Damrath, 2012). During the development of the Toyota Production System, the modern prototype of a lean company, Taiichi Ohno classified and defined the seven forms of waste that are also known as seven Ohno seedlings. Waste can result from overproduction, waiting time, transportation, inventory, processing, movement and product defects (see Figure 5).

Later, however, an eighth residue was added to Ohno's original list by other authors (see Figure 6), namely as "underutilized people" or unused human resources (Natasya et al., 2013).

Figure 5. The seven types of waste
(Melton, 2005)

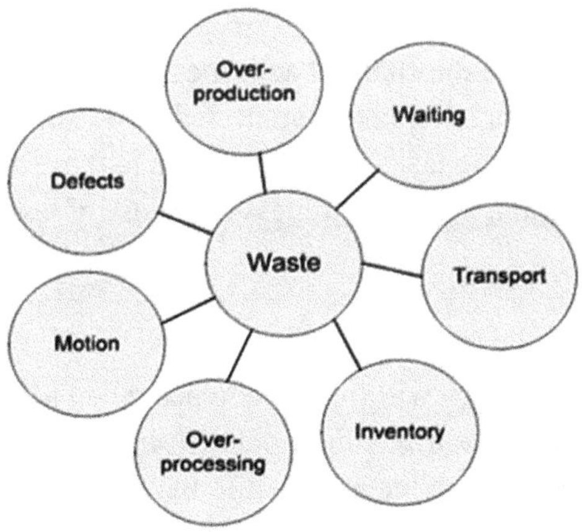

Make Visible

Figure 6. The eight types of waste
(Adapted from the website https://www.moresteam.com/University)

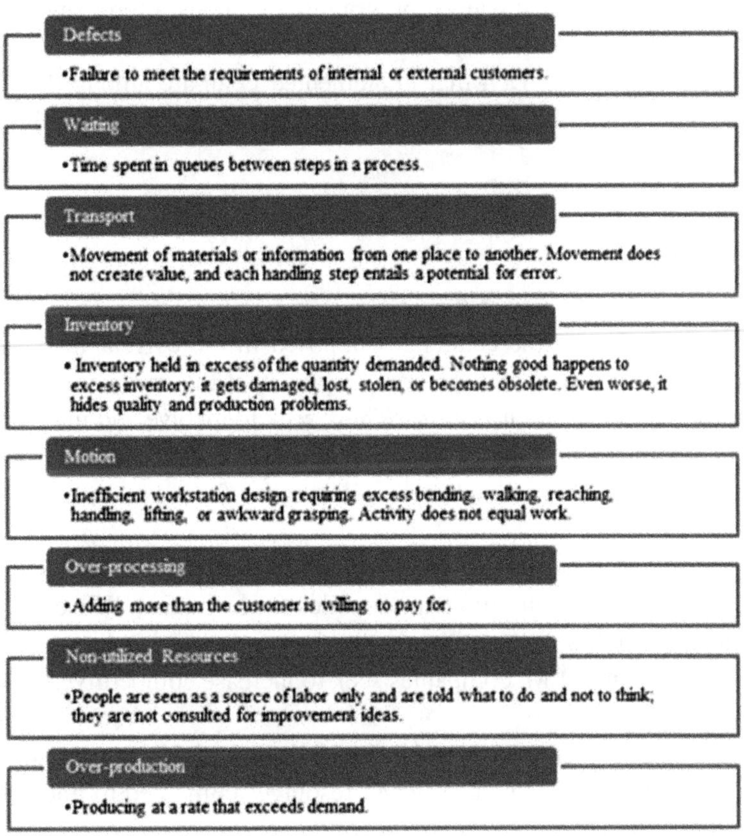

After identifying and eliminating waste, there follows the stage where it is necessary to make the work and consequently the entire process visible in order to be available to everyone - "out of sigth, out of mind" (Locher, 2011).

Using effective techniques to make the chain of activities as transparent as possible, it will allow for improved performance and communication between all, reduced task execution time and less effort to manage processes. It is important to emphasize that in addition to these advantages presented, it is above all essential that all stakeholders initially gain awareness and sense of responsibility for the role they play.

Continuous Improvement

The last step - continuous improvement - will only take place when the lean culture is deeply assumed by all employees, making this initiative a common practice in daily life, showing respect towards all parties involved (customers, suppliers, colleagues) while making this philosophy sustainable. In fact, continuous improvement is nothing but the constant search for more waste (Bob, 2008), expanding the reach of lean for everyone involved in the business value chain.

A successful transition requires a deep understanding of Lean principles and practices combined with extensive training at all levels in the organization.

Dennis (2002) argues that the increase in productivity, quality and cycle time cannot always be positively correlated with the application of Lean principles. In fact, many companies struggle to implement the lean system as a whole. The choice of suitable tools allows the necessary combination for the implementation of Lean principles. For example, management may choose to implement the 5S tool that is not very comprehensive, an incisive Kaizen program (continuous improvement) and perhaps some TPM (Total Productive Maintenance) (Dennis, 2002).

Companies like Ota, GE. FedEx, Dell that implemented Lean are among the most profitable and respected companies in the world, largely due to their commitment to lean, that is to say with the philosophy itself (Bob, 2008).

LEAN PRODUCTION

The competitiveness demanded by the challenges imposed in the current market, above all, by the improvement of the level of products and services, implies that the organizations necessarily seek to redefine and reorganize their production systems. These seek to involve and integrate not only production, but all parts of an organization, with the aim of eliminating waste (Ghinato, 2000). Worldwide, the lean transformation initiative has become a business imperative for most organizations and in virtually all industrial sectors.

In this context, the Lean Manufacturing (LM) concept has since been widely implemented throughout the manufacturing industry, ranging from automobiles to electronics. Wilson (2010) mentions LM as being a set of techniques and tools that allow improving quality and reducing production times and costs. With the implementation of LM, companies seek to increase competitiveness and organizational performance.

The theory of Lean Manufacturing, developed in the 1950s by Taiichi Ohno, father of TPS (McKenzie, 2014), features a production practice that uses fewer resources compared to traditional manufacturing

(Lynch, 2005). The goal is to provide the customer with the highest quality product at the lowest cost in the shortest possible time (Lynch, 2005).

Lynch (2005) refers to authors such as Dennis (2002), Liker (2004), Ohno (1997) and Schonberger (1986) to demonstrate that the practice of introducing LM methods has become known for significant savings in all aspects of production, for example, reduction of cycle times, costs, stocks and several other sources of waste (Fukuzawa, 2019). Worley & Doolen (2006) also point out other benefits associated with gaining greater quality, flexibility and customer satisfaction.

On the one hand, LM requires the reduction of any activity that does not add value to the customer using less human effort than traditional production. On the other hand, Achanga et. al (2006) refer that, as in any other productivity improvement initiative, it is believed that there are numerous difficulties. In fact, Thilmany (2005) states that companies still struggle to make LM work.

McKenzie (2014) quotes Worley and Doolen (2006) to state that many variables can impact successful Lean implementation. Especially considering that, for Worley and Doolen (2006), establishing a Lean philosophy for management and employees can be quite challenging. The most critical and common challenge that industrialists face in this context is to achieve continuous improvement effectively (Leong; 2019).

Morgan and Brenig-Jones (2009) talk about balance - "Lean is focused on people" - and the question is how can we improve the environment for people who are doing a certain task, providing them with resources (robots and automation in general) that allow them to execute and scale tasks in a Lean way.

The effects of digitalization of production are translated by the massive accumulation of data via IIoT (Internet Industrial of Things), fed essentially through ERPs and managed by specific processes. The data that is produced through devices allocated to the production processes is as good as what they can tell an operator (Connor, 2019). Therefore, the way to use this data and the consequent decisions of its evaluation are the next way to be lean. The focus is on how we use technology to make these processes clearer, more effective, consistent and therefore more Lean.

OBJECTIVES AND METHODOLOGIES

The objective of this study, as mentioned in the introduction, was to analyze and evaluate the adoption of lean culture at multinational company, by reviewing key processes and successfully implementing appropriate solutions for the studied reality.

One of the paradoxes of lean is that its execution depends essentially on people's adherence (Asnan et al., 2015). Thus, it was intended to clarify the real contribution and perception of employees in an attempt to create, in the medium/long term, a sustainable lean structure and guided by processes.

This work was based on a qualitative study (case study), where the necessary information was gathered through the bibliographic research on the subject and on the research methodologies, for the technical application of participant observation with simultaneous application of another method of research/ data collection (Focus Group). The interdepartamental team sought to contribute to the knowledge base necessary for the adoption of lean thinking and the redesign of key processes for the company. The steps followed in the study, for conducting the research, were those shown in the table below (See Table 1).

The purpose of Step 1 was above all to be able to review all the documentation made available by the company, obtained essentially through reports generated by the sales platform and by the reports of each Lean Driver (members of the Focus Group) regarding the difficulties experienced in the execution

Table 1. Study steps for conducting the research

Stages	Description
1	Data collection with the interdepartamental team
2	Data analysis to study possible improvement porposals
3	Presentation of proposals for improvement and action planning
4	Implementation and monitoring of actions evaluation of results
5	Evaluation of results

of a certain key intra or interdepartmental processes. In this way, we had the opportunity to observe the behavior of some indicators, namely in the sectors of financial-logistics, sales and services. It should be noted that, during Stage 1, dates were also established for the training needed to introduce and become familiar with the lean theme.

With regard to Step 2, a set of activities is also highlighted whose objective was to understand the real state of the company in relation to the management of processes. In this stage, the research objectives were defined, namely: all possibilities of intervention in the company were signaled, more specifically the review of processes considered critical for operational activities (based on the survey carried out in the previous step), in an attempt to understand which are related and that together they can be improved.

In the meetings that followed, it was stipulated that the objective would be to present and discuss some proposals as a result of the analyzed processes as well as the planning of the necessary actions. In this step (Step 3), there was a need to apply several management tools with a focus on eliminating waste from the revised key processes.

During Step 4, it was possible to effectively define those responsible for implementing and monitoring the actions. In Step 5, the results of the implementations carried out were evaluated in order to verify the improvements achieved in relation to the performance of the operational activities.

ANALYSIS AND EVALUATION OF RESULTS

After several meetings held with the Focus Group as well as the meetings held by each Lean Driver with the respective work teams, it was possible for the identified key processes to eliminate disturbances and small wastes caused by crucial daily operations of the company, namely in relation to the processes which involved customer ordering of equipment, requests for repair and warranty.

Regarding the ordering process, there was a better coordination between the departments involved, sharing accurate information on the sales platform - resulting in fewer errors in the processing of orders and compliance with delivery dates for customers.

As for the guarantee management process, it was noted that the lack of standardization / alignment of some procedures were some of the reasons identified when reviewing the current process. When customers contact the company, whether by email, telephone, a business visit or even through the platform that provides remote support to customers, they want to be provided with new equipment or repair service under the warranty. The fact is that this process did not present an answer as immediate, effective and satisfactory as the one that the client was expecting because it involves and affects several stakeholders and it was necessary to review the contribution and weight of each one. With the exhaustive review of this process, the response time and the interaction between the owners of each stage improved and above all it allowed the information to flow correctly, emphasizing the fact that the customer is always aware of the actions taken to solve his problem.

On the other hand, there was a clear decrease in the number of telephone calls received to the Services Department to question the equipment sent for repair. In this specific case, all records of entries of equipment for repair are now regularly monitored and the customer is always informed. The fact that a maximum limit of five working days for response has been established has reduced the number of complaints regarding the response time for equipment intervention.

In general for the company, it was noted that for the solutions presented, there were significant improvements in the level of service provided and in the quality of response to customer requirements. The processes became clearer for all stakeholders in the value chain and the most efficient and effective action for identifying waste, surgical alteration of a given component of the process to return to the standardized and optimized situation previously defined and reviewed.

The other solutions presented and implemented resulted in the elimination of "old habits" and the awareness of employees about the need to police their own behavior in favor of a more Lean environment.

CONCLUSION

The actions that were carried out after a survey of the key processes and respective revision allowed the elimination of disturbances and waste that impacted some daily actions of Endress+Hauser Portugal.

The constituted interdepartmental team (Focus Group) was able to clarify which initiatives are necessary to introduce the lean theme in the company as well as the application of some tools that helped in the adoption of the concept itself.

Significant improvements were clearly noted in the way in which everyone came to face "persistent problems" and small disturbances that particularly affected one or more departments simultaneously, such as response times for operations, cadence of actions, information flow, decision-making, whose resolution effectively came to be seen as a collective commitment.

Aware that the implementation of the lean philosophy is still a long way off, the Focus Group agreed that these first reviews will serve as a basis for the reevaluation and reengineering of other, more comprehensive and optimized processes. In general this work allowed to infer about the advantages and the real obstacles for the adoption of lean thinking in the company under study.

The application of lean culture in a multinational company aims to simplify the processes involved, through the possibility of intervening in activities that obstruct the flow of operations, always seeking to reduce costs by eliminating waste and, at the same time, maximizing the added value to the customer.

The conclusions of this case study suggest that, the company is starting to consider crucial the adoption of lean concept as an organizational culture focused on change and knowledge management. In fact to build it, they realized that it´s very important a base in parallel through communication, training/development and support to administrative leadership.

The focus from now on is to continue promoting teamwork, monitoring new projects based on the search for a sustainable adoption of lean, together with the creation of the concept of ownership and responsibility.

REFERENCES

Achanga, P., Shehab, E., Roy, R., & Nelder, G. (2006). Critical success factors for Lean implementation within SMEs. *Journal of Manufacturing Technology Management*. Consulted on: Febraury 16 2020, on: https://www.researchgate.net/publication/200552235_Critical_success_factors_for_lean_implementation_within_SMEs

Asnan, R., Nordin, N., & Othman, S. N. (2015). *Managing Change on Lean Implementation in Service Sector*. 2nd Global Conference on Business and Social Science, GCBSS-2015, Bali, Indonesia. Consulted on: april 4 2020, on: https://www.sciencedirect.com/science/article/pii/S187704281505380X

Atkinson, P. (2010). 'Lean' is a cultural issue. *Journal of the Institute of Management Services*.

Bob, V. (2008). Which way do you lean? *Plant Engineering*. Consulted on: may 20 2020, on: https://www.plantengineering.com/articles/which-way-do-you-lean/

Connor, P. (2019). Combining Lean manufacturing and Industry 4.0. *Manufacturers' Monthly*. Consulted on January 14 2019, on: https://www.manmonthly.com.au/Combining+Lean+manufacturing+and+Industry+4.0

Damrath, F. (2012). *Increasing competitiveness of service companies: developing conceptual models for implementing Lean Management in service companies*. Politecnico di Milano.

Dennis, P. (2002). *Lean production simplified*. Productivity Press.

Dunn, A. (2009). *Implementation of lean manufacturing in General MotorsManufacturing Luton (GMML). Warwick*. University of Warwick.

Fukuzawa, M. (2019). Critique on the Lean Production System Research. *Annals of Business Administrative Science, 18*, 85–101.

Grove, A., Meredith, J., MacIntyre, M., Angelis, J., & Neailey, K. (2010). UK health visiting: Challenges faced during lean implementation. *Leadership in Health Services, 23*(3), 204–218. doi:10.1108/17511871011061037

Hines, P., Holweg, M., & Rich, N. (2004). Learning to evolve: A review of contemporary lean thinking. *International Journal of Operations & Production Management, 24*(10), 994–1011. doi:10.1108/01443570410558049

Justa, M., Barreiros, N. (2009). Técnicas de Gestão do Sistema Toyota de Produção. *Revista Gestão Industrial, 5*(1), 1-17.

Learning Objectives - Lean Fundamentals - Let's Start Lean. (n.d.). Consulted on: August 8 2019, on: https://www.moresteam.com/University

Liker, J. K., & Meier, D. (2005). *The Toyota Way Fieldbook*. McGraw-Hill.

Locher, D. (2011). *Lean Office and Service Simplified The Definitive How to Guide*. Academic Press.

Lynch, L. (2005). *The relationship of lean manufacturing 5S principles to quality, productivity, and cycle time*. Walden University, ProQuest Dissertations Publishing.

Mann, D. (2005). *Creating a lean culture: tools to sustain lean conversion.* New York: Productivity Press. Consulted on: July 5 2019, on: https://books.google.com.br/books?hl=ptPT&lr=&id=X_CsBAAAQBAJ&oi=fnd&pg=PP1&dq=lean+culture+change+management&ots=2YzJ3ivs2t&sig=ULpofWRXBuyT0temxNxb0QKvos#v=onepage&q=lean%20culture%20change%20management&f=false

McKenzie, L. (2014). *Exploring the competitiveness of manufacturing organizations utilizing lean processes: A case study* (Doctoral Dissertation). Argosy University, Atlanta Campus College of Business.

Morgan, J., & Brenig-Jones, M. (2009). *Lean six-sigma for dummies.* West.

Natasya, A., Wahaba, A., Mukhtara, M., & Sulaiman, R. (2013). A Conceptual Model of Lean Manufacturing Dimensions. *The 4th International Conference on Electrical Engineering and Informatics (ICEEI).* Consulted on: October 10 2020, on: https://www.sciencedirect.com/science/article/pii/S2212017313004817

Ohno, T. (1997). *Toyota Production System.* Productivity Press.

Teixeira, E. (2012). *Graus de maturidade da cultura lean do pólo metal-mecânico do nordeste de Santa Catarina* (Master's dissertation). Programa de Pós-Graduação do Instituto Superior Tupy IST/SOCIESC Sociedade Educacional de Santa Catarina, Joinville.

Teixeira, E., & Melim, J. (2014). *V Congresso de Sistemas LEAN 23 e 24 de maio de 2014.* UFRGS.

Testani, M. V., & Ramakrishnan, S. (2012). Lean Leadership Readiness for Change: A Methodology for Lean Change Readiness and Continuous Improvement. *Proceedings of the 2012 Industrial and Systems Engineering Research Conference.*

Thilmany, J. (2005). *Thinking Lean.* Journal University of Missouri-Rolla.

Womack, J. (2004). *A Lean Walk Through.* Academic Press.

Womack, J. P., & Jones, D. T. (1996). *Lean Thinking: Banish Waste and Create Wealth in Your Corporation.* Simon & Schuster.

Womack, J. P., Jones, D. T., & Roos, D. (1990). *The machine that changed the world.* Simon & Schuster.

Worley, J., & Doolen, T. L. (2006). The role of communication and management support in a Lean manufacturing. *Management Decision, 44*(2), 228–245. doi:10.1108/00251740610650210

Chapter 10
A Lean-Kaizen Implementation:
A Case Study in the Food Retail Industry

Pedro Silva
CIICESI, ESTG, Politécnico do Porto, Portugal

Alexandra Braga
CIICESI, ESTG, Politécnico do Porto, Portugal

Sara Mota
CIICESI, ESTG, Politécnico do Porto, Portugal

Miguel Soares
CIICESI, ESTG, Politécnico do Porto, Portugal

Marisa R. Ferreira
CIICESI, ESTG, Politécnico do Porto, Portugal

ABSTRACT

Sustainable development is one of the greatest challenges facing our generation and the next, and achieving this goal will force society to continuously challenge and overcome itself. In order to attain the required sustainable objectives, many companies are investing in new methodologies, such as the Kaizen-Lean methodology. This chapter focuses on a case study in the food retail industry, a strategic and one of the largest and oldest industries in the world able to thrive even in the face of substantial adversity. The authors systematized the case study in three different stages via an action-research intervention. In a first stage, they identified the most sensitive areas, which enabled them to detect and target the intervention. In a second stage, they implemented and monitored several actions supported by the Kaizen/Lean methodologies. In a third stage, a survey was applied to workers whose work areas had changed in order to analyze and assess the impact of the implemented measures.

DOI: 10.4018/978-1-7998-7452-2.ch010

INTRODUCTION

In a very short period of time, the global pandemic triggered by the new coronavirus has caused severe limitations to the daily life of people and companies. The COVID-19 pandemic has forced governments around the world to impose lockdown measures aimed at curbing the spread of the virus and which has nearly brought the entire world economy to a standstill (Lin, Li, Luo, & Benitez, 2020), affecting a huge number of companies (Kraus, Clauss, Breier, Zardini, & Tiberius, 2020).

Besides the current hostile context, the globalization phenomenon and the consequent search for competitiveness have led companies to revamp their strategies and invest on evolving their working methods to foster better services and cost-benefit optimization to their customers. Globalization expands markets and facilitates trade, but it also leads to higher competition. Now consumers have at their disposal a greater variety of products and services, which generates a greater, and more sophisticated, demand. As a consequence, in the last decade, due to growing global competition, companies have been forced to rethink their manufacturing practices (Modarress, Ansari, & Lockwood, 2005). These facts, combined with technological advances, lead companies to face difficulties and seek solutions to avoid that their products lose value during the production process.

Sustainable development is not only one of the hottest topics of the last decade (Broman & Robèrt, 2017; Patzelt & Shepherd, 2011), but also a possible path, and it will probably be one of the most important topics for our generation and future ones, forcing society to continuously challenge and overcome itself. Sustainable development can be considered a proposal of development at a global scale, promoting equal chance of justice and thus leading to global cohesion both in social, economic and ecological sphere (Płachciak, 2009). Broman and Robèrt (2017) state that sustainable development allows companies to gradually reduce their negative impact on ecological and social systems by strengthening their organization through the creation of innovation opportunities and new business models, by exploring new markets, winning new market shares and reducing operational risks and costs.

Faced with this need to invest in new methodologies, many companies are currently using Kaizen-Lean methodologies. These methodologies aim at the continuous improvement of all processes, via a constant effort of waste reduction, methods of space organization and definition of operating standards, so Lean tools are used to improve quality, increase productivity, speed and reliability, while reducing inventories and costs (Belekoukias, Garza-Reyes, & Kumar, 2014). In our industrial world, continuous improvement of production processes has become necessary for companies to remain competitive and retain their share of the global market. As such, the implementation of the Kaizen methodology fosters this enhancement of the performance of activities, cost reduction and quality (Singh & Singh, 2009). According to Glover, Farris, Van Aken e Doolen (2011), Kaizen events have produced positive changes in business and human resources. According to Thessaloniki (2006), Kaizen is a management philosophy that forces higher standards at all levels of the organization, encouraging continuous improvement in all processes. This approach is based on the premise that there is no perfection in any process, because no structure, product or system reaches the ideal point. The Kaizen methodology stresses the importance of organizations optimizing each process to avoid being outdone by their competitors and thus remain active in the market, ensuring the satisfaction of their customers' needs and retaining them as their business partners, for they are central for the company's survival.

Our chapter worked a case study, a specific branch inside the food retailing industry, a strategic industry and one of the largest and oldest in the world, able to thrive even in the face of substantial adversity. We systematized our case study in three different stages through a research-action intervention.

Firstly, we identified the most sensitive areas; secondly, we implemented and monitored several actions supported by Kaizen and Lean methodologies; and finally, after the implementation of tools, a survey was carried out to the employees whose work areas had changed, in order to analyze and evaluate the impact of the implemented activities.

BACKGROUND

Lean Methodology

Lean production theory and techniques have been widely applied in companies to improve process efficiency by reducing waste and increasing value in value streams (Shou, Wang, Wu, & Wang, 2020). Over the past few decades, organizations from almost all sectors have used the Lean methodology as a fundamental method to transform management approaches, enhance results and take advantage of human potential. This methodology is widely used in interdisciplinary sectors and several definitions of it are available (Abu, Gholami, Mat Saman, Zakuan, & Streimikiene, 2019). Due to its high efficiency in reducing complexity and concentrating on value-added tasks, the Lean concept continues to be successful (Kolberg, Knobloch, & Zühlke, 2017).

Lean production has emerged in recent decades as one of the most popular topics and is the most widely used production paradigm in the industry today. Lean means production without waste, with a focus on efficiency and with the objective of manufacturing products and services at the lowest cost and the fastest possible pace (Maske & Valunjkar, 2020; Rahman, Sharif, & Esa, 2013). Lean methodology is often considered as a set of practices that can be used to achieve high operational performance (Haider & Bhat, 2020) and is characterized by five principles that facilitate the prevention of pollution, reduction and use/waste of resources reduction of waste, thus helping to improve a company's environmental performance (Dieste, Panizzolo, Garza-Reyes, & Anosike, 2019).

According to Chahala and Narwal (2017), the main objective of lean manufacturing is to help manufacturers who wish to improve their industrial operations to obtain the best product/service quality and ensure customer satisfaction. But this philosophy goes beyond a mere uncomplicated vision, as it emphasizes the determination of each process's value by distinguishing between value-added and non-value added activities, thus eliminating all steps that do not add value to the product (Jiju, 2011).

According to Aslam, Gao, & Smith (2020), although lean philosophies are emerging phenomena in waste reduction and improved sustainability, the industry does not always use all its benefits, either because of lack of awareness or complicated implementation strategies. According to these authors, companies experiencing difficulties in implementing lean processes tend to abandon such practices in the future. Although lean methodologies were initially seen as a means to improve efficiency by reducing operating costs, today they also incorporate the concept of sustainability (Peña-Montoya, Bouzon, Torres-Lozada, & Vidal-Holguin, 2016). Sustainability is one of the most critical issues facing manufacturers today. As such, it is essential that industries develop new and innovative approaches to ensure sustainability across all domains, economic, environmental and social (Venugopal & Saleeshya, 2019).

Lean implementation is one of the operational strategies that companies can apply to contribute to more sustainable industries via preventive measures in order to reduce environmental pollution while reducing costs (Zhang, Niu, & Liu, 2020). The lean methodology focuses on the complete change of the business model, from production to management and even the way employees perform their daily tasks

(Melton, 2005). When deciding to adopt lean manufacturing, it is imperative to investigate where and how lean practices are most needed to influence production and business performance. Such research becomes indispensable when lean thinking must be considered in a production arrangement different from a conventional, repetitive, high-volume, stable demand and discrete manufacturing environment (Panwar, Jain, Rathore, Nepal, & Lyons, 2018). In short, this management method is based on creating value for customers through the elimination or reduction of all activities that do not contribute to a competitive advantage.

Kaizen Methodology

The term Kaizen is a combination of two Japanese words that mean "continuous improvement": Kai means "change" and *Zen* means "for the better", indicating a process of continuous improvement of the standard way of work. In today's industrial world, continuous improvement of production processes has become essential for companies to remain competitive and retain their participation in the global market. As such, the application of the Kaizen methodology seeks to improve the performance of activities, reduce costs and increase quality (Singh & Singh, 2009).

According to Thessaloniki (2006), improving starts by recognizing the need for improvement. This author defines Kaizen as a management philosophy that forces the existence of higher standards of work at all levels of the organization, encouraging continuous improvement in all processes. This approach is based on the premise that there is no perfection in any process, because no structure, product or system reaches the ideal point. The application of the Kaizen methodology is based on the idea that small, continuous and conscious changes lead to major changes and transformations in all processes. The Kaizen methodology emphasizes the importance of organizations seeking to optimize each process to avoid being overtaken by their competitors, remain active in the market, and guarantee the satisfaction of their clients' needs, so that they can retain them as business partners, for they are fundamental for the company's survival.

The Kaizen method and technique are valuable instruments that can be used to increase productivity, obtain competitive advantage and increase the overall business performance on competitive markets. In general, Kaizen is a useful concept to facilitate workflow and improvements, being considered as an umbrella concept since it aggregates several different concepts, such as total quality control, customer orientation, automation or even productivity improvement (Imai, 1986).

There is a standard Kaizen methodology that can be used in different fields, such as manufacturing, engineering, management and other supporting processes in the organization, and it is developed in 8 steps. This methodology is presented in a cycle, as these are processes of continuous improvement, starting a process as soon as the previous one ends. Kaizen will help people to implement methodologies that allow them to perform tasks quickly, to identify and reduce/eliminate waste in the selected processes.

For the application of the Kaizen methodology, we can identify 10 basic rules:

1. Deconstruct conventional preconceived ideas about production;
2. Focus on how to do this, not why it can't be done;
3. Don't find excuses. Question current practice;
4. Don't look for perfection. Do this immediately, even if you only reach 50% of the goal;
5. Correct errors immediately;
6. Don't spend money on Kaizen;

7. Wisdom is revealed when we face difficulties;
8. Ask "why" 5 times and look for the root causes of the problem;
9. Look for the wisdom of 10 people instead of the knowledge of 1;
10. Kaizen ideas are endless.

Although there are no standard techniques/instruments for implementing Kaizen, several tools can be used (Wittenberg, 1994):

1. PDCA Cycle;
2. Elimination of 7 wastes (Muda);
3. 5S (Workplace organization);
4. 5 Why Technique;
5. 7 QC Tools;
6. Jidoka (Automation);
7. Poka-Yoke;
8. Andon.

In the next section, we will present our case study, split into three stages: (1) characterization of the company and diagnosis of the current situation; (2) implementation of continuous improvement actions; and (3) evaluation of the actions implemented.

PRACTICAL APPROACH

Characterization of the Company and Diagnosis of the Current Situation

E. Leclerc

The E. Leclerc distribution group was set up in 1949, in Landerneau, France. Independence is one of the group's central concepts. E. Leclerc promotes individual initiative and the autonomy of each store, always in line with this project's motto: making goods and services accessible to as many people as possible. E. Leclerc distinguishes itself from competitors by implementing a policy of independent commercial operator, a strategy that offers employees the possibility to become owners of their stores based on their merit, commitment and skills. According to the company itself, E. Leclerc is the only European group that allows its employees, who have made their apprenticeship in the group's stores, to one day become owners of their own stores.

The group is constantly growing, operating in areas other than distribution, such as jewellery, petrol stations, travel agencies and car repair centers. In 1992, the group opened its first store outside France, in Pamplona, Spain. Since then, the company has grown to several foreign markets, including Poland, Portugal, Slovenia and Italy.

The E. Leclerc group opened its first store in Portugal (Valongo) in 1995, followed by the opening of 20 more stores in Portuguese territory. The group opened its store in Lousada in November 2007, which is strategically located in the center of the city, thus being able to serve the various neighboring municipalities. This strategic location allows them to serve about 50,000 people. The proximity of this store to other similar competitors (e.g., Pingo Doce, Continente and Intermaché) allows it to benefit from the advantages of geographic market concentration.

The E. Leclerc store in Lousada is divided into two areas: an area for product sale, integrating the areas for product display and sales, and the storage area.

Diagnosis of the Initial Situation

After analyzing the E. Leclerc store in Lousada, we identified two critical areas that need continuous improvement actions: (i) the supply house, and (ii) the process of receiving and storing fresh and frozen products.

1. Supply House

In this section are stored products for the company's own consumption, such as office supplies, cleaning products, plastic bags for product packaging, labeling rolls, among other supplies. These products are used by different sections and so the costs associated with them need to be distributed among the different sections.

Plastic bags are used in these sections to package fruit and for the transport of fish and meat. Therefore, it is important to understand the number of products used by each section in order to make the correct allocation of quantities and costs, and thus avoid potential errors.

Currently, after being received, the products are distributed among the different sections and their preparation lies with each section employee. This distribution is done intuitively and is not based on the consumption history of previous periods. The cost of the products is distributed in percentage terms among the different sections in a way that is not very robust, nor consistent.

In short, the company has no control over the distribution of products by sections or the costs of distribution. This is where the core issue really lies, since the cost that is attributed to each section is not the real one; this factor directly influences the profit margin that each section achieves and may often affect the final sales price. Another negative factor arises from the way the products are stored, since the company does not have a defined area for storage, and sometimes products are randomly distributed in several different locations.

2. The Process of Receiving and Storing Fresh and Frozen Products

Another critical area that requires the implementation of continuous improvement actions is the fresh and frozen products section. This section encompasses OSSP (operation of self-service products), fruit and vegetables, frozen products, charcuterie, bakery, butchery and fishmongery.

Given the characteristics of the products in this section (short shelf life, temperature control of frozen products), it is important to describe the entire process of receiving and checking the products, as well as the process of storing the fresh products in an industrial freezer.

Figure 1 presents the process of receiving and checking the products, from the initial order to the suppliers to their preparation in the store or in the warehouse.

In point 1, the person responsible for the orders of each section sends the order to the supplier, who then sends the products to the store. In point 2, the warehouse manager deals with the reception and confirmation/conference of the products received. Whenever an error is found, the warehouse manager asks the supplier to correct it (point 3). In point 4, the accounting department performs the accounting

Figure 1. Reception of frozen products.

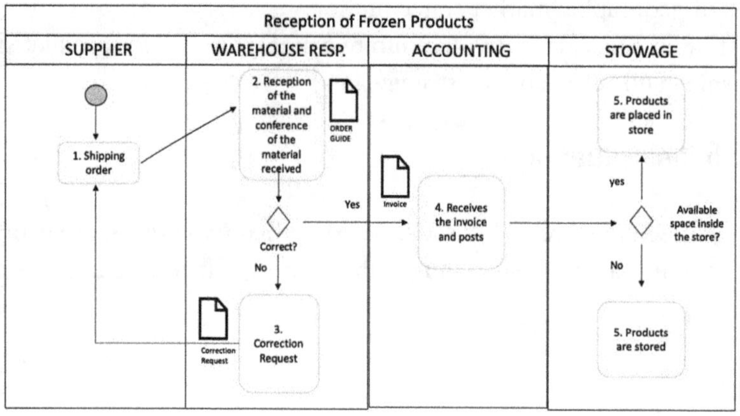

treatment and posts the invoice. In point 5, the employee goes to the store and places the products in their predestined areas. Products that do not fit in the store are stored in the warehouse: in the fresh products warehouse or in the industrial freezer.

The fresh products warehouse is shown on the left side of the map in Figure 2, which describes how the industrial freezer is organized. The blank areas are corridors, and the parts with double line are doors.

Figure 2. Fresh products warehouse.

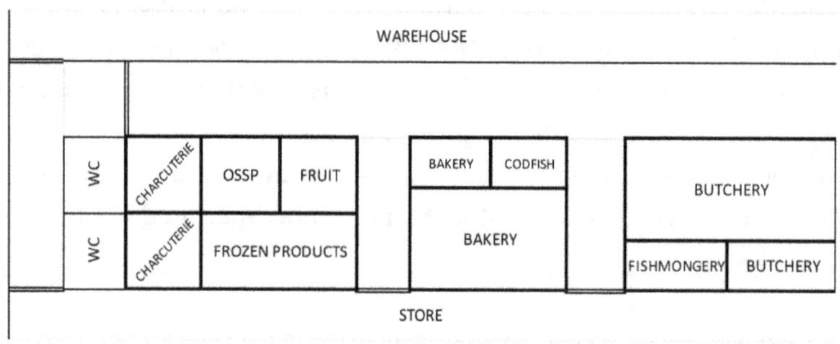

The industrial freezer is one of the most important areas of storage. Due to its specificity, it cannot be replaced by another form of storage. The industrial freezer area is used by different sections, namely butchery, charcuterie, bakery/pastry, OSSP and fishmongery. It is important to emphasize that it might be harmful to a worker's safety and health to be exposed for too long to the extreme cold temperatures inside the industrial freezer, and so employees should avoid spending more time than strictly required for specific tasks inside the industrial freezer. In order to minimize the risk, a system placed in the freezer emits a warning sound when a worker is exceeding the time limit.

In a first stage, it was found that there was no structured plan for product storage in the industrial freezer, with the employees of each section being responsible for storing the products wherever they considered to be most the convenient places — an obviously unsystematic method, always dependent on the individual's decision. This lack of planning meant that the industrial freezer was regularly disorganized and messy, which negatively affected the performance of all inherent activities.

It is also important to mention that the employee who stored the products inside the industrial freezer was not always the same one, and so there were different persons placing different products inside the freezer, which reinforced the need to define a pattern and a layout inside the industrial freezer.

The process defined so far corresponds to the reception and storage of products that are in accordance with what has been ordered, namely the quality of the products, packaging integrity, expiry dates, among others; however, the products do not always reach the company respecting all the characteristics pre-defined in the order.

Below are presented the various processes for addressing potential non-conformities. Non-conforming products are all those that at a given moment cannot be sold due to some kind of anomaly: for example, products with defective packaging at the time of receipt, products damaged during transport, products with unusual characteristics/properties, products still within the validity period but showing unexpected colors and/or textures.

When non-conforming products are found on the transport pallet, the warehouse manager adopts the following procedures: he photographs the occurrence and sends the photos together with a complaint guide to the central purchasing department, where a person is allocated to perform this specific process. This information is accompanied by a document (a delivery note) to the accounting department, which is then responsible for receiving the refund.

After detecting a non-conforming product, a treatment process divided into 4 phases is triggered:

- In a first stage, the employee detects the product anomaly and puts it in a box (B);
- Then, the section manager photographs the product and sends it to the central. After that, the product is transferred to another box (C);
- In a third stage, the supplier may choose to go to the store and exchange this product or to make a refund. When one of these situations happens, the product is moved to another box (A) meant for products that will be destroyed;
- Finally, the non-conforming product may also be placed in a different box (D). For these products, a different and specific document is sent directly to the supplier instead of the central. After that, the supplier manager goes to the store and directly replaces the damaged/non-conforming product.

Implementation of Continuous Improvement Actions

After analyzing the processes and identifying the main problems, changes were made, based on the Kaizen and Lean principles, in order to improve workflow, making it faster, more effective and more careful.

Some changes were implemented in the storage warehouse to make the process more efficient. As a starting point, instead of a warehouse for each section, there would be only a central warehouse, which workers from all sections would use to supply all the products.

The implementation of this change entailed a new work dynamic among the employees: the products had to be ordered the day before from the central warehouse. On the same day, the morning shift employee was responsible for verifying that the material requested in the previous day was enough for that working day; and in the event of stock rupture or shortage, the employee responsible must request the products in need to the central warehouse.

Bearing in mind the need for product control by section – which also facilitates accounting and control of associated costs –, it was defined that this central warehouse would be located in an area close to the warehouse manager workplace, who is the responsible person for the registration of all material outputs for the different sections. For this new organization, an exit document/guide was created, in which the warehouse manager must describe all material outputs, duly mentioning the section, the specific employee, the products and the quantities; the document must be signed after having verified that all information is correct.

In a second stage, it was essential to reorganize this new warehouse. For this purpose, existing furniture was used, which until now served only to store broken machines that were waiting for repair. This allowed storing all the material used in the different sections in the same space. In addition to these improvements, it is important to highlight the fact that all this work was carried out using materials that already existed in the company, thus minimizing inherent costs.

In addition to clear improvements in terms of planning and organization, the process of purchasing products became more expeditious. The employee responsible for issuing the order forms no longer needed to go through all the sections to check for possible material shortages, because now there is a centralization of products, and it is possible to visually check which products are in shortage or out of stock and thus place a specific order. A description of the product was placed next to each stored product. This description includes the name and code of the product, as well as its specific location. Thus, a storage pattern was defined, which considerably facilitates now access to all employees. In addition to the description, a bar code was placed for each product, because the description is sometimes very similar among some products. Whenever there is a need for ordering, the use of the code significantly facilitates and simplifies the operation.

Regarding the industrial freezer, it was decided to carry out a comprehensive overhaul of the previous working methods. The initial stage consisted in obtaining a better perception of the employees' way of

Figure 3. Industrial freezer.

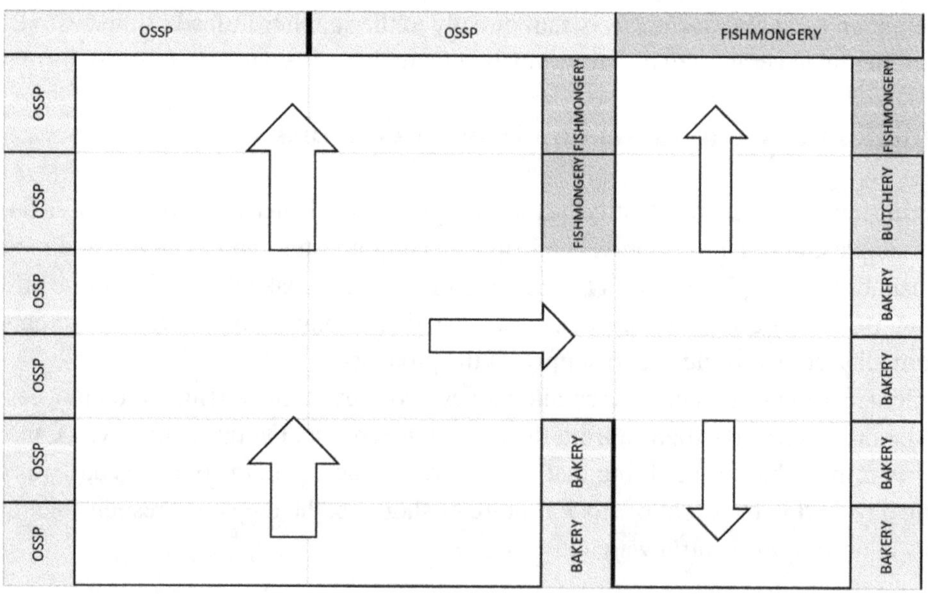

working, in order to assess errors and the main issues. This process started by assigning a storage location for each section's products, so that each section was aware of the storage location for products in shortage.

Circulation corridors were created inside the industrial freezer to ensure movement of workers and products, and to facilitate access to storage shelves. With a focus on improving organization processes and establishing storage standards, each section was further subdivided by product typology, as shown in Figure 4.

Figure 4. Industrial freezer subdivision.

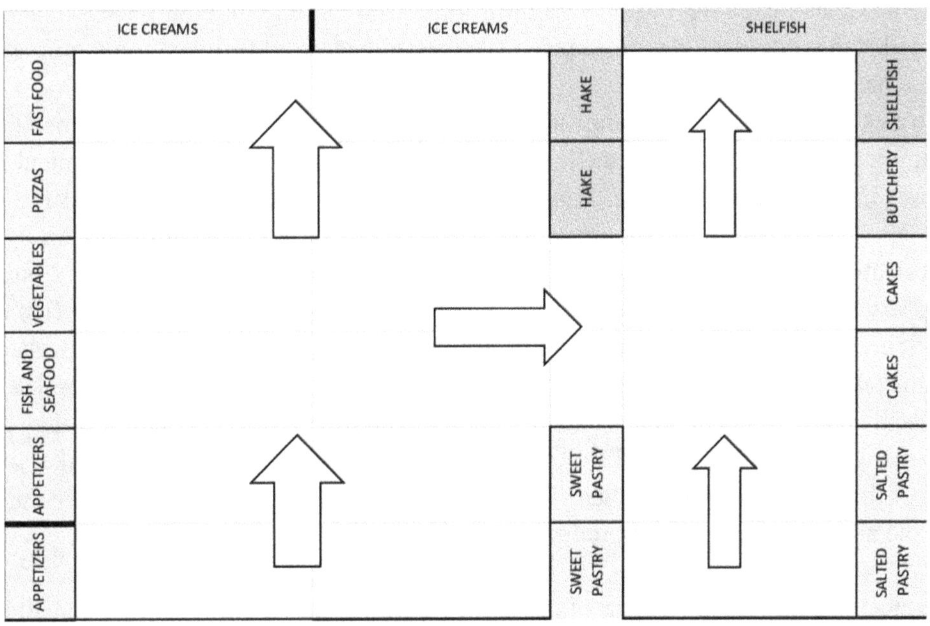

The second stage was the implementation of the changes previously described. The employees were informed through simple messages placed on the storage shelves which products should be stored on each shelf. This change provided greater speed in the store supply process, since the employee can easily detect the placement of a specific product and more assertively check the existence of the product.

In the present implementation, the PDCA ((Plan-Do-Check-Act) cycle methodology was adopted. Among the various sets of quality tools and lean management methodology, the PDCA is one of the most used dynamic models in continuous improvement processes (Chakraborty, 2016; Kholif, Abou El Hassan, Khorshid, Elsherpieny, & Olafadehan, 2018). Initially, the planning (corrective actions) was carried out to improve the section's daily functioning. In a second stage, action was taken (Do) where the previously planned measures were put into practice. At the stage of verification (Check), it was checked whether what had initially been developed was demonstrating the expected efficiency, and additional measures were also implemented. It was suggested that employees should start placing all the labels inherent to each box facing forward; and in the boxes where it was barely noticeable previously, they should place the product's expiration date inside the marker. The fourth and last stage of this tool (Action) should be conducted regarding issues that did not meet what was planned in the first stage. The cleaning was carried out as stipulated, but sometimes some employees failed to follow the plan and had to be alerted to make this correction, which they quickly accepted and implemented.

Considering the treatment of non-compliant products, a need was identified, and it was decided that the information related to non-compliant products should be communicated to the supplier, so that the process could be more agile and effective. In the analysis carried out, it was found that the predestined place for this type of products was quite untidy; there was no description of the place where each product should be placed at each stage and on the same shelf there were products unfit for consumption, thus confusing employees. Initially, the box used for storage of non-compliant products did not mention the condition of the products that were kept inside, nor the product's main purpose. The normal procedure was that the products inside the boxes were unfit for consumption, while all those outside the boxes were still marketable products; the proximity of these products could trigger some problems such as erroneous exchanges of products.

To facilitate the perception and organization of workflow in this section, it was defined that the best tool to be applied was the 5S. The 5S methodology is the most effective way to implement fundamental continuous improvement programs through visible change in the workplace (Maske & Valunjkar, 2020). This application mainly aims to make the work area more practical and agile through cleaning and standardization. According to this tool, in a first stage, the sorting (Seiri) is carried out, where all the unnecessary products are removed from the work area. Then it is necessary to define a place for each item (Seiton); next we have the cleaning (Seiso) of the workspace, which makes it easier to check for gaps in the labor process. After these steps, it is essential to create work standards (Seiketsu), that is, to define visual standards (visual management), so that employees can easily check if they are making mistakes in the way they are working. Lastly, the work team must be disciplined (Shitsuke) to guarantee the success of the previously defined plan. The following results were obtained with the application of this tool in the area of non-compliant products:

- All products that would not be part of the non-conforming batch were removed and all boxes were identified with simple but very assertive information regarding its contents.
- In addition to the changes mentioned above, a description of all the stages that the products must go through until they are completely destroyed was placed next to the place where these products are found. With this information, it became easier for newly hired employees, or for employees who were unfamiliar with the process, to quickly understand how to proceed.

Evaluation of the Implemented Activities

As a methodology for assessing the impact of this project implementation, a survey was developed in order to assess the global opinion of the employees. The questionnaire was completed by the 17 employees directly involved in the implementation of the Kaizen and Lean methodologies in their working areas.

Through the analysis of the questionnaires, it was found that all respondents stated that the changes regarding product storage allowed reducing search time for products in that specific work area. In addition to this perception, respondents positively quantified the search time reductions observed: it was observed that the majority of respondents (about 53%) responded that the current product disposal allowed a time saving between 20% and 40%.

Then workers were asked whether the changes implemented had positively impacted them, and if it was now easier to identify and locate the products in need. Their answers were very positive, with all respondents reporting that the whole process was more systematized and simpler. The changes implemented allowed reducing the search time for products, with a total of 64% of respondents reporting a time reduction between 20% and 40%.

The next questions were about a potential reduction in the number of shortages and a greater ease in finding products about to expire. The respondents answered very positively, stating that the changes implemented were beneficial for the daily work of the section, resulting in simpler, faster processes and promoting task efficiency.

The final questions addressed storage efficiency and speed and whether the work area became more methodical and organized after the implemented changes. The employees considered that their work area had significantly improved as a result of the changes made.

Generally, we can say that the implementation of the Kaizen and Lean methodologies brought benefits to all the sections where changes were implemented. In all areas, the employees mentioned benefits in terms of time saving, organization, cleanliness, and overall efficiency in performing daily tasks, fundamentally by reducing wasted time.

CONCLUSION

With the theoretical support of Kaizen-Lean methodologies, it was possible to implement tools aimed at the continuous improvement of currently existing methods in all areas, as well as the reduction of waste generated during the production process.

Initially, an analysis of the company's existing working methods was carried out, and then several procedures were developed, based on the methodologies under study, to change the issues that were not being properly enhanced. A map of implementations was then elaborated to change the current functioning of the company. A plan was created with a focus on improving tidiness, organization and cleaning, in order to create a more efficient and standardized work environment.

After this first analysis, the plan was implemented in the different target sections. In this sense, the product storage areas have undergone changes. The area for placing non-compliant products for sale was also a target for intervention using the 5S tool as a basis, creating a cleaner and more organized and methodical area. The interior of the store was also a target for interventions, such as improving the organization of frozen products for sale.

In the final stage, as a way of obtaining an evaluation of the implementations, a survey was carried out to the employees working in the sections that had been subjected to interventions. The survey yielded very positive results regarding the changes implemented to improve the daily work in the sections. In all sections, there were time savings (between 20% and 40%). Finally, is very important to highlight the positive attitude and commitment of all employees responsible for all the changes implemented in the company.

REFERENCES

Abu, F., Gholami, H., Mat Saman, M. Z., Zakuan, N., & Streimikiene, D. (2019). The implementation of lean manufacturing in the furniture industry: A review and analysis on the motives, barriers, challenges, and the applications. *Journal of Cleaner Production*, *234*, 660–680. doi:10.1016/j.jclepro.2019.06.279

Aslam, M., Gao, Z., & Smith, G. (2020). Exploring factors for implementing lean construction for rapid initial successes in construction. *Journal of Cleaner Production*, *277*, 123295. doi:10.1016/j.jclepro.2020.123295

Belekoukias, I., Garza-Reyes, J. A., & Kumar, V. (2014). The impact of lean methods and tools on the operational performance of manufacturing organisations. *International Journal of Production Research*, *52*(18), 5346–5366. doi:10.1080/00207543.2014.903348

Broman, G. I., & Robèrt, K. H. (2017). A framework for strategic sustainable development. *Journal of Cleaner Production*, *140*, 17–31. doi:10.1016/j.jclepro.2015.10.121

Chahala, V., & Narwal, M. S. (2017). An empirical review of lean manufacturing and their strategies. *Management Science Letters*, *7*(7), 321–336. doi:10.5267/j.msl.2017.4.004

Chakraborty, A. (2016). Importance of PDCA cycle for SMEs. *International Journal of Mechanical Engineering*, *3*(5), 30–34. doi:10.14445/23488360/IJME-V3I5P105

Dieste, M., Panizzolo, R., Garza-Reyes, J. A., & Anosike, A. (2019). The relationship between lean and environmental performance: Practices and measures. *Journal of Cleaner Production*, *224*, 120–131. doi:10.1016/j.jclepro.2019.03.243

Glover, W. J., Farris, J. A., Van Aken, E. M., & Doolen, T. L. (2011). Critical success factors for the sustainability of Kaizen event human resource outcomes: An empirical study. *International Journal of Production Economics*, *132*(2), 197–213. doi:10.1016/j.ijpe.2011.04.005

Haider, S., & Bhat, J. A. (2020). Does total factor productivity affect the energy efficiency: Evidence from the Indian paper industry. *International Journal of Energy Sector Management*, *14*(1), 108–125. doi:10.1108/IJESM-11-2018-0010

Imai, M. (1986). *Kaizen: The Key To Japan's Competitive Success*. Retrieved from https://books.google.pt/books?id=tCu1AAAAIAAJ

Jiju, A. (2011). *Six Sigma vs Lean Six Sigma: Some Perspectives from Leading Academics and Practitioners*. Purdue University.

Kholif, A. M., Abou El Hassan, D. S., Khorshid, M. A., Elsherpieny, E. A., & Olafadehan, O. A. (2018). Implementation of model for improvement (PDCA-cycle) in dairy laboratories. *Journal of Food Safety*, *38*(3), e12451. doi:10.1111/jfs.12451

Kolberg, D., Knobloch, J., & Zühlke, D. (2017). Towards a lean automation interface for workstations. *International Journal of Production Research*, *55*(10), 2845–2856. doi:10.1080/00207543.2016.1223384

Kraus, S., Clauss, T., Breier, M., Zardini, A., & Tiberius, V. (2020). The economics of COVID-19: initial empirical evidence on how family firms in five European countries cope with the corona crisis. *International Journal of Entrepreneurial Behaviour and Research*.

Lin, J., Li, L., Luo, X., & Benitez, J. (2020). How do agribusinesses thrive through complexity? The pivotal role of e-commerce capability and business agility. *Decision Support Systems*, *135*(June), 113342. doi:10.1016/j.dss.2020.113342 PMID:32834263

Maske, N. B., & Valunjkar, S. (2020). Lean Construction Tool – A Literature Review. *International Research Journal of Engineering and Technology*, *7*(10), 143–145.

Melton, T. (2005). The benefits of lean manufacturing: What lean thinking has to offer the process industries. *Chemical Engineering Research and Design, 83*(6A), 662–673. doi:10.1205/cherd.04351

Modarress, B., Ansari, A., & Lockwood, D. L. (2005). Kaizen costing for lean manufacturing: A case study. *International Journal of Production Research*, *43*(9), 1751–1760. doi:10.1080/00207540500034174

Panwar, A., Jain, R., Rathore, A. P. S., Nepal, B., & Lyons, A. C. (2018). The impact of lean practices on operational performance–an empirical investigation of Indian process industries. *Production Planning and Control*, *29*(2), 158–169. doi:10.1080/09537287.2017.1397788

Patzelt, H., & Shepherd, D. A. (2011). Recognizing opportunities for sustainable development. *Entrepreneurship Theory and Practice*, *35*(4), 631–652. doi:10.1111/j.1540-6520.2010.00386.x

Peña-Montoya, C., Bouzon, M., Torres-Lozada, P., & Vidal-Holguin, J. (2016). Lean Manufacturing and Sustainability: An Integrated View. *IFIP Advances in Information and Communication Technology*, 659–666. doi:10.1007/978-3-319-51133-7

Płachciak, A. (2009). Sustainable development - The way of building just society. *Economia e Sociologia*, *2*(1), 105–110. doi:10.14254/2071-789X.2009/2-1/10

Rahman, N. A. A., Sharif, S. M., & Esa, M. M. (2013). Lean Manufacturing Case Study with Kanban System Implementation. *Procedia Economics and Finance, 7*(Icebr), 174–180. doi:10.1016/S2212-5671(13)00232-3

Shou, W., Wang, J., Wu, P., & Wang, X. (2020). Lean management framework for improving maintenance operation: Development and application in the oil and gas industry. *Production Planning and Control*, *0*(0), 1–18. doi:10.1080/09537287.2020.1744762

Singh, J., & Singh, H. (2009). Kaizen Philosophy: A Review of Literature. *ICFAI Journal of Operations Management*, *8*(2), 51–72.

Thessaloniki. (2006). *A concept and tool for employees involvement*. Author.

Venugopal, V., & Saleeshya, P. G. (2019). Manufacturing system sustainability through lean and agile initiatives. *International Journal of Sustainable Engineering*, *12*(3), 159–173. doi:10.1080/19397038.2019.1566411

Wittenberg, G. (1994). Kaizen—The many ways of getting better. *Assembly Automation*, *14*(4), 12–17. doi:10.1108/EUM0000000004213

Zhang, B., Niu, Z., & Liu, C. (2020). Lean tools, knowledge management, and lean sustainability: The moderating effects of study conventions. *Sustainability (Switzerland)*, *12*(3), 956. Advance online publication. doi:10.3390u12030956

Chapter 11
Work 4.0:
The Future of Ethics in Professions in Portugal

Nuno Cruz
Polytechnic Institute of Setúbal, Portugal

Ana Carvalho
Polytechnic Institute of Setúbal, Portugal

Sandra Duarte
Polytechnic Institute of Setúbal, Portugal

ABSTRACT

This study aims to analyze the concerns of the largest companies operating in the Portuguese market regarding technological developments and artificial intelligence in the context of replacing human work with machines. More specifically, this study targets the reference to these concerns in these companies' codes of ethics and/or codes of conduct. The codes of ethics of 20 large companies operating in Portugal were thus analysed and classified according to their turnover, adopting an analytical method based on three dimensions identified as relevant for the respective evaluation: social responsibility, technological innovation, and commitments to employees. The conclusions from this study are that the companies analysed do not show in their codes of ethics any concern in mentioning the safeguarding of jobs if these are ever to be replaced by machines.

INTRODUCTION

"It was in this year (1943) that the wages of the average American peaked. Measured in 2013 dollars, an average worker, that is, from a universe of non-supervisory production workers in the private sector that represents well over half of the American labor force, earned about $767 per week in 1973. The following year, average real wages experienced a precipitous drop from which they would never fully recover. Four decades later, a similar worker earns just $64, a drop of nearly 13 percent" (Ford, 2015).

DOI: 10.4018/978-1-7998-7452-2.ch011

This is the starting point for a work that intends to be a comparative analysis of a set of codes of ethics/conduct of the main companies operating in the Portuguese market, in order to understand if they present references as to how companies view the replacement of human work by robotic machines.

The first paragraph of the introduction, an example from the USA, is a reflection of a paradigm shift that took place in the mid-1970s and started to have more repercussions in the 1980s, with companies launching a race to acquire machines that aided in-line production in their plants, as was the case, for example, in the automotive industry.

Only later do most companies become aware of the need to comply with a set of norms that, by societal pressure or legislative imposition, becomes essential for their social recognition in the territory where they operate. It is somewhat in this context that Codes of Ethics emerge structured according to specific rules. These Codes not only reveal a set of concerns regarding their employees but also seek to demonstrate how they, managers, suppliers, and partners who collaborate with the organization, should relate to each other.

At the end of the paper, we will present the conclusions we consider relevant to the study carried out.

THEORETICAL FRAMEWORK

It is important, and as a starting point, to present some definitions and discussions on the topic under study, incorporating the opinions/approaches of several authors, through the literature review. We begin, then, by presenting some concepts of Ethics.

The term Ethics derives from the Greek ethos (character, a person's way of being). One of the most important works on this subject is "Ethics demonstrated in the manner of geometers", published in 1677, and written by the Dutch philosopher of Portuguese origin, Baruch Spinoza. Another important work is "Nicomachaean Ethics" by the Greek philosopher Aristotle.

For Valls (2014) "ethics is one of those things that everyone knows what it is, but it is not easy to explain when someone asks." "Ethics is the normative science of human behaviors, it is like a set of norms, which human beings must follow in order to be respected in society" (Ourives 2006, *apud* Edmundo 2007).

For Reale, 1999, cited by Cosenza & Chamovitz, 2007 ethics "is the normative science of human behavior". In Weber's perspective, the ethical dimension related to intimate beliefs is of little use and, in certain cases, even harmful to decision making. For him, "[...] all activity oriented according to Ethics can be subordinated to two entirely different and irreducibly opposed maxims. It can be oriented according to the Ethics of responsibility or the Ethics of conviction. This does not mean that the Ethics of conviction is equivalent to the absence of responsibility, and the Ethics of responsibility to the absence of conviction. It is not that, of course. Nevertheless, there is a profound opposition between the attitude of one who conforms to the maxims of the Ethics of conviction - we would say, in religious language - The Christian does his duty and, as for the results of the action, trusts in God - and the attitude of one who is guided by the Ethics of responsibility, which says: "We must answer for the foreseeable consequences of our actions" (Weber, 2002).

We can conclude that Ethics is a set of moral values and principles that regulate human conduct in society. Ethics allows for balance and good social functioning, so that no one is harmed. In this sense, ethics is related to the feeling of social justice. Therefore, to be ethical is to always seek the good, to fight vices and weaknesses, to cultivate virtues, to protect and preserve life and nature. But what if we want to contextualize ethics in the business environment? This approach leads us to the concept of business ethics. However, it is important to define the word that is at the origin of the business concept, i.e., business.

Etymologically, the word company "is derived from the Latin *prehensus*, from *prehendere* (to undertake, to practice)", and has the sense of undertaking or investment for the achievement of a goal (Silva, 2002 *apud* Souza 2004).

"A company has been understood, doctrinally, as an organized economic activity, exercised professionally by the entrepreneur, through the establishment" (Bulgarelli, 1985). Already for Souza (2004) the concept company "offers varied senses, and not only the legal or economic sense, as is usual, but following other sociological, political and anthropological concerns that involve it." He also adds that "private or nationalized, small or large, updated or in technological decline, local or multinational, companies involve, in our days, the life of people, territories and cities."

This author tells us that companies involve people's lives, that is, there is here an approach in the sense of highlighting the concern with the human being. This design leads us to the central issue we are studying in this article.

However, and still regarding the concept of company, companies in Portugal may be classified, among other methods, according to their size. Since for this specific work we intend to analyze the codes of ethics in large companies, these are, according to INE - National Statistics Institute, and based on a European Commission Recommendation of May 6, 2003, companies which employ more than 250 workers, or have a turnover greater than 50 million euros and net assets greater than 43 million euros.

We can recognize that a company is like an economic-social entity made up of people, material goods and technicians, which has the objective of obtaining profits through partaking in the market of goods and services.

However, let's understand what some authors think about the subject of business ethics.

For Moreira (1999), it is "the behavior of the company understood to be profitable when it acts in conformity with moral principles and the rules of good procedure, accepted by society (ethical rules)." In Denny's (2001, p.134) definition, business ethics consists "in the pursuit of the common interest, that is, of the businessman, the consumer and the worker."

There is a widespread opinion that terms like "ethics" and "business" are difficult, if not impossible, to put together. There are several arguments that try to prevent this "marriage", but we must try to understand the reason for this conflict.

According to Cortina (2005), "(...) the company is governed by strategic rationality, while ethics is governed by communicative rationality, (...). Only if we overcome such obstacles by exposing the reasons why business ethics is possible and necessary, can we continue with our task." "What is business ethics?" [...] In the absence of a precise definition, texts evoke intuitive connotations that speak for themselves (good/bad, good/bad, fair/unfair ...), others offer a catalog of virtues [...] (honesty, integrity, respect, excellence, responsibility, etc.). [...] beyond the wave of 'anything goes' definitions, one problem remains unresolved: on what foundations, so non-rigorous, could the rules of business ethics be based?" Padioleau, (1989, p 84).

"The business of business is to make a profit [...] it is easier to deal with dollars than value judgments. People are more comfortable discussing business problems in terms of their financial impact than in terms of their ethical impact [...] Most people in business are probably not very well trained in ethical analysis, nor familiar with its language and concepts [...] If the problem is truly that of ethical ignorance, then some exposure to the concepts and issues should help [...] The study of business ethics assumes that people are moral beings who want to do the 'right' thing, but that there is often much confusion about what would be morally appropriate actions and practices" Buchholz (1989).

Business ethics, a narrower term than ethics, refers specifically to the relationship between companies and all parties within their scope of action: employees, customers, the public, competitors, the community, etc., commonly referred to as *stakeholders*. Business ethics is guided by legal principles, of a legal nature, and by principles of good coexistence, of a social nature, in accordance with the organization's values, which concern the individual responsibility of those who are part of it, and the social values that concern the social culture in which the company is inserted. The thought of business ethics is, in conceptual and historical terms, heir to the doctrine of social responsibility.

Here it is important to define social responsibility in business concretely. "A socially responsible company is one that can create methods, plans, and incentives so that, internally and externally, it is identified as a citizen-company." (Focus Social, 2004). In the opinion of Mattos (2005), a Business Strategy consultant, "social responsibility is a basic requirement to the attitude and ethical behavior, through practices that show that the company has a soul, whose preservation implies solidarity and social commitment." In his work, Drucker (2002, p. 207) reinforces the importance of a company's impact on the community: "increasingly, in our pluralistic society of organizations, the community's fundamental concern for the qualitative aspects of life, i.e., economic goods and services, must be joined by concern for the quality of life, i.e., the physical, human, and social environment of modern man and the modern community." In addition, and emphasizing the perspective of commitment to its employees, Gomes, Duarte & Neves (2011) say that "The managers of organizations, particularly those responsible for human resources should be aware that social responsibility policies can represent precious allies in the strategies of development and retention of their human resources. A clear bet on the complementarity between HRM (Human Resource Management) and social responsibility policies, or rather, in the development of socially responsible HRM policies, seems to be able to materialize in interesting benefits for the organization."

Nowadays, it is essential that a company has a well-established component of social responsibility in its mission, which shows, on the one hand, concern with the community and the qualitative aspects of people's lives, solidarity and social commitment. On the other hand, the commitment to its employees, through their appreciation, respect and dignity, promotion of equality and good working conditions, are unequivocally sources which contribute to the personal and professional growth of employees and the team itself, helping organizations to become more productive, and equally, socially responsible.

We now turn to the central theme of this article: codes of ethics, their definition and use.

Codes of ethics are an eminently American practice and were born based on legal, disciplinary, and punitive aspects as a result of external stakeholder demands: government, society, and consumers (Cressey & Moore, 1983).

Weaver (1993) defines code of ethics as "the distinct formal document that specifies conscious ethical obligations for organizational conduct (...) It is not part of operating procedure manuals and policies, even though it contains items of moral behavior." The author defines code of ethics as a document that should not be confused with annual reports, organizational mission, procedure manuals and other documents, which express values of the organization.

For Paine (1994), the code of ethics is any document of the organization that instills values of ethical integrity to guide and forge ethical behavior and decision making by employees, no matter its form, as long as its focus is on values or aspirations: code of conduct, vision statement, purposes, beliefs, principles or values. The Ethos Institute (2000) reiterates: "The code of ethics or social commitment is an instrument for realizing the company's vision and mission, which guides its actions and explains its social stance to all those with whom it maintains relations.

Some research conducted to analyze the content of the codes of ethics showed that (Cressey & Moore, 1983) it paid more attention to unethical conduct that affected the companies' profits than to reinforcing ethical conduct that could increase it. They were built on authority principles. As for orientation, 90% of them were *compliance-oriented*, that is, *top-down* control procedures in the hierarchical structure and punishments (Cressey & Moore, 1983). "(...) alone, the code of ethics is not capable of building the ethical and legal environment." Mathews (1987). Instruments are needed to support it, embedded in a consistent program to enable the internalization of values for the formation of ethical culture (Mathews & Weber, 1993 *apud* Charmen & Tomei, 2005).

Codes of ethics act as a "hat" that guides the way decisions are made by professionals in an organization, based on ethical values and behaviors. The organizations' code of ethics should relate these behaviors to day-to-day activities.

In Portugal, two guide standards were created by APEE (Associação Portuguesa de Ética Empresarial) – Portuguese Association for Business Ethics. The NP 4460-1:2007: Ethics in organizations, which defines the guidelines for the process of preparation and implementation of codes of ethics in organizations, and NP 4460-2:2010, with the guide for the preparation of these codes of ethics. These two standards, which complement each other, are intended to be practical tools for improving ethical performance in organizations, whatever their genesis, purpose or sector of activity.

And are ethical codes protective of human labor? Is the 4th Industrial Revolution, or Industry 4.0, evident in codes of ethics? What about innovation and artificial intelligence? These are questions that make perfect sense to be asked given recent developments in technological evolution.

Starting with Industry 4.0, whose advances were considered strategic moves by Germany to sediment its positioning as one of the countries investing the most in research and development and to stand out against other world powers, the concept was created in 2011 and adopted in 2013 as *Industrie 4.0.* (European Commission, 2017).

"The origin of this process is attributable to the situation in which a large number of technologies, by virtue of various factors, have become simultaneously cost-effective, minimally invasive and quantitatively widespread" (Celaschi, 2017 *apud* Souza, 2018).

When we refer to Industry 4.0 (Germany/European Union) or smart manufacturing (United States), we cannot help but link such concepts to the industrial revolutions that have occurred in history (Thoben, *et al.*, 2017, *apud* Souza, 2018). The first three industrial revolutions arose from the result of the mechanization of processes, the use of electricity, and the emergence of information technology (IT), respectively. The driving technologies of this industrial revolution are "the internet of things, Big Data, robotics, artificial intelligence, new materials, 3D printer, nanotechnology, biotechnology, energy storage, quantum computing, and autonomous vehicles. In the economy, its impact will affect all macroeconomic variables, such as GDP (gross domestic product), inflation, investments, consumption, trade and employment" (CNI, 2016 *apud* Souza, 2018). For Peters (2016), Industry 4.0 may generate the decrease in the number of jobs.

With the fourth industrial revolution, changes in the labor market are foreseen, with the disappearance of some jobs that are more routine and manual, especially in positions requiring lower degrees of qualification, while other jobs will be created, namely those associated with the creation, maintenance, and administration of new technologies, as well as jobs related to creative intelligence, organizational manipulation, or social intelligence. While human, social and organizational efficiency tends to improve with the fourth industrial revolution, human freedom needs to be maintained, especially on the new ethical issues that arise. To this end, regulation play a key role, as well as proper individual and organizational use of technology, so that it functions as an enabler of human lives and organizations, rather than making them slaves to those technologies (VER, 2019).

When we talk about industrial revolution, we certainly talk about innovation, because any of the industrial revolutions lived until today, always had the concept of innovation associated. For the OECD - Organisation for Economic Co-operation and Development (2004) innovation is "the implementation of a new or significantly improved product (good or service), or a process, or a new marketing method, or a new organizational method in business practices, workplace organization, or external relations." Grizendi (2011) and Bessant & Tidd (2009) (*apud* Bisneto & Lins, 2016), report that innovation does not occur by chance or in isolation, emphasizing the need to integrate it into the context of the organization, linking it to procedures ranging from stimulating creativity, learning and knowledge, to the formation of partnerships and organizational development aligned to the organization's strategy. Bisneto & Lins (2016) ask us several questions: "How to innovate? How to do new and different in a reality that surrounds everyone and everywhere? How to solve everyday problems for the benefit of society? This is the great challenge that hangs over the heads of those who want and need innovation as the essence of their organizations, contributing significantly to the achievement of results and their missions."

We can then conclude that an innovation can be defined as something new or improved, and that generates value for people and for organizations, through increasing turnover, cost reduction, improvement in working conditions, among others.

For its part, the concept of Artificial Intelligence, which is not easy to define, has, over time, passed through different lines of thought. "The new and interesting effort to make computers think (...) machines with minds, in the full and literal sense" (Haugeland, 1985 *apud* Batista, 2016). "The art of creating machines that perform functions that require intelligence when performed by people" (Kurzwei, 1990).

Artificial intelligence is the science that seeks to study and understand the phenomenon of intelligence and, at the same time, a branch of engineering that seeks to build tools to support human intelligence. Together, science and engineering aim to enable machines to perform tasks that, when performed by humans, require the use of intelligence. In practice, artificial intelligence invests in the search for the way humans think with the objective of elaborating theories and models of intelligence as computer programs. An artificial intelligence system, besides being able to store and manipulate data, can also acquire, represent, and manipulate knowledge. This manipulation refers to the ability to deduce or infer new knowledge from existing knowledge and to use methods of representation and manipulation to solve complex problems (Informant, 2018).

If on the one hand some authors define artificial intelligence as the process of thinking and reasoning, others define it as behavior, measuring success in terms of fidelity to human performance, or success by comparing it to an ideal concept of intelligence, rationality. We can define artificial intelligence, as the ability of machines to think like human beings: to learn, perceive and decide which paths to follow, rationally, when faced with certain situations. But can we affirm that artificial intelligence can be as rational as a human being?

METHODOLOGY

The study presented here aims, essentially, to find references about the relationship between the work done by humans and their possible future replacement by machines, in certain functions, through research, analysis and comparison of some Codes of Ethics/Conduct of certain organizations.

As mentioned in the framework, codes of ethics guide the decisions of those in charge of an organization and are based on ethical values and behaviors, seeking to relate these behaviors to the company's daily life activities.

In this sense, we decided to choose twenty large companies, according to their recorded turnover in 2019, operating in the Portuguese market. Research was carried out through the *websites* of each company, and the respective Codes of Ethics were downloaded.

After careful reading of the aforementioned documents of each of the twenty companies identified which belong to completely different sectors of activity, we carried out an analysis of their contents, based on a comparative evaluation of the elements that fit the dimensions we considered relevant to answer the pressing question: "Are codes of ethics protective of human labor?"

To this end, we believe that a comparative analysis of the codes of ethics would be fundamental, studying their approach and their focus on the following dimensions: social responsibility, technological innovation, and commitment to employees.

CODES OF ETHICS OR CONDUCT OF LARGE COMPANIES OPERATING IN PORTUGAL

To be able to reach some results and some conclusions regarding how organizations are planning and preparing for possible changes related to the robotization of functions and the replacement of jobs hitherto held by humans, and as already mentioned in the Methodology chapter, we, then, established a comparative analysis of the codes of ethics or conduct of twenty large companies operating in Portugal, according to the national ranking of the 500 largest companies.

As already explained in the Framework chapter, we recall that large companies are those that employ more than 250 workers or have a turnover greater than 50 million euros and net assets greater than 43 million euros, based on a European Commission Recommendation of May 6, 2003.

Some of the companies considered in this study are national companies, other companies are multinationals, headquartered in Portugal and belonging to completely different sectors of activity. Thus, we considered the codes of ethics or conduct of the companies listed in table 1.

After consulting the *websites* of each of the companies, the codes of ethics were located and downloaded, and then a comparative analysis of the contents was carried out from the standpoint of the dimensions identified by us as relevant to the question that guides our research, related to the protection of human labor, and which are: social responsibility, technological innovation, and commitment to employees.

Social responsibility because it represents the concern with the community where the company is located and with people's quality of life, especially that of its employees, in accordance with values of solidarity and social commitment; technological innovation, for the concern revealed with the innovation of processes and products through the development or introduction of new technologies, with a view to improving performance and results; commitment to employees, through the measures and actions developed and implemented to invest in their training and enrichment, their involvement and encouragement

Table 1. Table of companies selected for study

Company	Sector of Activity
ANA - AEROPORTOS OF PORTUGAL	Activities pertaining to air transportation
AUCHAN RETAIL PORTUGAL	Retail trade in supermarkets and hypermarkets
AUTOEUROPA - GRUPO VOLKSWAGEN	Manufacture of motor vehicles
BOSCH	Manufacture of radio receivers and similar consumer goods
BP PORTUGAL	Wholesale of petroleum products
BRISA – AUTOESTRADAS DE PORTUGAL	Land transport infrastructure management
COCA-COLA PORTUGAL	Manufacture of soft drinks and other non-alcoholic beverages
CONTINENTAL	Tire and tube manufacturing
EDP COMERCIAL	Electricity Trading
EDP DISTRIBUIÇÃO	Electricity Distribution
ENDESA	Electricity production from hydropower
GALP	Manufacture of refined petroleum products
INFRAESTRUTURAS DE PORTUGAL	Land transport infrastructure management
JERÓNIMO MARTINS (GRUPO)	Retail trade in supermarkets and hypermarkets
NAVIGATOR COMPANY	Wholesale of other intermediate goods
NOS	Wireline telecommunications activities
REPSOL	Wholesale of petroleum products
SONAE	Retail trade in supermarkets and hypermarkets
TAP (GRUPO)	Passenger air transport
VODAFONE (GRUPO)	Wireless Telecommunications Activities

Source: Prepared by the authors.

of participation in the life and decisions of the company, the improvement of their working conditions, respect for their differences, among others.

We then set out to discover the codes of ethics or codes of conduct of each of the companies identified, through research on their *websites,* in order to understand how they show their concerns in the three dimensions identified - social responsibility, technological innovation and commitment to employees - so that, in this way, it is possible to highlight some kind of approach to the central question that guides our work, i.e., how are companies preparing for the eventual replacement of man by machine in an increasing number of functions and tasks; how are they facing the much talked about 4th Industrial Revolution, the so-called Industry 4.0? Are the current professions in Portuguese companies at risk? Is man being replaced by artificial intelligence in companies? How is this issue being dealt with in large Portuguese companies? Are these concerns identified and expressed in their codes of ethics and conduct?

Through analyzing in detail and with enough attention all the documentation to which we were able to have access, there are a number of considerations that should be noted and that are important for our study.

Virtually all codes of ethics and/or conduct begin with a reference to the mission, vision, values, objectives and/or guiding ethical principles, with the exception of the documents of seven of the companies or groups analyzed. We make this distinction because, for example, regarding EDP Comercial and EDP Distribuição, the code of ethics of the entire EDP Group was considered. Therefore, we have an analysis of nineteen documents for a universe of twenty companies.

As far as mission, objectives, and values are concerned, it is important to clarify what these three concepts represent in the context of strategic planning. The mission of a company constitutes "it's starting point and reflects (...) the reason for its existence (...)." It must be "(...) unambiguous as to the overall goals and purposes of the organization. It establishes the direction that everyone within the organization should follow (...)" (Carvalho *et al.*, 2020). The objectives have to do with defining what must be done to fulfill the mission, meaning "(...) it is not enough to know where one wants to get to, one must know what one is going to do to get there" (Carvalho *et al.*, 2020). The company values are "(...) the attitudes and behaviors that the founders/owners/managers consider to be the most important to succeed in the mission (...)" (Carvalho, 2013).

Thus, we found that of the twelve documents that address them, there is one company that does not reflect any of the three dimensions relevant to our study in its strategic formulation: COCA-COLA PORTUGAL.

ANA - AEROPORTOS DE PORTUGAL has showed concerns with social responsibility, by stating "(...) contribute to the economic, social and cultural development of the regions in which it operates", and with commitments related to employees presented in its mission statement as follows "(...) and ensuring high levels of professional qualification and motivation of its employees."

AUCHAN RETAIL PORTUGAL, in its ten principles of ethical and responsible management, pays attention to social responsibility, identifying "solidarity and social intervention" and "protection of the environment", the commitment to employees, through "Respect for Human Rights", and also to technological innovation, identifying "Innovation and continuous improvement."

BP PORTUGAL only highlights social responsibility in its principles by stating "We are committed to safety, environmental protection and respect for the communities where we operate. We are committed to avoiding environmental damage among other consequences to the communities."

GALP refers, in terms of values, "Trust - As an expression of our ethics, transparency and integrity. We trust our people and their work, we share information and we develop solutions together", regarding the commitments with its employees; as well as "Agility - Of thought and action. We respond to change with a positive attitude, adapt quickly to new situations and show willingness to learn new ways of working and achieving goals" and "Innovation - Dynamic with the boldness to innovate, undertake, transform and create value. We promote new ideas and use them to develop new processes, methods, systems, products or services. We question the status quo, seek creative solutions and apply new solutions to achieve and exceed Galp's objectives", regarding the dimension of technological innovation.

INFRAESTRUTURAS PORTUGAL has represented the focus on social responsibility, by evidencing in its principles "the pursuit of public interest according to which the activity of the organization and its employees is pursued based on the prevalence of community and citizens' interest over private interest; social responsibility and environmental awareness which enable the economic and social progress of the community where the IP Group companies are located and stimulate the civic participation of its employees."

Also, JERÓNIMO MARTINS assumes in its mission a clear tendency towards a constant concern with social responsibility, as it refers "is (…) as well as contribute to the economic growth and sustainable development of the regions where it operates", and in its principles and values reinforces it when it refers to "Respect for the Law - (...) respect for the compliance with the applicable laws in the countries where it operates" and "Corporate Social Responsibility - (...) manage in a balanced way the relation between the necessary economic prosperity and the active contribution to the social development and environmental preservation in the regions where we are present."

As for NAVIGATOR COMPANY, we can see in its mission and fundamental objectives, the interest in the issue of social responsibility, on the one hand, when it says "(....) to position the Group's business at the forefront of the markets where it operates, maintaining a policy of sustainable management of natural resources, mitigation of environmental impacts, adopting principles and practices of social responsibility and fostering the social development of the areas where it does business" and, on the other hand, on the issue of commitments to employees when it mentions that "The fundamental aims pursued by The Navigator Company Group are based (...) also on recruiting, motivating and developing the best and most competent professionals. The Navigator Company Group will always promote a meritocratic culture that enables the personal and professional development of its employees (...)". Technological innovation is also present in the company's values through "Entrepreneurship - We have passion for what we do, we like to get out of our comfort zone, we have the courage to make decisions and take risks responsibly" and "Innovation - We promote the knowledge and creative potential of everyone to do the impossible."

REPSOL's values also include the dimension of social responsibility, when it identifies "Responsibility: We materialize our challenges, taking into account the global impact of our decisions and actions on people, the environment and the planet", and technological innovation, "Innovation: We believe that the key to our competitiveness and evolution lies in our ability to generate ideas and put them into practice, in an environment of collective and continuous collaboration and learning."

SONAE evidence all of the three dimensions in the company's values: social responsibility, through an "(...) active sense of social responsibility and we try to contribute to the improvement of the society in which we are inserted. We guide our conduct by environmental concerns and sustainable development policies. Co-operation and Independence - We remain open and willing to co-operate with governments (always with the aim of improving the regulatory, legislative and social framework), whilst being independent from central or local government. Value Creation: Sonae conducts its businesses with a view to creating long term value, respecting the principles of sustainability and corporate social and environmental responsibility"; commitment to employees placing "People at the heart of our success - Constant challenges and the willingness to change are fundamental to attract ambitious people. Our employees are key drivers of performance in all the markets where we operate. Therefore, in order to continuously enrich our culture, we invest in developing their skills and competencies", and technological innovation when it states that innovation "(...) is at the core of our business. We know that innovating involves risks, but we are aware of the importance of foreseeing and monitoring them in order to keep them within reasonable standards, so that we can grow continuously and sustainably.

Finally, TAP focuses its attention on its commitments to its employees, both with regard to the essential objectives when it refers to "Work, valuing its employees in their personal and professional skills" as one of them, and to the values, highlighting Professional Development in the following sentence "The employees of the TAP Group must, throughout their professional life in the Company, dedicate the best of their commitment to fulfilling the tasks entrusted to them and always seek to improve and update their knowledge."

Furthermore, and in an attempt to summarise the analysis in terms of the values defined by the companies that we were able to ascertain from a reading of their codes of ethics or codes of conduct, those most frequently repeated are responsibility, trust, excellence, integrity, innovation and social responsibility.

By analyzing all the codes of ethics and/or conduct by dimension - social responsibility, technological innovation, and commitments to employees - we registered some conclusions that we would like to highlight.

Regarding social responsibility issues and after having already identified which companies highlight it in their missions, objectives or values, we now highlight the companies that practically do not address the issue.

BRISA - AUTOESTRADAS DE PORTUGAL restricts itself to issues related to the environment and its Environmental Policy Statement.

CONTINENTAL also only addresses the issue by stating that "We are committed to the preservation of resources through the continuous adaptation of our production, the quality and performance of our products in terms of their environmental impact and the reduction of energy consumption, water, raw materials and consumables."

NOS limits its concern with social responsibility to the environment, committing to "(...) adopt the best environmental practices, promoting eco-efficient management, minimising the environmental impacts arising from the activity (...)", the concern with reducing the ecological footprint, the contribution to the promotion of more sustainable lifestyles, cooperation with civil society and the community in the place where they operate and respect for legislation and international conventions.

The remaining codes of ethics and/or conduct give special attention to various issues related to social responsibility, highlighting more commonly, the promotion and preservation of the welfare of populations, particularly the environment in which they operate, and the promotion of sustainable development. Some also mention, as a practice, the collaboration with local communities with a view to the economic, social and cultural development of the populations, the promotion of volunteer actions with the participation of its human resources, the contribution to the development of the national and regional economy, giving preference to local and national suppliers, the promotion of campaigns to raise goods and financial support, among other initiatives.

As far as the technological innovation dimension is concerned, only eight of the nineteen documents analyzed in this study make direct reference to the subject.

ANA - AEROPORTOS DE PORTUGAL indicates that they are in permanent "search for innovative solutions aimed at improving satisfaction levels", whereas AUCHAN RETAIL PORTUGAL addresses the matter in the ten principles of ethical and responsible management already mentioned above. AUTOEUROPA - VOLKSWAGEN GRUPO describes as company policy the design of "(...) advanced and efficient technologies, compatible with the environment (...)" and the implementation of these "(...) technologies throughout the life cycle of (...) products."

GALP, besides mirroring the concern with the issue at the level of the company's values, as previously identified, is the one that perhaps goes the furthest in its approach to the central issue that interests us, despite still being far from a direct approach, by indicating that one of their commitments is related to research and technology, considering that they are aware that the "(...) development and well-being of the communities in which we operate, present and future, is also developed through the contribution to innovation and technological research and the sharing of knowledge." Thus, they commit to "(...) cooperate with various institutions of this nature to promote technological development and more sustainable technologies that serve the present needs of local communities without compromising the ability of future generations to meet theirs as well."

NAVIGATOR COMPANY, REPSOL and SONAE have explicit indications on the issue in the values identified by their respective companies, as mentioned above.

As for the third and last dimension considered within the scope of our study, commitments to employees, we would like to highlight the following as the most addressed issues: respect for the dignity and rights of people; equitable treatment, countering situations of undue favouritism and inequality and meritocracy. NOS is one of those that goes further on this matter in its code of ethics when it states as a company commitment "(...) treating each employee fairly, in particular through a rigorous, transparent and constructive performance assessment based on merit."

Within the promotion of communication, sharing and interaction scope with a view to maximizing individual and collective performance we highlight what the code of ethics of COCA-COLA PORTUGAL refers to, regarding its objective of seeking to promote the best in each individual, i.e. to promote "(...) an internal culture that brings out the best in each individual. Within it, there is no room for leaders who are only good at doing their job; they also need to be good at maximizing the personal and professional development of their team members."

Also commonly mentioned are the stimulation of professional development namely through training and encouraging participation; the commitment to the creation of health, hygiene, and safety conditions at work the commitment to non-discrimination and equal opportunities; the guarantee of freedom of association and collective bargaining; the protection of personal data and privacy of employees. In this regard, VODAFONE's code of conduct states that the "(...) security (...) of employees (...) is crucial to fulfill our promise of creating a secure digital future. (...) The *Cyber Code* is the pillar that sets out how we expect all Vodafone employees to behave and work in order to safeguard our cyber security."

As far as those mentioning a work environment free from harassment and discrimination, EDP's code of ethics tells us about this premise that the company "(...) seeks to protect employees and does not tolerate acts of psychological violence and moral coercion - such as insults, threats, isolation, invasion of privacy or professional limitation - with the objective or effect of embarrassing the person, affecting his/her dignity or creating an intimidating, hostile, degrading, humiliating or destabilizing environment (...)".

We also found two specific situations, at BOSCH and ENDESA, respectively, which we found somewhat interesting and worth noting, related to employee turnover within the organization. In the case of ENDESA, the code of ethics states that "in case of reorganization of work activities, the value of human resources should be safeguarded by providing, whenever necessary, training and/or professional retraining actions. (...) in case that it is necessary to manage new or unforeseen situations, a collaborator may assign different tasks to previously developed ones, safeguarding at all times their professional competences." As for BOSCH, the business code of conduct dictates that "(...) in sensitive areas, such as Purchasing and Sales, we seek to effect, as a *matter* of principle, a regular rotation of personnel (*job rotation*)."

Following the in-depth analysis of the nineteen codes of ethics and/or conduct, the main records of which we have listed here, we, nevertheless, found that none of them makes any direct reference to the central premise of our study and/or to how the challenge will be presented and circumvented in the near future within their organizations.

CONCLUSION

Conducting a study that involves ethics, business, labor, humans and robots is a real challenge, all the more so in an age when the clash of values and principles concerning the sociological changes occurring in societies which stems from the rampant technological progress and many people question when assessing its impact on the quality of life, is evident.

Table 2. The three dimensions in the codes of ethics and conduct

	Social Responsibility	Technological Innovation	Commitments to Employees
ANA – AEROPORTOS DE PORTUGAL	MISSION: (...) contribute to the economic, social, and cultural development of the regions in which it operates.	Search for innovative solutions oriented to improve satisfaction levels - PASSENGERS, AVIATION COMPANIES, NON-AVIATION CUSTOMERS, CARGO CUSTOMERS.	MISSION: (...) and ensuring high levels of professional qualification and motivation of its employees. THE EMPLOYEES: 1. respect for people's dignity and rights; 2. equal treatment, counteracting situations of undue favoritism; 3. disclosure of all the information necessary for their motivation (...); 4. encouragement of individual and collective creativity; 5. encouragement of professional development; 6. commitment to creating conditions of health, hygiene and safety at work; 7. commitment to non-discrimination and equal opportunities; 8. guarantee of freedom of association and collective bargaining.
AUCHAN RETAIL PORTUGAL	10 principles of ethical and responsible management: Solidarity and social intervention; Environmental protection. ETHICS AND TRANSPARENCY: Promotion of social responsibility and transparency in the value chain; Responsible employability; Promotion of healthy and responsible consumption. COMMUNITY RELATIONSHIP: One of the principles that characterize Auchan's activity is the strong involvement with the communities where the stores are located. Auchan contributes to the development and improvement of the living conditions of local communities through various ways.	10 principles of ethical and responsible management: Innovation and continuous improvement.	10 principles of ethical and responsible management: Respect for Human Rights. EMPLOYEES: Safeguard of treatment with dignity, respect and equality; Health and safety conditions in the workplace; the right to a living wage in line with national regulations and the sector agreement; compliance with national regulations and sector agreements regarding the organization of working time; the right to freedom of association and the right to collective bargaining.
AUTO EUROPA - GRUPO VOLKSWAGEN	COMPANY POLICY: We make donations of monetary and material goods to the following areas: science and research, training, charitable purposes, sports, culture, churches and church institutions. In addition, donations are only given to non-profit institutions recognized as such or authorized to receive donations according to specific rules.	COMPANY POLICY: We design advanced and effective technologies that are compatible with the environment and implement them throughout the entire life cycle of our products.	COMPANY POLICY: We do not discriminate against anyone, nor do we tolerate any discrimination on the basis of ethnic origin or nationality, gender, religion, beliefs, age, disability, sexual orientation, skin color, political opinions, social background or other characteristic protected by law. We value diversity, and actively strive for inclusion. We hire, promote and develop our employees on the basis of their qualifications and abilities. We preserve and promote the health, skills and job satisfaction of our employees. We protect employees' personal data. Maintaining a professional relationship with the workers' representative body is an essential part of our corporate culture.
BOSCH	Social responsibility: On our own initiative and in the interests of our company, we act responsibly, also taking our impact on society and the environment into consideration. Donations: The Robert Bosch Foundation is active in the areas of international relations, health, education, science and culture.		Conduct toward employees: We respect and protect the personal dignity of each individual. We encourage diversity and do not tolerate any discrimination or harassment against or by our employees. In sensitive areas such as purchasing and sales, we aim to have regular job rotation as a matter of principle. In many cases, this also serves to further our professional development.
BP PORTUGAL	Our principles: We are committed to safety, environmental protection, and respect for the communities where we operate. We are committed to preventing environmental damage and other consequences to communities. Our expectations: Interacting with communities and respecting their rights and dignity. We want to be a trusted neighbor in the communities where we operate and live. Maintaining an open, ethical and respectful attitude towards diversity, local cultures and customs makes a positive difference. We encourage participation in the local community.		Threats, intimidation, and violence will not be tolerated. Diversity and inclusion are the foundation for teamwork and success. We value the unique contribution that each person brings to BP. Equal opportunity is a matter of fairness, respect and dignity. Provide a work environment free of harassment and bullying. We do not tolerate any form of abuse or harassment. BP respects the privacy of its employees. Commitment to human rights: We conduct our business in a manner that respects the human rights and dignity of people.

continued on following page

Table 2. Continued

	Social Responsibility	Technological Innovation	Commitments to Employees
BRISA – AUTOESTRADAS DE PORTUGAL	Environment: Promotion of biodiversity and promotion of natural resources, the environment and cultural heritage. Investment in the development of environmental management and scientific projects, new conservation systems, monitoring of differentiated environmental indicators, and technologies for energy efficiency and reduction of pollutant emissions. Rationalization in waste management (reduction, reuse and recovery), and the adoption of innovative solutions (construction techniques, choice of materials and equipment) that allow the reduction of energy, water and fuel consumption.	Professionalism and Responsibility: Brisa's employees should always dedicate their best effort in the fulfilment of the tasks entrusted to them, continuously seeking to develop and update their knowledge and skills, with a view to improving their professional capabilities and perfecting the functions they perform. Brisa encourages interaction and open and effective communication between its employees and this should promote a work environment that stimulates innovation, creativity and results through teamwork.	Equal Opportunities: Promoting an environment that values diversity and the conscious desire to achieve understanding, respect, dignity, social inclusion, as well as learning and constant professional development for all its Employees. Decisions should be based exclusively on the qualifications of the Employee. Brisa expressly forbids any form of discriminatory treatment. Respect for Fundamental Rights: Brisa undertakes the commitment to respect and ensure respect for human rights as recognized by national legislation and international conventions. Safety, Hygiene and Health at Work: Brisa undertakes the commitment to guarantee a safe work environment, scrupulously following all rules and practices.
COCA-COLA PORTUGAL	Acting globally and locally: Knows how to act on a planetary scale and how to embrace local culture, establishing lasting relationships with the communities in which it operates. Applying the circular economy to packaging management: Collect one can or bottle for every drink it puts on the market so that they do not end up as waste and can recycle and reuse more. Achieving water balance: The company has achieved this globally five years ahead of schedule, returning 100% of the water in its beverages to nature through various environmental interventions and projects. Reducing our carbon footprint: Iberia-wide, between 2010 and 2015, our carbon footprint in beverage manufacturing processes decreased by 67%, and we also improved our energy efficiency by replacing equipment with new ones.		Investing in the personal growth and talent of employees: Coca-Cola promotes an internal culture that brings out the best in each individual. Within it, there is no room for leaders who are not only good at doing their jobs; they also need to be good at maximizing the personal and professional development of their team members. Empower, promote equal opportunities, and be more inclusive: The company aspires to be as diverse as the consumers it serves. In this way, investing in young people is investing in social wealth. They are the future. So it offers them unforgettable experiences that stimulate their learning and maturity, so that they face the future with confidence, whether through creative writing, theater, or professional training.
CONTINENTAL	We are committed to preserving resources by continuously adapting our production, the quality and performance of our products in terms of their environmental impact, and reducing our consumption of energy, water, raw materials, and consumables.		Respect for human rights and fair working conditions: All employees enjoy freedom of association and the right to have their interests defended by elected representatives. We firmly repudiate any form of child or forced labor. We do not tolerate any form of harassment or physical or psychological abuse. We are collectively committed to creating a work environment free from any form of discrimination based on gender, age, race, skin color, social or ethnic origin, nationality, sexual orientation, religious or political beliefs, or any other characteristic protected by law. Health, safety, environment, and product integrity: It is our obligation to take measures for the protection of health and safety, to comply with work regulations and instructions and to use legally required protective equipment.
GRUPO EDP	EDP undertakes to act in full compliance with the legislation and regulations in force in the regions where it operates and to provide the authorities with all the collaboration within its reach Corporate social responsibility: EDP assumes its contribution to Sustainable Development and responsibility for the economic, environmental and social impacts resulting from its decisions and activities. Community: to maintain a close relationship with the communities in the regions where it operates, establishing a regular, open and frank dialogue, seeking to know their needs, respecting their cultural integrity and seeking to contribute to improving the living conditions of local populations.		Respect the Universal Declaration of Human Rights and international conventions, treaties, or initiatives. Respect for freedom of trade union association and recognition of the right to collective bargaining. EDP seeks to protect employees and does not tolerate acts of psychological violence and coercion. Guides its labour policies and procedures to prevent unjustified discrimination and differentiated treatment. It gives priority to the safety, health and well-being of employees. Employees: contribute to high levels of satisfaction and professional achievement, paying fair remuneration; promote respect for equal opportunities; promote correctness, friendliness, and professional pride in relations between employees; promote personal and professional improvement of employees; invest in the balance between professional and personal life of employees; value volunteering, encouraging employees to participate in civic affairs.

continued on following page

Table 2. Continued

	Social Responsibility	Technological Innovation	Commitments to Employees
ENDESA	Responsibility towards the community: Endesa aims to make its investments in an environmentally sustainable manner, respecting local and national communities, and to support initiatives of cultural and social value in order to enhance its own reputation and social acceptance. Environmental protection: Endesa programs its activities seeking a balance between economic initiatives and essential environmental needs. Aid and sponsorship: Endesa supports, through sponsorship activities and by formalizing specific agreements, initiatives that can be related to social, environmental, sports, entertainment and art, scientific and technological dissemination with events that offer quality assurance, that are national in nature or respond to specific territorial needs.		Endesa's employees are an indispensable factor for its success. Fairness of authority: Endesa guarantees that authority does not become the exercise of a power that is detrimental to the dignity and autonomy of the employee. Integrity of the person: Endesa guarantees the physical and moral integrity of its employees, working conditions that respect individual dignity, the rules of good manners and safe and healthy working environments. Personnel selection: (...) considering whether the profiles of the candidates correspond to those expected and the various business needs, respecting the principle of equal opportunities for all interested parties. Personnel management: Endesa avoids any form of discrimination with respect to its own employees. Endesa provides all employees with internal and remote information and training tools to enhance their specific skills and maintain the professional value of its employees. The involvement of employees in the development of their work is encouraged, promoting their participation in debates and functional decisions to achieve the company's objectives.
GALP	Compliance with the law and regulation: we observe and develop the appropriate diligence for compliance with the legal and regulatory duties applicable in each jurisdiction where Galp is present. Human rights: we commit ourselves in the communities where we develop our activities to minimize the negative impact that these have or may have. We respect the right of the communities to be heard before we start any activity that may have this impact. Environment: to ensure environmental protection in projects, undertakings and products throughout their life cycle, as well as the efficient use of energy and the incorporation of safe and innovative technologies in the management of activities. Corporate responsibility: to contribute to the promotion of quality of life and socio-economic development in the communities where we operate.	VALUES Agility: We respond to change with a positive attitude, adapt quickly to new situations, and show a willingness to learn new ways of working and achieving goals. Innovation: We promote new ideas and use them to develop new processes, methods, systems, products, or services. We question the status quo, seek creative solutions, and apply new solutions to achieve and exceed Galp's objectives. Research and technology: we are aware that the development and well-being of the communities in which we operate is also developed through the contribution to innovation and technological research and the sharing of knowledge. We are committed to cooperating with various institutions of this nature to promote technological development and more sustainable technologies that serve the present needs of local communities without compromising the ability of future generations to meet theirs as well.	VALUES We trust our people and their work, sharing information and developing solutions together. Safety: we choose to protect the lives and safety of people and property as the primary concern of our business. Health, hygiene, and well-being: We implement active policies to promote the health, hygiene and well-being of our people in the workplace. Non-discrimination: We do not discriminate against our own people or against anyone else. Harassment: Our working environment should be based on mutual respect, sharing experience and knowledge, and helping each other, so we do not tolerate any behavior that could constitute harassment. Equal opportunities: we hold our people accountable and value them based on merit. Privacy and personal data protection: compliance with the data protection legislation in force. Training: We provide appropriate training for people.
INFRAESTRUTURAS DE PORTUGAL (IP)	PRINCIPLES: prevalence of the community and citizens' interest over private interest; social responsibility and environmental awareness that enable the economic and social progress of the community where the IP Group companies are located and stimulate the civic participation of its employees. STANDARDS OF CONDUCT: (...) promoting and participating in initiatives that aim at the economic, social and cultural development of the populations. SOCIAL RESPONSIBILITY: act with awareness that its activity and decisions have an impact on the sustainability of future generations; favor the use of non-polluting technologies and energies; disseminate social responsibility practices including elements related to the identification of social, environmental and reputational risks; promote and participate in projects or actions of a civic, cultural or scientific nature that contribute to the well-being of society.		STANDARDS OF CONDUCT: equality in treatment, mutual respect and the rejection of any discriminatory behavior, as well as others that may constitute any form of harassment or abuse of power; perform their duties with professional pride, seeking to keep up to date in the areas relevant to the exercise of these duties, namely through training actions promoted within the scope of the IP Group; observe objective criteria in performance evaluation processes; comply with health and safety standards at work; respect the freedom of union association and recognize the right to collective bargaining; PREVENTION AND FIGHT AGAINST HARASSMENT AT WORK: This theme has merited autonomous treatment and developed in the internal normative "Policy for the Prevention and Combat of Harassment at Work" to which reference is made. PROTECTION OF PERSONAL DATA: The company recognizes privacy and the protection of personal data as fundamental values.

continued on following page

Table 2. Continued

	Social Responsibility	Technological Innovation	Commitments to Employees
JERÓNIMO MARTINS	MISSION: (...) to contribute to the economic growth and sustainable development of the regions in which it operates. Respect for the Law: to conduct its business in compliance with the applicable laws of the countries where it operates; to respect Human Rights, within the framework of the Universal Declaration of Human Rights and comply with the international treaties to which the countries where it operates are party. Corporate Social Responsibility: to manage in a balanced way the relationship between the necessary economic prosperity and the active contribution to social development and environmental preservation in the regions where we are present. Five transversal pillars present in the culture of the Jerónimo Martins Group: Promote Health through Food; Respect the Environment; Buy Responsibly; Support Communities; Be a Reference Employer.		OUR EMPLOYEES: guaranteeing a healthy and pleasant work environment, fair and adequate remuneration, in order to promote their motivation for work and a feeling of personal and professional accomplishment. Career Development and Non-Discrimination: to guarantee a personal and professional development based on merit, on qualifications and on equal opportunities; to promote their personal and professional development, to standardize training programs, especially in the distribution sector, to foster the sharing of experiences and to consolidate a Group culture. Safety, Health and Well-Being: ensures a safe and healthy working environment and conditions, prohibiting all forms of harassment. Freedom of Association: recognizes the various forms of freedom of association of its employees, namely those of a professional, recreational and socio-cultural nature. Respect for the Intimacy of the Employee's Private Life: ensures all employees the right to privacy and confidentiality regarding their private life.
NAVIGATOR COMPANY	MISSION AND FUNDAMENTAL OBJECTIVES: (...) to position the Group's business at the forefront of the markets where it operates, maintaining a policy of sustainable management of natural resources, mitigation of environmental impacts, adopting principles and practices of social responsibility and fostering the social development of the areas in which it carries on its business activities. SOCIAL RESPONSIBILITY AND SUSTAINABLE DEVELOPMENT: it assumes its social responsibility with the communities where it develops its business activities in order to contribute to their progress and well-being; it commits to adopt, comply with and promote a Sustainability and Environmental Protection Policy.	VALUES Entrepreneurship - We have passion for what we do, we like to get out of our comfort zone, we have courage to make decisions and take risks responsibly; Innovation - We promote the knowledge and creative potential of everyone to do the impossible;	MISSION AND FUNDAMENTAL OBJECTIVES: (...) recruitment, motivation, and development of the best and most competent professionals. The Navigator Company Group will always promote a meritocratic culture that enables the personal and professional development of its Employees (...) SAFETY AND WORKING CONDITIONS: The Navigator Company Group will never employ child or forced labor, nor will it collude with such practices. The safety and health of its employees is a priority. PROEFESSIONAL DEVELOPMENT AND PROGRESSION: it provides adequate training to its employees and encourages continuous training as an element that promotes motivation and better performance; the selection, hiring, remuneration and professional progression policies adopted are guided by merit criteria. NON-DISCRIMINATION AND COHESION: Any conduct that may constitute a form of coercion, namely through moral offenses, mobbing, moral or sexual harassment, or bullying, is expressly forbidden. PROTECTION OF PERSONAL DATA: Comprises the preponderant role of privacy and the protection of personal data.
NOS	SOCIETY: To adopt the best environmental practices, promoting an eco-efficient management, minimizing the environmental impacts resulting from the Group's activity and using the natural resources rationally; To promote the use of information and communication technologies that contribute to sustainable development, namely in reducing the ecological footprint and promoting quality of life in society; To cooperate and collaborate with civil society organizations and associations in the spirit of solidarity and mutual aid with the community where we operate. LEGISLATION: respect and promote international norms and conventions.		COMMITMENTS TO EMPLOYEES: To base the human resources management policy on respect for diversity, rights of each person and non-discrimination; not to condone any form of harassment or any other form of assault on dignity; to treat everyone fairly, namely through a rigorous, transparent and constructive performance assessment based on merit; to foster equal opportunities for personal and professional development; to respect the balance between professional and personal life; to create a good working environment, ensuring compliance with the applicable health and safety standards; to promote team spirit, the sharing of common goals. PRIVACY: protect all personal data that allows individual identification or characterization.

continued on following page

Table 2. Continued

	Social Responsibility	Technological Innovation	Commitments to Employees
REPSOL	OUR VALUES: Responsibility: We meet our challenges, taking into account the global impact of our decisions and actions on people, the environment and the planet. HUMAN RIGHTS: In addition to complying with the requirements of local legislation, Repsol is committed to respecting internationally recognized Human Rights. COMMUNITY RELATIONS: to establish solid and long-lasting relationships with local communities. ENVIRONMENTAL MANAGEMENT: We make our best efforts to prevent the company's actions from damaging the environment. POLITICAL ACTIVITIES AND DONATIONS: Repsol does not make any political donations, either in cash or in kind. Institutional contributions may be made.	OUR VALUES Innovation: We believe that the key to our competitiveness and evolution lies in our ability to generate ideas and put them into practice, in an environment of collective and continuous learning and collaboration.	Occupational Health and Safety: Provide a safe and healthy work environment; Harassment-Free Workplace: We all have the right to work in an environment free from intimidation, harassment, and abuse. Equal opportunities: Repsol brings together employees with a wide variety of career paths, skills and cultures. Discrimination is prohibited. Diversity and inclusion: We value the unique contribution that each person makes to Repsol. Personal information: For Repsol, privacy has always been a matter of trust. The right of employees to exercise freedom of expression and to participate in political activities is recognized.
SONAE	VALUES: Social Responsibility - We have an active sense of social responsibility and try to contribute to the improvement of the society in which we operate. Our conduct is guided by environmental concerns and sustainable development policies. Co-operation and Independence - We remain willing and open to co-operate with governments (always with the aim of improving the regulatory, legislative, and social framework), whilst adopting a position of independence in relation to central or local government. COMMUNITIES: Sonae develops a policy of active Social Responsibility and of contributing towards the improvement of Communities where its businesses operate, with a strong concern for the environment, economic and social well being and the development of human knowledge. ENVIRONMENT: adopts and encourages the responsible use of natural resources and the preservation of the environment, namely by promoting an eco-efficient management that minimizes the environmental impacts resulting from the companies' activities.	VALUES Innovation is at the core of our business. We know that innovating involves risks, but we are aware of the importance of foreseeing and monitoring them in order to keep them within reasonable standards, so that we can grow continuously and sustainably.	VALUES: People at the center of our success - Our people are key drivers of performance in all the markets where we operate. Therefore, and in order to continuously enrich our culture, we invest in the development of their skills and competencies. EMPLOYEES: Personal Development and Professional Progression - permanent training as an element that enhances their best performance and motivation. The selection, remuneration and professional progression policies adopted are guided by merit criteria. Protection of Rights: Sonae observes the principles and values set out in national and international legislation concerning Human and Social Rights. Discriminatory behaviours are not permitted, equal opportunities are promoted, and integrity and dignity are ensured in the workplace. Health and Safety: Sonae provides a healthy, safe and pleasant work environment that promotes well-being and productivity. Participation: Sonae values and encourages the participation of its employees.
TAP	The TAP Group companies base their actions on criteria of excellence and commitment to the community, which is why one of their objectives is to respect the quality of life of the communities in which they operate. Rules for Sponsorship: Sponsorships aim to combine the promotion of a brand with the development and enrichment of various events of social, sporting, or cultural scope. ENVIRONMENT: Its sustained growth presupposes the compatibility of economic performance with the responsibility it assumes towards society and the environment. SOCIAL RESPONSIBILITY: promotion of company policies that develop social responsibility, both internally and externally; participation in social intervention projects, civic, social, and cultural activities within the communities where they are located; making their skills available in community projects, namely through volunteer work.		ESSENTIAL OBJECTIVES: Work, valuing its employees in their personal and professional skills. GENERAL VALUES: Professional Development - employees should always seek to improve and update their knowledge. Relations with Employees: dignity of the person, not allowing discriminatory practices; recognition of merit as a factor in productivity gains and professional enhancement; continuous professional training of all employees and valuing free initiative; recruitment, selection and improvement of employees based on transparent and objective criteria. Protection of Personal Rights: guaranteeing equal opportunities; principle of non-discrimination; the right to privacy. Safety and Well-Being in the Workplace: a healthy and safe work environment, aimed at enhancement and well-being, promoting trust, respect, justice, and stimulating innovations.
VODAFONE	Business Principles | Communities and Society: We aim to provide products and services that can transform people's lives and contribute to greater sustainability by empowering individuals, contributing to broader development goals, and reducing environmental impacts. Environment: We are committed to protecting the environment. We invest in energy efficiency measures to mitigate the effects of climate change and we reduce, reuse and recycle telecommunications equipment to reduce waste through careful planning, design, installation and maintenance and end-of-life processes.		SECURITY: crucial to delivering on our promise to create a secure digital future. The Cyber Code is the cornerstone of how we expect all Vodafone employees to behave and work to safeguard our cyber security. HEALTH & SAFETY: We expect everyone at Vodafone to always behave in a safe and responsible manner. Business Principles | Employees: Respect for individuals and their human rights. We do not tolerate child labor. We do not accept any form of discrimination, harassment, or bullying. We promote equal opportunity and inclusion of all employees through our hiring policies and practices. Avoid harassment and bullying.

Source: Prepared by the authors.

Robots have been around for several decades and there is no doubt that not only are they here to stay, but they are also recognizably important in our lives. If we think that much of hospital technology that today helps operate people was only possible thanks to the justified means of production of hospital equipment, we realize that both technological development and its ability to develop increasingly perfect machines can be a real contribution to society. Nevertheless, as in almost all industrial revolutions, there are also consequences that, in essence, end up being the social price to pay for having these same technologies available.

Companies are perhaps one of the main drivers, if not the main driver, for the speed with which we see new technologies being developed today. Take the military industry, for example, which, in its aim to secure the best contracts with major governments, is now presenting increasingly powerful weapons full of technology, including AI-based technology.

Focusing the conclusion on the subject under discussion, that is, on the relationship between codes of ethics and the safeguarding of jobs that are being replaced by more productive and profitable machines, the result of our study is that there is no need within companies, at least for the time being, to mention the issue in their codes of ethics, nor is it expected to happen in the short term.

The main conclusion we reach, which, in our opinion, constitutes one of the reasons for the absence of any reference to job protection in the codes, is related to the perception that businesspeople, and the scientific society itself, have on the subject. At the moment the discussion centers on the effects of the introduction of new technologies on the current professions. There are two identified and opposing currents of thought as to the results of these changes, and they do not converge in their opinion. One clearly recognizes that there is a problem, which will worsen in the future, considering that a part of the current professions may disappear. It adds that, in addition to this disappearance, new professions will require other levels of knowledge, which may not be sufficient to fill all the lost jobs.

A second line of thought, more focused on demonstrating the benefits of technological advances in industry, clearly defends the idea that such technological introductions will result in economic and social benefits for the population, based on a criterion that advocates an increasing production of wealth, as well as a decrease in production costs and, finally, a reduction in the prices of goods that will lead to an increase in demand, with the results for companies. We cannot, nor is it the objective of this work, study the effects that will arise from the fourth industrial revolution, which is very different from previous ones in its essence, since it is based less on industrial production capacity and more on the capacity to produce data and store knowledge.

Basically, companies have social concerns, regardless of their goal of maximizing profits; there are concerns that are reflected in their codes of ethics, such as, for example, concerns for the community where they operate or the surrounding environment. Therefore, we believe that the time gap until the concerns are centered on the goal of maximizing the use of human labor tends to be closing, either by virtue of the pressure from communities, or the respect for imposed norms (e.g. World Labor Organization), or even labor regulations to be decreed by governments, which sooner or later will end up happening.

REFERENCES

Administradores (2021). Retrieved March 6, 2021, from https://administradores.com.br/artigos/etica-moral-e-responsabilidade-social

Alencastro, M. (2009, January/June). Hans Jonas e a proposta de uma ética para a civilização tecnológica. Desenvolvimento e Meio Ambiente. *Editora UFPR*, (19), 13–27.

Ana – Aeroportos de Portugal SA. (2021). Retrieved January 3, 2021, from http://www.dgtf.pt/

Associação Portuguesa de Ética Empresarial. (2020). Retrieved December 18, 2020, from https://www.apee.pt/2019-02-05-19-45-24/ethical-code-compliance-overview

Auchan Retail Portugal. (2021). Retrieved January 3, 2021, from www.auchan-retail.pt

Autoeuropa – Grupo Volkswagen. (2021). Retrieved January 3, 2021, from https://www.volkswagen-autoeuropa.pt/

Batista, G. (n.d.). *Inteligência Artificial – Introdução*. Retrieved December 18, 2020, from https://auto-ciencia.blogspot.com/2016/07/inteligencia-artificial-introducao.html

Bisneto, J., & Lins, O. (2016). Gestão da inovação: uma aproximação conceitual. *Revista Brasileira de Gestão e Inovação – Brazilian Journal of Management & Innovation, 3*(2), 86. Retrieved December 18, 2020, from http://www.ucs.br/etc/revistas/index.php/RBGI/index

Bosch. (2021). Retrieved January 3, 2021, from https://www.bosch.pt/

BP Portugal. (2021). Retrieved January 3, 2021, from https://www.bp.com/

Brisa – Autoestradas de Portugal SA. (2021). Retrieved January 3, 2021, from https://www.brisa.pt/

Buchholz, R. (1989). *Fundamental concepts and problems in business ethics*. Prentice Hall.

Bulgarelli, W. (1985). *A teoria jurídica da empresa* (R. dos Tribunais, Ed.; 1st ed.).

Carvalho, J. M. (2013). Planeamento Estratégico. O seu guia para o sucesso (2nd ed.). Porto: Vida Económica – Editorial, SA.

Carvalho, L., Bernardo, M., Sousa, I., & Negas, M. (2020). *Gestão das organizações. Uma abordagem integrada e prospetiva* (2nd ed.). Lisboa: Edições Sílabo.

Cherman, A., & Tomei, P. (2005). Códigos de Ética Corporativa e a Tomada de Decisão Ética: Instrumentos de Gestão e Orientação de Valores Organizacionais. *Revista de Administração Contemporânea, 9*(3), 99–120. doi:10.1590/S1415-65552005000300006

Coca-Cola Portugal. (2021). Retrieved January 3, 2021, from https://www.cocacolaportugal.pt/

Continental. (2021). Retrieved January 3, 2021, from https://www.continental.com/

Cortina, A. (2005). *Ética de la empresa. Claves para uma nueva cultura empresarial*. Madrid: Editorial Trotta, S.A.

Cosenza, O., & Chamovitz, I. (2007, October). *Ética, Ética Empresarial E Responsabilidade Social: Reflexões E Recomendações*. Paper presented at the XXVII Encontro Nacional de Engenharia de Produção, Foz do Iguaçu, Brasil.

Cressey, D., & Moore, C. (1983). *Managerial Values and Corporate Codes of Ethics*. California Management Review. doi:10.2307/41165032

Denny, A. (2001). *Ética e sociedade*. Capivari. Opinião E.

Dinheiro Vivo. (2021). Retrieved January 3, 2021, from https://ranking-empresas.dinheirovivo.pt/ranking-nacional-empresas

Duarte, A. P., & Neves, J. G. (2011). *Relação entre responsabilidade social percebida e satisfação no trabalho: O papel mediador da imagem organizacional. Percursos da investigação em psicologia social e organizacional*. Colibri.

Economia e Finanças. (2020). Retrieved December 16, 2020, from https://economiafinancas.com/2016/definicao-grande-media-pequena-microempresa/

EDP. (2021). Retrieved January 3, 2021, from https://www.edp.pt/

Endesa. (2021). Retrieved January 3, 2021, from http://www.fedecundi.com/

European Commission. (2017). Retrieved December 18, 2020, from https://ec.europa.eu/

Ford, M. (2015). *Robôs: A Ameaça de um futuro sem emprego*. Bertrand Editora.

Galp. (2021). Retrieved January 3, 2021, from https://www.galp.com/

Infraestruturas De Portugal, S. A. (IP). (2021). Retrieved January 3, 2021, from https://www.infraestruturasdeportugal.pt/

Instituto Ethos. (2020). Retrieved January 8, 2021, from https://www.ethos.org.br/

Jerónimo Martins. (2021). Retrieved January 3, 2021, from https://www.jeronimomartins.com/

Kurzweil, R. (1990). *The Age of Intelligent Machines*. MIT Press.

Moreira, J. M. (1999). *Ética, economia e política*. Lello & Irmãos Editores.

NOS. (2021). Retrieved January 3, 2021, from https://www.nos.pt/

OECD - Organisation for Economic Co-operation and Development. (n.d.). Retrieved March 7, 2021, from https://www.oecd.org/

Padioleau, J. (1989). *L'E'thique est-elle un Outil de Gestion?* Revue Française de Gestion. Juin-Julliet-Aout.

Paine, L. (1994). *Managing for Organizational Integrity*. Harvard Business Review.

Peters, M. A. (2016). Technological unemployment: Educating for the fourth industrial revolution. *Educational Philosophy and Theory*, *49*(1), 1–6. Retrieved January 8, 2021, from. doi:10.1080/00131857.2016.1177412

Racy, J., Moura, A., & Scarano, P. (n.d.). O Desenvolvimento Do Conceito De Empresa Na Teoria Econômica: Uma Revisão Das Principais Contribuições. *Revista de Economia Mackenzie, 3*(3), 154-17. Retrieved January 8, 2021, from https://biblat.unam.mx/hevila/RevistadeeconomiaMackenzie/2005/vol3/no3/7.pdf

Repsol. (2021). Retrieved January 3, 2021, from https://www.repsol.pt/

Revista critica de Ciências Sociais. (2021). Retrieved December 18, 2020, from https://journals.openedition.org/rccs/956

Sonae. (2021). Retrieved January 3, 2021, from https://www.sonae.pt/

Souza, M. (2018). *Como o impacto da utilização do Waze e Uber na Cidade de São Paulo, Brasil explica o fenómeno da quarta revolução industrial* (Tese de Mestrado, ISCTE Business School). Retrieved January 18, 2021, from https://repositorio.iscteiul.pt/bitstream/10071/18786/1/master_marcelo_anderson_souza.pdf

Souza, O. (2003). *Ética Individual & Ética Profissional* (Vol. 3). ABC.

Souza, W. (2004). Conceito de Empresa: um Desafio que Persiste? *Revista do Tribunal Regional Federal da 1ª Região, 16*(5). Retrieved December 18, 2020, from https://core.ac.uk/download/pdf/16048427.pdf

TAP. (2021). Retrieved January 3, 2021, from https://www.tapairportugal.com/pt/

The Navigator Company. (2021). Retrieved January 3, 2021, from http://www.thenavigatorcompany.com/

Valls, Á. L. M. (2014). O que é ética. *Revista Eletrônica Espaço Teológico, 8*(14), 308-314. Retrieved December 18, 2020, from https://revistas.pucsp.br/index.php/reveleteo

VER - Valores, ética e responsabilidade. (n.d.). Retrieved December 18, 2020, from https://www.ver.pt/os-desafios-da-4a-revolucao-industrial-na-empregabilidade-e-no-apoio-as-pessoas-vulneraveis/

Vodafone. (2021). Retrieved January 3, 2021, from https://www.vodafone.com/

Weaver, G. R. (1993). *Corporate Codes of Ethics: Purpose, Process and Content Issues*. Business and Society.

Weber, M. (2002). *Ciência e política: duas vocações*. Martin Clare.

Chapter 12
Information Systems Governance and Industry 4.0:
People as a Central Link

Pedro Fernandes Anunciação
https://orcid.org/0000-0001-7116-5249
Polytechnic Institute of Setúbal, Portugal

Fernando Gonçalves
Polytechnic Institute of Setúbal, Portugal

João Pimenta
Congelagos, Portugal

ABSTRACT

The information society requires governance. The complexity of the markets is bringing complexity to the functioning of economic organizations. The pressure of technological innovation challenges the need for governance on organizational systems, in particular on information systems. But the role of technological innovation is pressing for the re-qualification and re-balance of jobs and professions themselves. This process has come to assert itself as a result of the affirmation of Industry 4.0, where, evidently, technologies accelerate the replacement of human presence in the production system.

INTRODUCTION

The challenges of Information Systems Governance are, in most cases, transversal to different natures of organizations and sectors of activities. The business processes, common to any other organization, and particularly in industrial organizations, are characterized by the presence of specific production processes where industrial control systems take over, along with the business processes present in any other organization, a decisive impact on its governance.

DOI: 10.4018/978-1-7998-7452-2.ch012

In this sense, we can assume that the organization and industrial functioning constitute two indissoluble realities. The productive processes support, in an increasingly visible way, the factors of competitive differentiation, in that they must have the capacity to process massive amounts of data in increasingly short periods, from frequently distinct and unstructured sources. The recent trend towards one-size-fits-all production has been forcing. The transition from mass production to a more personalized one, supported by a set of technologies that provide a growing autonomy, requires differentiated strategies according to the specificity of market segments and a greater capacity for monitoring and inclusion of the most innovative technologies associated with their operation.

What we have generally agreed to call Industry 4.0 is currently a complex web of «communicating vessels» where numerous suppliers, physical flows of raw materials, subsidiary materials, energy resources and computing capacity converge for the execution of materials transformation processes in products. It is in this networked model, which underlies a process of transformation from a traditionally physical to digital environment, that SI governance emerges in most economic organizations, regardless of the sector, and that allows to anticipate the existence of particularities associated with IS governance in industrial organizations.

Information Systems Governance in industrial organizations has had a limited application when it comes to infrastructure planning and productivity increases in factories. However, recent technological innovations in the industrial field have highlighted the need for a more holistic approach to the traditional management of industrial units. Technologies such as Cyber-Physical systems (CPS), Internet of Things (Iot), Cloud Computing, among others, provide new opportunities and dynamics in the industrial field, even having opened the opportunity to classify a new phase of development in this sector called the 4th industrial revolution (Santos *et al.*, 2018). Industry 4.0 marks a new paradigm in economic history. Industry 4.0 promises to bring traditional industry into the era of artificial intelligence, where digital technologies will be an integral part of industrial production processes (Horváth, 2018). More stakeholders, more resources, more technologies, more technical and scientific interdisciplinarity will be realities associated with this new paradigm.

In this context, industrial competitiveness is now conditioned, from an internal perspective, by the availability and allocation of resources to investment, and, from an external perspective, by the ability to respond to time-to-market, among other examples, among other aspects. This new performance framework associated with technological innovation tends to significantly alter the traditional status quo with the polarization of production processes around automation and evolution to a "proto-cognitive" capacity at the factory level.

Even making projections only with current technology and its expected evolution, the transformation will have a very diverse range between geographies and sectors of activity, merging what is now distinct, changing combinations and opening deep cleavages in what is now continuous.

New paradigms of collaboration between people and machines/software, which are perspective, will be catalysts of the design of innovative infrastructures and the relationship between the parts of an Organization, and between organizations, requiring negotiation of new commitments, read, a new Governance, where high technology (IT) will function as a building block elementary.

While the current debate has highlighted the potential of a social crisis, resulting from unemployment generated by increasing automation, and relegated to secondary plan the challenge of population aging, the exclusion of people with limitations, the inability to integrate refugees and the scarcity of people able to meet the new challenges of companies in the more developed economies, the essence of the discussion of this theme, should take into account the opportunity to address the ethical dramas of the Society to a new level, through the transformation of processes and the framing of new solutions for the empowerment of people and their valorization to new levels of development.

These levels increasingly pass-through models of organization of society that, in the limit, translate into the economy of sharing and the emergence of "prosumers" - a term coined to designate consumers who, at the same time, contribute as producers to the system. These are, to a large extent, the proposals advocated by Jeremy Grifkin in his work "The Zero Marginal Cost Society" (2014, p. 17) and stemming from the connected economy – Internet of things or galaxy internet – the latter expression, which is the subject of one of the International Conferences of the European Club for the Governance of Information Systems – Portugal and whose impact on industry, economy and society is still, at least in part, truly unpredictable.

THE WORLD 4.0: INDUSTRY, PRODUCTIVITY AND ECONOMY

The extraordinarily long development cycles that characterized industry were particularly affected by the speed of digital transformation which, much more quickly, imposed a new dynamism on society and the economy. In a brief historical retrospective, we can recall that the First Industrial Revolution, which began between the end of the eighteenth century and the beginning of the nineteenth century, corresponded to the introduction of mechanical production systems, using water and steam, in companies. The Second Industrial Revolution, which began at the end of the 19th century, gave rise to mass production, through the use of electricity, providing new capacity to respond to the demands of the economy. The Third Industrial Revolution, which took place in the mid-20th century, introduced automation and microelectronics technology in production, advances very associated with information and communication technologies. It is at this stage that technological innovation, particularly in the field of ICT, begins to assume a central importance in the processes of changes in the production paradigm. There are several examples that could be mentioned in this 3rd Revolution, namely computer numerical control (computer numerical control – CNC) and industrial robots, which made possible flexible production systems (Flexible manufacturing systems – FMS's), technologies supporting industrial design (computer-Aided design – CAD), computer-assisted production (computer-Aided manufacturing – CAM) and computer-assisted planning (computer-Aided Processing Planning – CAPP) which enabled integrated computer production (computer Integrated manufacturing – CIM) (Feng, Li & Cen 2001).

Several authors consider that we are currently experiencing the Fourth Industrial Revolution. This was born in 2013, as a German strategic initiative, essentially focused on the aspects of connectivity, interoperability, and integration of the production process in the universe of the value chain. Almost simultaneously, China launches the Made in China 2025 initiative and the Taiwan Island the Productivity 4.0 initiative, the latter adding to the premises of Industry 4.0 aspects related to the organization of sectoral clusters and the appreciation and promotion of talent.

Industry 4.0 is described as a fourth industrial revolution since the first industrial revolution in the late 18th century (Xu, Xu & Li, 2018) and describes the increasing digitization of the industrial environment, or associated with it, by creating digital value chains that enable communication between products, their environment and business partners (Lasi *et al.*, 2014; Dallasega, Rauch & Linder, 2018). We have entered the era of the digital factory (Agis *et al.*, 2010).

Industry 4.0 or 4th Industrial Revolution expresses this new reality and that, in a synthetic way, corresponds to the implementation of "smart" Videos add a new dimension of «intelligence» to the value chain in general and to production lines. This new context is characterized by the potential associated with technologies such as Cyber-Physical systems (CPS), which represent a significant leap in the dynamics of industrial operation, in that they facilitate the self-organization of systems, monitoring processes or creating a virtual copy of the real world; Internet of Things (IoT), which connects machines, objects and people in real time; Cloud Computing, which offers storage solutions, as well as enabling access to information and decision-making, allowing production processes and businesses to be combined creating value for organizations (Anunciação, Esteves & Dinis, 2021) (Santos *et al.*, 2018) (Moeuf *et al.*, 2017) (Hermann, Pentek & Otto, 2016) (Lasi *et al.*, 2014) (Kagermann, Wahlster & Helbig, 2013) (Jasperneite, 2012).

CPS are systems with computational and physical capabilities, capable of interacting with humans, being directly connected to a physical environment. The CPS correspond to any system or product who has knowledge of its own, its creation, status, purposes, destination, and so on, allowing other systems to communicate with it and be aware of that information (Smart products are CPS's by definition) (Anunciação, Esteves & Dinis, 2021). They can be applied in process controls, medical devices, energy control, traffic control, aviation, advanced automated systems, and intelligent structures (Pires, 2016). These provide new demands in the industrial field namely in reliability, Maintenance, availability, safety and real-time operation. The characteristics of CPS are real-time information sharing between industrial machines, supply chains, suppliers, business systems, customers, and any other object/technology, as well as control, adaptation, monitoring, interaction, and personalization of any necessary area. These systems enable an extensive integration of customers and partners in business processes, the generation of added value and a better connection between production and high-quality standards (Vieira *et al.*, 2018) (Kagermann, Wahlster & Helbig, 2013).

Additive Manufacturing (AM) is the current term for the concept of rapid prototyping (RP - Rapid Prototyping) or what is popularly called 3D printing. RP has been used in various industries for the rapid creation of a system or parts prior to their production or final marketing. However, the RP being used in the creation of prototypes and final physical parts, using directly the data of the digital model, originated its evolution to the term additive manufacturing (Gibson, Rosen & Stucker, 2015).

Additive manufacturing, by allowing the direct manufacture of models generated through three-dimensional computer-aided design system (3D CAD) is seen as a set of disruptive technologies that are changing the way od products designed and businesses development strategies. The fact that less time is needed for the construction of the parts and for the transfer of information to the AM system significantly reduces the concern with the conversion and interpretation of the data (Gibson, Rosen, & Stucker, 2015). Another feature is the reduction of process steps, as the part is performed in only one step and the great versatility to allow coupling various support technologies (drill bits, silicone rubbers, etc.) making it possible to manufacture a wide range of parts with different characteristics. This opportunity makes it possible to overcome the limitations of traditional industry.

Cloud computing has been receiving a lot of attention over the years from organizations and industry in general, due to its flexibility and for its strong scalability around the growth of the organizations. Cloud computing provides convenient sharing of computational resources (networks, servers, storage, applications, and services) that can be quickly made available to organizations. Provides greater agility, scalability, and skill to enterprise organizations allowing them to adapt to business fluctuations thus enabling potential cost optimization (Hashizume *et al.*, 2013).

The IoT refers to a new paradigm that allows the connection of physical objects and the execution of certain actions, providing a new economic and social reality in which equipment can communicate with people or even with each other. It integrates a network that connects anything to the Internet based on protocols stipulated through certain equipment and information sensors. These serve to detect, inform, and communicate, with the aim of achieving intelligent recognitions, positioning, tracking, monitoring, and administration (Patel & Patel, 2016). The specific characteristics are: Inter-connectivity (connectivity between different objects and between different networks), training (additional characteristics to common objects), heterogeneity (diversity of objects, platforms, and networks), dynamism (ability to dynamically change device context), scalability (possibility of connectivity growth and integration into different networks).

AI corresponds to the computing capacity that approximates the action of technologies to human behavior, namely as regards the human capacity to reason, to make decisions, and to solve problems. AI addresses the phenomenon of intelligence allied to engineering, seeking to build instruments to support human intelligence, and to perform human tasks that require the use of intelligence (Lab, 2018).

In the context of the stages of industrial development, three important strands in the field of governance stand out. The first, conceptual basis, corresponds to the assumption that the evolutionary paradigm of economics has a close relationship with technological innovation, which has originated that is being carried out in shorter and shorter periods of time. The second, competitive base, corresponds to the need for vision and preparation of managers to minimize the associated impacts. The third, strategic base, corresponds to the assumption that innovation is increasingly transversal and that it is integrated with several sectors of activity, opening new opportunities. And the fourth, structural base, corresponds to a deeper change in that it is foreseen a restructuring of the productive system that will adopt a digital base, in which the industrial units will integrate into a digital ecosystem marked by new realities such as the additive manufacturing, augmented reality, big data and analytics, autonomous robots, simulation, horizontal and vertical systems integration, industrial internet of things, cybersecurity and cloud computing.

This is a movement that will cross all industrial sectors of economic activity. Take the case of the textile sector in Portugal where, in a prospective study carried out in 2001 on the industry up to 2020, the impact of technological innovation on the sector was anticipated, by identifying the customized manufacture of meshes, the use of prototyping technologies, 3D printing, e-textiles with colors and formats controlled by iPhone applications and with health signal monitoring devices distributing, via wireless, vital information to smartphones, among other examples (Agis *et al.*, 2010).

This is a technological development that continues to place people at the center of development and innovation as consumers, but at the same time contributes to reducing human intervention in manufacturing processes. The integration of technologies with the economy and society is increasingly evident and profound, and the focus of product innovation has led to the optimization and sophistication of the entire value chain, from production to materials, from marketing to logistics, from traditional applications to the development of new areas of application.

Welcoming these realities, the European Club for the Governance of Information Systems (CEGSI) - Portugal broadened the range of reflection, welcoming the theme of Economy 4.0 at its International Conference of 2017[1], that, as the President of CEGSI states in his intervention under that initiative, "intends to be the ICT Economy, "Artificial Intelligence", "Learning machines", Digital Transformation, Robotics, Companies without People, of machines with emotions and feelings, of "intelligent equipment" [...] (Oliveira, 2017, p.15).

It is clear that, without any doubt about the benefits of this new industry largely driven by ubiquity, by (near) real-time data transfer and by the integrated vision of the entire value chain, the individual remains at the center of this whole transformational process. It is in him that lies the intelligence, the ability to decide, the gift of governance.

In the industrial context, the World 4.0 forms itself in the combination of three determining dimensions: the most advanced technologies of communication, computational and data analysis; the completeness of the supply chain and value of each product or component; and, not least, the management and decision-making capacity arising from the two previous dimensions.

THE SOCIETY OF THE FUTURE

According to IT pioneer Alain Kay, "the best way to predict the future is to invent it" (Nadella, Shaw & Nichols, 2018, p. 206). Technological transformations and revolutions have indelibly marked the way societies organize and progress.

As we move progressively from feudal societies, predominantly rural and agricultural, to industrialization and services, trades and manual labor were progressively losing their importance, overwhelmed by serial production and the decreasing marginal costs of increasingly overwhelming production scales and potentially global markets.

This reality, however, seems to give signs of change. The economy of sharing, in which individuals engage in direct exchanges as in the distant past, the replacement of the possession of the goods by their use or the auto production, made possible by technologies such as 3D printers or domestic energy generation equipment are already daily themes with significant impact on the functioning of the economy (Grifkin, 2014) opening to new economic and, consequently, social challenges.

THE FUTURE OF THE INDUSTRIAL ORGANIZATION

The organization of the industry has been conditioned to the big investments and the intellectual property developed with sophisticated internal resources as protection against the entrance of new competitors. There is an extensive literature on the management of innovation understood as a competitiveness tool with the aim of breaking the rigidity of the organizations that were assembled around the concept of efficiency.

From the beginnings of the approaches to innovation, as a disciplined action and as an alternative to chance (Eureka moment), through Peter Drucker who has based management on innovation as a competitive tool that can be formalized, taught, trained, developed and constantly perfected, up to the most avant-garde theories about how the brain works and how to take greater advantage of its potential (Damásio, 2011), they all try to solve the dilemma between the need for a disruptive product/service and the predictability of continuous product improvement.

The new paradigms try to combine a method of obtaining the high profitability product before the competition with the exploitation of the maximum return on investments already made. In the recent past, huge investments were made in factories where competitiveness factors were at scale, process optimization and low operating costs. In this phase, theories around efficiency such as Lean, World Class Manufacturing and Activity Base Costing and Total Quality Management had the foreground of attention. Successive mergers and acquisitions were promoted until what was called the Globalization Movement in which the productive elements were moved to remote regions where the costs of production factors were minimized (Brazil, Russia, India and China).

This movement of global optimization generated a decoupling between the creative process and the production process, which was initially considered virtuous, but turned out to be pernicious in some aspects. The concept, in its genesis, seemed to have benefits upstream and downstream. On the one hand, it allowed more advanced countries to evolve their societies to a higher level of income around creation, design, and customer service activities whereas, downstream, the middle class of several hundred million people in formerly disadvantaged areas were given opportunities to ascend through large-scale migrations from subsistence farming to new industries, in a movement similar to what had happened during the 18th century industrial revolution.

Hence resulted in an unexpected blocking situation (deadlock) where large investments in highly optimized factories did not have the flexibility to accommodate the increasingly short life cycles of products created when large organizations specialized in design. Another counterproductive effect has also been superimposed on this deadlock situation, which is the result of the fact that the creative process itself depends on the know-how. When this knowledge dissociated for very long periods, the ability to innovate reduced pace by going to incremental improvement or reformulation of previous concepts (vintage look on cars, fusion of adjacent area like cookies and chocolates, etc).

The prolongation of this blockade has increased the fears of the incumbents about the emergence of a radical innovation coming:

1. from an unexpected sector that brought the giants to their knees, as they were unable to reorientate their highly organized corporations and were held hostage by intricate manufacturing networks (clusters of supply companies);
2. of a new competitor with a domain of technology, which allows him to achieve speed, scale, and coverage without significant investments in assets.

The movement of new entrants (disruptors such as Google, Tesla, Uber, etc.) began to show itself, capturing important slices of profitability of sectors without need of assets, though resorting to capital-intensive stock exchanges and the mass extinction of organizations in various areas (Kodak, Blockbuster, British automobile industry, Yahoo, Nokia, etc.).

As a reaction, the incumbents (dominant companies in sectors such as General Electric, Nike, Walmart, etc.) also seek to integrate in their operations the concept of platforms. On these platforms, initially known as Apple's Market Places (App Store, etc.), the coordination of the actors in a Cluster was done more efficiently, supported in sophisticated information systems, until the concept evolved to also include Customers and Distributors. This allowed large organizations to change the direction of absolute control of resources (coffee, steel, cocoa, etc.) and internal optimization of costs and processes to a paradigm where the new competitiveness factors are:

1. excellence in resource coordination.
2. sustainability in its use.
3. the recognition/identification of consumers with the trademark.

This new type of organization is allowing competitive advantages vis-à-vis traditional Competitors by creating the network effect, that is, benefiting from the contribution of Customers as communities of loyal Customers as opposed to the Customer Supplier relationship (Parker, Van Alstyne & Choudary, 2016):

1. make it difficult for customers to switch to new experiences offered by new entrants by promoting dynamics in the Customer communities that hold them back (successive discounts, etc.).
2. use these Client communities as co-creators of new concepts in a new creative process better adapted to local specificities or more skilled in detecting global trends (Zara Confections).
3. superior level of quality of service through a closer connection to the Customer with more powerful profiles databases and consumption histories fed by the Customers themselves.
4. use of new generation interaction tools (service bots, community leaders, etc).

NEW WAYS OF CREATING VALUE

In the past, the value of a given company was intrinsically linked to the valuation of its tangible assets: buildings, machinery, shops. Progressively, new components were added – intangible – whose relative weight in the balance came to accentuate significantly: software, royalties, brands, ideas, knowledge.

The value of the data assumes an unparalleled dimension, reflected in the nature of the most valuable companies in the world. Since 2016, the world's top 5 companies have been active in the field of data and/or intangible assets economics. Only 5 years earlier, 4 out of 5 of these companies were in the banking or oil business.

Technological developments in fields such as robotics, automatic storage, artificial vision, data analysis and machine Learning or blockchain are completely transforming the industry and, in particular, industrial processes.

Considered one of the great threats to factory jobs, robotics has, perhaps somewhat surprisingly, contributed to the increase of production in areas previously relocated from developed countries to countries with cheaper labor. The offshoring movement, typically originating in the search for cheap labor, has progressively given way to reshoring, with a double positive impact on the labor market of developed countries: creation of direct jobs by the recovery of previously delocalized and indirect productions due to the need to provide maintenance to robotic lines.

In April 2012, the Boston Consulting Group conducted a survey of US manufacturing executives and concluded that about half of companies with sales above US$10 billion were actively transferring or considering transferring their factories to United States of America (Ford, 2015, p. 9).

That movement, whose tendency has spread far beyond North America, has had the immediate effect of increasing unemployment in countries where cheap labor was once a competitive factor that boosted relocation. Initiatives such as Made in China 2025, in which the main priority is to replace undifferentiated low-cost production with the creation of Chinese brands associated with quality and research and development of new technologies and materials. The program has prioritized the following industrial domains (Li, 2017, p. 2-3): Information Technologies; Cutting-edge Automation Technology; Industrial Process Control Machinery; Aerospace and Aviation Equipment; Equipment in maritime engineering; Production of high-tech vessels; Low-consumption vehicles; New materials; Biomedicine and high-performance medical devices; and Agricultural equipment.

We will see later that this path has as its obverse the accentuation of the difficulties of employability and re-qualification of the age groups of the less qualified population, especially in countries less able to win the fight of literacy and well-being economic and social welfare for their populations in general. In any case, in this equation of value creation, supply-side variables must necessarily match on the demand side and vice versa, otherwise they cancel each other out.

Also artificial vision, data analysis and machine Learning are contributing to the elimination of some of the most complex paradoxes in the domain of many of the highly robotized factories. As Rodney Brooks of MIT pointed out, observing factories with a high degree of sophistication and highly robotic, "people are scarce, but they are not absent. And much of the work they do is repetitive and undifferentiated" (Brynjolfsson & McAfee, 2014, p. 53). Challenges of high complexity for robots, although repetitive and undifferentiated for humans, are being directed towards solutions based on the combination of artificial vision and algorithms "able to learn" (learners) or, in the limit explored by Pedro Domingos, "a single algorithm that combines the key functionalities of all of them: the master algorithm" (Domingos, 2015, p. 16).

THE CHALLENGES OF RECRUITMENT: DIVERSITY, AGEING, TALENT AND DIGITALIZATION

As Frances Cairncross says, "for as long as there is memory, networks have been the way in which individuals locate experts. The beauty of questioning a person instead of reading a book or searching a database lies in the fact that, if that person doesn't have the answer, he or she may give clues to someone who does." (Cairncross, 2002, p. 29).

This reality is now apparently enhanced by the facilitated access to, and large-scale processing of, data and by allegedly infinite communication and dissemination networks and media. Cities have never been so populated and flooded with telecommunications infrastructure, and loneliness and aging are so much discussed.

Differences in education levels, mathematical skills, problem solving, and basic computer skills are also very significant depending on the region, country, age group or even gender. And of these, the combination of robotization and aging is an overwhelming mix and a major challenge for states and society in general in the coming years: robotization and aging. In an OECD study on adult skills (OECD, 2016, p. 56), around 55% of adults who reported having no computer experience were in the 55-65 age group.

Do we run the risk of seeing a complete replacement of humans? The natural end of humans is running out?

CONCLUSION

As mentioned by the Information Systems Governance European Club, there are several areas of focus of the Governance of Information Systems, namely in the area of investments in Information Systems, the definition of the Organization of IS model and its insertion into the Institution's Macro Structure and the characterization of the IS Management model and practices (Urbanism, Architecture and IS Planning), in the acquisition and implementation of SI solutions, in the economic and financial analysis of SI investments, in the form of organization and mode of exploitation of IS, and also in the control of SI performances, among others.

However, in the area under consideration, industry will continue to be one of the forms of wealth creation in societies but will evolve to accommodate the way communities interact and consume resources.

If the governance of information systems is today a critical factor for the success of organizations, by ensuring the best conversion of strategy into systems architectures, robust processes, and effective team building, in the future will be decisive and in industry.

Today's industry coordinates an ecosystem of physical material suppliers that is as efficient as its logistics chain and effective in tuning in with internal media. The most successful organizations have maturity levels of information systems governance and are preparing the next step.

In the industry of the future, both incumbents and disruptors, success will continue to be determined by excellence in coordination, but in a broader context and the governance of information systems will be indispensable as is an essential function of the cognitive system of a body that coordinates different organs and driving elements:

1. The coordination of external processes, supported in the information systems, will go beyond the physical limits of the factories not only for the logistic integration of the Suppliers, but of other areas such as the internalization in the company of the upstream Customer experience and the sustainability of the downstream Suppliers.
2. 2 The depth of automation and its sophistication (artificial intelligence, IOT, autonomous robotics) will depend even more on advanced external information systems (IBM Watson, Google IOT and Tensor Flow, etc.) that blurs the boundary of internal/external information systems.
3. The attraction of the best talent will require to constitute more diverse teams, in broader geographies and with more fluid communication. The teams will be smaller and/or with variable geometry in time requiring a more careful management of the knowledge generated by these teams and maintained in the information systems.
4. Signs of a reorganization of global power are already being anticipated in which the new economic blocs will compete in the digital dimension (Internet-supported business systems, manipulated news, mobile devices and applications, advanced encryption and combat systems) in addition to the 4 classical dimensions (land, air, sea and space). As in the past, conflicts will affect civil society and industry is one of the main targets so that information systems security will have a greater preponderance in the governance of information systems.

REFERENCES

Agis, D., Bessa, D., Gouveia, J., & Vaz, P. (2010). *Wearing the future. Micro trends for the Textile, Clothing and Fashion Industries until 2020*. Portuguese Textile and Clothing Association. (in Portuguese)

Anunciação, P. F., Dinis, V., & Esteves, F. M. (2021). *Preventive Maintenance as a Critical Success Factor in Industry 4.0. In Handbook of Research on Digital Transformation and Challenges to Data Security and Privacy*. IGI-Global.

Brynjolfsson, E., & McAfee, A. (2014). *The Second Machine Age: Work, Progress and Prosperity in a Time of Brilliant Technologies.* W. W. Norton & Company.

Cairncross, F. (2002). *The Company of The Future: How Communications Revolution Is Changing Management.* Harvard Business School Press.

Dallasega, P., Rauch, E., & Linder, C. (2018). Industry 4.0 as an enabler of proximity for construction supply chains: A systematic literature review. *Computers in Industry, 99*, 205–225. doi:10.1016/j.compind.2018.03.039

Damásio, A. (2011). *The Error of Descartes: Emotion, Reason and Human Brain.* Círculo de Leitores Publishing. (in Portuguese)

Domingos, P. (2015). *The Master Algoritm: How the Quest for the Ultimate Learning Machine Will Remake Our World.* Penguin Random House.

Feng, S., Li, L., & Cen, L. (2001). An Object-oriented Intelligent Design Tool to Aid the Design of Manufacturing Systems. *Knowledge-Based Systems, 14*(5–6), 225–232. doi:10.1016/S0950-7051(01)00100-9

Ford, M. (2015). *Rise of the Robots: Technology and the Threat of a Jobless Future. Nova Iorque.* Basic Books.

Gibson, I., Rosen, D., & Stucker, B. (2015). Additive Manufacturing Technologies - 3D Printing, Rapid Prototyping, and Direct Digital Manufacturing. New York: Springer Science + Business Media.

Grifkin, J. (2014). *The Zero Marginal Cost Society.* Palgrave Macmillan.

Hashizume, K., Rosado, D., Medina, E., & Fernandez, E. (2013). *An analysis of security issues for cloud computing.* SpringerLink. doi:10.1186/1869-0238-4-5

Hermann, M., Pentek, T., & Otto, B. (2016). Design Principles for Industrie 4.0 Scenarios. *Proceedings of 2016 49th Hawaii International Conference on Systems Science.* 10.1109/HICSS.2016.488

Horváth, B. (2018). The Recognition of resource use through industrial development from a social perspective. Studia Mundi–Economica, 5(1). doi:10.18531/Studia.Mundi.2018.05.01.68-78

Jasperneite, J. (2012). Was Hinter Begriffen Wie Industrie 4.0 Steckt. *Computers and Automation, 12*, 24–28.

Kagermann, H., Wahlster, W., & Helbig, J. (2013). *Recommendations for Implementing the Strategic Initiative Industrie 4.0: Final Report of the Industrie 4.0 Working Group.* Acatech-National Academy of Science and Engineering.

Lab, O. (2018). *Inteligência Artificial.* Retrieved Jan 20, from https://observador.pt/explicadores/inteligencia-artificial/

Lasi, H., Peter, F., Thomas, F., & Hoffmann, M. (2014). Industry 4.0. *Business & Information Systems Engineering, 6*(4), 239–242. doi:10.100712599-014-0334-4

Li, L. (2017). China's manufacturing locus in 2025: With a comparison of "Made-in-China 2025" and "Industry 4.0". *Technological Forecasting and Social Change*. Advance online publication. doi:10.1016/j.techfore.2017.05.028

Moeuf, A., Pellerin, R., Lamouri, S., Tamayo-Giraldo, S., & Barbaray, R. (2017, September 8). The Industrial Management of SMEs in the Era of Industry 4.0. *International Journal of Production Research*. Advance online publication. doi:10.1080/00207543.2017.1372647

Nadella, S., Shaw, G., & Nichols, T. (2018). *Make Refresh: Microsoft's Soul Rediscovery and Creating a Better Future*. Vogais Publishing. (in Portuguese)

OECD. (2016). *Skills Matter: Further Results from the Survey of Adult Skills. OECD Skills Studies*. OECD Publishing. doi:10.1787/9789264258051-

Oliveira, A. (2017). *Information Systems Governance in Economy 4.0 - Who (and how) is in charge for the Information Systems Governance in Economy 4.0 - really?* Intervention in the context of the 9th International Conference of the European Club for the Governance of Information Systems, Lisbon, Portugal.

Parker, G., Van Alstyne, M., & Choudary, S. (2016). *Platform Revolution: How Networked Markets Are Transforming the Economy and How to Make Them Work for You*. W. W. Norton & Company.

Patel, K. K., & Patel, S. M. (2016). Internet of Things-IOT: Definition, Characteristics, Architecture, Enabling Technologies, Application & Future Challenges. *International Journal of Engineering Science and Computing*.

Pires, L. (2016). *Cyber-physical systems: the future of Industrial Maintenance?* Retrieved Nov 13, from https://www.researchgate.net/profile/Luis_Pires12/publication/309780775_Sistemas_ciber-fisicos_o_futuro_da_Manutencao_Industrial/links/5bfe8355a6fdcc1b8d4872ff/Sistemas-ciber-fisicos-o-futuro-da-Manutencao-Industrial.pdf

Santos, B. P., Alberto, A., Lima, T. D. F. M., & Charrua-Santos, F. M. B. (2018). Indústria 4.0: Desafios e Oportunidades. *Revista Produção e Desenvolvimento*, *4*(1), 111–124.

Vieira, M., Nicola, F. M., Junior, M. V., Simon, A. T., & Correr, I. (2018). The Application of Cyber-Physical Systems (CPS) in Manufacturing Systems: A Bibliometric Study. *Conference: National Meeting of Production Engineering*. 10.14488/ENEGEP2018_TN_STO_258_478_36385

Xu, L. D., Xu, E. L., & Li, L. (2018). Industry 4.0: State of the art and future trends. *International Journal of Production Research*, *56*(8), 2941–2962. doi:10.1080/00207543.2018.1444806

ENDNOTE

1 The 9th International Conference of CEGSI, which took place in Lisbon on October 10, 2017, was subject to the theme "Governance of Information Systems & Economy 4.0".

Chapter 13
Industrial Maintenance Entering the Industry 4.0 Era: A Roadmap Proposal

Pedro Fernandes Anunciação
https://orcid.org/0000-0001-7116-5249
Polytechnic Institute of Setúbal, Portugal

Vitor Manuel Lemos Dinis
https://orcid.org/0000-0003-4016-3851
Cibersur, Portugal

Francisco Madeira Esteves
Polytechnic Institute of Setúbal, Portugal

ABSTRACT

Industry 4.0 marks the beginning of the so-called fourth industrial revolution. The new emerging information technologies, such as internet of things, cloud computing, machine learning, artificial intelligence, among others, have challenged the management and organization of industrial companies. They have now shorter market response times, higher quality requirements, and customization needs, which challenges many industrial areas from production to maintenance, from design to asset management. The maintenance and asset management condition and the reliability of production lines are closely linked and constitute key areas of good industrial operation. This work seeks to present a roadmap proposal for the management of industrial assets from maintenance management. In addition, it seeks to identify the key elements for a roadmap design and proposes a set of management questions to assess maintenance maturity.

DOI: 10.4018/978-1-7998-7452-2.ch013

INTRODUCTION

Industry 4.0 is a major milestone in today's industry. Industry 4.0 promise to be the era of artificial intelligence, where digital technologies will prosper (Horváth, 2018). Although it can be assumed as a natural evolution of previous industrial systems, this evolution represents new levels of knowledge and learning that, supporting the consolidation of the knowledge held and linking them to technological innovation, open new prospects for the economic and social development of humanity. Without ruptures and conflicts, the evolution has been carried out in a search of answers to the market, in the mechanization of work, and in the automation of production, among other aspects.

Industry 4.0 brings several opportunities and benefits, such as highly flexible mass production, real-time coordination of the production system, value chain optimization, cost savings derived from complexity, or the creation of new services and business models. These industry-wide innovations put pressure on all other related activities in a push-pull logic. For example, regarding logistics, some experts say that industry 4.0 can only exist if logistics is able to supply production systems at the right time, in the right quantity, with the right quality and in the right place. So, however promising the "fourth industrial revolution" maybe there are still several challenges, risks, and barriers to overcome for its implementation. It will be necessary to deconstruct traditional management approaches, reorganize value creation processes, make changes within and between enterprises, define appropriate infrastructure and standards, ensure data security and educate employees so that a positive outcome of this change can be achieved (Hofmann & Rüsch, 2017).

Industry 4.0 or 4th Industrial Revolution are some of the terms used to describe the implementation of "smart" devices that can communicate autonomously along the value chain. It is in this context that technologies such as Cyber-Physical systems (CPS) have emerged, which represent a significant leap in the dynamics of industrial operation, in that they facilitate the self-organization of systems, monitoring processes or creating a virtual copy of the real world; Internet of Things (IoT), which connects machines, objects and people in real time; Cloud Computing, which offers storage solutions, as well as enabling access to information and decision-making, allowing production processes and businesses to be combined creating value for organizations (Santos *et al.*, 2018).

In the field of industrial management, the current challenge is very different from previous times. Equipment currently incorporates systems with intelligence characteristics and industrial units have become organizations with sufficient flexibility to meet the specific needs of demand, according to the response times that the market requires. The equipment communicates with each other and the sharing of data in real time opens opportunities for an automotive monitoring of systems, products, and processes. The systems control themselves and allow higher degrees of reliability. Customers require increasingly customized products in small batches, which would be impossible and unsustainable under the previous traditional production paradigm (Alkaya et al., 2015).

This new era of industrial is thus marked by the fusion between the physical and digital world, providing a new context of action characterized by a communication between products and machines and a symbiosis between organization and dynamics. An unprecedented autonomy in production and a convergence between different «worlds» (physical, digital, and biological world) is expected in an action guided by multi-disciplinarity and complementarity of knowledge.

This will be a new industrial and, at the same time, economic universe, marked by new information and communication technologies such as cloud computing, horizontal and vertical integration of management systems, AI, IoT, 3D printing and augmented reality or by new paradigms in the information society like Big Data. Let's look at the most targeted technologies.

The CPS has emerged as a new reality of industrial functioning, challenging organizations to change through a link between the real and the virtual world. CPS are systems with computational and physical capabilities, capable of interacting with humans, being directly connected to a physical environment. The CPS correspond to any system or product who has knowledge of its own, its creation, status, purposes, destination, and so on, allowing other systems to communicate with it and be aware of that information (Smart products are CPS's by definition) (Dinis, Esteves & Anunciação, 2021). They can be applied in process controls, medical devices, energy control, traffic control, aviation, advanced automated systems, and intelligent structures (Pires, 2016). These provide new demands in the industrial field namely in reliability, Maintenance, availability, safety and real-time operation. The characteristics of CPS are real-time information sharing between industrial machines, supply chains, suppliers, business systems, customers, and any other object/technology, as well as control, adaptation, monitoring, interaction, and personalization of any necessary area. These systems enable an extensive integration of customers and partners in business processes, the generation of added value and a better connection between production and high-quality standards (Vieira *et al.*, 2018) (Kagermann, Wahlster, & Helbig, 2013).

Additive Manufacturing (AM) is the current term for the concept of rapid prototyping (RP - Rapid Prototyping) or what is popularly called 3D printing. RP has been used in various industries for the rapid creation of a system or parts prior to their production or final marketing. However, the RP being used in the creation of prototypes and final physical parts, using directly the data of the digital model, originated its evolution to the term additive manufacturing (Gibson, Rosen, & Stucker, 2015).

Additive manufacturing, by allowing the direct manufacture of models generated through three-dimensional computer-aided design system (3D CAD) is seen as a set of disruptive technologies that are changing the way od products designed and businesses development strategies. The fact that less time is needed for the construction of the parts and for the transfer of information to the AM system significantly reduces the concern with the conversion and interpretation of the data (Gibson, Rosen, & Stucker, 2015). Another feature is the reduction of process steps, as the part is performed in only one step and the great versatility to allow coupling various support technologies (drill bits, silicone rubbers, etc.) making it possible to manufacture a wide range of parts with different characteristics. This opportunity makes it possible to overcome the limitations of traditional industry.

Cloud computing has been receiving a lot of attention over the years from organizations and industry in general, due to its flexibility and for its strong scalability around the growth of the organizations. Cloud computing provides convenient sharing of computational resources (networks, servers, storage, applications, and services) that can be quickly made available to organizations. Provides greater agility, scalability, and skill to enterprise organizations allowing them to adapt to business fluctuations thus enabling potential cost optimization (Hashizume *et al.*, 2013).

The IoT refers to a new paradigm that allows the connection of physical objects and the execution of certain actions, providing a new economic and social reality in which equipment can communicate with people or even with each other. It integrates a network that connects anything to the Internet based on protocols stipulated through certain equipment and information sensors. These serve to detect, inform, and communicate, with the aim of achieving intelligent recognitions, positioning, tracking, monitoring, and administration ((Patel & Patel, 2016). The specific characteristics are: Inter-connectivity (connectivity between different objects and between different networks), training (additional characteristics to common objects), heterogeneity (diversity of objects, platforms, and networks), dynamism (ability to dynamically change device context), scalability (possibility of connectivity growth and integration into different networks).

AI corresponds to the computing capacity that approximates the action of technologies to human behavior, namely as regards the human capacity to reason, to make decisions, and to solve problems. AI addresses the phenomenon of intelligence allied to engineering, seeking to build instruments to support human intelligence, and to perform human tasks that require the use of intelligence (Lab, 2018).

In this context, it is possible to observe increasing and simultaneously significant degrees of autonomy in software and robots, providing them with the ability to automate processes. This is an area with a strong impact on the functioning of enterprises and significant future social impacts, as it is expected that active workers will be strongly replaced by artificial intelligence systems, particularly in the industrial sector.

Russell & Norvig (2016) presents several domains where artificial intelligence is present, namely: robotic vehicles (vehicle that can identify the environment around it and circulate safely); voice recognition (devices that can recognize the voice of the user and, through commands, perform actions); robotics (inserted into robots, allowing to replace man in certain situations).

The term Big Data expresses the exponential volumetry of data that are generated by the technological devices applied in various contexts, and that require significant capacities at the level of the Information Systems regarding their processing and storage, due to its volume dimensions, characteristics, and variety (Nascimento *et al.*, 2017). Big Data thus reflects the emergence of innovative technology that offers alternatives for massive data processing, offering new ways to reuse and extract value from information (Akerkar, 2014). Thus, there are three characteristics associated with Big Data: volume, speed, and variety (Zikopoulos & Eaton, 2012). Schonberger & Cukier (2013) also added the value, associated with scarcity, uncertainty, and data diversity. The opportunities associated with Big Data provide greater possibilities for segmentation, experimentation, support of human decision-making through automated algorithms and innovation in products, services, and businesses (Manyika *et al.*, 2011).

Industry 4.0 thus presents a path for a new industrial management framework based on self-knowledge, self-supply, self-comparison, self-reconfiguration and self-maintenance, which relies on intelligent analytics through Big Data and CPS (Lee, Kao & Yang, 2014). This is a new reality to which industrial enterprises must pay special attention. Since the German government presented Industry 4.0 as one of its main initiatives to take the lead in technological innovation, numerous academic publications, articles, and conferences discuss this topic (Bauernhansl *et. al.*, 2014) industrial enterprises have been challenged to develop skills associated with intelligence, from products to production lines, from organization to competitiveness.

The impacts of these technological innovations put pressure not only on production specifically, but also on other areas such as maintenance and asset management. So, the imminent changes of Industry 4.0 and new technologies are expected to bring to an excellent opportunity rises in the field of company's maintenance performance improvement by reducing costs and assuring higher production uptime and higher profitability, through integration and development of preventive maintenance practices (Dinis, Esteves & Anunciação, 2021). Associated with maintenance is the concept of Asset Management (AM), which has been a growth of relevance. Although it was born in the financial sector, it encompasses the management of assets to their maintenance and profitability. In capital intensive industries AM is used to identify how an industrial organization deals with the management of its physical assets through their life cycle to achieve its strategy (El-Akruti &Dwight, 2013).

OBJECTIVES AND METHODOLOGIES

This work has as its general objective the elaboration of a roadmap proposal that facilitates the management of assets in industrial companies. To this end, it will be based on the principles identified by Rojas & Davis (2008) and, from this, will seek the identification of the most relevant dimensions of analysis associated with each of the aspects mentioned by this author. From this identification we will try to establish an evaluation framework that can be used in future research work to assess the maturity of the industry in this field.

This is an exploratory study with a qualitative approach (Lima, 2005) (Alves-Mazzotti & Gewandsznajder, 2004) (Godoy, 1995) in which an inductive inference is presented, with an interpretative objective, with the purpose of describing and understanding various realities, captures of everyday life and human perspectives. The reality investigated is objective and complex, focusing on the nature of the study object. This analysis explores the whole context of reality and seeks, from the interaction with the participants, analysis information, knowledge and experiences with a view to defining a roadmap and a evaluation framework.

The nature of this study and analysis is based on a theoretical and practical problem which supports the objective of research, management and preservation of industrial assets, and that it will guide the process of collecting empirical information with a view to characterizing and critically analyzing reality in the light of the theoretical-methodological assumptions that were at its basis (Marques, 2019).

With a view to a pragmatic validation of the coherence and relevance of the highlighted dimensions, the application of the technique of participant observation (Focus Group) was sought as a way of analyzing and assessing the usefulness of the dimensions identified in the evaluation of asset management. The Focus group comprised 8 specialists responsible for industrial maintenance in large industrial companies, 3 teachers in the field of information systems and industrial engineering and a top manager of systems services and information technologies company specializing in the development of software for industrial activity.

This type of methodological procedure of qualitative approach aimed to provide greater involvement with the problem and make it more explicit to the various participants, as stated Yin (2018). This approach also facilitates the identification the best way to implement and manage the respective impacts associated with change, through the development of a “how” and “why” strategy (Cavalcanti & Moreira, 2010).

ASSET MAINTENANCE MANAGEMENT

Asset Maintenance Management (AMM) has been around for quite some time and it has undergone continual name changes as well as changes to its overall definition. Rojas & Davis (2008) identify a set of relevant dimensions in this field, which will be learned and adopted in this work. Consider that an Asset Maintenance Management System (AMMS) can be characterized as a system that provides “a continuous process optimization strategy for improving availability, safety, reliability and longevity of physical assets” (i.e., systems, facilities, equipment, and processes).

Asset Maintenance Management System Components

An AMMS has to be viewed as belonging to and involving the entire organization, not just the maintenance department. The primary purpose of an AMMS and its accompanying components (programs, tasks, activities, etc.) is to:

1. Know exactly what assets organizational have (i.e., those that are responsible for operating, monitoring and/or maintaining);
2. Know precisely where the assets are located:
3. Know what condition organizational assets are in at any given time;
4. Understand the design criteria of organizational assets and how they are to be properly operated and under what conditions;
5. Develop an asset care, or maintenance, program that assures that each asset performs reliably (referred to as reliability) when it is needed (referred to as availability);
6. Acknowledge and perform all the above activities to optimize the costs of operating organizational assets and to extend their useful life at least to, if not beyond, what the initial design and installation specified.

Identifying Assets

Usually, it may be found that identifying what assets one has is not as simple as one might think, especially considering the large amount of infrastructure most companies maintain and operate. One asset registry must be developed for each facility. Those registries should be designed to be completed at each facility by the operations staff following the site treatment process train. An indispensable effort should be made to have a detailed inventory data for every asset in the facilities.

Also, every asset should have its location well defined, and quite often one has to dig out drawings, or track down the last person(s) who worked on a given asset. Frequently, assets that used to be easily locatable were now hidden under a sidewalk, street or any other structure.

Asset Condition

Knowing the asset condition of a certain item can be a challenge, especially when is hidden from normal sight (i.e., vaulted, underground or remotely located). Therefore, a process or procedure is necessary that enables workers to perform the necessary inspections, preventive maintenance, or predictive tasks whenever the opportunity arises to do so, and that would completely and accurately capture, document, and store all related information for easy access and review at any future point. This information typically comes from operators, maintenance crews, contractors, and engineers, reinforcing that a good AMMS is not just a maintenance department initiative.

Actual asset condition assessment regimen can be designed as a relatively course filter for the first inventory, with the expectation that it would be refined each time the inventory is reassessed. As a guide to operations staff, condition assessment ratings should be established for assignment to all asset components.

In addition to knowing what assets are owned and where they are located, a unique asset number must be assigned to each and every one, as well as a replacement or rehabilitation value, and an evaluation of remaining life. This data should be in a format that can be downloaded to the AMMS.

Asset Design Criteria

To monitor the facility situation, a company needs to know their asset's design specifications, document them, ensure that the equipment was operating within those specifications, and maintain equipment accordingly. For monitoring this type of data and information company will use information from different systems, namely DCS, MES, Uptime, and so on.

Asset Care Program

Once the assets identified, where they are, and how to properly utilize or operate them, a company must integrate a basic care program to ensure that those assets will be ready to use and, once engaged, would operate at or near the designed specification parameters until disengaged.

To accomplish this, a company needs a clear understanding of how it is expected to run its maintenance program. A company should operate in a more proactive maintenance environment, as opposed to a reactive one. Operating in a reactive mode (meaning that equipment is fixed after it breaks down) generally costs two to three times more (e.g., in labor, parts and materials, and loss of service) than operating in a proactive environment, in which regular inspections, effective preventive maintenance, and other predictive technologies find problems before they occur so that they can be fixed prior to actual failure. These tasks take some structure and continuous monitoring.

A proactive asset environment should include all the technologies mentioned above, along with effective planning and scheduling, as well as work orders feedback loops to provide asset history. This will eventually allow its maintenance planners to perform data mining, statistical process control (SPC), failure modes and effects analysis (FMEA), and root cause failure analysis (RCFA) when one of those unexpected failures occurs.

Because it is extremely challenging to keep this kind of data up to date, accurate and available, a company should install a computerized maintenance management system (CMMS).

Optimizing Operation Costs

Responsibility for achieving this objective fell primary to supervisory and management staff. There are two basic requirements:

1. To establish key performance indicators (KPIs) for the asset care process to monitor and determine such things as jobs in backlog, emergency jobs completed, percentage of emergency jobs, scheduled jobs completed, and schedule compliance.
2. To collect the right kinds of data, at the right time, in a consistent format that would allow company to make data-informed decisions versus best guesses. To know where and how asset care (maintenance) financial resources were being spent, company would need enough information in sufficient detail to decide whether to repair, refurbish, or replace a given asset.

Putting All Together

The fundamental components company must address as part of its asset maintenance management strategy are not always simple to enact, especially since organizations tended to be somewhat lax in incorporating many of these elements in the past. Companies in general recognize that they need to retain the services of a professional Asset Maintenance consulting company to assist with implementing the desired changes and getting employees up to speed so that they could realize the true benefit of an AMMS.

As a result, companies have successfully begun its journey towards a sound, effective and efficient AMMS by putting in place best business practices and incorporating them into the configuration and set-up of its new CMMS (computerized maintenance management system), which can be defined as a program to manage and control plant and equipment maintenance in modern manufacturing and service industries.

A CMMS comprises a large set of functionalities for maintenance management, namely, work requests, approvals, planning of preventive maintenance actions, work scheduling activities considering available resources and planned production, management of spare parts, analysis of data to reduce the occurrence of failures, work reporting, data management, equipment history, information management, cost accounting and for improving the performance of the maintenance function (Lopes, 2016).

The documented best business practices, coupled with the new CMMS system, will allow company to reduce maintenance costs, minimize unscheduled downtime, improve service reliability, and extend the lifecycle of its assets.

Basics of Sound Asset Care Maintenance

A sound maintenance asset management strategy has six basic components:

1. Work identification and control
2. Job planning
3. Work order scheduling
4. Preventive / predictive optimization
5. Materials coordination
6. Schedule outage / shutdown coordination

Work Identification and Control

Work identification and control is the most important component of the six listed above. Without this basic function in place, optimization of any of the others is virtually impossible. Remember the three cardinal rules:

1. No Work Order, No Work - this is the most basic procedure, meaning that never should a work be performed on any asset (by our people or a contractor) without a properly generated and approved work order.
2. No Work Order, No Parts.
3. No Parts, No Work.

This is important because equipment history files, in the form of work orders, collected through a CMMS system will become a source for accurate and relevant information regarding the condition and cost of maintaining each asset and will indicate whether to repair, refurbish or replace that asset.

Job Planning

An effective job planning process provides the following benefits:

1. Quicker repairs on prescheduled work, projects and other tasks
2. Better quality repairs and other work
3. More efficient wrench time from technicians and maintainers
4. Improved parts and materials costs and usage
5. Improved safety on the job
6. Less downtime, more uptime of systems and equipment

Job planning involves more than just identifying parts, it also involves Work Order Scheduling.

Work Order Scheduling

After identifying the work and planning the job, the next task is to decide when the work should be completed. Scheduling generally falls into three major groupings:

1. Right now – emergencies, unplanned outages (i.e., systems off-line), environmental or safety hazards, etc.
2. Near future – sometime within the next few hours or days
3. Distant future – more than a week out

Emergencies and unplanned outages, in a way, schedule themselves and allow little time, if any, for planning. Preventive maintenance, predictive maintenance and other RCM-related tools can help minimize these reactive situations.

Near future jobs typically allow a little more time to plan and schedule the work needed, but do not provide the effectiveness and efficiency allowed by more distant future jobs.

The most desirable scheduling situation is typically distant future projects (more than a week out). Under these conditions, there is time to effectively plan all aspects of the job to minimize the time, materials, and downtime requirements necessary to get the right work done right, at the right cost, and at the right time.

Preventive / Predictive Optimization

Although preventive and predictive maintenance activities help promote more proactive maintenance, it is important to balance and optimize priorities and, therefore, provide value for the time and effort they require. This can require a lot of resource to accomplish, particularly if such efforts have not been previously – or regularly – performed.

Materials Coordination

Parts and materials required to do a job contribute significantly to the cost of any work undertaken, as does maintaining these items in inventory. Having too much or too little inventory can result in increased storage and handling costs, spot buying, overnight freight charges and downtime.

In a reactive maintenance environment, it's difficult to know what to stock – until something breaks down. Identifying truly critical equipment as part of a CMMS equipment / asset hierarchy set-up can help determine which parts to keep in a stock and which parts can be ordered later. That, along with operations, maintenance and engineering departments working together as partners with the purchasing functions, can optimize materials coordination.

ASSET MANAGEMENT 4.0 PROPOSAL

The development of the Industry 4.0 framework, described by the Reference Architectural Model Industrie 4.0 (RAMI4.0, IEC PAS 63088:2017) brought unseen possibilities in maintenance, reliability and condition monitoring through new technologies such as Industrial Internet of Things (IIoT), Big Data, Machine Learning (Provost, 2013), Predictive Analytics (Sharda, 2018), and others, where fundamentals in operations, maintenance and asset management reinforce each other in order to achieve higher equipment reliability and cost performance, and particularly in asset intensive industries.

The opportunities for optimizing OPEX (Operational Expenditure), with the implementation of industry 4.0 and IIoT (to consider just these two new technologies), are huge when crucial data can be extracted out of the machines. A new era has arrived where data is processed by AI (Artificial Intelligence) at the edge (Shi, 2016), has a distributed processing and application over networked fog computing (Yi, 2015), and in the cloud in a real-time basis.

One important aspect in this new live AI-systems is the fact that AI-systems degrade over time if context information is not considered. And this demands that context information, which is seen by a human, must be fed into the AI-systems on a regular basis.

This is part of the new extremely important human role in I4.0 as a supervisor of all systems. Other important functions included in human AI-systems supervision are a regular AI-systems testing, the creative activities of modeling and simulating new environments, in order for the AI-systems to have additional context information and be prepared to decide soundly upon need for systems conditions quick, predicted or not, changes, in such trivial conditions as a fast consumer change as we experience so frequently.

In a I4.0 environment Preventive Maintenance is going to encompass intelligent AI-systems, built upon Digital Twins and Smart Sensors feeding information to the classical AMMS systems. Digital Twins also require from humans their continuous development through modeling, simulation, and training, in order for them to intelligently manage all assets, forecasting the failures and proposing optimized schedules for maintenance operations, taking in consideration the productivity and availability of the production facility.

Preventive Maintenance Model for I4.0

We have previously developed a Preventive Maintenance Model (PMM) for I4.0, shown below on Figure 1, which presents all the components that an AMMS must integrate for Industry 4.0 (Dinis, Esteves & Anunciação, 2021).

This model was built taking in consideration established standard practices based on ISA-95, as maintenance definitions, capacity, responses, and requests information rendering to corporate maintenance software, which incorporate the functionalities of above described AMMS. The model also presents the relevant information flow between PM / classical AMMS and all components, stakeholders, and digital twins (orchestrator and digital sections) needed for the migration to an Asset Management 4.0.

Model includes the man as an integral and essential partner at all level activities, integrates newly possible different business models as expert services, and makes a strong usage of models, simulations, custom usages and projects as results from the manageability and intelligence now available to all systems, which become AI-systems.

Figure 1. Preventive maintenance model
(Dinis, Esteves & Anunciação, 2021) (Cibersur, 2020)

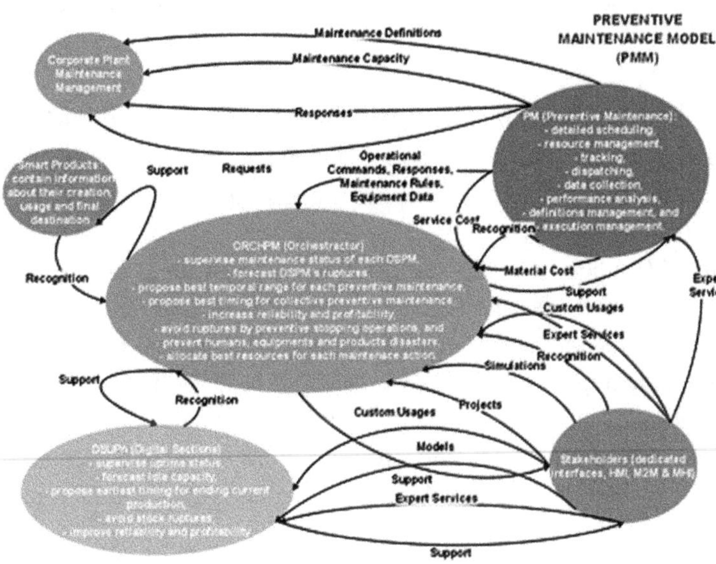

It is clear from the model that the new profile of the HUMAN SUPERVISION, part of the stakeholders directly involved in I4.0 operation, is a focal point in this new maintenance work organization, extending the AMMS conception.

Other focal points are the DIGITAL TWINS, namely on our nomenclature the Digital Sections and the Orchestrator. One should also make specific mention as focal points in maintenance for I4.0 the SMART SENSORS that will be capturing and evaluating DATA at the edge, maintaining status control of the assets in question, and can trigger control corrective actions immediately.

These focal points in fact extend and optimize the components of a classical AMMS, making maintenance more responsive and contributing efficiently to reliability and productivity. The main success critical factors are focus on data (capture and analysis), focus on human (supervision and training), focus on smart sensors (and actuators), and focus on digital twins (modeling and simulation).

- **Focus on Data:** The first aspect to recognize as a focal point is the integration of data in all processes. The availability of deep learning, massive processing power, cheap sensors and IIoT makes that today we can monitor our assets like never before, stream vast amounts of data to huge storage space and have best-in-class algorithms to try to make sense of this pile of data. In addition to sensor data, also the binary data that is produced by the programmable logic controller's (PLC) software of machines and assembly lines, can be used to improve the Overall Equipment Effectiveness (OEE) using statistical techniques and artificial intelligence. This improvement is obtained in several ways:
    - identifying and removing the reasons for slower throughput,
    - faster investigation of unplanned stops and thus shorter mean time to recovery, and
    - early detection of slow-downs and upcoming failures.
- **Focus on Human Supervision:** Although human technicians always were responsible for detecting a pending failure, with data from sensors and other systems, in I4.0 they become a focal point essential to a sound operation. Men now have at his disposal smart sensors which integrate control routines to analyze in real time the data they gather and trigger alerts and reactions before failure.

That data and alerts are collected in HMI (human machine interfaces) dashboards which analyze them, define trends, and calculate relevant KPIs (knowledge performance indicators), allowing men to take more well documented intime and online optimal decisions to order service, parts, materials and to schedule preventive maintenance.

As humans become I4.0 supervisors they need training in new areas and technologies now at their disposal. This training needs to go far and behind the classical technological background of their specializations, namely they seek an additional strong training in using and interpreting the data provided by their smart sensors and aggregated by their new dashboards, as well as training in using a toolbox of forecasting, modeling and simulation tools they now must use on a daily basis.

Also, the engineering schools must develop strong training and capabilities to pass on those maintenance concepts, and in general the Industry 4.0 culture, technologies and increment application laboratories (smart labs) for training.

- **Focus on Smart Sensors:** A third focal point is the usage of AI within the predictive maintenance industry by making use of historical process sensor data and analyzing it to find anomalies. This approach can be complemented, for instance, by vibration measurements, a technique that has been around for a while, and together one can confirm the forecasts of the other.

Nevertheless, both approaches usually have limitations and might fail to deliver on their promises, mainly due to sensors not being as easy to install and often requiring replacement programs that only add to the hassle.

The actual most promising tendency is to incorporate in sensors, located at the equipment, local AI intelligence to analyze immediately the data recovered and trigger immediate corrective actions, creating a new breed of sensors designated as Smart Sensors.

- **Focus on Digital Twins:** Companies across different sectors are implementing digital twins as an essential tool for optimizing the manufacturing value chain and innovative new products.

Large amounts of data are captured by sensors, actuators, and PLCs, and are analyzed across production lines, machines, etc., where all information can be structured with a digital twin.

Digital twins are software models representing objects, like a machine, a human organ or a process, examples being the climate or a production line. The definition of a Digital Twin, provided by the Digital Twin Consortium (Digital Twin Definition, 2021), as a recommended preferred definition is the following: "a digital twin is a virtual representation of real-world entities and processes, synchronized at a specified frequency and fidelity".

The Digital Twin concept was elaborated and introduced by Michael Grieves and John Vickers, and their concept contains three main parts (Grieves, 2014):

1. Physical products in 'Real Space',
2. Virtual digital products in 'Virtual Space', and
3. The connections of data and information that ties the virtual and real products together.

The permanent communication between the real and virtual world is a crucial point.

By studying the behavior of the (digital) twin it is possible to understand and forecast the behavior of its real-world counterpart and forecast / resolve problems before they occur.

Digital twins only become successful when they perform actions for the created insights in the most advanced case where machines become e.g., self-adjusting and self-optimizing.

For an industrial process we would typically use historical data to build the physical model / digital twin of the equipment we designate as a digital section.

With the experience and in-depth knowledge of the industrial process and the machines, we should be able to build the model / digital twin of an equipment solely based on these operational data.

This model / digital twin may already be used to train personnel and for data reduction purposes. The next step is the application of a data acquisition and analysis device at the machine to execute said functions of self-adjusting and self-optimizing.

Finally, we developed an orchestrator application, which is another digital twin, to model the production line, collecting data from all digital sections, allowing for the adjusting and optimization of the work order scheduling to the entire production line requirements, better ensuring reliability and profitability, keeping in the loop the Asset Maintenance Management System, and in this process making it intelligent.

A Roadmap Proposal to Asset Management 4.0

As established, focal points for an Asset Management 4.0 system are:

1. Focus on data (capture and analysis),
2. Focus on human (supervision and training),

3. Focus on smart sensors (and actuators),
4. Focus on digital twins (modeling and simulation).

To carry an AMMS into I4.0 it is needed a roadmap fully adjusted to the reality and objectives of the company. Such roadmap would require answers to questions defining:

- Where one company is in each of those focal points, and
- How it intends to invest in modifying its maintenance culture.

Because it is important not to lose focus on the point of it all: building stronger business.

Get it right and Industry 4.0 can play a big role in helping to scale human expertise, improve asset reliability and productivity of the maintenance teams.

Focus on Data-Driven Asset Management

Typical recurrent situations in daily asset management, like the following examples, are symptoms the need of a data-driven asset management:

- Are you spending 2-3 hours a day searching for the correct data of your technical assets?
- Do you waste valuable resources on keeping asset data current and validated when audits take place?

Many organizations deal with challenges such as fragmented and outdated CAD drawings, misaligned asset data and confusing and inconsistent asset standards.

In the fuzz of Big Data and Deep Learning, people tend to forget about Master Data (non- transactional data), and the fact that data cleansing and integration tends to be 80% of the work in a data science project.

Frequently forgotten are the architectural approaches required to integrate master data, transactional data, and measurements/sensor data, how they are deployed, the need to elaborate on data governance to guarantee that data requirements are met, and the exploration of the specific context of failure prediction in case of rare failures.

Rare failures are what we should strive to, but the absence of enough relevant failure data for those cases calls for specific approaches, and for bringing together a unified model architecture, governance, and algorithmic approach.

RAMI4.0 has already a unified model architecture, which includes data architecture, and stipulates the usage of semantic databases to comply with the needs of online (correct) data. On the other end, RAMI4.0 implements an IT and data governance model through the standards it is compliant with on data and IT levels.

RAMI4.0 has no restrictions on the algorithmic approach used for data processing. For instance, there is no restriction in implementing a Weibull analysis to diagnose the root cause of specific design failures, or unanticipated or premature failures, or even to understand the time and rate at which items fail, contributing to other reliability analyses such as failure modes, effects, and criticality analysis, fault tree analysis, reliability growth testing, reliability centered maintenance, and spares analysis.

A suggested set of questions for a company to analyze its actual focus on data:

1. Company has a AMMS system?
2. Is it owned by maintenance?
3. Is it up to date?
4. Does maintenance own its budget?
5. What is the current maintenance philosophy?
6. Do company want to change the current maintenance philosophy?
7. What are the changes foreseen?
8. What results are expected?
9. Are all company productive assets managed by the AMMS?
10. Are all productive assets technically described in AMMS?
11. Are all productive assets classified in AMMS?
12. Does company have an asset inspection program in the AMMS?
13. Are there standard instructions to inspect and / or test the different components of all assets in the AMMS?
14. Does company have a maintenance care program in the AMMS?
15. Are there standard instructions to repair the different components of all assets in the AMMS?
16. Is there an historical archive of all work orders and their work reports for all assets in the AMMS?
17. Do work reports show or link to man hours, materials and spares used?
18. Is there a interconnection for the warehouse stock consultations?
19. Is there a stock parts and materials management system accessible to maintenance?
20. Does maintenance get involved in defining all stock parts and materials order levels, minimum stocks and relevant parts and materials stock sheets?
21. Does maintenance get to revise all stock parts and materials acquisitions?
22. Does maintenance get to approval all stock parts and materials acquisitions?
23. What is the relative percentage and cost of corrective maintenance in the total maintenance activities?
24. What is the relative percentage and cost of preventive (programmed) maintenance in the total maintenance activities?
25. What is the relative percentage and cost of predictive maintenance in the total maintenance activities?
26. What is the regularity of programmed general shutdowns, why and what are their costs?
27. Does company have a architectural data model and qualified personnel in data cleansing and integration of master data, transactional data and measurements and / or sensor data?
28. Does company have a data governance policy in usage and accessible to maintenance?
29. Does company have personnel with algorithm skills to run Weibull analysis of failure data?

Focus on Human Supervision

Automation and digitalization are long-term evolutionary processes. As such they cause progressive and continuous transformation of occupations and job profiles. Research revision on these topics (Sima & al., 2020) shows the new directions in education associated with shifting the work environment, and the drivers for human capital development and consumer behavior under the influence of I4.0. In the digital age the workforce must be highly qualified and ready to develop new skills. The changes generated by the industry 4.0 revolution require the adoption of new business models, production processes, and new curriculums in academic programs.

Industry 4.0 will be accompanied by changing tasks and demands for the human in the factory and, as he is the most flexible entity in cyber-physical production systems, workers will be faced with a large variety of jobs ranging from specification and monitoring to verification of production strategies. Through technological support it is guaranteed that workers can realize their full potential and adopt the role of strategic decision-makers and flexible problem-solvers, mainly by, but not exclusively, implementing the representation of cyber-physical systems and therein occurring interactions in the form of intelligent user interfaces (Gorecky *et al.*,2014).

Nevertheless, it has been shown that, to date, current research on I4.0 technologies and implementation have broadly ignored the humans in the I4.0 system. The systematic consideration and attention to human factors in the digital transformation of work can avoid negative consequences for individual employees, production organizations, and for society. Research and practitioners need a systematic approach to incorporate human factors in the ongoing transformation and ensure their I4.0 investments overcome the challenges of the digital transformation of work and satisfy and motivate a diverse workforce with expanding capabilities suited to working in the I4.0 environment (Newmann *et al.*, 2021).

A suggested set of questions for a company to analyze its actual focus on human resources:

1. Company has a human factors transformation policy in place?
2. Does that policy evaluate beforehand the human resources training needs for new or transformation projects?
3. Does human factors transformation policy include evaluation of the skills needed to support a future I4.0 scenario?
4. Does company foresee looking in the market for personnel trained in I4.0 culture, technologies, and concepts?
5. Does company have a plan to evaluate its possible I4.0 human resources future scenarios?
6. Does company foresee what will be their actual personnel training needs to accommodate them to an I4.0 scenario?
7. Does company provide information to engineering schools on what might their future I4.0 technologies be?
8. Is company collaborating with engineering schools letting them know their future skills needs?
9. Does company provide information or other material support to engineering schools for them to create I4.0 laboratories to train future needed skills in technologies and their concepts?
10. Does company run internships with engineering schools on I4.0 technologies and concepts?

Focus on Smart Sensors

The evolution of machine-to-machine (M2M) technologies and the IoT are examples of application domains where infrastructural technologies are utilizing sensors to advance the current state of the art. New revenue streams will emerge by fitting sensors to existing products and to new product ranges. The data can then be used to support improved client services and enhanced product development (McGrath, 2013).

As everything is getting smarter, data generated at all levels of the production process are used to improve product quality, flexibility, and productivity. This is being possible with smart sensors, generating data and allowing further functionality from self-monitoring and self-configuration to condition monitoring of complex processes. Condition monitoring is a primary paradigm for introducing smart sensors and data analysis in manufacturing processes (Schütze, A. et al., 2018).

Smart sensors are regular sensors with an embedded microprocessor that allows processing directly within the sensor package to provide additional functions and connectivity (Festo, 2019).

Sensors are an essential building block of IIoT. Some of the most common smart sensors that are shaping the future of industry are (Kundinger, 2017): pressure sensors (monitoring pipelines, altitude, force or other metrics), level sensors (monitoring real-time level in tanks and vessels for inventory management and process control), aquatic sensors (monitoring water treatment and rainwater quality), temperature sensors (monitoring machine temperature in industrial setting and alerting operator or shut it off in emergency in overheating), infrared sensors (monitoring heat leaks), and proximity sensors (monitoring location and motion in installations).

Connectivity is a key characteristic of smart sensors. They make the data collected and processed available through all layers of the industry network (PLCs, SCADA, MES, ERP, Cloud) using a communication protocol. Smart sensors bring about new tasks that require new skills. A thorough understanding of the advantages and characteristics of smart sensors, in addition to industrial network communication and IT skills, is necessary in order to reap their full benefits, which means an additional need to train professionals in these new smart sensors and their industrial applications completing and extending automation training and control and bringing new local intelligent capabilities to equipment (Festo, 2021).

A suggested set of questions for a company to analyze its actual focus on smart sensors:

1. Company is considering a transformation of processes into the paradigm of I4.0?
2. Is company creating a new revenue maintenance stream by using smart sensors?
3. Is company supporting improved client maintenance services using smart sensors?
4. Is company seeking to improve product quality, flexibility or productivity by using smart sensors?
5. Said transformation requires new sensor types and capabilities? Why?
6. Can company list new smart sensors, with types and control functions, in the context of the upgrade of the existing automation and control system?
7. Does company recognize that the new smart sensors must have an adequate network to transmit sensors data to the operational management dashboard, namely to preventive maintenance dashboard application they already use?
8. Does company consider upgrading their preventive maintenance dashboards to show and treat smart sensors data to provide forecasts and procedural optimizations?
9. Is company aware of the needs to collect, storage, treat and analyze all the new data provided by the smart sensors?
10. Do company consider the training, recruitment or subcontracting needs required to have qualified personnel to maintain smart sensors?
11. Do company consider the training, recruitment or subcontracting needs required to have qualified personnel to treat data from smart sensors and extract failure and other relevant maintenance data from them?
12. Do company consider the need to have spare smart sensors or parts for them?
13. Do company consider the need to have an adequate smart sensor laboratory bench for repair and testing?

Focus on Digital Twins

The permanent communication between the real and virtual world is the crucial point in the conceptualization of a digital twin. Before, the concept of a Digital Twin was more a 'simple' digital mapping of an object. Their concept referred to engineered objects, which are accordingly described by engineering data as Computer Aided Design (CAD) and Computer Aided Manufacturing (CAM), (Kritzinger, 2018).

The digital twin is increasingly being explored as a means of improving the performance of physical entities through leveraging computational techniques, themselves enabled through the virtual counterpart.

Today, an engineering-oriented digital twin is used for design, manufacturing, and maintenance of the physical object (Jones, 2020).

The digital twin is increasingly being explored as a means of improving the performance of physical entities through leveraging computational techniques, themselves enabled through the virtual counterpart.

Companies embed their physical assets with sensors to produce the data necessary to inform a digital twin, to track and monitor the physical piece of machinery.

To qualify for inclusion in the Digital Twin category, a product must (Enterprise Asset Management):

- Provide a digital representation of a physical asset,
- Track data produced by the physical asset via sensors,
- Allow users to optimize performance of the physical asset based on the data produced by the asset.

Key Benefits of Digital Twin Software:

- Detect equipment issues remotely and proactively,
- Minimize downtime and costly process failures,
- Increase production yield and overall supply chain outcomes,
- Make informed decisions toward design and engineering of machines.

Some specific roles or teams that can benefit most directly from digital twin technology in their daily job functions are:

- Mechatronics engineers,
- Machinists / machine operators,
- Production managers,
- Maintenance managers,
- Prevention managers.

Digital twin software main features, requiring the implementation of IoT sensors within physical assets being replicated, are:

- Remote asset monitoring, is taking one step further with digital twins with detailed visualizations of machinery, full extent of monitoring and maintenance needs,
- Predictive maintenance and analytics, allowing for remote diagnostic and proactive maintenance decisions, before sudden downtime or critical damage, and custom alerts and analytics configuration,

- IoT prototyping and computer-aided design CAD for machines and updates,
- Event and product simulations.

Predictive maintenance and analytics are a key benefit of digital twin technology. Sudden machine failures can result in substantial losses, as well as delays in production and employee frustrations. The various analytics made possible through different software solutions allow users to anticipate the litany of issues that might arise with machine systems and devices, while monitoring overall performance metrics to shape continuous improvements of processes and designs. Data generated on these products might also assist with predictive waste reduction and predictive quality control of completed products, as well as general optimization of resources. Additionally, if any machine or process issues are identified, users can investigate their root causes by exploring virtual models and the data gathered across embedded sensors.

Digital twins will be useful for manufacturing teams using in their business Manufacturing Execution Systems / Manufacturing Operations Management (MES/MOM), by offering capabilities complementing those platforms (Enterprise Asset Management).

A suggested set of questions for a company to analyze its actual focus on digital twins in maintenance:

1. Company is considering an I4.0 transformation of processes through the definition of digital twins?
2. Company is considering said transformation to allow digital twins online and intime data being used by maintenance?
3. Company has a CMMS in current usage and updated?
4. Company has implemented a preventive maintenance care program for all its assets?
5. Company is considering maintenance usage of digital twin data for preventive maintenance forecasts and work decisions?
6. Company is considering maintenance usage of digital twin data for predictive maintenance analytics and future planning?
7. Company is considering maintenance usage of digital twin data for predictive assets end-of-live optimization?

CONCLUSION

Industry 4.0 is a challenge for industrial companies and for the entire value chain in which they operate. The introduction of new information technologies results in new demands, to which management should not remain indifferent. The effects are not limited only to one type of technology but to the combination of the various, which have marked this new stage of development.

It is important to manage the introduction of these technologies in companies and, at the same time, to develop a holistic approach to all areas where their impacts can be reflected. One of the areas where reflective action is, and will continue to be needed, is reflection on the effects of technologies in maintenance. The transition from mass production to more personalized production, the application of technological devices that allow greater autonomy of the equipment requires maintenance a more demanding intervention and greater monitoring in the face of the most prominent technological nature associated with the respective operation. Preventive maintenance is also of greater importance in general in the maintenance of industrial equipment since, in view of the high degree of integration of industrial equipment and devices, any unavailability not foreseen in any of the equipment compromises the whole Industrial System.

This importance of maintenance highlights the importance of managing industrial assets. Maintenance is generally a critical success factor for equipment availability and longevity. This means, in another perspective, that the unavailability or deterioration of equipment represents increased costs associated with its operation or replacement, economic and commercial opportunity costs should also be considered in the absence of activity.

These and other reasons underline the need for industrial managers to have management tools and mechanisms to allow control over equipment and its operation. As stated by Rojas & Davis (2008) there are four dimensions that should be considered, namely, Identifying Assets, Asset Condition, Asset Design Criteria, and Asset Care Program.

The relevance of this approach will allow the optimization of operating costs, a holistic view of the role of each equipment in the production dynamics and the identification of the respective criticality in the value chain. Thus, it will be easier to develop a sound maintenance asset management strategy in its various domains, namely, work identification and control, job planning, work order scheduling, preventive / predictive optimization, materials coordination, and schedule outage / shutdown coordination.

However, each of these dimensions should be more detailed with a view to a complete understanding of its impact on each of the industrial production areas of each of the companies. The different natures of production must require adjustments in the application of these perspectives to the existing reality.

Thus, the need for a roadmap for the management of the assets in this 4.0 context, namely through a focus at various levels: data (capture and analysis), human resources (supervision and training), smart sensors (and actuators), and digital twins (modeling and simulation).

REFERENCES

Akerkar, R. (2014). Big data computing. CRC Press: Taylor & Francis Group, LLC.

Alkaya, E., Bogurcu, M., Ulutas, F., & Demirer, G. N. (2015). Adaptation to climate change in industry: emproving resource efficiency through sustainable production applications. Water Environment Research, 87(1), 14–25.

Bauernhansl, T., Ten Hompel, M., & Vogel-Heuse, B. (2014). *Industrie 4.0 in Produktion, Automatisierung und Logistik-Anwendung, Technologien und Migration*. Alemanha: Springer Vieweg.

Digital Twin Definition. (2021). *Digital Twin Consortium*. https://www.digitaltwinconsortium.org/hot-topics/defining-digital-twin.htm

El-Akruti, K., & Dwight, R. (2013, October). A framework for the engineering asset management system. *Journal of Quality in Maintenance Engineering*, *19*(4), 398–412. Advance online publication. doi:10.1108/JQME-01-2012-0002

Enterprise Asset Management. (2021). Retrieved online on 15.03.2021 from https://www.g2.com/categories/enterprise-asset-management-eam

Festo Didactic, S. E. (2021). *Build Smart Sensors Skills for Industry 4.0 Workers*. https://www.festo-didactic.com/int-en/highlights/smart-sensors-for-industry-4.0

Festo Didactic, S. E. (2019). *Fundamental Principles of Smart Sensors*. https://www.festo-didactic.com/ov3/media/customers/1100/smart_sensors_infographic_a3_en.pdf

Gibson, I., Rosen, D., & Stucker, B. (2015). Additive Manufacturing Technologies - 3D Printing, Rapid Prototyping, and Direct Digital Manufacturing. New York: Springer Science + Business Media.

Gorecky, D., Schmitt, M., Losskyll, M., & Zuhlke, D. (2014). Human-machine-interaction in the industry 4.0 era. *Conference: 2014 12th IEEE International Conference on Industrial Informatics (INDIN)*.

Grieves, M. (2014). *Digital Twin: Manufacturing Excellence through Virtual Factory Replication*. https://www.researchgate.net/publication/275211047_Digital_Twin_Manufacturing_Excellence_through_Virtual_Factory_Replication

Grieves, M. (2021). *Intelligent Digital Twins: The Role of AI and ML in the Future of Digital Twins*. https://www.researchgate.net/publication/349042364

Hashizume, K., Rosado, D., Medina, E., & Fernandez, E. (2013). *An analysis of security issues for cloud computing*. SpringerLink. doi:10.1186/1869-0238-4-5

Hofmann, E., & Rüsch, M. (2017). Computers in Industry. Industry 4.0 and the current status as well as future prospects on logistics, 23-34.

Horváth, B. (2018). The Recognition of resource use through industrial development from a social perspective. Studia Mundi–Economica, 5(1). doi:10.18531/Studia.Mundi.2018.05.01.68-78

Jones, D., Snider, C., Nassehi, A., Yon, J., & Hicks, B. (2020). Characterizing the Digital Twin: A systematic literature review. *CIRP Journal of Manufacturing Science and Technology, 29*(A), 36-52.

Kagermann, H., Wahlster, W., & Helbig, J. (2013). *Recommendations for implementing the strategic initiative INDUSTRIE 4.0*. Obtido de https://www.din.de/blob/76902/e8cac883f42bf28536e7e8165993f1fd/recommendations-for-implementing-industry-4-0-data.pdf

Kritzinger, W., Karner, M., Traar, G., Henjes, J., & Sihn, W. (2018). Digital Twin in manufacturing: A categorical literature review and classification. *IFAC-PapersOnLine, 51*(11), 1016–1022. doi:10.1016/j.ifacol.2018.08.474

Kundinger. (2017). *6 Common Smart Sensors and Their IIoT Applications*. https://kundinger.com/6-common-smart-sensors-iiot-applications/

Lab, O. (2018). *Observador*. Obtido de Inteligência Artificial: https://observador.pt/explicadores/inteligencia-artificial/

Lee, J., Kao, H.-A., & Yang, S. (2014). Service innovation and smart analytics for Industry 4.0 and big data environment. *Procedia CIRP*, (16), 3-8. Obtido em 2020, de https://www.sciencedirect.com/science/article/pii/S2212827114000857?via%3Dihub

Lopes, I., Senra, P., Vilarinho, S., Sá, V., Teixeira, C., Lopes, J., Alves, A., Oliveira, J. A., & Figueiredo, M. (2016). Requirements specification of a computerized maintenance management system – a case study. *Procedia CIRP, 52*, 268–273. www.sciencedirect.com. doi:10.1016/j.procir.2016.07.047

Manyika, J., Chui, M., Brown, B., Bughin, J., Dobbs, R., Roxburgh, C., & Byers, A. H. (2011). *Big data: The next frontier for innovation, competition, and productivity*. McKinsey & Company. Obtido em 2020, de https://www.mckinsey.com/business-functions/mckinsey-digital/our-insights/big-data-the-next-frontier-for-innovation

McGrath, M. J., Scanaill, C. N., & Intel Labs Europe. (2013). *Sensor Technologies – Healthcare, wellness and environmental applications*. Apress Open. https://link.springer.com/content/pdf/10.1007%2F978-1-4302-6014-1.pdf

Nascimento, C., Hsu, P., Meneghatti, M., & Barzotto, L. (2017). *Inovação nos negócios por meio da Análise de Big data*. Obtido em 2020, de https://singep.org.br/6singep/resultado/333.pdf

Neumann, W. P., Winkelhaus, S., Grosse, E. H., & Glock, C. H. (2021) (2021). Industry 4.0 and the human factor – A systems framework and analysis methodology for successful development. *International Journal of Production Economics*, 233.

Pires, L. (2016). *Sistemas ciber-físicos: o futuro da Manutenção Industrial?* Obtido em 2020, de https://www.researchgate.net/profile/Luis_Pires12/publication/309780775_Sistemas_ciber-fisicos_o_futuro_da_Manutencao_Industrial/links/5bfe8355a6fdcc1b8d4872ff/Sistemas-ciber-fisicos-o-futuro-da-Manutencao-Industrial.pdf

Russell, S. J., & Norvig, P. (2016). *Artificial Intelligence - A Modern Approach*. Pearson Education Limited.

Santos, B. P., Alberto, A., Lima, T. D. F. M., & Charrua-Santos, F. M. B. (2018). Indústria 4.0: Desafios e Oportunidades. *Revista Produção e Desenvolvimento*, *4*(1), 111–124.

Schütze, A., Helwig, N., & Schneider, T. (2018). Sensors 4.0 – smart sensors and measurement technology enable Industry 4.0. *Journal of Sensor Systems*, *7*, 359–371.

Sima, V., Gheorghe, I. G., Subic, J., & Nancu, D. (2020). *Influences of the Industry 4.0 Revolution on the Human Capital Development and Consumer Behavior: A Systematic Review*. Academic Press.

Vieira, M., Nicola, F. M., Junior, M. V., Simon, A. T., & Correr, I. (2018). *A Aplicação de Sistemas Ciber-Físicos (CPS) em Sistemas de Manufatura: Um Estudo Bibliométrico*. Academic Press.

Zikopoulos, P. C., Eaton, C., deRoos, D., Deutsch, T., & Lapis, G. (2012). *Understanding Big Data: Analytics for Enterprise Class Hadoop and Streaming Data*. The McGraw-Hill.

Chapter 14
Change Management in Digital Transformation:
Business Model Concepts

Nuno Geada
https://orcid.org/0000-0003-3755-0711
Polytechnic Institute of Setúbal, Portugal

ABSTRACT

Digital transformation is a process in which entities make use of technology to improve their performance, reach, and guarantee better results. It is a structural change in organizations, giving an essential role to the technology. Digital transformation engages processes where organizational actors engage in digital innovation and transform their organizations in order to respond to change in their business and technology environments. So, just like all changes must have models and frameworks that support transition, it is a path in this case, under constant pressure, to achieve goals and have efficient management of the processes that it contains.

INTRODUCTION

In the last decade, the emergence of a diverse set of powerful digital technologies, digital platforms and digital infrastructures has transformed, throw well organized projects of change, both innovation and entrepreneurship in significant ways with broad organizational and policy implications (Nambisan *et al*, 2019). Organizations are facing daily with environments that are resistant to change, and specifically about health organizations, human resources have a greater tendency to exercise greater resistance to changing processes (Direção Geral Saúde, 2012), which is why it is necessary create control mechanisms for change management that allow, through the implementation of methodologies, to reduce operations and processes without added value, through methods, techniques and tools.

According to Rance *et al* (2011), the implementation of methodologies requires the application of changes in the scope of the transition, namely in terms of people's mentality, and of the organization's processes, since in most cases the greatest entropy in the application of change is usually triggered by

DOI: 10.4018/978-1-7998-7452-2.ch014

its stakeholders included in the process, instead of the complexity of implementing the methodology itself. Determining the best path to digital transformation is not smooth and easy, because technologies are evolving very faster. Many organizations are constantly under pressure to move to digital transformation without a defined methodology model and strategy as well. So, the difficult is to coordinate the strategy from planning to implementation to create engaging and consistent digital experiences. The major challenge faced by organizations today is how to adopt the ability to promote digital transformation is in large part determined by a clear digital strategy enabled by a culture of change, risk-taking and innovation, with constant disruptions, leveraging technology to simultaneously drive growth and efficiency that constitutes a challenge.

To embrace a digital mindset, demanding different mindsets and skill sets, it has been necessary a conceptual and real dimensions of project change management, methodologies, and frameworks so it can be easier to achieve the defined objectives and prevent disruptions (Geada & Anunciação, 2019). Besides, it is necessary to control, with support of models and frameworks, the four variables which according to Wirtz (2019) influence digital business: *Convergence and Technology, Customer Empowerment, Digitalization, and Innovation dynamics*, and finally the *market complexity*. Therefore, when an organization launches a digital transformation project, must be consider what methodology to use in which models we will use to manage the entire process. Although, it will be a process of change that will involve both technological and human resources, assuming the need for a change management.

DOES THE DIGITAL TRANSFORMATION IMPLY THE NEED FOR CHANGE MANAGEMENT?

Like the word "*transformation*" indicates, when applied it will change something, so we will have to manage change, relating use of technologies, changes in value creation, structural changes, and financial aspects (Figure 1). According to Matt et al (2015), if all these four dimensions are considered as part of

Figure 1. Digital transformation framework: balancing four transformational dimensions
Source from (Matt, Hess, & Benlian, 2015)

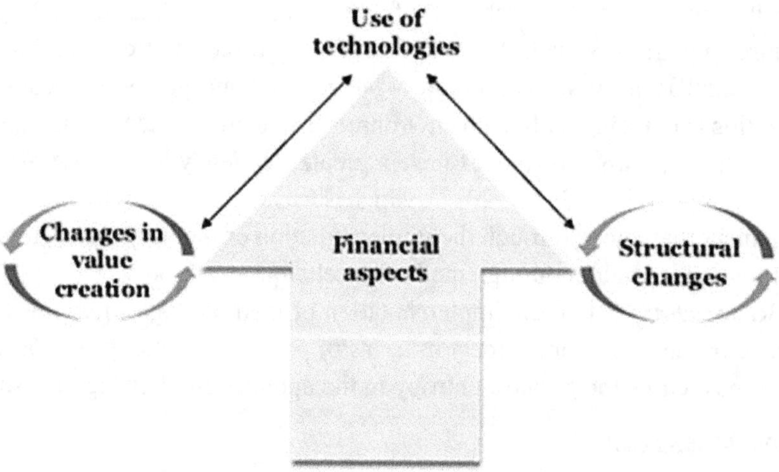

the framework, this will support firms in the assessment of their current abilities and the formulation of a digital transformation strategy.

Referring formulation of a digital transformation strategy, the organizational change introduced by the Information Systems is basically reflected in the changes made at the level of process reengineering. Reengineering is what Hammer & Champy (1994) presents as a reaction to the practices of the industrial era, through the reunification of tasks in business processes.

The authors use four keywords to define this change:

- Fundamental;
- Radical;
- Drastic;
- Procedural.

These keywords mean that the most basic forms of the organization's functioning must be questioned, disregarding all existing structures and procedures, and inventing completely new ways of doing the job. Another component of introducing IS in organizations is the need that arises to create job skills. So, digital transformation is a macro process, that inflicts change, and this change must be manage and controlled under pain of causing a great disruption in organizations, and even if the process goes less well the company can permanently close.

Associated to change we have sustainability that is a concept related to sustainable development, that is, formed by a set of ideas, strategies and other ecologically correct, economically viable, socially just and culturally diverse attitudes and serves as an alternative to guarantee the survival of the organization natural resources, while allowing people and societies create a development solution.

DOES CHANGE MANAGEMENT AFFECTS ORGANIZATIONAL SUSTAINABILITY?

Corporations are central to the realization of sustainable development, but to contribute to the sustainable development agenda, they must change drastically and become sustainable themselves. Recognizing the need for sustainable development requires a type of organizational change that advances sustainable development in the corporate context and is generally known as organizational change for corporate sustainability (Benn, Dunphy, & Griffiths, 2014) (Irimiás & Mitev, 2020). Organizations can no longer operate without taking the cross connection between society, their environment, and their economic aspirations.

Organizational change for corporate sustainability affects the organization's internal and external environment and requires new ways of thinking that can hold varying logics. These logics arise from the ethical, cultural, social, religious, political, civil, and legal changes that arise from sustainability issues. This complexity is usually accompanied by dissonance and anxiety, which create a great leadership opportunity for individuals and teams within organizations to lead and reinforce the change for corporate sustainability even if they are ordinary members. It takes much courage to step up to the sustainability leadership challenge, particularly in large organizations where change encounters politicized resistance from the various internal and/ or external stakeholder groups (Burnes, 2015) (Benn, Dunphy, & Griffiths, 2014) (Abad-Segura, González-Zamar, Infante-Moro, & García, 2020).

According to Bansal & DesJardine (2014) corporate sustainability is a concept that is fast becoming fashionable in strategic management, and yet its meaning is often elusive, rooted in the macro notion of sustainable development put forth by the Brundtland *Report of the World Commission on Environment and Development*. Corporate sustainability is realized when social, environmental, and economic considerations are pursued and integrated in strategic organizational management (Baumgartner & Rauter, 2016). A company is a process environment that transforms resources into value that leads to services as into unwanted by-products, waste, and emissions. In order to do so, the company must deliver appropriate returns to those who provide the company with resources (Figure 2). Management coordinates internal activities as well as its relationships with customers, shareholders, suppliers, partner companies, authorities, society, and the stakeholders in general.

Figure 2. Diagram of process of a company as a system for transforming resources.
Source from (Baumgartner & Rauter, 2016)

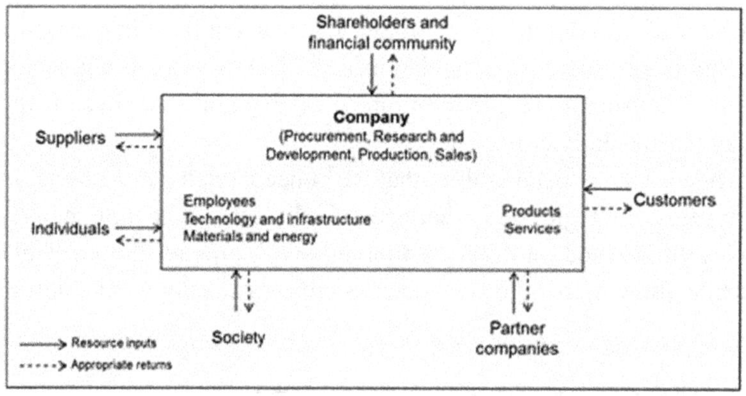

In order to realize sustainable development through corporate sustainability, it is imperative for organizations to be able to institutionalize changes for corporate sustainability effectively. Digital Transformation is an efficient tool to support sustainable environmental, social, and economic development. Information and communication technologies can improve and support emission reduction, waste management thought frameworks and good practices. Technology is rapidly progressing and evolving every second as we speak, organizations are confronted with enormous changes (Colbert, *et al* 2016). The new digital business models are affected by several digital developments, although at the same time the increasing and successful application of these digital business models (predominantly by new entrants, such as Amazon) affect markets and firms.

How Does the Digital Transformation Affect Organizations?

The focus of the marketing discipline might be more on the consequences rather than on the drivers of digital business models (Verhoef & Bijmolt, 2019). In recent years, the business model concept has become a popular tool in business practice because it can help to successfully analyze and handle these complexities (Wirtz, 2019).

According to Wirtz (2019) there are tree business research streams of the business model concept:

- Information Technology;
- Organizational Theory;
- Strategic Management.

In figure 3 is it possible to observe the correlation and detail of each other.

Figure 3. Research streams of the business model concept
Source from (Wirtz, 2019)

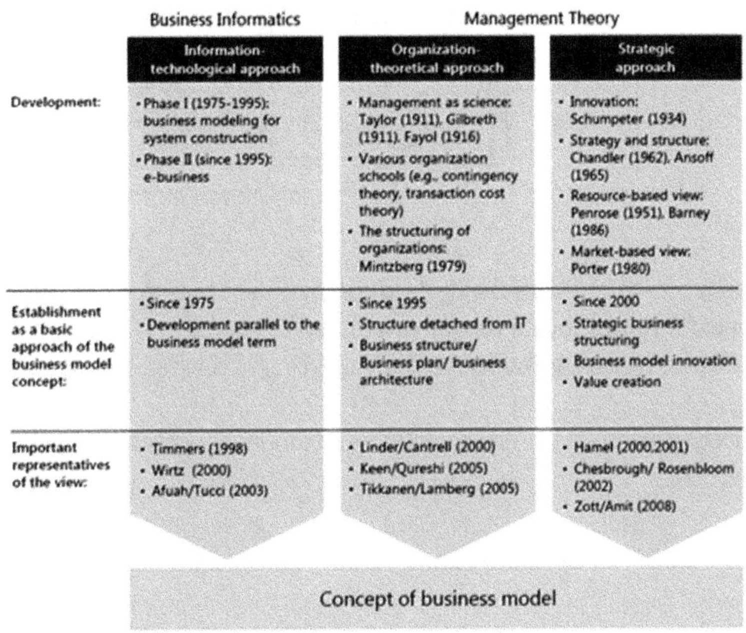

According to the authors Verhoef & Bijmolt (2019) after applying the digital transformation they assume that the new digital business model will have direct effects on the market and on firms (Figure 4). Following diffusion and disruption theory, these market-level effects can be small initially, but when business models become successful and take off, strong effects may occur. New digital business models can affect competition, and, in some markets, digital giants take over large parts of the market, leading to monopolistic markets, for an example, the hegemony of Microsoft within world.

So, in order to minimize the less good impact generated by the need to make changes, there is a proposal for a methodological model as shown in Figure 5, called "Methodology for Implementation of Improvement Ideas (MIII) (Geada, 2019).

Details:

- **Define Improvement Strategy** (DIS): Definition of the goals and requirements of the improvement envisaged;

Figure 4. Conceptual model on the impact of new digital business models on markets and firms
Source from (Verhoef & Bijmolt, 2019)

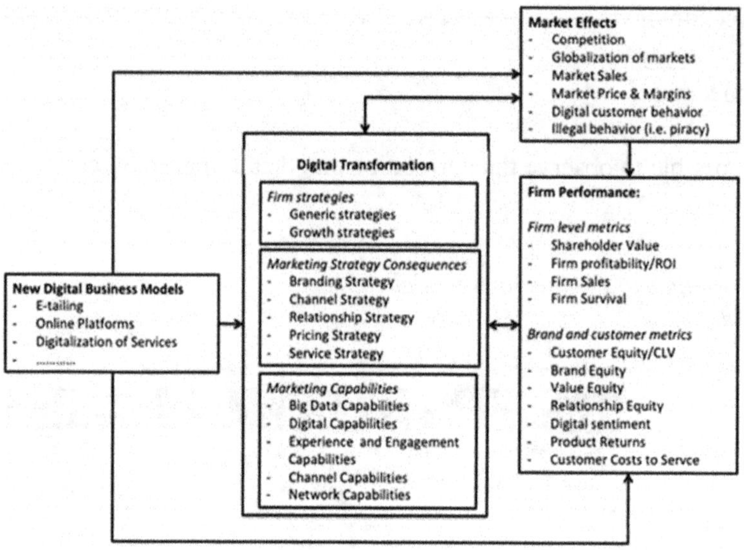

- **Improvement Design** (ID): After the collection of all the necessary data, it is developed the design to be adopted for the implementation of the improvement;
- **Improvement Design Consolidation** (IDC): Validation of all variables designed and designed to operationalize;
- **Improvement Operation** (IO): Implementation of improvement, based on knowledge and consolidated design.

Figure 5. Implementation methodology improvement ideas scheme
Source from (Geada, 2019)

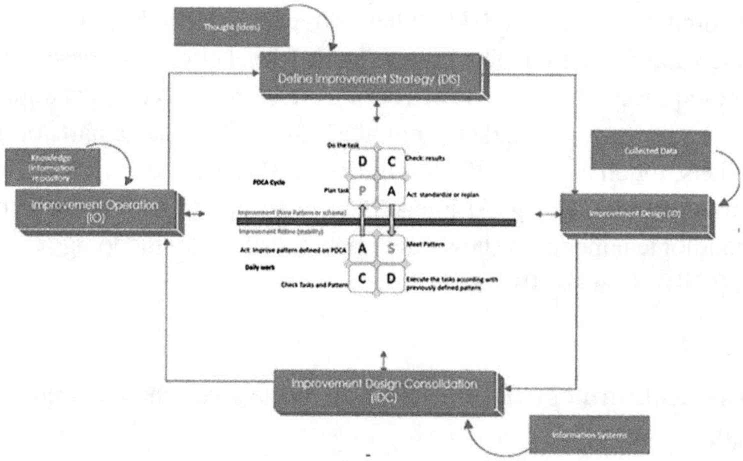

Finally, as regards the control to motivate the continuous improvement, the PDCA + SDCA tool must be applied at all stages. This tool, applied within the methodology x, allows to minimize the impact, together with the three important variables of change, people, the environment, and processes, so the following premises must be considered:

- Choose the terms used to describe the concepts in the scope, namely rather than call change or change, the term "Idea of Improvement" (IM) because it has a more positive impact, when it is transmitted the information that a change is going to happen;
- Ensure that the continuous improvement process is applied in all phases of the IM, and not only in the latter;
- We should always involve all people in the improvement process;
- Always adapt to the surrounding environment.

So, the organizational information systems management transformations are aligned with the transformation of operational processes in order to facilitate the attainment of certain business and organizational goals, namely, to be more efficient, effective, and reliable in the different paths of its operational process and value offerings (Wessel et al., 2020). Digital transformation merges a company towards developing tools that are characteristic of a company that creates and delivers digital value propositions as part of its offerings as well as leverages digital technologies in its operational processes (Legner et al., 2017; Wessel et al., 2020).

According to Westerman, *et al* (2014) executives in every industry must be awake to the opportunities and threats of rapid digital evolution and be ready to reinvent business models as needed. Business model reinvention sometimes involves radically shifting what you sell, how you sell it, or how you make money from it. Reinvention may involve reimagining the nature of competition in your industry or reconfiguring your value chain to deliver at a substantial efficiency advantage against their competitors.

Figure 6. Focus on culture during digital transformation
Source Hemerling et al, (2018)

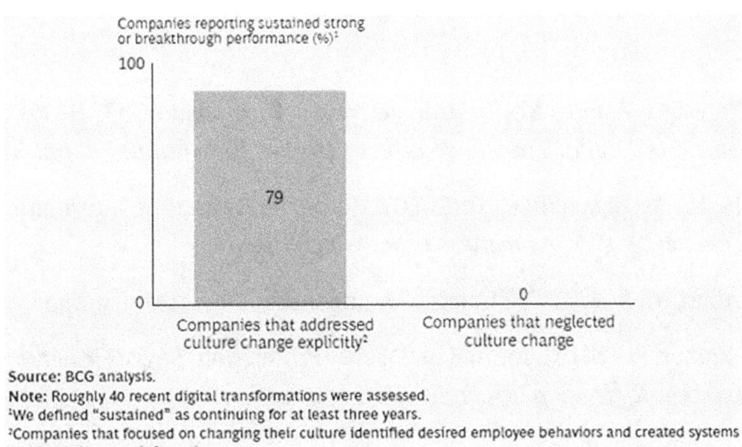

Although for this to work properly the culture of organizations must be installed for this scope. Culture comprises the values and characteristic set of behaviors that define how things get done in organizations. By ignoring the variable culture, it may inflict risks of failure in digital transformation.

According to Hemerling *et al*, (2018) study, they accessed roughly 40 digital transformations and found that the proportion of companies reporting breakthrough or strong financial performance was five times greater (90%), among those that focused on culture than it was among those neglected culture (17%).

The focus on digital culture has an indicator of 79% (Figure 6) of the organizations that focused on culture sustained strong or breakthrough performance. If we control digital culture, we have a high probability of success during the process of transformation.

CONCLUSION

With this chapter, it is possible to provide an overview on the changes resulting from the digital transformation for work design and leadership and at the same time give structure to the highly fragmented existing literature. Additionally, change dimensions emerged, providing valuable directions for future research, and helping organizations to prepare for the requirements of the digital age that will embrace all humankind for good. As soon as the strategy is defined, guidelines and standards are established to facilitate its implementation, thus ensuring quality in service delivery, process optimization, productivity, customer satisfaction, and growth, thus contributing to stability and survival of the organizations.

With the introduction of new business models or changing and improving the existing ones is a particularly difficult task for companies in crisis, as the majority of assets are earmarked for short-term financial restructuring, which cannot guarantee further existence and development without change in other areas of the company, whereas surprisingly less attention and envisaged activities are devoted to development and technological fields.

Finally, the impact of changes is reduced with the application of tools/models that help to unleash good practices in controlling change arising from digitization processes. There are no correct ways or a predefined methodology to follow a default path through IS services to manage transformation. But it will be possible to implement new, globally competitive business models, which will include digital transformation with knowledge management processes, on the basis of the technological restructuring

REFERENCES

Abad-Segura, E., González-Zamar, M.-D., Infante-Moro, J., & García, G. R. (2020). Sustainability. *Sustainable Management of Digital Transformation in Higher Education: Global Research Trends.*

Baiyere, A., Salmela, H., & Tapanainen, T. (2020). European Journal of Information Systems. *Digital transformation and the new logics of business process management.*

Bansal, P., & DesJardine, M. R. (2014). Strategic Organization. *Business sustainability: It is about time.*

Baumgartner, R., & Rauter, R. (2016). Journal of Cleaner Production. *Strategic perspectives of corporate sustainability management to develop a sustainable organization.*

Benn, S., Dunphy, D., & Griffiths, A. (2014). Enabling Change for Corporate Sustainability: An Integrated Perspective. *Australasian Journal of Environmental Management.*

Colbert, A., Yee, N., & George, G. (2016). The Digital Workforce and the Workplace of the Future. *The Academy of Management Journal.*

Direção Geral Saúde. (2012). *Plano Nacional de Saúde (PNS) 2012-2016.* Obtido de https://pns.dgs.pt/pns-2012-2016/

Gagliardi, D., Psarra, F., Wintjes, R., Trendafili, K., Pineda Mendoza, J., Haaland, K., & Niglia, F. (2020). *New Technologies and Digitisation: Opportunities and Challenges for the Social Economy and Social Enterprises.* European Commission, Executive Agency for SMEs.

Geada, N. (2019). Change Management in the Digital Economy: Model Proposal. *International Journal of Innovation in the Digital Economy, 11*(3), 4.

Geada, N., & Anunciação, P. (2019). Change Management Projects in Information Systems: The impact of the Methodology Information Technology Infrastructure Library (ITIL). In Handbook of Research on Emerging Technologies for Effective Project Management. IGI Global.

Hammer, M., & Champy, J. (1994). *Reengineering the Corporation: A manifesto for business revolution.* Nicholas Brealy.

Hemerling, J., Kilmann, J., Danoesastro, M., Stutts, L., & Ahern, C. (2018). *It's Not a digital Tansformation without a Digital Culture.* The Boston Consulting Group.

Irimiás, A., & Mitev, A. (2020). *Sustainability. Change Management, Digital Maturity, and Green Development: Are Successful Firms Leveraging on Sustainability?* Academic Press.

Legner, C., Eymann, T., & Hess, T. (2017). *Digitalization: opportunity and challenge for the business and information systems engineering community.* Academic Press.

Matt, C., Hess, T., & Benlian, A. (2015). Digital Transformation Strategies. *Business & Information Systems Engineering, 57*(5), 339–343. doi:10.100712599-015-0401-5

Nambisan, S., Wright, M., & Feldman, M. (2019). *The digital transformation of innovation and entrepreneurship: Progress, challenges and key themes.* Academic Press.

Rance, S., Rudd, C., Lacy, S., & Hanna, A. (2011). *ITIL Service Management* - (2011 Edition). TSO - The Stationery Office.

Schwarzmüller, T., Brosi, P., Duman, D., & Welpe, I. M. (2018). *How Does the Digital Transformation Affect Organizations? Key Themes of Change in Work Design and Leadership.* NOMOS. doi:10.5771/0935-9915-2018-2-114

Thakhathi, A., le Roux, C., & Davis, A. (2019). Sustainability Leaders' Influencing Strategies for Institutionalising Organisational Change towards Corporate Sustainability: A Strategy-as-Practice Perspective. *Journal of Change Management*, 246–265. doi:10.1080/14697017.2019.1578985

Verhoef, P., & Bijmolt, T. H. (2019). Marketing perspectives on digital business models: A framework and overview of the special issue. *International Journal of Research in Marketing.*

Wessel, L., Baiyere, A., Ologeanu-Taddei, R., Cha, J., & Jensen, T. (2020). Unpacking the Difference between Digital Transformation and IT-enabled Organizational Transformation. *Journal of the Association for Information Systems*.

Westerman, G., Bonnet, D., & Mcafee, A. (2014). *Turning Technology into Business Transformation*. Harvard Business Review Press.

Wirtz, B. W. (2019). *Digital business models. Concepts, models, and the alphabet case study*. Springer. doi:10.1007/978-3-030-13005-3

Zhang, Y., Khan, U., Lee, S., & Salik, M. (2019). Sustainability. *The Influence of Management Innovation and Technological Innovation on Organization Performance. A Mediating Role of Sustainability*. Academic Press.

Chapter 15
Change Management:
Application of a Simplified APQP Model With a "Gate Release" System for Change Management in an SME

Ricardo Jorge Travassos
Polytechnic Institute of Setúbal, Portugal

Nuno Sérgio Martins
Polytechnic Institute of Setúbal, Portugal

João Pedro Sousa
Polytechnic Institute of Setúbal, Portugal

Ricardo Barata Mota
Polytechnic Institute of Setúbal, Portugal

ABSTRACT

The present markets affect organizations by triggering the need for change. However, in addition to flexibility, it is considered the implementation of procedures to alleviate the 'weather'. So, change management is fundamental in organizations that move in innovative and disruptive environments. The present work seeks to provide a tool that will allow the collection and structuring of the constituent data necessary for the management of new projects/products, creating relevant information to strategic decision makers, stating that the exploratory cycle of the process intends to create organizational knowledge that will 'situate' all team members within the various projects. It will consist of a literary review followed by the presentation of a case study, which can be applied in an SME due to its technical simplicity. The objective is to support the proposal as a promoter of information and knowledge management. The work ends with a critical analysis of the contents, exposure of limitations, and suggestions for possible future work associated with the current theme.

DOI: 10.4018/978-1-7998-7452-2.ch015

INTRODUCTION

To (Kotler, Kartajaya, & Setiawan, 2017) the world is changing, presenting features of increasing horizontality, inclusion, and socializing. Globalization is responsible for the phenomena of " Hyperconnectivity ", increasing innovation and technological disruption. Consequently, we are today highly informed and demanding consumers, however, the authors warn that the 'Tsunami' of available data and information, destroyed the "romanticism" of diversity. Due to the significant reduction in associated costs, there are efforts to homogenize consumption and experiences. In this way, they point out as a current paradox, the individual reaction that we all must combat this diligence by demanding exclusivity and personalization of our goods and services.

Toumi, (2001) *as cited in* Rossetti & Morales, 2007) stating that 'business success' depends to a large extent on innovation and knowledge, and this fact changes the traditional perceptions of business management.

For management, this presupposes, the need to consider the collection and processing of data systems, possible to generate information as a precedent of knowledge, enabling target markets and adapt portfolios of products and services, where there is greater profitability. In addition, the specificities presented, show that the competitiveness in the markets is high and growing, and for this reason, the productive efficiency associated with flexibility is a constant in decision making.

At the present, we are witnessing a high level of competition, largely due to the responsibility of globalization, because we may have competitors on the other side of the planet, as well as on the other side of the corner, and for these reasons, organizations must become flexible and capable readjust itself quickly and continuously to compete and guarantee advantages in the market in which they operate. (Machado & Neiva, 2017)

The systems of ICT (information and communication technologies), are presented as crucial to the contemporary management, allowing assertiveness for the strategic choice, and as a departmental integrator, intend to create an organizational knowledge, and help to the people change to.

Rossetti & Morales (2007) emphasize ICT, pointing out its importance as "… an instrument to support the incorporation of knowledge, as the main aggregator of value to products, processes and services delivered by organizations to their customers." But the authors, indicate that the intrinsic value of Information does not come from ICT *itself,* generally managers spend large amount of money on ICT, but then translate into unfounded investments, as the focus on information and information systems has not been clearly assumed.

We will introduce a procedure developed by the team '*Launch Management* ' in a big car industry company, the reduced size of the built *Budgets* associated, and operation. Motivated by the need for team cohesion, and the generation of knowledge across all departments. It is important to emphasize the importance of considering information systems as integrators, and transversal to the various departments of an organization, especially when it comes to managing changes. Thus, the architecture of the systems, and all associated elements, should not be a solitary and imposing task on the part of the project manager, and those responsible for ICT.

In this sense, leadership associated with the change process is also relevant, defined not as the coordination and management of subordinates' activities, maintaining a relationship of authority with them (Rosari, 2019), but rather, as a relationship – leadership presupposes four elements, first that leadership is practiced between leaders and followers, second that the relationship of members is based on mutual influence, third that both want real changes, and fourth that leaders and followers develop mutual purposes. (Rost, 1993 *as cited in* Rosari 2019).

Emphasizing the possibility of increasing scanning the same as later stage, where it is expected to clear evidence of benefit even in the above-described value.

It is intended to fill three referenced aspects: 1st - the need for change associated with market dynamics; 2nd - the imperative to emphasize information and IS as a value of operational efficiency, of the offer; and the creation of organizational knowledge; 3rd - the presentation of a low-cost procedure that supports this valuation, allowing managers to bet on the technological progression phase in a reasoned manner.

OBJECTIVES AND METHODOLOGY

The main objective of this study is related to the facility in applying an information and knowledge system, through a system of "gate releases " capable of helping an SME in a changing situation, more and more dynamic and complex. As already mentioned, change is inevitable and is an obligation to ensure the survival of companies. That said, it is important to define and apply systems and methodologies that add value to the organization and that imply minimal expenses and barriers for the organization simultaneously.

The collection of data oversaw using the focus group technique to a management board of a multinational car company, composed of 5 directors (quality, logistics, finance, production, and general director). All of them contributed to the presentation of their opinion on the subject in question and that they provided important inputs for the application of the referred model.

According to Morgan (1996 and 1997) as cited in (Silva et al., 2014) the focus group allows the collection of qualitative data on a given topic through the interaction of the researcher in the dynamization of the discussion, having this group chosen, a set of characteristics that can give a fundamental contribution to the theme Casey (2009) as cited in (Silva et al., 2014)

In view of the problems associated with the use of this methodology, namely the possibility of individuals not answering a certain question due to the thought that the group may have or because it is uncomfortable or due to the fact that there are individuals with less propensity to expose their ideas (Sim & Waterfield, 2019), it will be up to the interviewer to overcome these difficulties, which is why the responsible interviewer is the individual with the academic degree and experience at the level of the interviewees in order to better explore the concepts and be able to challenge all individuals to participate actively.

THEORETICAL FRAMEWORK

Creation of Organizational Knowledge

In the process of translating information into knowledge, quality weighs more than quantity, because in this knowledge creation process, we add value, which makes knowledge more expensive. In most Western countries, industry has been losing weight in the Gross Domestic Product (GDP), being replaced by the services sector, typically the result of the transformation of industrial society into information society, and information technology has completely revolutionized the world. as we know it, just as the new sources of energy went to successive industrial revolutions (Castells, 1999; Rascão, 2008). This effort is only possible with the adoption of concepts related to knowledge management, with the application of efficient models, where the presence of all the *stakeholders* is a basic premise, as a way to accept the sharing of this knowledge as something natural, a product of knowing what to do and knowing how to do it, allowing evolution through the efficient application of knowledge, which generates innovation that allows the optimization of processes and procedures (Coelho, 2003).

From the perspective of organizations and taking into account the diverse views of knowledge presented by Von Krogh et al. (2001), two distinct views stand out: the "Distributed" ones, where each individual, group or department of an organization can develop its own idea of knowledge, allowing a high degree of commitment and understanding with the organization, however with a lack of coordination between the many views that may exist in the organization; and the "Visionaries" called 360º, who present themselves as the best way to create knowledge, allowing to satisfy all the criteria, where the vision of knowledge is instilled by the entire organization, and these visions require coordination so that it is possible to exercise a significant impact on the business vision.

Data, Information and Knowledge

Since information is the key to knowledge management, we can consider that information is a set of data that, accompanied by a certain meaning, define it. According to Wiliam Zikmund (2000), knowledge management is defined as a process that allows the creation of an understandable organizational memory with easy access, called the intellectual capital of the organization, being also understood by Rascão (2008, p. 70), as being: "… The organization of intellectual capital in a formal structure that is easy to use", and as such requires relevant information, intelligence, and quick communication so that a certain person can make decisions.

To understand how knowledge is processed, we will first have to address the basic concepts that allow knowledge to be generated. The terms "Information" and "Knowledge" are often used and even confused, with a clear distinction between these two terms. We can understand information as a flow of messages or meanings that can add or change knowledge, where the information results from the analysis of data that are important productive factors for information and, consequently, for knowledge. When knowledge is understood in the context of experience and learning and taking into account that the creation of knowledge is dependent on information, the development of relevant information requires the application of previously acquired knowledge. This interactive dynamic configures the relationship between information and knowledge, where the methods of analysis and instruments can influence the knowledge created, which results from the tacit learning process, and which is associated with the environment and the experience that each individual has acquired over the years. lo n go of time (Chaffey & Wood, 2005; Martins, 2010; Nonaka, 1994).

For those who share and follow this vision, knowledge is described through a hierarchical pyramid, which includes from the bottom to the top the following elements, as discussed in Figure 1, with the "Data", the "Information", the " Knowledge" and finally "Wisdom", the latter element being able to assess the understanding and the reason for things (Ackoff, 1989; Martins, 2010; Newell et al., 2009). In this way, Ackoff (1989) demonstrates, through the hierarchy of knowledge, the increase in the degree of connectedness between the different dimensions, thus allowing to reach the level of perception of the individual in relation to his surroundings.

Information has a variety of connotations between different fields of knowledge, with biology and psychology as examples, where information is used in different ways, that is, while some analyze information as a basic property of the universe, others understand as a variable of sensory perception or human understanding. The notion of information is widely associated with messages, which can take on different interpretations, with different theoretical treatments, and can be assumed in an orderly or extremely complex way. Information is currently understood in a radically different way from the ideas that initially defined it, recognizing knowledge and information as being the dominant characteristics of our time.

Knowledge is seen as a dynamic cluster of experiences, values, contextual information, and experienced *insight,* allowing a new basis for the Knowledge Management Model in the Context of an Organization.

Since knowledge is something that arises from a person's cognitive ability, when he relates complex structures of information, taking into account his experience and values, then knowledge cannot be shared, at least in its purest aspect. However, it is possible to share the technique and components that produce new information for understanding by another person. It is in the attempt to proceed with the transmission of knowledge, derived from the duality of the attempt to store this knowledge and its passage from person to person, that the difficulty in the treatment and management of that knowledge arises (Davenport & Prusak, 1998; Rascão, 2008).

SECI Model in the Creation of Knowledge in Organizations

In order to enable organizations to create knowledge, Nonaka & Konno (1998) developed a knowledge conversion model using tacit knowledge (skills, intuitions, judgments, among others) and explicit knowledge (all the facts and skills that can be documented). This model, called the SECI process, is divided into four actions defined as Socialization (tacit – tacit), Externalization (tacit – explicit), Combination (explicit – explicit) and Interiorization (explicit – tacit).

The knowledge creation process needs a specific context, for whom, and how it participates in the generation of it, where the creation and renewal of "Ba"[1] provide the energy, the quality and the place so that it is possible to carry out the individual conversions in order to advance the spiral of knowledge that complements the SECI model. Therefore, "Ba" is the space, not exclusive to a physical space, it can be virtual (communication software), and the time when information is interpreted to become knowledge (Martins, 2010).

There are 4 types of "Ba", which fit the SECI model (Nonaka & Konno, 1998):

1. Origin of "Ba": which consists of individual and direct interactions, being a place where individuals share experiences, feelings, emotions and mental models, being associated with a context of socialization;
2. Dialogue in "Ba": which consists of direct and collective interactions, it is the place where the aptitudes and mental models of individuals are shared, converted into common terms and articulated as concepts, in a context of externalization;
3. "Ba" System: it consists of virtual and collective interactions, presenting a context of combination of existing explicit knowledge, since it can be easily transmitted;
4. Exercise in "Ba": consisting of virtual and individual interactions, in a context of internalization where individuals incorporate the explicit knowledge transmitted through manuals or simulators;

Knowledge assets are the inputs, outputs and moderating factors in the knowledge creation process. Unlike other assets, these are intangible, specific to the organization and change dynamically. The essence of knowledge assets is that they must be built and used internally so that their full value is realized. Not only does it mean knowledge already created, but it also includes knowledge to create knowledge, such as the organizational capacity to innovate (Nonaka & Toyama, 2005).

They are divided into four types:

1. empirical knowledge assets, which consist of shared tacit knowledge built through organizational experiences;
2. conceptual knowledge assets, consisting of explicit knowledge articulated through images, symbols and language;
3. systemic knowledge assets, consisting of systematizations and packages;
4. routine knowledge assets, which consist of tacit knowledge that is routine and incorporated into actions and practices. To conduct the knowledge creation process, top and middle managers are identified as the key people to work on the four elements of the process. They must provide the vision of knowledge, develop and promote the sharing of knowledge resources, create and stimulate Ba and continue the knowledge creation spiral (Vorakulpipat & Rezgui, 2008).

In a succinct way, using existing knowledge assets, an organization creates knowledge through the SECI process that takes place in Ba, where the new knowledge, once created, becomes, in turn, the basis for a new spiral of creation of the knowledge. The first action of conversion, socialization, arises from the interaction of tacit-to-tacit knowledge and is a difficult process to manage, since it involves the conversion of tacit / personal knowledge. It is a process that involves sharing common experiences, discussing opinions and skills. It can be helped using tools, such as videoconferences, for providing a meeting in a virtual space simulating a face-to-face interaction, or, following the example of Japanese organizations, holding informal meetings outside the workplace.

The wealth of tacit knowledge fosters the creation of knowledge, becoming the motivating force for its generation. The reach of this type of knowledge can be obtained through others without using language, as is the case of organizational learning (Nonaka & Konno, 1998; Sabherwal & Becerra-Fernandez, 2003).

The second action of conversion, externalization, appears in the transformation of tacit knowledge into explicit. It is the transition from tacit knowledge to explicit concepts, for example, when an employee tries to transmit his knowledge, experience, and technical skills to a manual. His knowledge is transferred to a set of words that explicitly tries to reveal his erudition (Sabherwal & Becerra-Fernandez, 2003). For Nonaka, Toyama & Byosière (2001), of the four conversion actions, externalization is the key to knowledge creation, as it creates new and explicit concepts of tacit knowledge, and when this happens, it can be shared by others and can make the basis for new knowledge.

The third conversion action, combination, occurs during the transfer of explicit knowledge to explicit knowledge. Key issues are the processes of communication and diffusion, and the systematization of knowledge. It is a process of linking distinct elements of explicit knowledge into a series of systematic knowledge (Nonaka & Konno, 1998; Sabherwal & Becerra-Fernandez, 2003). Such conversion is carried out through the exchange and combination of knowledge between individuals, in a simple exchange of telephone conversation, in meetings, e-mail or documents.

The fourth conversion action, internalization of newly created knowledge, corresponds to the transition from explicit knowledge to tacit knowledge of the organization. This forces the individual to identify the knowledge relevant to himself within the organizational knowledge. It is facilitated by expert systems, digitized manuals, and technological networks. It can be summed up by learning by doing (Nonaka & Konno, 1998; Sabherwal & Becerra-Fernandez, 2003). Explicit knowledge, in order to be internalized, can be provided through online manuals, videos, *Frequently Asked Questions* (FAQ) lists, online narrative tools, online discussion groups.

Spiral of Knowledge

An organization cannot create knowledge on its own. Much of what is done in knowledge management is based on successive passages from tacit to explicit knowledge and vice versa, in the so-called knowledge spiral, which demonstrates that new knowledge originates in people and refers to different ways of conversion of knowledge that occurred through interactions between an individual's tacit knowledge and his explicit knowledge (Eliufoo, 2008; Nonaka & Takeuchi, 1995; Sabherwal & Becerra-Fernandez, 2003; Vorakulpipat & Rezgui, 2008). The knowledge spiral starts again, after being completed, but at ever higher levels, thus expanding the application of knowledge in other areas of the organization (Nonaka & Takeuchi, 1995)

According to Nonaka (1994), knowledge creation focuses on the construction of tacit and explicit knowledge and, more importantly, on the exchange between these two aspects of knowledge through internalization and externalization. If the process of dialogue between tacit and explicit knowledge fails, we will have serious problems, because resorting only to a pure application of combination and socialization presents disadvantages in the application of knowledge, except eventually in the specific context for which it was created. Thus, it is important to safeguard the transfer of tacit knowledge in the form of explicit knowledge, with dialogue and the individual's mental model being important in the process of externalizing tacit knowledge in explicit (Nonaka et al., 2000). One of the concepts implicit in the study of Nonaka, consists of the " *knowledge network* ", which represents a network of knowledge data of the organization, and during its creation phase, the concept created, clarified and justified in the organization is then integrated into the database. knowledge of this organization, which basically comprises a network of organizational knowledge, easy access to the organization's memory and which is often called the organization's intellectual capital (Nonaka, 1991; Sousa et al., 2013; Zikmund, 2000).

This organizational knowledge base is reorganized, through a process of interaction between the established organizational vision and the concept of the newly created one.

Knowledge Management Activities

Knowledge management can be described as a collective process, of an interactive nature, which presupposes a sharing of information and attitudes in the various stages of knowledge development. To transform knowledge into a valuable organizational asset, knowledge, experience and expertise must be formalized, distributed and applied. Knowledge management is thus considered the fundamental part of the strategy to use knowledge to create sustainable competitive advantages (Bloodgood & Salisbury, 2001; Grant, 2006; Gray & Meister, 2006; Sher & Lee, 2004). According to Serrano & Fialho (2003), knowledge management is a systematic, articulated, and intentional process, supported by the creation, codification, dissemination, and appropriation of knowledge, with the objective of achieving organizational excellence. Through the identification and management of the organization's knowledge assets and sharing the best practices and technologies that drive these processes, knowledge management disseminates and generates new knowledge to obtain competitive advantage. Matusik (2002) states, in summary, that the knowledge levels of organizations are influenced by four processes, in which each of them will affect the level of global knowledge of the organization:

1. knowledge creation;
2. absorption of relevant (external) public knowledge;
3. knowledge transferred within the organization;
4. dissemination in the external environment of the knowledge organization belonging to it.

According to some authors, the main activities of knowledge management are the generation of knowledge (creation or acquisition), the codification of knowledge (or storage) and the transfer of knowledge (Silva & Neves, 2003; Franco & Mariano, 2007).

Process Change Management

Definition of Change - Aversion to Change

Change Management is the English term for change management, it is essential to start by defining the concept of change, in the organizational scope, since it is a theme that has different meanings, varying from author to author.

According Kissil (1998), the change can be defined as a process involving people, organizations and social systems; It is necessary to know the reason for changing the destabilizing forces of the current state in which things are; and needs to know what you want to change, it just ignores knowing where you are starting from, and where you want to get to; and demands to organize and manage the change process; who has authority the decision to change.

For Herzog (1991), in an organizational context, the change includes changes to human behavior, work patterns and values in response to changes or anticipating strategic, resource or technology changes (Wood, 2000).

Basil & Cook (1974) consider the main elements of organizational change: Technology; social behavior; and institutions and structures. According to the authors, most organizations resort to change in response to crises (Wood, 2000). Changes can then be defined as a process where the structure and mode of operation of an organization can be changed, to make more competitive organization (Fernandes, 2005).

The change, in one way or another, is associated with objects of contestation, and this fact can be explained by the conservative tendency of the human being. The change can sometimes be the target of resistance, meaning that there may be a factor that can significantly affect the functioning of the organization. In an organizational context, the manifestation of resistance can be expressed in different ways, explicit and immediate or concealed and deferred in time, revealing different types of behavior, which can be easily identified through clear manifestations or difficult to be identified through situations of implicit resistance and temporally out of phase.

For these reasons, it is essential to acquire knowledge of the organizational and individual factors that are the source of manifestations of resistance. This knowledge must be considered as essential, since it helps in the understanding and management of manifestations, contributing to avoid the occurrence of situations of conflict and rupture.

According to Robbins (2008), the individual factors associated with resistance are: fear of the unknown or the exchange of a situation taken for granted by an uncertain one; the need for security and the fear of taking risks; economic factors generally associated with the idea that the change can lead to a reduction or loss of income; habit, in the sense that we depend on established behavioral patterns and routines to deal with complexity, which in the face of a changing situation must be reorganized; the selective perception that we use to manage information and shape the world is, in a context of change, generally used to ignore information that may affect that same world.

Moreover, Robbins (2008) also notes that organizational factors are: the structural inertia, used to produce stability and act as a counterweight when facing change; the focus of change, in the sense that the more circumscribed the space affected by the change, the greater the resistance felt at other organizational levels that will exert pressure to cancel it; the group inertia works as conditioning element of individual acceptance of change; the threat to resources relating to certain groups or departments, which will inevitably lead to manifestations of resistance to change as a means of safeguarding them; and the threat to established power, which will provoke the resistance of those interested in safeguarding their sphere of power.

Change Management

The above considerations are related to the contextual environment and transactional market, features to change the definition companies or organizations, always, that in small or large scale, had changing needs. It has also referred to the perceived uncertainty and complexity of our society.

However, due to the contextualization transmitted by the previous sections, it is stated that information and knowledge management is a strategic resource and an asset for companies, playing a fundamental role in managing change. Intrinsic knowledge in companies is recognized as a necessity and an advantage to keep organizations competitive in the market and improve their performance (Luchesi, 2012).

Organizations have been developing activities in an environment that is characterized by a knowledge-based, technology-intensive, and constantly changing economy. Knowledge has become an advantage for economic growth and improved productivity. This knowledge serves for companies to deal with increasing competitiveness, and to be able to face the permanent needs of innovation (Guadamillas & Donate, 2006).

In view of this, organizations face the challenge of responding, changing the organization's structures, and in turn, the way of negotiating, using new management techniques. Thus, the organizational capacity to acquire information, transform it into knowledge, incorporate it as learning, share it quickly and implement it where, how, and when necessary, is the most important to deal with turbulences (Grant, 1996). It is for this reason that information and knowledge are considered as a source of competitive advantage, since they stimulate economic development, creativity, invention and application of new products, services, and processes, which generate value creation and increase productivity and profitability. Thus, organizations are better prepared to manage change if there is a need.

Organizational change is a theme that involves various interventions, human actions, communication, and interaction activities, and cannot be considered a static theme. Therefore, this organizational change can be characterized as a process (Jian & Sydow, 2011), and it can evolve in both progressive and retrograde directions (Ambos & Birkinshaw, 2010). However, according to several authors, there is the possibility of control and monitoring of the change, by the managers. Thus, the term Change management can be referred to the possibility of planning, controlling, and monitoring human action in this process (Rao, 2015).

Change management involves monitoring and managing human emotions and reactions, with the objective of reducing inevitable falls in productivity, which are the consequences of change processes (Maurer, 2001). The conscious use of systematic strategies and methods are characteristics of change management that ensure that the organization changes in the direction of the desired results and that guarantee its effectiveness (Hayes, 2007).

Stoner, Freeman & Gilbert (2009) state that this process is not just about applying rules, whether they are hard or fast, but rather directing an unpredictable process. That is, where strategies can lead to intentional and unintended results. However, change management is not only emerging, as it can also be frustrating and discouraging, with 70% of change programs failing, according to the authors (Balogun, 2006; Burke, 2011).

Several authors then emphasize that change management must be perceived in terms of practices. According to Sande (2015), successful change processes show the best management practices. Rao (2015) demonstrates that during the change process, people's acceptance of what is proposed, as an incentive system, focus on technology, learning, team building and leaders, commitment to organizational goals, vision and strategy, and communication shared by the changes, they generate short-term victories, because they connect the subjects' beliefs, providing a clear idea of where to be in the next phase.

According to Van de Ven (1994), change can be implemented in 2 different ways:

- Linear and continuous incremental form.
- Deep, multidimensional, and radical form.

In relation to the first case, it is a change that is planned in terms of a process of permanent evolution, which is sustained in a short-term, progressive, and localized cycle, of adaptations and changes. In other words, an adaptation of the organization to the surrounding reality. This change is directly related to a car will operating casing with respect to procedures, structures, or technology, which will have a short-term effect on the organization's activity, but which exerts extreme behavior importance.

Regarding the second case, the change is usually forced by the need to adapt quickly to environmental changes that cause threats to the organization and seeks to cause a break with previous standards of action, in order to generate lasting and irreversible effects.

Companies are therefore subject to change on a daily basis. Changes that can be processed too quickly and in very complex ways. We are currently experiencing a moment in which the challenges brought about by economic globalization and which can affect organizations are experienced on a daily basis. They deal more and more with resistance to change, in a more recurrent and complex way and try to manage it in a more adequate way, having new strategies.

Operationality of the Change Management Process

The objectives explicit in the introduction, show the intention to present a system and / or procedure based on an APQP system, and of " g *until release process* " as an integral part of it, and the present section will focus on the definition of both, so that the reader can analyze the case study under these definitions.

APQP System – Quality Tool Associated With Change Management

The APQP (Advanced Product Quality Planning) can be considered a structured method, which is established to guarantee the attendance of the level of qualities, within the deadlines defined by the client. This method aims to have an effective interface between all sectors involved in the planning and development of the product, creating a synergy between all components of the multi-functional groups, which come to be formed in this process. The groups are structured with the objective of carrying out all stages of the APQP process, within the timeframes foreseen in the schedule, in search of a reduction or even the elimination of possible modes of failure with quality and the minimization of risks of poor quality at product launch. APQP is also an essential process for directing resources through customer satisfaction, identifying changes in requirements in advance, avoiding changes in product development and after its launch, and achieving product quality in the shortest time at minimum cost (APQP, 2019).

Therefore, APQP can be summarized as follows:

- Focus – launching quality, that is, determining consumer satisfaction and continuous improvement;
- Five phases – definition and planning of the program; product development and design; process development and design; product and process validation; evaluation and continuous improvement.
- Five activities – planning; project; develop; validate; produce.
- Seven elements – customer comprehension; projection within the capabilities of the process; control special / critical features; project avoidance; verification and validation of the process; the analysis and treatment of failures and continuous improvement.

Regarding the stages of the process, these involve:

- Planning: phase in which all customer needs are defined, through direct contact between the organization and the customer, *benchmarks* (research and comparison process for applying best practices), product / process reliability studies and information provided by the customer;
- Product design and development: phase that consists of a critical review of the requirements, deadlines, objectives and goals of the process, based on an analysis that considers all factors of the project, even if they are the property of the client, in order to complete the evaluation on the viability of production;
- Process design and development: phase in which all activities of the stage (critical review and survey of potential problems) and the stage (commitment of the team to the viability and support of the management) will be finalized. In this phase, one of the most important stages will then be elaborated, the team's commitment to the viability and support of management;
- Product and process validation: phase in which it is validated whether the developed product meets the customer's needs and evaluated the results if they are in accordance with the customer's expectations;
- Feedback and corrective action analysis: phase related to continuous improvement and customer satisfaction.

Gate Release Process and Stage Gate System

In view of the growing demand for new and innovative products on the market, it is necessary and essential for companies to adopt work organization systems and methodologies that encourage, control, and accelerate the innovation process. These methodologies and systems aim to make the entire innovation process from its genesis to its placement in the form of a product on the market, with a view to a more efficient and effective process for the company, which downstream will translate into greater reduction of expenses (time and money) and will bring greater profitability, necessary to ensure the company's success in the market and its long-term survival.

However, innovation without knowledge is an empty bag of nothing. (Cunha, Cunha, Rego, Neves, & Cardoso, 2016) say that innovation requires a break that allows reconfiguring knowledge beyond what is known today. Innovation presupposes a paradigmatic rupture and not just the addition of new technologies or small innovations, that is, it involves, therefore, a change in the way of understanding knowledge. At the base of knowledge is the information that is perceived today as a main source of development and that leads to the appearance of several competitive advantages in companies for the achievement of organizational success (Gómes, Serna, & Badenes, 2009). Thus, a good information processing system is able to provide the company's strategic decision maker with information on technological, social, technological and process aspects (Boel & CecezKecmanovic, 2015), which allow the company to be provided with organizational knowledge, that is, what it needs to be known for something to be done (Newey, Verreynne & Griffiths, 2012). This knowledge will translate into an increase in creativity, sharing and leverage of the company's business and that it endows important tools to be successful in the market, namely, in the significant reduction of risk in decision making and allows the continuity of innovation in the company, crucial for the development and survival of the company.

The technologies are perceived as the pillar for innovations, however, without a solid knowledge management that allows to link the written knowledge with the practice using the technology will not be more of costs and inefficiency for the companies. This is why the use of the methodology *stage – gate process* will efficiently contribute to knowledge to be effectively used in hand with the technology as a condition judicious innovation processes can lead to the emergence of new products to market better performance or bring important reductions in the structure of expenses for the company (Newey, Verreynne & Griffiths, 2012).

The *stage – gate* system is a "conceptual as well as operational system for promoting a product, from idea to launch. It is a plan to manage a product process to improve its efficiency and effectiveness" (Cooper, 1990, p. 44). This system applies several control points and quality criteria throughout the process of developing and implementing a product on the market.

Cooper (1990) stated that in a traditional product development process there are 5 phases: Preliminary Evaluation (proceeds to product evaluation, market evaluation and preposition of product value); Construction and preparation of the business plan (critical phase where more resources and energy are allocated in order to assess the product's viability - structure of expenses and profitability. It contains the following activity-definition and analysis of the product, construction of the business model and the product design and product feasibility analysis); Development (development and design of the product, definition of the marketing processes associated with the products and the first test units created); Test and validation (the test reports of the prototypes are determined and the product development process and project profitability are once again analyzed) and Product Production and Launch (definition of the marketing – *mix* strategy of the product and it is placed on the Marketplace).

Between each Stage there are associated gates. These gates have very demanding quality assessment criteria that continually attest to the viability of the business and where decisions are made to advance / stop / endure / recycle the project, that is, the decision making takes into account the "(...) quality of the inputs and outputs of each phase, evaluation of the quality of the project from an economic and business point of view that culminates in a decision to advance / stop / hold / recycle the project and approve the action plan for the next phase (in case of progress)) and allocate the necessary resources "(Cooper, 1990, p. 46).

The use of this system presupposes several positive points for companies, specifically and according to (Cooper, 1990):

- Focus in building quality product development programs (the criteria built the gates ensure that no crucial activity in the process is omitted, the existence of an action plan at each gate, involvement and participation of project leaders and top management into the process, which ensures a complete product development process);
- Focus in market orientation (the company carries out various actions involving consumers in the product development process and know what they need / want, such as market research and prototype testing by consumers);
- Investment in pre-development activities (resources are allocated in order to assess the entire project in view of its feasibility, profitability, target consumer, value preposition, project costs, so as not to place "weak" products on the market that put the company at risk);
- Development time reduction (in this system during the various stages and gates are developed several tasks simultaneously which results in less time spent from the generation of the idea to its market launch, and to ensure that everything is done right at the first time);
- Waste reduction (as all activities in the process are detailed carefully there is therefore a greater awareness and control in the allocation of resources to the project to avoid waste of resources and weak investment in products);
- Involvement of the various hierarchical levels (there is a need of involvement of top management and all the leaders in order to design a deep knowledge of the whole process, their specificities and needs to take responsibility responsible for their decisions and can bring the experience component, combined with important *soft* and *hard skills* to achieve the success of the process) and *visible road map* (the *stage- getaway* system is simple and presents itself as a process map that is easy to understand and interpret due to the its SMART objectives and the description of tasks and activities about what is expected by the agents, knowing all the participating agents where the project is, where it is going and what needs to be done next) and Process control (prevents anarchy) carrying out the various activities and processes that culminate in high levels of inefficiency and uncontrolled development expenditures).

CASE STUDY

Starts the presentation of the case study, noting that it is a procedure developed in the company's industry Automobile, and directed to the industrialization stages of changes that affect the production process. The emphasis given to this phase, is since there are dimensional limitations of the present development, and because it is in this phase that the greatest quality risks are denoted. Represented their application, one added value to managers of SMEs, which sought, to reduce the risk and costs associated with the change.

The overall objective of the procedure can be segmented as follows:

- Subject: Procedure for managing changes that influence the serial process and any of its stakeholders. The following changes are assigned to this procedure: new projects; changes to Serial projects (running *changes)*; internal releases of new equipment or tools; release of tools at suppliers that require customer approval.
- Goal: This procedure aims to define the methodology, documentation, and the steps to be followed to manage the typologies of designated changes. The *Sharepoint* directory structure to be used is also described in the present. The present proposal and the document that may come from it, are alive, to the extent that if there is a contingent need or due to customer requirements, they may be subject to change. However, such changes will have to be previously approved either by the *launch manager*, or by the *gate keepers*, after consensus of the project team. D under the continuous improvement, also affect the improvements derived from experimentation, and the lessons learned during the project.
- Scope: Applies to production units that, due to their exploratory cycle, are affected by market dynamics, needing to change their product in terms of design and operation, or introduce new technologies that need approval from their customers.
- Necessary documents for the execution of the process: Structured procedure with its description, flowchart and *RASI chart* (table of responsibilities); Sharing point or 'Sharing place', known 'digitally' as *Sharepoint* and structured with a directory 'tree'; *Check-list* APQP (Change *Management check-list)*; Project schedule; Global action plan; association of possible Indicators allocated to the *checklists*, global action plan or schedules.

Above, the need for a *Sharepoint* (sharing point), a tool currently available, for the installation of any operating system and cost framed by an SME is explicit. What this means, is that there is a virtual "place" shared by all team members, where mutual interaction in the consultation and storage of documents is allowed, allowing also, whoever wishes, to check the status of each of the projects to be carried out. level of scheduling and assessing progress.

This points a "open" when team members need, or in their regular meetings, and together validate, the needs of the various departmental valences. It is noted here the presence of a horizontality and inclusion posture affects the procedure. Corroborating Von Krogh et al. (2001), and the "Visionary" perspective of 360° knowledge creation. The coordination requirement cited by the authors is presented in this proposal for intervention *Launch Manager* (Project Manager) and *Gate keepers* (any leader who has decision-making power within the company). The project manager ensures the coordination of projects, the transition of the various phases, and there is a need to intervene reactively one of the stages, the latter representing the hierarchical power that will boost the action of members lack.

The procedure itself in its creation and revision will respect the transversal nature of all the company's areas of expertise. For this purpose, it will be created through a series of meetings, where it is intended that all members designated within the team within the project team, introduce their inputs and discuss the expectations of outputs. Only after global agreement will it be possible to start its execution. It is also mentioned that the procedure is itself affected by the change, and that the integrative and transversal line of thought should last whenever there is a need to update it.

The visualization of the sharing point (*Sharepoint*) is aided by the presentation of a proposal for the layout of directories (Figure 1), which will allow team members to 'get used' to fetch the information they need at the correct 'place', i.e., to collect the necessary inputs and the to discuss the expectations of the outputs. In this example, it is corroborated that the quality of the information is obtained through the coherence of the functions associated with its production and availability (acquisition, storage, processing, recovery, transmission, distribution, and dissemination of information). Implying in this case that the information is made available in a timely manner.

Various *Sharepoint* possibilities currently exist on the market, and associated with operating systems, for example *MS Teams,* it allows associating a *Sharepoint* to virtual meetings, allowing a totally personalized configuration, for consulting the most varied files.

The Sharepoint should be structured as a directory that represents the needs of the team, for example, if there are needs to consult drawings, one of the folders should be designated as 'drawings', which in turn can be subdivided into several other folders, designating different drawings needed for the project. In this way, the team members find the right way to consult a certain input, indispensable to their collaboration. So, it should be for any input necessary for the correct management of change. As already mentioned, the success of the sharing point, part of the team's agreement on its architecture, and the name of the various constituent portfolios.

The proposal presented here is based, as explained above, on a *stage gate process system,* this process focuses on the industrialization phases after the design of the new product, but the construction logic of it should be applied holistically, if that is the scope of the company that wants to use it. A sequence of gates called Gate 60.70, 80 and 90 is thus presented (just because it is the name used in the company that created it, and the gates can be designated in the way that the work team understands). The relevance is based on the fact that each of these 'Gates' effectively represents a distinct and complementary phase from the previous phase, which will guide the team to the global positioning of the project, and which must be 'signed' by *Gate Keeper s* to "close a gate »and proceed with the process (next phase and next gate).

The first gates (Gate 60 and 70) represent the execution of all preliminary requirements, and the actual execution and / or implementation of the project on the "shop floor". As a result of these two phases, the physical 'parts' which, after internal approvals, are considered able to be sent to the client as prototypes, and which need final approval, to designate the desired SOP (Start *of Production).* To reduce costs associated with approval, some customers delegate the validation of certain characteristics to the supplier, if it presents previously agreed documentation, which is why it is important that this information package is highly systematized and validated within the 'Gate' (Gate 80).

At the last gate (*Gate* 90) it is desired that the first series productions are controlled, making use of tighter inspections of the products resulting from the ' *ramp up* ' period, then a safe start of the ' *Safe* ' series takes place. But it is also intended to make an exercise of lessons learned, that is, all team members will discuss what are good practices to continue, and where there may be opportunities for improvement, this represents, the closing of the quality cycle, or also the so-called closure of the continuous improvement cycle. It should be emphasized that this practice contributes to increase organizational knowledge, regarding project management, where we will try to use everyone's tacit knowledge about the project in conjunction with explicit knowledge and promote improvements to the procedure and constituent documents.

To start the change process, a *Kick-off* meeting will have to be organized to distribute an initial information package that will guide the team in the preliminary steps to start the Project (drawings, timings, specifications).

Figure 1. Directory "tree" Sharepoint.
Source: own elaboration.

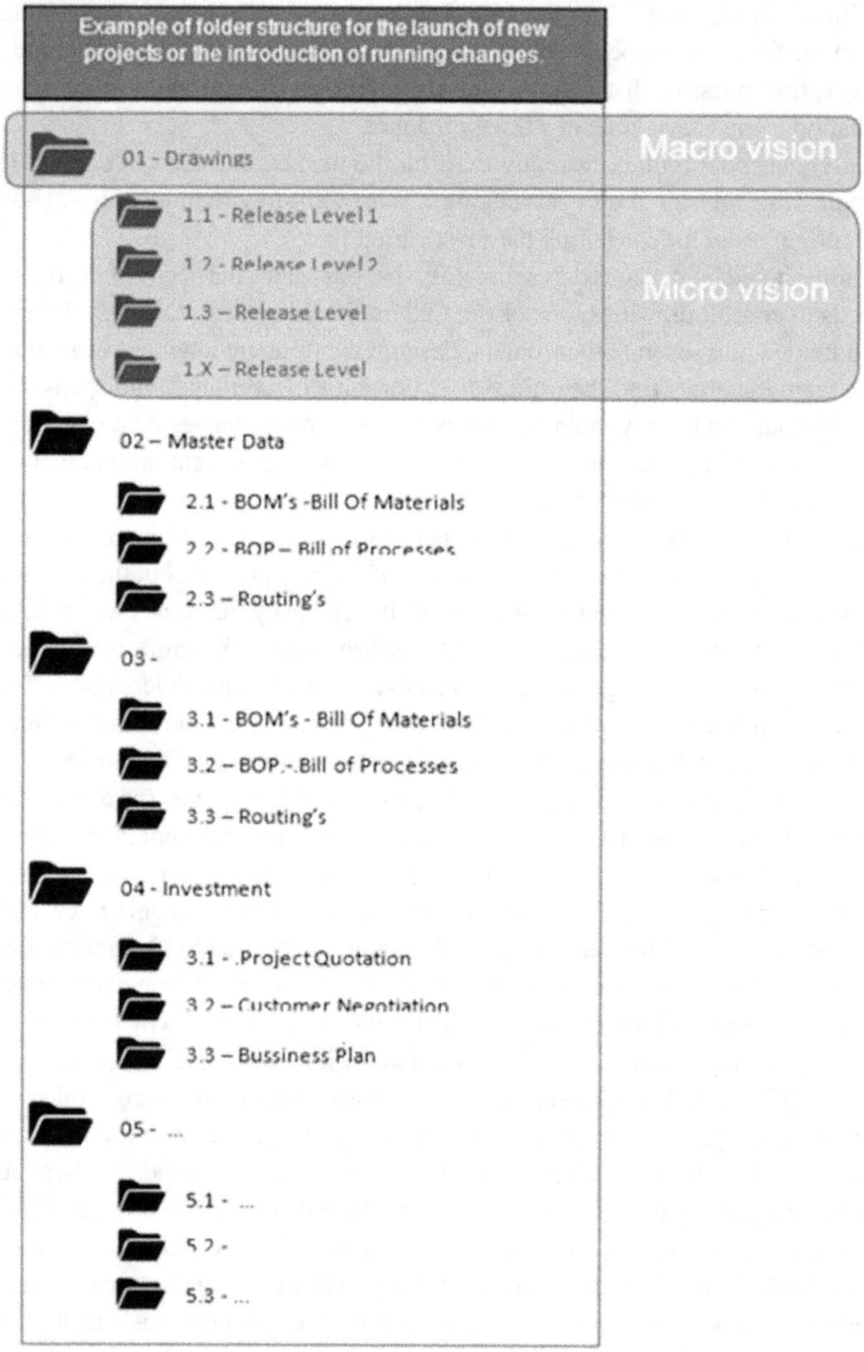

Then all the documentation relevant to the project will have to be prepared as well as the beginning of the procurement of tools necessary for the project, whether they are internal to the production process or external (supplier tools), with all conditions in place for a closing meeting of *Gate* 60. marked for validation of the initial conditions and start of the industrialization process.

This phase represents the industrialization execution phase, in this phase, it is necessary to guarantee the supply and approval of components necessary for the pre-series that will serve to validate the process.

The engineering team, after receiving all the necessary tools, proceeds to implement them and validate the processes with quality and production (e.g. pre-series manufacturing, capabilities - R & R.Cpk, capacity validation -R @ R and process audit).

From these validations, a machine acceptance protocol is signed that will lead to an acknowledgment by the quality team, that the process is capable of being presented to the customer. Parts in *off-tool / off-process* conditions will also come out of this phase, for the purposes of laboratory tests and shipments to customers (functional tests).

Training for equipment operators is given during this phase to prepare them for *ramp-up* and series production. It is also important that the approval agreement with the customer is signed if it is not made explicit through the procedure. After all the above conditions have been met, a Gate 70 closing meeting will have to be organized and all the points described above are validated. After this *Gate* 70 is closed, customer approval processes (Gate 80) begin.

Having the internal processes validated, it is possible to proceed with the submission of the documentation previously agreed with the customer, so that the same can give its approval, establishing the beginning of the series production. In this phase, it is already possible to guarantee, with suppliers, the serial deliveries (Schedule *ordering*) of the components already approved. After the information package approved by the client, the team will have to be notified of the start of the Project's series, and there may be some mismatch here to what was initially planned. Having met the conditions described above, a meeting to close the *Gate* 80 process will have to be organized, and all points validated. Once closed, proceed to the *Gate* 90 process.

This process is already in a series production reality, and we will have to have *safe launch* results associated with the *ramp-up* productions. At this stage, a meeting of lessons learned will have to be organized to remove or not learn lessons to be implemented in future projects. It is during this phase that possible lessons are transmitted to the company's central database. After all the conditions described above have been met, a closing meeting of *Gate* 90 will have to be organized and thus the end of the entire change management process.

We always must take into account that if there is a fault condition that blocks the closure of any of the *Gates,* a reaction action plan is signed immediately with the *gate keepers* that are present at the closing meetings.

It should also be noted that projects often lack continuity of monitoring during the series period, and even the EOP (*End of production*), as the transition from an ' old *part-number* ' to a new project starts the cycle, and the need for an assertive *cut- point* reduces costs and obsolescence due to the transition.

Sequential exposure above proposal is the core of system of *gate stage process*, which should be represented in the form of flow chart when the procedure creation, for the graphical representation of the 'text' is a considerable help to facilitate the interpretation of all information associated with the procedure. It can be as complex, as necessary. Below presents an example of the simplified flowchart of the procedure (Figure 2), and according to the requirements associated to the gates, which are Aaron listed in the designated *Change Management check-list (APQP check-list).*

Figure 2. Simplified flowchart of the change management procedure
Source: own elaboration.

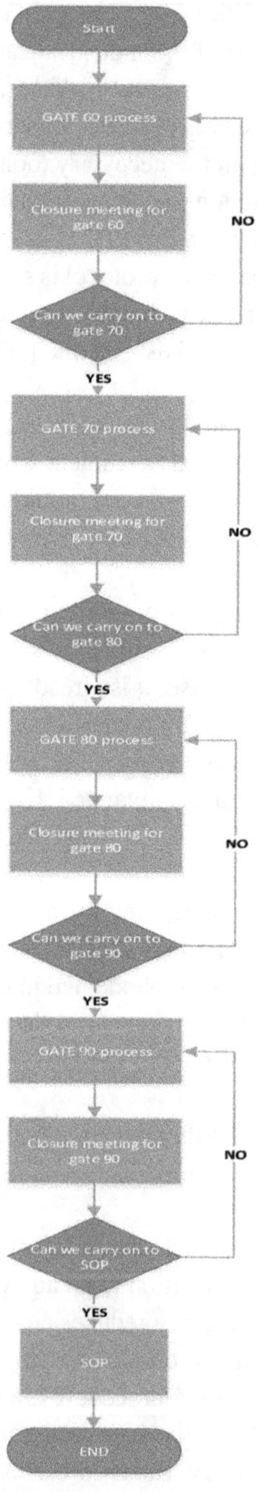

The change management checklist, the overall project schedule, and the global action plan or open task list are three complement to those who complete the "documentary structure" of the proposed process.

The first one uses the APQP methodology and lists all the requirements that the team considered necessary for the various phases of the project, so that a certain gate can be closed, and move on. This document is presented in the form of an *Excel* sheet, due to its simplicity of construction and low associated cost. The *Excel* allows some programming on the database and on the sheet itself. Objective that the responsible appointed by the allocation of a document and / or the execution of certain task, do the validation that / the same / a is finished / and the / a confirm and the *Chek-list*, the end date of your obligation. You should also allocate a Hyperlink in your line of action, allowing any user to go to the folder, within *Sharepoint*, where the receipt is, without having to completely open the path in the «tree» of directories, saving time in the consultation.

It must be constructed in such a way as to have a heading, or some form of presentation of the project, briefly describing the motivation and nature of the change, and any type of identification that the team finds pertinent. It should be followed by a visual field, where you can check the overall *status* of the project. A 'traffic light' is recommended where the *GYRstatus* (*Green, Yellow, Red)* can be visualized, making it clear in the procedure that in case the project is 'red' there is a need for hierarchical escalation, directed to the *gate keepers*, so that an emerging action plan is triggered. A 'yellow' *status* represents risk, and an action plan should also be triggered, but still within the team. The situation of "cruising speed" is expressed by the *status* in green, in this case the project is continued without the need for complementary interventions.

If a project is at risk with a yellow or even red status, the phase designation, shown in the visual status field, will allow the team to view the task (line) in red, which is the root cause of such status, and the name of the guardian in default with his contribution.

Below are examples of excerpts from the *Check-list* (Figures 3, 4, 5) which is in the Annex (Annex 1).

Figure 3. Proposal of a change management checklist.
Source: own elaboration.

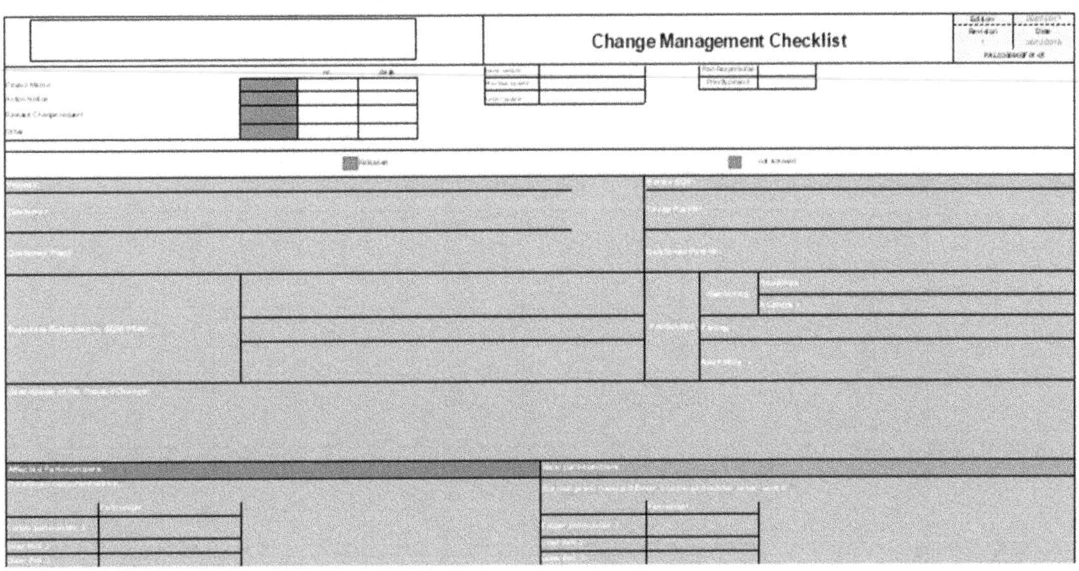

Figure 4. Proposal of status and information about team members of the project
Source: own elaboration.

Affected Part-numbers:		New part-numbers:	
The affected component will be...		The change will mean a different .3 caliper part-number as well as new...	
	Part-number		Part-number
Caliper part-number .3		Caliper part-number .3	
Inner Pad .2		Inner Pad .2	
Outer Pad .2		Outer Pad .2	

Project Team

	Name	Department	Phone	e-mail
Coord.	Ricardo Barata Mota	IE - NPL - Team Leader	+351934200138	ricardo.mota@continental-corporation.com
	Ricardo Pereira	IE - NPL	+351932113247	ricardo02.pereira@continental-corporation.com
	To be defined	PM - Central	To be defined	To be defined
	Ricardo Tavares	IE - Assembly	+351935485004	ricardo.tavares@continetal-corporation.com
	Miguel Lopes	IE - Machining	+351212387586	miguel.lopes@continental-corporation.com
	Sonia Andrade	Quality Planner - Ass.	+351212387562	sonia.andrade@continental-corporation.com
	Marília Fernandes	IE - Capacity, Process	+351934200241	marilia.fernandes@continental-corporation.com
	Miguel Cabo	Machining Segment leader	+351932100003	miguel.cabo@continental-corporation.com
	Tiago Ricardo	Foreman Machining	+351932001853	tiago.ricardo@continental-corporation.com
	Ricardo Ferreira	Assembly Segment leader	+351932009195	ricardo02.ferreira@continental-corporation.com
	Antonio Pinto	Foreman Assembly	+351932113984	antonio.pinto@continental.corporation.com
	To be defined	SCM - Customer Relations	To be defined	To be defined
	Paulo Moreira	SQM - Customer coordinator	+351212387577	paulo.moreira@continental-corporation.com
	Francisco Cortez	Laboratory	+351932113798	francisco.cortez@continental-corporation.com
	Vitor Maneta	Assembly Technologist	+351932012847	vitor.maneta@continental-corporation.com
	Ricardo Gomes	Purchase Manager	+351212387542	Ricardo.Gomes@continental-corporation.com
	Mário Martins	Metrology Area	+351212387511	mario.martins@continental-corporation.com
	Alexandre Magalhães	Finance - Controlling	+351212387504	alexandre.magalhaes@continental-corporation.com
	Marta Pereira	Quality Planner - Mach.	+351932001877	marta.pereira@continental-corporation.com
	Fernando Jacinto	Responsible of the 3D machine	+351212387511	fernando.jacinto@continental-corporation.com

GYR STATUS	MLC Status
G Y R	Gate Status
G On-track	
Y Actions needed	
R Escalation needed	

The second document is no more than the Project's timeline (schedule), where the '*milestone* ' and the main '*deadlines* ' are explicit, the expected delivery dates for the documents, the closing of the various gates, and the expected date of SOP. It is, therefore, a graphical representation of the APQP *Chek-list* (*Change management check-list*), and should also be available as a preparation requirement, essential for closing *gate* 60. It is suggested to use the *MSproject* or, if it is not possible, another sheet *and excel*, in the shape of graphic Gantt, easily accessible and free of charge on the Internet. Below is an example figure (Figure 6) of the two hypotheses. Attached (Annex 2) is the proposal of *Excel* because it is the most accessible for a possible implementation of the procedure.

Figure 5. Proposal for listing the requirements necessary for the gate 60 release.
Source: own elaboration.

Gate	N.º		Item	Required (Y-Yes N-No)	Status	Program Need Date	Real Date	Δ	Resp.	Share point Link	Remarks
Gate 55 - Design Stable	1		Preliminary PFEMA Machining						Marília Fernandes		
	2		Preliminary PFMEA assembly						Marília Fernandes		
	3		MLC55-Release						por definir		
	Closure Status									Due Date:	Status: 100 %
Gate 60 - Design Validated - Ok to Go for industrialization	4	P-FMEA	Process FMEAs Machining						Marília Fernandes		
	5		Process FMEAs Assembly						Marília Fernandes		
	6	Internal Distribution	Internal Release - Kick off meeting						por definir		
	7		Internal Industrialization Plan available						por definir		
	8		Internal Drawing Distribution						por definir		
	9	Documentation update	Packaging Definition in clarification with Customer						Helena Costa		
	10		Ramp up controls sheet						Tomas Sedmak		
	11		APQP supplier List						Bruno Carvalho		
	12		Control Plan update Machining						Marta Pereira		
	13		Control Plan update Assembly						Sónia Andrade		
	14		Process flow						por definir		
	15		Safe launch documentation Assembly						Sónia Andrade		
	16		Zeiss Machine Program approved						Fernando Jacinto		
	17		Quality Instructions for Machining						Marta Pereira		
	18		Quality intsructions for Assembly						Sonia Andrade		
	19		Working instructions for Machining						Miguel Lopes		
	20		Working Instructions for Assembly						Ricardo Tavares		
	21		Packaging Instructions done						Helena Costa		
	22	Master Data Creation	Create Material Master on SAP system		0				Ricardo Mota		
	23		BOM creation						por definir		
	24		Production version creation - Machining						Eugénio Estevão		
	25		Production version creation - Assembly						Tiago Trindade		
	26		Costing						Alexandre Magalhães		
	27	Tooling Procurement	eCR release - WBS elements created						Rafael Campos		
	28		Drawing to Suppliers via Supply - on						Ricardo Gomes		
	29		Purchase Order release for Assembly toolings & fixtures.						Ricardo Tavares		
	30		Purchase Order release for Maching toolings & fixtures.						Miguel Lopes		
	31		Purchase Order release for supplier tooling						Ricardo Gomes		
	32		Quality Gauges Purchase order release						Francisco Cortez		
	33		Internal Gate 60 Release						por definir		
	34		MLC60- Release						por definir		
	Closure Status									Due Date:	Status: 100 %

Figure 6. Proposed schedules to be used for the execution of the procedure.
Source: own elaboration

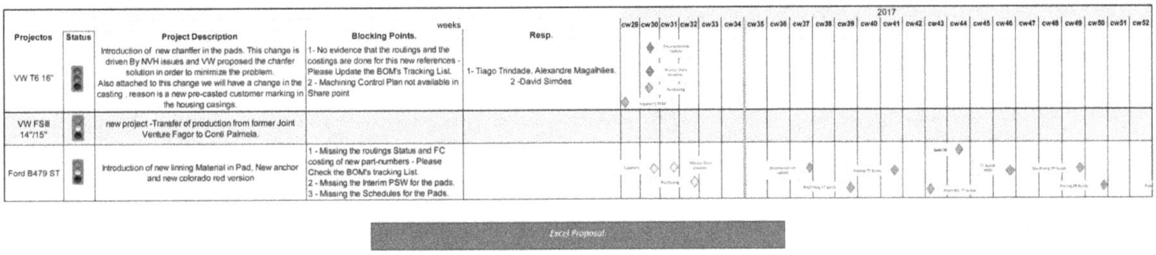

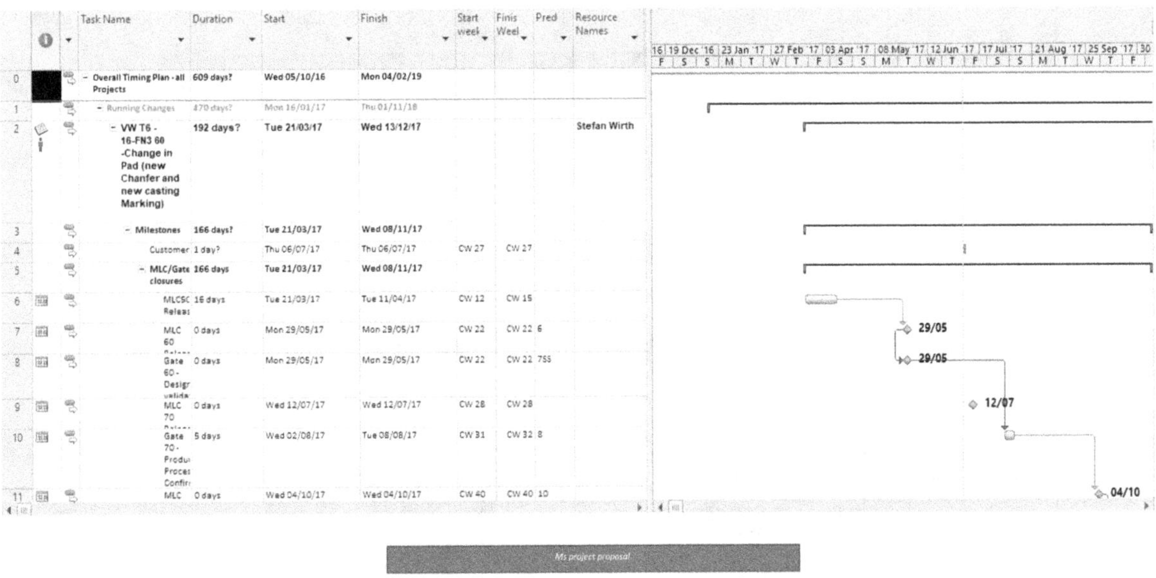

It should consider the possibility, of a member of the team, may have multiple tasks simultaneously on multiple projects, so, instead of seeking out its tasks in varied *Change management checklist's,* the worker through the *Sharepoint* consult the Plan global stock market. This proposal is no more than a table structured where each team member can filter his name and check all the tasks incumbent upon it and respective dates *terminus.* In addition, *gate keepers can* associate the *status* of projects to those responsible, who have overdue tasks, facilitating the perception of lack of commitment or excess of tasks. Thus, it allows strategic decision making within its teams, without compromising the progress of projects.

It should be noted that the proposed Global Action Plan is accompanied by a 'set' of KPIs or indicators. These are intended to assess the team's contribution in respect of the commitments varied, they are: meeting deadlines; respect for expected budgets; assertiveness in the delivery of tasks (doing well at first); trends related to task execution delays; etc.

Below are excerpts from the attached document (Annex 3), which shows two different sheets, one with the global action plan and the other with the associated indicator *dashboard* (Figure 7).

These documents portfolios associated with indicators, guide the team in accessing and structuring the information, aiming to create organizational knowledge on the conduct of the projects, and also cre-

Figure 7. Proposal of global action plan and management control indicators.
Source: own elaboration.

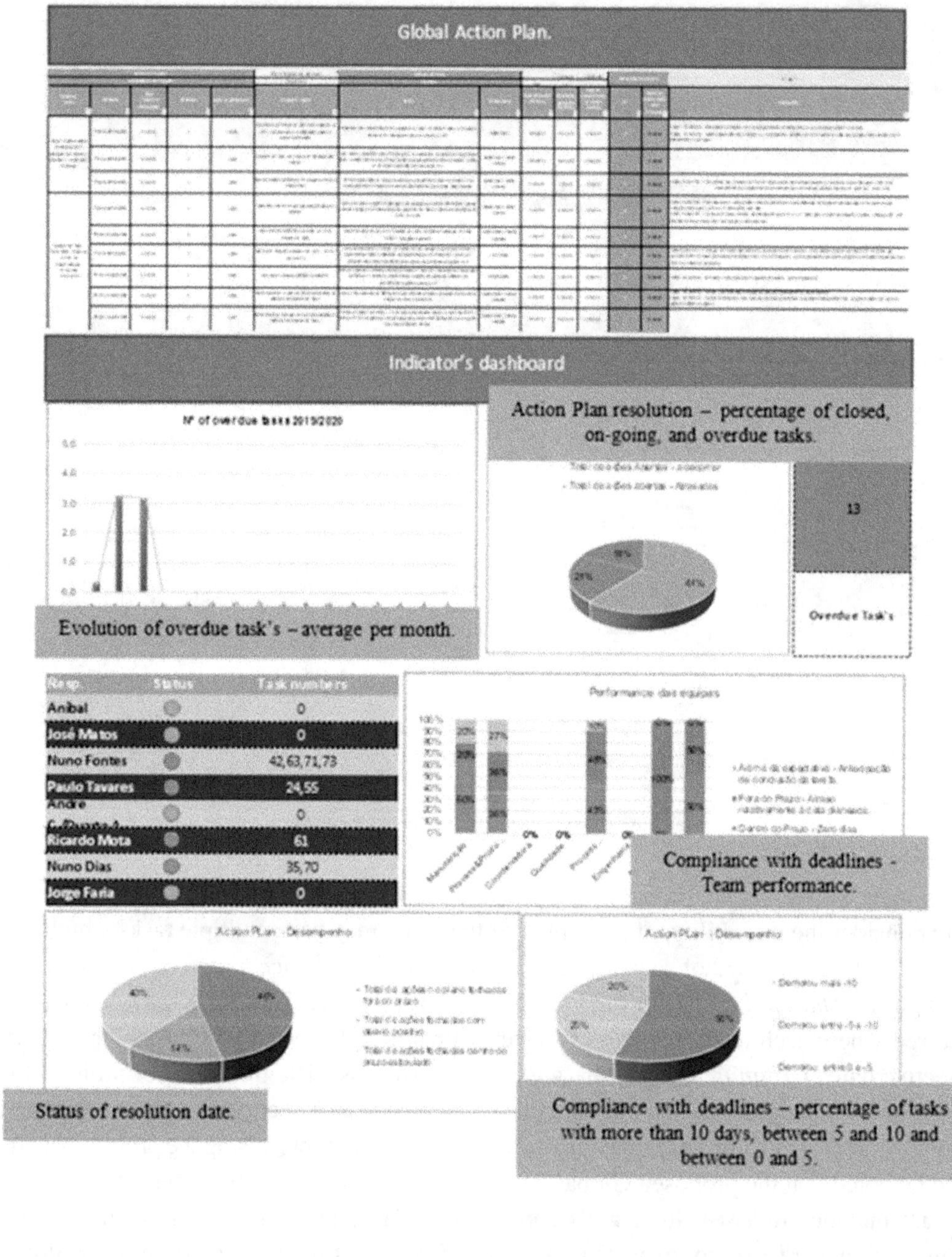

ate foreknowledge, how is forecasted the organization of new releases, as well as the forecast times and budgets associated with each of the phases.

As already mentioned, when the cycle is *closed* (*Gate* 90), team members will tend to be increasingly able to discuss the failures present in the various phases of the project, being also better able to

Figure 8. IS architecture proposal.
Source: own elaboration.

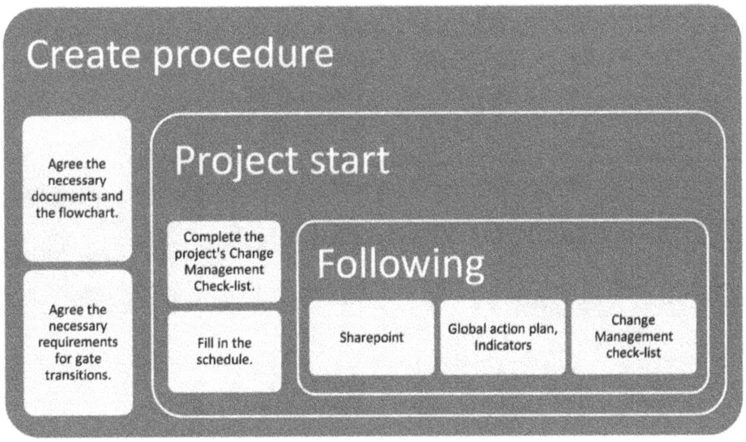

suggest improvements that allow for a reduction in time. and associated costs, making the process and documents increasingly assertive and easy to understand.

Below is an 'architecture' of the proposed System, followed by a structure of periodic meetings, which will allow the team the necessary interactions to monitor the projects and generate the desired organizational knowledge.

In a cyclical perspective, the procedural proposal can be represented as shown below, referring to the PDCA cycle (*Plan, Do, Check, Act*) as the basis of « *Lean* » thinking, also inherent to information and knowledge management.

Appeared a process based on a "formal structure easy to use" Rascão (2008, p. 70) capable of organizing intellectual capital where the various IS entities may consult relevant information and interact allowing taking decisions agreed in the course of change management. This corroborates the definition

Figure 9. Matrix of meetings associated with the procedure.
Source: own elaboration.

Frequency	Meeting	Duration	Topics addressed	Documents/resources	Attendees
one-off	Kick off meeting	1h	Presentation of the project, presentation of the timing plan, presentation of the change management checklist, discussion of the necessary actions to be contemplated in the checklist	Change Management checklist, timing plan, global action plan meeting room (virtual or Physic).	Launch Manager, Project team, Gate keepers
Weekly	Project Status meeting	2h	Revision of Global action plan, revision of the indicator's, necessarys updates in documentation	Change Management checklist, timing plan, global action plan meeting room (virtual or Physic).	Launch Manager, Project team
one-off	Gate 60 meeting	1h	Revision of the requirements for gate 60 pass-over, indicator's revision.	Change Management checklist, timing plan, global action plan meeting room (virtual or Physic).	Launch Manager, Project team, Gate keepers
one-off	Gate 70 meeting	1h	Revision of the requirements for gate 70 pass-over, indicator's revision.	Change Management checklist, timing plan, global action plan meeting room (virtual or Physic).	Launch Manager, Project team, Gate keepers
one-off	Gate 80 meeting	1h	Revision of the requirements for gate 80 pass-over, indicator's revision.	Change Management checklist, timing plan, global action plan meeting room (virtual or Physic).	Launch Manager, Project team, Gate keepers
one-off	Gate 90 meeting	1h	Revision of the requirements for gate 90 pass-over, indicator's revision.	Change Management checklist, timing plan, global action plan meeting room (virtual or Physic).	Launch Manager, Project team, Gate keepers
one-off	Reaction meeting	1h	Change management checklist revision, global action plan revision, introduction of reactive actions.	Change Management checklist, timing plan, global action plan meeting room (virtual or Physic).	Launch Manager, Project team, Gate keepers

Figure 10. PDCA cycle associated with the proposed procedure.
Source: own elaboration.

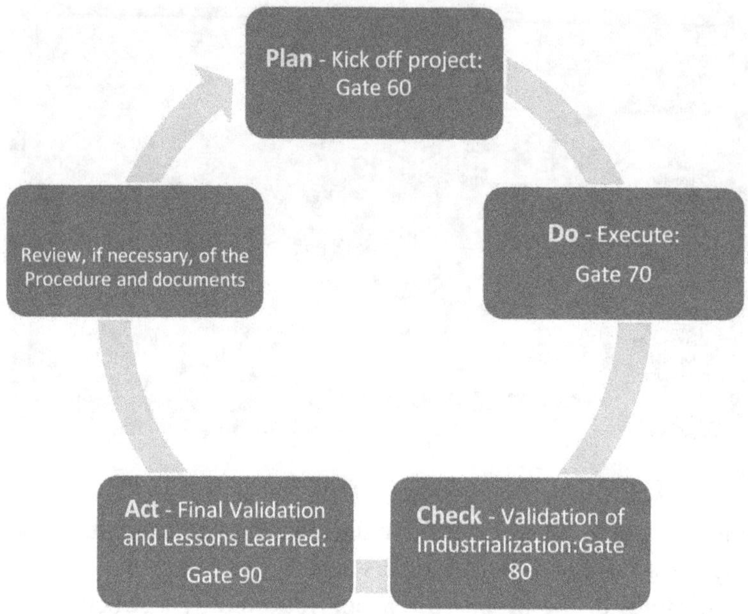

of knowledge management as a process that creates an understandable organizational memory with easy access (Wiliam Zikmund, 2000).

It appears that the case study presents a management model that fits the model of creation of knowledge (Nonaka & Konno, 1998), prevails ing a specific context, for whom, and how to participate in the generation of knowledge.

The 4 types of "Ba", which fall under the SECI model (Nonaka & Konno, 1998), are explicit in the proposal as follows:

1. Source "Ba": individual and direct interactions of the team members, sharing experiences, feelings, emotions and mental models, during the construction of the procedure, the establishment and subsequent validation of the necessary requirements to gates transitions, as well as the existing interactions in the elaboration of reaction plans and the lessons learned related to the closing of the cycle, the context of socialization is thus associated, reinforced by the necessary periodic and occasional meetings;
2. Dialogue in "Ba": the place where the aptitudes and mental models of individuals are shared, presented in the form of a point of sharing (*Sharepoint*), and of meetings allowing direct and collective interactions of the team members.
3. System "Ba": the virtual and collective interactions, features of the form of the procedure itself, the *sharepoint*, the regular meetings, and documents that allow the combination of knowledge 're quote the existing explicit.
4. Exercise "Ba": presents itself through the interactions of the members of the project team, the relationship Cycle *PDCA,* which is incorporated in an internalization of context, explicit knowledge

transmitted through d the practice of the procedure itself, and the filling the *Change Management checklist*, plan of global actions and timelines.

There are also the presence of four types of knowledge assets, across organizational experiences that the members have in the course of the projects prevailing de potential of tacit knowledge and sharing (assets of empirical knowledge), the existence of flow associated the procedure and structured documents is evidence of articulation of explicit knowledge, articulated in the form of images, symbols and language (conceptual knowledge assets), the practice of the APQP system and the PDCA cycle of the procedure in the form of *gate stage process*, shows the presence of systemic knowledge assets; the routine of executing the procedure and filling in the documents, will allow the incorporation of tacit knowledge into actions and practices (routine knowledge assets).

One can also corroborate the validity of the proposal, describing the change management procedure as "a collective process, of an interactive nature, which presupposes a sharing of information and attitudes in the various stages of knowledge development", where the experience is formalized and the knowledge of team members, and for that reason knowledge is transformed into a valuable organizational asset.

By the definition of (APQP, 2019), one of the key documents to the process is validated, the *Change Management checklist*. This, in its structured methodology, meets the level of qualities, within the deadlines defined by the client, and allows interaction and synergy between all team members.

It is effectively a plan to manage a process of introducing a new product, equipment... that will allow to improve the efficiency and effectiveness of the necessary change, applying "... several control points and quality criteria throughout the development and implementation process..." (Cooper, 1990, p. 44).

It is also stated that by applying it, it is possible to mitigate: the individual factors associated with resistance to change, by reducing the risk associated with the practice of management routines, and by horizontality and transversality; and, organizational factors such as group inertia, as the interaction affects the procedure allows for intense group dynamics in the company. Corroborating in this way the definitions set out above by Robbins (2008).

The case study ends, suggesting that the present proposal is an initial phase to the total digitalization of the procedure, that is, there is potential for optimization of the procedure when considering an integrating *software,* where the document portfolios are automatically interconnected and accessible on the same system, and where the point of sharing exist in the same domain. This phase to be built, benefits from the knowledge that comes from the practice of the previous procedure, because the company that wants to evolve in order to digitize the management of changes, will have already obtained affectionate organizational knowledge, and all the team members involved, will understand more ease the validity of the implementation, and more easily collaborate in the architecture of such a system.

CONCLUSION

In conclusion, we introduced an open and dynamic system of information considering that an organization or company is also one system dynamic open, governed by the principles of causality, stability, and repeatability. We consider thus the presence of four properties: summative and constitutive, dynamic, self-organization, entropy, which are features of its structure, d relationships between their constituent parts d of the maintained with other systems, and as is its temporal evolution.

The great competitiveness of the markets, forces organizations to improve and differentiate their services and/or products in relation to their competitors, therefore, they need to innovate (mainly SMEs). This innovation requires organizations to adopt new methods of acting, such as knowledge management. The intangible assets that organizations have, especially knowledge, are fundamental for their growth and for obtaining competitive advantages, resulting in the greatest interest on the part of organizations.

Through the application of focus group methodology and obtaining important qualitative data, we can apply this proposal to an SME, allowing differentiation in high-risk processes, fulfilling the need for change associated with current business dynamics, in a type of innovation designated as incremental and organizational innovation, framed by the investment limitations of small companies. It allows to emphasize the information and the IS as values of the operational efficiency, of the offer, and the creation of organizational knowledge. It is corroborated by several authors the potential that the proposal has in the valorization of information and knowledge.

The creation of the procedure is of low cost, considering that its construction is supported by *software* proper to the usual and current operating systems. It has the flexibility to be applied to a spectrum of complexity that is desired by managers and teams, and the constituent documents are easy to perceive and apply.

By the above designation of an open and dynamic system, it is possible to adapt it, temporarily, to any type of contingency that may occur.

In this way, the proposed objectives are fulfilled, by presenting a change management procedure, which can be applied to an SME, which promotes the structuring of information, consequently increasing organizational knowledge, and enhancing differentiation in a business group, little concerned with similar procedures.

To conclude, it should be noted that the associated leadership is extremely important, and that the SMEs should invest in training the leadership of workers, as this attitude allows to accentuate the spirit of horizontality and inclusiveness essential to the proper functioning of the procedure.

LIMITATIONS AND FUTURE WORK

It is considered that the development of the case study was carried out from a Macro perspective, due to the limitations associated with the size of the text. Since a better understanding of the proposal would benefit from the detail in the description of some of the documents presented (Micro perspective), namely the *Change management checklist,* the global action plan, and the management control *dashboard.*

The presentation of indicators was also limited, proposing to the reader only those that are considered essential to change management, but the control of the procedure would be further enriched by the presentation of complementary indicators that would enable a better perception of the associated management control.

No evidence of the effectiveness of such a procedure was presented in the case study, that is, there is no evidence of the result, exposed in the form of *KPI's,* after the implementation compared to the previous reality.

That is why it is suggested that future work may focus on the in-depth and detailed development of the procedure, looking for its practical application, to show clear indicators that prove its efficiency in an SME. Basically, to show that before the application, the change management was less efficient, and that the organizational knowledge is promoted after the implementation, obtaining this confirmation from the workers and managers of the company.

REFERENCES

Ackoff, R. L. (1989). From data to wisdom. *Journal of Applied Systems Analysis, 16*(1), 3–9.

Antunes, S. M. (n.d.). *A mudança organizacional e a gestão da mudança organizacional.* Academic Press.

APQP. (2019). *APQP - Planeamento Avançado da Qualidade do Produto.* Obtido de https://apqp.com.br/#fases-do-apqp

Bloodgood, J. & Salisbury, W. (2001). Understanding the influence of organizational change strategies on information technology and knowledge management strategies. *Decision Support Systems, 31*(1), 55-69.

Boel, S. K., & Cecez-Kecmanovic, D. (2015). *What is an Information System.* Academic Press.

Castells, M. (1999). *A sociedade em Rede-A era da informação: economia, sociedade e cultura* (Vol. 1). Paz E Terra.

Chaffey, D., & Wood, S. (2005). Business Information Management: Improving Performance Using Information Systems (1st ed.). Pearson Education (Prentice Hall).

Cooper, R. G. (1990). Stage-Gate Systems: A new tool for Managing new Products. *Business Horizons.*

Cunha, M. P., Cunha, R. C., Rego, A., Neves, P., & Cardoso, C. C. (2016). *Manual de Comportamento Organizacional e Gestão* (8th ed.). Editora RH.

Davenport, T. H., & Prusak, L. (1998). What do we talk about when we talk about knowledge. *Working Knowledge: How Organizations Manage What They Know.*

Eliufoo, H. (2008). Knowledge creation in construction organizations: a case approach. *The Learning Organization, 15*(4), 309-325.

Fernandes, E. A. (2005). *Gestão da Mudança Organizacional.* Academic Press.

Franco, M. & Mariano, S. (2007). Information Technology Repositories and Knowledge Management Processes. *Journal of Information and Knowledge Management Systems, 37*(4), 440-451.

Gómes, H. G., Serna, M. D., & Badenes, R. F. (2009). *Evolución Y Tendencias de los Sistemas de Información para la Gestión de la Empresa: El M-Business.* Academic Press.

Grant, R. (2006). The Knowledge-Based View of the Firm. In Strategy: A Strategy Overview and Competitive Strategy. Oxford University Press. doi:10.1093/oxfordhb/9780199275212.003.0008

Gray, P. & Meister, D. (2006). Knowledge Sourcing Methods. *Information and Management, 43*(2), 142-156.

Kotler, P., Kartajaya, H., & Setiawan, I. (2017). *Marketing 4.0.* Conjuntura Atual.

Luchesi, E. S. (2012). *Gestão do Conhecimentos nas organizações.* Academic Press.

Machado, L., & Neiva, E. (2017). *Práticas de gestão da mudança: Impacto nas atitudes e nos resultados percebidos*. Academic Press.

Martins, J. (2010). *Gestão do Conhecimento: Criação e Transferência de Conhecimento*. Edições Sílabo.

Matusik, S. (2002). Managing Public and Private Firm Knowledge within the context of Flexible Firm Boundaries. In C. W. Choo & N. Bontis (Eds.), *The strategic management of intellectual capital and organizational knowledge* (pp. 605–617). Oxford University Press.

Newell, S., Robertson, M., Scarbrough, H., & Swan, J. (2009). *Managing knowledge work and innovation*. Palgrave Macmillan. doi:10.1007/978-0-230-36641-1

Newey, L. R., Verreynne, M.-L., & Griffiths, A. (2012). The relationship between dynamic and operating capabilities as a stage-gate process: insights from radical innovation. *Journal of Management & Organization*.

Nonaka, I. (1991). A empresa criadora de conhecimento. *Harvard Business Review*, 11.

Nonaka, I. (1994). A dynamic theory of organizational knowledge creation. *Organization Science*, *5*(1), 14–37. doi:10.1287/orsc.5.1.14

Nonaka, I., & Takeuchi, H. (1995). *The Knowledge Creating Company: How Japanese Companies create the dynamics of innovation*. Oxford University Press.

Nonaka, I. & Toyama, R. (2005). The theory of the knowledge-creating firm: subjectivity, objectivity and synthesis. *Industrial and Corporate Change, 14*(3), 419-436.

Rascão, J. P. (2008). Novos desafios da gestão da informação. Lisboa: Edições Sílabo.

Romero, F., & Araújo, J. (2015). *A gestão da informação do conhecimento organizacional das empresas*. Academic Press.

Rosari, R. (2019). Leadership Definitions Applications for Lectures' Leadership Development, *Journal of Leadership in Organizations*. doi:10.22146/jlo.42965

Rossetti, A., & Morales, A. B. (2007). O papel da tecnologia da informação na gestão do conhecimento. *Ciência da Informação*. doi:10.15900100-19652007000100009

Sabherwal, R. & Becerra-Fernandez, I. (2003). An Empirical Study of the Effect of Knowledge Management Processes at Individual, Group, and Organizational. *Decision Sciences, 34*(2), 225-260.

Serrano, A., & Fialho, C. (2003). *Gestão do Conhecimento – o novo paradigma das organizações*. FCA – Editora de Informática.

Sher, J. & Lee, C. (2004). Information Technology as a Facilitator for Enhancing Dynamic Capabilities through Knowledge Managements. *Information and Management, 41*(8), 933-945.

Silva, I. S., Veloso, A. L., & Keating, J. B. (2014). Focus group: Considerações teóricas e metodológicas. *Revista Lusófona de Educação*, 26.

Silva, R., & Neves, A. (2003). *Gestão de Empresas na Era do Conhecimento*. Edições Sílabo.

Sim, J., & Waterfield, J. (2019). Focus group methodology: Some ethical challenges. *Quality & Quantity*, *53*(6), 3003–3022. Advance online publication. doi:10.100711135-019-00914-5

Von Krogh, G., Ichijo, K., & Nonaka, I. (2001). *Facilitando a Criação de Conhecimento: reiventando a empresa com o poder da inovação contínua*. Campus.

Von Krogh, G., Nonaka, I., & Ichijo, K. (2000). *Enabling Knowledge Creation: How to Unlock the Mystery of Tacit Knowledge and Release the Power of Innovation*. Oxford University Press. doi:10.1007/978-1-349-62753-0

Vorakulpipat, C., & Rezgui, Y. (2008). Value creation: the future of knowledge Management. The Knowledge Engineering Review, 23(3), 283-294.

Zikmund, G. W. (2000). *Business research methods*. Oklahoma State University.

ENDNOTE

1 The term "Ba" was established by the Japanese philosopher Kitaro Nishida and, later, worked more closely on KM by the Japanese also Nonaka and Konno, represents the context in which the creation, transmission and use of knowledge of an organization has the ideal characteristics to be leveraged. This context can deal with a physical space (offices, meeting room), virtual (e-mail, video calls), mental (shared experiences) or, even, a union of the three.

APPENDIX 1

Figure 11. Change management check-list.
Source: own elaboration.

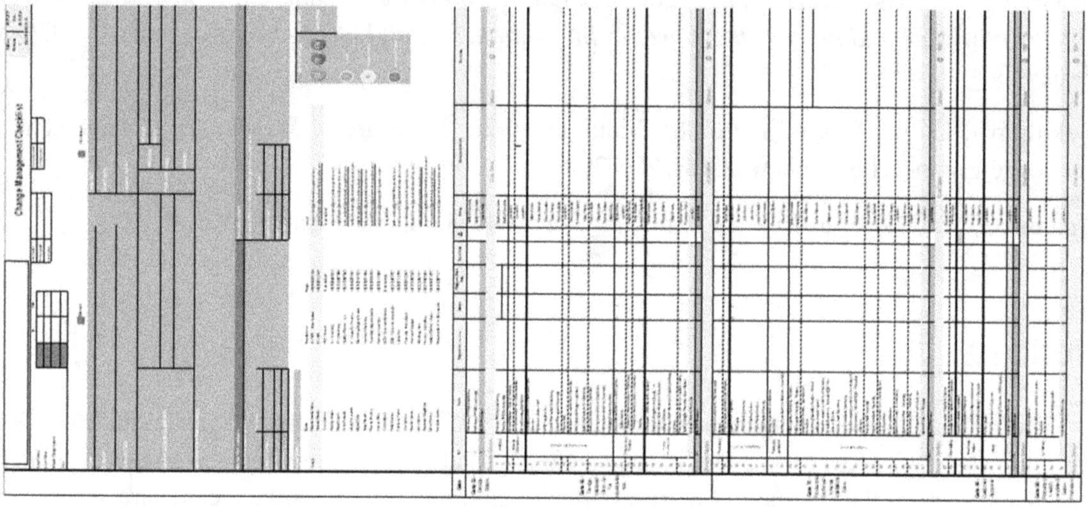

APPENDIX 2

Figure 12. Schedule of projects in Excel.
Source: own elaboration.

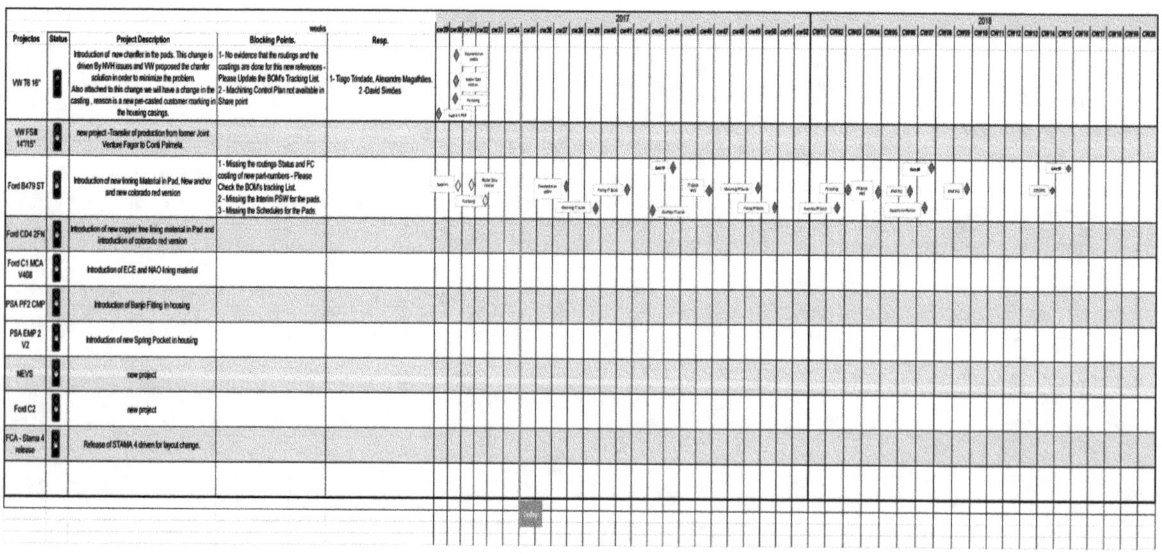

Projectos	Status	Project Description	Blocking Points.	Resp.
VW T6 16"		Introduction of new chanfer in the pads. This change is driven By NVH issues and VW proposed the chanfer solution in order to minimize the problem. Also attached to this change we will have a change in the casting, reason is a new pre-casted customer marking in the housing casings.	1- No evidence that the routings and the costings are done for this new references - Please Update the BOM's Tracking List. 2 - Machining Control Plan not available in Share point	1- Tiago Trindade, Alexandre Magalhães. 2-David Simões
VW FS8 14"/15"		new project -Transfer of production from former Joint Venture Fagor to Conti Palmela.		
Ford B479 ST		Introduction of new lining Material in Pad, New anchor and new colorado red version	1 - Missing the routings Status and FC costing of new part-numbers - Please Check the BOM's tracking List. 2 - Missing the Interim PSW for the pads. 3 - Missing the Schedules for the Pads.	
Ford CD4 2FN		Introduction of new copper free lining material in Pad and introduction of colorado red version		
Ford C1 MCA V408		Introduction of ECE and NAO lining material		
PSA PF2 CMP		Introduction of Banjo Fitting in housing		
PSA EMP 2 V2		Introduction of new Spring Pocket in housing		
NEVS		new project		
Ford C2		new project		
FCA - Stama 4 release		Release of STAMA 4 driven for layout change.		

APPENDIX 3

Figure 13. Sheet x - Global action plan.
Source: own elaboration.

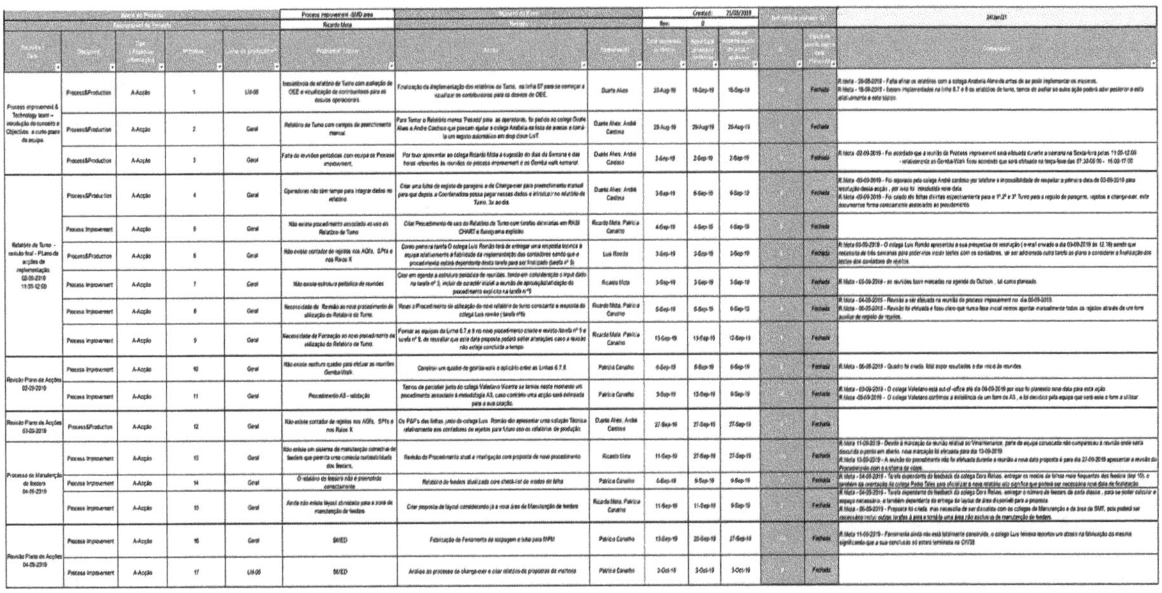

[illegible]					Process improvement -SMD area	[illegible]		Created:	21/08/2019		[illegible]		[illegible]
[illegible]					Ricardo Mota	[illegible]		Rev:	0				
[illegible]	[illegible]	[illegible]	[illegible]	[illegible]	[illegible]	[illegible]	[illegible]	[illegible]	[illegible]	[illegible]	[illegible]	[illegible]	[illegible]
Process improvement & Technology team – introdução do conceito e Objectivos a curto prazo da equipa	Process&Production	A-Acção	1	LM-06	Inexistência de relatório de Turno com avaliação de OEE e visualização de contribuintes para os desvios operacionais.	[illegible]	Duarte Alves	20-Aug-19	16-Sep-19	16-Sep-19	[illegible]	Fechada	[illegible]
	Process&Production	A-Acção	2	Geral	Relatório de Turno com campos de preenchimento manual.	[illegible]	Duarte Alves; André Cardoso	23-Aug-19	29-Aug-19	26-Aug-19	[illegible]	Fechada	
	Process&Production	A-Acção	3	Geral	Falta de reuniões periódicas com equipa de Process improvement.	[illegible]	Duarte Alves; André Cardoso	2-Sep-19	2-Sep-19	2-Sep-19	[illegible]	Fechada	[illegible]
Relatório de Turno - revisão final - PLano de acções de implementação. 02-09-2019 11:05-12:00	Process&Production	A-Acção	4	Geral	Operadores não têm tempo para integrar dados no relatório.	[illegible]	Duarte Alves; André Cardoso	3-Sep-19	6-Sep-19	9-Sep-19	[illegible]	Fechada	[illegible]
	Process Improvement	A-Acção	5	Geral	Não existe procedimento associado ao uso do Relatório de Turno	[illegible]	Ricardo Mota; Patrícia Carvalho	4-Sep-19	4-Sep-19	4-Sep-19	[illegible]	Fechada	
	Process&Production	A-Acção	6	Geral	Não existe contador de rejeitos nos AOIs, SPIs e nos Raios X	[illegible]	Luis Romão	3-Sep-19	3-Sep-19	3-Sep-19	[illegible]	Fechada	[illegible]
	Process Improvement	A-Acção	7	Geral	Não existe estrutura periódica de reuniões	[illegible]	Ricardo Mota	3-Sep-19	3-Sep-19	3-Sep-19	[illegible]	Fechada	[illegible]
	Process Improvement	A-Acção	8	Geral	Necessidade de Revisão ao novo procedimento de utilização do Relatório de Turno.	[illegible]	Ricardo Mota; Patrícia Carvalho	6-Sep-19	6-Sep-19	6-Sep-19	[illegible]	Fechada	[illegible]
	Process Improvement	A-Acção	9	Geral	Necessidade de Formação ao novo procedimento de utilização do Relatório de Turno.	[illegible]	Ricardo Mota; Patrícia Carvalho	13-Sep-19	13-Sep-19	12-Sep-19	[illegible]	Fechada	
Revisão Plano de Acções 02-09-2019	Process Improvement	A-Acção	10	Geral	Não existe nenhum quadro para efetuar as reuniões Gemba Walk.	[illegible]	Patrícia Carvalho	6-Sep-19	6-Sep-19	6-Sep-19	[illegible]	Fechada	[illegible]
	Process Improvement	A-Acção	11	Geral	Procedimento A3 - validação	[illegible]	Patrícia Carvalho	3-Sep-19	13-Sep-19	6-Sep-19	[illegible]	Fechada	[illegible]
Revisão Plano de Acções 03-09-2019	Process&Production	A-Acção	12	Geral	Não existe contador de rejeitos nos AOIs, SPIs e nos Raios X	[illegible]	Duarte Alves, André Cardoso	27-Sep-19	27-Sep-19	27-Sep-19	[illegible]	Fechada	
Processo de Manutenção de feeders 04-09-2019	Process Improvement	A-Acção	13	Geral	Não existe um sistema de manutenção correctiva de feeders que permita uma correcta rastreabilidade dos feeders.	[illegible]	Ricardo Mota	11-Sep-19	27-Sep-19	27-Sep-19	[illegible]	Fechada	[illegible]
	Process Improvement	A-Acção	14	Geral	O relatório de feeders não é preenchido correctamente	[illegible]	Patrícia Carvalho	6-Sep-19	9-Sep-19	9-Sep-19	[illegible]	Fechada	[illegible]
	Process Improvement	A-Acção	15	Geral	Ainda não existe layout otimizado para a zona de manutenção de feeders	[illegible]	Ricardo Mota, Patrícia Carvalho	11-Sep-19	11-Sep-19	9-Sep-19	[illegible]	Fechada	[illegible]
Revisão Plano de Acções 04-09-2019	Process Improvement	A-Acção	16	Geral	SMED	[illegible]	Patrícia Carvalho	13-Sep-19	20-Sep-19	27-Sep-19	[illegible]	Fechada	[illegible]
	Process Improvement	A-Acção	17	LM-06	SMED	[illegible]	Patrícia Carvalho	3-Oct-19	3-Oct-19	3-Oct-19	[illegible]	Fechada	

APPENDIX 4

Figure 14. Sheet y - Indicators Dashboard
Source: own elaboration.

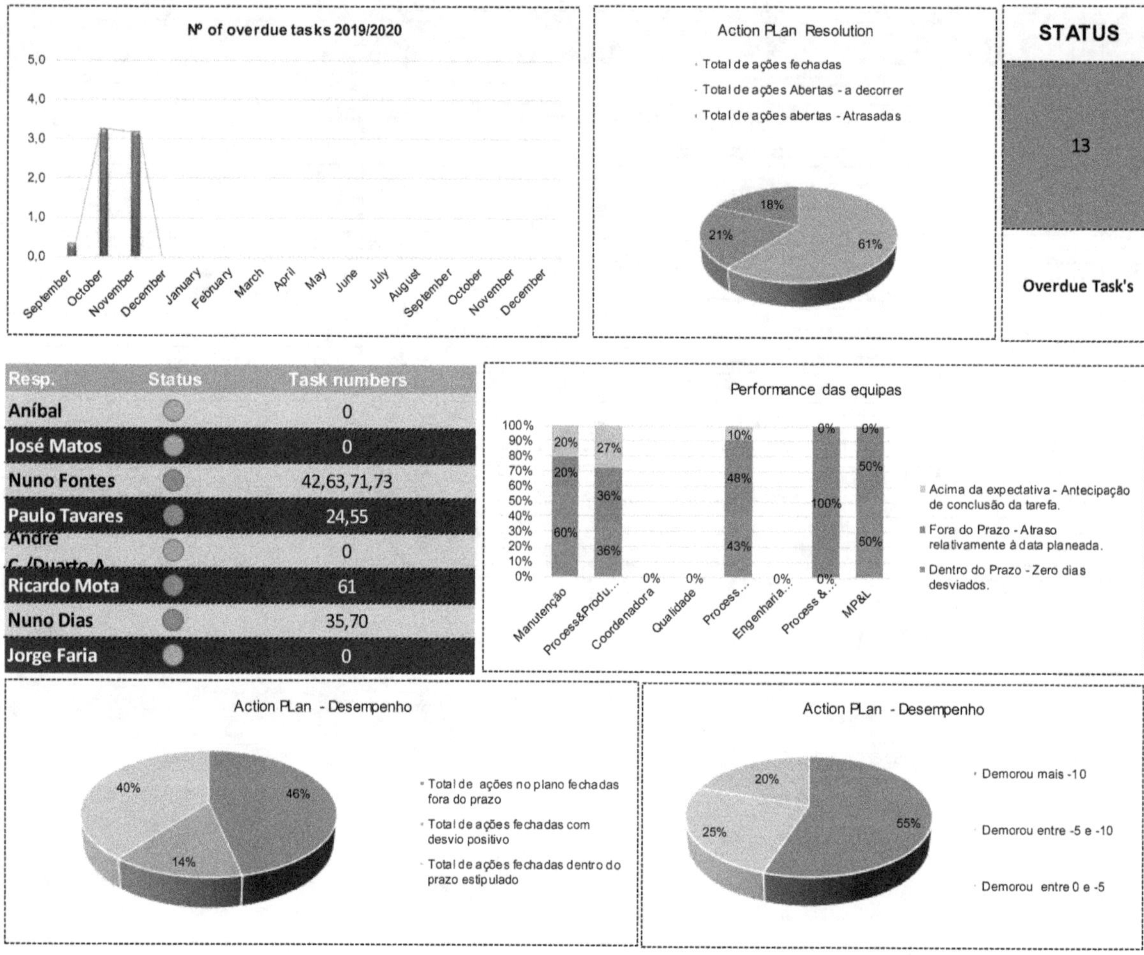

Chapter 16
Analysis of Research on Knowledge Management in Universities

Mariana D. Gonzalez-Zamar
https://orcid.org/0000-0003-1187-8970
University of Almeria, Spain

Emilio Abad-Segura
https://orcid.org/0000-0001-8624-103X
University of Almeria, Spain

ABSTRACT

The teaching management of higher education institutions (HEIs) has traditionally focused on processing compliance with regulated curricular conditions rather than normalizing the learning and knowledge developed to be transferred to society. The motivation of knowledge management in HEIs should be oriented to the strengthening of knowledge preservation strategies. In recent decades, this model has been a growing interest on the part of academics and academic institutions at the international level. The main objective of this study is to analyze the research trends on knowledge management in HEIs worldwide during the period 2000-2019. Bibliometric techniques were applied to a sample of 1,836 articles from scientific journals selected from the Scopus database. The study documented a rapidly growing knowledge base, mostly written by academics located in developed societies. This chapter provides a point of reference for future research on this topic, as well as revealing the intellectual structure of this interdisciplinary field.

INTRODUCTION

Over time, the educational management of some higher education institutions (HEIs) has been in charge of managing compliance with regulated curricular conditions, rather than processing and standardizing the learning and knowledge formed, to be transferred to society (Orr, 2019).

DOI: 10.4018/978-1-7998-7452-2.ch016

So, exploring alternatives to contribute to management, allows promoting the development of strategies to recognize and accredit the knowledge and learning that is created in the different university processes, with the intention that they can be used strategically. For this reason, it is necessary to bear in mind that knowledge is considered an intangible asset in society, that it works as a competitive tool, and that it needs to be properly managed (Huisman & Mampaey, 2018).

Knowledge management refers to the provision of explicit and empirical knowledge institutions, in an orderly, practical, and effective way, to optimize productivity and performance. On the other hand, it will also make use of methodological resources of knowledge management, to recognize and accredit learning and knowledge, and create value (Mukhtar et al., 2020). In this line, strategies will be designed to efficiently implement knowledge management, which will contribute to the process of creating, documenting, and communicating tacit and explicit information in the organization (Walker II, 2016). These will allow create, codify, appropriate, share and reuse knowledge so that they enable the development of collective work, and contribute to the acquisition of skills at all levels of the organization. Therefore, knowledge management refers to the design and implementation of actions in different organizational processes, in addition to the work system that supports and promotes the storage, transfer and application of knowledge (Harrison, & Luckett, 2019).

In this context, knowledge management in HEIs refers to directing cognitive assets as strategic assets that generate opportunities for the development of activities, such as teaching, research, extension and social projection. In addition, it will generate and maintain institutional quality, because this model is filtered in all processes (Archer-Brown, & Kietzmann, 2018).

Therefore, knowledge management links people and technologies that promote policies and practices to share knowledge. The HEIs have formalized knowledge management based on the study of contexts, to implement actions that stimulate environments that generate, learn, and share knowledge, in addition to improving teaching, internationalization, and research functions. In this way, knowledge management models insert mechanisms to collect data and information from the educational institution, which in turn can be shared between individuals, groups and departments, and develop a culture of knowledge management and propose strategies (Lee, & Kuzhabekova, 2019).

The purpose of this research chapter was to examine the evolution of scientific knowledge based on knowledge management in universities. Thus, the research questions that arise refer to determining (1) how scientific production has evolved, (2) how the main driving agents of the study theme cooperate, and (3) what the current lines of research and future are.

Consequently, the main objective of this study is to analyze research trends on knowledge management in HEIs globally during the period 2000-2019. To obtain answers to the research questions, a sample of 1836 articles from scientific journals selected from the Scopus database was analyzed. This study uses bibliometric techniques to synthesize the knowledge base on teaching and knowledge management in HEIs.

The results showed the contributions of this line of research, which has allowed identifying the main driving agents, their future trends, and revealing certain gaps in critical knowledge.

Finally, it should be noted that among the lines of research that are currently being developed in relation to the subject of the study, these refer, among others, to those related to the holistic concept of university, knowledge-based systems, knowledge transfer, knowledge management, teaching, information management, and learning.

Likewise, new terms associated with the study of knowledge management in the field of HEIs have been detected, which will lead to the development of this topic in the future, such as educational ecosystems, wellbeing, data analysis software, program evaluation, and organizational performance.

FRAMEWORK

The study of knowledge management in HEIs is supported by the analysis of a series of theoretical principles that together with the basic concepts define the frame of reference in this field of research. In this way, these explanatory theoretical elements delimit the way about how a set of phenomena behave to later generalize and carry out a separate abstraction of the particular cases.

Theoretical Principles

This research topic is supported by various theoretical principles of educational theory, as a reflective dimension of Pedagogy. Although it arises from classical times, with philosophy, mainly from Plato and Aristotle, in this context it refers to the science of education from its Kantian origins.

To give education a scientific character, it is considered that it must have certain axes that support it. Among the various meanings of the theory, it is conceived as an instrument for reasoned explanation and prediction, as well as the attempt to account for a set of hypotheses or laws of nature by submerging them in a more general explanation (Tizkar, & Abdul, 2018). The theory focuses on the interest of giving an explanation about some belief regarding education and uses the concept of prediction, that is, announcing something educational that is going to happen.

Educational theory is the product of practice, that is, it is built in the context in which it is lived, with an objective centered on the man who wishes to be trained. Henceforth, the main objective in doing science is to capture the truth about the world and express that truth in the form of laws of nature (Jøranli, 2018).

Education is considered as a set of activities that are interrelated and that are carried out at different levels. The levels are considered as logical differences, that is, one level depends on another: demonstrate and punish; then we build the principles, advice and recommendations that are given at the first level; and, finally, there is philosophy, which is essential to classify the concepts that occur at the second level, giving consistency and validity to the first (Wald, & Harland, 2019).

Each educational theory is built from the context in which it is lived, from the needs of society, from the ideal of man that one wants to form. Hence, educational theory measures the progress of practice through the evolution of humanity, provides categories of analysis, helps to know which elements were highlighted and when they were given importance. This coincides with Marx's idea of historical materialism, where it is argued that learning to analyze the past will help solve present problems (Ryabova, 2019).

Conceptual Framework

In this way, a series of interrelated terms are described that allows conceptualizing the study in the field of knowledge and consolidating the purpose of the research.

In the first place, the basis of this study is education, which refers to the cultural and learning process through which people develop cognitive capacities, physical abilities and base the values and beliefs that we act as good citizens. Thus, access to education is a right that all people have, which bases its importance in the various areas of human development (Atapattu, 2018). For this reason, education goes beyond acquiring or reinforcing knowledge, since it is also a cultural process that allows us to better understand our context. In this sense, education encompasses different transversal axes such as culture, values, cognitive development, and social integration (Gulua, 2019).

Therefore, the purpose of education is the general development of individuals so that they can function in society, generate critical thoughts, propose ideas or projects based on the common welfare and fairer and more balanced societies.

Consequently, higher education is that which contemplates the last phase of the academic learning process, that is, that which comes after the secondary stage. It is taught in universities, higher institutes, or technical training academies. The teaching offered by higher education is at the professional level (Hamilton, & Mostert, 2019), here are other modes of teaching such as the informal one that occurs throughout our lives and the non-formal one that does not have a structured character.

Knowledge Management

In the line of education, it is necessary to contextualize the term of knowledge. In view of that, this refers to the process by which reality is reflected and reproduced in human thought. It is the product of different types of experiences, reasoning, and learning. It is a complex concept, which has been dealt with by numerous traditions of thought throughout history, and which has always been elusive (Wu, & Hu, 2018).

In fact, it is difficult to define knowledge succinctly or to establish its limits, since it always depends on the philosophical and theoretical perspective from which it is based. Hence, there is knowledge related to each branch of human knowledge, and even to each area of their experience. It is not easy to find a concept of knowledge. Traditionally, knowledge belongs only to the human being; it depends on reason, which is a complex way of acquiring knowledge of the environment (Jøranli, 2018; Tizkar, & Abdul, 2018).

Therefore, knowledge is one of the most important assets for organizations, so that due to its management it adds value to the products or services it produces, allowing the development of technologies, methodologies, and strategies (Mukhtar et al., 2020).

In this sense, the management concept refers to the correct management of the resources that a certain organization has. This term can cover a long list of activities, but it always focuses on the efficient use of these resources, to the extent that their returns must be maximized (Orr, 2019).

For all this, management is defined as the action and effect of administering, and includes the ideas of governing, arranging to direct, ordering or organizing a situation. Likewise, it refers to the process by which the manager determines the actions to be followed by the organization and establishes the strategies and goals to be achieved (Van Beveren, 2002).

Knowledge management is a discipline whose purpose is to improve the performance of individuals and organizations, to maintain and take advantage of the present and future value of knowledge assets. It can also be considered as an integration of numerous efforts and fields of study (Wald, & Harland, 2019).

For this reason, knowledge management is a process that supports organizations to find relevant information, select, organize and communicate it to all active personnel; this cycle is necessary for actions such as problem solving, learning dynamics and decision making. In addition, it can improve the performance of the organization to achieve an intelligent organization. Therefore, this involves the planning of strategies and the establishment of policies and also the collaboration of all the personnel of the organization, a high sense of commitment to execute their work and acceptance of the management process (Nechaev et al., 2017; Veer-Ramjeawon, & Rowley, 2019).

Furthermore, knowledge management is a trend in the modern economy, which is gradually becoming the key success factor for organizations and seeks the application of technological tools for manipulating the organization's data and information (Laihonen, & Mäntylä, 2018).

In this line, this management is inspired by strategic objectives of generating, sharing, and innovating; Knowledge management practitioners must know the epistemological foundations of knowledge theory to determine its implications for organizational knowledge, identify types of knowledge; as well as the interactions that occur between the two (Cheng, & Chang, 2019; Durst, & Zieba, 2018).

Knowledge Management in Higher Education Institutions

Higher education institutions are entities that have, according to legal regulations, official recognition as providers of the public service of higher education, and their classification is based on the type of education they provide: university (public and private) and non-university (Lebedyk, 2020).

In this sense, the university refers to the institution of higher education, divided into faculties according to the specialties of study that it can offer. The term also applies to the building for higher education (Freeman, 1974). It is an institution organized for the mutual benefit and legal protection of this group (Menon, 2020).

These teaching centers exist to train future professionals in different areas, and to promote free thought on various topics, from religious, sociological and political. It is a space for each person to find themselves, note their potential and the level of courage they have to face each test that comes their way (Shevchenko, Puchkina, & Tolstov, 2019; White, & Lee, 2019).

Management, mainly, consists of making things happen in any area of knowledge; However, when we say knowledge management we are talking about the creation, transfer, storage, application and use of knowledge itself; what should be considered is a very important element: intellectual capital (Effeney, 2019; Ashour, 2020). In any area of knowledge, and even more so in education, intellectual capital is involved.

In recent years, concern arose in higher education for knowledge management; Few HEIs have managed to take advantage of the richness of this type of management, when it is in higher education that knowledge is gestated or should be gestated (Khalil, & Shea, 2012; Teichler, 2002). To implement knowledge management in HEIs, it is essential to start by showing some of its approaches in the university context. Knowledge management is identified as a main component for service companies, where it determines the skills to offer new services and generate recognition in the market; For this, investment in research is decisive, which serves to measure productivity levels in organizations and, thus, be competitive in the long and medium term (Ryabova, 2019).

On the other hand, this management model is recognized as one of the most important assets for any business or academic institution, as the process to store, capture, share and use knowledge to achieve competitive advantages (Baporikar, & Smith, 2019). This is achieved through the development of a knowledge-intensive culture; therefore, the promotion of processes that facilitate interaction and knowledge exchange should be sought (Lo, & Tang, 2019; Bamber, & Elezi, 2020). Research can increase its productivity through knowledge management with spaces for interaction, discussion, renewal and updating, since needs to be solved to improve the social environment are indicated, and for this, information and communication technologies are tools to diversify knowledge and achieve its capture and transfer (Jung, 2019; Khalil, & Shea, 2012).

The HEIs are distinguished by the United Nations Educational, Scientific and Cultural Organization (UNESCO) as dynamizers of the social, economic and personal capacities, both of their members and of society. Due to their conditions, HEIs enable the transmission, distribution and generation of knowledge, an essential resource to participate in the resolution of global challenges: food security, climate change, water management, among others. These processes must be managed and ordered in an ideal way in order to produce the expected results (Williams, 2019; Hauke, 2019).

In this sense, HEIs together with other actors contribute to the innovative development of a country, being the engine of change, they are also fundamental for the circulation and dissemination of knowledge, since they have the task of training the human capital in charge of developing and innovating the solutions of the planet, it is therefore necessary that in the HEIs management strategies are designed, which allow incorporating actions that make it possible for the knowledge generated in them, be it scientific, organizational, technological, or of another nature, to result in the development of capacities and learning for the institution (Sutton, 2018).

Therefore, a knowledge-based organization implies a general search for traditional management approaches, personnel selection, recruitment and management of workers; but with a new business approach that manages to combine information with human resources to generate an advance in the organizational culture (Wald, Harland, 2019).

METHODOLOGY

Bibliometric analysis has been carried out using mathematical, statistical, and mapping tools. Thus, it has been possible to identify and analyze the main elements of the research topic, represent the metadata available in the different repositories and determine the trends in a specific field of research (Bornmann, & Mutz, 2015).

Through this methodology, it can be presented how interest in the subject matter of the study has evolved, reflecting the authors, countries, journals, and most relevant keywords in recent years (Abad-Segura, González-Zamar, 2019). Likewise, the most important collaboration and bonding relationships between them are presented, through an analysis of co-authorship and co-occurrences.

Several databases of scientific works related to the subject we have been dealing with have been consulted, such as Scopus, Web of Science or Google Scholar. Finally, the information from Scopus has been selected, as it is the largest repository of scientific articles and with a greater number of journals and authors, with peer review, compared to the rest of the databases (Yeo et al., 2008). In addition, it is the database with more detail in the treatment of the information corresponding to each author, institution, and country, of how many have been consulted.

In the search for articles, the terms that define this field of research have been used as search parameters in Scopus: "higher education", "university" and "knowledge management". The search has focused on the fields of title, abstract and keywords and a period of 20 years, from 2000 to 2019, as reflected in other bibliometric works (Abad-Segura, et al., 2020; López- Meneses et al., 2020; González-Zamar et al., 2020).

The final sample included a total of 1836 articles, with a wide variety of variables to analyse for each record, such as: the year of publication, the journal, the subject area, the author and co-authors of the work, the institutional affiliation of the authors, as well as the country of affiliation and, not least, the keywords that define the article. Regarding the scientific production indicators, the evolution of the number of articles published, the language used in the writing of the articles, the thematic areas where the articles are classified, the most productive journals are presented.

For the structural indicators, the VOSviewer software (version 1.6.15., University of Leiden, Leiden, The Netherlands), which offers data on the interactions and the evaluation of subject-matters, was applied to measure the activities of research networks. This tool allows analysis from the visualization of relationship maps and network links between journals, authors, institutions, countries, and keywords. That is, network maps have been used to provide values on international collaboration and trends in this field of research (Van Eck, & Waltman, 2009).

ANALYSIS OF THE RESULTS

This section presents and analyses the results obtained after applying the methodology to the sample of selected articles.

Analysis of Scientific Production

During the period analyzed (2000-2019), the interest in research on knowledge management in HEIs globally has been increasing, as seen in Figure 1, especially in the last 10 years, corresponding to the period 2010 -2019, where 1353 articles have been published, that is, 73.69% of the total for the last 20 years. In addition, 613 articles (33.38%) have been published in the last five years. The year 2019 corresponds to the year with the highest number of publications, with 209 (11.38%).

The first article on this topic was published in 2000, under the title "The viable system model and knowledge management", by author affiliated with the Toronto, ON, Canada, Leonard, A., and published in the Journal Kybernetes (Leonard, 2008).This article was about the Integrated Academic (Advanced) Information Management System (IAIMS) concept and the logical integration of the information that comes from databases in the areas of administration, clinical care, education, libraries and research.

On the other hand, the most cited article on knowledge management in HEIs during the period analyzed was published in 2013, with the title "Academic engagement and commercialization: A review of the literature on university-industry relations" by the authors Perkmann, M. et al., in the journal Research Policy. It has 882 citations and reviewed the academic participation of academic scientists in activities such as collaborative research, contract research, consulting, and informal relationships for knowledge transfer between university and industry.

It is followed among the most cited, with 364 citations, the article "Analyzing knowledge transfer channels between universities and industry: To what degree do sectors also matter?" Authors Bekkers, R., Bodas Freitas, I.M., and published in 2008 by the journal Research Policy (Bekkers, & Freitas, 2008). This interesting work analyses the channels through which knowledge and technology are transferred between universities and industry.

Articles on this research topic have been written in 14 different languages. Most of the articles are written in English (89.87%), since it broadens their audience, as fundamentally happens in the searches carried out in the Scopus database (Albarillo, 2014). In addition, the writing in other languages stands out, such as Spanish (5.61%), Chinese (1.36%), German (1.25%), or Portuguese (1.20%), while in the rest of the languages it does not reach 1% of the total contributions.

The most productive journal in global research on knowledge management in HEIs has been the American Journal of Technology Transfer, with 44 published articles, which represents 2.99% of the period analyzed. This journal presents an SJR index (SCImago Journal Rank) of 1.66 in 2019. It is followed in productivity by the Smart Innovation Systems and Technologies with 36 (1.96%), Journal of Knowledge Management with 33 (1.80%), and Research Policy with 29 (1.58%).

Figure 1. Evolution in the publication of articles (2000-2019).

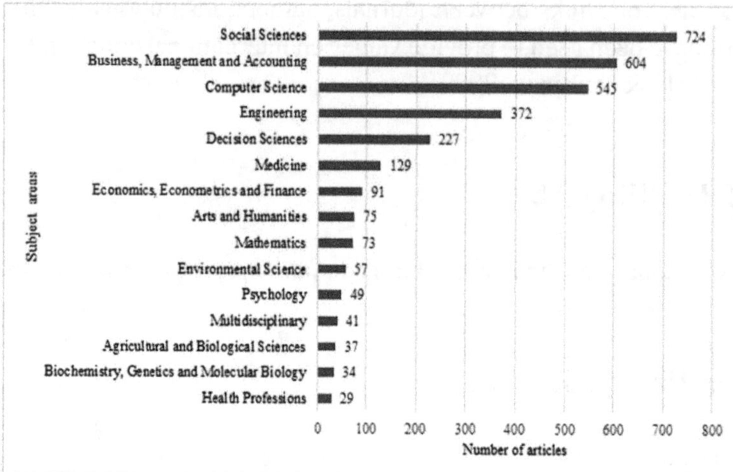

According to the Scopus database, articles are classified into 26 different subject areas. It is necessary to indicate that the same article can be classified in more than one discipline, depending on the interest of the author or the publisher.

In the field of study research, the main subject area in which the articles are grouped is Social Sciences, with 724, which represents 39.34% of the total. They are followed, in order of importance, by Business, Management and Accounting, with 604 articles (32.89%); Computer Science, with 545 (29.68%); Engineering, with 372 (20.26%) and Decision Sciences, with 227 (12.36%). Each of the other thematic areas groups less than 10% of the total articles on knowledge management in universities.

Analysis of Authors, Organizations, and Countries

According to Scopus database, the authors who have contributed the most to this topic have been Rowley, J., and Ugwu, C.I., with 7 articles, Akhavan, P., with 6, and Chang, C.C. and Tirado, A.U., with 5 each of them.

Figure 2 shows the collaboration map between the main authors who have published on knowledge management in HEIs, based on the co-authorship method. The different colours represent the different components formed by the working groups in the production of articles, while the size of the circle varies depending on the number of articles of each author. The main authors are grouped into four clusters.

Cluster 1 (pink color), the most numerous, presents the collaboration between Bode A., Broy M., Daniel H., Feussner H., Gradinger R., Hauner H., Holzmann B., Horsch A., Höfler H., Kemper A. or Ziegler S. Cluster 2 associates, among others, Clevert D.-A, Dugas M., Glaser C., Küttner B., Lucke A., Pander E., Reiser M., Treitl M., Trumm C., Weinzierl S. or Wirth S. Cluster 3 (red color) links Knoll A., Kochs E.F., Krcmar H., Kuhn K.A. or Lange R. Cluster 4 (yellow) associates, among other authors, Molls M., Navab N., Nüsslin F., Peschel C., Ring J. or Rummeny E.J.

In relation to the most prolific research institutions in knowledge management in universities, they have been: University of Tehran, with 20 articles, University of Antioquia, with 15, followed by a group of two institutions with 12 articles each published. (University of South Africa, Universidade Federal

Figure 2. Cooperation network between authors based on co-authorship.

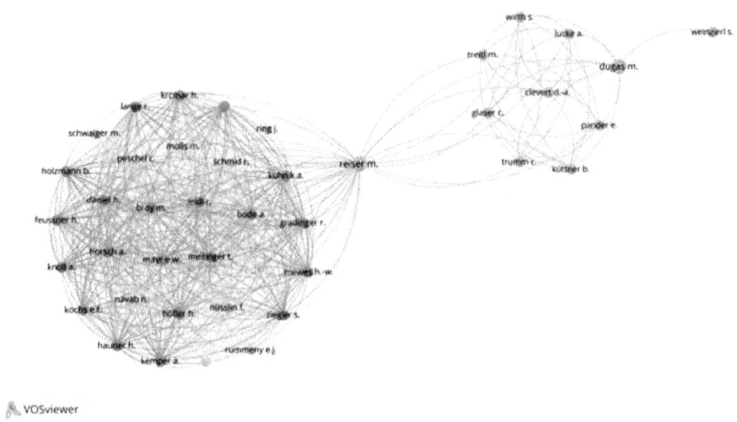

de Santa Catarina, Universiti Teknologi Malaysia, University of Technology Sydney, and Universidad Autónoma de Madrid); another group of three institutions (Universitat Politècnica de València, University of South Africa, and University of Cambridge) with 11 each; and three institutions with 10 articles (Universiti Sains Malaysia, Università degli Studi di Torino, and Multimedia University). The rest of the institutions at the international level do not reach 10 articles.

On the other hand, United States is the most productive country, with 245 articles; followed by United Kingdom (230), China (125), and Spain (107). Figure 3 shows the network map of collaboration between the main countries based on the co-authorship analysis. The different colours represent the different clusters formed by the country groups, and the size of the circle varies depending on the number of articles in each country. Hence, the larger the country's circle, the greater the number of articles it represents. They have been grouped into four clusters.

Cluster 1, led by United States, includes 48 countries, among which are: Italy, Spain, Germany, France, Netherlands, Australia, Denmark, Sweden, Canada, and China. Group 2, the largest along with cluster 1, is led by Malaysia, which shares work with Taiwan, Ireland, India, Iran, Pakistan, Portugal, Turkey, Jordan, Nigeria, Chile, and Peru, among others. Cluster 3 is led by United Kingdom, and includes countries such as Ghana, Mauritius, Philippines, Romania and Sri Lanka. Finally, cluster 4 is headed by the Spain and includes Colombia, Cuba, Ecuador, and Venezuela.

These territories collaborate in the development of the publications for different reasons, such as the language, the continent, the historical international relations between certain countries, or because of the access to funds that finance the studies (Rousseau &Ye, 2012). Basically, during the period examined, these contributions have revolved around, among other aspects, e-learning, knowledge management, educational innovation, student satisfaction, or collaborative learning (Schnitzler, 2019). All of them are key questions to plan university action strategies for referring to the management.

Analysis of Keywords

The software tool has identified seven clusters of keywords, which are linked to the same lines of research in the period analyzed (2000-2019). Each of these differentiated schools of thought are associated with the keywords with the most occurrences within each of the groups. -

Figure 3. Cooperation network between countries based on co-authorship.

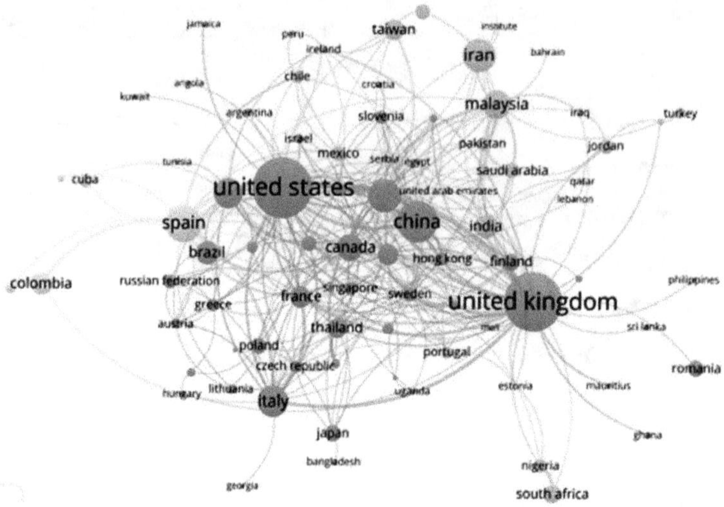

The first cluster (pink), the most numerous, is led by University and groups terms such as decision making, internet, information dissemination, leadership, organizational culture, organization, organization and management, information retrieval, software, communication, quality control, training, information processing, information system, personnel training, procedures, social network, methodology, or decision support system. The first line of research identified has contributed to developing the concept of university in relation to knowledge management, as the educational institution dedicated to higher education and research, empowered to deliver academic degrees and professional degrees (Eraut, 1985; Hordern, 2014).

The second cluster (green), headed by Knowledge based systems, groups terms such as information technology, e-learning, knowledge acquisition, management, knowledge engineering, knowledge management system, curriculum, human resource management, semantics, information systems, design, education computing, collaboration, knowledge base, project management, or information and communication technologies. This second line studies the development of knowledge management systems, which allow the reuse of information stored in the organization and its incorporation into functional and operational processes, integrating existing information systems and allowing the durability of information and knowledge (Košir, 2014). Cluster 3 (red), led by Knowledge transfer, associates terms such as societies and institutions, knowledge, innovation, research, technology transfer, sustainable development, economics, university sector, regional planning, patents and inventions, management science, knowledge exchange, university industries, academic entrepreneurship, or industrial research. The third line of thought contributes to the transfer of knowledge, as one of the elements of social responsibility of universities, which tries to return to society the investment that citizens make in the university system (Kramer, & Braxton, 2017).

Cluster 4 (Yellow), headed by Knowledge management, links to terms such as knowledge sharing, higher education, intellectual capital, knowledge-sharing, higher education institutions, competition, design/methodology/approach, organizational learning, social networking (online), knowledge creation, tacit knowledge, academic libraries, developing countries, competitive advantage, university libraries, knowledge workers, or virtual reality. The fourth line of research, related to one of the search terms in the Scopus database, studies knowledge management in HEIs from different perspectives such as the one that provides the focus on the economy of organizations and it is assumed that Universities are a type of organization, in which there are permanent links beyond the market relations between the agents that comprise it; economic agents who have limited rationality and whose decisions, moreover, can be opportunistic without due structural and legal safeguards (Bibi, Padhi, & Dash, 2020; Woodfield, 2018).

The fifth cluster (purple), led by Teaching, groups terms such as human computer interaction, collaborative learning, university students, controlled study, user interfaces, computer simulation, networks, user-computer interface, machine learning, decision trees, or educational organizations.

The fifth line of research studies university teaching, exploring the different pedagogical uses of technological tools, to identify conditioning factors and their associated variables (Yanaprasart, 2020). They also develop publications on teaching practices, mediated by teachers' pedagogical concepts and beliefs, and by the technological uses that influence and transform these concepts.

Cluster 6 (blue), headed by Information management, is associated with learning systems, technology, data mining, artificial intelligence, mathematical models, algorithms, database systems, efficiency, decision support systems, information analysis, administrative data processing, or algorithm. This line of research develops publications that revolve around information management systems that integrate information resources; in addition to supporting operations and managing information and documentation in an organization for decision-making (Chedid et al., 2019).

Finally, the seventh cluster (orange), led by the term Learning, is associated with other keywords, such as sustainability, economic and social effects, management practice, culture, quality assurance, resource management, industrial economics, social aspects, information and communication technology, problem-based learning, or resource allocation (Yagodzinski, 2003; Lawler, & Sillitoe, 2013). This line of thought develops studies on the intrinsic purpose of education and learning, which contributes to the

Figure 4. Keyword's network based on co-occurrences.

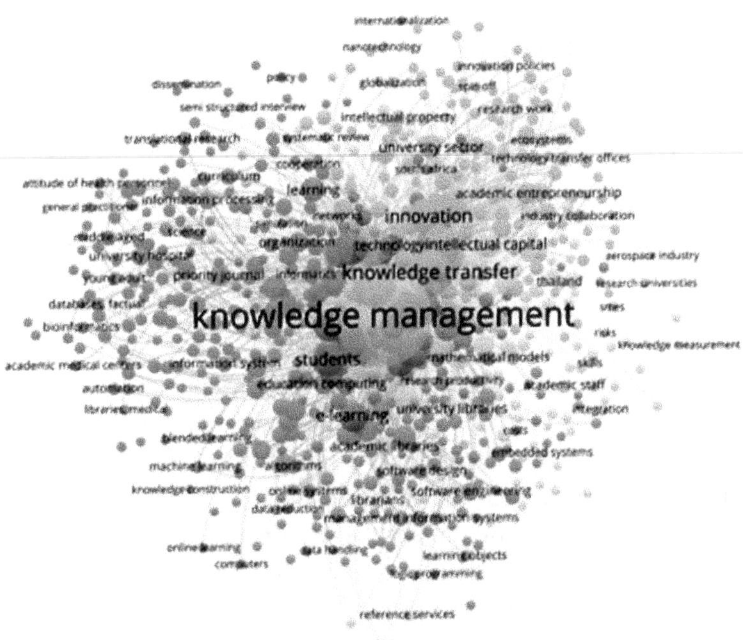

full development of the person and her/his dignity. Education, therefore, will be relevant if it promotes the learning of the competences and capacities necessary to fully participate in the different spheres of human life, face the demands and challenges of society, access decent employment, and develop a project of life in relation to others.

CONCLUSION

The objective of this study was to analyze research trends on knowledge management in HEIs globally during the last 20 years. Bibliometric techniques have been applied to a sample composed of 1836 articles obtained from the Scopus database. The number of articles published per year, the languages in which they have been published, the subject areas, the journals, the authors, the organizations, and the most productive countries in the publications on this field of research have been identified.

The number of scientific articles per year during the period 2000-2019 has increased, especially in the last ten years where 1353 articles have been published, representing 73.69% of contributions on this research topic. These articles are published in English mostly.

The Social Sciences thematic area is the main one, since it groups 39.43% of the articles, followed by Business, Management and Accounting with 32.90%, and Computer Science with 29.68%.

The most outstanding journal, with 44 published articles, has been the Journal of Technology Transfer, which represents 2.39%.

According to Scopus, the most prolific authors have been Rowley, J. and Ugwu, C.I; while they were grouped into six clusters due to the similarity of their lines of research. Likewise, the countries that have contributed the most in this period have been the United States and the United Kingdom, with more than 200 articles published.

In the period analysed, the main driving agents of this field of study have developed, fundamentally, seven differentiated lines of thought, related to the university, knowledge-based systems, knowledge transfer, knowledge management, teaching, information management, and learning.

However, this research has a set of limitations that can be used for future research, such as the Scopus database chosen to select the sample of documents; the terms or variables chosen to extract the documents; the period of analysis; applied bibliometric techniques; even the research questions posed. However, a variation of these variables would suppose the obtaining of other results, which would make possible the comparison with those obtained in this study.

Likewise, new terms associated with the study of knowledge management in the field of HEIs have been detected, which will lead to the development of this field of research with future contributions related to educational ecosystems, wellbeing, data analysis software, program evaluation, and organizational performance.

This research has identified the latest trends related to knowledge management in HE. As in other sectors, knowledge institutions must consider aspects such as sustainable development as a priority, while addressing the economic, social and environmental effect that this entails. The results of this review reinforce the determining role that educational and academic institutions will play in the global effort to achieve the SDGs, assuming a role that strengthens the implementation, monitoring and review of these objectives. This is reaffirmed when observing the growing trend in the literature on Sustainable Development Goals in HEIs, their interdisciplinary composition, the high number and quality of the journals that they publish in this field of research, as well as the academics who have joined and committed.

Finally, it has been observed that international research on knowledge management in HEIs presents an upward trend, derived mainly from the publication of the number of articles and lines of research, which indicates the growing interest in the academic community and scientific.

REFERENCES

Abad-Segura, E., & González-Zamar, M.-D. (2019). Effects of Financial Education and Financial Literacy on Creative Entrepreneurship: A Worldwide Research. *Education Sciences*, *9*(3), 238. doi:10.3390/educsci9030238

Abad-Segura, E., González-Zamar, M.-D., Infante-Moro, J. C., & Ruipérez García, G. (2020). Sustainable Management of Digital Transformation in Higher Education: Global Research Trends. *Sustainability*, *12*(5), 2107. doi:10.3390u12052107

Albarillo, F. (2014). Language in Social Science Databases: English Versus Non-English Articles in JSTOR and Scopus. *Behavioral & Social Sciences Librarian*, *33*(2), 77–90. doi:10.1080/01639269.2014.904693

Archer-Brown, C., & Kietzmann, J. (2018). Strategic knowledge management and enterprise social media. *Journal of Knowledge Management*, *22*(6), 1288–1309. doi:10.1108/JKM-08-2017-0359

Ashour, S. (2020). Quality higher education is the foundation of a knowledge society: Where does the UAE stand? *Quality in Higher Education*, *26*(2), 1–15. doi:10.1080/13538322.2020.1769263

Atapattu, M. (2018). High performance work practices and knowledge workers' propensity for knowledge management processes. *Knowledge Management Research and Practice*, *16*(3), 356–365. doi:10.1080/14778238.2018.1493365

Bamber, C., & Elezi, E. (2020). Knowledge Management Evaluation in British Higher Education Partnerships. *Journal of Information & Knowledge Management*, *19*(02), 2050005. doi:10.1142/S0219649220500057

Baporikar, N., & Smith, A. (2019). Talent Management in Higher Education Institution. *International Journal of Applied Management Sciences and Engineering*, *6*(2), 36–57. doi:10.4018/IJAMSE.2019070103

Bekkers, R., & Freitas, I. M. B. (2008). Analysing knowledge transfer channels between universities and industry: To what degree do sectors also matter? *Research Policy*, *37*(10), 1837–1853. doi:10.1016/j.respol.2008.07.007

Bibi, G., Padhi, M., & Dash, S. S. (2020). Theoretical necessity for rethinking knowledge in knowledge management literature. *Knowledge Management Research and Practice*, 1–12. doi:10.1080/14778238.2020.1774433

Bornmann, L., & Mutz, R. (2015). Growth rates of modern science: A bibliometric analysis based on the number of publications and cited references. *Journal of the Association for Information Science and Technology*, *66*(11), 2215–2222. doi:10.1002/asi.23329

Chedid, M., Caldeira, A., Alvelos, H., & Teixeira, L. (2019). Knowledge-sharing and collaborative behaviour: An empirical study on a Portuguese higher education institution. *Journal of Information Science*. Advance online publication. doi:10.1177/0165551519860464

Cheng, Q., & Chang, Y. (2019). Influencing factors of knowledge collaboration effects in knowledge alliances. *Knowledge Management Research and Practice*, 1–14. doi:10.1080/14778238.2019.1678412

Durst, S., & Zieba, M. (2018). Mapping knowledge risks: Towards a better understanding of knowledge management. *Knowledge Management Research and Practice*, *17*(1), 1–13. doi:10.1080/14778238.2018.1538603

Effeney, G. (2019). Risk in work integrated learning: A stakeholder centric model for higher education. *Journal of Higher Education Policy and Management*, 1–16. doi:10.1080/1360080X.2019.1701852

Eraut, M. (1985). Knowledge creation and knowledge use in professioal contexts. *Studies in Higher Education*, *10*(2), 117–133. doi:10.1080/03075078512331378549

Flavin, M., Zhou Chen, T., & Quintero, V. (2019). Size matters: An analysis of UK higher education institution mission statements. *Journal of Higher Education Policy and Management*, *42*(3), 285–299. doi:10.1080/1360080X.2019.1658839

Freeman, L. D. (1974). The Management of Knowledge. *The Journal of Higher Education*, *45*(2), 81. doi:10.2307/1980554

González-Zamar, M. D., Ortiz Jiménez, L., Sánchez Ayala, A., & Abad-Segura, E. (2020). The Impact of the University Classroom on Managing the Socio-Educational Well-being: A Global Study. *International Journal of Environmental Research and Public Health*, *17*(3), 931. doi:10.3390/ijerph17030931 PMID:32028598

Goryaeva, I. A. (2019). Stakeholder management as a factor of higher education institution development. *Vestnik Universiteta*, (3), 11–17. doi:10.26425/1816-4277-2019-3-11-17

Grybauskienė, I., Jankauskienė, Ž., & Kubilienė, E. (2019). The Impact of Knowledge Management on Sustainable Activities Of Higher Education Institution. *EUREKA: Social and Humanities*, *3*, 17–29. doi:10.21303/2504-5571.2019.00891

Guerrero, M., Herrera, F., & Urbano, D. (2019). Strategic knowledge management within subsidised entrepreneurial university-industry partnerships. *Management Decision*, *57*(12), 3280–3300. Advance online publication. doi:10.1108/MD-10-2018-1126

Gulua, E. (2019). Management of Process and Infrastructure in Higher Education Institution. *European Journal of Interdisciplinary Studies*, *5*(1), 27. doi:10.26417/ejis.v5i1.p27-46

Hamilton, L., & Mostert, C. L. (2019). Investigating the Factors Inhibiting Entrepreneurial Activity amongst Business Management Students at a South African Higher Education Institution. *Polish Journal of Management Studies*, *19*(1), 157–169. doi:10.17512/pjms.2019.19.1.12

Harrison, N., & Luckett, K. (2019). Experts, knowledge and criticality in the age of "alternative facts": Re-examining the contribution of higher education. *Teaching in Higher Education*, *24*(3), 259–271. doi:10.1080/13562517.2019.1578577

Hauke, E. (2019). Understanding the world today: The roles of knowledge and knowing in higher education. *Teaching in Higher Education*, *24*(3), 378–393. doi:10.1080/13562517.2018.1544122

Henry, J. (1990). Enriching Prior Knowledge: Enhancing Mature Literacy in Higher Education. *The Journal of Higher Education*, *61*(4), 425–447. doi:10.1080/00221546.1990.11780723

Hordern, J. (2014). Management studies educational knowledge: Technical, elite or political? *Teaching in Higher Education*, *19*(4), 385–396. doi:10.1080/13562517.2013.860112

Jøranli, I. (2018). Managing organisational knowledge through recruitment: Searching and selecting embodied competencies. *Journal of Knowledge Management*, *22*(1), 183–200. doi:10.1108/JKM-12-2016-0541

Jung, J. (2019). The fourth industrial revolution, knowledge production and higher education in South Korea. *Journal of Higher Education Policy and Management*, *42*(2), 134–156. doi:10.1080/1360080X.2019.1660047

Khalil, O. E. M., & Shea, T. (2012). Knowledge Sharing Barriers and Effectiveness at a Higher Education Institution. *International Journal of Knowledge Management*, *8*(2), 43–64. doi:10.4018/jkm.2012040103

Khalil, O. E. M., & Shea, T. (2012). Knowledge Sharing Barriers and Effectiveness at a Higher Education Institution. *International Journal of Knowledge Management*, *8*(2), 43–64. doi:10.4018/jkm.2012040103

Košir, S. (2014). The Role of Knowledge Management and Internal Communication for a Better Quality Assurance in Higher Education Institution. *Literacy Information and Computer Education Journal*, *5*(3), 1641–1648. doi:10.20533/licej.2040.2589.2014.0219

Kramer, J. W., & Braxton, J. M. (2017). Contributions to Types of Professional Knowledge by Higher Education Journals. *New Directions for Higher Education*, *2017*(178), 9–20. doi:10.1002/he.20230

Laihonen, H., & Mäntylä, S. (2018). Strategic knowledge management and evolving local government. *Journal of Knowledge Management*, *22*(1), 219–234. doi:10.1108/JKM-06-2017-0232

Lawler, A., & Sillitoe, J. (2013). Facilitating "organisational learning" in a "learning institution.". *Journal of Higher Education Policy and Management*, *35*(5), 495–500. doi:10.1080/1360080X.2013.825415

Lebedyk, L. (2020). Measures of Pedagogical Competence Teachers of Higher Education Institution. *Image of The Modern Pedagogue*, *1*(1), 29–33. doi:10.33272/2522-9729-2020-1(190)-29-33

Lee, J. T., & Kuzhabekova, A. (2019). Building local research capacity in higher education: A conceptual model. *Journal of Higher Education Policy and Management*, *41*(3), 342–357. doi:10.1080/1360080X.2019.1596867

Lo, W. Y. W., & Tang, H.-H. H. (2019). Chasing Phantoms? Innovation policy, higher education and the pursuit of a knowledge economy in Hong Kong. *Journal of Higher Education Policy and Management*, *42*(2), 178–193. doi:10.1080/1360080X.2019.1687268

López-Meneses, E., Vázquez-Cano, E., González-Zamar, M.-D., & Abad-Segura, E. (2020). Socioeconomic Effects in Cyberbullying: Global Research Trends in the Educational Context. *International Journal of Environmental Research and Public Health*, *17*(12), 4369. doi:10.3390/ijerph17124369 PMID:32570762

Menon, S. (2020). Organizational Agility Assessment for Higher Education Institution. *Journal of Research on the Lepidoptera*, *51*(1), 561–573. doi:10.36872/LEPI/V51I1/301050

Mukhtar, M., Sudarmi, S., Wahyudi, M., & Burmansah, B. (2020). The Information System Development Based on Knowledge Management in Higher Education Institution. *International Journal of Higher Education*, *9*(3), 98. doi:10.5430/ijhe.v9n3p98

Nechaev, V. V., Bogoradnikova, A. V., Panchenko, V. M., … Chumak, V. M. (2017). Psychological factor of objective knowledge control analysis. *Educational Resources and Technology*, 8–14. doi:10.21777/2312-5500-2017-1-8-14

Nnazor, R., & Borrero, A. (1996). The University as an Institution Today. *The Journal of Higher Education*, *67*(4), 476. doi:10.2307/2943808

Orr, S. (2019). Democratizing Knowledge in Art and Design Education. Art. *Design & Communication in Higher Education*, *18*(2), 131–133. doi:10.1386/adch_00001_2

Penrod, J. I., & Witte, R. (1988). IAIMS infrastructure: Technological base. *Journal of the American Society for Information Science*, *39*(2), 118–125. doi:10.1002/(SICI)1097-4571(198803)39:2<118::AID-ASI10>3.0.CO;2-R PMID:10286231

Perkmann, M., Tartari, V., McKelvey, M., Autio, E., Broström, A., D'Este, P., ... Krabel, S. (2013). Academic engagement and commercialisation: A review of the literature on university–industry relations. *Research Policy*, *42*(2), 423–442. doi:10.1016/j.respol.2012.09.007

Rehman, U. U., & Iqbal, A. (2020). Nexus of knowledge-oriented leadership, knowledge management, innovation and organizational performance in higher education. *Business Process Management Journal*, *26*(6), 1731–1758. Advance online publication. doi:10.1108/BPMJ-07-2019-0274

Rousseau, R., & Ye, F. (2012). Basic independence axioms for the publication-citation system. *Journal of Scientometric Research*, *1*(1), 22–27. doi:10.5530/jscires.2012.1.6

Ryabova, Z. (2019). Knowledge Management in Development of a Project-Oriented Education Institute. *Image of The Modern Pedagogue*, *1*(5), 25–28. doi:10.33272/2522-9729-2019-5(188)-25-28

Schnitzler, T. (2019). The Bridge Between Education for Sustainable Development and Transformative Learning: Towards New Collaborative Learning Spaces. *Journal of Education for Sustainable Development*, *13*(2), 242–253. doi:10.1177/0973408219873827

Shevchenko, I., Puchkina, E., & Tolstov, N. (2019). Shareholders' and Managers' Interests: Collisions in Russian Corporations. *Higher School of Economics Economic Journal*, *23*(1), 118–142. doi:10.17323/1813-8691-2019-23-1-118-142

Sutton, H. (2018). Be proactive to make your institution fully accessible. *Disability Compliance for Higher Education*, *23*(10), 1–5. doi:10.1002/dhe.30431

Teichler, U. (2002). Diversification of higher education and the profile of the individual institution. *Higher Education Management and Policy*, *14*(3), 177–188. doi:10.1787/hemp-v14-art24-en

Tizkar Sadabadi, A., & Abdul Manaf, A. (2018). IKML approach to integrating knowledge management and learning for software project management. *Knowledge Management Research and Practice*, *16*(3), 343–355. doi:10.1080/14778238.2018.1474165

Van Beveren, J. (2002). A model of knowledge acquisition that refocuses knowledge management. *Journal of Knowledge Management*, *6*(1), 18–22. doi:10.1108/13673270210417655

Van Eck, N. J., & Waltman, L. (2009). Software survey: VOSviewer, a computer program for bibliometric mapping. *Scientometrics*, *84*(2), 523–538. doi:10.100711192-009-0146-3 PMID:20585380

Veer-Ramjeawon, P., & Rowley, J. (2019). Embedding knowledge management in higher education institutions (HEIs): A comparison between two countries. *Studies in Higher Education*, 1–17. doi:10.1080/03075079.2019.1608431

Wald, N., & Harland, T. (2019). Graduate attributes frameworks or powerful knowledge? *Journal of Higher Education Policy and Management*, *41*(4), 361–374. doi:10.1080/1360080X.2019.1613310

Walker, E. G. II. (2016). Predicting higher education outcomes and implications for a postsecondary institution ratings system. *Journal of Higher Education Policy and Management*, *38*(4), 422–433. doi:10.1080/1360080X.2016.1181886

White, P. M., & Lee, D. M. (2019). Geographic Inequalities and Access to Higher Education: Is the Proximity to Higher Education Institution Associated with the Probability of Attendance in England? *Research in Higher Education*. Advance online publication. doi:10.100711162-019-09563-x

Williams, R. (2019). National higher education policy and the development of generic skills. *Journal of Higher Education Policy and Management*, *41*(4), 404–415. doi:10.1080/1360080X.2019.1606690

Woodfield, S. (2018). International HE in the UK: Leveraging the policy-institution-expert nexus in uncertain times. *Journal of Higher Education Policy and Management*, *40*(6), 629–647. doi:10.1080/1360080X.2018.1530424

Wu, I.-L., & Hu, Y.-P. (2018). Open innovation-based knowledge management implementation: A mediating role of knowledge management design. *Journal of Knowledge Management*, *22*(8), 1736–1756. doi:10.1108/JKM-06-2016-0238

Yagodzinski, E. (2003). eSocrates Knowledge Management System and e-Learning Company. *The Internet and Higher Education*, *6*(1), 105–107. doi:10.1016/S1096-7516(02)00167-7

Yanaprasart, P. (2020). Language of knowledge and knowledge of language. Towards plurilingual sciences? *European Journal of Higher Education*, 1–19. doi:10.1080/21568235.2020.1777450

Yeo, W.-D., Sohn, E.-S., Jung, E.-S., & Lee, C.-H. (2008). Identification of Emerging Research at the national level: Scientometric Approach using Scopus. *Journal of International Management*, *39*(3), 95–113. doi:10.1633/JIM.2008.39.3.095

Zaim, H., Muhammed, S., & Tarim, M. (2018). Relationship between knowledge management processes and performance: Critical role of knowledge utilization in organizations. *Knowledge Management Research and Practice*, *17*(1), 24–38. doi:10.1080/14778238.2018.1538669

Compilation of References

Abad-Segura, E., González-Zamar, M.-D., Infante-Moro, J., & García, G. R. (2020). Sustainability. *Sustainable Management of Digital Transformation in Higher Education: Global Research Trends.*

Abad-Segura, E., & González-Zamar, M.-D. (2019). Effects of Financial Education and Financial Literacy on Creative Entrepreneurship: A Worldwide Research. *Education Sciences*, *9*(3), 238. doi:10.3390/educsci9030238

Abad-Segura, E., González-Zamar, M.-D., Infante-Moro, J. C., & Ruipérez García, G. (2020). Sustainable Management of Digital Transformation in Higher Education: Global Research Trends. *Sustainability*, *12*(5), 2107. doi:10.3390u12052107

Abu, F., Gholami, H., Mat Saman, M. Z., Zakuan, N., & Streimikiene, D. (2019). The implementation of lean manufacturing in the furniture industry: A review and analysis on the motives, barriers, challenges, and the applications. *Journal of Cleaner Production*, *234*, 660–680. doi:10.1016/j.jclepro.2019.06.279

Accelerating Digitalization. (2020). *Critical Actions to Strengthen the Resilience of the Maritime Supply Chain.* World Bank Group (WB), International Association of Ports and Harbours (IAPH), World Ports Sustainability Program (WPSP).

Achanga, P., Shehab, E., Roy, R., & Nelder, G. (2006). Critical success factors for Lean implementation within SMEs. *Journal of Manufacturing Technology Management.* Consulted on: Febraury 16 2020, on: https://www.researchgate.net/publication/200552235_Critical_success_factors_for_lean_implementation_within_SMEs

Ackoff, R. L. (1989). From data to wisdom. *Journal of Applied Systems Analysis*, *16*(1), 3–9.

Administradores (2021). Retrieved March 6, 2021, from https://administradores.com.br/artigos/etica-moral-e-responsabilidade-social

Agis, D., Bessa, D., Gouveia, J., & Vaz, P. (2010). *Wearing the future. Micro trends for the Textile, Clothing and Fashion Industries until 2020.* Portuguese Textile and Clothing Association. (in Portuguese)

Ahadi, S. (2011). Relationship between empowerment and organizational learning among academics in Malaysian research universities. *Journal of Business and Management*, *22*(2), 226–241.

Ahrne, G., & Brunsson, N. (2006). Organizing the world. In M.L. Djelic & K. Sahlin-Andersson (Eds.), Transnational Governance: Institutional Dynamics of Regulation. Cambridge, UK: Cambridge University Press.

Akerkar, R. (2014). Big data computing. CRC Press: Taylor & Francis Group, LLC.

Alaerds, R., Grove, S., Besteman, S., & Bilderbeek, P. (2017). *The Foundations of our Digital Economy.* Wouter Pegtel & Splend.

Alaqra, F., & Leveau, P. (2018). *Management of intrinsic competencies for sustainable organizational growth The study of the Swedish construction industry* (Master's thesis). 15 HE Business Administration Master Programme in Business Administration (MBA).

Alavi, M., & Leidner, D. E. (2001). Knowledge management and knowledge management systems: Conceptual foundations and research issues. *Management Information Systems Quarterly*, *25*(1), 107–136. doi:10.2307/3250961

Albarillo, F. (2014). Language in Social Science Databases: English Versus Non-English Articles in JSTOR and Scopus. *Behavioral & Social Sciences Librarian*, *33*(2), 77–90. doi:10.1080/01639269.2014.904693

Alberti, F. G., & Varon Garrido, M. A. (2017). Can profit and sustainability goals co-exist? New business models for hybrid firms. *The Journal of Business Strategy*, *38*(1), 3–13. doi:10.1108/JBS-12-2015-0124

AldrichJ. (2019, February 1). Retrieved from https://www.invisionapp.com/inside-design/remote-life-whats-it-all-about/

Alencastro, M. (2009, January/June). Hans Jonas e a proposta de uma ética para a civilização tecnológica. Desenvolvimento e Meio Ambiente. *Editora UFPR*, (19), 13–27.

Al-Hosseini, H. (2002). *Organizational Development*. Bahariye Press.

Alkaya, E., Bogurcu, M., Ulutas, F., & Demirer, G. N. (2015). Adaptation to climate change in industry: improving resource efficiency through sustainable production applications. Water Environment Research, 87(1), 14–25.

Allen, C., & Clouth, S. (2012). Green economy, green growth, and low-carbon development – history, definitions and a guide to recent publications. *UNDESA: A Guidebook to the Green Economy*. Retrieved from https://sustainabledevelopment.un.org/content/documents/GE%20Guidebook.pdf

Ana – Aeroportos de Portugal SA. (2021). Retrieved January 3, 2021, from http://www.dgtf.pt/

Anand, G. a. (2009). Development of a framework for lean manufacturing systems. *International Journal of Services and Operations Management*, *5*(5), 687–716.

Anand, G. a. (2010). Analysis of lean manufacturing frameworks. Advanced Manufacturing Systems, 9(1), 1–30.

Andreassen, T. W., Lervik-Olsen, L., Snyder, H., Van Riel, A. C. R., Sweeney, J. C., & Van Vaerenbergh, Y. (2018). Business model innovation and value-creation: The triadic way. *Journal of Service Management*, *29*(5), 883–906. doi:10.1108/JOSM-05-2018-0125

Angelopoulos, M., Kontakou, C., & Pollalis, Y. (2019, August 12). *Digital Transformation and Lean Management. Challenges in the Energy Industry of Utilities. A Review*. MPRA.

Antonaras, A., & Kostopoulos, A. (2017). Stakeholder agriculture: Innovation from farm to store. In Driving agribusiness with technology innovations (pp. 125-147). doi:10.4018/978-1-5225-2107-5.ch008

Antunes, S. M. (n.d.). *A mudança organizacional e a gestão da mudança organizacional*. Academic Press.

Anunciação, P. F., Dinis, V., & Esteves, F. M. (2021). *Preventive Maintenance as a Critical Success Factor in Industry 4.0. In Handbook of Research on Digital Transformation and Challenges to Data Security and Privacy*. IGI-Global.

Anunciação, P., & Zorrinho, C. (2006). *Urbanismo Organizacional: Como Gerir o Choque Tecnológico nas Empresas*. Edições Silabo.

APQP. (2019). *APQP - Planeamento Avançado da Qualidade do Produto*. Obtido de https://apqp.com.br/#fases-do-apqp

Archer-Brown, C., & Kietzmann, J. (2018). Strategic knowledge management and enterprise social media. *Journal of Knowledge Management*, *22*(6), 1288–1309. doi:10.1108/JKM-08-2017-0359

Ardley, B., & May, C. (2020). Ethical marketer and sustainability: Facing the challenges of overconsumption and the market. *Strategic Change*, *29*(6), 617–624. doi:10.1002/jsc.2372

Argyris, C. (1998). Organizational behavior: Production of knowledge for action in the world of practice. In J. McKelvey & M. Neufeld (Eds.), *Industrial relations at the dawn of the new millennium* (pp. 54–61). New York State School of Industrial and Labor Relations.

Ashour, S. (2020). Quality higher education is the foundation of a knowledge society: Where does the UAE stand? *Quality in Higher Education*, *26*(2), 1–15. doi:10.1080/13538322.2020.1769263

Aslam, M., Gao, Z., & Smith, G. (2020). Exploring factors for implementing lean construction for rapid initial successes in construction. *Journal of Cleaner Production*, *277*, 123295. doi:10.1016/j.jclepro.2020.123295

Asnan, R., Nordin, N., & Othman, S. N. (2015). *Managing Change on Lean Implementation in Service Sector*. 2nd Global Conference on Business and Social Science, GCBSS-2015, Bali, Indonesia. Consulted on: april 4 2020, on: https://www.sciencedirect.com/science/article/pii/S187704281505380X

Associação Portuguesa de Ética Empresarial. (2020). Retrieved December 18, 2020, from https://www.apee.pt/2019-02-05-19-45-24/ethical-code-compliance-overview

Atapattu, M. (2018). High performance work practices and knowledge workers' propensity for knowledge management processes. *Knowledge Management Research and Practice*, *16*(3), 356–365. doi:10.1080/14778238.2018.1493365

Atkinson, P. (2010). 'Lean' is a cultural issue. *Journal of the Institute of Management Services*.

Attias, D., & Mira-Bonnardel, S. (2016). Extending the scope of partnerships in the automotive industry between competition and cooperation. In The Automobile Revolution: Towards A New Electro-Mobility Paradigm (pp. 69-85). doi:10.1007/978-3-319-45838-0_5

Auchan Retail Portugal. (2021). Retrieved January 3, 2021, from www.auchan-retail.pt

Autoeuropa – Grupo Volkswagen. (2021). Retrieved January 3, 2021, from https://www.volkswagenautoeuropa.pt/

Axelos. (n.d.). Retrieved from https://www.axelos.com/: https://www.axelos.com/

Azharul, K.-U.-Z. (2013). A methodology for effective implementation of lean strategies and its performance evaluation in manufacturing organizations. Business Process Management Journal, 19, 169-196.

Baiyere, A., Salmela, H., & Tapanainen, T. (2020). European Journal of Information Systems. *Digital transformation and the new logics of business process management*.

Baldassarre, B., Konietzko, J., Brown, P., Calabretta, G., Bocken, N., Karpen, I. O., & Hultink, E. J. (2020). Addressing the design-implementation gap of sustainable business models by prototyping: A tool for planning and executing small-scale pilots. *Journal of Cleaner Production*, *255*, 120295. Advance online publication. doi:10.1016/j.jclepro.2020.120295

Balmer, J. M., & Gray, E. R. (1999). Corporate identity and corporate communications: Creating a competitive advantage. *Corporate Communications*, *4*(4), 171–177.

Balogun, J., Hailey, V. H., & Gustafsson, S. (2015). *Exploring strategic change* (4th ed.). Pearson Education.

Bamber, C., & Elezi, E. (2020). Knowledge Management Evaluation in British Higher Education Partnerships. *Journal of Information & Knowledge Management*, *19*(02), 2050005. doi:10.1142/S0219649220500057

Banda, G., Mittra, J., Tait, J., Watkins, A., & Omidvar, O. (2019). Understanding the emergence and evolution of new business models in the UK regenerative medicine sector. *Technology Analysis and Strategic Management*. Advance online publication. doi:10.1080/09537325.2019.1685087

Bank of Ireland. (2021). Retrieved from https://www.bankofirelanduk.com/about/responsible-business/colleagues/

Bansal, P., & DesJardine, M. R. (2014). Strategic Organization. *Business sustainability: It is about time.*

Baporikar, N. (2018a). Innovation and Sustainability in SMEs. In R. Perez-Uribe, C. Salcedo-Perez, & D. Ocampo-Guzman (Eds.), *Handbook of Research on Intrapreneurship and Organizational Sustainability in SMEs* (pp. 163–181). IGI Global. doi:10.4018/978-1-5225-3543-0.ch008

Baporikar, N. (2018b). *Global Practices in Knowledge Management for Societal and Organizational Development.* IGI Global. doi:10.4018/978-1-5225-3009-1

Baporikar, N. (2019). Knowledge Management Dynamics and Public Sector Organization Development. In Y. Albastaki, A. Al-Alawi, & S. Abdulrahman Al-Bassam (Eds.), *Handbook of Research on Implementing Knowledge Management Strategy in the Public Sector* (pp. 55–71). IGI Global. doi:10.4018/978-1-5225-9639-4.ch003

Baporikar, N. (2020a). Learning Link in Organizational Tacit Knowledge Creation and Dissemination. *International Journal of Sociotechnology and Knowledge Development, 12*(4), 70–88. doi:10.4018/IJSKD.2020100105

Baporikar, N. (2020b). Sustainability of Social Enterprises. In J. Saiz-Álvarez & J. Gámez-Gutiérrez (Eds.), *Senior Entrepreneurship and Aging in Modern Business* (pp. 148–169). IGI Global., doi:10.4018/978-1-7998-2019-2.ch009

Baporikar, N., & Smith, A. (2019). Talent Management in Higher Education Institution. *International Journal of Applied Management Sciences and Engineering, 6*(2), 36–57. doi:10.4018/IJAMSE.2019070103

Barley, S. R., & Tolbert, P. S. (1997). *Institutionalization and structuration: Studying the links between action and institution.* Retrieved from Cornell University, ILR School site: http://digitalcommons.ilr.cornell.edu/articles/130/

Barney, J. (1991). Firm resources and sustained competitive advantage. *Journal of Management, 17*(1), 99–120.

Barney, J. B. (1986). Strategic Factor Markets: Expectations, Luck and Business Strategy. *Management Science, 32*(10), 1231–1241. doi:10.1287/mnsc.32.10.1231

Barni, A., Montini, E., Menato, S., Sorlini, M., Anaya, V., & Poler, R. (2018, June). Integrating agent-based simulation in the design of multi-sided platform business model: a methodological approach. In *2018 IEEE International Conference on Engineering, Technology, and Innovation (ICE/ITMC)* (pp. 1-9). IEEE. 10.1109/ICE.2018.8436360

Barth, H., & Melin, M. (2018). A green lean approach to global competition and climate change in the agricultural sector – A Swedish case study. *Journal of Cleaner Production, 204*, 183–192. doi:10.1016/j.jclepro.2018.09.021

Basl, J., Buchalcevova, A., & Gala, L. (2012). Conceptual model of the impact of enterprise information systems innovation on sustainability. *Advances in Enterprise Information Systems, II*, 27–34. doi:10.1201/b12295-5

Batista, G. (n.d.). *Inteligência Artificial – Introdução.* Retrieved December 18, 2020, from https://autociencia.blogspot.com/2016/07/inteligencia-artificial-introducao.html

Bauernhansl, T., Ten Hompel, M., & Vogel-Heuse, B. (2014). *Industrie 4.0 in Produktion, Automatisierung und Logistik-Anwendung, Technologien und Migration.* Alemanha: Springer Vieweg.

Baumgartner, R., & Rauter, R. (2016). Journal of Cleaner Production. *Strategic perspectives of corporate sustainability management to develop a sustainable organization.*

Baumgartner, R.J., & Korhonen, J. (2010). *Strategic thinking for sustainable development.* Academic Press.

Bekkers, R., & Freitas, I. M. B. (2008). Analysing knowledge transfer channels between universities and industry: To what degree do sectors also matter? *Research Policy, 37*(10), 1837–1853. doi:10.1016/j.respol.2008.07.007

Belekoukias, I., Garza-Reyes, J. A., & Kumar, V. (2014). The impact of lean methods and tools on the operational performance of manufacturing organisations. *International Journal of Production Research*, *52*(18), 5346–5366. doi:10.1080/00207543.2014.903348

Bell, S. (2006). *Lean Enterprise Systems: Using IT for Continuous Improvement*. John Wiley & Sons.

Bell, S. C., & Orzen, M. A. (2012). *Lean IT: Enabling and Sustaining Your Lean Transformation*. BP Trends.

Belui Essimengane, J., Mushiri, T., & Mbohwa, C. (2016). Improving the management of operations at the "office des ports et RAdes du Gabon" (OPRAG). The road to achieve and sustain quality service delivery. *Proceedings of the International Conference on Industrial Engineering and Operations Management*, 1004-1007.

Ben-Eli, M. (2015). Sustainability: Definition and five core principles a new framework the sustainability laboratory. Academic Press.

Benn, S., Dunphy, D., & Griffiths, A. (2014). Enabling Change for Corporate Sustainability: An Integrated Perspective. *Australasian Journal of Environmental Management*.

Beraldo, D., & Milan, S. (2019). From data politics to the contentious politics of data. *Big Data & Society*, *6*(2), 1–11. doi:10.1177/2053951719885967

Berrone, P., & Gomez-Mejia, L.R. (2009). Environmental performance and executive compensation: an integrated agency-institutional perspective. *Academy of Management Journal, 52*(1), 103-126.

Bharadwaj, A., El Sawy, O. A., Pavlou, P. A., & Venkatraman, N. (2013). Digital business strategy: Toward a next generation of insights. *Management Information Systems Quarterly*, *37*(2), 471–482. doi:10.25300/MISQ/2013/37:2.3

Bianchi, C. (2012). Enhancing performance management and sustainable organizational growth through system-dynamics modelling. In *Systemic management for intelligent organizations* (pp. 143–161). Springer Berlin Heidelberg.

Bianchi, C. (2016). Fostering Sustainable Organizational Development Through Dynamic Performance Management. In *Dynamic Performance Management. System Dynamics for Performance Management* (Vol. 1). Springer.

Bibi, G., Padhi, M., & Dash, S. S. (2020). Theoretical necessity for rethinking knowledge in knowledge management literature. *Knowledge Management Research and Practice*, 1–12. doi:10.1080/14778238.2020.1774433

Bisneto, J., & Lins, O. (2016). Gestão da inovação: uma aproximação conceitual. *Revista Brasileira de Gestão e Inovação – Brazilian Journal of Management & Innovation, 3*(2), 86. Retrieved December 18, 2020, from http://www.ucs.br/etc/revistas/index.php/RBGI/index

Bloodgood, J. & Salisbury, W. (2001). Understanding the influence of organizational change strategies on information technology and knowledge management strategies. *Decision Support Systems, 31*(1), 55-69.

Bob, V. (2008). Which way do you lean? *Plant Engineering*. Consulted on: may 20 2020, on: https://www.plantengineering.com/articles/which-way-do-you-lean/

Bocken, N. M., & Geradts, T. H. (2020). Barriers and drivers to sustainable business model innovation: Organization design and dynamic capabilities. *Long Range Planning*, *53*(4), 101950. doi:10.1016/j.lrp.2019.101950

Boel, S. K., & Cecez-Kecmanovic, D. (2015). *What is an Information System*. Academic Press.

Bogers, M., Chesbrough, H., & Strand, R. (2020). Sustainable open innovation to address a grand challenge: Lessons from Carlsberg and the green fiber bottle. *British Food Journal*, *122*(5), 1505–1517. doi:10.1108/BFJ-07-2019-0534

Bohns, V. K. (2017, April 17). *Harvard Business Review.* Retrieved from https://hbr.org/: https://hbr.org/2017/04/a-face-to-face-request-is-34-times-more-successful-than-an-email

Bornmann, L., & Mutz, R. (2015). Growth rates of modern science: A bibliometric analysis based on the number of publications and cited references. *Journal of the Association for Information Science and Technology, 66*(11), 2215–2222. doi:10.1002/asi.23329

Bosch. (2021). Retrieved January 3, 2021, from https://www.bosch.pt/

Bouma, J. J., & Wolters, T. (2018). *Corporate sustainability: Inclusive business approaches contributing to a sustainable world.* Routledge., doi:10.4324/9781315639185

Bounfour, A. (2003). *The management of intangibles: The organisation's most valuable assets* (Vol. 16). Psychology Press.

Boyd, B., Henning, N., Reyna, E., Wang, D. E., Welch, M. D., & Hoffman, A. J. (2017). Hybrid organizations: New business models for environmental leadership. doi:10.4324/9781351279246

Boyett, J.H., (2001). *Lo mejor de los gurús. Las ideas clave de Covey, Drucker, Bennis, Champy, Hammer, Kaplan, Mintzberg, Peters, Porter, Senge y los demás gurús del management.* Academic Press.

BP Portugal. (2021). Retrieved January 3, 2021, from https://www.bp.com/

Brandt, C. (2019). I Heard You Paint Houses. The Irishman. In The Strategic Management of Intellectual Capital and Organizational Learning. Oxford University Press.

Breinbauer, A., Leitner, J., & Becker, K. (2019). Sustainable location development: How do investment promotion agencies go about attracting sustainable foreign direct investment? In Emerging market multinationals and Europe: Challenges and strategies (pp. 143-158). doi:10.1007/978-3-030-31291-6_9

Brekke, K. A., & Nyborg, K. (2008). Attracting responsible employees: Green production as labor market screening. *Resource and Energy Economics, 30*(4), 509–526.

Brendzel-Skowera, K. (2019). Circular economy in the development of sustainable entrepreneurship. *33rd International Business Information Management Association Conference, IBIMA 2019: Education Excellence and Innovation Management Through Vision*, 8390–8399.

Brisa – Autoestradas de Portugal SA. (2021). Retrieved January 3, 2021, from https://www.brisa.pt/

Broman, G. I., & Robèrt, K. (2017). A framework for strategic sustainable development. *Journal of Cleaner Production, 140*, 17–31. doi:10.1016/j.jclepro.2015.10.121

Brown, D. R., & Harvey, D. F. (2011). *An experiential approach to organization development.* Academic Press.

Brulin, G., & Svensson, L. (2012). *Managing Sustainable Development Programmes: A Learning Approach to Change.* Gower Publishing.

Brynjolfsson, E., & McAfee, A. (2014). *The Second Machine Age: Work, Progress and Prosperity in a Time of Brilliant Technologies.* W. W. Norton & Company.

Buchholz, R. (1989). *Fundamental concepts and problems in business ethics.* Prentice Hall.

Buhanist, P. (2000). *Organisational Change, Development Efforts and Action Research. HUT Industrial Management and Work and Organizational Psychology. Report 12.* Helsinki University of Technology.

Bulgarelli, W. (1985). *A teoria jurídica da empresa* (R. dos Tribunais, Ed.; 1st ed.).

Burnes, B. (2014). *Managing Change* (6th ed.). Harlow, UK: Pearson Education.

Cairncross, F. (2002). *The Company of The Future: How Communications Revolution Is Changing Management*. Harvard Business School Press.

Campbell, H. (1996). A Social Interactionist Perspective on Computer Implementation. *Journal of the American Planning Association, 62*(1), 99–107. doi:10.1080/01944369608975673

Canetta, L., Fontana, A., Foletti, M., & Tschanen, M. (2018). Sustainability assessment of various circular economy scenarios in the consumer electronics sector. *2018 IEEE International Conference on Engineering, Technology, and Innovation, ICE/ITMC 2018 – Proceedings*. 10.1109/ICE.2018.8436270

Carbone, V., & de Martino, M. (2003). *The Changing role of ports in supply-chain management: an empirical analysis*. Taylor & Francis.

Cardoso, F. (2016). Citizens: the new urban leaders. *Smart Cities*.

Cardoso, L. (2007). *Requiem for the lone navigator*. Don Quixote.

Cartlidge, A., Hanna, A., Rudd, C., Macfarlane, I., Windebank, J., & Rance, S. (2007). *An Introductory overview of ITIL*. The UK Chapter of the itSMF.

Carvalho, J. M. (2013). Planeamento Estratégico. O seu guia para o sucesso (2nd ed.). Porto: Vida Económica – Editorial, SA.

Carvalho, J. M. S. (2017). Social innovation and entrepreneurship: The case of Porto region. In Entrepreneurship: Concepts, methodologies, tools, and applications (pp. 850-887). doi:10.4018/978-1-5225-1923-2.ch036

Carvalho, L., Bernardo, M., Sousa, I., & Negas, M. (2020). *Gestão das organizações. Uma abordagem integrada e prospetiva* (2nd ed.). Lisboa: Edições Sílabo.

Castells, M. (1996), The rise of the network society. Oxford: Blackwell.

Castells, M. (1999), The network society (2nd ed., vol. 1). São Paulo: Peace and Earth.

Castells, M. (2003). The Internet Galaxy: Reflections on the Internet, Business and Society. Rio de Janeiro: Jorge Zahar Ed.

Castells, M. (1999). *A sociedade em Rede-A era da informação: economia, sociedade e cultura* (Vol. 1). Paz E Terra.

Castells, M. (2007). *The network society*. Peace and Earth.

Castells, M. (2010). *Networking: the age of information, economy, society and culture*. Peace and Earth.

Castells, M. (2013). *Networks of indignation and hope: social movements in the internet age*. Zahar.

Castells, M. (2015). *The power of communication*. Peace and Earth.

Ch, F. A., Holland, A., & Fathi, M. (2010, September). Advanced knowledge management concept for sustainable environmental integration. In *2010 IEEE 9th International Conference on Cybernetic Intelligent Systems* (pp. 1-7). IEEE.

Chaffey, D., & Wood, S. (2005). Business Information Management: Improving Performance Using Information Systems (1st ed.). Pearson Education (Prentice Hall).

Chahala, V., & Narwal, M. S. (2017). An empirical review of lean manufacturing and their strategies. *Management Science Letters, 7*(7), 321–336. doi:10.5267/j.msl.2017.4.004

Chakraborty, A. (2016). Importance of PDCA cycle for SMEs. *International Journal of Mechanical Engineering, 3*(5), 30–34. doi:10.14445/23488360/IJME-V3I5P105

Chandler, A. D. (1962). *Strategy and structure: Chapters in the history of the industrial empire*. MIT Press.

Chedid, M., Caldeira, A., Alvelos, H., & Teixeira, L. (2019). Knowledge-sharing and collaborative behaviour: An empirical study on a Portuguese higher education institution. *Journal of Information Science*. Advance online publication. doi:10.1177/0165551519860464

Cheng, Q., & Chang, Y. (2019). Influencing factors of knowledge collaboration effects in knowledge alliances. *Knowledge Management Research and Practice*, 1–14. doi:10.1080/14778238.2019.1678412

Cherman, A., & Tomei, P. (2005). Códigos de Ética Corporativa e a Tomada de Decisão Ética: Instrumentos de Gestão e Orientação de Valores Organizacionais. *Revista de Administração Contemporânea, 9*(3), 99–120. doi:10.1590/S1415-65552005000300006

Chinta, R., & Kloppenborg, T. J. (2010). Projects and processes for sustainable organizational growth. *S.A.M. Advanced Management Journal, 75*(2), 22.

Choi, H. R., Le, T. M. H., Alfaro, L. A., Cho, M. J., & Kim, C. S. (2015). Challenges and opportunities for port logistics in using BPAAS based on the TCO model. *International Journal of Economic Research, 12*(3), 559–581.

Choo, C. W. (2002b). *Information Management for the Intelligent Organization: The Art of Scanning the Environment* (3rd ed.). Information Today, Inc.

Choo, C. W. (2008). *Social use of information in organizational groups, information management: Setting the scene* (A. Huizing & E. J. De Vries, Eds.). Elsevier.

Chow, W. S., & Chen, Y. (2012). Corporate sustainable development: Testing a new scale based on the mainland Chinese context. *Journal of Business Ethics, 105*(4), 519–533. doi:10.100710551-011-0983-x

Christmann, P. (2000). Effects of "bestpractices" of environmental management on cost advantage: The role of complementary assets. *Academy of Management Journal, 43*(4), 663–680.

Clegg, S., & Hardy, C. (1996). *Handbook of Organisational Studies*. Sage Publications Ltd.

Coca-Cola Portugal. (2021). Retrieved January 3, 2021, from https://www.cocacolaportugal.pt/

Colbert, A., Yee, N., & George, G. (2016). The Digital Workforce and the Workplace of the Future. *The Academy of Management Journal*.

Comin, L. C., Aguiar, C. C., Sehnem, S., Yusliza, M., Cazella, C. F., & Julkovski, D. J. (2019). Sustainable business models: A literature review. *Benchmarking, 27*(7), 2028–2047. doi:10.1108/BIJ-12-2018-0384

Comissão europeia. (2017). Livro Branco sobre o futuro da europa, reflexões e cenários para a EU – 27 em 2025

Connor, P. (2019). Combining Lean manufacturing and Industry 4.0. *Manufacturers' Monthly*. Consulted on January 14 2019, on: https://www.manmonthly.com.au/Combining+Lean+manufacturing+and+Industry+4.0

Continental. (2021). Retrieved January 3, 2021, from https://www.continental.com/

Cooper, R. G. (1990). Stage-Gate Systems: A new tool for Managing new Products. *Business Horizons*.

Cooperrider, D., & Srivastva, S. (1987). Appreciative inquiry in organizational life. In R. Woodman & W. Pasmore (Eds.), Research in organizational change and development (Vol. 1, pp. 129–169). Academic Press.

Cortez, L. A. B., & Baldassin, R. (2016). Policies towards bioethanol and their implications: Case brazil. Global bioethanol: Evolution, risks, and uncertainties (pp. 142-162) doi:10.1016/B978-0-12-803141-4.00006-X

Cortina, A. (2005). *Ética de la empresa. Claves para uma nueva cultura empresarial.* Madrid: Editorial Trotta, S.A.

Cosenza, O., & Chamovitz, I. (2007, October). *Ética, Ética Empresarial E Responsabilidade Social: Reflexões E Recomendações.* Paper presented at the XXVII Encontro Nacional de Engenharia de Produção, Foz do Iguaçu, Brasil.

Cressey, D., & Moore, C. (1983). *Managerial Values and Corporate Codes of Ethics.* California Management Review. doi:10.2307/41165032

Crossan, M. M., & Berdrow, I. (2011). Organizational learning and strategic renewal. *Strategic Management Journal, 24*(11), 1087–1105.

Cummings, T. G., & Worley, C. G. (2014). *Organization development and change.* Cengage Learning.

Cunha, M. P., Cunha, R. C., Rego, A., Neves, P., & Cardoso, C. C. (2016). *Manual de Comportamento Organizacional e Gestão* (8th ed.). Editora RH.

Czarniawska, B., & Sevón, G. (1996a). Introduction. In B. Czarniawska & G. Sevón (Eds.), *Translating (organizational change)* (pp. 1–12). DeGruyter.

Czarniawska, B., & Sevón, G. (Eds.). (1996). *Translating Organizational Change.* New York, NY: Walter de Gruyter.

Dahlberg, I. (1978). Theory of concept. Information Science, 7(2).

Dahlberg, I. (2006). Feature: Interview with Integrant Dahlberg, December 2007. *Knowledge Organization, 35*(2/3).

Dallasega, P., Rauch, E., & Linder, C. (2018). Industry 4.0 as an enabler of proximity for construction supply chains: A systematic literature review. *Computers in Industry, 99*, 205–225. doi:10.1016/j.compind.2018.03.039

Daly, H. E. (1996). 14 sustainable growth: an impossibility theorem. *Valuing the earth: Economics, ecology, ethics,* 267.

DamaniM. D.KhairaS. (2020, December). Retrieved from https://www.wipro.com/business-process/proliferating-new-age-digital-technologies-to-boost-mental-health-and-wellbeing/

Damásio, A. (2011). *The Error of Descartes: Emotion, Reason and Human Brain.* Círculo de Leitores Publishing. (in Portuguese)

Damrath, F. (2012). *Increasing competitiveness of service companies: developing conceptual models for implementing Lean Management in service companies.* Politecnico di Milano.

Davenport, T. H. (1998). Ecology of Information: why technology alone is not enough for success in the information age (6th ed.). São Paulo: Futura.

Davenport, T. H., & Prusak, L. (1998). What do we talk about when we talk about knowledge. *Working Knowledge: How Organizations Manage What They Know.*

Davenport, T. H., & Glaser, J. (2002). Just-in-time delivery comes to knowledge management. *Harvard Business Review, 80*(7), 107–111. PMID:12140850

Davenport, T. H., & Prusak, L. (1998). *Business knowledge: how organizations manage their intellectual capital.* Campus.

De Fátima Ferreiro, M., & Salavisa, I. (2019). *Innovation and business models towards a sustainable food system.* Paper presented at the Proceedings of the European Conference on Innovation and Entrepreneurship. doi:10.34190/ECIE.19.119

De Filippo, M., Colangelo, D., & Farnia, L. (2017). Innovation and new business models in tourism. *Rivista di Studi sulla Sostenibilità*, (1), 149–168. doi:10.3280/RISS2017-001010

De Mul, J. (2015). Database Identity: Personal and Cultural Identity in the age of Global Datafication. In *Crossroads in new media, identity, and law: the shape of diversity to come* (pp. 97–118). Palgrave Macmillan. doi:10.1057/9781137491268_6

de Ven, A. V., & Hargrave, T. (2000). Social, Technical, and Institutional Change. Academic Press.

Dean, J. (2005). Communicative Capitalism: Circulation and the foreclosure of politics. *Cultural Politics*, *1*(1), 51–74. doi:10.2752/174321905778054845

Dechant, K. and Altman, B. (1994). Environmental leadership: from compliance to competitive advantage. *The Academy of Management Executive*, *8*(3), 7-20.

Decreto-Lei n.º 53/2019 de 17 de abril. Diário da República nº 76, Série I - Presidência do Conselho de Ministros – "Estabelece o conceito de porto seco e define as regras, os procedimentos e a desmaterialização necessários para a sua implementação

Decreto-Lei nº 158/2019 de 22 de outubro. Diário da República nº 203, Serie I – Presidência do Conselho de Ministros – "Cria a Janela Única Logística, transpondo a Diretiva n.º 2010/65/EU"

Deloitte. (2020). Retrieved from https://www2.deloitte.com/content/dam/Deloitte/global/Documents/About-Deloitte/RECOVER-TAL-STRAT-Reimagine-talent-strategy-op-modelPDF1.pdf

Denison, D. R., & Spreitzer, G. M. (1991). Organizational culture and organizational development: A competing values approach. *Research in Organizational Change and Development*, *5*(1), 1–21.

Dennis, P. (2002). *Lean Production Simplified - A Plain Language Guide to the World's Most Powerful Production System*. Productivity Press.

Dennis, P. (2002). *Lean production simplified*. Productivity Press.

Denny, A. (2001). *Ética e sociedade*. Capivari. Opinião E.

DESA-UN. (2018, April 4). *The Sustainable Development Goals Report 2017*. https://undesa.maps.arcgis.com/apps/MapSeries/index.html

Devlin, K. (1991). *Logic and Information*. Cambridge University Press.

Devlin, K. (1999). *Info Sense: turning information into knowledge*. W. H. Freeman and Company.

Di Vaio, A., Palladino, R., Pezzi, A., & Kalisz, D. E. (2021). The role of digital innovation in knowledge management systems: A systematic literature review. *Journal of Business Research*, *123*, 220–231. doi:10.1016/j.jbusres.2020.09.042

Dias, J. C. Q. (2003). *Integração Logística em Tempo de Globalização: Que Estratégias e Políticas para Portugal*. Camarate, Cargo Edições.

Dieste, M., Panizzolo, R., Garza-Reyes, J. A., & Anosike, A. (2019). The relationship between lean and environmental performance: Practices and measures. *Journal of Cleaner Production*, *224*, 120–131. doi:10.1016/j.jclepro.2019.03.243

Digital Twin Definition. (2021). *Digital Twin Consortium*. https://www.digitaltwinconsortium.org/hot-topics/defining-digital-twin.htm

Dinheiro Vivo. (2021). Retrieved January 3, 2021, from https://ranking-empresas.dinheirovivo.pt/ranking-nacional-empresas

Direção Geral Saúde. (2012). *Plano Nacional de Saúde (PNS) 2012-2016*. Obtido de https://pns.dgs.pt/pns-2012-2016/

Diretiva 2010/65/EU do parlamento Europeu e do conselho – Formalidades de declaração exigidas aos navios à chegada e/ou à partida dos portos dos Estados-Membros e que revoga a Diretiva 2002/6/CE

Domingos, P. (2015). *The Master Algoritm: How the Quest for the Ultimate Learning Machine Will Remake Our World.* Penguin Random House.

Donner, M., & de Vries, H. (2021). How to innovate business models for a circular bio-economy? *Business Strategy and the Environment*, *30*(4), 1932–1947. Advance online publication. doi:10.1002/bse.2725

Downing, J. D. H. (2002). *Radical media: rebellion in communications and social movements*. Editora Senac.

Duarte, A. P., & Neves, J. G. (2011). *Relação entre responsabilidade social percebida e satisfação no trabalho: O papel mediador da imagem organizacional. Percursos da investigação em psicologia social e organizacional*. Colibri.

Dunn, A. (2009). *Implementation of lean manufacturing in General MotorsManufacturing Luton (GMML). Warwick.* University of Warwick.

Dupada, S., Gedela, R. K., Aryasri, R. C., & Acharya, R. (2013). Building value chain through actionable benchmarking for sustainability and excellence. *Proceedings of the 2013 2nd International Conference on Information Management in the Knowledge Economy,* 24-30.

Du, Q., & Kang, J. T. (2016). Tentative ideas on the reform of exercising state ownership of natural resources: Preliminary thoughts on establishing a state-owned natural resources supervision and administration commission. *Jiangxi Social Science*, *6*, 160.

Durst, S., & Zieba, M. (2018). Mapping knowledge risks: Towards a better understanding of knowledge management. *Knowledge Management Research and Practice*, *17*(1), 1–13. doi:10.1080/14778238.2018.1538603

Economia e Finanças. (2020). Retrieved December 16, 2020, from https://economiafinancas.com/2016/definicao-grande-media-pequena-microempresa/

EDP. (2021). Retrieved January 3, 2021, from https://www.edp.pt/

Effeney, G. (2019). Risk in work integrated learning: A stakeholder centric model for higher education. *Journal of Higher Education Policy and Management*, 1–16. doi:10.1080/1360080X.2019.1701852

Eisenhardt, K. M., & Bourgeois, L. J. (1988). Politics of strategic decision making in high- velocity environments: Toward a midrange theory. *Academy of Management Journal.*

El-Akruti, K., & Dwight, R. (2013, October). A framework for the engineering asset management system. *Journal of Quality in Maintenance Engineering*, *19*(4), 398–412. Advance online publication. doi:10.1108/JQME-01-2012-0002

Elg, M., Ellström, P., Klofsten, M., & Tillmar, M. (2020). *Sustainable development in organizations*. Downloaded from Elgar Online.

Elia, V., Gnoni, M. G., & Tornese, F. (2019). Exploring the benefits of productization in public services utilities. *Proceedings of the Summer School Francesco Turco*, *1*, 41–45.

Eliufoo, H. (2008). Knowledge creation in construction organizations: a case approach. *The Learning Organization, 15*(4), 309-325.

Elkington, J. (2006). Governance for sustainability, Corporate Governance. *International Review (Steubenville, Ohio)*, *14*(6), 522–529.

Endesa. (2021). Retrieved January 3, 2021, from http://www.fedecundi.com/

EngageRocket. (2020). Retrieved from https://www.engagerocket.co/hubfs/Resilience%20of%20SG%20workforce%20Whitepaper_Aug%2020_EngageRocket.pdf

Enterprise Asset Management. (2021). Retrieved online on 15.03.2021 from https://www.g2.com/categories/enterprise-asset-management-eam

Eraut, M. (1985). Knowledge creation and knowledge use in professioal contexts. *Studies in Higher Education, 10*(2), 117–133. doi:10.1080/03075078512331378549

Erhabor, N. I., & Don, J. U. (2016). Impact of Environmental Education On the Knowledge and Attitude of Students Towards the Environment. *International Journal of Environmental and Science Education, 11*(12), 5367–5375.

European Commission. (2017). Retrieved December 18, 2020, from https://ec.europa.eu/

Evans, S., Vladimirova, D., Holgado, M., Van Fossen, K., Yang, M., Silva, E. A., & Barlow, C. Y. (2017). Business model innovation for sustainability: Towards a unified perspective for creation of sustainable business models. *Business Strategy and the Environment, 26*(5), 597–608. doi:10.1002/bse.1939

Evers, B. A. (2018). *Why adopt the Sustainable Development Goals? The case of multinationals in the Colombian coffee and extractive sector* (Master Thesis). Erasmus University Rotterdam.

Fane, G. R., Vaghefi, M. R., Deusen, C., & Woods, L. A. (2003). Competitive advantage the Toyota way'. *Business Strategy Review, 14*(4), 51–60. doi:10.1111/j..2003.00286.x

Farias, C., & Farias, G. (2010). Cycles of poverty and consumption: The sustainability dilemma. *Competitiveness Review, 20*(3), 248–257. doi:10.1108/10595421011047433

Feng, S., Li, L., & Cen, L. (2001). An Object-oriented Intelligent Design Tool to Aid the Design of Manufacturing Systems. *Knowledge-Based Systems, 14*(5–6), 225–232. doi:10.1016/S0950-7051(01)00100-9

Fernandes, E. A. (2005). *Gestão da Mudança Organizacional.* Academic Press.

Festo Didactic, S. E. (2019). *Fundamental Principles of Smart Sensors.* https://www.festo-didactic.com/ov3/media/customers/1100/smart_sensors_infographic_a3_en.pdf

Festo Didactic, S. E. (2021). *Build Smart Sensors Skills for Industry 4.0 Workers.* https://www.festo-didactic.com/int-en/highlights/smart-sensors-for-industry-4.0

Fidan, F. Ş., Aydoğan, E. K., & Uzal, N. (2021). An integrated life cycle assessment approach for denim fabric production using recycled cotton fibers and combined heat and power plant. *Journal of Cleaner Production, 287*, 125439. Advance online publication. doi:10.1016/j.jclepro.2020.125439

Filice, M., & Young, S. (2012). From mainstage to movies to media: Sustaining the live and performing arts through artistic convergence and the Balaban and Katz philosophy of continuous performance. *International Journal of Arts Management, 14*(2), 48–56.

Flavin, M., Zhou Chen, T., & Quintero, V. (2019). Size matters: An analysis of UK higher education institution mission statements. *Journal of Higher Education Policy and Management, 42*(3), 285–299. doi:10.1080/1360080X.2019.1658839

Floridi, L. (2010). The philosophy of information: ten years later. *Metaphilosophy, 41*(3), 402-419.

Floridi. (2014a). *The fourth revolution: how the infosphere is reshaping human reality.* Oxford University Press.

Floridi. (2014b). *What is the philosophy of information.* Academic Press.

Ford, M. (2015). *Rise of the Robots: Technology and the Threat of a Jobless Future. Nova Iorque*. Basic Books.

Ford, M. (2015). *Robôs: A Ameaça de um futuro sem emprego*. Bertrand Editora.

Foresight Mental Capital and Wellbeing Project. (2008, October). Retrieved from https://assets.publishing.service.gov.uk/government/uploads/system/uploads/attachment_data/file/292453/mental-capital-wellbeing-summary.pdf

Framework for Improving Critical Infrastructure Cybersecurity. (2018). *Nacional Institute os Information and Communications Technology*. NIST.

Franco, M. & Mariano, S. (2007). Information Technology Repositories and Knowledge Management Processes. *Journal of Information and Knowledge Management Systems, 37*(4), 440-451.

Freeman, L. D. (1974). The Management of Knowledge. *The Journal of Higher Education, 45*(2), 81. doi:10.2307/1980554

Fuchs, C. (2016). Towards a Marxist problem of internet studies. *Marxist Criticism*, (43), 67–93.

Fuchs, C., & Chandler, D. (2019). *Digital Objects. Digital Subjects. Interdisciplinary perspectives on capitalism, labour and politics in the age of Big Data*. University Westminster Press.

Fukuzawa, M. (2019). Critique on the Lean Production System Research. *Annals of Business Administrative Science, 18*, 85–101.

Gabriel, C., Bortsie-Aryee, N. A., Apparicio-Farrell, N., & Farrell, E. (2018). How supply chain choices affect the life cycle impacts of medical products. *Journal of Cleaner Production, 182*, 1095–1106. doi:10.1016/j.jclepro.2018.02.107

Gagliardi, D., Psarra, F., Wintjes, R., Trendafili, K., Pineda Mendoza, J., Haaland, K., & Niglia, F. (2020). *New Technologies and Digitisation: Opportunities and Challenges for the Social Economy and Social Enterprises*. European Commission, Executive Agency for SMEs.

Galp. (2021). Retrieved January 3, 2021, from https://www.galp.com/

Galpin, T. J. (1996). *The Human Side of Change: A Practical Guide to Organization Redesign*. Academic Press.

Garetti, M., & Taisch, M. (2012). Sustainable manufacturing: Trends and research challenges. *Production Planning and Control, 23*(2-3), 83–104. doi:10.1080/09537287.2011.591619

Gartner. (2020, October 21). *Smarter With Gartner*. Retrieved from www.gartner.com: https://www.gartner.com/smarterwithgartner/how-successful-chinese-companies-adapted-to-covid-19/

Gattorna, J. (2016). *Dynamic supply chain alignment: A new business model for peak performance in enterprise supply chains across all geographies*. Routledge. doi:10.4324/9781315578316

Geada, N., & Anunciação, P. (2019). Change Management Projects in Information Systems: The impact of the Methodology Information Technology Infrastructure Library (ITIL). In Handbook of Research on Emerging Technologies for Effective Project Management. IGI Global.

Geada, N. (2019). Change Management in the Digital Economy: Model Proposal. *International Journal of Innovation in the Digital Economy, 11*(3), 4.

Geissdoerfer, M., Vladimirova, D., & Evans, S. (2018). Sustainable business model innovation: A review. *Journal of Cleaner Production, 198*, 401–416. doi:10.1016/j.jclepro.2018.06.240

Genpack Research Institute. (2017). *Putting Digital to Work - The Lean Digital Way*. Author.

Gholami, H., Rezaei, G., Saman, M. Z. M., Sharif, S., & Zakuan, N. (2016). State-of-the-art green HRM system: Sustainability in the sports center in Malaysia using a multi-methods approach and opportunitiesforfutureresearch. *Journal of Cleaner Production, 124*, 142–163. www.sciencedirect.com/science/journal/09596526/124?sdc=1

Gibson, I., Rosen, D., & Stucker, B. (2015). Additive Manufacturing Technologies - 3D Printing, Rapid Prototyping, and Direct Digital Manufacturing. New York: Springer Science + Business Media.

Gils, B. V., & Weigand, H. (2020). Towards sustainable digital transformation. *Proceedings - 2020 IEEE 22nd Conference on Business Informatics, CBI 2020,* 104-113. 10.1109/CBI49978.2020.00019

Gino, F., & Staats, B. (2015). Why organizations don't learn. *Harvard Business Review, 11*(November). https://hbr.org/2015/11/why-organizations-dont-learn

Ginzberg, M. J. (1981). Early diagnosis of MIS implementation failure: Promising results and unanswered questions. *Management Science, 27*(4), 459–478. doi:10.1287/mnsc.27.4.459

Girotra, K., & Netessine, S. (2013). Business model innovation for sustainability. *Manufacturing & Service Operations Management, 15*(4), 537–544. doi:10.1287/msom.2013.0451

Gjøsæter, Å. S., Kyvik, Ø., Nesse, J. G., & Årethun, T. (2021). Business models as a framework for sustainable value-creation: Strategic and operative leadership challenges. *International Journal of Innovation and Sustainable Development, 15*(1), 50–74. doi:10.1504/IJISD.2021.111549

Gloet, M. (2006). Knowledge management and the links to HRM. *Management Research News, 29*(7), 402–413. doi:10.1108/01409170610690862

Glover, W. J., Farris, J. A., Van Aken, E. M., & Doolen, T. L. (2011). Critical success factors for the sustainability of Kaizen event human resource outcomes: An empirical study. *International Journal of Production Economics, 132*(2), 197–213. doi:10.1016/j.ijpe.2011.04.005

Gómes, H. G., Serna, M. D., & Badenes, R. F. (2009). *Evolución Y Tendencias de los Sistemas de Información para la Gestión de la Empresa: El M-Business*. Academic Press.

Gonçalves, N. C. (2015). *Strategic knowledge management: case study at the Federal Institute of Brasília. Course Completion Work (Graduation in Business Administration).* IESB University Center.

González-Zamar, M. D., Ortiz Jiménez, L., Sánchez Ayala, A., & Abad-Segura, E. (2020). The Impact of the University Classroom on Managing the Socio-Educational Well-being: A Global Study. *International Journal of Environmental Research and Public Health, 17*(3), 931. doi:10.3390/ijerph17030931 PMID:32028598

Google. (2020). Retrieved from https://services.google.com/fh/files/misc/2020_covidadsplaybook_en-us.pdf

Gopal, P. R. C., & Thakkar, J. (2016). Analyzing critical success factors to implement sustainable supply chain practices in the Indian automobile industry: A case study. *Production Planning and Control, 27*(12), 1005–1018. doi:10.1080/09537287.2016.1173247

Gorecky, D., Schmitt, M., Losskyll, M., & Zuhlke, D. (2014). Human-machine-interaction in the industry 4.0 era. *Conference: 2014 12th IEEE International Conference on Industrial Informatics (INDIN).*

Goryaeva, I. A. (2019). Stakeholder management as a factor of higher education institution development. *Vestnik Universiteta,* (3), 11–17. doi:10.26425/1816-4277-2019-3-11-17

Gossling-Goidsmiths, J. (2018). *Sustainable development goals and uncertainty visualization* (Master's thesis). University of Twente.

Gössling, S., & Michael Hall, C. (2019). Sharing versus collaborative economy: How to align ICT developments and the SDGs in tourism? *Journal of Sustainable Tourism, 27*(1), 74–96. doi:10.1080/09669582.2018.1560455

Grant, R. (2006). The Knowledge-Based View of the Firm. In Strategy: A Strategy Overview and Competitive Strategy. Oxford University Press. doi:10.1093/oxfordhb/9780199275212.003.0008

Grant, R. (1991). The Resource-based Theory of Competitive Advantage: Implications for Strategy Formulation. *California Management Review, 33*(3), 114–135. doi:10.2307/41166664

Gray, P. & Meister, D. (2006). Knowledge Sourcing Methods. *Information and Management, 43*(2), 142-156.

Gray, R. (2010). Is accounting for sustainability actually accounting for sustainability … and how would we know? An exploration of narratives of organizations and the planet. *Accounting, Organizations and Society, 35*(1), 47–62. doi:10.1016/j.aos.2009.04.006

Greenan, N. (2003). Organisational change, technology, employment and skills: an empirical study of French manufacturing. *Cambridge Journal of Economics, 27*(2), 287–316.

Grieves, M. (2014). *Digital Twin: Manufacturing Excellence through Virtual Factory Replication.* https://www.researchgate.net/publication/275211047_Digital_Twin_Manufacturing_Excellence_through_Virtual_Factory_Replication

Grieves, M. (2021). *Intelligent Digital Twins: The Role of AI and ML in the Future of Digital Twins.* https://www.researchgate.net/publication/349042364

Grifkin, J. (2014). *The Zero Marginal Cost Society*. Palgrave Macmillan.

Grove, A., Meredith, J., MacIntyre, M., Angelis, J., & Neailey, K. (2010). UK health visiting: Challenges faced during lean implementation. *Leadership in Health Services, 23*(3), 204–218. doi:10.1108/17511871011061037

Gruchmann, T., & Seuring, S. (2018). Explaining logistics social responsibility from a dynamic capabilities perspective. *International Journal of Logistics Management, 29*(4), 1255–1278. doi:10.1108/IJLM-08-2017-0200

Grybauskienė, I., Jankauskienė, Ž., & Kubilienė, E. (2019). The Impact of Knowledge Management on Sustainable Activities Of Higher Education Institution. *EUREKA: Social and Humanities, 3*, 17–29. doi:10.21303/2504-5571.2019.00891

Guerci, M., & Carollo, L. (2016). A paradox view on green human resource management: Insights from the Italian context. *International Journal of Human Resource Management, 27*(2), 212–238.

Guerrero, M., Herrera, F., & Urbano, D. (2019). Strategic knowledge management within subsidised entrepreneurial university-industry partnerships. *Management Decision, 57*(12), 3280–3300. Advance online publication. doi:10.1108/MD-10-2018-1126

*Guidelines on Maritime Cyber Risk Management – ISM (*MSC-FAL.1/Circ.3)

Gulua, E. (2019). Management of Process and Infrastructure in Higher Education Institution. *European Journal of Interdisciplinary Studies, 5*(1), 27. doi:10.26417/ejis.v5i1.p27-46

Gumora, G., & Arsenio, W. F. (2002). Emotionality, emotion regulation, and schoolperformance in middle school children. *Journal of School Psychology, 395*, 413.

Günther, W. A., Mehrizi, M. H. R., Huysman, M., & Feldberg, F. (2017). Debating big data: A literature review on realizing value from big data. *The Journal of Strategic Information Systems, 26*(3), 191–209. doi:10.1016/j.jsis.2017.07.003

Habermas, J. (1987). Technique and science as ideology (70th ed.). Academic Press.

Habermas. (2017). *The post-national constellation: political essays*. doi:10.5433/2178-8189.2017v21n3p323

Habermas, J. (1978). *Raison et legitimité: problèmes de légitimation dans le capitalisme avancé*. Payot.

Haider, S., & Bhat, J. A. (2020). Does total factor productivity affect the energy efficiency: Evidence from the Indian paper industry. *International Journal of Energy Sector Management*, *14*(1), 108–125. doi:10.1108/IJESM-11-2018-0010

Hák, T., Janoušková, S., & Moldan, B. (2016). Sustainable development goals: A need for relevant indicators. *Ecological Indicators*, *60*(1), 565–573. doi:10.1016/j.ecolind.2015.08.003

Hamilton, L., & Mostert, C. L. (2019). Investigating the Factors Inhibiting Entrepreneurial Activity amongst Business Management Students at a South African Higher Education Institution. *Polish Journal of Management Studies*, *19*(1), 157–169. doi:10.17512/pjms.2019.19.1.12

Hammer, M., & Champy, J. (1994). *Reengineering the Corporation: A manifesto for business revolution*. Nicholas Brealy.

Han, S. H., Kim, D. Y., Jang, H. S., & Choi, S. (2010). Strategies for contractors to sustain growth in the global construction market. *Habitat International*, *34*(1), 1–10.

Hansen, M. T., Nohria, N., & Tierney, T. (2005). What's your strategy for managing knowledge. *Knowledge Management: Critical Perspectives on Business and Management, 77*(2), 322.

Harrison, N., & Luckett, K. (2019). Experts, knowledge and criticality in the age of "alternative facts": Re-examining the contribution of higher education. *Teaching in Higher Education*, *24*(3), 259–271. doi:10.1080/13562517.2019.1578577

Hashizume, K., Rosado, D., Medina, E., & Fernandez, E. (2013). *An analysis of security issues for cloud computing*. SpringerLink. doi:10.1186/1869-0238-4-5

Hatch, M., Ji, B., & Shu, O. (1997, September). Do Standing, Lifting, Climbing, or Long Hours of Work during Pregnancy Have an Effecton Fetal Growth? *Epidemiology (Cambridge, Mass.)*, *8*(5), 530–536.

Hauke, E. (2019). Understanding the world today: The roles of knowledge and knowing in higher education. *Teaching in Higher Education*, *24*(3), 378–393. doi:10.1080/13562517.2018.1544122

Hayes, P., & Poel, V. D. (2020, September). Algorithms and values in justice and security. *AI & Society*, *35*(3), 533–555. Advance online publication. doi:10.100700146-019-00932-9

Hedstrom, G. S. (2018). *Sustainability: What it is and how to Measure it.* Walter de Gruyter GmbH & Co KG. doi:10.1515/9781547400423

Hemerling, J., Kilmann, J., Danoesastro, M., Stutts, L., & Ahern, C. (2018). *It's Not a digital Tansformation without a Digital Culture.* The Boston Consulting Group.

Henry, J. (1990). Enriching Prior Knowledge: Enhancing Mature Literacy in Higher Education. *The Journal of Higher Education*, *61*(4), 425–447. doi:10.1080/00221546.1990.11780723

Hermann, M., Pentek, T., & Otto, B. (2016). Design Principles for Industrie 4.0 Scenarios. *Proceedings of 2016 49th Hawaii International Conference on Systems Science*. 10.1109/HICSS.2016.488

Hersi, P. & Blanchard, K. (1988). *Management of Organizational Behavior – Utilizing Human Resources* (5th ed.). Prentice-Hall Inc.

Hess, T., Matt, C., Benlian, A., & Wiesböck, F. (2016). Options for formulating a digital transformation strategy. *MIS Quarterly Executive*, *15*(2).

Hewitt., & Associates. (2010). Hewitt and Associates establishes strong relationship between employee engagement and CSR. Academic Press.

Hi bob Inc. (n.d.). Retrieved from https://www.hibob.com/guides/hybrid-working-model-advantages/

Hill, R. C., & Bowen, P. A. (1997). Sustainable construction: Principles and a framework for attainment. *Construction Management and Economics, 15*(3), 223–239.

Hines, P., Holweg, M., & Rich, N. (2004). Learning to evolve: A review of contemporary lean thinking. *International Journal of Operations & Production Management, 24*(10), 994–1011. doi:10.1108/01443570410558049

Hitchcock, D., & Willard, M. (2006). *The Business Guide to Sustainability: Practical Strategies and Tools for Organizations*. Earthscan.

Hofmann, E., & Rüsch, M. (2017). Computers in Industry. Industry 4.0 and the current status as well as future prospects on logistics, 23-34.

Høgevold, N. M., Svensson, G., Wagner, B., Petzer, D. J., Klopper, H. B., Varela, J. C. S., ... Ferro, C. (2014). Sustainable business models: Corporate reasons, economic effects, social boundaries, environmental actions, and organizational challenges in sustainable business practices. *Baltic Journal of Management, 9*(3), 357–380. doi:10.1108/BJM-09-2013-0147

Holbrook, M.B. & Hirschman, E.C. (1982). *The experiential aspects of consumption*. Academic Press.

Hordern, J. (2014). Management studies educational knowledge: Technical, elite or political? *Teaching in Higher Education, 19*(4), 385–396. doi:10.1080/13562517.2013.860112

Horváth, B. (2018). The Recognition of resource use through industrial development from a social perspective. Studia Mundi–Economica, 5(1). doi:10.18531/Studia.Mundi.2018.05.01.68-78

Hotho, J.J., Lyles, M.A., & Easterby-Smith, M. (2015). The mutual impact of global strategyand organizational learning: current themes and future directions. *Glob. Strat. J.,* 85–112.

Hoveskog, M., Halila, F., Mattsson, M., Upward, A., & Karlsson, N. (2018). Education for sustainable development: Business modeling for flourishing. *Journal of Cleaner Production, 172*, 4383–4396. doi:10.1016/j.jclepro.2017.04.112

How to Develop a Port Community System Guide. (2015). International Port Community System Association (IPCSA).

Iasevoli, G., & Massi, M. (2012). The relationship between sustainable business management and competitiveness: Research trends and challenge. *International Journal of Technology Management, 58*(1/2), 32–48. doi:10.1504/IJTM.2012.045787

Imai, M. (1986). *Kaizen: The Key To Japan's Competitive Success*. Retrieved from https://books.google.pt/books?id=tCu1AAAAIAAJ

Imai, M. (1997). *Gemba Kaizen: A Commonsense, Low-Cost Approach to Management*. McGraw Hill Professional.

Imai, M. (2006). *Gemba Kaizen*. MT Biznes.

Infraestruturas De Portugal, S. A. (IP). (2021). Retrieved January 3, 2021, from https://www.infraestruturasdeportugal.pt/

Instituto Ethos. (2020). Retrieved January 8, 2021, from https://www.ethos.org.br/

Irimiás, A., & Mitev, A. (2020). *Sustainability. Change Management, Digital Maturity, and Green Development: Are Successful Firms Leveraging on Sustainability?* Academic Press.

Itami, H. (1987), Mobilizing Invisible Assets. Harvard University Press.

Ivan, C., Mukta, R., Sudeep, C., & Burak, C. (2015). Long-term sustainable sustainability in luxury. Where else? In Handbook of Sustainable Luxury Textiles And Fashion (pp. 17-34). doi:10.1007/978-981-287-742-0_2

Iveroth, E. (2010). Inside Ericsson: A framework for the practice of leading global IT-enabled change. *California Management Review*, *53*(1), 136–153. doi:10.1525/cmr.2010.53.1.136

Jabbour, C. J. C., Jabbour, A. B. L. D. S., Sarkis, J., & Filho, M. G. (2019). Unlocking the circular economy through new business models based on large-scale data: An integrative framework and research agenda. *Technological Forecasting and Social Change*, *144*, 546–552. doi:10.1016/j.techfore.2017.09.010

Jackson, S.E. & Seo, J. (2010), The greening of strategic HRM scholarship. *Organization Management Journal*, *7*(4), 278-290.

Jaeger, W. (1962). *Early Christianity and Greek Paideia. Cambridge (Mass.): Harvard University Press.* Oxford University Press.

Jahmurataj, V. (2015). Impact of culture on organizational development: Case study Kosovo. *Acad. J. Interdis. Stud*, *4*, 206–210.

Jameel, A. L. (2018). *Four Principles Management Consulting FZ-LLC.* Lean Digital Transformation.

James, L. R., Choi, C. C., Ko, C. H. E., McNeil, P. K., Minton, M. K., Wright, M. A., & Kim, K. I. (2008). Organizational and psychological climate: A review of theory and research. *European Journal of Work and Organizational Psychology*, *17*(1), 5–32.

Jasperneite, J. (2012). Was Hinter Begriffen Wie Industrie 4.0 Steckt. *Computers and Automation*, *12*, 24–28.

Jerónimo Martins. (2021). Retrieved January 3, 2021, from https://www.jeronimomartins.com/

Jiju, A. (2011). *Six Sigma vs Lean Six Sigma: Some Perspectives from Leading Academics and Practitioners.* Purdue University.

Johannsdottir, L. (2014). Transforming the linear insurance business model to a closed-loop insurance model: A case study of Nordic non-life insurers. *Journal of Cleaner Production*, *83*, 341–355. doi:10.1016/j.jclepro.2014.07.010

Johnson, G., Scholes, K., Whittington, R., Angwin, D., & Regner, P. (2018). *Fundamentals of Strategy* (4th ed.). Pearson Education.

Jones, D., Snider, C., Nassehi, A., Yon, J., & Hicks, B. (2020). Characterizing the Digital Twin: A systematic literature review. *CIRP Journal of Manufacturing Science and Technology*, *29*(A), 36-52.

Jones, G. (2007). *Organisational Theory, Design, and Change.* Pearson Prentice.

Jøranli, I. (2018). Managing organisational knowledge through recruitment: Searching and selecting embodied competencies. *Journal of Knowledge Management*, *22*(1), 183–200. doi:10.1108/JKM-12-2016-0541

Jung, J. (2019). The fourth industrial revolution, knowledge production and higher education in South Korea. *Journal of Higher Education Policy and Management*, *42*(2), 134–156. doi:10.1080/1360080X.2019.1660047

Justa, M., Barreiros, N. (2009). Técnicas de Gestão do Sistema Toyota de Produção. *Revista Gestão Industrial*, *5*(1), 1-17.

Kagermann, H., Wahlster, W., & Helbig, J. (2013). *Recommendations for implementing the strategic initiative INDUSTRIE 4.0.* Obtido de https://www.din.de/blob/76902/e8cac883f42bf28536e7e8165993f1fd/recommendations-for-implementing-industry-4-0-data.pdf

Kagermann, H., Wahlster, W., & Helbig, J. (2013). *Recommendations for Implementing the Strategic Initiative Industrie 4.0: Final Report of the Industrie 4.0 Working Group.* Acatech-National Academy of Science and Engineering.

Kankaanpää, T., Shamsuzzoha, A., Carneiro, L., Almeida, R., Helo, P., Fornasiero, R., ... Chiodi, A. (2016). Methodology for non-hierarchical collaboration networks for complex products manufacturing. *2010 IEEE International Technology Management Conference, ICE 2010*. 10.1109/ICE.2010.7477018

Karlusch, A., Sachsenhofer, W., & Reinsberger, K. (2018). Educating for the development of sustainable business models: Designing and delivering a course to foster creativity. *Journal of Cleaner Production*, *179*, 169–179. doi:10.1016/j.jclepro.2017.12.199

Katzenbach, J. R., & Smith, D. K. (1993). The Discipline of Teams. *Harvard Business Review, 71*(2), 111-20.

Keen & Scott-Morton. (1978). *Decision Support Systems*. Addison-Wesley.

Kerem, K., & Sternad, D. (2011). Deal of the day at cherry. *Emerald Emerging Markets Case Studies*, *1*(3), 1–13. doi:10.1108/20450621111170630

Khalil, O. E. M., & Shea, T. (2012). Knowledge Sharing Barriers and Effectiveness at a Higher Education Institution. *International Journal of Knowledge Management*, *8*(2), 43–64. doi:10.4018/jkm.2012040103

Khanna, M., & Anton, W.R.Q. (2002). Corporate environmental management: regulatory and market base dincentives. *Land Economics*, *78*(4), 539-558.

Kholif, A. M., Abou El Hassan, D. S., Khorshid, M. A., Elsherpieny, E. A., & Olafadehan, O. A. (2018). Implementation of model for improvement (PDCA-cycle) in dairy laboratories. *Journal of Food Safety*, *38*(3), e12451. doi:10.1111/jfs.12451

Kissflow. (2020, June 8). Retrieved from https://kissflow.com/news/kissflow-launches-remoteplus/

Kling, R., & Lamb, R. (1999, Setembro). IT and Organiacional Change in Digital Economies. *A Socio-Technical Approach*, 17-25.

Kolberg, D., Knobloch, J., & Zühlke, D. (2017). Towards a lean automation interface for workstations. *International Journal of Production Research*, *55*(10), 2845–2856. doi:10.1080/00207543.2016.1223384

Košir, S. (2014). The Role of Knowledge Management and Internal Communication for a Better Quality Assurance in Higher Education Institution. *Literacy Information and Computer Education Journal*, *5*(3), 1641–1648. doi:10.20533/licej.2040.2589.2014.0219

Kotler, P., Kartajaya, H., & Setiawan, I. (2017). *Marketing 4.0*. Conjuntura Atual.

Kotter, J. P. (2012). Accelerate! *Harvard Business Review*, *90*(11), 44–52. PMID:23155997

Kraemmerand, P., Møller, C., & Boer, H. (2003). ERP implementation: An integrated process of radical change and continuous learning. *Production Planning and Control*, *14*(4), 338–348. doi:10.1080/0953728031000117959

Kramer, J. W., & Braxton, J. M. (2017). Contributions to Types of Professional Knowledge by Higher Education Journals. *New Directions for Higher Education*, *2017*(178), 9–20. doi:10.1002/he.20230

Kraus, S., Clauss, T., Breier, M., Zardini, A., & Tiberius, V. (2020). The economics of COVID-19: initial empirical evidence on how family firms in five European countries cope with the corona crisis. *International Journal of Entrepreneurial Behaviour and Research.*

Kriegesmann, B., Kley, T., & Schwering, M. G. (2005). Creative errors and heroic failures: capturing their innovative potential. *Journal of Business Strategy, 26*(3), 57-64. doi:10.1108/02756660510597119

Kritzinger, W., Karner, M., Traar, G., Henjes, J., & Sihn, W. (2018). Digital Twin in manufacturing: A categorical literature review and classification. *IFAC-PapersOnLine*, *51*(11), 1016–1022. doi:10.1016/j.ifacol.2018.08.474

Kryger Aggerholm, H., Esmann Andersen, S., & Thomsen, C. (2011). Conceptualising employer branding in sustainable organisations. *Corporate Communications*, *16*(2), 105–123. https://doi.org/10.1108/13563281111141642

Kumar, V., Loonam, J., Allen, J. P., & Sawyer, S. (2016). Exploring enterprise social systems & organisational change: Implementation in a digital age. *Journal of Information Technology*, *31*(2), 97–100. doi:10.1057/jit.2016.13

Kundinger. (2017). *6 Common Smart Sensors and Their IIoT Applications*. https://kundinger.com/6-common-smart-sensors-iiot-applications/

Kurzweil, R. (1990). *The Age of Intelligent Machines*. MIT Press.

Kwon, H., & Hong, P. (2015). Comparative efficiency assessment and strategic benchmarking of smartphone providers with data envelopment analysis. *International Journal of Productivity and Quality Management*, *15*(2), 185–202. doi:10.1504/IJPQM.2015.067762

Lab, O. (2018). *Inteligência Artificial*. Retrieved Jan 20, from https://observador.pt/explicadores/inteligencia-artificial/

Lab, O. (2018). *Observador*. Obtido de Inteligência Artificial: https://observador.pt/explicadores/inteligencia-artificial/

Lacy, P., Haines, A., & Hayward, R. (2012). Developing strategies and leaders to succeed in a new era of sustainability: Findings and insights from the United Nations global compact-accenture CEO study. *Journal of Management Development*, *31*(4), 346–357. doi:10.1108/02621711211218997

Ladan, M. T. (2012). The imperatives of industrial harmony and academic excellence in a productive educational system. The National Orientation Agency, University of Calabar.

Laihonen, H., & Mäntylä, S. (2018). Strategic knowledge management and evolving local government. *Journal of Knowledge Management*, *22*(1), 219–234. doi:10.1108/JKM-06-2017-0232

Lasi, H., Peter, F., Thomas, F., & Hoffmann, M. (2014). Industry 4.0. *Business & Information Systems Engineering*, *6*(4), 239–242. doi:10.100712599-014-0334-4

Laudon, K. C., & Laudon, J. P. (2014). Managment Information Systems - Managing the Digital Firm (13th ed.). Pearson.

Laudon, K. C., & Laudon, J. P. (2002). *Management information systems*. Pearson Publications.

Lawler, A., & Sillitoe, J. (2013). Facilitating "organisational learning" in a "learning institution.". *Journal of Higher Education Policy and Management*, *35*(5), 495–500. doi:10.1080/1360080X.2013.825415

Learning Objectives - Lean Fundamentals - Let's Start Lean. (n.d.). Consulted on: August 8 2019, on: https://www.moresteam.com/University

Lebedyk, L. (2020). Measures of Pedagogical Competence Teachers of Higher Education Institution. *Image of The Modern Pedagogue*, *1*(1), 29–33. doi:10.33272/2522-9729-2020-1(190)-29-33

Lee, J., Kao, H.-A., & Yang, S. (2014). Service innovation and smart analytics for Industry 4.0 and big data environment. *Procedia CIRP*, (16), 3-8. Obtido em 2020, de https://www.sciencedirect.com/science/article/pii/S2212827114000857?via%3Dihub

Lee, I. (2011). Overview of emerging web 2.0-based business models and web 2.0 applications in businesses: An ecological perspective. *International. Journal of Business Research*, *7*(4), 1–16. doi:10.4018/jebr.2011100101

Lee, J. T., & Kuzhabekova, A. (2019). Building local research capacity in higher education: A conceptual model. *Journal of Higher Education Policy and Management*, *41*(3), 342–357. doi:10.1080/1360080X.2019.1596867

Lee, S. Y. (2008). Drivers for the participation of small and medium-sized suppliers in green supply chain initiatives. *Supply Chain Management*, *13*(3), 185–198.

Legner, C., Eymann, T., & Hess, T. (2017). *Digitalization: opportunity and challenge for the business and information systems engineering community*. Academic Press.

Lieberwitz, R. L. (2005). What social responsibility for the corporation? A report on the united states. *Managerial Law*, *47*(5), 4–19.

Liker, J. F. (2004). *The Toyota Way - 14 Management Principles from the World's Greatest Manufacturer*. McGraw-Hill.

Liker, J. F., & Meirer, D. P. (2007). *Toyota Talent - Developing your People The Toyota Way*. McGraw-Hill.

Li, L. (2017). China's manufacturing locus in 2025: With a comparison of "Made-in-China 2025" and "Industry 4.0". *Technological Forecasting and Social Change*. Advance online publication. doi:10.1016/j.techfore.2017.05.028

Li, M., & Lin, K. A. (2011). New Paradigm of Organizational Transformation: Enacting Wholeness Praxis in the Oneness of Problem and Possibility. *Systemic Practice and Action Research*, *24*, 107–132. https://doi.org/10.1007/s11213-010-9179-z

Lindblom, C. E. (1959). The science of 'muddling through'. *Public Administration Review*, *19*(2), 79–88.

Lin, J., Li, L., Luo, X., & Benitez, J. (2020). How do agribusinesses thrive through complexity? The pivotal role of e-commerce capability and business agility. *Decision Support Systems*, *135*(June), 113342. doi:10.1016/j.dss.2020.113342 PMID:32834263

Link, K. (2005). *Magic for Beginners*. Small Beer Press.

Lisichkina, N.V., & Goloktionova, Y. G. (2015). Synergetics as a way to solve forecast problems of complex social-economic systems. *Fundamental Research*, *7*(2), 413 – 417.

Lobo, M.-J., Pietriga, E., & Appert, C. (2015). An evaluation of interactive map comparison techniques. In *Proceedings of the 33rd Annual ACM Conference on Human Factors in Computing Systems - CHI '15* (pp.3573–3582). ACM Press. 10.1145/2702123.2702130

Locher, D. (2011). *Lean Office and Service Simplified The Definitive How to Guide*. Academic Press.

Lojkine, J. (2002). *The Informational Revolution*. Cortez.

Loonam, J., Eaves, S., Kumar, V., & Parry, G. (2018). Towards digital transformation: Lessons learned from traditional organizations. *Strategic Change*, *27*(2), 101–109. doi:10.1002/jsc.2185

Loonam, J., Kumar, V., Mitra, A., & Abd Razak, A. (2018). Critical success factors for the implementation of enterprise systems: A literature review. *Strategic Change*, *27*(3), 185–194. doi:10.1002/jsc.2194

Loonam, J., McDonagh, J., Kumar, V., & O'Regan, N. (2014). Top managers & information systems:'Crossing the Rubicon'! *Strategic Change*, *23*(3-4), 205–224. doi:10.1002/jsc.1971

Loonam, J., Zwiegelaar, J., Kumar, V., & Booth, C. (2020). Cyber-Resiliency for Digital Enterprises: A Strategic Leadership Perspective. *IEEE Transactions on Engineering Management*, 1–14. doi:10.1109/TEM.2020.2996175

Lopes de Sousa Jabbour, A. B. (2019). Going in circles: New business models for efficiency and value. *The Journal of Business Strategy*, *40*(4), 36–43. doi:10.1108/JBS-05-2018-0092

Lopes, I., Senra, P., Vilarinho, S., Sá, V., Teixeira, C., Lopes, J., Alves, A., Oliveira, J. A., & Figueiredo, M. (2016). Requirements specification of a computerized maintenance management system – a case study. *Procedia CIRP*, *52*, 268–273. www.sciencedirect.com. doi:10.1016/j.procir.2016.07.047

López-Meneses, E., Vázquez-Cano, E., González-Zamar, M.-D., & Abad-Segura, E. (2020). Socioeconomic Effects in Cyberbullying: Global Research Trends in the Educational Context. *International Journal of Environmental Research and Public Health, 17*(12), 4369. doi:10.3390/ijerph17124369 PMID:32570762

Losey, M., Meisinger, S., & Ulrich, D. (2005). *The Future of Human Resource Management, Hoboken.* John Wiley and Sons, Inc.

Lo, W. Y. W., & Tang, H.-H. H. (2019). Chasing Phantoms? Innovation policy, higher education and the pursuit of a knowledge economy in Hong Kong. *Journal of Higher Education Policy and Management, 42*(2), 178–193. doi:10.1080/1360080X.2019.1687268

Luchesi, E. S. (2012). *Gestão do Conhecimentos nas organizações.* Academic Press.

Ludema, J., Cooperrider, D., & Barrett, F. (2001). Appreciative inquiry: The power of the unconditional positive question. Reason and Bradbury, 189–208.

Lupton, D. (2015). *Digital Sociology.* Routledge Taylor & Francis Group.

Lupton, D. (2016). The Diverse Domains of Quantified Selves: Self-tracking Modes and Dataveillance. *Economy and Society, 45*(1), 101–122. doi:10.1080/03085147.2016.1143726

Lupton, D. (2017). Williamson, Ben., (2017b) The Datafile child: The dataveillance of children and implications for their rights. *New Media & Society, 19*(5), 780–794. doi:10.1177/1461444816686328

Lupton, D. (2019a). "It's made me a lot more aware": A new materialist analysis of self-tracking health. *Media International Australia, 171*(1), 1–14. doi:10.1177/1329878X19844042

Lupton, D. (2019b). Data mattering and self-tracking: What can personal date do? *Continuum (Perth).* Advance online publication. doi:10.1080/10304312.2019.1691149

Lupton, D., & Michael, M. (2017a). 'Depends on Who's Got the Data': Public Understandings of Personal Digital Dataveillance. *Surveillance & Society, 15*(2), 254–268. doi:10.24908s.v15i2.6332

Lynch, L. (2005). *The relationship of lean manufacturing 5S principles to quality, productivity, and cycle time.* Walden University, ProQuest Dissertations Publishing.

Machado, L., & Neiva, E. (2017). *Práticas de gestão da mudança: Impacto nas atitudes e nos resultados percebidos.* Academic Press.

Madison, J., (2017). *Life Before the Presidency—Miller Center.* millercenter.org

Mahal, P. K. (2009). Organizational culture and organizational climate as a determinant of motivation. *IUP Journal of Management Research, 8*(10), 38.

Mahoney, J., & Pandian, J. R. (1992). The Resource-Based View Within The Conservation of Strategic Management. *Strategic Management Journal, 13*, 363–380. doi:10.1002mj.4250130505

Majidi, M. A. (1998). *Effect of Displacement on Organizational Commitment and Job Satisfaction.* Tarbiyat Modarres Press.

Malone, T. W., & Laubacher, R. J. (1999). The Dawn of the E-Lance Economy. *Wirtschaftsinformatik Proceedings, 2.* https://aisel.aisnet.org/wi1999/2

Mann, D. (2005). *Creating a lean culture: tools to sustain lean conversion*. New York: Productivity Press. Consulted on: July 5 2019, on: https://books.google.com.br/books?hl=ptPT&lr=&id=X_CsBAAAQBAJ&oi=fnd&pg=PP1&dq=lean+culture+change+management&ots=2YzJ3ivs2t&sig=ULpofWRXBuyT0temxNxb0QKvos#v=onepage&q=lean%20culture%20change%20management&f=false

Manyika, J., Chui, M., Brown, B., Bughin, J., Dobbs, R., Roxburgh, C., & Byers, A. H. (2011). *Big data: The next frontier for innovation, competition, and productivity*. McKinsey & Company. Obtido em 2020, de https://www.mckinsey.com/business-functions/mckinsey-digital/our-insights/big-data-the-next-frontier-for-innovation

March, J. G., & Olsen, J. P. (1976). *Ambiguity and Choice in Organizations*. University Press of Norway.

March, J. G., & Simon, H. A. (1958). *Organizations*. Wiley.

Marín-García, A., Gil-Saura, I., & Ruíz-Molina, M. E. (2020). How do innovation and sustainability contribute to generate retail equity? Evidence from Spanish retailing. *Journal of Product and Brand Management*, *29*(5), 601–615. doi:10.1108/JPBM-12-2018-2173

Markey, R., McIvor, J., & Wright, C. F. (2016). Employee participation and carbon emissions reduction in Australian workplaces. *International Journal of Human Resource Management*, *27*(2), 173–191.

Markus, M. L., & Benjamin, R. I. (1997). The magic bullet theory in IT-enabled transformation. *Sloan Management Review*, *38*(2), 55–68.

Markus, M. L., & Robey, D. (1988). Information Technology and Organisational Change: Causal Structure in Theory and Research. *Management Science*, *34*(5), 583–598. doi:10.1287/mnsc.34.5.583

Marques, P. C., & Cunha, P. F. (2014). Integrating product-service systems with new business models definition for manufacturing industries. *International Journal of Service Science, Management, Engineering, and Technology*, *5*(2), 66–86. doi:10.4018/ijssmet.2014040105

Martins, H. (2020). *Communications in times of crisis*. Popular Expression, Rosa Luxembourg Foundation.

Martins, J. (2010). *Gestão do Conhecimento: Criação e Transferência de Conhecimento*. Edições Sílabo.

Marx, K. (2008), Contribution to the critique of political economy (2nd ed.). São Paulo: Popular Expression.

Marx, G. T. (2015). Surveillance Studies. In N. J. Smelser & P. B. Baltes (Eds.), *International Encyclopedia of the Social & Behavioral Sciences* (2nd ed., pp. 733–741). Elsevier. doi:10.1016/B978-0-08-097086-8.64025-4

Marx, G. T. (2016). *Windows into the Soul: Surveillance and Society in at Age of High Technology. Chicago, Chicago, Chicago*. The University of Chicago Press. doi:10.7208/chicago/9780226286075.001.0001

Marx, K. (1976). *Le Capital, Critique de l'économie politique*. Socialeditions. (Original work published 1875)

Marx, K. (2011). *Grundrisse*. Boitempo.

Marx, K. (2013). *The capital: critique of political economy. Book I*. Boitempo.

Maske, N. B., & Valunjkar, S. (2020). Lean Construction Tool – A Literature Review. *International Research Journal of Engineering and Technology*, *7*(10), 143–145.

Maslach, C., & Leiter, M. P. (1997). *The truth about burnout: How organizations cause personal stress and what to do about it*. Jossey-Bass.

Mathapati, C. M. (2013). Green HRM: A strategic facet. *Tactful Management Research Journal*, *2*(2), 1–6.

Matt, C., Hess, T., & Benlian, A. (2015). Digital Transformation Strategies. *Business & Information Systems Engineering, 57*(5), 339–343. doi:10.100712599-015-0401-5

Matusik, S. (2002). Managing Public and Private Firm Knowledge within the context of Flexible Firm Boundaries. In C. W. Choo & N. Bontis (Eds.), *The strategic management of intellectual capital and organizational knowledge* (pp. 605–617). Oxford University Press.

McFarlan, F. W. (Ed.). (1984). *The information systems research challenge: Proceedings*. Harvard Business School Press.

McGrath, M. J., Scanaill, C. N., & Intel Labs Europe. (2013). *Sensor Technologies – Healthcare, wellness and environmental applications*. Apress Open. https://link.springer.com/content/pdf/10.1007%2F978-1-4302-6014-1.pdf

McKenney, J. L., & McFarlan, F. W. (1982). The information archipelago-maps and bridges. *Harvard Business Review, 60*(5), 109–119.

McKenzie, L. (2014). *Exploring the competitiveness of manufacturing organizations utilizing lean processes: A case study* (Doctoral Dissertation). Argosy University, Atlanta Campus College of Business.

McKinsey Global Institute. (2020, July 7). Retrieved from https://www.mckinsey.com/business-functions/organization/our-insights/reimagining-the-postpandemic-workforce

McKinsey Global Institute. (2020, November 23). Retrieved from https://www.mckinsey.com/featured-insights/future-of-work/whats-next-for-remote-work-an-analysis-of-2000-tasks-800-jobs-and-nine-countries

Meier, D., & Liker, J. (2005). *The Toyota Way Fieldbook*. McGraw Hill Professional.

Melton, T. (2005). The benefits of lean manufacturing: What lean thinking has to offer the process industries. *Chemical Engineering Research and Design, 83*(6A), 662–673. doi:10.1205/cherd.04351

Menard, A. (2017). *How can we recognize the real power of the Internet of Things?* McKinsey Consulting.

Menon, S. (2020). Organizational Agility Assessment for Higher Education Institution. *Journal of Research on the Lepidoptera, 51*(1), 561–573. doi:10.36872/LEPI/V51I1/301050

Mensah, J., & Enu-Kwesi, F. (2018). Implication of environmental sanitation management in the catchment area of Benya Lagoon, Ghana. *Journal of Integrative Environmental Sciences*.

Mercer, T. G., Kythreotis, A. P., Stolte, T., Robinson, Z. P., George, S. M., & Haywood, S. K. (2017). The use of educational game design and play in higher education to influence sustainable behaviour. *International Journal of Sustainability in Higher Education*.

Meulen, R. v., & Pettey, C. (2018, January 25). *Gartner*. Retrieved from www.gartner.com/en: https://www.gartner.com/en/newsroom/press-releases/2018-01-25-gartner-says-self-service-analytics-and-bi-users-will-produce-more-analysis-than-data-scientists-will-by-2019

Michellone, G., & Zollo, G. (2000). Competencies management in knowledge-based firms. *International Journal of Manufacturing Technology and Management, 1*(1), 20–41.

Mintzberg, H., Simons, R., & Basu, K. (2002). Beyond selfishness. *MIT Sloan Management Review, 44*(1), 67-74.

Mintzberg, H. (1990). The design school: Reconsidering the basic premises of strategic management. *Strategic Management Journal, 11*(3), 171–195. doi:10.1002mj.4250110302

Mir-fakhrae, T. (20009. Song of the silent discourse of advertising. In *Advertising Industry Conference Proceedings Persian*. Tehran: Ministry of Culture and Islamic Guidance, Propaganda Department.

Mishra, P. (2017). Green human resource management: A framework for sustainable organizational development in an emerging economy. *The International Journal of Organizational Analysis, 25*(5), 762–788. https://doi.org/10.1108/IJOA-11-2016-1079

Modarress, B., Ansari, A., & Lockwood, D. L. (2005). Kaizen costing for lean manufacturing: A case study. *International Journal of Production Research, 43*(9), 1751–1760. doi:10.1080/00207540500034174

Moeuf, A., Pellerin, R., Lamouri, S., Tamayo-Giraldo, S., & Barbaray, R. (2017, September 8). The Industrial Management of SMEs in the Era of Industry 4.0. *International Journal of Production Research.* Advance online publication. doi:10.1080/00207543.2017.1372647

Moghimi, M. (1999). *Organization and Management: a Research Approach.* Termeh Publication.

Montaldo, C. R. B. (2013). *Sustainable Development Approaches for Rural Development and Poverty Alleviation & Community Capacity Building for Rural Development and Poverty Alleviation.* Academic Press.

Moore, A. F., & Hawarden, V. (2020). Discovery digital health strategy: COVID-19 accelerates online health care in South Africa. *Emerald Emerging Markets Case Studies, 10*(3), 1–18. doi:10.1108/EEMCS-06-2020-0197

Moore, S. B., & Manring, S. L. (2009). Strategy development in small and medium sized enterprises for sustainability and increased value creation. *Journal of Cleaner Production, 17*(2), 276–282.

Moreira, J. M. (1999). *Ética, economia e política.* Lello & Irmãos Editores.

Morgan, G. (1997). *Images of Organisation.* SAGE.

Morgan, J., & Brenig-Jones, M. (2009). *Lean six-sigma for dummies.* West.

Motwani, J. (2003). business process change framework for examining lean manufacturing: Case study'. *Industrial Management & Data Systems, 103*(5), 339–346. doi:10.1108/02635570310477398

Mukhtar, M., Sudarmi, S., Wahyudi, M., & Burmansah, B. (2020). The Information System Development Based on Knowledge Management in Higher Education Institution. *International Journal of Higher Education, 9*(3), 98. doi:10.5430/ijhe.v9n3p98

Mumford, E. (1996). *Systems Design: Ethical Tools for Ethical Change.* Macmillan. doi:10.1007/978-1-349-14199-9

Murto, K. (1991). *Towards the well functiong community. Studies in education, psychology and social research.* University of Jyväskylä.

Nadella, S., Shaw, G., & Nichols, T. (2018). *Make Refresh: Microsoft's Soul Rediscovery and Creating a Better Future.* Vogais Publishing. (in Portuguese)

Nambisan, S., Wright, M., & Feldman, M. (2019). *The digital transformation of innovation and entrepreneurship: Progress, challenges and key themes.* Academic Press.

Narang, R. (2008). Some issues to consider in lean production. *2008 First International Conference on Emerging Trends in Engineering and Technology*, 749–753.

Nascimento, C., Hsu, P., Meneghatti, M., & Barzotto, L. (2017). *Inovação nos negócios por meio da Análise de Big data.* Obtido em 2020, de https://singep.org.br/6singep/resultado/333.pdf

Nasution, A. H., Aula, M., & Ardiantono, D. S. (2020). Circular economy business model design. *International Journal of Integrated Supply Management, 13*(2-3), 159–177. doi:10.1504/IJISM.2020.107848

Natasya, A., Wahaba, A., Mukhtara, M., & Sulaiman, R. (2013). A Conceptual Model of Lean Manufacturing Dimensions. *The 4th International Conference on Electrical Engineering and Informatics (ICEEI).* Consulted on: October 10 2020, on: https://www.sciencedirect.com/science/article/pii/S2212017313004817

Nechaev, V. V., Bogoradnikova, A. V., Panchenko, V. M., … Chumak, V. M. (2017). Psychological factor of objective knowledge control analysis. *Educational Resources and Technology*, 8–14. doi:10.21777/2312-5500-2017-1-8-14

Negri, E., Holgado, M., Wagner, D., Grefrath, C., & Macchi, M. (2013). Life cycle-based and triple bottom line assessment of sustainability impacts in product-service systems. *Proceedings of the Summer School Francesco Turco*, 139-144.

Neumann, W. P., Winkelhaus, S., Grosse, E. H., & Glock, C. H. (2021) (2021). Industry 4.0 and the human factor – A systems framework and analysis methodology for successful development. *International Journal of Production Economics*, 233.

Newell, S., Robertson, M., Scarbrough, H., & Swan, J. (2009). *Managing knowledge work and innovation.* Palgrave Macmillan. doi:10.1007/978-0-230-36641-1

Newey, L. R., Verreynne, M.-L., & Griffiths, A. (2012). The relationship between dynamic and operating capabilities as a stage-gate process: insights from radical innovation. *Journal of Management & Organization.*

Ng, A. W., Wong, A. K. L., & Wut, T. M. (2016). Second-movers' advantage of utilizing big data to enhance sustainability performance: The case of the elevator industry. *Proceedings of the International Conference on Industrial Engineering and Operations Management*, 2569-2579.

NICE. (2009, November 5). Retrieved from https://www.nice.org.uk/guidance/ph22/chapter/1-Recommendations

Niosi, J., & McKelvey, M. (2018). Relating business model innovations and innovation cascades: The case of biotechnology. *Journal of Evolutionary Economics*, *28*(5), 1081–1109. doi:10.100700191-018-0561-9 PMID:30613125

Nissenbaum, H. (2010). *Privacidad amenazada. Tecnología, política y la integridad de la vida social.* Ocean.

Nnazor, R., & Borrero, A. (1996). The University as an Institution Today. *The Journal of Higher Education*, *67*(4), 476. doi:10.2307/2943808

Nonaka, I. & Toyama, R. (2005). The theory of the knowledge-creating firm: subjectivity, objectivity and synthesis. *Industrial and Corporate Change, 14*(3), 419-436.

Nonaka, I. (1991). A empresa criadora de conhecimento. *Harvard Business Review*, 11.

Nonaka, I. (1994). A dynamic theory of organizational knowledge creation. *Organization Science*, *5*(1), 14–37. doi:10.1287/orsc.5.1.14

Nonaka, I., & Takeuchi, H. (1995). *The Knowledge Creating Company: How Japanese Companies create the dynamics of innovation.* Oxford University Press.

Nonaka, I., & Takeuchi, H. (1995). *The knowledge-creating company: How Japanese companies create the dynamics of innovation.* Oxford university press.

NOS. (2021). Retrieved January 3, 2021, from https://www.nos.pt/

Nosratabadi, S., Mosavi, A., Shamshirband, S., Kazimieras Zavadskas, E., Rakotonirainy, A., & Chau, K. W. (2019). Sustainable business models: A review. *Sustainability*, *11*(6), 1663. doi:10.3390u11061663

Novikova, E. N. (2013). *The rule of law as a challenge of time.* Thought.

O'Brien, J., & Marakas, G. M. (2011). *Management Information Systems.* Mcgraw-Hill.

O'Donohue, W., & Torugsa, N. (2016). The moderating effect of 'green' HRM on the association between proactive environmental management and financial performance in small firms. *International Journal of Human Resource Management, 27*(2), 239–261.

O'Neill, D. W., Fanning, A. L., Lamb, W. F., & Steinberger, J. K. (2018). A good life for all within planetary boundaries. *Nature Sustainability, 1*(2), 88–95. doi:10.103841893-018-0021-4

OECD - Organisation for Economic Co-operation and Development. (n.d.). Retrieved March 7, 2021, from https://www.oecd.org/

OECD. (2016). *Skills Matter: Further Results from the Survey of Adult Skills. OECD Skills Studies*. OECD Publishing. doi:10.1787/9789264258051-

Ohno, T. (1988). *Toyota Production System: Beyond Large-Scale Production*. CRC Press.

Ohno, T. (1997). *Toyota Production System*. Productivity Press.

Oliveira, A. (2017). *Information Systems Governance in Economy 4.0 - Who (and how) is in charge for the Information Systems Governance in Economy 4.0 - really?* Intervention in the context of the 9th International Conference of the European Club for the Governance of Information Systems, Lisbon, Portugal.

Ones, D. S., & Dilchert, S. (2012). Environmental sustainability at work: A call to action. *Industrial and Organizational Psychology: Perspectives on Science and Practice, 5*(4), 444–466.

Opatha, H. H. D. N. P., & Arulrajah, A. A. (2014). Green human resource management: Simplified general reflections. *International Business Research, 7*(8), 101.

Orlikowski, W. J., & Baroudi, J. J. (1991). Studying information technology in organizations: Research approaches and assumptions. *Information Systems Research, 2*(1), 1–28. doi:10.1287/isre.2.1.1

Orr, S. (2019). Democratizing Knowledge in Art and Design Education. Art. *Design & Communication in Higher Education, 18*(2), 131–133. doi:10.1386/adch_00001_2

Osterloh, M., & Frey, B. S. (2000). Motivation, knowledge transfer, and organizational forms. *Organization Science, 11*(5), 538–550.

Padioleau, J. (1989). *L'E'thique est-elle un Outil de Gestion?* Revue Française de Gestion. Juin-Julliet-Aout.

Paillé, P., Chen, Y., Boiral, O., & Jin, J. (2014). The impact of human resource management on environmental performance: an employee-level study. *Journal of Business Ethics, 121*(3), 451-466.

Paine, L. (1994). *Managing for Organizational Integrity*. Harvard Business Review.

Pajula, T., Behm, K., Vatanen, S., & Saarivuori, E. (2017). Managing the life cycle to reduce environmental impacts. In Dynamics of long-life assets: From technology adaptation to upgrading the business model (pp. 93-113). doi:10.1007/978-3-319-45438-2_6

Panwar, A., Jain, R., Rathore, A. P. S., Nepal, B., & Lyons, A. C. (2018). The impact of lean practices on operational performance–an empirical investigation of Indian process industries. *Production Planning and Control, 29*(2), 158–169. doi:10.1080/09537287.2017.1397788

Papadopoulos, I., Karagouni, G., Trigkas, M., & Beltsiou, Z. (2014). Mainstreaming green product strategies why and how furniture companies integrate environmental sustainability? *EuroMed Journal of Business, 9*(3), 293–317. doi:10.1108/EMJB-12-2013-0058

Parker, G. G., Van Alstyne, M. W., & Choudary, S. P. (2016). *Platform revolution: How networked markets are transforming the economy and how to make them work for you.* WW Norton & Company.

Parker, G., Van Alstyne, M., & Choudary, S. (2016). *Platform Revolution: How Networked Markets Are Transforming the Economy and How to Make Them Work for You.* W. W. Norton & Company.

Parr, A. N., & Shanks, G. 2000, January. A taxonomy of ERP implementation approaches. In *Proceedings of the 33rd Annual Hawaii International Conference on System Sciences.* IEEE. 10.1109/HICSS.2000.926908

Patel, K. K., & Patel, S. M. (2016). Internet of Things-IOT: Definition, Characteristics, Architecture, Enabling Technologies, Application & Future Challenges. *International Journal of Engineering Science and Computing.*

Patterson, M. G., West, M. A., Shackleton, V. J., Dawson, J. F., Lawthom, R., Maitlis, S., Robinson, D. L., & Wallace, A. M. (2005). Validating the organizational climate measure: Links to managerial practices, productivity and innovation. *Journal of Organizational Behavior, 26*(4).

Patzelt, H., & Shepherd, D. A. (2011). Recognizing opportunities for sustainable development. *Entrepreneurship Theory and Practice, 35*(4), 631–652. doi:10.1111/j.1540-6520.2010.00386.x

Pedersen, E. R. G., Earley, R., & Andersen, K. R. (2019). From singular to plural: Exploring organizational complexities and circular business model design. *Journal of Fashion Marketing and Management, 23*(3), 308–326. doi:10.1108/JFMM-04-2018-0062

Pedersen, E. R. G., & Netter, S. (2015). Collaborative consumption: Business model opportunities and barriers for fashion libraries. *Journal of Fashion Marketing and Management, 19*(3), 258–273. doi:10.1108/JFMM-05-2013-0073

Peña-Montoya, C., Bouzon, M., Torres-Lozada, P., & Vidal-Holguin, J. (2016). Lean Manufacturing and Sustainability: An Integrated View. *IFIP Advances in Information and Communication Technology*, 659–666. doi:10.1007/978-3-319-51133-7

Penrod, J. I., & Witte, R. (1988). IAIMS infrastructure: Technological base. *Journal of the American Society for Information Science, 39*(2), 118–125. doi:10.1002/(SICI)1097-4571(198803)39:2<118::AID-ASI10>3.0.CO;2-R PMID:10286231

Penrose, E. (1959). *The Theory of the Growth of the Firm.* Basil Blackwell.

Perkmann, M., Tartari, V., McKelvey, M., Autio, E., Broström, A., D'Este, P., ... Krabel, S. (2013). Academic engagement and commercialisation: A review of the literature on university–industry relations. *Research Policy, 42*(2), 423–442. doi:10.1016/j.respol.2012.09.007

Peters, M. A. (2016). Technological unemployment: Educating for the fourth industrial revolution. *Educational Philosophy and Theory, 49*(1), 1–6. Retrieved January 8, 2021, from. doi:10.1080/00131857.2016.1177412

Petrini, M., De Freitas, C. S., & Da Silveira, L. M. (2017). A proposal for a typology of sharing economy. *Revista De Administracao Mackenzie, 18*(5), 39–62. doi:10.1590/1678-69712017/administracao.v18n5p39-62

Pettigrew, A. M., Woodman, R. W., & Cameron, K. S. (2001). Studying organizational change and development: Challenges for future research. *Academy of Management Journal, 44*(4), 697–713.

Pfeffer, J. (1994). *Competitive Advantage through People Unleashing the Power of the Workforce.* Harvard Business School Press.

Phillips, L. (2007). Go green to gain the edge over rivals. *People Management*, p. 9. Available at: www2.cipd.co.uk/pm/peoplemanagement/b/weblog/archive/2013/01/29/gogreentogaintheedgeoverrivals-2007-08.aspx

Pinto, J. P. (2010). Gestão de Operações Na Indústria e nos Serviços (3rd ed.). Lisboa: Lidel -Edições Tecnica Lda.

Pinto, C. J. (2016). *Impactos organizacionais, informacionais e tecnológicos da implementação da Diretiva 2010/65/EU (dissertação de mestrado).* Instituto Politécnico de Setúbal. Escola Superior de Ciências Empresariais.

Pinto, J. P. (2014). *Pensamento Lean-A filosofia das organizações vencedoras.* Lidel.

Pires, L. (2016). *Cyber-physical systems: the future of Industrial Maintenance?* Retrieved Nov 13, from https://www.researchgate.net/profile/Luis_Pires12/publication/309780775_Sistemas_ciber-fisicos_o_futuro_da_Manutencao_Industrial/links/5bfe8355a6fdcc1b8d4872ff/Sistemas-ciber-fisicos-o-futuro-da-Manutencao-Industrial.pdf

Pires, L. (2016). *Sistemas ciber-físicos: o futuro da Manutenção Industrial?* Obtido em 2020, de https://www.researchgate.net/profile/Luis_Pires12/publication/309780775_Sistemas_ciber-fisicos_o_futuro_da_Manutencao_Industrial/links/5bfe8355a6fdcc1b8d4872ff/Sistemas-ciber-fisicos-o-futuro-da-Manutencao-Industrial.pdf

Pitt, M., Tucker, M., Riley, M., & Longden, J. (2009). Towards sustainable construction: Promotion and best practices. *Construction Innovation, 9*(2), 201–224.

Płachciak, A. (2009). Sustainable development - The way of building just society. *Economia e Sociologia, 2*(1), 105–110. doi:10.14254/2071-789X.2009/2-1/10

Plenert, G. (2007). Reinventing Lean: Introducing Lean Management into the Supply Chain. Elsevier.

Plewnia, F., & Guenther, E. (2018). Mapping the sharing economy for sustainability research. *Management Decision, 56*(3), 570–583. doi:10.1108/MD-11-2016-0766

Polesie, T., & Birkin, F. (Eds.). (2019). *Intrinsic Capability: Implementing Intrinsic Sustainable Development for an Ecological Civilisation.* World Scientific. doi:10.1142/9789813225589

Popescu, D. I., Popa, I., Ştefan, S. C., & Vlăsceanu, C. (2016). Innovative Business Models and Responsible Consumption–Case Study. *28th IBIMA Conference, Vision 2020: Innovation Management, Development Sustainability, and Competitive Economic Growth*, 4275-4290.

Porter, M. E. (1993). A Vantagem Competitiva das Nações. Rio de Janeiro: Campus.

Porter, M.E. (1998). On competition. Boston: Harvard Business School Publishing.

Porter, M.E., & Millar, V.E. (1985). *How information gives you competitive advantage.* Academic Press.

Porter, M. E., & Heppelmann, J. E. (2014). How smart, connected products are transforming competition. *Harvard Business Review, 92*(11), 64–88.

Porter, M. E., & Heppelmann, J. E. (2015). How smart, connected products are transforming companies. *Harvard Business Review, 93*(10), 96–114.

Postmes, T. (2003). A social identity approach to communication in organizations. *Social identity at work: Developing theory for organizational practice, 81*, 191-203.

Powell, L., & Tilt, C. (2017). The examination of power and politics in a conservation organization. *Accounting, Auditing & Accountability Journal, 30*(3), 482–509. doi:10.1108/AAAJ-01-2015-1933

Racy, J., Moura, A., & Scarano, P. (n.d.). O Desenvolvimento Do Conceito De Empresa Na Teoria Econômica: Uma Revisão Das Principais Contribuições. *Revista de Economia Mackenzie, 3*(3), 154-17. Retrieved January 8, 2021, from https://biblat.unam.mx/hevila/RevistadeeconomiaMackenzie/2005/vol3/no3/7.pdf

Rahman, N. A. A., Sharif, S. M., & Esa, M. M. (2013). Lean Manufacturing Case Study with Kanban System Implementation. *Procedia Economics and Finance, 7*(Icebr), 174–180. doi:10.1016/S2212-5671(13)00232-3

Ramanathan, R., Duan, Y., Ajmal, T., Dong, F., Ransbeeck, S. V., Valverde, J. M. M., & Valverde, S. B. (2019). IoT sensors in aquaculture-barriers and facilitators for sustainability in the brazilian context. *Proceedings of the International Conference on Industrial Engineering and Operations Management*, 465-467.

Ramus, C. A. (2002). Encouraging innovative environmental actions: What companies and managers must do. *Journal of World Business*, *37*(2), 151–164.

Rance, S., Rudd, C., Lacy, S., & Hanna, A. (2011). *ITIL Service Management* - (2011 Edition). TSO - The Stationery Office.

Rantala, T., Ukko, J., Saunila, M., & Havukainen, J. (2018). The effect of sustainability in the adoption of technological, service, and business model innovations. *Journal of Cleaner Production*, *172*, 46–55. doi:10.1016/j.jclepro.2017.10.009

Rascão, J. P. (2008). Novos desafios da gestão da informação. Lisboa: Edições Sílabo.

ReadM. (2020, April 29). Retrieved from https://www.wpp.com/-/media/project/wpp/images/investors/2020/annual-report/download-files/wpp_annual_report_2019_strategic_report-2.pdf?la=en

Recommendation and Guidelines on establishing a Single Window. (2005). United Nations Centre for Trade Facilitation and Electronic Business.

Redington, I. (2005). Making CSR Happen: the contribution of people management. In C. I. O. P. A. Development (Ed.), *The Virtuous Circle*. Chartered Institute of Personnel and Development.

Rehman, U. U., & Iqbal, A. (2020). Nexus of knowledge-oriented leadership, knowledge management, innovation and organizational performance in higher education. *Business Process Management Journal*, *26*(6), 1731–1758. Advance online publication. doi:10.1108/BPMJ-07-2019-0274

Reich, B. H., & Benbasat, I. (2000). Factors that influence the social dimension of alignment between business and information technology objectives. *Management Information Systems Quarterly*, *24*(1), 81–113. doi:10.2307/3250980

Repsol. (2021). Retrieved January 3, 2021, from https://www.repsol.pt/

Requeijo, J. F., & Pereira, Z. L. (2008). *QUALIDADE: Planeamento e Controlo Estatístico de Processos*. Prefácio.

Resolução do conselho de ministros nº 175/2017 Diário da República – Nº 227/2017, Série I de 2017-11-24. Estratégia para o aumento da competitividade da rede de portos comerciais do continente – Horizonte 2026

Retamal, M. (2019). Collaborative consumption practices in Southeast Asian cities: Prospects for growth and sustainability. *Journal of Cleaner Production*, *222*, 143–152. doi:10.1016/j.jclepro.2019.02.267

Retchless, D. P., & Brewer, C. A. (2016). Guidance for representing uncertainty on global temperature change maps. *International Journal of Climatology*, *36*(3), 1143–1159. doi:10.1002/joc.4408

Revista critica de Ciências Sociais. (2021). Retrieved December 18, 2020, from https://journals.openedition.org/rccs/956

Rezaeian Fordoie, S. (2014). *Innovation, Innovation System and Needs*. Secretary of the High Council of the Cultural Revolution.

Rickards, T., Smaje, K., & Sohoni, V. (2015). *'Transformer in chief': The new chief digital officer*. McKinsey Consulting.

Rifkin, J. (2000). *The Age of Access*. Puntnam.

Robertson, J. L., & Barling, J. (2013). Greening organizations through leaders' influence on employees' pro environmental behaviors. *Journal of Organizational Behavior*, *34*(2), 176–194.

Rohrbeck, R., Konnertz, L., & Knab, S. (2013). Collaborative business modeling for systemic and sustainability innovations. *International Journal of Technology Management, 63*(1-2), 4–23. doi:10.1504/IJTM.2013.055577

Romero, F., & Araújo, J. (2015). *A gestão da informação do conhecimento organizacional das empresas*. Academic Press.

Roome, N., & Louche, C. (2016). Journeying toward business models for sustainability: A conceptual model found inside the black box of organizational transformation. *Organization & Environment, 29*(1), 11–35. doi:10.1177/1086026615595084

Roos, S., Zamani, B., Sandin, G., Peters, G. M., & Svanström, M. (2016). A life cycle assessment (LCA)-based approach to guiding an industry sector towards sustainability: The case of the Swedish apparel sector. *Journal of Cleaner Production, 133*, 691–700. doi:10.1016/j.jclepro.2016.05.146

Rosa, P., Sassanelli, C., & Terzi, S. (2018). Circular economy in action: uncovering the relation between Circular Business Models and their expected benefits. In 23rd Summer School" Francesco Turco"-Industrial Systems Engineering 2018 (pp. 228-235). Academic Press.

Rosari, R. (2019). Leadership Definitions Applications for Lectures' Leadership Development, *Journal of Leadership in Organizations*. doi:10.22146/jlo.42965

Rosário, A. (2021). Research-Based Guidelines for Marketing Information Systems. *International Journal of Business Strategy and Automation, 2*(1), 1–16. doi:10.4018/IJBSA.20210101.oa1

Rosário, A., & Cruz, R. (2019). Determinants of Innovation in Digital Marketing, Innovation Policy and Trends in the Digital Age. *Journal of Reviews on Global Economics, 8*, 1722–1731. doi:10.6000/1929-7092.2019.08.154

Rosário, A., Fernandes, F., Raimundo, R., & Cruz, R. (2021). Determinants of Nascent Entrepreneurship Development. In A. Carrizo Moreira & J. G. Dantas (Eds.), *Handbook of Research on Nascent Entrepreneurship and Creating New Ventures* (pp. 172–193). IGI Global. doi:10.4018/978-1-7998-4826-4.ch008

Rossetti, A., & Morales, A. B. (2007). O papel da tecnologia da informação na gestão do conhecimento. *Ciência da Informação*. doi:10.15900100-19652007000100009

Rousseau, R., & Ye, F. (2012). Basic independence axioms for the publication-citation system. *Journal of Scientometric Research, 1*(1), 22–27. doi:10.5530/jscires.2012.1.6

Røvik, K. A. (2011). From fashion to virus: An alternative theory of organizations' handling of management ideas. *Organization Studies, 32*(5), 631–653.

Russell, S. J., & Norvig, P. (2016). *Artificial Intelligence - A Modern Approach*. Pearson Education Limited.

Ryabova, Z. (2019). Knowledge Management in Development of a Project-Oriented Education Institute. *Image of The Modern Pedagogue, 1*(5), 25–28. doi:10.33272/2522-9729-2019-5(188)-25-28

Sabaté, F. T. (1989). *Fundamentals of Economics de la Empresa* (2nd ed.). Librería Hispano Americana.

Sabherwal, R. & Becerra-Fernandez, I. (2003). An Empirical Study of the Effect of Knowledge Management Processes at Individual, Group, and Organizational. *Decision Sciences, 34*(2), 225-260.

Sacavém, A., Cruz, R., Sousa, M., & Rosário, A. (2019). An integrative literature review on leadership models for innovative organizations, innovation policy and trends in the digital age. *Journal of Reviews on Global Economics, 8*, 1741–1751. doi:10.6000/1929-7092.2019.08.156

Santos, A. D. G. (2018). Interview given to Paulo Victor Melo. *Eptic: network of political economy of information, communication, and culture*. Available in: http://eptic.com.br/entrevista-com-anderson-santos-presidente-da-ulepicc-brasil/

Santos, F. R. L. (2017), Intellectual vices and social networks: does constant access to information make us intellectually vicious? Veritas, 62(3), 657-682.

Santos, A. D. G., & Mota, J. S. (2020). 10 years of ULEPICC-Br: Contributions to EPC from its events and its praxis. *EPTIC Magazine*, *16*(1), 57–75. doi:10.18617/liinc.51222

Santos, B. P., Alberto, A., Lima, T. D. F. M., & Charrua-Santos, F. M. B. (2018). Indústria 4.0: Desafios e Oportunidades. *Revista Produção e Desenvolvimento*, *4*(1), 111–124.

Santos, E. A. (2013). Credit to death: The decomposition of capitalism and its criticisms, by Anselm Jappe. *Plural*, *20*(2), 219–222. doi:10.11606/issn.2176-8099.pcso.2013.76370

Savitz, A. W., & Weber, K. (2006). *The triple bottom line*. Jossey-Bass.

Say, A. L., Guo, R., & Chen, C. (2018). Disruption or new order? The emergence of the unicorn bike-sharing entrepreneurship in china. *PICMET 2018 - Portland International Conference on Management of Engineering and Technology: Managing Technological Entrepreneurship: The Engine for Economic Growth, Proceedings*. 10.23919/PICMET.2018.8481864

Schein, E. H. (1999). *Process consultation revisited: Building the helping relationship*. Addison-Wesley.

Schmiedinger, B., Valentin, K., & Stephan, E. (2005). Competence based business development-organizational competencies as basis for successful companies. *Journal of Universal Knowledge Management*, *1*, 13–20.

Schnitzler, T. (2019). The Bridge Between Education for Sustainable Development and Transformative Learning: Towards New Collaborative Learning Spaces. *Journal of Education for Sustainable Development*, *13*(2), 242–253. doi:10.1177/0973408219873827

Schoenherr, T. (2012). The role of environmental management in sustainable business development: A multi-country investigation. *International Journal of Production Economics*, *140*(1), 116–128. doi:10.1016/j.ijpe.2011.04.009

Schumacher, S., Bildstein, A., & Bauernhansl, T. (2020). The Impact of the Digital Transformation on Lean Production Systems. *53rd CIRP Conference on Manufacturing System*. 10.1016/j.procir.2020.03.066

Schütze, A., Helwig, N., & Schneider, T. (2018). Sensors 4.0 – smart sensors and measurement technology enable Industry 4.0. *Journal of Sensor Systems*, *7*, 359–371.

Schwarzmüller, T., Brosi, P., Duman, D., & Welpe, I. M. (2018). *How Does the Digital Transformation Affect Organizations? Key Themes of Change in Work Design and Leadership*. NOMOS. doi:10.5771/0935-9915-2018-2-114

Sebastian, I., Ross, J., Beath, C., Mocker, M., Moloney, K., & Fonstad, N. (2017). How big old companies navigate digital transformation. *MIS Quarterly Executive*, *16*(3).

Sen, S. K., & Ongsakul, V. (2017). Emerging frontiers in entrepreneurship through retail-E-business: 'centripetal momentum' engaged product life cycle model. *The Journal of Business and Retail Management Research*, *12*(1), 13–25. doi:10.24052/JBRMR/V12IS01/EFIETREBCMEPLCM

Seow, C., Hillary, R., Robinson, H. S., Anumba, C. J., Carrillo, P. M., & Al-Ghassani, A. M. (2006). STEPS: A knowledge management maturity roadmap for corporate sustainability. *Business Process Management Journal*.

Seppänen-Järvelä, R. (1999). Kehittämistyön luonne sosiaali- ja terveysalalla. Tutkimuksia 104, Helsinki: Stakes.

Serrano, A., & Fialho, C. (2003). *Gestão do Conhecimento – o novo paradigma das organizações*. FCA – Editora de Informática.

Shang, S., & Seddon, P. B. (2000). A comprehensive framework for classifying the benefits of ERP systems. AMCIS 2000 Proceedings, 39.

Shapiro, C., & Varian, H. R. (1999). *Information Rules - a Strategic Guide to the Network Economy*. Harvard Business School Press.

Sher, J. & Lee, C. (2004). Information Technology as a Facilitator for Enhancing Dynamic Capabilities through Knowledge Managements. *Information and Management, 41*(8), 933-945.

Shevchenko, I., Puchkina, E., & Tolstov, N. (2019). Shareholders' and Managers' Interests: Collisions in Russian Corporations. *Higher School of Economics Economic Journal, 23*(1), 118–142. doi:10.17323/1813-8691-2019-23-1-118-142

Shingo, S., & Ohno, T. (2017). *Fundamental Principles of Lean Manufacturing*. Productivity Press.

Shou, W., Wang, J., Wu, P., & Wang, X. (2020). Lean management framework for improving maintenance operation: Development and application in the oil and gas industry. *Production Planning and Control, 0*(0), 1–18. doi:10.1080/09537287.2020.1744762

Shrivastava, P. (1995). The role of corporations in achieving ecological sustainability. *Academy of Management Review, 20*(4), 936–960.

Silva, I. S., Veloso, A. L., & Keating, J. B. (2014). Focus group: Considerações teóricas e metodológicas. *Revista Lusófona de Educação*, 26.

Silva, R., & Neves, A. (2003). *Gestão de Empresas na Era do Conhecimento*. Edições Sílabo.

Sima, V., Gheorghe, I. G., Subic, J., & Nancu, D. (2020). *Influences of the Industry 4.0 Revolution on the Human Capital Development and Consumer Behavior: A Systematic Review*. Academic Press.

Sim, J., & Waterfield, J. (2019). Focus group methodology: Some ethical challenges. *Quality & Quantity, 53*(6), 3003–3022. Advance online publication. doi:10.100711135-019-00914-5

Singh, J., & Singh, H. (2009). Kaizen Philosophy: A Review of Literature. *ICFAI Journal of Operations Management, 8*(2), 51–72.

Slee, C., & Slovin, M. (1997). Legacy asset management. *Information Systems Management, 14*(1), 12–21. doi:10.1080/10580539708907024

Somogyi, E. K., & Galliers, R. D. (1987). Applied information technology: From data processing to strategic information systems. *Journal of Information Technology, 2*(1), 30–41. doi:10.1177/026839628700200107

Sonae. (2021). Retrieved January 3, 2021, from https://www.sonae.pt/

Sonnichsen, R. (2000). *High Impact Internal Evaluation. A Practitioner's Guide to Evaluating and Consulting Inside Organizations*. Sage.

Souza, M. (2018). *Como o impacto da utilização do Waze e Uber na Cidade de São Paulo, Brasil explica o fenómeno da quarta revolução industrial* (Tese de Mestrado, ISCTE Business School). Retrieved January 18, 2021, from https://repositorio.iscteiul.pt/bitstream/10071/18786/1/master_marcelo_anderson_souza.pdf

Souza, W. (2004). Conceito de Empresa: um Desafio que Persiste? *Revista do Tribunal Regional Federal da 1ª Região, 16*(5). Retrieved December 18, 2020, from https://core.ac.uk/download/pdf/16048427.pdf

Souza, O. (2003). *Ética Individual & Ética Profissional* (Vol. 3). ABC.

Srnicek, N., & Sutter, F. L. (2016). Platform Capitalism. Polity Press.

Starace, F. (2020). From national champion to global player. In The Italian Utilities Industry: Success Stories and Future Perspectives (pp. 71-83). doi:10.1007/978-3-030-37677-2_4

Stern, M.J., Powell, R.B. & Hill, D. (2014), Environmental education program evaluation in the new millennium: what do we measure and what have we learned? *Environmental Education Research, 20*(5), 581-611.

Stoddart, H., Schneeberger, K., Dodds, F., Shaw, A., Bottero, M., Cornforth, J., & White, R. (2011). *A pocket guide to sustainable development governance.* Stakeholder Forum 2011.

Stringer, L. (2009). *The Green Workplace: Sustainable Strategies That Benefit Employees, the Environment, and the Bottom Line*. Macmillan.

Subramanian, N., Abdulrahman, M. D., Wu, L., & Nath, P. (2016). Green competence framework: Evidence from China. *International Journal of Human Resource Management, 27*(2), 151–172.

Sun, W. (2008). Lean changes mindsets. *Industrial Engineering (American Institute of Industrial Engineers), 40.*

Sustainability for future growth: A key element of successful business strategies. (2012). *Strategic Direction, 28*(8), 6-8. doi:10.1108/02580541211249538

Sutton, H. (2018). Be proactive to make your institution fully accessible. *Disability Compliance for Higher Education, 23*(10), 1–5. doi:10.1002/dhe.30431

Svensson, L., & Brulin, G. (2013). Effects of programmes and projects. In L. Svensson, G. Brulin, S. Jansson, & K. Sjöberg (Eds.), *Capturing Effects of Projects and Programmes* (pp. 15–33). Studentlitteratur.

Symons, V. (1991). Impacts of Information Systems: Four Perspectives. *Information and Software Technology, 33*(3), 181–190. doi:10.1016/0950-5849(91)90132-U

Tadeu, H. F. B., & Silva, J. T. M. (2018). Improving productivity by adopting existing technologies and sustainability. In Handbook of Research on Strategic Innovation Management for Improved Competitive Advantage (pp. 331-341). doi:10.4018/978-1-5225-3012-1.ch018

Tan, M., & Morales-Arroyo, M. (2014). Understanding distributional disruptions in the interactive digital media eco-system. *International Journal of Electronic Business, 11*(1), 42–62. doi:10.1504/IJEB.2014.057900

TAP. (2021). Retrieved January 3, 2021, from https://www.tapairportugal.com/pt/

Tapscott. (2014). *The Digital Economy Anniversary Edition: Rethinking Promise and Peril in the Age of Networked Intelligence*. McGraw-Hill.

Tapscott, D., & Tapscott, A. (2016). *Blockchain Revolution: How the chnology behind bitcoin is changing Money, business, and the world.* Penguin Random House LLC.

Tariq, S., Jan, F. A., & Ahmad, M. S. (2016). Green employee empowerment: A systematic literature review on state-of-art in green human resource management. *Quality & Quantity, 50*(1), 237–269.

Teichler, U. (2002). Diversification of higher education and the profile of the individual institution. *Higher Education Management and Policy, 14*(3), 177–188. doi:10.1787/hemp-v14-art24-en

Teixeira, E. (2012). *Graus de maturidade da cultura lean do pólo metal-mecânico do nordeste de Santa Catarina* (Master's dissertation). Programa de Pós-Graduação do Instituto Superior Tupy IST/SOCIESC Sociedade Educacional de Santa Catarina, Joinville.

Teixeira, E., & Melim, J. (2014). *V Congresso de Sistemas LEAN 23 e 24 de maio de 2014.* UFRGS.

Teixeira, J. F. (1998). *Minds and machines: an introduction to cognitive science*. Medical Arts.

Teixeira, R. A., & Rotta, T. N. (2012). Valueless knowledge-commodities and financialization: Productive and financial dimensions of capital automatization. *The Review of Radical Political Economics*, *44*(4), 448–467. doi:10.1177/0486613411434387

Teresko, J. (2006). *Learning From Toyota - Again' Rebuilding U.S. Manufacturing* (Vol. 225). www.industryweek.com

Testani, M. V., & Ramakrishnan, S. (2012). Lean Leadership Readiness for Change: A Methodology for Lean Change Readiness and Continuous Improvement. *Proceedings of the 2012 Industrial and Systems Engineering Research Conference*.

Thakhathi, A., le Roux, C., & Davis, A. (2019). Sustainability Leaders' Influencing Strategies for Institutionalising Organisational Change towards Corporate Sustainability: A Strategy-as-Practice Perspective. *Journal of Change Management*, 246–265. doi:10.1080/14697017.2019.1578985

The Navigator Company. (2021). Retrieved January 3, 2021, from http://www.thenavigatorcompany.com/

Thessaloniki. (2006). *A concept and tool for employees involvement*. Author.

Thilmany, J. (2005). *Thinking Lean*. Journal University of Missouri-Rolla.

Thomas, C. F. (2015). *Naturalizing Sustainability Discourse: Paradigm, Practices and Pedagogy of Thoreau, Leopold, Carson and Wilson* (PhD Thesis). Arizona State University.

Tideman, S. G., Arts, M. C., & Zandee, D. P. (2013). Sustainable leadership: Towards a workable definition. *Journal of Corporate Citizenship*, *2013*(49), 17–33. doi:10.9774/GLEAF.4700.2013.ma.00004

Tieman, M. (2015). Halal clusters. *Journal of Islamic Marketing*, *6*(1), 2–21. doi:10.1108/JIMA-05-2014-0034

Tizkar Sadabadi, A., & Abdul Manaf, A. (2018). IKML approach to integrating knowledge management and learning for software project management. *Knowledge Management Research and Practice*, *16*(3), 343–355. doi:10.1080/14778238.2018.1474165

Tjarve, B., & Zemīte, I. (2016). The Role of Cultural Activities in Community Development. *Acta Universitatis Agriculturae et Silviculturae Mendelianae Brunensis*, *64*(6), 2151–2160.

Toma, S., & Tohanean, D. (2019). Green business models: The case of a German automaker. *Quality - Access to Success*, *20*(S2), 635–640.

Toosi, M. A. (2002). Organizational Development. Publication of the Center for Scientific Management Training.

Tosun, J., & Leininger, J. (2017). *Governing the inter-linkages between the sustainable development goals: Approaches to attain policy integration*. Global Challenges.

Trist, E., & Emery, F. (2005). Socio-technical systems theory. *Organizational Behavior 2: Essential Theories of Process and Structure, 169*.

Trivelli, L., Apicella, A., Chiarello, F., Rana, R., Fantoni, G., & Tarabella, A. (2019). From precision agriculture to industry 4.0: Unveiling technological connections in the agrifood sector. *British Food Journal*, *121*(8), 1730–1743. doi:10.1108/BFJ-11-2018-0747

Turing, A. M. (1950). Computing machinery and intelligence. *Mind*, *59*(236), 433–460. doi:10.1093/mind/LIX.236.433

Uber x Taxi. (2018). Understand the differences in costs and services between taxi and the app. *G1 News*. Available in: http://especiais.g1.globo.com/saopaulo/2015/uber-x-taxi/

Ugwu, O. O., & Haupt, T. C. (2007). *Key performance indicators and assessment methods for infrastructure sustainability—a South African construction industry perspective*. Academic Press.

UN/CEFACT, recomendação nº 33 (2005)

UNCTAD. (2019). *Review of Maritime Transport*. United Nations Publications.

Ustundag, A., & Cevikcan, E. (2018). *Industry 4.0: Managing The Digital Transformation*. Springer. doi:10.1007/978-3-319-57870-5

Vallone, C., & Veglio, V. (2019). Customer perceptions of the albergo diffuso concept: What makes the difference in terms of service excellence? *Tourism Analysis*, *24*(3), 367–375. doi:10.3727/108354219X15511864843902

Valls, Á. L. M. (2014). O que é ética. *Revista Eletrônica Espaço Teológico, 8*(14), 308-314. Retrieved December 18, 2020, from https://revistas.pucsp.br/index.php/reveleteo

Van Beveren, J. (2002). A model of knowledge acquisition that refocuses knowledge management. *Journal of Knowledge Management*, *6*(1), 18–22. doi:10.1108/13673270210417655

Van de Ven, A. H., Angle, H. L., & Poole, M. S. (Eds.). (2000). *Research on the Management of Innovation: The Minnesota Studies*. Oxford University Press.

Van Eck, N. J., & Waltman, L. (2009). Software survey: VOSviewer, a computer program for bibliometric mapping. *Scientometrics*, *84*(2), 523–538. doi:10.100711192-009-0146-3 PMID:20585380

Van Haren - Publishing. (2011). *ITIL Foundations - Best Practice*. Author.

Van Kleef, J. A., & Roome, N. J. (2007). Developing capabilities and competence for sustainable business management as innovation: A research agenda. *Journal of Cleaner Production*, *15*(1), 38–51. doi:10.1016/j.jclepro.2005.06.002

Van Loon, P., & Van Wassenhove, L. N. (2020). Transition to the circular economy: The story of four case companies. *International Journal of Production Research*, *58*(11), 3415–3422. doi:10.1080/00207543.2020.1748907

Vanegas, J. A., DuBose, J. R., & Pearce, A. R. (1996, November). Sustainable technologies for the building construction industry. *Proceedings, Symposium on Design for the Global Environment*.

Vansina, L. (1998). The Individual in Organisations: Rediscovered or Lost Forever? *European Journal of Work and Organizational Psychology*, *7*(3), 265–282.

Veer-Ramjeawon, P., & Rowley, J. (2019). Embedding knowledge management in higher education institutions (HEIs): A comparison between two countries. *Studies in Higher Education*, 1–17. doi:10.1080/03075079.2019.1608431

Venugopal, V., & Saleeshya, P. G. (2019). Manufacturing system sustainability through lean and agile initiatives. *International Journal of Sustainable Engineering*, *12*(3), 159–173. doi:10.1080/19397038.2019.1566411

VER - Valores, ética e responsabilidade. (n.d.). Retrieved December 18, 2020, from https://www.ver.pt/os-desafios-da-4a-revolucao-industrial-na-empregabilidade-e-no-apoio-as-pessoas-vulneraveis/

Verenikin, A. O., Makhankova, N. A., Finley, J. T., & Verenikina, A. Y. (2020). Evaluation of sustainable development of Russian largest companies. *ICITM 2020 - 2020 9th International Conference on Industrial Technology and Management*, 37-41. 10.1109/ICITM48982.2020.9080388

Verhoef, P., & Bijmolt, T. H. (2019). Marketing perspectives on digital business models: A framework and overview of the special issue. *International Journal of Research in Marketing*.

Vial, G. (2019). Understanding digital transformation: A review and a research agenda. *The Journal of Strategic Information Systems*, *28*(2), 118–144. doi:10.1016/j.jsis.2019.01.003

Vieira, M., Nicola, F. M., Junior, M. V., Simon, A. T., & Correr, I. (2018). *A Aplicação de Sistemas Ciber-Físicos (CPS) em Sistemas de Manufatura: Um Estudo Bibliométrico*. Academic Press.

Vieira, M., Nicola, F. M., Junior, M. V., Simon, A. T., & Correr, I. (2018). The Application of Cyber-Physical Systems (CPS) in Manufacturing Systems: A Bibliometric Study. *Conference: National Meeting of Production Engineering*. 10.14488/ENEGEP2018_TN_STO_258_478_36385

Vodafone. (2021). Retrieved January 3, 2021, from https://www.vodafone.com/

Von Krogh, G., Ichijo, K., & Nonaka, I. (2001). *Facilitando a Criação de Conhecimento: reiventando a empresa com o poder da inovação contínua*. Campus.

Von Krogh, G., Nonaka, I., & Ichijo, K. (2000). *Enabling Knowledge Creation: How to Unlock the Mystery of Tacit Knowledge and Release the Power of Innovation*. Oxford University Press. doi:10.1007/978-1-349-62753-0

Vorakulpipat, C., & Rezgui, Y. (2008). Value creation: the future of knowledge Management. The Knowledge Engineering Review, 23(3), 283-294.

Wald, N., & Harland, T. (2019). Graduate attributes frameworks or powerful knowledge? *Journal of Higher Education Policy and Management*, *41*(4), 361–374. doi:10.1080/1360080X.2019.1613310

Walker, E. G. II. (2016). Predicting higher education outcomes and implications for a postsecondary institution ratings system. *Journal of Higher Education Policy and Management*, *38*(4), 422–433. doi:10.1080/1360080X.2016.1181886

Wanamaker, C. (2018). *The Environmental, Economic, and Social Components of Sustainability: The Three Spheres of Sustainability*. U.S. Army Corps of Engineers. https://soapboxie.com/social-issues/The-Environmental-Economic-and-Social-Components-of-Sustainability

Wang, Y., & Pettit, S. (2016). *E-Logistics – Managing Your Digital Supply Chains For Competitive Advantage*. London: Kogan Page.

Waterman, R. H. Jr, Peters, T. J., & Phillips, J. R. (1980). Structure is not organization. *Business Horizons*, *23*(3), 14–26. doi:10.1016/0007-6813(80)90027-0

Weaver, G. R. (1993). *Corporate Codes of Ethics: Purpose, Process and Content Issues*. Business and Society.

Weber, M. (2002). *Ciência e política: duas vocações*. Martin Clare.

Weick, K. E., & Quinn, R. E. (1999). Organizational change and development. *Annual Review of Psychology*, *50*(1), 361–386.

Weick, K., & Quinn, R. (1999). *Organizational Change and Development. Annual Revision Psychology*.

Weldy, T. G. (2009). Learning organization and transfer: Strategies for improving performance. *The Learning Organization*, *16*(1), 58–68.

Weldy, T. G., & Gillis, W. E. (2010). The learning organization: Variations at different levels. *The Learning Organization*, *17*, 455–470.

Wessel, L., Baiyere, A., Ologeanu-Taddei, R., Cha, J., & Jensen, T. (2020). Unpacking the Difference between Digital Transformation and IT-enabled Organizational Transformation. *Journal of the Association for Information Systems*.

Westerman, G., Bonnet, D., & McAfee, A. (2014). *Leading digital: Turning technology into business transformation.* Harvard Business Press.

Westerman, G., Bonnet, D., & Mcafee, A. (2014). *Turning Technology into Business Transformation.* Harvard Business Review Press.

White, P. M., & Lee, D. M. (2019). Geographic Inequalities and Access to Higher Education: Is the Proximity to Higher Education Institution Associated with the Probability of Attendance in England? *Research in Higher Education.* Advance online publication. doi:10.100711162-019-09563-x

Whomack, J. P., & Jones, D. T. (1996-2003). *Lean Thinking.* Free Press.

Wiggins, R. R., & Ruefli, T. W. (2002, January–February). Sustained Competitive Advantage: Temporal Dynamics and the Incidence and Persistence of Superior Economic Performance. *Organization Science, 13*(1), 63–105.

Wiig, K. M. (1997). Knowledge management: An introduction and perspective. *Journal of Knowledge Management, 1*(1), 6–14. doi:10.1108/13673279710800682

Wilburn, K., & Wilburn, R. (2014). The double bottom line: Profit and social benefit. *Business Horizons, 57*(1), 11–20. doi:10.1016/j.bushor.2013.10.001

Williamson, B. (2017). The Datafile child: The dataveillance of children and implications for their rights. *New Media & Society, 19*(5), 780-794.

Williamson, O. E. (2002). The Theory of the firm as governance structure: from choice to contract. *Journal of Economic Prospective, 16*(3).

Williamson, O. E. (1975). *Markets and Hierarchies: Analysis and antitrust implications.* The Free Press.

Williamson, O. E. (1999). Strategy Research: Governance and Competence Perspectives. *Strategic Management Journal, 20*(12), 1087–1108. doi:10.1002/(SICI)1097-0266(199912)20:12<1087::AID-SMJ71>3.0.CO;2-Z

Williams, R. (1979). *Marxism and Literature.* Zahar.

Williams, R. (2019). National higher education policy and the development of generic skills. *Journal of Higher Education Policy and Management, 41*(4), 404–415. doi:10.1080/1360080X.2019.1606690

Winter, M., Smith, C., Morris, P., & Cicmil, S. (2006). Directions for future research in project management: The main findings of a UK government- funded research network. *International Journal of Project Management, 24*(8), 638–649.

Wirawan, C., Yudoko, G., & Lestari, Y. D. (2018). Developing a conceptual framework of product-service system management toward firms' sustainability for Indonesian industrial estate firms. *Advances in Science, Technology and Engineering Systems, 3*(5), 128–139. doi:10.25046/aj030517

Wirawan, C., Yudoko, G., & Lestari, Y. D. (2020). Determining an appropriate product-service system management to encourage firms' sustainability: A conceptual framework (case for Indonesian industrial estate firms). *International Journal of Public Sector Performance Management, 6*(4), 488–507. doi:10.1504/IJPSPM.2020.109300

Wirtz, B. W. (2019). *Digital business models. Concepts, models, and the alphabet case study.* Springer. doi:10.1007/978-3-030-13005-3

Witkamp, M. J., Raven, R. P. J. M., & Royakkers, L. M. M. (2011). Strategic niche management of social innovations: The case of social entrepreneurship. *Technology Analysis and Strategic Management, 23*(6), 667–681. doi:10.1080/09537325.2011.585035

Wittenberg, G. (1994). Kaizen—The many ways of getting better. *Assembly Automation, 14*(4), 12–17. doi:10.1108/EUM0000000004213

Wójcik, E. B., & Olejko, K. (2019). Legal and ethical aspects of CSR: Potential in new business models development. In Networked Business Models in the Circular Economy (pp. 200-223). Academic Press.

Womack, J. (2004). *A Lean Walk Through.* Academic Press.

Womack, J. P., & Jones, D. T. (1996). *Lean Thinking: Banish Waste and Create Wealth in Your Corporation.* Simon & Schuster.

Womack, J. P., Jones, D. T., & Roos, D. (1990). *The machine that changed the world.* Simon & Schuster.

Womark, J. P., Jones, D., & Ros, D. (1990). *The Machine that Changed the World.* Macmillan Publishing Company.

Woodfield, S. (2018). International HE in the UK: Leveraging the policy-institution-expert nexus in uncertain times. *Journal of Higher Education Policy and Management, 40*(6), 629–647. doi:10.1080/1360080X.2018.1530424

World Bank. (2017). *Atlas of sustainable development goals 2017.* World Development Indicators.

World Health Organization. (n.d.). *World Heath Organization.* Retrieved from https://www.who.int/emergencies/diseases/novel-coronavirus-2019/donate

Worley, J., & Doolen, T. L. (2006). The role of communication and management support in a Lean manufacturing. *Management Decision, 44*(2), 228–245. doi:10.1108/00251740610650210

Wu, I.-L., & Hu, Y.-P. (2018). Open innovation-based knowledge management implementation: A mediating role of knowledge management design. *Journal of Knowledge Management, 22*(8), 1736–1756. doi:10.1108/JKM-06-2016-0238

Xiao, Y., & Watson, M. (2019). Guidance on conducting a systematic literature review. *Journal of Planning Education and Research, 39*(1), 93–112. doi:10.1177/0739456X17723971

Xu, L. D., Xu, E. L., & Li, L. (2018). Industry 4.0: State of the art and future trends. *International Journal of Production Research, 56*(8), 2941–2962. doi:10.1080/00207543.2018.1444806

Yagodzinski, E. (2003). eSocrates Knowledge Management System and e-Learning Company. *The Internet and Higher Education, 6*(1), 105–107. doi:10.1016/S1096-7516(02)00167-7

Yanaprasart, P. (2020). Language of knowledge and knowledge of language. Towards plurilingual sciences? *European Journal of Higher Education*, 1–19. doi:10.1080/21568235.2020.1777450

Yang, L. X. (2019). From general principles of civil law to general provisions of civil law: A historical leap in contemporary Chinese civil law. *Social Sciences in China, 2*, 85–91.

Yang, M., Evans, S., Vladimirova, D., & Rana, P. (2017). Value uncaptured perspective for sustainable business model innovation. *Journal of Cleaner Production, 140*, 1794–1804. doi:10.1016/j.jclepro.2016.07.102

Yao, D. A. (1988). Beyond the Reach of the Invisible Hand: Impediments to Economic Activity, Market Failures and Profitability. *Strategic Management Journal, 9*, 59-70.

Yarahmadi, M., & Higgins, P. G. (2012). Motivations towards environmental innovation: A conceptual framework for multiparty cooperation. *European Journal of Innovation Management, 15*(4), 400–420.

Yeo, W.-D., Sohn, E.-S., Jung, E.-S., & Lee, C.-H. (2008). Identification of Emerging Research at the national level: Scientometric Approach using Scopus. *Journal of International Management, 39*(3), 95–113. doi:10.1633/JIM.2008.39.3.095

Zaim, H., Muhammed, S., & Tarim, M. (2018). Relationship between knowledge management processes and performance: Critical role of knowledge utilization in organizations. *Knowledge Management Research and Practice*, *17*(1), 24–38. doi:10.1080/14778238.2018.1538669

Zehir, C., Zehir, M., & Zehir, S. (2019). New strategies for evolution of business eco-systems: Platform strategies. In Handbook of Research on Strategic Fit and Design In Business Eco-Systems (pp. 98-122). doi:10.4018/978-1-7998-1125-1.ch005

Zhai, T. T., & Chang, Y. C. (2019). Standing of environmental public-interest litigants in China: Evolution, obstacles and solutions. *Journal of Environmental Law*, *30*(3), 369–397. doi:10.1093/jel/eqy011

Zhang, Y., Khan, U., Lee, S., & Salik, M. (2019). Sustainability. *The Influence of Management Innovation and Technological Innovation on Organization Performance. A Mediating Role of Sustainability*. Academic Press.

Zhang, B., Niu, Z., & Liu, C. (2020). Lean tools, knowledge management, and lean sustainability: The moderating effects of study conventions. *Sustainability (Switzerland)*, *12*(3), 956. Advance online publication. doi:10.3390u12030956

Zibarras, L. D., & Coan, P. (2015). HRM practices used to promote pro-environmental behavior: A UK survey. *International Journal of Human Resource Management*, *26*(16), 2121–2142.

Zijm, H., & Klumpp, M. (2015). Logistics and supply chain management: Developments and trends. *Logistics and Supply Chain Innovation: Bridging the Gap between theory into practice*, 1–20. doi:10.1007/978-3-319-22288-2_1

Zikmund, G. W. (2000). *Business research methods*. Oklahoma State University.

Zikmund, W. G. (2000). *Business. In Research Methods* (6th ed.). Dryden Press Harcourt College Publishers.

Zikopoulos, P. C., Eaton, C., deRoos, D., Deutsch, T., & Lapis, G. (2012). *Understanding Big Data: Analytics for Enterprise Class Hadoop and Streaming Data*. The McGraw-Hill.

About the Contributors

Nuno Geada has a Master degree in Systems Information Management by Polytechnic Institute of Setúbal, School of Business Sciences and Management, Setúbal; degree in Industrial Management and Technology by Polytechnic Institute of Setúbal, School of Technology of Setubal. He has written chapters and papers about topics regarding information technology management and strategic change management. Main research interests in information systems management, strategy, knowledge management, change management, and information technology management adoption in business contexts throw models and frameworks. He also works as an IT Director.

Pedro Anunciação is a professor of Information Systems at Polytechnic Institute of Setúbal, Co-ordinator of Research Center in Business Administration, General-Secretary of Information Systems Governance, European Club Portuguese Chapter.

* * *

Neeta Baporikar is currently Professor (Management) at Harold Pupkewitz Graduate School of Business (HP-GSB), Namibia University of Science and Technology, Namibia. Prior to this, she was Head-Scientific Research, with the Ministry of Higher Education CAS-Salalah, Sultanate of Oman, Professor (Strategic Management and Entrepreneurship) at IIIT Pune and BITS India. With more than a decade of experience in the industry, consultancy, and training, she made a lateral switch to research and academics in 1995. Prof Baporikar holds D.Sc. (Management Studies) USA, Ph.D. in Management, the University of Pune INDIA with MBA (Distinction) and Law (Hons.) degrees. Apart from this, she is an external reviewer, Oman Academic Accreditation Authority, Accredited Management Teacher, Qualified Trainer, FDP from EDII, Doctoral Guide, and Board Member of Academic and Advisory Committee in accredited B-Schools. She has to her credit many conferred doctorates, is a member of the international and editorial advisory board, reviewer for Emerald, IGI, Inderscience, etc, published numerous refereed papers, and authored books in the area of entrepreneurship, strategy, management, and higher education.

Ana Carvalho has a Degree in Sociology, by UNL/FCSH, Post-Graduation in Event Management, by INP.

Nuno Cruz has a Degree in Sports Science, by IPS/ESE.

Vitor Dinis is CEO of Cibersur.

Sandra Duarte has a Degree in Distribution and Logistics Management, by IPS/ESCE, Post-Graduation in Quality Management, by ISEC.

Francisco Esteves is an Invited Professor of Information Systems at Polytechnic Institute of Setúbal; Member of Research Center of Business Sciences.

Fernando Gonçalves is Global Information Systems Director at Grupo Nabeiro, Delta Cafés Visiting Professor at Polytechnic Institute of Setúbal, President of the Board of GUSP, Portuguese SAP User Member of ceGSI, Information Systems Governance European Club, Portuguese chapter.

John Loonam is an Assistant Professor of Strategy at DCU Business School. He holds a Bachelor of Arts in European Studies and a Masters of Business Studies from the University of Limerick. He received his PhD in Business Studies from Trinity College, Dublin. He teaches Business Strategy to both Undergraduate and Postgraduate students. His research focuses on Strategic Leadership & Digital Transformation.

Nuno Martins was born in Lourenço Marques (Mozambique). Graduated in Agroindustrial Engineering at Escola Superior Agrária de Beja, post-graduated in Management and Information Systems at ISTEC Business School and Master in Business Sciences - Logistics Management by the Escola Superior de Ciências Empresariais do Instituto Politécnico de Setúbal. Currently director of the commercial department of Santiago do Cacém at the company Delta Cafés.

Ricardo Mota was born in Lisbon (Portugal). Degree in electromechanical engineering from the Escola superior de tecnologia no Instituto Politécnico de Setúbal and a master's in business sciences - Management of Small and Medium Enterprises from the Escola Superior de Ciências Empresariais do Instituto Politécnico de Setúbal. Currently Engineering Director of the automotive industry at Aptiv and trainer in Lean management.

João Pimenta is CEO, Congelagos S.A. Member of ceGSI, Information Systems Governance European Club, Portuguese chapter.

Jose Poças Rascão (PhD, ISCTE / ULI) is a Professor of Management Information Systems at the Polytechnic Institute of Setubal, Graduate School of Business Sciences, Portugal. It is research in the Research Unit in the development of enterprise (UNIDE) at the Lisbon University Institute (ISCTE / ULI). Since 2000 he has published 15 books and over 80 research papers in international scholarly academic journals, about on management strategy and management of information. Under his supervision, 17 Masters Theses have been successfully from 2007 to 2018. From 2010 to 2015 was Director of Course Management of Distribution and Logistics. From 2013 to 2014 was Coordinator of Research Center, Polytechnic Institute of Setubal, Graduate School of Business Sciences. From 2000-2004 was Information Systems Management Course Coordinator Polytechnic Institute of Setubal, Graduate School of Business Sciences. He also works the private Management Consultant for large and medium-sized enterprises. He worked the Management Consult at Price Waterhouse and Coopers & Lybrand between 1989 and 1995.

Albérico Travassos Rosário, Ph.D. Marketing and Strategy of the Universities of Aveiro (UA), Minho (UM) and Beira Interior (UBI). With affiliation to the GOVCOPP research center of the University of Aveiro. Master in Marketing and Degree in Marketing, Advertising and Public Relations, degree from ISLA Campus Lisbon-European University I Laureate International Universities. Has the title of Marketing Specialist and teaches with the category of Assistant Professor at IADE-Faculty of Design, Technology and Communication of the European University and as a visiting Associate Professor at the Santarém Higher School of Management and Technology (ESGTS) of the Polytechnic Institute of Santarém. He taught at IPAM-School of Marketing I Laureate International Universities, ISLA- Higher Institute of Management and Administration of Santarém (ISLA-Santarém), was Director of the Commercial Management Course, Director of the Professional Technical Course (TeSP) of Sales and Commercial Management, Chairman of the Pedagogical Council and Member of the Technical Council and ISLA-Santarém Scientific Researcher. He is also a marketing and strategy consultant for SMEs.

Ana Silva graduated in Information Systems Management from Polytechnic Institute of Setubal, Consultant in the Area of Analytics and Cognitive in Deloitte Portugal, and master student of Statistics and Information Management in NOVA Information Management School.

Miguel Soares graduated in Sports from the Faculty of Sports of the University of Porto in 2010 and graduated in Business Sciences from the School of Management and Technology at Polytechnic Institute of Porto in 2016. Attending a PhD in Management at the University of Beira Interior. Teacher in the area of management at the School of Management and Technology at Polytechnic Institute of Porto in 2017.

João Sousa was born in Barreiro (Portugal), Degree in Business Management from the at Escola Superior de Gestão e Tecnologia de Santarém and Master in Business Sciences - Management of Small and Medium Enterprises from the Escola Superior de Ciências Empresariais do Instituto Politécnico de Setúbal. Currently with administrative functions in the commercial department of Setúbal, at the company Delta Cafés.

Ricardo Travassos was born in Barreiro (Portugal), graduated in Human Resources Management by the Escola Superior de Ciências Empresariais do Instituto Politécnico de Setúbal and Master in Business Sciences, Management of Small and Medium Enterprises by the Escola Superior de Ciências Empresariais do Instituto Politécnico de Setúbal. Currently involved in academic projects.

José G. Vargas-Hernández, M.B.A., Ph.D., Member of the National System of Researchers of Mexico and a research professor at University Center for Economic and Managerial Sciences, University of Guadalajara. Professor Vargas-Hernández has a Ph. D. in Public Administration and a Ph.D. in Organizational Economics. He has undertaken studies in Organisational Behaviour and has a Master of Business Administration, published four books and more than 200 papers in international journals and reviews (some translated to English, French, German, Portuguese, Farsi, Chinese, etc.) and more than 300 essays in national journals and reviews. He has obtained several international Awards and recognition.

Index

F

G

H

I

K

L

M

N

O

P

R

S

T

U

W

www.ingramcontent.com/pod-product-compliance
Lightning Source LLC
LaVergne TN
LVHW062122300926
849161LV00010B/2519